Student Well-Being in Higher Education Institutions

Peter Jo Aloka
University of the Witwatersrand, South Africa

A volume in the Advances in Higher Education and Professional Development (AHEPD) Book Series

Published in the United States of America by
IGI Global
Information Science Reference (an imprint of IGI Global)
701 E. Chocolate Avenue
Hershey PA, USA 17033
Tel: 717-533-8845
Fax: 717-533-8661
E-mail: cust@igi-global.com
Web site: http://www.igi-global.com

Copyright © 2024 by IGI Global. All rights reserved. No part of this publication may be reproduced, stored or distributed in any form or by any means, electronic or mechanical, including photocopying, without written permission from the publisher.
Product or company names used in this set are for identification purposes only. Inclusion of the names of the products or companies does not indicate a claim of ownership by IGI Global of the trademark or registered trademark.

Library of Congress Cataloging-in-Publication Data

CIP DATA PENDING

ISBN13: 9798369344170
Isbn13Softcover: 9798369344217
EISBN13: 9798369344187

British Cataloguing in Publication Data
A Cataloguing in Publication record for this book is available from the British Library.

All work contributed to this book is new, previously-unpublished material.
The views expressed in this book are those of the authors, but not necessarily of the publisher.

For electronic access to this publication, please contact: eresources@igi-global.com.

Table of Contents

Preface xvi

Chapter 1
An Exploration of Mental Well-Being Among Students in Higher Learning Institutions in Western Kenya 1
    Monica Anne Achieng Oyoo, Maseno University, Kenya

Chapter 2
Nursing Students Mental Well-Being During COVID-19 Pandemic: A Rapid Review... 31
    Nestor Tomas, University of Namibia, Namibia
    Takaedza Munangatire, University of Namibia, Namibia
    Hileni Nangulohi Niikondo, University of Namibia, Namibia

Chapter 3
Childhood Loneliness: A Step Towards Maladaptive Well-Being 55
    Ganesh Kumar J., Christ University, India
    Arnisha Aman, Christ University, India

Chapter 4
Student Well-Being in Higher Education Institutions: Academic Pressures 81
    Mary Jebii Chemagosi, Pwani University, Kenya

Chapter 5
Influence of Neuroticism and Locus of Control on Anxiety Among Students in Higher Education Institutions 107
    Sreeja Gangadharan, Christ University, India
    Anuradha Sathiyaseelan, Christ University, India
    Harshita Kumaran Dharam, Christ University, India
    Dalya Verma, Christ University, India
    Deepa K. Damodaran, Jain University, India

Chapter 6
Exploring Protective Factors for Stress Among University Students: A Theoretical Perspective 127
    Anna Niitembu Hako, University of Namibia, Namibia

Chapter 7
Coping Mechanisms for Stress Among Students at Universities 157
    S. C. Vetrivel, Kongu Engineering College, India
    T. P. Saravanan, Kongu Engineering College, India
    R. Maheswari, Kongu Engineering College, India
    V. P. Arun, JKKN College of Engineering and Technology, India

Chapter 8
Coping Mechanisms for Stress Among Students in Universities 187
    Damaris Auma Ochanda, Masinde Muliro University of Science and Technology, Kenya

Chapter 9
Stress Among the Undergraduate Students in Public Universities in Kenya 213
    Peter Omae Onderi, Maseno University, Kenya
    Samson N. O. Moracha, Maseno University, Kenya
    Christine Mwajuma Opondo, Maseno University, Kenya
    Justine Momanyi Omare, Jaramogi Oginga Odinga University of Science and Technology, Kenya

Chapter 10
A Systematic Literature Review for Identifying the Factors Causing Prevalences of Suicide Among Youths in India 237
    Priya Baluni, Department of Humanities and Social Sciences, Graphic Era University (Deemed), Dehradun, India
    Rishima Bhutani, Department of Humanities and Social Sciences, Graphic Era University (Deemed), Dehradun, India
    Ravindra Singh, Department of Psychology, Magadh University, Bodh Gaya, India
    Ajay Kumar Singh, Department of Humanities and Social Sciences, Graphic Era University (Deemed), Dehradun, India

Chapter 11
Study on Vulnerability to Maladjustment and Addictions in the Early Years of Student Life 267
    Cristina-Georgiana Safta, Petroleum-Gas University of Ploiesti, Romania
    Silvian Suditu, Petroleum-Gas University of Ploiesti, Romania

Chapter 12
Transition From Virtual to Reality in Post-Pandemic Academic Environment:
Challenges of Students' Well-Being 289
    N. Elangovan, Christ University, India
    E. Sundaravel, Christ University, India

Chapter 13
Impact of Social Media on Student Wellbeing in Kenyan Universities 317
    Peter Omae Onderi, Maseno University, Kenya
    Moses Oginda, Maseno University, Kenya

Chapter 14
Social Networking Platforms and Academic Performance of Students: A
Correlation Tests Approach 343
    Kapil Kumar Aggarwal, Chandigarh University, India

Chapter 15
Spatial Dimension of Students' Well-Being: A Gender-Sensitive Approach 359
    Susana Rosado, University of Lisbon, Portugal
    Vitória Rodrigues Jeronimo, University of Lisbon, Portugal

Chapter 16
Financial Well-Being of Students at Higher Education Institutions: A Study
of Northern Zone, Tanzania 399
    Kennedy Omondi Otieno, St. Augustine University of Tanzania, Arusha,
        Tanzania
    Loishiye Lengaram Saiteu, Institute of Accountancy, Arusha, Tanzania

Chapter 17
The Impetus of Monetary Intelligence on Financial Satisfaction and Security:
A Preliminary Survey on University Students from India 423
    K. Madhu Kishore Raghunath, GITAM University, Visakhapatnam,
        India
    Adil Khan, GITAM University, Visakhapatnam, India

Compilation of References 449

About the Contributors 541

Index 549

Detailed Table of Contents

Preface xvi

Chapter 1
An Exploration of Mental Well-Being Among Students in Higher Learning
Institutions in Western Kenya 1
    Monica Anne Achieng Oyoo, Maseno University, Kenya

Mental well-being is a vital factor which determines an individual's level of general health and productivity. According to WHO, mental health problems are increasing and about 25% of people suffer from mental illness globally. Depression, anxiety and stress are the most common particularly among students in higher learning institutions. In Kenya studies on mental well-being have concentrated on students in secondary schools. One among the few studies conducted in a university in Nairobi Region found the prevalence of depression to be 35.7%. The purpose of the study therefore was to explore mental well-being among students in universities in Western Kenya. Objectives of the study were to determine prevalence of depression, anxiety and stress, explore socio-demographic correlates of depression, anxiety and stress.

Chapter 2
Nursing Students Mental Well-Being During COVID-19 Pandemic: A Rapid Review... 31
    Nestor Tomas, University of Namibia, Namibia
    Takaedza Munangatire, University of Namibia, Namibia
    Hileni Nangulohi Niikondo, University of Namibia, Namibia

Student well-being is a top priority in higher education policy. However, recent research has shown that at least three out of five adolescents have psychiatric disorders by the age of 21 during the school life. This is inclusive of nursing students who are experiencing high levels of stress as they try to meet their academic demands. Most rapid reviews on mental well-being during COVID-19 have focused on the healthcare workforce, with little attention given to specific groups like nursing students. This review aims to consolidate knowledge and provide actionable evidence on the mental well-being of nursing students during the COVID-19 pandemic. A scoping review was conducted on English articles from various databases, following the PRISMA checklist. The synthesis includes different well-being strategies implemented by nursing students between 2019 and March 2024. This review provides swift evidence and guidance from Cochrane and the World Health Organization on conducting rapid reviews to address the urgent need for policy planning related to nursing student well-being.

Chapter 3
Childhood Loneliness: A Step Towards Maladaptive Well-Being 55
    Ganesh Kumar J., Christ University, India
    Arnisha Aman, Christ University, India

A growing concern among school children in recent years has been understanding the impact of loneliness on mental health and overall well-being. This chapter will explore the distinct and complex interplay between the varied social relationships and the wider societal influences that contribute to childhood loneliness. This research aims to explore the different underpinnings towards this growing concern by analysing parent-child relationships, familial relationships, family structures, the socioeconomic status of the family, the school environment, and most importantly, the detrimental impact of epidemics.

Chapter 4
Student Well-Being in Higher Education Institutions: Academic Pressures 81
Mary Jebii Chemagosi, Pwani University, Kenya

This chapter examines the factors impacting students' well-being within university settings, drawing on contemporary research and theoretical frameworks. Psychological factors, such as anxiety, depression, and academic pressure, exert effects on students' mental health and well-being. Social factors, encompassing interactions with peers, faculty, and staff, shape students' sense of belonging, support systems, and satisfaction with university life. Academic factors like workload, performance expectations, and perceived competence significantly impact students' well-being. Environmental factors, comprising physical surroundings, campus amenities, safety measures, and resource accessibility, play a pivotal role in shaping students' well-being. Societal factors, such as socioeconomic status, cultural background, family dynamics, and societal norms, intricately shape students' perceptions, values, and coping strategies within their university experiences. By fostering a supportive and empowering university culture, institutions can promote the well-being and success of their students.

Chapter 5
Influence of Neuroticism and Locus of Control on Anxiety Among Students in Higher Education Institutions 107
Sreeja Gangadharan, Christ University, India
Anuradha Sathiyaseelan, Christ University, India
Harshita Kumaran Dharam, Christ University, India
Dalya Verma, Christ University, India
Deepa K. Damodaran, Jain University, India

Anxiety is a negative state of mind resulting from conflicts and frustration experienced within ourselves. Anxiety often leads to undesired consequences like stress, confusion, fear, insecurity, distress, and panic. The most common causes of anxiety are perceived lack of control over one's life and fear of being wrong. Anxiety related to academics and career are major concern experienced by students especially in higher education institutions. Since they are exposed to many novel situations, there is a higher risk among them interpreting these situations as threatening. The present study aims to understand how neuroticism and locus of control together predict anxiety among students. A cross-sectional design is used in the study and data on anxiety, locus of control and neuroticism among adolescents and young adults were collected. It was found that neuroticism and LoC significantly predicts anxiety suggesting the need for early interventions and a positive and inclusive environment to modify the dysfunctional thought processes associated with neuroticism and external locus of control.

Chapter 6
Exploring Protective Factors for Stress Among University Students: A
Theoretical Perspective 127
    Anna Niitembu Hako, University of Namibia, Namibia

The chapter explores protective factors that can reduce stress in university students, highlighting cultural differences in stress responses. Using a literature review and document analysis method, it emphasizes holistic stress management, highlighting the importance of resilience, self-care, social support, coping abilities, and financial stability. The study suggests creating a welcoming campus environment, promoting social interactions, and providing resources to safeguard students' well-being.

Chapter 7
Coping Mechanisms for Stress Among Students at Universities 157
    S. C. Vetrivel, Kongu Engineering College, India
    T. P. Saravanan, Kongu Engineering College, India
    R. Maheswari, Kongu Engineering College, India
    V. P. Arun, JKKN College of Engineering and Technology, India

Stress is a prevalent issue among university students, stemming from academic pressures, social dynamics, financial concerns, and transitional challenges. This study explores the coping mechanisms employed by university students to manage stress and maintain mental well-being. Through a mixed-methods approach, including surveys and focus group discussions, The authors identify common stressors and categorize coping strategies. The chapter reveals that students use a combination of problem-focused coping, emotion-focused coping, and avoidance strategies. Problem-focused coping, such as time management and seeking academic support, is associated with reduced stress levels. Emotion-focused coping, including mindfulness and social support, also contributes positively to student well-being. However, reliance on avoidance strategies, like excessive gaming or substance use, often correlates with increased stress. The study underscores the need for university support systems that encourage adaptive coping strategies and reduce reliance on maladaptive ones.

Chapter 8
Coping Mechanisms for Stress Among Students in Universities 187
    Damaris Auma Ochanda, Masinde Muliro University of Science and
        Technology, Kenya

Students experience more psychological problems including stress compared to individuals of the same age and to any other population. Stress among students is related to different factors including transition to university and high academic expectations. The increasing stress has witnessed many students struggling to adjust and cope. For those not able to cope studies have shown linkage to poor mental health, suicidal tendencies and high drop out from the university. Through coping, one engages in intentional efforts to minimize the physical, psychological, or social harm of stress. Coping includes adaptive coping strategies such as problem-focused, emotion focused, meaning focused and social focused coping. Some students adapt maladaptive coping mechanisms. Understanding different coping mechanisms employed by university students will inform university administrators and stakeholders on how to design and implement programmes aimed at improving student's psychological health and minimize the negative effects of stress.

Chapter 9
Stress Among the Undergraduate Students in Public Universities in Kenya 213
    Peter Omae Onderi, Maseno University, Kenya
    Samson N. O. Moracha, Maseno University, Kenya
    Christine Mwajuma Opondo, Maseno University, Kenya
    Justine Momanyi Omare, Jaramogi Oginga Odinga University of
        Science and Technology, Kenya

Stress is an emotional feeling of tension. Stress is the body's reaction to a challenge or demand. The arising struggles of life in developing countries of the world has led to the increase of stress in instructions of higher learning. The purpose of this study is to find out the major causes of stress amongst students of higher learning in public universities in Kenya. The study investigated the causes of stress. The study sample consisted of undergraduate students from public universities. Based on the study findings university students face a lot of stress. The stressors are academic stress, financial stress, relationships, family conflicts, and uncertain future. The study recommended constant guidance and counseling for the students, parents, and guardians.

Chapter 10
A Systematic Literature Review for Identifying the Factors Causing
Prevalences of Suicide Among Youths in India 237
>	Priya Baluni, Department of Humanities and Social Sciences, Graphic
>		Era University (Deemed), Dehradun, India
>	Rishima Bhutani, Department of Humanities and Social Sciences,
>		Graphic Era University (Deemed), Dehradun, India
>	Ravindra Singh, Department of Psychology, Magadh University, Bodh
>		Gaya, India
>	Ajay Kumar Singh, Department of Humanities and Social Sciences,
>		Graphic Era University (Deemed), Dehradun, India

The prevalence of suicide rate is relatively higher among the youths in India as compared to other countries. However, limited studies could examine the prevalence of suicide rate and its leading factors among the youths in India. This chapter, therefore, explains the suicide rate of youths and its causing factors in India using a systematic literature review of previous studies. The statistical results showed that suicide has contributed to 12% of total deaths in the total population of India. It is also noticed that suicide cases have increased two times more among the male population in India in last five years. More comprehensive and inclusive data would be helpful for analyses and the development of suicide prevention measures in India. This chapter provides a significant scope for further research in the area of the suicide rate of youth and its causing factors in India.

Chapter 11
Study on Vulnerability to Maladjustment and Addictions in the Early Years
of Student Life 267
>	Cristina-Georgiana Safta, Petroleum-Gas University of Ploiesti,
>		Romania
>	Silvian Suditu, Petroleum-Gas University of Ploiesti, Romania

In a society characterized by an accentuated dynamic, by uncertainty and insecurity, with complex challenges and temptations at every step, the problem of students' well-being and the evaluation of their degree of vulnerability, respectively of the dimensions of that, represents a problem of major interest, with multiple implications both on an individual level and on a social level. This study therefore aims to evaluate the well-being and vulnerability of students in the first years of study, with the help of two standardized instruments, namely the vulnerability to maladjustment (VM) questionnaire and the vulnerability and resilience to addictions (VrA) questionnaire. The conclusions drawn from the analysis and interpretation of the results led to the formulation of a set of recommendations regarding the strategies that universities can develop with the aim of securing the emotional security of young people and cultivating well-being.

Chapter 12
Transition From Virtual to Reality in Post-Pandemic Academic Environment:
Challenges of Students' Well-Being 289
    N. Elangovan, Christ University, India
    E. Sundaravel, Christ University, India

The COVID-19 pandemic triggered a significant shift in academic settings. Post-pandemic normality prompted a return to traditional face-to-face classrooms from virtual and hybrid models. This chapter explores the multifaceted challenges students encounter during this transition, drawing on existing literature and empirical observations. Findings highlight the complexities of readjusting to classroom environments, managing academic expectations, and fostering peer interactions. Moreover, it emphasizes the critical need to address mental health concerns amid performance pressures. Practical implications underscore the importance of resilience, adaptability, and community support in empowering students. It calls for educational institutions to prioritize student well-being and academic success through robust support systems and open discourse on mental health. This chapter contributes to understanding the evolving academic landscape, offering insights for stakeholders to develop targeted interventions and support mechanisms for successful transitions in the post-pandemic era.

Chapter 13
Impact of Social Media on Student Wellbeing in Kenyan Universities 317
    Peter Omae Onderi, Maseno University, Kenya
    Moses Oginda, Maseno University, Kenya

Students who spend much of their time on social media are likely to struggle with time management and become less productive in their studies due to distractions by constant alerts, endless scrolling feeds, and the appeal of viral material. The chapter proposed to discuss, social networking sites, academic performance, social opportunities, and challenges. The findings were that social media helps university students get necessary information for their academic achievement, it creates stress, and it exposes them to cyberbullying, is addictive, causes sleep disorders and anxiety, and can help them make money online. The study recommended that the social media use at university should be restricted to academic use only and here should be provide adequate Wi-Fi hotspots within the universities.

Chapter 14
Social Networking Platforms and Academic Performance of Students: A
Correlation Tests Approach 343
    Kapil Kumar Aggarwal, Chandigarh University, India

Since college students use social media extensively, studying the link between social media use and academic achievement has become an important research topic. This study aimed to assess the impact of social networking platform usage on the academic performance of undergraduate and postgraduate students in the commerce and management fields. The chapter also aimed to determine the extent to which University students' usage of social networking sites influences their academic achievement. This chapter utilizes the correlation tests to assess and compare the impact of social networking sites on the academic achievement of the chosen students. The data has been collected from December 2023 to February 2024. This research examines the impact of social networking sites on students' academic achievement, specifically focusing on how students might utilize these platforms without negative consequences. Several tools on these platforms facilitate students in acquiring new learning techniques and exchanging thoughts and questions with students worldwide.

Chapter 15
Spatial Dimension of Students' Well-Being: A Gender-Sensitive Approach 359
    Susana Rosado, University of Lisbon, Portugal
    Vitória Rodrigues Jeronimo, University of Lisbon, Portugal

Human well-being depends on various factors, including the perception of spaces and architecture. For higher education students, well-being is closely linked to their experiences within institutional spaces, which affect them differently based on gender. This study focuses on students at the Lisbon School of Architecture, University of Lisbon, Portugal, to understand how physical and symbolic aspects of spaces facilitate or hinder their appropriation in a gender-sensitive manner. Using participatory methods like exploratory marches, collective maps, focus groups, and questionnaires, the authors examine how these spatial experiences impact student well-being. The research identifies deficiencies in comfort, security, and belonging, and suggests architectural improvements to enhance social well-being in higher education institutions.

Chapter 16
Financial Well-Being of Students at Higher Education Institutions: A Study
of Northern Zone, Tanzania... 399
    Kennedy Omondi Otieno, St. Augustine University of Tanzania, Arusha,
       Tanzania
    Loishiye Lengaram Saiteu, Institute of Accountancy, Arusha, Tanzania

The study investigated the relationship between financial well-being of students and grade point average (GPA) scored. The study adopted sequential explanatory design. A sample size involved 151 respondents; that is, five deans of students and ten non-academic staffs purposively sampled, 36 academic staffs (AS), and 100 undergraduate students. Data was obtained using stratified and simple random sampling techniques. Research experts determined content validity of instruments. Reliability for AS questionnaire (0.877) and students' questionnaire (0.777) was established using Cronbach's Alpha method. A statistically significant relationship (R =0. 762, R2 =0.581) between financial well-being of students and GPA scored was found. Increase in financial support to students was recommended since students facing financial hardship are more likely to drop out or score a low GPA.

Chapter 17
The Impetus of Monetary Intelligence on Financial Satisfaction and Security:
A Preliminary Survey on University Students from India 423
    K. Madhu Kishore Raghunath, GITAM University, Visakhapatnam,
      India
    Adil Khan, GITAM University, Visakhapatnam, India

One predominant factor which has had a great influence on financial wellbeing is monetary intelligence or love for money. Different parts of the world have different perceptions towards the aspect of money/monetary intelligence/love for money. Some perceive money as not so important factor in life, whereas others believe that money is the most important part of individuals life. The desired benefits of monetary intelligence on financial well-being also depends upon the levels of hierarchical needs that people would like to satisfy. Whereas financial well-being is an abstract theory that describes the general condition of a person or society, which further differs from individual to individual. The authors in the present study aim to analyse the impact of different dimensions of monetary intelligence on the financial wellbeing of young individuals in India. The dimensions of monetary intelligence, mainly cognitive, affective, and behavioural.

Compilation of References 449

About the Contributors 541

Index 549

Preface

In the contemporary landscape of higher education, institutions face an array of challenges and complexities in their quest to provide optimal teaching and learning environments. The well-being of university students has emerged as a significant priority for governments and educational bodies worldwide. Despite its importance, robust evidence supporting effective well-being initiatives has often been lacking. Higher well-being is intricately linked to better mental and physical health, heightened self-esteem, self-efficacy, and effective coping strategies.

University life introduces students to a myriad of new experiences, including relocating to unfamiliar environments, forming new social connections, managing finances, maintaining a household, and autonomously managing their time. These transitions, coupled with the shift towards academic independence, can profoundly impact students' well-being. The challenges they face can be daunting and often necessitate comprehensive support systems within higher education institutions.

Despite the critical importance of student well-being, there is a noticeable paucity of comprehensive resources addressing this subject in the context of higher education. Our book, *Student Well-Being in Higher Education Institutions*, aims to fill this gap by presenting a detailed examination of various aspects influencing student well-being.

This book is structured into chapters that delve into diverse dimensions of student well-being, providing valuable insights for scholars, doctoral students, university administrators, counselors, master's students, lecturers, and instructors. University counselors and administrators, in particular, will find this book instrumental in developing effective mechanisms to enhance the well-being of their students.

The chapters cover a range of topics including:

- The current state of student well-being in higher education institutions.
- Factors impacting student well-being in universities.
- Emotional well-being of students.
- Risk factors associated with student well-being.

- Protective factors fostering student well-being.
- Strategies for coping with well-being challenges.
- Intrinsic and extrinsic factors influencing student well-being.
- Social and psychological aspects of student well-being.
- Student stress and coping mechanisms in higher education.
- Protective strategies against stress for university students.

By providing a comprehensive exploration of these themes, our book aspires to contribute to the academic discourse on student well-being and serve as a valuable resource for enhancing the educational experiences and overall health of students in higher education institutions.

ORGANIZATION OF THE BOOK

Chapter 1: An Exploration of Mental Well-Being Among Students in Higher Learning Institutions in Western Kenya

This chapter delves into the critical issue of mental well-being among university students in Western Kenya, highlighting the prevalence of depression, anxiety, and stress within this demographic. Despite the global increase in mental health issues, as indicated by WHO, and the significant percentage of individuals suffering from mental illnesses, there is limited research focusing on university students in this region. A study in Nairobi found a 35.7% prevalence of depression among university students, underscoring the need for further exploration. This research aims to fill that gap by determining the prevalence of mental health issues and examining the socio-demographic factors that correlate with depression, anxiety, and stress among students in Western Kenya.

Chapter 2: Nursing Students' Mental Well-Being During COVID-19 Pandemic: A Rapid Review

The COVID-19 pandemic has significantly impacted the mental well-being of nursing students, a group that faces unique stressors compared to their peers. This chapter provides a rapid review of the mental well-being of nursing students during the pandemic, consolidating knowledge from English-language articles and synthesizing strategies employed by these students to manage their mental health. Using the PRISMA checklist, the review offers evidence and guidance from Cochrane and WHO on addressing the urgent mental health needs of nursing students, aiming to inform policy planning and enhance support mechanisms within educational institutions.

Chapter 3: Childhood Loneliness: A Step Towards Maladaptive Well-Being

Addressing the growing concern of childhood loneliness, this chapter explores the complex interplay between social relationships, societal influences, and mental health. It examines the impact of parent-child and familial relationships, family structures, socioeconomic status, school environment, and the effects of epidemics on childhood loneliness. By analyzing these factors, the chapter aims to understand the underpinnings of loneliness and its detrimental effects on children's well-being, providing insights into preventive measures and interventions to combat this issue.

Chapter 4: Student Well-Being in Higher Education Institutions: Academic Pressures

This chapter investigates the various factors influencing student well-being within university settings. It examines psychological factors such as anxiety and depression, social factors including peer and faculty interactions, academic factors like workload and performance expectations, environmental factors related to campus amenities and safety, and societal factors such as socioeconomic status and cultural background. By fostering a supportive and empowering university culture, the chapter highlights how institutions can promote student well-being and academic success.

Chapter 5: Influence of Neuroticism and Locus of Control on Anxiety Among Students in Higher Education Institutions

This chapter explores how neuroticism and locus of control predict anxiety among university students. Using a cross-sectional design, the study collected data on anxiety, locus of control, and neuroticism from adolescents and young adults. The findings reveal that both neuroticism and locus of control significantly predict anxiety, suggesting the need for early interventions and the creation of positive, inclusive environments to address dysfunctional thought processes associated with these traits.

Chapter 6: Exploring Protective Factors for Stress Among University Students: A Theoretical Perspective

Highlighting the importance of protective factors in stress management, this chapter reviews literature and documents to emphasize holistic approaches to stress reduction. It discusses the roles of resilience, self-care, social support, coping abilities, and financial stability in safeguarding students' well-being. The chapter suggests that creating a welcoming campus environment and promoting social interactions are crucial for mitigating stress and enhancing student well-being.

Chapter 7: Coping Mechanisms for Stress Among Students at Universities

This chapter examines the coping mechanisms university students use to manage stress. Through surveys and focus group discussions, the study identifies common stressors and categorizes coping strategies into problem-focused, emotion-focused, and avoidance strategies. It highlights the effectiveness of problem-focused coping in reducing stress and the positive impact of emotion-focused coping. However, it also warns against reliance on avoidance strategies, which often correlate with increased stress. The chapter underscores the need for university support systems to encourage adaptive coping strategies.

Chapter 8: Coping Mechanisms for Stress Among Students in Universities

This chapter explores the psychological problems, including stress, faced by university students and the coping mechanisms they employ. Stress related to the transition to university and high academic expectations can lead to poor mental health, suicidal tendencies, and high dropout rates. The chapter examines adaptive coping strategies such as problem-focused, emotion-focused, meaning-focused, and social-focused coping, as well as maladaptive mechanisms. It emphasizes the need for universities to design and implement programs that improve students' psychological health and reduce the negative effects of stress.

Chapter 9: Stress Among Undergraduate Students in Public Universities in Kenya

This chapter investigates the major causes of stress among undergraduate students in public universities in Kenya. Using a sample of undergraduate students, the study identifies academic stress, financial stress, relationship issues, family conflicts, and concerns about the future as primary stressors. The chapter recommends regular guidance and counseling for students, parents, and guardians to help manage these stressors and improve student well-being.

Chapter 10: A Systematic Literature Review for Identifying the Factors Causing Prevalences of Suicide Among Youths in India

This chapter addresses the high prevalence of suicide among youths in India by conducting a systematic literature review of previous studies. The statistical analysis reveals that suicide contributes to 12% of total deaths in India, with a significant increase in suicide cases among males in the past five years. The chapter highlights the need for comprehensive data to develop effective suicide prevention measures and provides a basis for further research on the factors contributing to youth suicides in India.

Chapter 11: Study on Vulnerability to Maladjustment and Addictions in the Early Years of Student Life

This chapter evaluates the well-being and vulnerability of students in the early years of university life using the VM (Vulnerability to Maladjustment) and VrA (Vulnerability and Resilience to Addictions) Questionnaires. The study identifies key vulnerabilities and provides recommendations for universities to develop strategies that secure emotional security and cultivate well-being among young students, addressing the challenges and temptations they face in a dynamic and uncertain society.

Chapter 12: Transition from Virtual to Reality in Post-Pandemic Academic Environment: Challenges of Students' Well-being

This chapter explores the challenges students face as they transition from virtual learning environments back to traditional classrooms post-pandemic. It highlights the complexities of readjusting to classroom settings, managing academic expectations, and fostering peer interactions. The chapter emphasizes the need to address mental health concerns and suggests practical implications for educational institutions to prioritize student well-being and academic success through robust support systems and open discourse on mental health.

Chapter 13: Impact of Social Media on Student Wellbeing in Kenyan Universities

This chapter examines the impact of social media on student well-being in Kenyan universities. It discusses how excessive social media use can lead to time management issues, distractions, stress, cyberbullying, addiction, sleep disorders, and anxiety. While social media can provide valuable information for academic achievement and offer financial opportunities, the chapter recommends that universities restrict social media use to academic purposes and provide adequate Wi-Fi hotspots to support this.

Chapter 14: Social Networking Platforms and Academic Performance of Students: A Correlation Tests Approach

This chapter investigates the correlation between social networking platform usage and academic performance among undergraduate and postgraduate students in commerce and management fields. Using "Correlation Tests," the study assesses the impact of social networking sites on academic achievement. The findings suggest that while social media can facilitate learning and global interaction, it is essential for students to use these platforms judiciously to avoid negative consequences on their academic performance.

Chapter 15: Spatial Dimension of Students' Well-Being: A Gender-Sensitive Approach

This chapter explores the spatial dimension of student well-being from a gender-sensitive perspective. Focusing on students at the Lisbon School of Architecture, it examines how physical and symbolic aspects of institutional spaces affect well-being differently based on gender. Using participatory methods such as exploratory marches, collective maps, focus groups, and questionnaires, the research identifies deficiencies in comfort, security, and belonging. The chapter suggests architectural improvements to enhance social well-being in higher education institutions.

Chapter 16: Financial Well-being of Students at Higher Education Institutions: A Study of Northern Zone, Tanzania

This chapter investigates the relationship between the financial well-being of students and their academic performance (GPA) in the Northern Zone of Tanzania. It explores how the financial status of students impacts their well-being, academic success, and overall performance. The chapter provides insights into the challenges faced by students from economically disadvantaged backgrounds and emphasizes the need for supportive financial policies to enhance student well-being and academic achievement.

Chapter 17: The Impetus of Monetary Intelligence on Financial Satisfaction and Security: A Preliminary Survey on University Student From India

The authors in the present study aim to analyze the impact of different dimensions of monetary intelligence on the financial wellbeing of young individuals in India. The dimensions of monetary intelligence mainly cognitive, affective and behavioral.

IN CONCLUSION

In concluding this exploration into the well-being of students in higher education institutions, we emphasize the critical importance of addressing the multifaceted aspects of student life. The well-being of students is not merely an adjunct to their academic performance but is integral to their overall success and development. As we have discussed throughout this book, higher well-being is correlated with better mental and physical health, higher self-esteem, increased self-efficacy, and more effective coping strategies.

The university experience, while rich with opportunities for growth and learning, also presents significant challenges. Students must navigate new social environments, manage financial responsibilities, and balance the demands of academic and personal life. These pressures can be overwhelming, and without adequate support, they can negatively impact a student's well-being.

Our comprehensive approach in this book provides a robust framework for understanding and improving student well-being. We have examined intrinsic and extrinsic factors, identified both risk and protective factors, and discussed various strategies for managing stress and promoting psychological and social health. This holistic perspective is essential for developing effective interventions and support systems within higher education institutions.

We hope this book serves as a valuable resource for scholars, doctoral students, university administrators, counselors, master's students, lecturers, and instructors. By fostering a deeper understanding of student well-being, we aim to inspire actionable strategies that can be implemented to create supportive, healthy, and thriving educational environments.

Ultimately, the well-being of students is a shared responsibility that requires concerted efforts from all stakeholders within the academic community. It is our hope that this book not only informs but also motivates meaningful changes that will enhance the educational experiences and life outcomes for students in higher education institutions. Through collective action and commitment, we can ensure that our universities are places where students can flourish both academically and personally.

Peter Jo Aloka
University of the Witwatersrand, South Africa

Chapter 1
An Exploration of Mental Well-Being Among Students in Higher Learning Institutions in Western Kenya

Monica Anne Achieng Oyoo
https://orcid.org/0009-0005-6276-1846
Maseno University, Kenya

ABSTRACT

Mental well-being is a vital factor which determines an individual's level of general health and productivity. According to WHO, mental health problems are increasing and about 25% of people suffer from mental illness globally. Depression, anxiety and stress are the most common particularly among students in higher learning institutions. In Kenya studies on mental well-being have concentrated on students in secondary schools. One among the few studies conducted in a university in Nairobi Region found the prevalence of depression to be 35.7%. The purpose of the study therefore was to explore mental well-being among students in universities in Western Kenya. Objectives of the study were to determine prevalence of depression, anxiety and stress, explore socio-demographic correlates of depression, anxiety and stress.

DOI: 10.4018/979-8-3693-4417-0.ch001

INTRODUCTION

Mental health is a state of mental well-being that enables people to cope with the stresses of life, realize their abilities, learn and work well. It is a basic human right which is crucial to personal, community and socio-economic development (WHO, 2022). Mental health problems on the other hand, are characterized by a significant disturbance in an individual's cognition or behaviour associated with distress or impairment in important areas of functioning (Kenya AIDS NGOs Consortium, 2021). There are various types of mental health problems namely: Neurodevelopmental disorders, Stress, Schizophrenia, Eating Disorders, Bipolar Disorder, Anxiety Disorders, Depression, Drugs and Substance Abuse. Prevalence of mental health problems are on the rise. According to Ferrari (2022) mental disorders increased from 654·8 million to 970·1 million cases between 1990 and 2019 globally. It is approximated that 25% of people suffer from mental illness globally (Tay, Tay & Yobus, 2018; WHO, 2019). Depression, stress and anxiety are reported to be the most common of the mental disorders, half of which manifest at the age of 14 (WHO, 2021). In 2019, 301 million people were living with an anxiety disorder and 280 million people were living with depression globally (Institute of Health Metrics and Evaluation Global Health Data Exchange, 2022). Depression was further reported to be affecting more than 350 million people in the world by 2023 (Bakesia, Olayo, Mengich et al., 2023).

The holistic approach to education encompasses the well-being of learners' minds, bodies, and spirits: psychological, social and mental aspects (Agrawal & Sharma, 2022). It is important to note that the life of students in higher institutions of learning has its challenges but at the same time, it acts as a bridge for their successful future. In other words, college years inculcate vital professional, vocational, and life skills in students. At the same time during these years, they develop a sense of themselves and their involvement in the world (Ozer & Schwartz, 2020). Thus, these years act as a foundation stone for their future success and accomplishment. Therefore, the well-being of students in higher education is a matter of attention and focus and higher education institutes can play a key role in the holistic development of students enrolled in higher institutions of learning. According to Botha et al. (2019), the overall well-being of the student population is reflected in their emotional, psychological, social, spiritual and physical well-being. Also, self-perception of well-being plays a vital role in improving the quality of a university student's life

Mental well-being is a vital factor as it determines individual's level of general health, productivity as well as social interactions. The World Health Organization on the other hand uses the term well-being to define mental health as 'a state of well-being in which an individual realizes his or her own abilities, can cope with the normal stresses of life, can work productively and is able to make a contribution to his or her community' (WHO, 2018). Mental health in this research is conceptualized as the continuum of neurophysiological and cognitive state that is related to emotion, mood, thinking and behaviour. Mental wellbeing has been argued to have both positive and negative dimension (Franke, et al., 2017). Positive dimension of mental wellbeing is considered as a complete state of cognitive functioning whereby the individual can cope with adversity, whereas, the negative dimension refer to the psychological distress and psychiatric disorder (Schütte, et al., 2014). The current study will focus on the negative dimension.

Various studies conducted on mental well-being among students in secondary schools show high prevalence of psychological distress. A study by Osborn, Venturo-Conerly & Gan (2021) found prevalence of 28.06% for clinical depression and 38% for anxiety. Studies conducted in Western Kenya by Bakesia et al. (2023) registered prevalence of depression of 44.8% and Nyayieka, Nyangwecha & Nzyuko (2020) found prevalence of 57% for depression and 49.4% for anxiety among adolescents in secondary schools. However, very little research is available about mental well-being of students in higher institutions of education particularly in Western Kenya. Othieno et al. (2014) also found that prevalence levels of depression among Kenyan university students was poorly understood. Besides, few studies have established the relationship between psychological distress and type of institution of learning. The purpose of the current study therefore was to explore mental well-being among students in higher learning institutions in Western Kenya. Objectives of the study were to determine prevalence of depression, anxiety and stress, explore socio-demographic correlates of depression, anxiety and stress and establish interventions to improve mental well-being of students in higher learning institutions in Western Kenya.

In the current study, higher education was conceptualized as any kind of formal training after secondary education in an organized institution. This includes Technical and Vocational Education and Training (TVET) which is critical for producing middle level manpower (Republic of Kenya, 2016). The TVET sector envisions providing skilled and globally competitive employable human resource with the right attitudes and values required for growth and prosperity of the various sectors of the economy of the country. Therefore, TVET is necessary for laying a foundation for the vocational skills required for socio-economic development, equipping students with entrepreneurial skills and positive attitudes for self or formal employment, and providing practical training that is responsive and relevant to the country's sustainable economic and industrial development (Technical and Vocational Education and Training Authority (TVETA), 2023). The right of access to higher education is mentioned in a number of international human rights instruments. The UN International Covenant on Economic, Social and Cultural Rights of 1966 declares, in Article 13, that "higher education shall be made equally accessible to all, on the basis of capacity, by every appropriate means, and in particular by the progressive introduction of free education (TVETA, 2023). This is the more reason mental well-being of students in higher learning institutions needs to be taken care of in order not to disadvantage them.

BACKGROUND

Mental Wellbeing of Students in Higher Institutions of Learning

Mental well-being is the experience of positive emotions such as happiness and contentment as well as the development of one's potential, having some control over one's life, having a sense of purpose and experiencing positive relationships (Ruggeri, Garcia-Garzon & Huppert, 2020). mental well-being can also be defined as an individual's ability to develop their potential, work productively and creatively and build strong and positive relationships with others and contribute to their community (de Cates, Stranges & Blake et al., 2015).

Psychological distress is a global health concern. Studies have also revealed increasing levels of stressors and hardship among higher education students especially in low and middle income countries making it necessary for higher education institutions to find out ways of providing robust and comprehensive support for students who experience stressors and hardship (Nyasanu, et al. (2020). Further, studies show that the prevalence of psychological distress is higher in students' population than in the general population (Mutinta, 2021).

In Pakistan, the frequency of depression, anxiety and stress among university students was found 75%, 88.4% and 84.4% respectively in a study by Asif, et al. (2020). The findings of the study showed the prevalence of depression within the range of normal (25%), mild (16%), moderate (35.8%), severe (14.6%) and extremely severe (8.6%). The prevalence of anxiety was found to be in the range of normal (11.6%), mild (4.4%), moderate (19.4%), severe (17.8%) and extremely severe (46.8%). Stress was normal (15.6%), mild (33.8%), moderate (35.4%), severe (13.2%) and extremely severe (2.8%). A Saudi study conducted by Sani et al. (2012) to investigate the prevalence of stress among medical students in Jizan University in Saudi Arabia also revealed the prevalence of stress among medical students was 71.9%, with females being more stressed (77%) than the males (64%).

In Africa, a study in South Africa by Visser et al. (2021) highlighted the emotional difficulties and low levels of mental health of students after 3months of lockdown during the COVID-19 pandemic. The scoring on the PHQ-4 indicated that almost half of the students (45.6%) had subjective experiences of anxiety during the month preceding the completion of the survey, whereas 35.0% had experiences of depression. Another study conducted in South Africa by Mutinta, (2021) found the prevalence of mental distress among students at 53.3% (95% CI 47.0%, 58.1%). Female students were more prone to mental distress than male students ([AOR]: 4.67; 95% CI 2.82, 7.72, $P=0.001$). Field of study ([AOR]: 3.9; 95% CI 1.74, 5.50, $P=0.010$), year of study ([AOR]: 4.29; 95% CI 0.86, 21.46, $P=0.002$), academic workload ([AOR]: 4.66; 95% CI 2.81, 7.71, $P=0.003$), poor sleep quality ([AOR]: 2.24; 95% CI 1.13, 3.67, $P=0.010$) and using cannabis ([AOR]: 3.10; 95% CI 1.755, 5.51, $P=0.020$) were other factors significantly correlated with students' mental distress. Further, a study by Bantjes, et al. (2023) found that prevalence estimates were higher for any anxiety disorder (37.1%) and any disruptive behaviour disorder (38.7%) than for any mood disorder (16.3%) or any substance use disorder (6.6%) among students in universities in South Africa.

In East Africa, Naijuka et al. (2021) conducted a study in Uganda to determine level of depression, anxiety, and stress among Ugandan university students during the COVID-19 lockdown. An online survey was carried out using the Depression Anxiety and Stress Scale (DASS-21). The prevalence of mental health symptoms among participants was 80.7%, 98.4%, and 77.9% for depression, high levels of anxiety, and stress, respectively. In Kenya, a random sample of 923 University of Nairobi students (525 male and 365 female) responded to a questionnaire where depressive symptoms were measured using Centre for Epidemiological Studies Short Depression Scale (CES – D 10). The overall prevalence of moderate depressive symptoms was 35.7% (33.5% males and 39.0% females) and severe depression was 5.6% (5.3% males and 5.1% female), (Othieno, et al., 2014). Mutiso, Ndetei & Muia et al.(2023) also conducted a study that aimed at determining the prevalence of stress, different types of stress and their severity among students in Kenyan university, college and high school students. Descriptive analysis for the prevalence of different types of stress and inferential analysis for stress and independent variables were done. The mean age of the respondents was 21.4 years (range 16–43). It was concluded that up to 30% of the students suffered from mild to severe stress. The next section will give a review of risk factors.

RISK FACTORS OF DEVELOPING PSYCHOLOGICAL DISTRESS

Psychological distress is a state of emotional suffering and also characterized by somatic symptoms (Belay, et al., 2021). In the current study, psychological distress was limited to depression, anxiety and stress. Various studies have shown that university students are more at risk of depression, stress and anxiety than their peers who go straight into work due to the financial strain of higher education, coupled with academic and social stressors. A systematic review conducted by Campbell, et al. (2022) found that factors most strongly and consistently associated with increased risk of developing poor mental health included students with experiences of trauma in childhood, those that identify as LGBTQ and students with autism. Factors that promote wellbeing include developing strong and supportive social networks. Students who are prepared and able to adjust to the changes that moving into higher education presents also experience better mental health. The study found that some behaviours associated with poor mental health include lack of engagement both with learning and leisure activities and poor mental health.

According to a systematic review by Flatt (2013), six factors lead to mental health disorders among university students. Academic pressure was the first factor, which elevates the stress level and leads to mental health problems (e.g., stress, anxiety and depression) because students fail to cope effectively with academic mis-achievement at university, and because of the difficulty to achieve the high grades they desire. Financial burden was the second factor leading to depression, anxiety, stress, and psychosis, as well as to academic failure among university students. This factor was the result of increased tuition fees, decreased governmental financial support, increased students loans with high interest rates and related causes. The third factor was limited accessibility to higher education for many minority group students from different cultural, social, and economic backgrounds. In addition, female students were found to have a higher risk for mental health disorders than male students. The negative or harmful effect of the overuse of technology was the fifth factor that was found to create mental health issues among university students. This includes internet addiction or problematic internet use, mobile phone use, and overuse of internet pornography which were found to be directly linked to depression, anxiety, social isolation, shyness, low self-esteem, and lack of social and emotional skills. The final factor was change in life style of students, which was found to lead to mental health problems such as depression, anxiety, and panic disorders, as well as physical health problems such as gaining body weight. Life style change includes eating unhealthy or poor diet, decreasing physical exercises, and neglecting managing stress and depression using effective coping mechanisms.

A study conducted among university and college students in UK by Campbell et al. (2022) found that factors most strongly and consistently associated with increased risk of developing poor mental health included students with experiences of trauma in childhood, those that identify as LGBTQ and students with autism. Factors that promote wellbeing include developing strong and supportive social networks. Students who are prepared and able to adjust to the changes that moving into higher education presents also experience better mental health. Some behaviours that are associated with poor mental health include lack of engagement both with learning and leisure activities and poor mental health literacy. In addition, the prevalence of depression among first year female students in Canada and United States was double that of their male counterparts: 14% and 7% respectively by Field, et al.

(2012). Their results were supported by a study conducted by Burris et al. (2009) who found that female students had perceived poorer mental health status compared to male students, and were at a greater risk for depression during university. Likewise, Vaez et al. (2008) found that female university students accessed health services in higher proportions when compared to male students. The proportion of females was significantly higher than that of males (64.8% compared with 35.2%). In Saudi Arabia, the major factors associated with perceived stress among students were "long hours of study, examinations and very tight time schedules, psychological and family issues, lack of entertainment in the campus; and the education system itself (Sani et al., 2012).

According to a study by Mohamad et al. (2021) among students in universities in Malaysia, the prevalence of students with the risk of anxiety was 29% based on the GAD-7 score. Race, residency, smoking status and alcohol consumption were significantly associated with the risk of anxiety. The risk of anxiety was shown to be higher among students with poor sleep quality than students who had better sleep quality. BMI was found to be statistically significant with the risk of anxiety, where the percentage of obese and underweight students who had a risk of anxiety were slightly higher in these groups as compared to other BMI groups. Wei et al. (2022) also conducted a study at a University in Malaysia. The prevalence of depressive symptoms was found to be between 26.4% and 36.8% with an average of 29.9%. The risk of depressive symptoms was higher among female students, those who were dependent on the family for financial support and those who were stressed.

Another study by Luo et al. (2024) found a relatively high (48.9%) prevalence of depression among college students in China. College students with higher grades (OR = 1.574, 95%CI: 1.369–1.810), profession of medicine and allied health sciences (OR = 1.779, 95%CI: 1.203–2.629), experiencing higher study stress (OR = 2.006, 95%CI: 1.601–2.514), and having poor physical condition (OR = 1.527, 95%CI: 1.247–1.869) were identified as risk factors for depressive tendency. The correlation between higher grades and increased learning pressure, coupled with poorer physical condition, heightens the vulnerability of college students to depression. Moreover, the more they attribute these experiences to achievement effort (OR = 0.897, 95%CI: 0.828–0.972), achievement ability (OR = 0.903, 95%*CI*: 0.838–0.972), and affiliation context (OR = 0.919, 95%CI: 0.860–0.982), the less likely they are to develop depression.

In a study conducted by (Memiah et al., 2022) the HIV burden in sub-Saharan Africa (SSA) equally affects adolescents' mental health during this transition period. It is evidenced that people living with HIV (PLHIV) report higher rates of mental health issues, including stress, depression, anxiety, and trauma. Prevalence estimates varied significantly by historical segregation status of institutions ($F_3 = 221.6, p < .001$), with prevalence consistently highest in Historically White Institutions (HWIs).

Across all institutions, risk of any disorder was lower among oldest than younger students (RR = 0.7, 95%CI = 0.7–0.8), and elevated among gender non-conforming (RR = 1.3, 95%CI = 1.1–1.4), female (RR = 1.2, 95%CI = 1.1–1.2), and sexual minority (RR = 1.2, 95%CI = 1.2–1.3) students. Black students attending HWIs had elevated risk of any disorder relative to White students (Bantjes et al., 2023).

In Zimbabwe, Nyasanu et al. (2020) examined students´ expression of their experience with stressors and problems of studying in higher education in the Eastern Highlands of Zimbabwe. Three institutions of higher education in the eastern border highlands of Zimbabwe were considered. Five overarching themes emerged from the analysis: (i) the stress of completing assessments without adequate learning materials. (ii) Unfair placement workload results into poor assessment outcomes. (iii) College-life is more difficult due to financial constraints. (iv) Marital problems interfering with college work: there is no mental health service available. (v) Enduring pains of bereavement with no emotional support or helpline. The study recommended the need to develop an inter-ministerial mental health strategy for institutions of higher learning with the view of implementing policies that address students suffering in Zimbabwean HE institutions. A study by Aina & Adebowale (2020) among a total of 400 students in College of Medicine University of Lagos, Nigeria found that prevalence of depression was 36.5% among the students out of which 18.2% portrayed severe depression.

A systematic reviewed carried out by Anbesaw et al. (2023) among a total number of 5207 university students in Ethiopia found a pooled prevalence of depression to be 28.13% (95% CI: 22.67, 33.59). In the sub-group analysis, the average prevalence was higher in studies having a lower sample size (28.42%) than studies with a higher sample; 27.70%, and studies that utilized other (PHQ-9, HADS); 30.67% higher than studies that used BDI-II; 26.07%. Being female (pooled AOR = 5.56) (95% CI: 1.51, 9.61), being a first-year (pooled AOR = 4.78) (95% CI: 2.21, 7.36), chewing khat (pooled AOR = 2.83) (95% CI: 2.32, 3.33), alcohol use (pooled AOR = 3.12 (95% CI:3.12, 4.01) and family history of mental illness (pooled AOR = 2.57 (95% CI:2.00, 3.15) were factors significantly associated with depression.

In East Africa, Naijuka et al. (2021) conducted a study in Tanzania and found a statistically significant association between mental health symptoms on multi-logistic regression with Males (depression=2.97[1.61–5.48] and stress=1.90[1.07–3.35]), engagement in leisure activity (depression=1.87[1.01–3.49] and stress=1.98[1.10–3.56]), and being finalist (stress=0.55[0.31– 0.97]). Use of addictive substances seemed to potentially alleviate symptoms of depression, anxiety and stress in the short term.

In Kenya, a study by Othieno et al. (2014) among students at the University of Nairobi found that depressive illness was significantly more common among the first year students, those who were married; those who were economically disadvantaged and those living off campus. Other variables significantly related to higher depression levels included year of study, academic performance, religion and college attended. Logistic regression showed that those students who used tobacco, engaged in binge drinking and those who had an older age were more likely to be depressed. No difference was noted with respect to gender. Another study conducted by Mutiso et al. (2023) among 9741 students in universities in Kenya found that money issues were the commonest stressors while alcohol and drug use were the least. The independent predictors of stress were females, college students and use of gas stove. In conclusion, up to 30% of the students suffer from mild to severe stress. The students indicated experiencing a wide range of stressors. The most important stressors included money and finances, family related problems and concerns about their future.

A similar study conducted by Kiarie-Makara & Ndegwa (2020) found out that several factors were associated with depression among university students. The study showed that students who had dependents were at a highest risk of getting depressed than their colleagues who had no dependents. In this study, there were 94 students from the TUK School of Engineering Science and Technology (N = 432) who had dependents. Out of the 94 students, 46 (48.94%) were suffering from depression. Out of the remaining 338 who had no dependents, only 87(25.74%) were depressed. At UON, there were 56 students (N = 430) who had dependents out of whom 45 (80.36%) were suffering from depression. Out of the remaining 364 students who had no dependents, only 91 (25%) were depressed. The study also established that being in leadership positions increases university students' likelihood of suffering from depression. There were 47 students from the TUK School of Engineering Science and Technology (N = 432) who were holding leadership positions. Out of the 47 students, 20 (42.55%) were suffering from depression. Of the rest 385 who were not in leadership positions, only 113 (29.35%) were suffering from depression. At UON, there were 20 students who were in leadership positions (N= 420). Out of these, 9 (45%) were suffering from depression. Of the remaining 400 students who were not in leadership positions, only 127 (31.51%) were suffering from depression. The study further found out that the more the friends that the students had, including friends of the opposite sex, the less likely to suffer depression. However, the correlation between gender and depression was not significant. The following section highlights method used in the research.

Mutiso, Ndetei & Muia et al. (2023) conducted a study that aimed at determining determinants of psychological distress among students in Kenyan university, college and high school students. Descriptive analysis for the prevalence of different types of stress and inferential analysis for stress and independent variables were done. The mean age of the respondents was 21.4 years (range 16–43). Money issues were the commonest stressors while alcohol and drug use were the least. The independent predictors of stress were females, college students and use of gas stove. It was concluded the most important stressors included money and finances, family related problems and concerns about their future.

Liverpool, Moinuddin & Aithal et al. (2023) conducted a study aimed to examine the mental health and wellbeing of further and higher education students and the associating factors after returning to face-to-face (in-person) learning after Covid-19 restrictions. A cross-sectional study informed by student consultations was conducted using a survey design. Mental health and wellbeing were assessed using self-report items on the Depression, Anxiety and Stress Scale (DASS-21) and the Short Warwick–Edinburgh Mental Wellbeing Scale (SWEMWBS). N = 1160 students participated; 69.6% between 16 and 25 years, 67.9% studying in the UK, 66.5% studying away from home, 60.2% identified as she/her, 59.8% studying at the undergraduate degree level, 42.5% belonging to non-White ethnic backgrounds, 29.6% identifying as having additional needs and 22.8% as sexual minority. Moderate anxiety (M = 13.67, SD = 9.92) and depression (M = 17.04, SD = 11.56) scores were mainly reported. Gender expression, sexuality, age, ethnicity, having additional needs and level and location of study was associated with mental health or wellbeing.

Furthermore, a study was conducted by Theurel, Witt & Shankland (2022) to assess the effectiveness of an 8-week online intervention, integrating a variety of evidence-based strategies for improving French university students' mental health. Students were assigned to: (1) the online self-help program ETUCARE (n = 53), or (2) the control condition (n = 50). All the participants completed pre- and post-intervention questionnaires that assessed mental health problems and psychological well-being. The findings revealed that, compared to the control group, participation in the online program was associated with higher levels of psychological well-being post-test and fewer clinical symptoms of psychological distress, anxiety, and alcohol consumption.

ASSOCIATION BETWEEN MENTAL HEALTH LITERACY AND MENTAL WELLBEING

Mental health literacy (MHL) has been found to have a great influence on mental well-being. MHL is the ability to recognize mental health problems, knowledge of mental health, resilience building strategies and attitude towards appropriate help-seeking behaviours (Tully, Hawes & Doyle et al., 2019; Bale, Grové & Costello, 2018). To begin with, a systematic review study carried out by Renwick, Pedley & Johnson (2022) established that MHL would help improve mental health as it would combat low levels of help-seeking and effective treatment receipt. Bjornsen et al. (2019) also conducted a study based on a cross-sectional survey of adolescents aged

15−21 years at five upper secondary schools in an urban area in mid-Norway. The study was intended to examine the relationship between positive MHL and mental well-being and 1,888 adolescents were sampled. The study established that MHL is a significant determinant of mental health. In a study carried out by Tullius et al. (2021) in Netherlands to determine relationship between MHL and help seeking behaviour, MHL was found to help prevent mental health problems. Online FGDs and interviews were used to collect data. A sample of 58 adolescents, ages 13-19 participated in the study. Another study was conducted to investigate MHL and mental well-being among secondary school students in Slovakia by Sokolova (2024). A convenient sample of 250 students responded to online survey. The findings showed that MHL determined the students' help-seeking behaviour thereby affecting their mental well-being.

In Africa, Korhonen, Axelin & Stein et al. (2022) conducted a study with a population of PHC workers (n = 250) in South Africa and Zambia with the aim to assess MHL and its impact on mental well-being. Results highlighted the need for improving MHL in order to help address mental health challenges. Alsaraireh, Al-Oran, Althnaibat et al. (2023) also conducted a study in Southern Jordan aimed to understand the relationship between MHL and the psychological state associated with depression among adolescents in schools. A cross sectional descriptive design was used with a sample of 450 adolescent students. The study concluded that levels of MHL significantly correlated with mental well-being.

In East Africa, Amone-P'Olak, Kakinda & Kibedi et al. (2023) conducted a study in Uganda to assess influence of MHL on depression among early adults. Data were collected from 56 students in two of the largest universities in Uganda using questionnaires. MHL significantly predicted depression. In Kenya, a study was conducted by Ayiro et al. (2023) to determine stress levels, coping strategies and MHL among students. A total of 400 students aged 16–22 years participated in the study. A questionnaire was used to collect data in the cross-sectional study. The respondents were drawn from the following counties: Nairobi, Bungoma, Kakamega, Uasin Gishu, Kisumu, Kisii, and Nakuru, Samburu, Turkana, Isiolo, Wajir, and Tana River. The study determined that MHL could be a protector from stress and other mental health problems.

INTERVENTIONS TO IMPROVE MENTAL WELLBEING

Much of research and public policy remain focused on mental illness and other pathologies, often disregarding the positive aspects of mental health and wellbeing. However, mental and psychological wellbeing are both desirable outcomes in themselves, as well as linked to a host of other positive outcomes, such as better physical health (Vazquez, Hervas & Rahona et al., 2009), improved performance at work or school, lower levels of absenteeism, and more satisfying and successful relationships (Diener, 2009). In essence, optimal wellbeing is linked to actively flourishing in all aspects of life (Seligman & Csikszentmihalyi, 2014). This can be achieved by the use of interventions as discussed in this section.

Several studies have come up with interventions to improve mental wellbeing among students. Physical activity (PA) is one of the interventions associated with improved mental health in higher education settings. A study was conducted among students in universities in the UK to establish PA-based interventions to improve mental health and wellbeing of students. Of 143 public UK universities identified, 125 (87%) responded. Of these, only 45 (36%) universities had PA provisions in place, with a total of 54 interventions available across the country, each delivered for between 6 and 12 weeks. Most interventions were tailored (82%) and used behaviour change techniques (BCTs) focused on instructing students on how to perform physical activity (61%), restructuring the environment to facilitate activity (54%) and behavioural goal setting (46%). It was concluded that only a minority of UK universities offered PA interventions to students. It was recommended that universities should consider offering greater PA provision to students, and address students' motivation to engage in PA (Malagodi, Dommett & Findon, 2024).

Further, a systematic review study was conducted by Worsley, Pennington & Corcoran (2020). Mindfulness-based interventions (MBI), cognitive behavioural therapy (CBT), and technology-delivered interventions appeared to be effective when compared to a passive controls (receiving no intervention). There was some evidence to suggest that the effects of CBT-related interventions are sustained over time. Recreation programmes were also found to be effective. In one high quality review, while both CBT and MBIs were found to be effective, other interventions (such as art, exercise, and peer support) were found to be more effective. The review-level evidence suggested that psycho-education interventions are not as effective as other intervention forms such as mindfulness-based interventions, cognitive-behavioural interventions, relaxation interventions, and meditation. In addition, the effects of psycho-education interventions did not appear to sustain over time.

Another systematic literature review was conducted by Bhavana & Otaki (2021) to find interventions aimed at alleviating the burden of mental health challenges faced by students and/ or at equipping them with coping mechanism that will foster their resilience. A total of 1,399 records were identified by the electronic search, out of which 40 studies were included in the study. The authors inductively identified four overlapping categories of interventions and coded them as follows: Mindfulness, Movement, Meaning, and Moderator. It was concluded that focusing on devising holistic, university-based interventions that embrace the individuality of students to improve their mental health through elements of mindfulness, movement, meaning, and moderator be encouraged.

Ferrari, Allan & Arnold (2022) also conducted a systematic review and meta-analysis aimed to assess digital interventions targeting psychological well-being among university students. A total of 13 eligible studies were identified, 10 (77%) of which were included in the meta-analysis. Mean pre-post effect sizes indicated that such interventions led to small and significant improvement in psychological well-being (Hedges g=0.32, 95% CI 0.23-0.4; P<.001). It was concluded that digital psychological interventions could help alleviate psychological distress among university students. Moreover, a cross-sectional study conducted by Liverpool et al. (2023) to establish interventions to improve mental well-being of students in universities in the UK. N = 1160 students participated and questionnaires were used to collect data. Specifically targeted interventions focusing on useful coping strategies and increasing self-efficacy and physical activity were found to be beneficial for students.

In Africa, Mabrouk, Mbithi & Chongwo et al. (2022) conducted a systematic review to establish evidence-based adolescent mental health interventions to reduce the risk and burden of mental health problems in Sub Saharan Africa (SAA). The 64 studies reviewed described a total of 57 unique mental health interventions comprising 40,072 adolescents. The interventions included various implementation strategies such as economic-based, family strengthening, psycho-education, interpersonal psychotherapy, CBT and resilience training among others. Most of the interventions were selective interventions that targeted adolescents at high risk of developing mental health problems including adolescents living with HIV, war-affected adolescents, orphans, adolescents from poorer backgrounds and survivors of sexual violence. Mthiyane, Rapulana & Harling et al. (2022) also conducted a systematic review to establish evidence of the effectiveness of community or family-level interventions on mental health disorders among adolescents in SSA. Studies were eligible for inclusion in the review if they were randomised controlled trials (RCTs) or controlled quasi-experimental studies conducted in sub-Saharan African countries and measured the effect of an intervention on common mental disorders in adolescents aged 10–24 years. Findings suggested that multi-level interventions comprise economic empowerment, peer-support, cognitive behavioural therapy were effective in improving mental health among vulnerable adolescents. Majority of studies that delivered interventions to community groups reported significant positive changes in mental health outcomes. It was concluded that multi-level interventions can reduce mental health disorders in adolescents.

METHOD

The study was anchored on Albert Bandura's Social Cognitive Theory and a conceptual framework showing relationship between socio-demographic factors and depression, anxiety and stress. Descriptive survey and correlational research designs were employed.

Theoretical Framework

Albert Bandura's Social Cognitive Theory (SCT) which identifies that people learn from their own experiences and by observing the experiences of others. The SCT focuses on the impact of an individual's social environment, expectations, observations, as well as their self-efficacy (Bandura, 1997). According to SCT, there are three major constructs that interact to influence behaviour. These are: personal factors such as gender, environmental factors including type of institution and aspects of the behaviour itself such as vigour of the behaviour, competence with the behaviour and outcomes achieved as a result of practicing the behaviour, Rottschaefer (1991). Therefore, SCT is relevant to this study as it explains how socio-demographics such as gender and type of institution interact with indicators of psychological distress (depression, anxiety and stress).

Conceptual Framework

Figure 1. A Conceptual Framework showing relationship between socio-demographic factors and fig distress

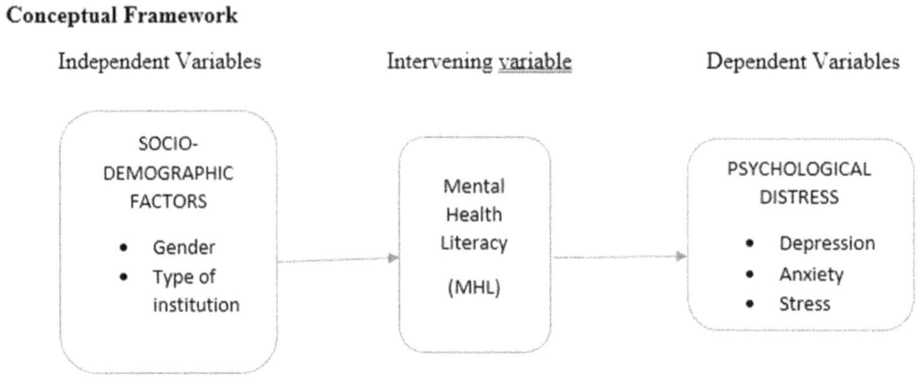

Conceptual Framework

Independent Variables	Intervening variable	Dependent Variables
SOCIO-DEMOGRAPHIC FACTORS • Gender • Type of institution	Mental Health Literacy (MHL)	PSYCHOLOGICAL DISTRESS • Depression • Anxiety • Stress

The study envisioned that socio-demographic factors such as gender and type of institution would have an influence on depression, anxiety and stress and MHL representing aspects and knowledge of psychological distress would be the intervening variable. Since gender differences influence personality and behaviour, it is expected that the same would influence mental wellbeing. Likewise, type of institution determines several factors including availability of mental health resources which may in turn affect mental wellbeing. Additionally, level of MHL is expected to be the intervening variable. As such, higher level of MHL is expected to lead to better mental wellbeing and vice-versa. The conceptual framework is similar to the theoretical framework as both explain the interaction between socio-demographic factors and mental wellbeing.

PARTICIPANTS

Convenience sampling was used to select 200 respondents from higher institutions in Western Kenya. The sample population was arrived at based on financial constraints. The area of study covers a total of eleven counties namely: Kisumu, Homabay, Migori, Kisii, Nyamira, Siaya, Vihiga, Busia, Kericho, Bomet and Kakamega. There several higher learning institutions in the region including middle level colleges (TVETs) including Kisumu National Polytechnic, Ober Kamoth Ramogi Institute and Technology, Mawego and universities such as Maseno, Jaramogi Oginga Odinga Science and Technology, Kabianga, Rongo, Kaimosi, Masinde Muliro, Tom Mboya and Kisii. A total of 146 students (105 from universities and 45 from TVETs) responded to the questionnaire giving a response rate of 73%. Only 34 (male) and 28 (female) declared their gender.

INSTRUMENTS

Data was collected using a questionnaire which had two sections. The first section collected data on socio-demographics which were limited to gender and type of institution in the current study. In the second section, the DASS-21 (Depression, Anxiety, Stress Scale) was used to measure level of depression, anxiety and stress. The DASS-21 is a widely used screening tool, which can separately measure depression, anxiety, and stress symptoms. It has three sub-scales, namely the depression subscale (DASS-D), Anxiety subscale (DASS-A) and stress subscale (DASS-S) (Moussa et al. 2017). The DASS-D measures an individual's hopelessness, positive affect and self-esteem. The DASS-A measures autonomic arousal, situational anxiety, musculoskeletal symptoms, the perceived experience of anxiety arousal and situation anxiety. DASS-S measures agitation, tension and negative affect (Tran, 2013). Each subscale comprises seven items that are scored from 0 (did not apply to me at all) to 3 (applied to me very much, or most of the time) for the week preceding the interview to reflect severity. The total score for each DASS-21 subscale ranges from 0 to 21. The items' scores are added and multiplied by two to obtain the total score that can be compared with the original DASS-42. A study by Moya, et al. (2022) established the overall Cronbach's alpha for DASS-21 at 0.74. The internal reliability (Cronbach's alpha) of EPDS was 0.74, with item-test correlation and item-specific alpha ranging from 0.30 to 0.81 and 0.67 to 0.76, respectively. The ordinal alphas for DASS-D, DASS-A and DASS-S subscales were 0.83, 0.74 and 0.87, respectively. Moreover, Bintabara et al. (2024) tested reliability of DASS 21 by calculating the overall Cronbach's alpha of the DASS 21 which was 0.92 and the Cronbach's alpha of each sub-scale (Depression=0.76, anxiety=0.86, and stress=0.87. A pilot study was carried out among 30 students and the reliability of DASS 21 was established at 0.91 using Pearson's r.

ETHICAL CONSIDERATIONS

Respondents were required to be 18years or above. The purpose of the study was explained to them. They were also made aware that completing the survey was voluntary and it was done anonymously. Contact details of an organization providing online consultation for students in distress were provided. The respondents were then given consent forms to sign. Data were filed using a password-protected providing only researcher access.

LIMITATIONS OF THE STUDY

The current findings were based on self-reports which may be affected by dishonesty by the respondents. The sample population was also small, limiting generalizability. The use of convenience sampling is also prone to sampling bias which may not be representative to the study population.

DATA ANALYSIS

Quantitative data were analyzed using means, percentages and independent t-test. IBM SPSS 20 was used to run the analysis. The results were presented in tables and bar graphs. The severity of psychological distress was determined based on suggested cut-off scores for conventional severity labels in DASS 21 as follows:

Table 1. Cut-off scores for severity labels in DASS 21

Severity	Depression	Anxiety	Stress
Normal	0–9	0–7	0–14
Mild	10–13	8–9	15–18
Moderate	14–20	10–14	19–25
Severe	21–27	15–19	26–33
Extremely severe	28+	20+	34+

RESULTS AND DISCUSSION

Psychological Distress

The means of psychological distress, depression, anxiety and depression are presented in table 2.

Table 2. Means of psychological distress, depression, anxiety and stress

		Psychological distress	Depression	Anxiety	Stress
N	Valid	146	146	146	146
	Missing	0	0	0	0
Mean		46.1301	14.3082	15.8904	15.9315
Std. Deviation		22.73544	9.50467	9.53189	8.78059
Minimum		.00	.00	.00	.00
Maximum		108.00	40.00	48.00	36.00

The average mean scores were as follows: psychological distress ($M = 46.13$, $SD = 22.73$) depression ($M = 14.31$, $SD = 9.50$) anxiety ($M = 15.89$, $SD = 9.54$) and stress ($M = 15.93$, $SD = 8.78$). These results show very high levels of mental health problems among students in higher institutions in Western Kenya. Among the indicators of psychological distress, stress had the highest mean followed by depression while depression had the lowest mean. This implies that even though the prevalence of psychological distress among students was high, the highest indicator was stress. The findings resonate with those of other researchers such as Asif et al. (2020); Sani et al. (2012) and Memiah et al. (2022) which indicated that the levels of psychological distress among students in higher learning institutions are very high.

The researcher further explored the prevalence of each of the mental health problems. These were analyzed using percentages and presented in bar graphs.

DEPRESSION

The following bar graph shows the prevalence of depression among students.

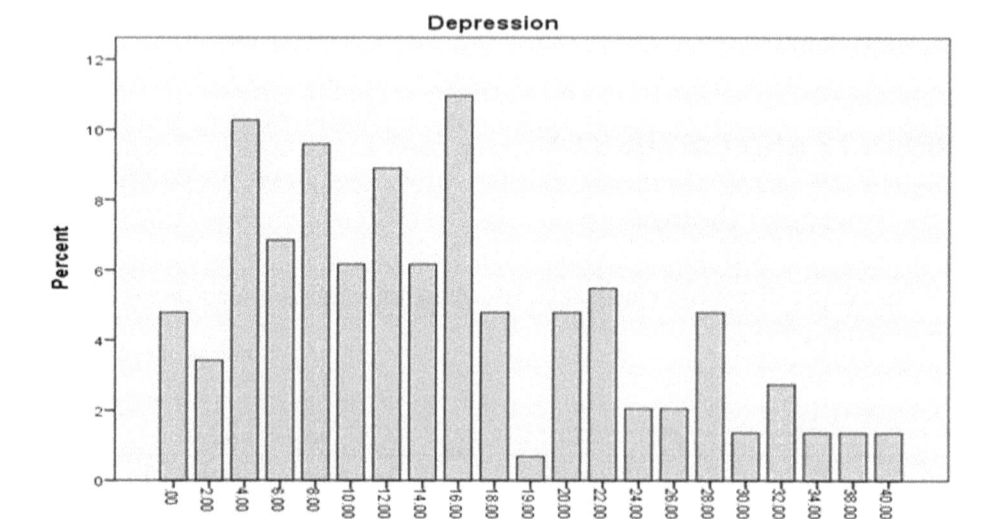

Figure 2. A bar graph showing prevalence of depression

Results in figure 2 show that depression ranged from 0-40 with a mean of ($M = 14.31, SD = 9.50$). Only 4.8 respondents reported no signs of depression, 34.9% reported normal depression, 15.1% mild, 27.4% moderate, 9.6% severe and 13% extremely severe. From the findings, it is clear that prevalence of depression among students in higher learning institutions is high. The findings support those by Kiarie-Makara, et al. (2020), Aina et al. (2020), Othieno et al. (2014), Luo et al. (2024), Wei et al. (2022) and Anbesaw, et al. (2023). Since these studies were conducted in different regions, it could be that there are similar issues that predispose the students to depression and it is therefore important for the administrators to establish the causes as well as preventive and corrective measures. This would help in reducing negative effects of depression which may interfere with the students' general health and also affect their academic achievement. The repercussions could even be worse going by the reports that depression was the leading cause of death among young adults aged 15 to 24 years in US, WHO (2021).

ANXIETY

The following bar graph shows the prevalence of anxiety among students.

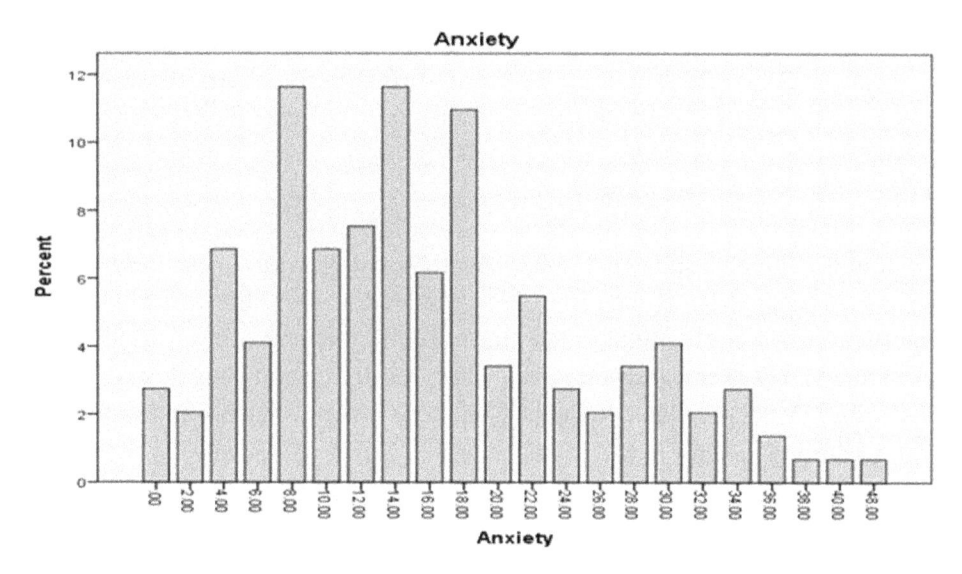

Figure 3. A bar graph showing prevalence of anxiety

Results in figure 3 show that anxiety ranged from 0-48 with a mean of $M = 15.89$, $SD = 9.54$ (severe). Only 2.7% reported no signs of anxiety. Normal 15.8%, Mild 11.6%, Moderate 26%, severe 17.1% extremely severe 29.5%. Likewise, Mohamad et al. (2021) found high levels of anxiety among students in higher institutions of learning.

STRESS

The following bar graph shows the prevalence of stress among students.

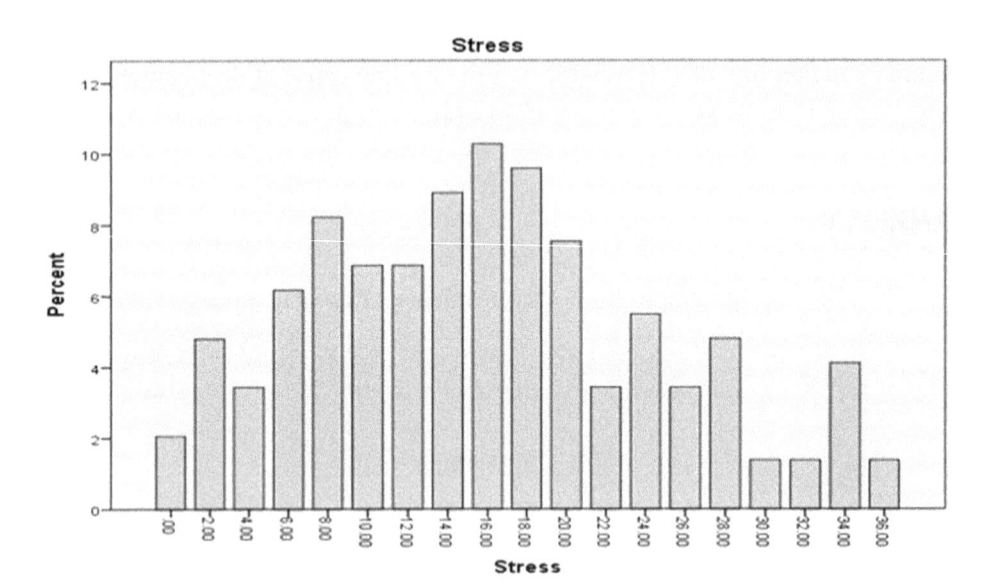

Figure 4. A bar graph showing prevalence of stress

Results in graph 3 show that stress ranged from 0-36 with a mean of $M = 15.93$, $SD = 8.78$. Only 2.1% of the respondents reported no signs of stress while 47.3% reported normal stress, 19.8% mild stress, 16.5% moderate stress, 10.9% severe stress and 5.5% extremely severe stress. These results are similar to those of Mutiso et al. (2023) who also found high levels of stress among students in institutions of higher learning in Kenya.

RELATIONSHIP BETWEEN DEMOGRAPHIC FACTORS AND PSYCHOLOGICAL DISTRESS.

The relationship between demographic factors and psychological distress was explored. The demographic factors in the study were gender and type of institution. Analysis was conducted using independent samples t-test.

Relationship Between Gender and Psychological Distress

According to the results, the average scores among boys were: psychological distress ($M = 41.12, SD = 21.57$), depression ($M = 14.41, SD = 10.23$), anxiety ($M = 10.76, SD = 7.12$) and stress ($M = 15.94, SD = 9.37$). Among girls the scores were: psychological distress ($M = 59.50, SD = 22.96$), depression ($M = 18.43, SD = 10.17$), anxiety ($M = 21.07$, $SD = 10.95$) and stress ($M = 20.00$, $SD = 7.66$). Independent t-test indicated strong statistically significant gender difference in psychological distress ($t(60) = .729$, $p = .002$) and anxiety ($t(60) = .007$, $p = .000$). However, there was no statistically significant gender difference in depression ($t(60) = .872$, $p = .128$) and stress($t(60) = .314$, $p = .071$). The findings the study resonate with those of Field et al. (2012) and Burris et al. (2009) that female students in higher education institutions had higher levels of mental health problems compared to their male counterparts. The findings are also similar to those of Kiarie-Makara et al. (2020) which indicated no statistically significant gender difference on prevalence of depression among students in universities in Kenya.

Relationship Between Type of School and Psychological Distress

The average scores among students in universities were: psychological distress ($M = 48.38$, $SD = 22.81$), depression ($M = 15.27$, $SD = 9.95$), anxiety ($M = 16.38$, $SD = 9.72$) and stress ($M = 16.65$, $SD = 8.49$). For students in TVETs, the scores were: psychological distress ($M = 40.89$, $SD = 22.12$), depression ($M = 12.10$, $SD = 7.89$), anxiety ($M = 14.49$, $SD = 9.08$) and stress ($M = 14.29$, $SD = 9.39$). There was a weak statistically significant difference in the type of institution and depression ($t(143) = .261, p = .046$). However, there was no statistically significant difference in the type of institution and psychological distress ($t(143) = .546$, $p = .75$); anxiety ($t(143) = .844$, $p = .283$) and stress ($t(143) = .321$, $p = .146$). The findings are similar to those by Othieno et al. (2014) which indicated that college attended was among the variables related to higher depression levels among students in the University of Nairobi.

CONCLUSION

Based on the findings, it was concluded that prevalence of psychological distress particularly anxiety among students in higher learning institutions in Western Kenya is high. Gender was found to be a determinant of level of psychological distress while the institution attended influenced level of depression. Moreover, findings suggested that multi-level interventions comprising economic empowerment, peer-support, cognitive behavioural therapy were effective in improving mental health among vulnerable adolescents. In addition, Mindfulness, Movement, Meaning, and Moderator, psycho-education, digital psychological interventions and physical activity were also found to be useful interventions in improving the students' mental wellbeing.

RECOMMENDATIONS

It is expected that these findings will provide insights for administrators, educators, and healthcare providers in academic institutions for both preventing mental illness and promoting mental health among students. This could be achieved by:

- Developing collaborative, multidimensional, and culturally sensitive preventive mental health programs.
- Using multi-level interventions to improve mental wellbeing comprising economic empowerment, peer-support, cognitive behavioural therapy were effective in improving mental health among vulnerable adolescents; Mindfulness, Movement, Meaning and Moderator, CBT, psycho-education, digital psychological interventions and physical activity.
- Employing tailored interventions in order to take care of gender as well as individual differences.
- Designing MHL programmes suited to the context of the institution to develop a generation of young adolescents who are more aware and free of mental disorders.

SUGGESTIONS FOR FUTURE RESEARCH

Based on the findings, it would be important for future studies to determine the following:

- Influence of institutional factors on students' mental wellbeing
- Interventions to reduce psychological distress among students in higher learning institutions in Western Kenya.
- The most effective intervention to improve mental wellbeing.
- Effect of type of course on students' mental wellbeing.
- Factors contributing to gender difference in psychological distress

REFERENCES

Agrawal, S., & Sharma, N. (2022). Barriers and Role of Higher Educational Institutes in Students' Mental Well-being: A Critical Analysis. In *2nd International Conference on Sustainability and Equity (ICSE-2021)*, (pp. 173–180). Atlantis Press.

Aina, B. A., & Adebowale, D. K. (2020). Knowledge and prevalence of depression among students on College of Medicine University of Lagos. *European Journal of Public Health, 30*(5), 166.

Amone-P'Olak, K., Kakinda, A. I., Kibedi, H., & Omech, B. (2023). Barriers to Treatment and Care for Depression among the Youth in Uganda: The Role of Mental Health Literacy. *Frontiers in Public Health*, 11, 1054918. 10.3389/fpubh.2023.1054918

Anbesaw, T., Zenebe, Y., Necho, M., Gebresellassie, M., Segon, T., Kebede, F. & Bete, T. Prevalence of Depression among Students at Ethiopian Universities and Associated Factors: A Systematic Review and Meta-Analysis. *Plos One. 12*(10).

Alsaraireh, F., Al-Oran, H., Althnaibat, H., & Leimoon, H. (2023). The Determinants of Mental Health Literacy among Young Adolescents in South of Jordan. *ASEAN Journal of Psychiatry*, 24(1), 1–15.

Asif, S., Mudassar, A., Shahzad, T. Z., Raouf, M., & Pervaiz, T. (2020). Frequency of Depression, Anxiety and Stress among University Students. *Pakistan Journal of Medical Sciences*, 36(5), 971–976.

Ayiro, L., Misigo, B. L., & Dingili, R. (2023). Stress levels, Coping Strategies, and Mental Health Literacy among Secondary School Students in Kenya. *Front. Educ. Sec. Educational Psychology*, 8, 1–10.

Bakesia, G., Olayo, R., Mengich, G., & Opiyo, R. (2023). Prevalence and Sociodemographic Predictors of Depression among Adolescents in Secondary Schools in Kakamega County, Kenya. *East African Medical Journal*, 100(8).

Bale, J., Grové, C., & Costello, S. (2018). A Narrative Literature Review of Child-Focused Mental Health Literacy Attributes and Scales. *JO-Mental Health and Prevention*, 12, 26–31.

Bandura, A. (1997). *Self-efficacy: The exercise of control*. New York: Freeman. https://Psycnet.apa.org

Bantjes, J., Kessler, M., & Lochner, C. (2023). The mental health of university students in South Africa: Results of the national student survey. *Journal of Affective Disorders*, 321, 217–226.

Belay, A. S., Guangul, M. M., Asmare, W. N., & Mesafint, G. (2021). Prevalence and Associated Factors of Psychological Distress among Nurses in Public Hospitals, Southwest, Ethiopia: A cross-sectional Study. *Ethiopian Journal of Health Sciences*, 31(6), 1247–1256.

Bhavana, N. & Otaki, F. (2021). *Promoting University Students' Mental Health: A Systematic Literature Review Introducing the 4M-Model of Individual-Level Interventions*. Front. Public Health, Sec. Public Mental Health.

Bintabara, D., Singo, J.B., Mvula, M., Jofrey, S. & Shayo, F.K. (2024). Mental Health Disorders among Medical Students during the COVID-19 Pandemic in the Area with No Mandatory Lockdown: A Multicenter Survey in Tanzania. *Sci Rep.*, *11* (1), 3451.

Bjørnsen, H. N., Espnes, G. A., Eilertsen, M.-E. B., Ringdal, R., & Moksnes, U. K. (2019). The Relationship between Positive Mental Health Literacy and Mental Well-Being among Adolescents: Implications for School Health Services. *The Journal of School Nursing: the Official Publication of the National Association of School Nurses*, 35(2), 107–116. 10.1177/1059840517732125

Botha, B., Mostert, K., & Jacobs, M. (2019). Exploring indicators of subjective well-being for first-year university students. *Journal of Psychology in Africa*, 29(5), 480–490.

Burris, J. L., Brechtin, E. H., Salsman, J., & Carlson, C. R. (2009). Factors Associated With the Psychological Well-Being and Distress of University Students. *Journal of American College Health*, 57(5), 536–543.

Campbell, F., Blank, L., Cantrell, A., Baxter, S., Blackmore, C., Dixon, J., & Goyde, E. (2022). Factors that Infuence Mental Health of University and College Students in the UK: A Systematic Review. *BMC Public Health*, 22, 1778.

Corley, L. (2013). Prevalence of Mental Health Issues among College Students: How Do Advisers Equip Themselves? *The Mentor*.

Diener, E. (2009). *Well-being for public policy. Series in positive psychology. NewnYork*. Oxford University Press.

Ferrari, M., Allan, S., Arnold, C., Eleftheriadis, D., Alvarez-Jimenez, M., Gumley, A., & Gleeson, J. F. (2022). Digital Interventions for Psychological Well-being in University Students: Systematic Review and Meta-analysis. *J Med Internet Res.*, *28*(9).

Field, T., Diego, M., Pelaez, M., Deeds, O., & Delgado, J. (2012). Depression and related problems in university students. *College Student Journal*, 46(1), 193–202.

Flatt, A. A. (2013). Suffering Generation: Six Factors Contributing to The Mental Health Crisis in North American Higher Education. *The College Quarterly*, 16(1).

Franke, F., Huffmeier, J., Montano, D., & Reeske, A. (2017). Leadership, followers' mental health and job performance in organizations: A comprehensive meta-analysis from an occupational health perspective. *Journal of Organizational Behavior*, 38(3), 327–350.

Hogan, V., Hogan, M., & Hodgins, M. (2016). A study of workaholism in Irish academics. *Occupational Medicine*, 66(6), 460–465. 10.1093/occmed/kqw032

Ibrahim, N., Al- Kharboush, D., El-Khatib, L., Al –Habib, A. & Asali, D. (2013). Prevalence and predictors of anxiety and depression among female medical students in King Abdulaziz University, Jeddah, Saudi Arabia. *Iranian Journal of Public Health*, 42(7), 726–736.

Khaldoun, M. A., Nasir, A. M., & Le Navenec, C. (2014). Mental Health among Undergraduate University Students: A Background Paper for Administrators, Educators and Healthcare Providers. *Universal Journal of Public Health*, 2(8), 209–214.

Kiarie-Makara, M., & Ndegwa, J. (2020). Factors Related to Depression among University Students in Nairobi County, Kenya. *International Journal of Humanities and Social Science*, 7, 35–41.

Korhonen, J., Axelin, A., Stein, J. D., Seedat, S., Mwape, L., Jansen, R., Groen, G., Grobler, G., & Jörns-Presentati, A. J., Katajisto & Lahti, M. (2022). Mental health literacy among primary healthcare workers in South Africa and Zambia. *Brain and Behaviour Journal.*, 12(12), 1–2.

Liverpool, S., Moinuddin, M., Aithal, S., Owen, M., Bracegirdle, K., & Caravotta, M. (2023). Mental health and wellbeing of further and higher education students returning to face-to- face learning after Covid-19 restrictions. *PLoS One*, 18(1), e0280689.

Luo, M., Hao, M., Li, X., Liao, J., Wu, M., & Wang, Q. (2024). Prevalence of Depressive Tendencies among College Students and the Influence of Attributional Styles on Depressive Tendencies in the Post-Pandemic Era. *Frontiers in Public Health*, 12.

Mabrouk, A., Mbithi, G., Chongwo, E., Too, E., Sarki, A., Namuguzi, M., Atukwatse, J., Ssewanyana, D., & Abubakar, A. (2022). Mental health interventions for adolescents in sub-Saharan Africa: A scoping review. *Frontiers in Psychiatry*, 13, 937723. 10.3389/fpsyt.2022.937723

Malagodi, F., Dommett, E., Findon, J. & Gardner, B. (2024). Physical activity interventions to improve mental health and wellbeing in university students in the UK: A service mapping study. JO - Mental Health and Physical Activity. VL - 26 SP – 100563.DO - 10.1016/j.mhpa.2023.100563

Memiah, P., Wagner, F. A., & Kimathi, R. (2022). Voices from the Youth in Kenya Addressing Mental Health Gaps and Recommendations. *International Journal of Environmental Research and Public Health*, 19(9), 5366.

Miller, E., & Chung, H. A. (2009). Literature Review of Studies of Depression and Treatment Outcomes among U.S. College Students since 1990. *Psychiatric Services (Washington, D.C.)*, 60(9), 1257–1260.

Mohamad, N. E., Sidik, S. M., & Akhtari-Zavare, M. (2021). The Prevalence Risk of Anxiety and its Associated Factors among University Students in Malaysia: A National Cross-Sectional Study. *BMC Public Health*, 21, 438.

Moussa, M. T., Lovibond, P., Laube, R., & Megahead, H. A. (2017). Psychometric Properties of an Arabic Version of the Depression Anxiety Stress Scales (DASS). *Research on Social Work Practice*, 27, 375–386.

Moya, E., Larson, L. M., & Stewart, R. C. (2022). Reliability and validity of depression anxiety stress scale (DASS)-21 in screening for common mental disorders among postpartum women in Malawi. *BMC Psychiatry*, 22, 352.

Mthiyane, N., Rapulana, A. M., & Harling, G. (2022). Effect of multi-level interventions on mental health outcomes among adolescents in sub-Saharan Africa: A systematic review. *BMJ (Clinical Research Ed.)*, 13, e066586. 10.1136/bmjopen-2022-066586

Mutinta, G. (2022). Mental distress among university students in the Eastern Cape Province, South Africa. *BMC Psychology*, 10, 204.

Mutiso,, V. N., Ndetei, D.M., Muia, E.N., Musyimi, C., Masake, M., Osborn, T. L., Sourander, A., Weisz, J..R & Mamah, D. (2023). Students Stress Patterns in A Kenyan Socio-Cultural and Economic Context: Toward A Public Health Intervention. *Sci Rep.*, *11*(1), 580.

Najjuka, S. M., Checkwech, G., Olum, R., Ashaba, S., & Kaggwa, M. M. (2021). Depression, anxiety, and stress among Ugandan university students during the COVID-19 lockdown: An online survey. *African Health Sciences*, 21(4), 1533–1543.

Newman, M.G, Llera, S. J., Erickson, T.M, Przeworski, A. & Castonguay, L.G. (2013). Worry and Generalized Anxiety Disorder: A Review and Theoretical Synthesis of Evidence on Nature, Etiology, Mechanisms, and Treatment. *DSM: Diagnostic and Statistical Manual of Mental Disorders*. APA.

Nyayieka, M. A., Nyagwencha, S., & Nzyuko, P. S. (2020). Prevalence of Clinical Depression and Anxiety among Adolescents in Selected Public Secondary Schools in Homabay County, Kenya. *African Journal of Clinical Psychology*, 3(01).

Nyashanu, M., Nuwematsiko, R., Nyashanu, W. & Jidong, D. E. (2020). Lived experiences of stressors and problems of higher education students on teacher education course in the Eastern Highlands of Zimbabwe. *Panafrican medical journal, 36*(289).

Oman, D., Shapiro, S. L., Thoresen, C. E., & Plante, T. G. (2008). Flinders T. Meditation Lowers Stress and Supports Forgiveness among College Students: A Randomized Controlled Trial. *Journal of American College Health*, 56(5), 569–578. 10.3200/JACH.56.5.569-578

Osborn, T., Venturo-Conerly, K., Gan, J., Rodriguez, M., Alemu, R., Roe, E., Arango, S., Wasil, A., Weisz, J., & Wasanga, C. (2021). Depression and Anxiety Symptoms amongst Kenyan Adolescents: Psychometric Properties, Prevalence, Psychosocial and Socio- Demographic Factors.DO-10.31234/osf.io/ze8tf.ResearchGate-https://www.researchgate.net/publication/348540829

Othieno, C. J., Okoth, R. O., Peltzer, K., Pengpid, S., & Malla, L. O. (2014). Depression among university students in Kenya. *Prevalence and Socio-demographic Correlates Journal of Affective Disorders*, 165, 120–125.

Ozer, S., & Schwartz, S. J. (2020). Academic motivation, life exploration, and psychological well-being among emerging adults in Denmark. *Nordic Psychology*, 72(3), 199–221.

Price, E. L., Mcleod, P. J., Gleich, S. S., & Hand, D. (2006). One-Year Prevalence Rates of Major Depressive Disorder in First-Year University Students. *Canadian Journal of Counselling*, 40, 68–81.

Renwick, L., Pedley, R., & Johnson, I. (2022). Mental health literacy in children and adolescents in low- and middle-income countries: A Mixed Studies Systematic Review and Narrative Synthesis. *European Child & Adolescent Psychiatry*. 022-01997-610.1007/s00787-

Republic of Kenya. (2016). *2017/18-2019/20 Education Sector Report*. Government Printers.

Rottschaufer, W. A. (1991). Some Philosophical Implications of Bandura's Cognitive Theory of Human Agency. *The American Psychologist*, 46(2), 153–155. 10.1037/0003-066X.46.153

Sani, M., Mahfouz, M. S., Bani, I., Alsomily, A. H., Alagi, D., Alsomily, N., & Asiri, S. (2012). Prevalence of stress among medical students in Jizan University, Kingdom of SaudiArabia. *Gulf Medical Journal*, 1(1), 19–25.

Schütte, S., Chastang, J. F., Parent-Thirion, A., Vermeylen, G., & Niedhammer, I. (2014). Social inequalities in psychological well-being: A European comparison. *Community Mental Health Journal*, 50(8), 987–990. 10.100710597-014-9725-8 PMID:24664367

Seedat, S., Stein, D., Jackson, P., Heeringa, S., Williams, D., & Myer, L. (2009). Life stress and mental disorders in the South African stress and health study. *South African Medical Journal*, 99(5), 375–382.

Seligman, M. E., & Csikszentmihalyi, M. (2014). Positive psychology: An Introduction. In Csikszentmihalyi, M. (Ed.), *Flow and the foundations of positive psychology* (pp. 279–298). Springer.

Sokolova, L. (2024). *Mental health literacy and seeking for professional help among secondary school students in Slovakia: A brief report*. Front. Public Health. Sec. *Public Mental Health.*, 12(10). 10.3389/fpubh.1333216

The American College Health Association. (2006). American College Health Association, National College Health Assessment. *Journal of American College Health*, 54(4), 195–206.

Theurel, A., Witt, A., & Shankland, R. (2010). Promoting University Students' Mental Health through an Online Multicomponent Intervention during the COVID-19 Pandemic. *International Journal of Environmental Research and Public Health*, 19, 10442.

Tran, T. D., Tran, T., & Fisher, J. (2013). *Validation of the depression anxiety stress scales (DASS) 21 as a screening instrument for depression and anxiety in a rural community-based cohort of northern Vietnamese women*. BioMed Central. http://www.biomedcentral.com/1471-244X/13/24

Tullius, J. & Beukema, L. (2021). Importance of Mental Literacy in times of Crisis: Adolescent Mental Health during the COVID – 19 pandemic. *European Journal of Public Health, 31*(3), 164.

Tully, L. A., Hawes, D. J., Doyle, F. L., Sawyer, M. G., & Dadds, M. R. (2019). A National Child Mental Health Literacy Initiative is needed to Reduce Childhood Mental Health Disorders. *The Australian and New Zealand Journal of Psychiatry*, 53(4), 286–290.

Vaez, M., & Laflamme, L. (2008). Experienced Stress, Psychological Symptoms, Self-rated Health and Academic Achievement: A Longitudinal Study of Swedish University Students. *Social Behavior and Personality*, 36(2), 183–196.

Vazquez, C. Hervas, G.R., Rahona, J., & i Gómez, D. (2009). Psychological well-being and health: Contributions from Positive Psychology. *Annu Clin Health Psychol*, 5, 15–27.

Visser, M., & Wyk, E. L. (2021). University students' mental health and emotional wellbeing during the COVID-19 pandemic and ensuing lockdown. *South African Journal of Psychology. Suid-Afrikaanse Tydskrif vir Sielkunde*, 51(2), 229–243.

Waghachavare, V. B., Dhumale, G. B., Kadam, Y. R., & Gore, A. D. (2013). A study of Stress among Students of Professional Colleges from an Urban Area in India. *Sultan Qaboos University Medical Journal*, 13(3), 429–436.

Wei, C., Karunanithy, D., Khairul, S., Mohan, S. & Kavitha, S. (2022). The prevalence of depression among students in higher education institution: a repeated cross-sectional study. *Journal of Public Mental Health, 21.* DO - .10.1108/JPMH-12-2021-0152

World Health Organization. (2018). *Mental Health Atlas 2017.* WHO Regional Office for the Eastern Mediterranean.

Worsley, J., Pennington, A., & Corcoran, R. (2020). What interventions improve college and university students' mental health and wellbeing? A review of review-level evidence. *J-O Students Mental Health, Vl,* 1(1), 1–54.

Chapter 2
Nursing Students Mental Well-Being During COVID-19 Pandemic:
A Rapid Review

Nestor Tomas
https://orcid.org/0000-0002-4769-2724
University of Namibia, Namibia

Takaedza Munangatire
University of Namibia, Namibia

Hileni Nangulohi Niikondo
https://orcid.org/0000-0001-8286-5654
University of Namibia, Namibia

ABSTRACT

Student well-being is a top priority in higher education policy. However, recent research has shown that at least three out of five adolescents have psychiatric disorders by the age of 21 during the school life. This is inclusive of nursing students who are experiencing high levels of stress as they try to meet their academic demands. Most rapid reviews on mental well-being during COVID-19 have focused on the healthcare workforce, with little attention given to specific groups like nursing students. This review aims to consolidate knowledge and provide actionable evidence on the mental well-being of nursing students during the COVID-19 pandemic. A scoping review was conducted on English articles from various databases, following the PRISMA checklist. The synthesis includes different well-being strategies implemented by nursing students between 2019 and March 2024. This review provides swift evidence and guidance from Cochrane and the World Health Organization

DOI: 10.4018/979-8-3693-4417-0.ch002

on conducting rapid reviews to address the urgent need for policy planning related to nursing student well-being.

INTRODUCTION

The field of nursing is widely recognized as a source of stress for students globally, as indicated by various studies (Cilar et al., 2019; Li & Hasson, 2020; Mulyadi et al., 2021; Tomas & Hausiku, 2024). Clinical education exposes nursing students to the practical realities of the profession, requiring them to care for acutely ill patients amidst challenges such as staff shortages and limited resources (Sterner et al., 2019; González-García et al., 2020). The precision and competency required to care for critically ill patients can often instill fear of making errors among nursing students (Wang, 2019; Aljohani et al., 2021; Baluwa et al., 2021). This fear is heightened by the demanding academic schedules that foster competitive and stressful learning environments (Wang, 2019; Aljohani et al., 2021; Baluwa et al., 2021).

Nursing students, who are often just beginning their professional journeys in the demanding field of healthcare, are routinely exposed to highly distressing situations, including the profound realities of death and the intricate care of dying patients, very early in their educational experiences. This exposure can be overwhelming as they navigate their studies, clinical placements, and personal lives simultaneously. Previous research has established a significant connection between the mental well-being of nursing students and various critical factors such as self-esteem, stress levels, and effective coping mechanisms (Karaca et al., 2019). On the other hand, a multitude of diverse factors—ranging from reduced educational attainment and childhood trauma to social isolation, systemic discrimination, chronic stress, economic hardships, persistent health issues, substance abuse challenges, and even genetic predispositions—have been identified as potential contributors to the poor mental health experienced by nursing students (Cilar et al., 2019). Recognizing these elements is essential in understanding the complex landscape of mental health within this population and the need for targeted support systems.

International research conducted during the global pandemic has unveiled concerning findings regarding the experiences of student nurses. Not only did they endure substantial psychological distress, but they also encountered numerous mental health challenges. These challenges encompassed emotional and social isolation, post-traumatic stress disorder, burnout, depression, and fatigue (Cobo-Cuenca et al., 2022; Labrague et al., 2021). The existing literature suggests that prolonged exposure to the intense stress of the pandemic can have an adverse impact on individuals' overall psychological well-being (Otu et al., 2020; Ceri & Cicek, 2021). The mental well-being of individuals, particularly those in demanding fields like healthcare, is crucial for the effective functioning of society. Those with a strong sense of well-being are better equipped to navigate stress and contribute more effectively to their communities. However, when confronted with unforeseen circumstances such as epidemics, natural disasters, or other crises, individuals, including student nurses, often confront significant challenges that can significantly impact their mental well-being. They must cope with the psychological ramifications of such extraordinary circumstances.

The promotion of emotional well-being among nursing students is a complex undertaking that involves two main approaches: emotion-centered coping strategies and problem-centered coping strategies (Labrague et al., 2024; Labrague, 2022; Park & Kim, 2018), each playing a critical role in fostering resilience and mental health. Problem-centered coping strategies involve proactive actions aimed at addressing the underlying causes of stress that nursing students often encounter, such as demanding academic requirements and clinical responsibilities. These strategies encompass various effective techniques, including problem-solving behaviors that empower students to confront challenges directly, self-assurance techniques that boost their confidence, goal setting that provides clear direction and motivation, and actively seeking appropriate social support from peers and mentors (Caparrós & Masferrer, 2021; De la Fuente et al., 2017; Labrague, 2022; Tomas & Hausiku, 2024). On the other hand, emotion-centered coping strategies involve intentional actions focused on managing an individual's emotional response to stressors, enabling students to navigate their feelings in a constructive manner. This may involve redirection, where students shift their attention away from stressors, avoidance behaviors that provide temporary relief, engaging in distracting activities that offer a mental break, and mental detachment that fosters a healthier perspective during overwhelming times (Labrague, 2022; Tomas & Hausiku, 2024). By integrating both strategies, nursing students can develop a strong framework for emotional resilience that enhances their overall well-being and academic success.

Rapid reviews are conducted as a preferred alternative to systematic reviews when there is a need for prompt information to inform policy and practice within a shorter timeframe (Martin et al., 2022). With the ongoing impact of the COVID-19 pandemic and the significant strain it has placed on healthcare professionals, there is a critical necessity for a timely consolidation of current research findings in this area. Additionally, majority of rapid reviews pertaining to mental well-being during COVID-19 have focused on the healthcare workforce, with limited emphasis on specific groups such as nursing students (Serrano-Ripoll et al., 2020; Preti et al., 2020; De Kock et al., 2021; Martin et al., 2022). In order to effectively care for vulnerable populations during COVID-19 and beyond, it was necessary to conduct a rapid review of nursing students' mental well-being.

AIM

The objective of this rapid review was twofold: i) to examine the effects of COID-19 pandemics on the mental health of nursing students; ii) to evaluate the efficacy of interventions aimed at mitigating the detrimental impact on the mental well-being of nursing students.

DESIGN

A rapid review methodology was utilized to synthesize information and produce practical evidence regarding the mental well-being of nursing students within a condensed timeframe (Eaton et al., 2023). This approach is well-suited for delivering swift evidence during urgent situations (O'Reilly et al., 2021), aligning with guidance from Cochrane and the World Health Organization (WHO) on conducting rapid reviews (Tricco et al., 2017; Garritty et al., 2020).

SEARCH METHODS

The current review included primary studies of both qualitative and quantitative study designs. These studies examined the well-being of nursing students amidst the COVID-19 pandemic. The focus was on the impact of COVID-19 on mental well-being and the interventions to mitigate its impacts. The review was limited to the following key words "(("Students, Nursing"[Mesh]) AND "Mental Health"[Mesh]) AND ("SARS-CoV-2"[Mesh] OR "COVID-19"[Mesh])" using the guidelines Preferred Reporting Items for Systematic Review and Meta-analysis (PRISMA). The following electronic databases were searched: PUBMED; PsycINFO; Scopus; Embase; Emcare and the Cochrane Library. The databases were selected based on their widespread use in the field of health, encompassing both single-discipline and multidisciplinary databases. In addition to this, backward referencing and a Google search were utilized to identify theses, dissertations, and governmental reports (Table 1). Inclusion criteria consisted of studies focusing on university nursing students' mental well-being during the COVID-19 pandemic, encompassing both quantitative and qualitative research designs, and not restricted by geographical location. Additionally, to expedite the review process, searches were limited to English language publications released between December 2019 and May 2024. Excluded from the review were secondary (reviews) studies focusing on graduate nurses or studies involved other health disciplines, as well as those not published in English.

DATA EXTRACTION

Data extraction was performed by a single reviewer (NT) and validated by two authors (MT & HN) using Rayyan online software for qualitative systematic reviews (Ouzzani et al., 2016). The application was also utilized to identify and eliminate any duplicates, as well as to choose suitable studies from the database findings and other resources. Two proficient reviewers (NT & MT) with expertise in conducting systematic reviews were responsible for selecting the eligible studies. Any discrepancies between reviewers regarding the inclusion or exclusion of studies were resolved by a third reviewer (NT). The three authors (NT, MT & HN) employed a structured form to extract pertinent data. The quality of cross-sectional studies was evaluated using the Joanna Briggs Institute tool (Joanna Briggs Institute, 2017; Tomas & Hausiku, 2024). This form encompassed details such as author, date, title, publication type, population, setting, and outcomes related to nursing students' well-being during the COVID-19 pandemic, along with the best practices for implementation.

METHODOLOGICAL QUALITY

The WHO checklist, a commonly utilized quality assessment instrument for rapid reviews, was employed to uphold the review's quality assurance (Tricco et al., 2017). This tool offers a standardized structure for assessing various research methodologies in rapid reviews (Table 2). To guarantee the methodological rigor of the incorporated studies, one reviewer (NT) evaluated the studies, while two additional reviewers (MT & HN) confirmed their accuracy in this review. Any disparities were addressed through collaborative discussion. All studies, irrespective of their quality outcomes, underwent data extraction and synthesis.

DATA SYNTHESIS

The extracted data in this review was synthesized through a narrative approach, which involves compiling and interpreting findings from various sources in textual form to provide a comprehensive understanding of the topic (Martin et al., 2022). The use of quantitative synthesis was deemed unsuitable due to the diverse study designs, contexts, and outcomes present in the literature. Thus, a narrative synthesis was employed to identify key themes and concepts across studies. In line with Popay et al.'s (2006) guidelines on narrative synthesis, the review took note of variations in outcomes, study designs, populations, and content, while also documenting relationships within and between studies. To ensure rigor, three authors (NT, MT & HN) were engaged in the data synthesis process. The eligible studies were independently reviewed multiple times by the authors to establish preliminary themes and the findings from individual eligible studies were organized into a table. These themes were subsequently deliberated upon and scrutinized by the entire research team against the complete dataset. The identification of key themes through a thorough review of primary data exemplifies an inductive methodology (O'Reilly et al., 2021).

The focus of the studies encompassed the well-being of nursing students during the COVID-19 pandemic and the effective strategies for implementing student well-being programs. The WHO checklist for rapid reviews was utilized to uphold the quality assurance of the review process (Table 1).

Table 1. Example of search strategy

Searchers	Results
1. "students, nursing"[MeSH Terms] OR Nursing students[Text Word]	31672
2. AND "Mental Health"[Mesh]	67157
3. "COVID 19"[All Fields] OR "COVID19"[MeSH Terms] OR "COVID19 Vaccines"[All Fields] OR "COVID19 Vaccines"[MeSH Terms] OR "COVID19 serotherapy"[All Fields] OR "COVID19 serotherapy"[All Fields] OR "COVID19 Nucleic Acid Testing"[All Fields] OR "covid19 nucleic acid testing"[MeSH Terms] OR "COVID19 Serological Testing"[All Fields] OR "covid19 serological testing"[MeSH Terms] OR "COVID19 Testing"[All Fields] OR "covid19 testing"[MeSH Terms] OR "SARS CoV2"[All Fields] OR "sars cov2"[MeSH Terms] OR "Severe Acute Respiratory Syndrome Coronavirus 2"[All Fields] OR "NCOV"[All Fields] OR "2019 NCOV"[All Fields]	428,073
1 and 2 and 3	43

Note: Data base searched on 15 May 2024

RESULTS

A total of 158 citations were retrieved and reviewed in accordance with the inclusion criteria, utilizing a study eligibility form to evaluate their titles and abstracts. This rigorous process led to the identification of 13 studies for a thorough assessment and a total of 10 articles in the final review after 3 articles were excluded during appraisal stage (Figure 1). Literature that focussed on the effects of COID-19 pandemics on the mental health of nursing students and on the efficacy of interventions aiming at mitigating the detrimental impact on the mental well-being of nursing students were of particular focus in this review (Table 2).

Table 2. WHO minimum reporting items for rapid reviews checklist

Category	Items to consider	Response
Protocol	Was a protocol used?	No
	If so, was the protocol made public, published in a journal, and/or registered (if so, provide reference and/or registration number, or link to protocol)?	No
Overall scope	Was the scope limited in any way?	No
	Were there a limited number of research or policy questions?	No
	Were the research questions of limited type (e.g. effectiveness only, specific populations)?	No
	Was the number of included studies limited?	No
Comprehensiveness	Was the search strategy limited in any way (e.g. number of databases, grey literature, date, setting, language)?	No
	Were there limits on the types of study designs included (e.g. existing systematic reviews, randomized controlled trials)?	No limit
	Was textual analysis limited (e.g. no full-text review and/or limits on the number of items extracted)?	No
Rigour and quality control	Was the process of dual study selection or dual data extraction modified or omitted?	No
	Was the internal or external review of the final research limited or omitted?	Yes
Synthesis	Was the assessment of risk of bias or quality of evidence limited or omitted?	No
	Was qualitative or quantitative analysis limited or omitted?	No
Other	When making statements about the findings of the rapid review, were the conclusions simplified or omitted?	No
	Is it appropriate to provide a disclaimer and/or limitations section in context with your findings?	Yes. Limitations of the review have been outlined.

Figure 1. Flow chart of searches and exclusions

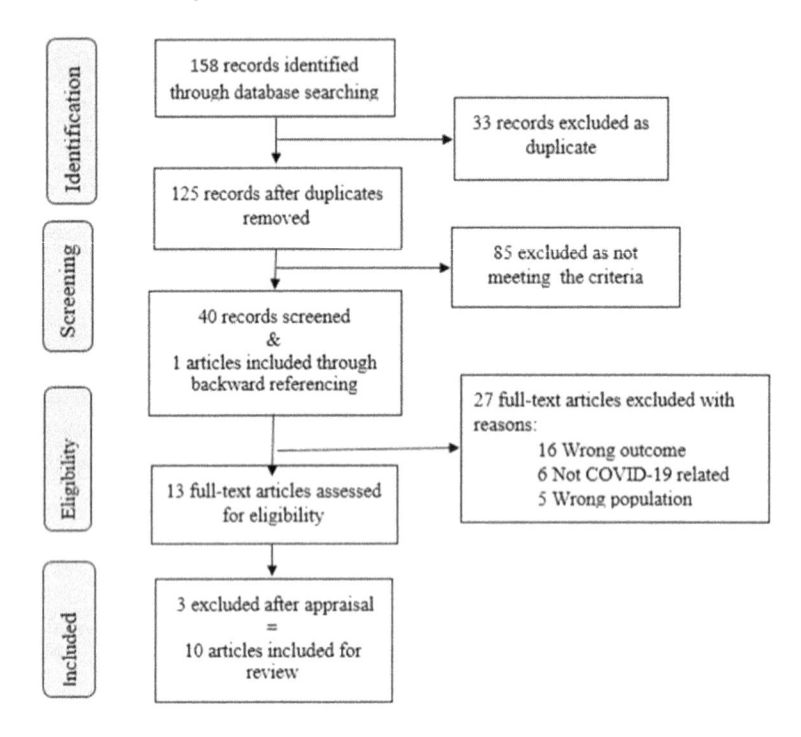

```
Identification:
  158 records identified through database searching
  → 33 records excluded as duplicate
  125 records after duplicates removed

Screening:
  → 85 excluded as not meeting the criteria
  40 records screened
  &
  1 articles included through backward referencing

Eligibility:
  → 27 full-text articles excluded with reasons:
     16 Wrong outcome
     6 Not COVID-19 related
     5 Wrong population
  13 full-text articles assessed for eligibility

Included:
  3 excluded after appraisal
  =
  10 articles included for review
```

NARRATIVE SYNTHESIS

Based on the objectives of the review two major themes emerged include the negative impact of COVID-19 on nursing students mental well-being and measures used to mitigate negative effects of COVID-19 (Table 3).

Negative Impact of COVID-19 on Nursing Students Mental Well-Being

A comprehensive review of nine recent academic studies conducted by various researchers (Usher et al., 2020; Kim et al., 2021; Patelarou et al., 2021; Reverté-Villarroya et al., 2021; Zhu et al., 2021; Albani et al., 2022; Cobo-Cuenca et al., 2022; Hung & Choi, 2022; Eweida et al., 2023) has revealed and shed light on the alarming and distressing levels of stress, anxiety, and depression that nursing students have experienced during the tumultuous times amidst and following the unprecedented COVID-19 pandemic. These meticulously conducted studies have uncovered a multitude of significant challenges faced by these dedicated students, which include the disruptive impacts on their academic schedules, the widespread cancellation of essential classes and exams, the abrupt loss of part-time jobs that many relied upon for financial stability, and the glaring lack of adequate support systems during this challenging period. Furthermore, it is important to emphasize that some courageous students have bravely put themselves at risk by coming into direct, often distressing, contact with infected patients and healthcare staff during their practical training experiences, all in the name of fulfilling their commitments to their education and the healthcare profession.

In a comprehensive study conducted by Kondo et al., (2021), it was observed that there has been a notable decline in preventive health behaviors among nursing students, a phenomenon attributed to a significant reduction in their daily hours of sleep, which is crucial for maintaining overall well-being. Meanwhile, Reverté-Villarroya et al., (2021) posit that the far-reaching impact of the COVID-19 pandemic has led nursing students to experience profound emotional exhaustion, a troubling decrease in self-esteem, and a diminished sense of coherence, making it increasingly difficult for them to navigate both their academic responsibilities and personal lives amidst the relentless challenges posed by this global health crisis. In light of these multifaceted stressors, nursing students are now grappling with the pervasive effects of post-traumatic stress, coupled with insufficient mental engagement (Usher et al., 2020; Cobo-Cuenca et al., 2022; Labrague, 2022). Thus, the compounding pressures from both academic and the COVID-19 pandemic have created a concerning environment for these future healthcare professionals.

Measures to Mitigate the Effects of COVID-19

Four recent studies conducted by various researchers have shed light on effective strategies to mitigate the negative effects of the COVID-19 pandemic. According to prior studies (Kim et al., 2021; Patelarou et al., 2021; Cobo-Cuenca et al., 2022; Labrague 2022), strong family dynamics, resilience, and robust spiritual support have been identified as crucial factors in mitigating the adverse impacts of the virus. Moreover, Usher et al., (2020) suggested key strategies such as prioritized academic leadership, nursing students' reflection on past experiences, and ensuring convenient access to accurate information regarding COVID-19. On the other hand, emphasized the significance of institutional support, psychological interventions, and guidance for affected students in coping with current and future disasters (Zhu et al., 2021; Kondo et al., 2021; Albani et al., 2022; Hung & Choi 2022).

Furthermore, recent research (Kondo et al., 2021), has shed light on additional measures that can significantly help mitigate the negative effects of the ongoing COVID-19 pandemic, which has affected countless individuals across the globe.

Among these essential measures are ensuring that individuals receive sufficient and restorative sleep, which is crucial for maintaining both physical and mental well-being, as well as providing much-needed financial support during these challenging and uncertain times when many people are struggling to make ends meet. Additionally, the implementation of Psychological First Aid (PFA), a supportive intervention designed to assist people in coping with the aftermath of traumatic events, has been shown to enhance the psychological health status and resilience capacity levels of pre-licensure nursing students during the COVID-19 crisis (Eweida et al., 2023). This intervention not only equips students with the necessary tools to navigate their own mental health challenges but also prepares them to better serve others in a healthcare setting, ultimately fostering a stronger, more compassionate healthcare workforce in the face of adversity.

Table 3. Summary of the selected studies

Authors and date of publication	Title	Region	Publication type	Main findings - Impact	Main findings - Interventions	Joanna Briggs Institute tool Quality appraisal
Kim et al., (2021).	Impacts of Coping Mechanisms on Nursing Students' Mental Health during COVID-19 Lockdown: A Cross-Sectional Survey.	San Diego, USA.	Quantitative	High levels of self-reported stress, accompanied by moderate-to-severe anxiety and depression.	• Strong family dynamics and resilience • Robust spiritual support	High
Labrague, (2022).	Specific coping styles and its relationship with psychological distress, anxiety, mental health, and psychological well-being among student nurses during the second wave of the COVID-19 pandemic.	Philippines	Quantitative	• Insufficient Mental Engagement	• Resilience	Medium

continued on following page

Table 3. Continued

Authors and date of publication	Title	Region	Publication type	Main findings - Impact	Main findings - Interventions	Joanna Briggs Institute tool Quality appraisal
Eweida et al., (2023).	Psychological first aid intervention: rescue from psychological distress and improving the pre-licensure nursing students' resilience amidst COVID-19 crisis and beyond	Egypt	quasi-experimental	• Psychological distress	• The implementation of Psychological First Aid (PFA) proved to be successful in aiding the recuperation of pre-licensure nursing students experiencing psychological distress due to COVID-19, as well as enhancing their resilience.	Medium
Patelarou et al., (2021)	Nursing students, mental health status during COVID-19 quarantine: evidence from three European countries	Greece, Spain and Albania	Quantitative design	• Mild depression	• Provisioning mental health interventions at universities should be a top priority.	High
Usher et al., (2020).	The mental health impact of COVID-19 on pre-registration nursing students in Australia.	Australia.	Editorial	• Class and examinations cancellations • Losing part-time jobs, or • Being at risk of exposure to infected patients and staff • Experiencing post-traumatic stress • Feeling a lack of support	• Convenient access to accurate information regarding COVID-19. • Academic leadership • Resilience. • Reflecting on past experience	High

continued on following page

Table 3. Continued

Authors and date of publication	Title	Region	Publication type	Main findings - Impact	Main findings - Interventions	Joanna Briggs Institute tool Quality appraisal
Reverté-Villarroya et al., (2021).	The influence of COVID-19 on the mental health of final-year nursing students: comparing the situation before and during the pandemic.	Spain	Quantitative designs	• Mental well-being self-esteem, emotional exhaustion, and sense of coherence.	• None	Medium
Albani et al., (2022).	The impact of mental health, subjective happiness and religious coping on the quality of life of nursing students during the covid-19 pandemic.	Greece	Quantitative designs	• Anxiety, • Depresssion	• Provide assistance and guidance	Medium
Kondo et al., (2021)	Perceived Control, Preventative Health Behaviors, and the Mental Health of Nursing Students During the COVID-19 Pandemic: A Cross-Sectional Study.	Japan	Quantitative	• Lower rates of preventive health behaviors were associated with shorter hours of sleep per day.	• Institutional support, • Ssufficient sleep, and financial support	High
Cobo-Cuenca et al., (2022).	Longitudinal Study of the Mental Health, Resilience, and Post-Traumatic Stress of Senior Nursing Students to Nursing Graduates during the COVID-19 Pandemic	Spain	Quantitative: prospective longitudinal cohort study	• Anxiety, depression, and post-traumatic stress disorder.	• Resilience	High

continued on following page

Table 3. Continued

Authors and date of publication	Title	Region	Publication type	Main findings — Impact	Main findings — Interventions	Joanna Briggs Institute tool Quality appraisal
Zhu et al., (2021).	An evaluation of mental health and emotion regulation experienced by undergraduate nursing students in China during the COVID-19 pandemic: A cross-sectional study.	China	Quantitative	• Anxiety, depression, or both anxiety and depression	• Psychological interventions	High

DISCUSSION

The recent analysis has brought to light several significant adverse impacts of COVID-19 on the mental well-being of nursing students. The COVID-19 pandemic has necessitated the enforcement of mandatory confinement measures, leading to the closure of universities and requiring substantial modifications in teaching approaches within the academic sector. This shift has prompted a widespread adoption of virtual learning formats (Reverté-Villarroya et al., 2021; Tomas et al., 2022; Maboe, & Tomas, 2023), which had negative effects on students mental well-being. Nursing and health sciences students have faced disruptions in their clinical training sessions due to decisions made by governmental bodies or university administrations in their respective regions (Reverté-Villarroya et al., 2021).

The predominant effects observed include elevated levels of stress, anxiety, and depression among nursing students during the COVID-19 crisis (Usher et al., 2020; Kim et al., 2021; Patelarou et al., 2021; Reverté-Villarroya et al., 2021; Zhu et al., 2021; Albani et al., 2022; Cobo-Cuenca et al., 2022; Hung & Choi, 2022; Eweida et al., 2023). Noteworthy is that the heightened stress, anxiety, and depression levels identified in this study were not exclusive to nursing students but were also reported in the general population (Aucejo et al., 2020; Burns et al., 2020; Son et al., 2020; Romeo et al., 2021). It is evident that students across various disciplines were equally affected by the challenges posed by the COVID-19 pandemic. The fear of contracting COVID-19, stay-at-home directives, and social distancing regulations have notably amplified stress levels among student nurses, who were already under significant pressure in their academic pursuits (Labrague, 2021). International research has shown that student nurses grappled not only with psychological distress but also with additional mental health issues during the pandemic, such as emotional and social isolation, post-traumatic stress disorder, burnout, depression, and fatigue (Cobo-Cuenca et al., 2022; Labrague et al., 2021). Studies have indicated varying levels of stress experienced by nursing students during the peak of the coronavirus crisis (Ersin and Kartal, 2020; Kim et al., 2021; Reverté-Villarroya et al., 2021), with younger and female students reporting higher stress levels (Tomas et al., 2024). Disruptions to academic schedules, class cancellations, inadequate support systems, and increased exposure to COVID-19 risks during patient interactions in clinical rotations have compounded the fear and stress levels among nursing students compared to their peers (Savitsky et al., 2020; Al Maqbali, 2021).

Consistent with the extensive body of research previously (Romero-Blanco et al., 2020; Al Maqbali 2021), this comprehensive review underscores the alarmingly substandard quality of sleep that nursing students have been experiencing, even in the face of allocating additional time for rest during the unprecedented lockdown period. This finding paints a troubling picture of the struggles faced by these future healthcare professionals. Conversely, Kondo et al., (2021) observed a concerning decrease in proactive health practices among nursing students, a trend that can be attributed to a notable and distressing decrease in their daily sleep duration, further exacerbating their overall health and academic performance. These diverse and compounding stressors arising from the myriad challenges posed by the COVID-19 pandemic highlight the pressing and urgent necessity for universities to prioritize the implementation of effective strategies aimed at mitigating post-traumatic stress and supporting the mental health of nursing students, who are already under tremendous pressure as they navigate their demanding academic and clinical responsibilities.

Dealing with anxiety and stress is crucial in managing their impact on health, as emphasized by recent research findings (Savitsky et al., 2020). Studies have highlighted the significance of strong family relationships, resilience, and robust spiritual support in mitigating the adverse effects of COVID-19 (Kim et al., 2021; Patelarou et al., 2021; Cobo-Cuenca et al., 2022; Labrague 2022). Particularly, strong spiritual support has been associated with a reduced risk of depression (Labrague, 2022). A review focusing on resilience, stress, and psychological well-being among nursing students underscored the role of resilience in lowering anxiety levels (Li & Hasson, 2020). Additionally, maintaining social connections and employing self-help techniques have been recognized as effective coping strategies (Hamadeh et al., 2021). Family social support, encompassing emotional encouragement, practical assistance, and a profound sense of connectedness, has proven to be a substantial protective factor for individuals contending with challenges or adversities. As emphasized by

Mariani et al., (2020), this supportive network cultivates resilience and enhances mental well-being, empowering individuals to navigate difficulties with heightened security and self-assurance. The existence of understanding family members can facilitate the development of effective coping strategies and ultimately contribute to improved health outcomes, underscoring the pivotal role that familial relationships play in an individual's ability to flourish.

Furthermore, it was found that prioritizing academic leadership, encouraging nursing students to reflect on past experiences, and ensuring easy access to accurate information about COVID-19 are essential. University academic leaders have been tasked with making critical decisions to safeguard the well-being of students, faculty, and academic communities amidst the rapid changes brought about by the pandemic. Consistent with recent research, institutional support, psychological interventions, and guidance for affected nursing students played a crucial role in coping during COVID-19 (Zhu et al., 2021; Kondo et al., 2021; Albani et al., 2022; Hung & Choi 2022). Providing access to mental health services at quarantine facilities during the pandemic has been linked to higher student satisfaction levels and improved mental well-being during extended periods of isolation (Gedney-Lose et al., 2022). These findings underscore the importance of prioritizing mental health interventions in university settings to effectively address the challenges posed by COVID-19.

Several comprehensive studies meticulously conducted during the ongoing global pandemic have demonstrated that nursing students, who are grappling with unprecedented challenges and mounting pressures in their demanding and rigorous field of study, have employed a diverse and innovative range of coping strategies to effectively navigate the complex mental and psychological hurdles that have arisen from this global crisis. These strategies encompass both problem-centered approaches, which are designed to directly tackle and address the source of stress and anxiety, as well as emotional-centered approaches that aim to manage feelings, enhance emotional well-being, and foster a sense of stability in tumultuous times (Ersin and Kartal, 2020; Kim et al., 2021; Tomas et al., 2024). Additionally, in a thorough and insightful study, Labrague (2022) conducted in-depth research that explored various problem-focused coping techniques, highlighting their significance as effective tools in alleviating debilitating symptoms of anxiety, stress, fear, and depression among nursing students. This research ultimately contributes to their resilience and equips them with the vital skills necessary to cope with and withstand the adverse effects of the ongoing healthcare situation, ensuring that they maintain their commitment to patient care and professional development in the face of adversity.

Nursing students frequently employ problem-solving approaches as coping behaviors, as emphasized by Labrague et al., (2017). This study indicates that these problem-based coping strategies are not only essential for managing the challenges and stresses encountered by nursing students but also have notable benefits for their overall learning experiences, clinical performance, and mental well-being. Conversely, the research indicates that emotion-based coping strategies, often involving avoidance or emotional repression, have been found to be detrimental to the health and academic success of these aspiring healthcare professionals. This highlights the importance of equipping nursing students with effective problem-solving skills to bolster their resilience and adaptability in the demanding field of healthcare.

The adverse effects of the COVID-19 pandemic on the mental well-being of nursing students necessitate universities to prioritize the mitigation of post-traumatic stress and emotional distress associated with the pandemic. This entails implementing robust mental health support systems, offering counseling services, and establishing safe spaces for students to openly express their experiences and emotions. These endeavors are crucial for nurturing resilience and ensuring the academic and personal flourishing of future healthcare professionals in the aftermath of such a global crisis.

STRENGTHS AND LIMITATIONS

In the context of the mental well-being of nursing students during the COVID-19 pandemic, a notable strength of this review is its capacity to provide a rapid synthesis of peer-reviewed articles from diverse settings. The findings from this review provide theoretical implications for policies regarding the provision of mental health services during COVID-19, as well as their replicability for future pandemics. However, the conclusion of this review is ultimately constrained by the quality of the primary studies that were reviewed. The recent review exclusively focused on peer-reviewed publications in English and may not have encompassed all relevant existing and emerging published or unpublished materials on the impact of COVID-19 on the mental well-being of nursing students, as well as the interventions used to mitigate the negative consequences of COVID-19. Finally, considering that the studies examining the mental well-being of nursing students during the COVID-19 pandemic were predominantly conducted in different countries around the world, it is crucial to exercise caution when attempting to generalize the findings to diverse cultural and contextual settings. The study recommends that future research investigate effective interventions to support the mental health of nursing students during and after the COVID-19 pandemic.

IMPLICATIONS ON NURSING EDUCATION AND PRACTICE

The implications of stress on nursing students are multifaceted, affecting both their academic performance and personal health. Heightened levels of stress can lead to a decrease in concentration, impaired decision-making abilities, and compromised critical thinking skills. This emotional decline not only affects the relationships between nurses and patients but also increases the likelihood of medical errors and compromises patient safety.

Indeed, stress among nursing students is a significant challenge that demands attention from educators, administrators, and mental health professionals. By recognizing the difficulties these students face and implementing supportive measures like counseling services and stress management programs, institutions can foster a healthier learning environment.

CONCLUSION

During the unprecedented COVID-19 crisis, nursing students across the globe have been experiencing significantly elevated levels of stress, anxiety, and depression, largely as a result of the chaotic and challenging circumstances surrounding the pandemic. The effects of this global health emergency have profoundly affected the mental health and overall well-being of nursing students, who have been on the front lines of patient care and public health response. The availability of mental health services is crucial in combating the negative psychological effects, including post-traumatic stress, that many students are grappling with. Therefore, it is imperative for universities to promptly and effectively prioritize addressing the post-traumatic stress related to the pandemic and its detrimental effects on the mental health and emotional resilience of nursing students. Future research should focus on exploring targeted interventions and best practices to support the mental health of nursing students during and after the pandemic.

REFERENCES

Al Maqbali, M. (2021). Sleep disturbance among frontline nurses during the COVID-19 pandemic. *Sleep and Biological Rhythms*, 19(4), 467–473. 10.1007/s41105-021-00337-634230810

Albani, E., Strakantouna, E., Vus, V., Bakalis, N., Papathanasiou, I. V., & Fradelos, E. C. (2022). The impact of mental health, subjective happiness and religious coping on the quality of life of nursing students during the COVID-19 pandemic. *Wiadomosci Lekarskie (Warsaw, Poland)*, 75(3), 678–684. 10.36740/WLek20220312035522878

Aljohani, W., Banakhar, M., Sharif, L., Alsaggaf, F., Felemban, O., & Wright, R. (2021). Sources of stress among Saudi Arabian nursing students: A cross-sectional study. *International Journal of Environmental Research and Public Health*, 18(22), 11958. 10.3390/ijerph182211195834831714

Asmar, A., & Hafiz, M. (2020). Improvement students' problem solving ability through problem centered learning (Pcl). *International Journal of Scientific & Technology Research*, 9(2), 6214–6217.

Aucejo, E. M., French, J., Araya, M. P. U., & Zafar, B. (2020). The impact of COVID-19 on student experiences and expectations: Evidence from a survey. *Journal of Public Economics*, 191, 104271. 10.1016/j.jpubeco.2020.10427132873994

Baluwa, M. A., Lazaro, M., Mhango, L., & Msiska, G. (2021). Stress and coping strategies among Malawian undergraduate nursing students. *Advances in Medical Education and Practice*, 12, 547–556. 10.2147/AMEP.S30045734093050

Burns, D., Dagnall, N., & Holt, M. (2020). Assessing the impact of the COVID-19 pandemic on student wellbeing at universities in the United Kingdom: A conceptual analysis. *Frontiers in Education*, 5, 582882. 10.3389/feduc.2020.582882

Ceri, V., & Cicek, I. (2021). Psychological well-being, depression and stress during COVID-19 pandemic in Turkey: A comparative study of healthcare professionals and non-healthcare professionals. *Psychology Health and Medicine*, 26(1), 85–97. 10.1080/13548506.2020.185956633320723

Chaudhry, S., Tandon, A., Shinde, S., & Bhattacharya, A. (2024). Student psychological well-being in higher education: The role of internal team environment, institutional, friends and family support and academic engagement. *PLoS One*, 19(1), e0297508. 10.1371/journal.pone.029750838271390

Chitanand, N., Rathilal, S., & Rambharos, S. (2018). Higher education well-being: A balancing Act. *South African Journal of Higher Education*, 32(6), 168–176.

Cilar, L., Barr, O., Štiglic, G., & Pajnkihar, M. (2019). Mental well-being among nursing students in Slovenia and Northern Ireland: A survey. *Nurse Education in Practice*, 39, 130–135. 10.1016/j.nepr.2019.07.01231476545

Cobo-Cuenca, A. I., Fernández-Fernández, B., Carmona-Torres, J. M., Pozuelo-Carrascosa, D. P., Laredo-Aguilera, J. A., Romero-Gómez, B., Rodríguez-Cañamero, S., Barroso-Corroto, E., & Santacruz-Salas, E. (2022). Longitudinal study of the mental health, resilience, and post-traumatic stress of senior nursing students to nursing graduates during the COVID-19 pandemic. *International Journal of Environmental Research and Public Health*, 19(20), 13100. 10.3390/ijerph19201310036293681

Cobo-Cuenca, A. I., Fernández-Fernández, B., Carmona-Torres, J. M., Pozuelo-Carrascosa, D. P., Laredo-Aguilera, J. A., Romero-Gómez, B., Rodríguez-Cañamero, S., Barroso-Corroto, E., & Santacruz-Salas, E. (2022). Longitudinal study of the mental health, resilience, and post-traumatic stress of senior nursing students to nursing graduates during the COVID-19 pandemic. *International Journal of Environmental Research and Public Health*, 19(20), 13100. 10.3390/ijerph19201310036293681

De Kock, J. H., Latham, H. A., Leslie, S. J., Grindle, M., Munoz, S. A., Ellis, L., Polson, R., & O'Malley, C. M. (2021). A rapid review of the impact of COVID-19 on the mental health of healthcare workers: Implications for supporting psychological well-being. *BMC Public Health*, 21(1), 1–18. 10.1186/s12889-020-10070-333422039

De la Fuente, J., Fernández-Cabezas, M., Cambil, M., Vera, M. M., González-Torres, M. C., & Artuch-Garde, R. (2017). Linear relationship between resilience, learning approaches, and coping strategies to predict achievement in undergraduate students. *Frontiers in Psychology*, 8, 1039. 10.3389/fpsyg.2017.0103928713298

Dodd, A. L., Priestley, M., Tyrrell, K., Cygan, S., Newell, C., & Byrom, N. C. (2021). University student well-being in the United Kingdom: A scoping review of its conceptualisation and measurement. *Journal of Mental Health (Abingdon, England)*, 30(3), 375–387. 10.1080/09638237.2021.187541933567937

Eaton, S. E., Pethrick, H., & Turner, K. L. (2023). Academic integrity and student mental well-being: A rapid review. *Canadian Perspectives on Academic Integrity*, 5(2), 34-58. 10.11575/cpai.v5i2.73748

Ersin, F., & Kartal, M. (2021). The determination of the perceived stress levels and health-protective behaviors of nursing students during the COVID-19 pandemic. *Perspectives in Psychiatric Care*, 57(2), 929–935. 10.1111/ppc.1263633090517

Eweida, R. S., Rashwan, Z. I., Khonji, L. M., Shalhoub, A. A. B., & Ibrahim, N. (2023). Psychological first aid intervention: Rescue from psychological distress and improving the pre-licensure nursing students' resilience amidst COVID-19 crisis and beyond. *Scientific African*, 19, e01472. 10.1016/j.sciaf.2022.e0147236506753

Garritty, C., Gartlehner, G., Nussbaumer-Streit, B., King, V. J., Hamel, C., Kamel, C., Affengruber, L., & Stevens, A. (2021). Cochrane Rapid Reviews Methods Group offers evidence-informed guidance to conduct rapid reviews. *Journal of Clinical Epidemiology*, 130, 13–22. 10.1016/j.jclinepi.2020.10.00733068715

Gedney-Lose, A., Daack-Hirsch, S., & Nicholson, A. (2022). Innovative Management of Nursing Student COVID-19 Cases and High-Risk Exposures. *The Journal of Nursing Education*, 61(4), 217–220. 10.3928/01484834-20220209-0735384764

González-García, M., Lana, A., Zurrón-Madera, P., Valcárcel-Álvarez, Y., & Fernández-Feito, A. (2020). Nursing students' experiences of clinical practices in emergency and intensive care units. *International Journal of Environmental Research and Public Health*, 17(16), 5686. 10.3390/ijerph1716568632781646

Hamadeh Kerbage, S., Garvey, L., Willetts, G., & Olasoji, M. (2021). Undergraduate nursing students' resilience, challenges, and supports during corona virus pandemic. *International journal of mental health nursing*, 30, 1407-1416. https://doi.org/10.1111/inm.12896

Jithoo, V. (2018). Contested meanings of mental health and well-being among university students. *South African Journal of Psychology. Suid-Afrikaanse Tydskrif vir Sielkunde*, 48(4), 453–464. 10.1177/0081246317731958

Joanna Briggs Institute. (2017). JBI critical appraisal checklist for analytical cross sectional studies. 2017. *Diakses Pada*, 22, 2019–05.

Karaca, A., Yildirim, N., Cangur, S., Acikgoz, F., & Akkus, D. (2019). Relationship between mental health of nursing students and coping, self-esteem and social support. *Nurse Education Today*, 76, 44–50. 10.1016/j.nedt.2019.01.02930769177

Kim, S. C., Sloan, C., Montejano, A., & Quiban, C. (2021). Impacts of coping mechanisms on nursing students' mental health during COVID-19 lockdown: A cross-sectional survey. *Nursing Reports*, 11(1), 36–44. 10.3390/nursrep1101000434968310

Kim, S. C., Sloan, C., Montejano, A., & Quiban, C. (2021). Impacts of coping mechanisms on nursing students' mental health during COVID-19 lockdown: A cross-sectional survey. *Nursing Reports*, 11(1), 36–44. 10.3390/nursrep1101000434968310

Kim, S. C., Sloan, C., Montejano, A., & Quiban, C. (2021). Impacts of coping mechanisms on nursing students' mental health during COVID-19 lockdown: A cross-sectional survey. *Nursing Reports*, 11(1), 36–44. 10.3390/nursrep1101000434968310

Kondo, A., Abuliezi, R., Naruse, K., Oki, T., Niitsu, K., & Ezeonwu, M. C. (2021). Perceived control, preventative health behaviors, and the mental health of nursing students during the COVID-19 pandemic: A cross-sectional study. *Inquiry*, 58, 00469580211060279. 10.1177/0046958021106027934915745

Labrague, L. J. (2021). Resilience as a mediator in the relationship between stress-associated with the Covid-19 pandemic, life satisfaction, and psychological well-being in student nurses: A cross-sectional study. *Nurse Education in Practice*, 56, 103182. 10.1016/j.nepr.2021.10318234508944

Labrague, L. J. (2022). Specific coping styles and its relationship with psychological distress, anxiety, mental health, and psychological well-being among student nurses during the second wave of the COVID-19 pandemic. *Perspectives in Psychiatric Care*, 58(4), 2707–2714. 10.1111/ppc.1311135582787

Labrague, L. J. (2024). Umbrella Review: Stress Levels, Sources of Stress, and Coping Mechanisms among Student Nurses. *Nursing Reports*, 14(1), 362–375. 10.3390/nursrep1401002838391073

Labrague, L. J., McEnroe-Petitte, D. M., Gloe, D., Thomas, L., Papathanasiou, I. V., & Tsaras, K. (2017). A literature review on stress and coping strategies in nursing students. *Journal of Mental Health (Abingdon, England)*, 26(5), 471–480. 10.1080/09638237.2016.124472127960598

Li, D., Zou, L., Zhang, Z., Zhang, P., Zhang, J., Fu, W., Mao, J., & Cao, S. (2021). The psychological effect of COVID-19 on home-quarantined nursing students in China. *Frontiers in Psychiatry*, 12, 652296. 10.3389/fpsyt.2021.65229633897502

Li, Z. S., & Hasson, F. (2020). Resilience, stress, and psychological well-being in nursing students: A systematic review. *Nurse Education Today*, 90, 104440. 10.1016/j.nedt.2020.10444032353643

Li, Z. S., & Hasson, F. (2020). Resilience, stress, and psychological well-being in nursing students: A systematic review. *Nurse Education Today*, 90, 104440. 10.1016/j.nedt.2020.10444032353643

Luescher, T. M., Schreiber, B., & Moja, T. (2018). Towards student well-being and quality services in student affairs in Africa. *Journal of Student Affairs in Africa*, 6(2). 10.24085/jsaa.v6i2.3317

Maboe, K. A., & Tomas, N. (2023). Online Assessments and COVID-19: A Qualitative Study of Undergraduate Nursing Students in Southern Africa. *International Journal of Africa Nursing Sciences*, 100590, 100590. 10.1016/j.ijans.2023.100590

Mariani, R., Renzi, A., Di Trani, M., Trabucchi, G., Danskin, K., & Tambelli, R. (2020). The impact of coping strategies and perceived family support on depressive and anxious symptomatology during the coronavirus pandemic (COVID-19) lockdown. *Frontiers in Psychiatry*, 11, 587724. 10.3389/fpsyt.2020.58772433281647

Martin, P., Tian, E., Kumar, S., & Lizarondo, L. (2022). A rapid review of the impact of COVID-19 on clinical supervision practices of healthcare workers and students in healthcare settings. *Journal of Advanced Nursing*, 78(11), 3531–3539. 10.1111/jan.1536035841328

Mulyadi, M., Tonapa, S. I., Luneto, S., Lin, W. T., & Lee, B. O. (2021). Prevalence of mental health problems and sleep disturbances in nursing students during the COVID-19 pandemic: A systematic review and meta-analysis. *Nurse Education in Practice*, 57, 103228. 10.1016/j.nepr.2021.10322834653783

O'Reilly, A., Tibbs, M., Booth, A., Doyle, E., McKeague, B., & Moore, J. (2021). A rapid review investigating the potential impact of a pandemic on the mental health of young people aged 12–25 years. *Irish Journal of Psychological Medicine*, 38(3), 192–207. 10.1017/ipm.2020.10632912358

Otu, A., Charles, C. H., & Yaya, S. (2020). Mental health and psychosocial well-being during the COVID-19 pandemic: The invisible elephant in the room. *International Journal of Mental Health Systems*, 14(1), 38. 10.1186/s13033-020-00371-w32514302

Ouzzani, M., Hammady, H., Fedorowicz, Z., & Elmagarmid, A. (2016). Rayyan—A web and mobile app for systematic reviews. *Systematic Reviews*, 5(1), 1–10. 10.1186/s13643-016-0384-427919275

Park, S. U., & Kim, M. K. (2018). Effects of campus life stress, stress coping type, self-esteem, and maladjustment perfectionism on suicide ideation among college students. *Korean Journal of Clinical Laboratory Science*, 50(1), 63–70. 10.15324/kjcls.2018.50.1.63

Patelarou, A., Mechili, E. A., Galanis, P., Zografakis-Sfakianakis, M., Konstantinidis, T., Saliaj, A., Bucaj, J., Alushi, E., Carmona-Torres, J. M., Cobo-Cuenca, A. I., Laredo-Aguilera, J. A., & Patelarou, E. (2021). Nursing students, mental health status during COVID-19 quarantine: Evidence from three European countries. *Journal of Mental Health (Abingdon, England)*, 30(2), 164–169. 10.1080/09638237.2021.187542033504241

Popay, J., Roberts, H., Sowden, A., Petticrew, M., Arai, L., Rodgers, M., & Duffy, S. (2006). Guidance on the conduct of narrative synthesis in systematic reviews. *A product from the ESRC methods programme Version, 1*(1), b92.

Preti, E., Di Mattei, V., Perego, G., Ferrari, F., Mazzetti, M., Taranto, P., Di Pierro, R., Madeddu, F., & Calati, R. (2020). The psychological impact of epidemic and pandemic outbreaks on healthcare workers: Rapid review of the evidence. *Current Psychiatry Reports*, 22(8), 1–22. 10.1007/s11920-020-01166-z32651717

Rasheed, N., Fatima, I., & Tariq, O. (2022). University students' mental well-being during COVID-19 pandemic: The mediating role of resilience between meaning in life and mental well-being. *Acta Psychologica*, 227, 103618. 10.1016/j.actpsy.2022.10361835588627

Reverté-Villarroya, S., Ortega, L., Lavedán, A., Masot, O., Burjalés-Martí, M. D., Ballester-Ferrando, D., Fuentes-Pumarola, C., & Botigué, T. (2021). The influence of COVID-19 on the mental health of final-year nursing students: Comparing the situation before and during the pandemic. *International Journal of Mental Health Nursing*, 30(3), 694–702. 10.1111/inm.1282733393201

Reverté-Villarroya, S., Ortega, L., Lavedán, A., Masot, O., Burjalés-Martí, M. D., Ballester-Ferrando, D., Fuentes-Pumarola, C., & Botigué, T. (2021). The influence of COVID-19 on the mental health of final-year nursing students: Comparing the situation before and during the pandemic. *International Journal of Mental Health Nursing*, 30(3), 694–702. 10.1111/inm.1282733393201

Romeo, M., Yepes-Baldó, M., Soria, M. Á., & Jayme, M. (2021). Impact of the COVID-19 pandemic on higher education: Characterizing the psychosocial context of the positive and negative affective states using classification and regression trees. *Frontiers in Psychology*, 12, 714397. 10.3389/fpsyg.2021.71439734539516

Romero-Blanco, C., Rodríguez-Almagro, J., Onieva-Zafra, M. D., Parra-Fernández, M. L., Prado-Laguna, M. D. C., & Hernández-Martínez, A. (2020). Sleep pattern changes in nursing students during the COVID-19 lockdown. *International Journal of Environmental Research and Public Health*, 17(14), 5222. 10.3390/ijerph1714522232698343

Savitsky, B., Findling, Y., Ereli, A., & Hendel, T. (2020). Anxiety and coping strategies among nursing students during the covid-19 pandemic. *Nurse Education in Practice*, 46, 102809. 10.1016/j.nepr.2020.10280932679465

Serrano-Ripoll, M. J., Meneses-Echavez, J. F., Ricci-Cabello, I., Fraile-Navarro, D., Fiol-deRoque, M. A., Pastor-Moreno, G., Castro, A., Ruiz-Pérez, I., Zamanillo Campos, R., & Gonçalves-Bradley, D. C. (2020). Impact of viral epidemic outbreaks on mental health of healthcare workers: A rapid systematic review and meta-analysis. *Journal of Affective Disorders*, 277, 347–357. 10.1016/j.jad.2020.08.03432861835

Son, C., Hegde, S., Smith, A., Wang, X., & Sasangohar, F. (2020). Effects of COVID-19 on college students' mental health in the United States: Interview survey study. *Journal of Medical Internet Research*, 22(9), e21279. 10.2196/2127932805704

Sterner, A., Hagiwara, M. A., Ramstrand, N., & Palmér, L. (2019). Factors developing nursing students and novice nurses' ability to provide care in acute situations. *Nurse Education in Practice*, 35, 135–140. 10.1016/j.nepr.2019.02.00530818117

Tomas, N., Awala-Nashima, A. N., & Tomas, T. N. (2024). Gender Differences in Stress Among Students of Higher Education During the COVID-19 Pandemic: A Textual Narrative Meta-Synthesis. In *Mental Health Crisis in Higher Education* (pp. 209-225). IGI Global. 10.4018/979-8-3693-2833-0.ch012

Tomas, N., & Hausiku, L. (2024). Stress and Coping Strategies Among Nursing Students at the University Campus in Namibia. In *Student Stress in Higher Education* (pp. 91–107). IGI Global. 10.4018/979-8-3693-0708-3.ch006

Tomas, N., Munangatire, T., & Iihuhua, S. N. (2022). Effectiveness of online assessments in higher education during the COVID-19 pandemic: Nursing students' reflections in Namibia. In *Teaching and Learning with Digital Technologies in Higher Education Institutions in Africa* (pp. 106–119). Routledge. 10.4324/9781003264026-9

Tricco, A. C., Langlois, E., Straus, S. E., & World Health Organization. (2017). *Rapid reviews to strengthen health policy and systems: A practical guide*. World Health Organization.

Usher, K., Wynaden, D., Bhullar, N., Durkin, J., & Jackson, D. (2020). The mental health impact of COVID-19 on pre-registration nursing students in Australia. *International Journal of Mental Health Nursing*. https://hdl.handle.net/1959.11/31619

Wang, A. H., Lee, C. T., & Espin, S. (2019). Undergraduate nursing students' experiences of anxiety-producing situations in clinical practicums: A descriptive survey study. *Nurse Education Today*, 76, 103–108. 10.1016/j.nedt.2019.01.01630776531

Zhu, Y., Wang, H., & Wang, A. (2021). An evaluation of mental health and emotion regulation experienced by undergraduate nursing students in China during the COVID-19 pandemic: A cross-sectional study. *International Journal of Mental Health Nursing*, 30(5), 1160–1169. 10.1111/inm.12867

Chapter 3
Childhood Loneliness:
A Step Towards Maladaptive Well-Being

Ganesh Kumar J.
Christ University, India

Arnisha Aman
https://orcid.org/0009-0007-5743-3017
Christ University, India

ABSTRACT

A growing concern among school children in recent years has been understanding the impact of loneliness on mental health and overall well-being. This chapter will explore the distinct and complex interplay between the varied social relationships and the wider societal influences that contribute to childhood loneliness. This research aims to explore the different underpinnings towards this growing concern by analysing parent-child relationships, familial relationships, family structures, the socioeconomic status of the family, the school environment, and most importantly, the detrimental impact of epidemics.

INTRODUCTION

Loneliness is a hurtful subjective experience wherein an individual lacks significant social relationship (Weiss RS, 1973). Although loneliness is a common human experience, research has shown that approximately one-tenth of school-aged children experience peer rejection and social isolation (Galanaki E, 2004; Junntila N & Vauras M, 2009). A significant factor of loneliness is that each individual has a distinct and unique experience associated with it and includes many factors in

DOI: 10.4018/979-8-3693-4417-0.ch003

terms of genetics, the immediate environment, and individual experiences (Bartels M et al., 2008). Recent research has tried to distinguish between the constructs of loneliness and aloneness, wherein the latter is deemed to be an objective state where an individual has no one else around and is also measured in terms of the number of contacts, the amount of time spent alone and the kinds of conversations that one engages with others (Jefferson et al., 2023). Loneliness is experienced more during the emerging adulthood period, and the relative emergence is attributed to the isolated experiences during childhood ages, wherein children of eight years of age have reported feelings of loneliness "very often" and "always" around 5% of the time (Lempinen et al., 2018). Individuals who experience prolonged loneliness from childhood to late adolescence have been shown to contribute towards negative attitudes towards school, academics, family and immediate surroundings along with progressive development of maladaptive psychological behaviours (Guay F et al., 1999; Kochenderfer BJ & Ladd GW; 1996; Benner AD, 2011; Frostad P et al., 2015).

In this essence, this study aims to analyse the different underpinnings that contribute significantly to such prolonged experiences of childhood loneliness. The different research questions which will be answered through this review paper are:

- Does the parent-child relationship induce the experiences of loneliness?
- How does the family structure play a significant role in ideating experiences of loneliness?
- How do relationships between and among family members play an influential role?
- Does a family's socioeconomic status influence the feelings of loneliness among children?
- Can a child's school environment play a significant role in imbibing feelings of loneliness?
- Can relative loneliness be a contributing factor towards maladaptive psychological well-being?
- How did COVID-19 impact the transformational process towards a virtual environment?

Loneliness has been widely defined by researchers as the cognitive awareness of deficiency in one's personal and social relationships that is known to ensue affective reactions of sadness, longing and emptiness (Asher & Paquette, 2003). There exists a wide consensus that the subjective experience of loneliness cannot be equated with the child's objective features like their peer experiences and how well they are accepted by their peer groups. It is suggested that children can have a robust circle of interpersonal relationships, yet they might experience loneliness (Asher

& Paquette, 2003). Thus, loneliness is considered to be an internal emotional state that can be strongly influenced by one's social life factors.

Loneliness can be an unbearable experience for many children and is always hidden, defended against, or expressed in disguise in many different forms. These forms can range from either being expressed in their childhood stages by being homesick, not willing to attend school, a sense of agitation or frustration from being around their peers or family, or it may also be expressed during their adult stages where they may cater to severe forms of alcohol or drug addiction or even develop a schizophrenic pattern of living (Peplau, 1955).

PARENTAL INFLUENCE AND CHILDHOOD LONELINESS

During early childhood, each child is known to make efforts to secure attention and attachment from their immediate adults either by engaging in activities or simply by being passive spectators in activities that help ignite their sense of curiosity. These efforts can often be misinterpreted or seen with indifference as the child's attention-seeking behaviour and also serve as a justification for the feelings of annoyance with the child (Sullivan, H.S, 1953). The child expresses his effort to seek an audience in order to see himself in relation to other people and also sees this as an opportunity to yield their increasing need to communicate meaningful experiences. Childhood is considered a period of invention whereby the child develops the capacity to invent and attach deeply valued personal meanings to events, and in this pursuit, as they seek attentive participation from adults, their ways of handling these scenarios with insignificance leave a hollow remark of meaninglessness that can be related to others (Peplau, 1955). In this essence, the child longs to find plausible explanations for the occurrences around them, and these intense feelings of helplessness, smallness, and the need to belong give way to a search for defences against loneliness. This wish to be accepted by their adults and the desire to be cooperative leads the way towards the usage of fantasies. Later, these become the source of difficulty when the child wants to maintain a distinction between what is real and what is fantasy. Therefore, yet again, the adult will not appreciate these mechanisms of defence and will draw a generalised consensus of the child as a liar or as a delinquent, drafting problems for the child as magnified (Reisman et al., 1950).

These regressed patterns of socializing at home make the child inadept towards the different developmental milestones of adjusting to peers. They become the objects of entertainment and fun spearheaded by their peers, and these stable anticipations of real or imagined threats, strengthened by the fears of making mistakes, deepen the sense of social isolation (Asher et al., 2001).

The understanding of childhood neglect becomes an important precursor towards the development of loneliness, wherein a child's health and well-being are negatively affected as their mental, emotional and physical needs are not met adequately (Sciarrino et al., 2018). It has been suggested that children who are neglected are more vulnerable to experiencing loneliness because of their inability to form warm, open and permanent relations with their parents (Rohner et al., 2020). Studies have shown that children who have been rejected by their parents experience a sense of insecurity, exhibit violent and aggressive behaviors and, in some scenarios, also cause feelings of guilt and shame Logan-Greene & Jones, 2015; Moore et al., 2020; Putnick et al., 2012). Such experiences aid in the development of self-perception, further forming their basis of self-assessment. Thus, when a parent meets their child's basic wants adequately and on time by showing love and acceptance, it nurtures a positive self (Birkeland et al., 2014; Mattanah et al., 2011).

In a study conducted on Turkish children and parents, it was found that there was a significant positive correlation between parental neglect and loneliness in children. There was also a significant negative correlation between parental neglect and self-esteem in children, which further indicates that poor child-parent relationship is associated with childhood depression (Ayhan & Beyazit, 2021). Studies have indicated that the mere remembrance of rejection by one's mother in childhood is linked with poor psychological adjustment in adulthood; additionally, the influence of paternal rejection seems to have a greater impact on children due to the perceived higher interpersonal power and prestige within families than do women (Rohner, 2014). Longitudinal studies offer an in-depth understanding of the progression from childhood to adolescence loneliness. In one study aiming to gain a perspective towards this developed a developmental psychopathology framework wherein they hypothesized that adolescent loneliness could have its roots in infancy, specifically during infant behavioural inhibition (BI), as higher levels of BI put an infant at risk of becoming more socially withdrawn (Fox et al., 2005; Rubin & Chronis-Tuscano, 2021; Rubin et al., 2009). Although BI has both direct and indirect ways of functioning, the indirect pathway is of more significance, which has been postulated to predispose a child to behave in a more fearful and avoidant manner in both social and non-social situations (Rubin et al., 2018). Negative parenting is suggested to moderate the stability of BI. When parents restrict their child's independence and beaviour and also try to control their child's activities, it leads to minimal opportunities for them to adjust themselves in social situations (Rubin et al., 2002, 2009). Utilizing this theoretical framework, a longitudinal study found that infants who experienced negative parenting increasingly became more withdrawn two years later (Verhagen et al., 2022). In addition, negative parenting in extremely emotionally arousing situations also contributed to infant inhibition (Verhagen et al., 2022).

Researchers are starting to move away from this unidimensional perspective wherein they are beginning to understand that the cause of a child's cause of loneliness can also be attributed to the perceived experiences of loneliness and stress parents experience in their adult life or have experienced as children. Stress is the demands one places in one's external environment, requiring constant adaptation or change. The varied theoretical underpinnings of stress have explained it how individuals perceive and cope with stress is inclusive of the relative perception of control one has over the stressor, the quality of social relationships and the parent's exposure to childhood trauma (Sapolsky, R.M, 2015; Brosschot et al., 2018). Findings have suggested that parents who have a high internal locus of control and perceive themselves as having quality and meaningful social relationships are less likely to experience loneliness (Hawkley et al., 2010; Cacioppo et al., 2018). Models of loneliness have represented this negative state as a psychological stress response to the social threat of lacking social relationships (Quadt et al., 2020). Such hypervigilance of social threat increases one's perception of stress in general, thereby increasing the likelihood of perceiving events and social interactions as threatening (Brosschot et al., 2018; Hawkley et al., 2010). Parents who undergo such chronic or extreme stress in their childhood, called early life stress, with a profound history of early childhood trauma, are hypersensitive to threats in their environment with marked disruption of the stress response system (Lupien et al., 2009; Kalsea J. et al., 2017). This sense of perceived control of threat and stress in their environment has been associated with positive parenting behaviour (Lippold et al., 2017) and in regulating their child's behaviour (Moreland et al., 2016; Caron et al., 2006). Parents with extreme exposure to childhood trauma develop negative and less sensitive parenting behaviour (Kim et al., 2010). In a study replicating these constructs found that the perceptions of control, loneliness and early stress significantly predicted the stress levels of caregivers, including socioeconomic factors like income, neighbourhood and education. Moreover, the study revealed that caregivers with higher resting parasympathetic cardiac measures moderated the relationship between perceptions of control and loneliness and perceived stress. Parents with high parasympathetic activity were more responsive to the stress-reducing effects of perceived control and were less affected by the stress-enhancing effects of loneliness (Smith et al., 2023).

FAMILY STRUCTURE AND CHILDHOOD LONELINESS

The ecological environment becomes imperative to understand an individual's mental and physical health (Kawachi & Berkman, 2001; Pachucki et al., 2015; Seeman, 1996). The examination of a child's family network provides a unique opportunity to gain insight into the family as a context for development. A family with tight-knit bounds might create an environment in which all members of the family experience safety, security and warmth (Heshmati et al., 2021). The family systems theory becomes an important theoretical framework while considering the stance on the significance of family structure contributing to childhood loneliness, which focuses on the interdependent subsystem functioning within families as organised wholes (Cox & Paley, 1997; Minuchin, 1985). It entails the importance of families to self-regulate and self-reorganise (Cox & Paley, 1997). Bretherton (1985) emphasised the relationships between children's internal representations of multiple family relationships, which signified the importance of considering families as wholes rather than as a group of individuals. Child development as an influence of family bidirectionality focused on factors like physical growth, autonomy and language development in children stems out of the kinds of interactions the child has with their family (Maccoby, 1984). With an increasing number of goals in their developmental milestones, children develop the ability to communicate with their family members and become more aware of their choices and family opinions (Newson & Newson, 1976). Expressing one's emotions becomes important as it enables the child to signify their wants and discomforts (Dunn & Munn, 1985). However, as this force of change is not unidirectional, parents in compliance with the multitude of changes with their children also develop and mend their ways of parental development by either adjusting or adopting different parenting and disciplinary styles (Kuczynski et al., 1987). As with this transactional family dynamics, behaviour systems within families have multiple, hierarchically ordered causes in which events at lower levels of hierarchy influence the higher systems (Schermerhorn & Cummings, 2006). This influential process begins with the actions of individual family members whose influence will impact the members nested with the dyads (Schermerhorn & Cummings, 2008). In this regard, an important, influential aspect that appears to dismantle the family is parent separation and divorce. The resultant parent-child relationship that develops thereafter is within a new family structure built through partnering (Pateels & Bastaits, 2020). After a relative separation, a child is expected to adapt and be flexible towards these dynamic family transitions wherein they are required to learn and cope with the varied norms and regulations of different households (Pateels & Bastaits, 2020). Bastaits and colleagues (2014) foregrounded the parental resource theory (Thomson & McLanahan, 2012; Thomson et al., 1994), wherein the presence of a stepparent as a second adult with their biological parent holds different meanings for the child and causes confusion in compliance to authority and in terms of seeking comfort, affecting the child's well-being, leading isolation. Additionally, according to the instability hypothesis proposed by Fomby and Cherlin (2007), children who experience family structure transitions have difficulty in progressing developmentally. The literature has been divided as researchers have tried to comprehend how parental divorce contributes to loneliness but precisely have followed two major theoretical orientations to guide their assumptions. The first is the stress relief hypothesis (Wheaton, 1990), which postulates that certain life events, instead of being stressful or problematic, can prove to be beneficial as it might offer an escape from a chronic stressful situation. For children who have observed poor parental relationships prior to the divorce, the separation can have a shifting impact from an aversive and stressful home environment (Booth & Amato, 2001; Strihschein, 2005). However, if a parental relationship is otherwise characterised as having low distress, it may prove to be detrimental for the child. Children who have been brought up in harmonious families often do not benefit from divorce as it involves a maladaptive upsurge to their normal standards of living where they have to shift to a novel society, school or may also involve losing complete contact with the non-custodial parent (Amato, 2010). Such unprecedented upsurges can contribute to being the leading precursors to loneliness, with Booth and Amato (2001), providing three plausible reasons towards this: children who never anticipated parental separation find it more difficult to accept the reasons for the separation if children are unable to comprehend such situations they are very likely to construct their own story around the minimal knowledge they possess, thereby increasing the risk that they are likely to blame themselves (Maes et al.m 2012), as such the inability to anticipate such events will contribute towards the feeling that they have less control over the events in their lives and anything they do would cause suffering around them; thus they may willingly choose to be alienated from the world (Bussel 1996, Kim et al., 1997). A study aimed to understand the long-term effects of unanticipated separation examined the influence of parental divorce on young adult relationships and on individual distress; individuals who experienced parental divorce had less parental regard; additionally, if children observed their parents having lower couple satisfaction, their attitudes of disregard is most likely to spill over to different interpersonal relationships, contributing to dissolution and distress (Johnson & Galambos, 2014; Roper et al., 2019).

SOCIOECONOMIC STATUS CONTRIBUTING TO CHILDHOOD LONELINESS

The well-being of children is dependent on varied domains, and studies have implied that the emotional development and adjustment of children are indicated by their family income. The Family Stress Model suggests that financial distress influences parents' psychological state and overall well-being, which directly affects the child (Conger et al., 2000, 2002). This model suggests that the hardships caused by economic pressures cause problems in marital relationships and can be marked by depression, hostility, and anxiety (Landers-Potts et al., 2015; O'Neal et al., 2015).

Such psychological distress can lead to the adoption of unsupportive or insensitive parenting (Newland et al., 2013), reduced quality of time spent, and less resources for social and cognitive enrichment (Nievar et al., 2014). These inconsistencies in parenting and in providing a nurturing environment can cause a culminated sense of frustration, resulting in externalised childhood problems of substance abuse, defiance of authority, poor academic achievements, conduct disorders and higher rates of dropouts (Masarik & Conger, 2017). Although the associations between parental nonemployment causing long-term spillover effects for children are less widely studied, the comprehension of the same has led to an understanding of its impact on the overall health and social isolation of children (Jimenez, 2023). In recent contexts, the economic recessions in countries have been implicated as important mediators for these consequences (Sevilla et al., 2020). In specificities concerning demographics, it was found that the mental well-being of female Australian children was worsened by parental unemployment (Bubonya et al., 2017). Moreover, data collected from the German Socio-Economic Panel (SOEP), paternal unemployment leads to a decreased sense of life satisfaction for male children as they reach their young adulthood stage (Kind & Haisken-DeNew, 2012). The intra-household resource allocation theory (Rosenweig & Schultz, 1983), an influential theory also utilised in the field of economics, explains parents can enhance or undermine their child's health with the help of different channels as a consequence of an income shock, which can persist in their adulthood (Currie, 2009; Mork et al., 2014; Chiappori & Meghir, 2014; Yi et al., 2015). On the contrary, studies from an optimistic perspective have suggested that parents who are unemployed and cater for their children's needs and combat their already existing difficulties can have a positive impact later in their lives with better interpersonal adjustments (Schaller & Zerpa, 2019).

PEER RELATIONS, SCHOOL ENVIRONMENT AND CHILDHOOD LONELINESS

The ecological environment stretches far beyond one's family structure to other areas of a child's socio-emotional development, the most important being the school environment. Children are expected to develop healthy peer relationships while at school, and the difficulties experienced in this regard put the child at risk for future maladjustment (Parker & Asher, 1987). Two distinct developmental pathways have been identified that lead to difficult peer relationships in childhood (Rubin et al., 1990). The first pathway is externalising aggressive, inappropriate behaviour, whereas the second pathway focuses on internalising behaviours in terms of inhibition, social withdrawal and shyness. Projection of such social behaviour can lead to a series of rejections from accompanying peers and classmates, contributing to their attributed sense of loneliness. The chronic experiences of loneliness for a child stem from the adverse adjustment outcomes and have been briefly explained by the transactional model of peer rejection, which suggests that loneliness arises from pervasive patterns of interactions between peers who express their dislike and how the child copes in the face of such rejection (Coie, 1999). These repeated exposure to rejection elicits emotional upheavals where they experience social exclusion and accelerate their negative emotions of sadness and distress (Ladd et al., 2014; Troop-Gorden & Ladd, 2005). There runs a considerable risk that the status of being rejected is maintained across their developmental milestones, causing an imbalance in their psychosocial well-being by making them more susceptible to anxiety and depression.

Social behaviour is known to play a crucial role in contributing to loneliness, promoting very few social interactions and friendships possible (Woodhouse et al., 2012). Olweus (1978), who has contributed significantly to the understanding of child bullying, suggested that children who are submissive and shy are frequent victims of peer bullying, and they hold relatively fewer sociometric nominations. The understanding of withdrawn behaviour has been well explained by Hart and colleagues (2000), wherein the primary observation was to comprehend cultural variations serving as a link between peer acceptance and withdrawal. In this regard, they have identified variations in school-age children across three cultural groups (Rubin et al., 1998). The first behaviour pattern is the "solitary passive" behaviour in which the child is indulged in quiet activity when they are playing, and this kind of behaviour do not directly imply the presence of psychopathology but the researchers believe that the extreme form of this behaviour might indicate the presence of lacking interest in social relationships. The second type is "solitary active" behaviour is when the child, although being present in peer groups, likes to be playing alone or be in a fantasy play, and the researchers have linked this kind of behaviour to rejection by peers. The third type is of "reticent" behaviour is when the child indulges in watching others play but will not be interested in playing with them, this kind of behaviour has been linked to the child having greater levels of anxiety and fearfulness as is associated with the child having a lower social preference. These varied patterns of behaviour projected by a child place them in unfavourable situations, especially when certain labels of reputation are attributed to them, by frequently placing them to be accountable for any ambiguous scenarios (Hymerl, 1986; Hymel, Wagner & Butler, 1990).

Researchers have used social cognition theories to highlight how a child's comprehension of the various psychological issues that their peers face directly influences how the child who is experiencing problems will have their attitudes or behaviours modelled in the social context. This understanding of peer exclusion has been interpreted in a variety of ways (Hennessy et al., 2007). The attribution theory, which is the first of these two views, holds that a child's troublesome behaviour results from their own personal traits that cause them to externalise their difficulties more and project them more outwardly in the community. According to empirical research on the subject, children who exhibit aggressive behaviour are more likely to be judged as having personal traits that are to blame for the behaviour. This, in turn, leads to the child displaying more anger, which further heightens feelings of social rejection (Graham & Hoehn, 1995). Furthermore, Juvonen (1991) discovered in a number of related experiments that when a peer judged a child's aberrant behaviour as the result of the child's personal responsibility, the youngster was thought to have less positive affect and more negative affect.

According to Giles (2003), psychological essentialism is the second hypothesis. It holds that an individual's behaviour is recognised to represent deep, permanent, and internal qualities of the individual. According to the theory, children frequently evaluate aggressive action from an essentialist perspective. This process gave children the capacity to understand social contexts and information about the characteristics or behaviours of those contexts. Although this understanding is not fully generalisable, it has been suggested that it is more prevalent in younger children and that situational factors can have a significant impact. Specifically, the degree of aggression exhibited by a child and the intention behind it, in addition to a variety of social and cultural factors, appear to have a significant impact on whether or not the behaviour displayed by a child who is having difficulties will be interpreted as a reflection of their personal characteristics (Giles & Heyman, 2003).

As such, these theoretical orientations have been successful in explaining and attributing the social and situational factors that can contribute to and maintain the factors of loneliness in children; there still exists a robust need to implement these into experimental stances in recent years.

Teachers' support within a classroom setting is considered to be crucial and encompasses varied dimensions, and researchers have distinguished between emotional and instrumental support (Federici & Skaalvik, 2014; Semmer et al., 2008). Emotional support refers to the student's perception of their teacher to be friendly, caring, trustworthy and empathetic, whereas instrumental support is where the student perceives that they would receive academic help and support from their teachers. This association between the teacher and the student has been based on the attachment theory, which is of the view that children's and adolescents' loneliness with three qualities of the teacher-child relationship- closeness, dependency and conflict (Birch & Ladd, 1997; Burgess et al., 1999). Closeness is defined to function as a form of support as it is characterised by an affectionate and warm relationship between the teacher and the child. Dependency, on the contrary, is when the child is known to exhibit overreliance on their teacher and demands constant attention and affection. However, such characterisations of dependency are said to be different from the child's secure attachment to an adult figure in which the latter, as explained by Bowlby (1969), allows the child to explore their environment and seek closeness but as and when the child is dependent on their teacher, they are less likely to exhibit exploratory behaviour in both interpersonal and academic domains in school. The loneliness-dependency relationship is known to be reciprocal because as the child feels lonely, which can be due to peer rejection, low parental support and low-quality friendships, the child inherently turns towards the teacher, who is perceived to be the only source of support in the school and as the child receives reinforcement for such behaviour they tend to exhibit "clingy" behaviour. A classroom setting can also be characterised by frequent and intense conflict in terms of reduced rapport and discordant interaction between the teacher and the child. Such conflicts can increase feelings of anxiety, anger, frustration and alienation, which predisposes the child to become more vulnerable to withdraw themselves from school activities and exist in complete isolation (Galankai, 2004).

A study (Morin, 2020) aimed to understand the diverse kinds of support that a teacher offers to students by examining how first-year upper secondary school students' perceptions of teacher support and found that there exists a positive relationship between instrumental and emotional teacher support and social classroom environment, but these relationships did not persist over time which suggested that these perceptions may be transient and situational. Instrumental support was indirectly related to loneliness through its positive impact on the social class environment, especially for boys. Additionally, the strongest predictor of school loneliness was students' perceptions of the school classroom environment, where students who perceived their classroom positively were less likely to experience loneliness.

Yet another study aimed to examine the relationship between teachers' attachment orientations and their ability to provide care to first-grade students (Lifshin et al., 2019). Teachers who possessed an avoidant attachment style had more negative effects on children's attachment in the classroom environment; the students in such scenarios perceived their teachers as less responsive, experiencing increased loneliness and decreased liking towards the school. Additionally, it was also found that teachers who are avoidant in nature play a significant role in demoralising even securely attached children.

The Office for National Statistics (ONS), UK, published its findings on loneliness (HM Government, 2018) and found that 11.3% of children aged 10 to 15 years of age report feeling lonely and having decreased satisfaction with their overall health. In this regard, a study conducted in England aimed to explore the relationship between socioemotional well-being, loneliness and school belongingness among primary school children (Palikara et al., 2021). The study is in alignment with the belongingness hypothesis (Baumeister & Leary, 1995), which suggests that school belonging mediates the relationship between socioemotional well-being and loneliness, further suggesting that interventions aimed at improving socioemotional well-being will affect the feelings of loneliness and enhance the child's sense of school belonging.

Future studies can improvise in the same essence to address the importance of socio-emotional competence, making it important to address how we recognise teachers who possess the characteristics of emotionally and socially competent individuals.

LONELINESS, PSYCHOLOGICAL WELL-BEING AND THE IMPACT OF COVID-19

Subjective well-being is considered to be an important indicator of positive mental health. The self-determination theory (Deci & Ryan, 2012) has focused significantly on child well-being, suggesting that the social environment offers opportunities to satisfy three psychological needs- competence, autonomy, and relatedness. When children experience competence autonomy and are socially accepted, they become intrinsically motivated to develop and enhance their self-regulation skills for the perseverance of positive behaviour.

Clinical anxiety is characterised by extreme worry and fear of one's surroundings, which is exacerbated by different stresses. Anxiety is one of the most common mental health issues that affect children. According to behavioural genetics studies, the concept of a "shared environment," which includes nervous parenting, controlling parents, and child-rearing techniques, plays a major role in explaining childhood anxiety and terror (Eley, 2001). In this regard, imbalances in mental health functioning, such as anxiety and depressive symptoms, are deemed to be internalised problems consisting of emotions like worry and sadness and are experienced within the individual (Blossom & Apsche, 2023). A variant of anxiety known as social anxiety disorder is characterised by extreme fear of more than one situation where one is concerned about their behavioural outlook in front of unfamiliar others and has been shown to be directly associated with prolonged experiences of loneliness in the future (American Psychiatric Association, 2013). This triadic association between loneliness, social anxiety, and depressive symptoms has been of interest to many researchers, wherein they have focused on understanding if these internalising problems function as risk factors for one another and if they potentially reinforce and maintain each other. In a comprehensive theoretical model study, understanding these dynamics found that loneliness, social anxiety symptoms and depression were related to each other in a unidirectional way (Danneel et al., 2019; Lim et al., 2016). A longitudinal study aimed at fulfilling the existing research gap found that loneliness and social anxiety symptoms co-develop across adolescents; moreover, the positive slope-slope correlations among these internalising problems show that children who develop any one of these symptoms are at higher risk of simultaneous experiences in other types of internalising problems. Explanations provided about this co-occurrence have been attributed to shared environmental risk factors, more specifically in the interpersonal domain, as in the case of victimisation by peers (Epkins & Heckler, 2011). Additionally, intra-individual risk factors in terms of cognitive biases result in negative interpretations of social situations (Spithoven et al., 2017) along with lower perceptions of self-esteem (Vanhalst et al., 2013).

The social relationships of children were adversely disrupted by the COVID-19 pandemic, wherein 90% of the world's children and adolescents were affected by school closures (UNESCO, 2021). The stay-at-home mandataries disrupted daily life and routines and made children and adolescents the most vulnerable populations to experience loneliness during the crisis (Goldberstein et al., 2020; Wang et al., 2020). An early survey conducted to assess the mental health needs of the youth in the UK found that 80% reported that the pandemic had worsened their mental health, and around 87% reported increased social isolation with reduced access to mental healthcare (YoungMinds, 2020). Longitudinal studies were conducted to assess the extent of increased internalising and externalising problems as a result of pandemic-related stressors (Rosen et al., 2021; Weissman et al., 2021), found that reduced physical activity, increased screen time, witnessing stress, anxiety in parents as well as exposure to increased information causing fear, uncertainty contributed to greater psychosocial difficulties (Fiorillo & Gorwood, 2020). To examine the impact of pandemic-induced loneliness on the quality of life among children in the United States, it was found that loneliness was associated with depression and anxiety, with long-term implications for children's mental health. Additionally, parental stress and distress negatively influenced children, whereas strong family relationships and better family functioning were found to be protective against declines in children's quality of life and an increased sense of loneliness (Skeens et al., 2022).

The closure of schools introduced a new normal for children, who continued their schoolwork digitally in the absence of physical contact (Larsen et al., 2022). The experiences of children vary regarding their ability to concentrate on their school work, meet deadlines and the perceived level of support they receive from their parents and teachers. For some students, it provided them with an increased sense of independence, while for others, they struggled to balance their motivation and self-discipline, while younger children coped with much more difficulty (Bubb S, Jones M-A, 2020; Brooks SK et al., 2020). Research conducted in the North American population found that worry related to COVID-19 and the stress associated with the amount of time spent digitally was associated with increased loneliness and depression in children (Ellis WE et al., 2020).

The disruption with regards to the division of labour led to reallocation of household tasks, children spending an inordinate amount of time at home, not being able to meet with friends, parents adjusting their work environment schedules at home, and children moving, shifting between households due to parental separation led to increased household tensions (Biroli et al., 2020) with increased interparental conflict (Lades et al., 2020). Longitudinal studies aimed at understanding the impact of screen time showed that homeschooling yielded a negative impact on the well-being of children with increased anxiousness and worry about the future; however, positive practices at home with a followed schedule were associated with fewer emotional and somatic/cognitive reactions. The inability to interact with friends physically was also linked with higher emotional reactions, underpinning the importance of peer support for children (Larsen et al., 2022).

At the outset, the flow of stress from parents to children's well-being has been magnified from a negative perspective; a negligible emphasis has been given towards how the potential shift to be at home gave an opportunity to bond and spend more time with one another, thereby reducing the risk of future stressors (Burning et al., 2020). In this regard, to understand the complexities of the pandemic towards the overall well-being of children, future studies should cater to the heterogeneity of experiences by focusing on a broad spectrum of reactions rather than having an emphasis only on psychopathologies (Wade et al., 2020). There is a need to understand these experiences from a developmental perspective as to how different ages accommodate and react to these experiences and while we try to analyse them, the utilisation of qualitative methods and longitudinal approaches can prove to be more effective.

SUMMARY AND CONCLUSION

Family relationships, socioeconomic conditions, the educational environment, and larger societal events such as the COVID-19 epidemic all have a significant impact on children's well-being and their experiences of loneliness. Divorce is a common problem for children from happy homes, which can result in unhealthy reactions and more loneliness. Financial difficulties and poor family income can lead to psychological anguish in parents, which can impact the quality of their parenting and the emotional development of their children. This can result in externalised problems such as substance misuse and scholastic difficulties. Peer interactions and teacher assistance are important factors in the socioemotional development of children in the school setting. Peer connection issues, which are frequently the result of aggressive or reclusive behaviour, cause social rejection and loneliness. While teacher support—both instrumental and emotional—can help reduce feelings of loneliness, its effects could be transitory and fleeting.

Children who experienced disruptions in their social contacts and routines due to COVID-19 were more likely to internalise difficulties such as despair and anxiety, which in turn made them feel even more alone. The pandemic's consequences brought to light how crucial it is to have supportive surroundings and strong family ties in order to protect children's mental health. Prolonged social isolation during the pandemic had a major negative impact on children's well-being, according to longitudinal research, underscoring the need for efficient interventions to improve children's mental health.

The results highlight the intricate interactions among familial, financial, and educational elements that influence kids' feelings of isolation. Economic pressures and divorce are important predictors of loneliness, which can have long-term effects on children's mental health. The Family Stress Model demonstrates how parental behaviour is impacted by financial hardship and how this impacts the development of the children. Comparably, the school setting is essential for reducing loneliness and promoting socio-emotional development, especially when it comes to peer relationships and teacher support.

COVID-19 brought attention to how easily children's social interactions can be disrupted, highlighting the importance of having strong support networks. The pandemic's effects exposed weaknesses in the current child mental health care systems, calling for all-encompassing approaches to deal with these problems.

REFERENCES

Amato, P. R. (2010). Research on Divorce: Continuing Trends and New Developments. *Journal of Marriage and Family*, 72(3), 650–666. 10.1111/j.1741-3737.2010.00723.x

American Psychiatric Association. (2013). *Diagnostic and statistical manual of mental disorders: DSM-5 (5th edition)*. APA.

Asher, S. R., & Paquette, J. A. (2003). Loneliness and Peer Relations in Childhood. *Current Directions in Psychological Science*, 12(3), 75–78. 10.1111/1467-8721.01233

Asher, S. R., Rose, A. J., & Gabriel, S. W. (2006). Peer Rejection in Everyday Life. *Interpersonal Rejection*, 104–142. 10.1093/acprof:oso/9780195130157.003.0005

Ayhan, A. B., & Beyazit, U. (2021). The Associations between Loneliness and Self-Esteem in Children and Neglectful Behaviors of their Parents. *Child Indicators Research*, 14(5), 1863–1879. 10.1007/s12187-021-09818-z

Birch, S. H., & Ladd, G. W. (1997). The teacher-child relationship and children's early school adjustment. *Journal of School Psychology*, 35(1), 61–79. 10.1016/S0022-4405(96)00029-5

Birkeland, M. S., Breivik, K., & Wold, B. (2013). Peer Acceptance Protects Global Self-esteem from Negative Effects of Low Closeness to Parents During Adolescence and Early Adulthood. *Journal of Youth and Adolescence*, 43(1), 70–80. 10.1007/s10964-013-9929-123435859

Biroli, P., Bosworth, S., Della Giusta, M., Di Girolamo, A., Jaworska, S., & Vollen, J. (2021). Family Life in Lockdown. *Frontiers in Psychology*, 12, 687570. 10.3389/fpsyg.2021.68757034421738

Blossom, P., & Apsche, J. (2013). Effects of loneliness on human development. *International Journal of Behavioral and Consultation Therapy*, 7(4), 28–29. 10.1037/h0100963

Booth, A., & Amato, P. R. (2001). Parental Predivorce Relations and Offspring Postdivorce Well-Being. *Journal of Marriage and Family*, 63(1), 197–212. 10.1111/j.1741-3737.2001.00197.x

Bowlby, J. (1969). *Attachment and Loss*. Hogarth Press.

Bretherton, I. (1985). Attachment theory: Retrospect and prospect. *Monographs of the Society for Research in Child Development*, 50(1/2), 3–35. 10.2307/3333824

Brooks, S. K., Smith, L. E., Webster, R. K., Weston, D., Woodland, L., Hall, I., & Rubin, G. J. (2020). The impact of unplanned school closure on children's social contact: Rapid evidence review. *Eurosurveillance*, 25(13). 10.2807/1560-7917.ES.2020.25.13.200018832265006

Brosschot, J., Verkuil, B., & Thayer, J. (2018a). Generalized Unsafety Theory of Stress: Unsafe Environments and Conditions, and the Default Stress Response. *International Journal of Environmental Research and Public Health*, 15(3), 464. 10.3390/ijerph1503046429518937

Brosschot, J., Verkuil, B., & Thayer, J. (2018b). Generalized Unsafety Theory of Stress: Unsafe Environments and Conditions, and the Default Stress Response. *International Journal of Environmental Research and Public Health*, 15(3), 464. 10.3390/ijerph1503046429518937

Bubb, S., & Jones, M.-A. (2020). Learning from the COVID-19 home-schooling experience: Listening to pupils, parents/carers and teachers. *Improving Schools*, 23(3), 209–222. 10.1177/1365480220958797

Bubonya, M., Cobb-Clark, D. A., & Wooden, M. (2017). Job loss and the mental health of spouses and adolescent children. *IZA Journal of Labor Economics*, 6(1), 6. 10.1186/s40172-017-0056-1

Bussell, D. A. (1996). A Pilot Study of African American Children's Cognitive and Emotional Reactions to Parental Separation. *Journal of Divorce & Remarriage*, 24(3-4), 1–22. 10.1300/J087v24n03_01

Cacioppo, J. T., & Cacioppo, S. (2018). The growing problem of loneliness. *Lancet*, 391(10119), 426. 10.1016/S0140-6736(18)30142-929407030

Caron, A., Weiss, B., Harris, V., & Catron, T. (2006). Parenting Behavior Dimensions and Child Psychopathology: Specificity, Task Dependency, and Interactive Relations. *Journal of Clinical Child and Adolescent Psychology*, 35(1), 34–45. 10.1207/s15374424jccp3501_416390301

Coie, J. D. (2004). The impact of negative social experiences on the development of antisocial behavior. *Children's Peer Relations: From Development to Intervention*, 243–267. APA. 10.1037/10653-013

Cox, M. J., & Paley, B. (1997). FAMILIES AS SYSTEMS. *Annual Review of Psychology*, 48(1), 243–267. 10.1146/annurev.psych.48.1.2439046561

Cummings, E. M., Schermerhorn, A. C., Davies, P. T., Goeke-Morey, M. C., & Cummings, J. S. (2006). Interparental Discord and Child Adjustment: Prospective Investigations of Emotional Security as an Explanatory Mechanism. *Child Development*, 77(1), 132–152. 10.1111/j.1467-8624.2006.00861.x16460530

Danneel, S., Bijttebier, P., Bastin, M., Colpin, H., Van den Noortgate, W., Van Leeuwen, K., Verschueren, K., & Goossens, L. (2019). Loneliness, Social Anxiety, and Depressive Symptoms in Adolescence: Examining Their Distinctiveness Through Factor Analysis. *Journal of Child and Family Studies*, 28(5), 1326–1336. 10.1007/s10826-019-01354-3

Deci, E. L., & Ryan, R. M. (2012). Motivation, Personality, and Development Within Embedded Social Contexts: An Overview of Self-Determination Theory. *The Oxford Handbook of Human Motivation*, 84–108. Oxford Press. 10.1093/oxfordhb/9780195399820.013.0006

Dodge, K. A., Lansford, J. E., Burks, V. S., Bates, J. E., Pettit, G. S., Fontaine, R., & Price, J. M. (2003). Peer Rejection and Social Information-Processing Factors in the Development of Aggressive Behavior Problems in Children. *Child Development*, 74(2), 374–393. 10.1111/1467-8624.740200412705561

Dunn, J., & Munn, P. (1985). Becoming a Family Member: Family Conflict and the Development of Social Understanding in the Second Year. *Child Development*, 56(2), 480. 10.2307/1129735

Ellis, W. E., Dumas, T. M., & Forbes, L. M. (2020). Physically isolated but socially connected: Psychological adjustment and stress among adolescents during the initial COVID-19 crisis. *Canadian Journal of Behavioural Science / Revue Canadienne. Science et Comportement*, 52(3), 177–187. 10.1037/cbs0000215

Epkins, C. C., & Heckler, D. R. (2011). Integrating Etiological Models of Social Anxiety and Depression in Youth: Evidence for a Cumulative Interpersonal Risk Model. *Clinical Child and Family Psychology Review*, 14(4), 329–376. 10.1007/s10567-011-0101-822080334

Evans, F. B. (2020). Interpersonal Theory of Psychiatry (Sullivan). *Encyclopedia of Personality and Individual Differences*, 2386–2394. Springer. 10.1007/978-3-319-24612-3_1390

Farrell, A. H., Vitoroulis, I., Eriksson, M., & Vaillancourt, T. (2023). Loneliness and Well-Being in Children and Adolescents during the COVID-19 Pandemic: A Systematic Review. *Children (Basel, Switzerland)*, 10(2), 279. 10.3390/children1002027936832408

Fiorillo, A., & Gorwood, P. (2020). The consequences of the COVID-19 pandemic on mental health and implications for clinical practice. *European Psychiatry*, 63(1), e32. 10.1192/j.eurpsy.2020.3532234102

Fomby, P., & Cherlin, A. J. (2007). Family Instability and Child Well-Being. *American Sociological Review*, 72(2), 181–204. 10.1177/000312240707200020321918579

Fox, N. A., Henderson, H. A., Marshall, P. J., Nichols, K. E., & Ghera, M. M. (2005). Behavioral Inhibition: Linking Biology and Behavior within a Developmental Framework. *Annual Review of Psychology*, 56(1), 235–262. 10.1146/annurev.psych.55.090902.14153215709935

Galanaki, E. (2004a). Are children able to distinguish among the concepts of aloneness, loneliness, and solitude? *International Journal of Behavioral Development*, 28(5), 435–443. 10.1080/01650250444000153

Galanaki, E. (2004b). Teachers and Loneliness. *School Psychology International*, 25(1), 92–105. 10.1177/0143034304041504

Giles, J. (2003). Children's essentialist beliefs about aggression. *Developmental Review*, 23(4), 413–443. 10.1016/S0273-2297(03)00039-X

Golberstein, E., Wen, H., & Miller, B. F. (2020). Coronavirus Disease 2019 (COVID-19) and Mental Health for Children and Adolescents. *JAMA Pediatrics*, 174(9), 819. 10.1001/jamapediatrics.2020.145632286618

Haisken-DeNew, J. P., & Kind, M. (2012). Unexpected Victims: How Parents' Unemployment Affects Their Children's Life Satisfaction. SSRN *Electronic Journal*. 10.2139/ssrn.2006040

Hart, C. H., Yang, C., Nelson, L. J., Robinson, C. C., Olsen, J. A., Nelson, D. A., Porter, C. L., Jin, S., Olsen, S. F., & Wu, P. (2000). Peer acceptance in early childhood and subtypes of socially withdrawn behaviour in China, Russia, and the United States. *International Journal of Behavioral Development*, 24(1), 73–81. 10.1080/016502500383494

Hawkley, L. C., & Cacioppo, J. T. (2010). Loneliness Matters: A Theoretical and Empirical Review of Consequences and Mechanisms. *Annals of Behavioral Medicine*, 40(2), 218–227. https://www.ncbi.nlm.nih.gov/pmc/articles/PMC3874845/. 10.1007/s12160-010-9210-820652462

Hennesy, S., Ruthven, K., & Brindley, S. (2005). Teacher perspectives on integrating ICT into subject teaching: Commitment, constraints, caution, and change. *Journal of Curriculum Studies*, 37(2), 155–192. 10.1080/0022027032000276961

Heshmati, S., Blackard, M. B., Beckmann, B., & Chipidza, W. (2021). Family relationships and adolescent loneliness: An application of social network analysis in family studies. *Journal of Family Psychology*, 35(2), 182–191. 10.1037/fam000066033871279

Hymer, S. (1986). The multidimensional significance of the look. *Psychoanalytic Psychology*, 3(2), 149–157. 10.1037/0736-9735.3.2.149

Jefferson, R., Barreto, M., Verity, L., & Qualter, P. (2023). Loneliness During the School Years: How It Affects Learning and How Schools Can Help. *The Journal of School Health*, 93(5), 428–435. Advance online publication. 10.1111/josh.1330636861756

Johnson, M. D., & Galambos, N. L. (2014). Paths to Intimate Relationship Quality From Parent-Adolescent Relations and Mental Health. *Journal of Marriage and Family*, 76(1), 145–160. 10.1111/jomf.12074

Junttila, N., & Vauras, M. (2009). Loneliness among school-aged children and their parents. *Scandinavian Journal of Psychology*, 50(3), 211–219. 10.1111/j.1467-9450.2009.00715.x19490524

Juvonen, J. (1991). Deviance, perceived responsibility, and negative peer reactions. *Developmental Psychology*, 27(4), 672–681. 10.1037/0012-1649.27.4.672

Kawachi, I., & Berkman, L. (2001). Social Ties and Mental Health. *Journal of Urban Health*, 78(3), 458–467. 10.1093/jurban/78.3.45811564849

Kim, H. K., Pears, K. C., Fisher, P. A., Connelly, C. D., & Landsverk, J. A. (2010). Trajectories of maternal harsh parenting in the first 3 years of life. *Child Abuse & Neglect*, 34(12), 897–906. 10.1016/j.chiabu.2010.06.00221030081

Kim, L. S., Sandler, I. N., & Tein, J.-Y. (1997).. . *Journal of Abnormal Child Psychology*, 25(2), 145–155. 10.1023/A:10257835130769109031

Klaczynski, P. A., & Daniel, D. B. (2005). Individual differences in conditional reasoning: A dual-process account. *Thinking & Reasoning*, 11(4), 305–325. 10.1080/13546780442000196

Koss, K. J., & Gunnar, M. R. (2017). Annual Research Review: Early adversity, the hypothalamic–pituitary–adrenocortical axis, and child psychopathology. *Journal of Child Psychology and Psychiatry, and Allied Disciplines*, 59(4), 327–346. 10.1111/jcpp.1278428714126

Kuczynski, L., & Kochanska, G. (1990). Development of children's noncompliance strategies from toddlerhood to age 5. *Developmental Psychology*, 26(3), 398–408. 10.1037/0012-1649.26.3.398

Ladd, G. W. (2006). Peer Rejection, Aggressive or Withdrawn Behavior, and Psychological Maladjustment from Ages 5 to 12: An Examination of Four Predictive Models. *Child Development*, 77(4), 822–846. 10.1111/j.1467-8624.2006.00905.x16942492

Lades, L. K., Laffan, K., Daly, M., & Delaney, L. (2020). Daily emotional well-being during the COVID-19 pandemic. *British Journal of Health Psychology*, 25(4), 902–911. 10.1111/bjhp.1245032573074

Landers-Potts, M. A., Wickrama, K. A. S., Simons, L. G., Cutrona, C., Gibbons, F. X., Simons, R. L., & Conger, R. (2015). An Extension and Moderational Analysis of the Family Stress Model Focusing on African American Adolescents. *Family Relations*, 64(2), 233–248. 10.1111/fare.12117

Larsen, L., Helland, M. S., & Holt, T. (2021). The impact of school closure and social isolation on children in vulnerable families during COVID-19: A focus on children's reactions. *European Child & Adolescent Psychiatry*, 31(8), 1–11. 10.1007/s00787-021-01758-x33770275

Lempinen, L., Junttila, N., & Sourander, A. (2017). Loneliness and friendships among eight-year-old children: Time-trends over a 24-year period. *Journal of Child Psychology and Psychiatry, and Allied Disciplines*, 59(2), 171–179. 10.1111/jcpp.1280728892142

Lifshin, U., Kleinerman, I. B., Shaver, P. R., & Mikulincer, M. (2019). Teachers' attachment orientations and children's school adjustment: Evidence from a longitudinal study of first graders. *Journal of Social and Personal Relationships*, 37(2), 559–580. 10.1177/0265407519874881

Lim, M. H., Rodebaugh, T. L., Zyphur, M. J., & Gleeson, J. F. M. (2016). Loneliness over time: The crucial role of social anxiety. *Journal of Abnormal Psychology*, 125(5), 620–630. 10.1037/abn000016227124713

Lippold, M. A., Glatz, T., Fosco, G. M., & Feinberg, M. E. (2017). Parental Perceived Control and Social Support: Linkages to Change in Parenting Behaviors During Early Adolescence. *Family Process*, 57(2), 432–447. 10.1111/famp.1228328271492

Logan-Greene, P., & Semanchin Jones, A. (2015). Chronic neglect and aggression/delinquency: A longitudinal examination. *Child Abuse & Neglect*, 45, 9–20. 10.1016/j.chiabu.2015.04.00325910418

Lupien, S. J., McEwen, B. S., Gunnar, M. R., & Heim, C. (2009). Effects of stress throughout the lifespan on the brain, behaviour and cognition. *Nature Reviews. Neuroscience*, 10(6), 434–445. 10.1038/nrn263919401723

Maccoby, E. E. (1984). Socialization and Developmental Change. *Child Development*, 55(2), 317. 10.2307/1129945

Maes, S. D., De Mol, J., & Buysse, A. (2011). Children's experiences and meaning construction on parental divorce: A focus group study. *Childhood*, 19(2), 266–279. 10.1177/0907568211421220

Martínez-Jiménez, M. (2023). Parental nonemployment in childhood and children's health later in life. *Economics and Human Biology*, 49, 101241. 10.1016/j.ehb.2023.10124137068451

Masarik, A. S., & Conger, R. D. (2017). Stress and child development: A review of the Family Stress Model. *Current Opinion in Psychology*, 13(13), 85–90. 10.1016/j.copsyc.2016.05.00828813301

Mattanah, J. F., Lopez, F. G., & Govern, J. M. (2011). The contributions of parental attachment bonds to college student development and adjustment: A meta-analytic review. *Journal of Counseling Psychology*, 58(4), 565–596. 10.1037/a002463521823789

Moore, S. M., Welsh, M. C., & Peterson, E. (2019). History of Childhood Maltreatment: Associations with Aggression and College Outcomes. *Journal of Aggression, Maltreatment & Trauma*, 1–18. 10.1080/10926771.2019.1637989

Moreland, A. D., Felton, J. W., Hanson, R. F., Jackson, C., & Dumas, J. E. (2016). The Relation Between Parenting Stress, Locus of Control and Child Outcomes: Predictors of Change in a Parenting Intervention. *Journal of Child and Family Studies*, 25(6), 2046–2054. 10.1007/s10826-016-0370-4

Morin, A. H. (2020). Teacher support and the social classroom environment as predictors of student loneliness. *Social Psychology of Education*, 23(6), 1687–1707. 10.1007/s11218-020-09600-z

Newland, R. P., Crnic, K. A., Cox, M. J., & Mills-Koonce, W. R. (2013). The family model stress and maternal psychological symptoms: Mediated pathways from economic hardship to parenting. *Journal of Family Psychology*, 27(1), 96–105. 10.1037/a003111223421837

Nievar, M. A., Moske, A. K., Johnson, D. J., & Chen, Q. (2014). Parenting Practices in Preschool Leading to Later Cognitive Competence: A Family Stress Model. *Early Education and Development*, 25(3), 318–337. 10.1080/10409289.2013.788426

O'Neal, C. W., Arnold, A. L., Lucier-Greer, M., Wickrama, K., & Bryant, C. M. (2015). Economic pressure and health and weight management behaviors in African American couples: A family stress perspective. *Journal of Health Psychology*, 20(5), 625–637. 10.1177/1359105315577979725903249

Pachucki, M. C., Ozer, E. J., Barrat, A., & Cattuto, C. (2015). Mental health and social networks in early adolescence: A dynamic study of objectively-measured social interaction behaviors. *Social Science & Medicine*, 125, 40–50. 10.1016/j.socscimed.2014.04.01524797692

Palikara, O., Castro-Kemp, S., Gaona, C., & Eirinaki, V. (2021). The mediating role of school belonging in the relationship between socioemotional well-being and loneliness in primary school age children. *Australian Journal of Psychology*, 73(1), 24–34. 10.1080/00049530.2021.1882270

Parkhurst, J. T., & Asher, S. R. (1992). Peer rejection in middle school: Subgroup differences in behavior, loneliness, and interpersonal concerns. *Developmental Psychology*, 28(2), 231–241. 10.1037/0012-1649.28.2.231

Pasteels, I., & Bastaits, K. (2020). Loneliness in Children Adapting to Dual Family Life. *Life Course Research and Social Policies*, 195–213. 10.1007/978-3-030-44575-1_10

Peplau, H. E. (1955). Loneliness. *The American Journal of Nursing*, 55(12), 1476. 10.2307/346954813268491

Putnick, D. L., Bornstein, M. H., Lansford, J. E., Chang, L., Deater-Deckard, K., Di Giunta, L., Gurdal, S., Dodge, K. A., Malone, P. S., Oburu, P. O., Pastorelli, C., Skinner, A. T., Sorbring, E., Tapanya, S., Tirado, L. M. U., Zelli, A., Alampay, L. P., Al-Hassan, S. M., Bacchini, D., & Bombi, A. S. (2012). Agreement in Mother and Father Acceptance-Rejection, Warmth, and Hostility/Rejection/ Neglect of Children Across Nine Countries. *Cross-Cultural Research*, 46(3), 191–223. 10.1177/1069397112440931 23024576

Quadt, L., Esposito, G., Critchley, H. D., & Garfinkel, S. N. (2020). Brain-body interactions underlying the association of loneliness with mental and physical health. *Neuroscience and Biobehavioral Reviews*, 116, 283–300. 10.1016/j.neubiorev.2020.06.01532610178

Rohner, R. P. (2014). Parental Power and Prestige Moderate the Relationship Between Perceived Parental Acceptance and Offspring's Psychological Adjustment. *Cross-Cultural Research*, 48(3), 197–213. 10.1177/1069397114528295

Rohner, R. P., & Rohner, E. C. (1980). Antecedents and consequences of parental rejection: A theory of emotional abuse. *Child Abuse & Neglect*, 4(3), 189–198. 10.1016/0145-2134(80)90007-1

Roper, S. W., Fife, S. T., & Seedall, R. B. (2019). The Intergenerational Effects of Parental Divorce on Young Adult Relationships. *Journal of Divorce & Remarriage*, 61(4), 1–18. 10.1080/10502556.2019.1699372

Rosen, M. L., Rodman, A. M., Kasparek, S. W., Mayes, M., Freeman, M. M., Lengua, L. J., Meltzoff, A. N., & McLaughlin, K. A. (2021). Promoting youth mental health during the COVID-19 pandemic: A longitudinal study. *PLoS One*, 16(8), e0255294. 10.1371/journal.pone.025529434379656

Rubin, K. H. & Bukowski, W. M. (2011). *Handbook of peer interactions, relationships, and groups*. Guilford.

Rubin, K. H., Burgess, K. B., & Hastings, P. D. (2002). Stability and Social-Behavioral Consequences of Toddlers' Inhibited Temperament and Parenting Behaviors. *Child Development*, 73(2), 483–495. 10.1111/1467-8624.0041911949904

Rubin, K. H., & Chronis-Tuscano, A. (2021). Perspectives on Social Withdrawal in Childhood: Past, Present, and Prospects. *Child Development Perspectives*, 15(3), 160–167. 10.1111/cdep.1241734434251

Rubin, K. H., Coplan, R. J., & Bowker, J. C. (2009). Social Withdrawal in Childhood. *Annual Review of Psychology*, 60(1), 141–171. 10.1146/annurev.psych.60.110707.16364218851686

Sapolsky, R. M. (2015). Stress and the brain: Individual variability and the inverted-U. *Nature Neuroscience*, 18(10), 1344–1346. 10.1038/nn.410926404708

Schermerhorn, A. C., & Mark Cummings, E. (2008). Transactional Family Dynamics: A New Framework for Conceptualizing Family Influence Processes. *Advances in Child Development and Behavior*, 36, 187–250. 10.1016/S0065-2407(08)00005-018808044

Sciarrino, N. A. (2018). *Understanding Child Neglect: Biopsychosocial Perspectives*. Springer International Publishing.

Seeman, T. E. (1996). Social ties and health: The benefits of social integration. *Annals of Epidemiology*, 6(5), 442–451. 10.1016/S1047-2797(96)00095-68915476

Sevilla, A., Phimister, A., Krutikova, S., Kraftman, L., Farquharson, C., Costa Dias, M., Cattan, S., & Andrew, A. (2020). *How are mothers and fathers balancing work and family under lockdown?* IFS. 10.1920/BN.IFS.2020.BN0290

Skeens, M. A., Hill, K., Olsavsky, A., Ralph, J. E., Udaipuria, S., Akard, T. F., & Gerhardt, C. A. (2023). Family functioning buffers the consequences of the COVID-19 pandemic for children's quality of life and loneliness. *Frontiers in Psychology*, 13, 1079848. 10.3389/fpsyg.2022.107984836710839

Smith, B., & Lim, M. (2020). How the COVID-19 pandemic is focusing attention on loneliness and social isolation. *Public Health Research & Practice*, 30(2). 10.17061/phrp302200832601651

Smith, K. E., Graf, E., Faig, K. E., Dimitroff, S. J., Rockwood, F., Hernandez, M. W., & Norman, G. J. (2023). Perceived control, loneliness, early-life stress, and parents' perceptions of stress. *Scientific Reports*, 13(1), 13037. 10.1038/s41598-023-39572-x37563259

Strohschein, L. (2005). Parental Divorce and Child Mental Health Trajectories. *Journal of Marriage and Family*, 67(5), 1286–1300. 10.1111/j.1741-3737.2005.00217.x

Thomson, E., Hanson, T. L., & McLanahan, S. S. (1994). Family Structure and Child Well-Being: Economic Resources vs. Parental Behaviors. *Social Forces*, 73(1), 221–242. 10.2307/2579924

Thomson, E., & McLanahan, S. S. (2012). Reflections on "Family Structure and Child Well-Being: Economic Resources vs. Parental Socialization.". *Social Forces*, 91(1), 45–53. 10.1093/sf/sos11923378674

Troop-Gordon, W., & Ladd, G. W. (2005). Trajectories of Peer Victimization and Perceptions of the Self and Schoolmates: Precursors to Internalizing and Externalizing Problems. *Child Development*, 76(5), 1072–1091. 10.1111/j.1467-8624.2005.00898.x16150003

UNESCO. (2020, March 4). *Education: From disruption to recovery*. UNESCO. https://en.unesco.org/covid19/educationresponse#durationschoolclosures

Verhagen, M., Derks, M., Roelofs, K., & Maciejewski, D. (2022). Behavioral inhibition, negative parenting, and social withdrawal: Longitudinal associations with loneliness during early, middle, and late adolescence. *Child Development*. 10.1111/cdev.1387436449019

Wade, M., Prime, H., & Browne, D. T. (2020). Why we need longitudinal mental health research with children and youth during (and after) the COVID-19 pandemic. *Psychiatry Research*, 113143, 113143. 10.1016/j.psychres.2020.11314332502829

Weiss, R. S. (1983). *The Experience of Emotional and Social Isolation*. Massachusetts Institute Of Technology.

Weissman, D. G., Rodman, A. M., Rosen, M. L., Kasparek, S., Mayes, M., Sheridan, M. A., Lengua, L. J., Meltzoff, A. N., & McLaughlin, K. A. (2021). Contributions of Emotion Regulation and Brain Structure and Function to Adolescent Internalizing Problems and Stress Vulnerability During the COVID-19 Pandemic: A Longitudinal Study. *Biological Psychiatry Global Open Science*, 1(4), 272–282. Advance online publication. 10.1016/j.bpsgos.2021.06.00134901918

Wheaton, B. (1990). Life Transitions, Role Histories, and Mental Health. *American Sociological Review*, 55(2), 209. 10.2307/2095627

Chapter 4
Student Well-Being in Higher Education Institutions:
Academic Pressures

Mary Jebii Chemagosi
Pwani University, Kenya

ABSTRACT

This chapter examines the factors impacting students' well-being within university settings, drawing on contemporary research and theoretical frameworks. Psychological factors, such as anxiety, depression, and academic pressure, exert effects on students' mental health and well-being. Social factors, encompassing interactions with peers, faculty, and staff, shape students' sense of belonging, support systems, and satisfaction with university life. Academic factors like workload, performance expectations, and perceived competence significantly impact students' well-being. Environmental factors, comprising physical surroundings, campus amenities, safety measures, and resource accessibility, play a pivotal role in shaping students' well-being. Societal factors, such as socioeconomic status, cultural background, family dynamics, and societal norms, intricately shape students' perceptions, values, and coping strategies within their university experiences. By fostering a supportive and empowering university culture, institutions can promote the well-being and success of their students.

DOI: 10.4018/979-8-3693-4417-0.ch004

INTRODUCTION

In the bustling corridors of higher education, students embark on a journey that extends far beyond academic pursuits. Within the walls of universities, a diverse tapestry of experiences, challenges, and triumphs shapes the holistic well-being of individuals (Smith, 2018). As scholars and practitioners delve into the intricacies of student life, it becomes evident that myriad factors intersect to influence their well-being. From social dynamics to academic pressures, and from financial constraints to mental health considerations, the landscape of students' well-being is multifaceted and ever-evolving (Jones & Johnson, 2019). At the heart of this exploration lies a profound recognition of the interconnectedness between various aspects of students' lives (Brown & Jones, 2020). As they navigate the transition from adolescence to adulthood, students grapple with a plethora of challenges that extend beyond the confines of lecture halls and libraries. The academic rigors of university life, while intellectually stimulating, can also exert immense pressure on individuals, impacting their emotional and psychological equilibrium. Moreover, the pursuit of knowledge is intricately intertwined with social interactions, extracurricular engagements, and personal development, all of which play pivotal roles in shaping students' well-being (Hurtado et al., 2019).

One of the fundamental pillars of students' well-being revolves around their mental health. The prevalence of stress, anxiety, and depression among university students has garnered increased attention in recent years, highlighting the imperative of fostering a supportive and inclusive campus environment (Smith et al., 2017). Academic demands, coupled with the challenges of adjusting to newfound independence, can exacerbate existing mental health concerns or precipitate the onset of psychological distress. Recognizing the significance of mental health literacy and destigmatizing seeking help are essential steps in promoting a culture of well-being within university communities (Adams & Brown, 2016). Furthermore, the socio-economic landscape significantly influences students' well-being trajectories. Financial constraints, affordability of education, and access to resources profoundly impact students' ability to thrive academically and personally (Jackson & Green, 2018). The intersectionality of socio-economic status with other identity markers such as race, gender, and ethnicity further complicates the equation, underscoring the importance of adopting an intersectional lens in addressing disparities in well-being outcomes among diverse student populations (Gonzalez et al., 2020).

In addition to internal factors, external contextual elements shape the contours of students' well-being experiences. Socio-cultural norms, institutional policies, and broader societal trends intersect to create a complex ecosystem within which students navigate their educational journey. From the prevalence of digital technologies to shifting cultural paradigms surrounding work-life balance, the external environment continuously evolves, presenting both opportunities and challenges for promoting students' well-being in universities (Turner et al., 2018). As we embark on this exploration of factors impacting students' well-being in universities, it is crucial to adopt a holistic perspective that transcends disciplinary boundaries. Interdisciplinary collaboration and dialogue offer invaluable insights into the intricate interplay between psychological, social, cultural, and environmental determinants of well-being (Brown et al., 2021). By embracing a multifaceted approach, scholars, practitioners, and policymakers can develop nuanced interventions that address the multifaceted needs of diverse student populations.

In the ensuing chapters, we will delve deeper into specific dimensions of students' well-being, examining the role of social support networks, academic engagement, campus environments, and institutional policies in shaping students' experiences (Taylor & Johnson, 2019). Through empirical research, theoretical frameworks, and practical strategies, we aim to enrich our understanding of students' well-being and empower stakeholders to cultivate nurturing environments conducive to holistic growth and development (Parker & Jones, 2020). By acknowledging the interconnectedness of various determinants and adopting a holistic perspective, we can unravel the intricacies of students' well-being experiences and pave the way for meaningful interventions that foster thriving and resilience in university communities (Smith & Brown, 2019).

BACKGROUND

Higher education institutions serve as hubs of intellectual discourse, academic inquiry, and personal development, shaping the trajectories of countless students across the country (Mugenda & Mugenda, 2016). Against the backdrop of a rapidly evolving educational landscape, understanding the factors impacting students' well-being in universities emerges as a pressing concern, with implications for individual flourishing and societal progress (Nzomo & Nthiga, 2020). Kenyan universities, like their global counterparts, grapple with a myriad of challenges that intersect to influence students' well-being (Musau, 2019). Academic pressures, exacerbated by the transition from secondary to tertiary education, contribute to heightened levels of stress and anxiety among students (Orodho, 2017). The competitive nature of academic environments, coupled with the emphasis on examination outcomes, places immense pressure on individuals, impacting their mental health and overall well-being (Njenga & Kiriti-Nganga, 2018). Gaps remain in our understanding of the nuanced factors impacting students' well-being in the universities. Research efforts aimed at unraveling the complex interplay between academic, socio-economic, and socio-cultural determinants of well-being are essential for informing evidence-based interventions and policy reforms (Orodho, 2017). By leveraging insights from local and international research, scholars, practitioners, and policymakers can develop holistic strategies that address the unique needs of the students and foster environments conducive to thriving and resilience.

FACTORS INFLUENCING ON THE STUDENT'S WELL-BEING IN NIVERSITIES

Academic Pressures

Academic pressure is a pervasive phenomenon in educational institutions, characterized by the stress and strain experienced by students due to the demands of academic performance. This pressure stems from a variety of sources, including rigorous coursework, high expectations, and societal norms regarding achievement and success in academia. The consequences of academic pressure extend beyond the classroom, affecting students' mental and physical well-being, as well as their social connections and overall quality of life. The academic pressure paradigm within universities is complex and multifaceted, emanating from various sources that contribute to the overall burden on students. Rigorous coursework, with demanding assignments, extensive readings, and challenging exams, forms the backbone of academic pressure. Deadlines for submissions and exams add a sense of urgency, exacerbating the stress experienced by students. Moreover, the high expectations set by peers, professors, and oneself create a competitive environment where the fear of failure looms large.

Numerous studies have highlighted the detrimental effects of academic pressure on students' mental health. The constant pursuit of academic success can lead to heightened levels of anxiety, depression, and burnout among students. According to a study by Mokhtari et al. (2019), academic stressors significantly predict symptoms of depression and anxiety among university students. Additionally, the stigma surrounding mental health issues further compounds the problem, as students may be hesitant to seek help due to fear of judgment or adverse consequences on their academic standing (Eisenberg et al., 2007). In addition to its impact on mental health, academic pressure also takes a toll on students' physical well-being. Irregular sleep patterns, unhealthy dietary habits, and lack of exercise are common consequences of prioritizing academic pursuits over self-care. These lifestyle factors can lead to fatigue, weakened immune systems, and chronic illnesses, further hindering students' academic performance and overall quality of life (Hershner & Chervin, 2014). Furthermore, academic pressures often isolate students from their social support networks. The demands of coursework and extracurricular activities leave little time for meaningful social interactions, leading to feelings of loneliness and alienation. The competitive nature of academic environments may foster mistrust and rivalry among peers, hindering the formation of genuine connections and support systems (Wang et al., 2020).

Institutional Policies

A policy, in the context of universities, refers to a set of rules, regulations, and guidelines established by the institution to govern various aspects of student life and academic affairs. These policies serve as frameworks for decision-making and behavior, shaping the environment in which students learn and interact. Institutional policies encompass a wide range of areas, including academic conduct, campus safety, diversity, and student support services, all of which contribute to the overall well-being of students in universities. Academic policies are among the most influential factors shaping the educational experience and well-being of students. Grading policies, for example, dictate how students' academic performance is assessed and evaluated. Research indicates that high-stakes assessments and rigid grading curves can contribute to academic anxiety and feelings of inadequacy among students (Johns et al., 2019). Conversely, implementing flexible grading schemes and providing academic support resources can alleviate student stress and foster a positive learning environment (Roberts & Styron, 2018). Additionally, institutional policies related to academic integrity and plagiarism detection can impact student well-being. While upholding academic integrity is crucial, excessively punitive measures may deter students from seeking help or admitting mistakes, leading to heightened stress and fear of failure (Bretag et al., 2018). Therefore, universities should strive to balance deterrence with educational interventions and support services to promote a culture of honesty and accountability without compromising student well-being.

Ensuring campus safety is paramount for promoting student well-being and fostering a conducive learning environment. Campus safety policies encompass measures such as emergency response protocols, security personnel presence, and preventive initiatives. A study by Fisher and Sloan (2019) found that students' perceptions of safety significantly influence their overall well-being and academic performance. Strict enforcement of safety policies can enhance students' sense of security and reduce anxiety levels, contributing to improved mental health outcomes. However, overly restrictive security measures or incidents of racial profiling can undermine students' trust in the institution and exacerbate feelings of marginalization among minority groups (Schlosser & Groesz, 2019). Therefore, universities must implement inclusive and culturally sensitive safety policies that prioritize the well-being and dignity of all students while maintaining a safe campus environment. Promoting diversity and inclusion is essential for fostering a supportive and enriching learning environment in universities. Diversity and inclusion policies encompass initiatives such as affirmative action, cultural competency training, and inclusive curriculum development. Research suggests that diverse learning environments enhance students' cognitive skills, critical thinking abilities, and empathy, contributing to their overall well-being and academic success (Hurtado et al., 2019).

Conversely, the absence of inclusive policies or incidents of discrimination can have detrimental effects on student well-being, leading to feelings of alienation, isolation, and psychological distress (Turner et al., 2020). Therefore, universities must prioritize the development and implementation of inclusive policies that celebrate diversity, address systemic inequalities, and create a sense of belonging for all students. Access to comprehensive student support services is crucial for addressing the diverse needs and challenges faced by students in universities. Institutional policies governing student support services encompass provisions such as counseling, academic advising, healthcare, and financial aid. Research indicates that adequate support services contribute to higher retention rates, improved academic performance, and enhanced overall well-being among students (King et al., 2018). However, budgetary constraints or insufficient resources may limit the availability and effectiveness of support services, particularly for marginalized or underrepresented student populations (Bridges et al., 2020). Therefore, universities must prioritize funding and resource allocation to ensure equitable access to support services for all students, regardless of their background or circumstances.

Socio-Economic Factors

Socio-economic factors play a crucial role in shaping student well-being in universities across various aspects of academic, social, and emotional life. These factors encompass elements such as financial resources, family background, employment status, and access to support services, all of which can significantly impact students' experiences and outcomes in higher education. Financial constraints often present significant challenges for students from lower socio-economic backgrounds. The cost of tuition, textbooks, housing, and other expenses can create financial stress and limit access to essential resources. Research has shown that financial strain can negatively affect students' mental health, academic performance, and overall well-being (Gonzalez, 2016). High levels of student debt and the need to work part-time or full-time jobs to support themselves financially can further exacerbate stress and fatigue, impacting students' ability to fully engage in their studies and participate in campus life (Browning et al., 2017).

Moreover, students from lower socio-economic backgrounds may face additional barriers to accessing support services and resources available on campus. Limited financial resources may restrict their ability to afford counseling services, academic tutoring, or extracurricular activities that contribute to a well-rounded university experience. As a result, these students may feel isolated and disconnected from the campus community, leading to feelings of alienation and low self-esteem (Ryder et al., 2020). Family background also influences student well-being in universities. Students from disadvantaged backgrounds may lack the academic support and encouragement needed to navigate the challenges of higher education successfully. They may come from families with limited educational attainment or face cultural expectations that prioritize immediate financial stability over pursuing higher education. These factors can contribute to feelings of imposter syndrome and self-doubt among students, particularly when they encounter academic difficulties or face social pressures to conform to societal norms (Stephens et al., 2012).

Furthermore, employment status can significantly impact student well-being in universities. Many students, particularly those from lower socio-economic backgrounds, work part-time or full-time jobs to support themselves financially while attending school. Balancing work and academic responsibilities can be challenging, leading to increased stress, fatigue, and time constraints. Research has shown that students who work more than 20 hours per week are at higher risk of experiencing burnout and lower academic performance (Cotten & Wilson, 2006). Additionally, working long hours may limit students' opportunities for social engagement and extracurricular involvement, further isolating them from the university community. Access to support services is another critical aspect affected by socio-economic factors. Students from disadvantaged backgrounds may face barriers in accessing counseling, academic advising, and other support services due to financial constraints or lack of awareness about available resources. Limited availability of affordable mental health services on campus can exacerbate stress and anxiety among students, particularly those experiencing financial hardship or academic pressure (Soria et al., 2013). Moreover, stigma surrounding mental health issues may deter students from seeking help, further exacerbating the negative impact on their well-being.

Ways Through Which University Students Misuse Their Finances

o Excessive Spending on Non-Essentials: Students may overspend on non-essential items such as entertainment, dining out, or clothing, leading to financial strain.
o Impulse Buying: Impulse buying, especially with the availability of online shopping platforms, can quickly drain a student's finances without careful consideration of budgetary constraints.
o Ignoring Budgeting: Many students fail to create and adhere to a budget, which can result in overspending or neglecting essential expenses like textbooks, rent, or utilities.

- o Using Credit Cards Irresponsibly: Some students may rely on credit cards without understanding the implications of high-interest rates and accumulating debt. Carrying balances on credit cards can lead to long-term financial difficulties.
- o Not Taking Advantage of Student Discounts: Failure to utilize student discounts and deals on various services and products can result in missed opportunities for saving money.
- o Skipping Meals or Eating Out Too Often: Students may skip meals due to budget constraints or spend excessively on dining out rather than opting for more affordable meal options.
- o Ignoring Financial Aid Opportunities: Some students may overlook available financial aid opportunities such as scholarships, grants, or work-study programs, which could help alleviate financial pressure.
- o Borrowing Money from High-Interest Sources: In times of financial need, students may resort to borrowing money from high-interest sources such as payday lenders or loan sharks, which can lead to a cycle of debt.

Socio-Cultural Dynamics

Universities are dynamic environments where students from diverse socio-cultural backgrounds come together to pursue higher education. Socio-cultural factors encompass elements such as cultural norms, societal expectations, family dynamics, and social support networks, all of which can significantly influence student well-being in universities. This essay explores how socio-cultural factors affect various aspects of student well-being, including academic performance, mental health, social integration, and sense of belonging, highlighting the importance of recognizing and addressing these factors to create a supportive and inclusive campus environment.

Impact on Academic Performance

Socio-cultural factors can have a profound impact on students' academic performance in universities. Cultural expectations regarding education, family dynamics, and socio-economic status can shape students' attitudes towards learning, motivation levels, and study habits. Research has shown that students from collectivist cultures, where family obligations and social harmony are prioritized, may face challenges in adapting to the individualistic and competitive academic environment prevalent in many Western universities (Hong et al., 2017). Moreover, students from marginalized or underrepresented communities may encounter systemic barriers that impede their academic success. For example, first-generation college students and students from low-income backgrounds may lack access to educational resources and support networks, hindering their ability to excel academically (Stephens et al., 2012). Similarly, students from minority groups may experience discrimination or macroaggressions in academic settings, leading to feelings of alienation and diminished self-confidence (Harper, 2012).

Impact on Mental Health

Socio-cultural factors also play a significant role in shaping students' mental health and well-being in universities. Cultural attitudes towards mental health, stigma surrounding help-seeking behavior, and access to culturally competent care can all influence students' willingness to seek support for mental health concerns. Research suggests that students from certain cultural backgrounds may be less likely to disclose mental health issues or seek professional help due to cultural norms emphasizing self-reliance and resilience (Hwang et al., 2015).

Impact on Social Integration

Socio-cultural factors influence students' social integration and sense of belonging within the university community. Cultural differences, language barriers, and social identity dynamics can affect students' ability to form meaningful connections with their peers and engage in campus life. International students, for example, may experience challenges in navigating cultural nuances and building social networks in a foreign academic environment (Ward et al., 2016).

Additionally, students from minority or underrepresented groups may face exclusion or marginalization within social and academic spaces on campus. Discriminatory attitudes, lack of representation in curricular and extracurricular activities, and macroaggressions can contribute to feelings of isolation and disconnection among these students (Museus et al., 2011). Therefore, universities must prioritize inclusive programming, cultural competency training, and intercultural dialogue to promote social cohesion and foster a sense of belonging among all students.

Impact on Sense of Belonging

Socio-cultural factors profoundly influence students' sense of belonging and identity development in universities. Cultural identity, social identity, and intersectionality shape students' perceptions of themselves and their place within the university community. Students from marginalized or underrepresented backgrounds may grapple with issues of identity negotiation, imposter syndrome, and cultural adjustment as they navigate the complexities of higher education (Hurtado et al., 2019). Moreover, institutional culture and campus climate can either reinforce or challenge students' sense of belonging. Universities that prioritize diversity, equity, and inclusion initiatives create environments where students feel valued, affirmed, and empowered to fully participate in academic and social life (Strayhorn, 2012). Conversely, institutions that perpetuate systemic inequities or fail to address issues of diversity and inclusion may inadvertently contribute to feelings of isolation and marginalization among certain student groups.

CAMPUS ENVIRONMENT

The campus environment plays a pivotal role in shaping the well-being of students in universities. From physical infrastructure and safety measures to social support networks and access to healthcare services, various aspects of the campus environment contribute to students' overall health and happiness. This essay explores how the campus environment influences student well-being, examining its effects on physical safety, social connectedness, and access to healthcare services and wellness programs, emphasizing the importance of creating a supportive and conducive environment for student success.

Physical Infrastructure and Safety

The physical infrastructure of a university campus, including buildings, grounds, and amenities, significantly impacts students' sense of safety and well-being. Well-maintained facilities, adequate lighting, and clear signage contribute to a welcoming and secure environment, while dilapidated buildings and poorly maintained grounds can evoke feelings of discomfort and insecurity among students (Pascarella & Terenzini, 2005). Moreover, safety measures such as surveillance cameras, emergency call boxes, and security patrols play a crucial role in ensuring the physical safety of students on campus. Research has shown that students' perceptions of campus safety influence their overall well-being and academic performance (Fisher & Sloan, 2019). Therefore, universities must prioritize investments in campus infrastructure and safety measures to create an environment where students feel protected and can focus on their academic pursuits without fear of harm.

Social Support Networks and Community Engagement

The campus environment also shapes students' social support networks and community engagement, which are essential components of their overall well-being. Opportunities for social interaction, peer support, and involvement in campus organizations contribute to students' sense of belonging and connectedness (Tinto,

2012). Research has demonstrated that students who are actively engaged in campus life report higher levels of satisfaction and well-being (Kuh, 2009). Furthermore, the presence of supportive faculty and staff members who provide mentorship and guidance enhances students' social support networks and contributes to their academic and personal development (Hurtado et al., 2012). Therefore, universities should foster a culture of inclusivity and community engagement by offering diverse programming, promoting student leadership opportunities, and facilitating meaningful interactions between students and faculty outside the classroom.

Access to Healthcare Services and Wellness Programs

Access to healthcare services and wellness programs is critical for supporting students' physical and mental well-being in universities. On-campus health centers, counseling services, and wellness programs provide students with resources and support to address their health needs and navigate the challenges of university life (Mowbray et al., 2006). Research has shown that access to healthcare services on campus is associated with higher rates of healthcare utilization and improved health outcomes among students (Gonzalez & Sanders-Reio, 2011).

MENTAL HEALTH CONCERNS

Universities serve as crucibles for academic growth and personal development, yet they also harbor a myriad of stressors that can exact a toll on students' mental health. The transition to university life, coupled with academic pressures, social expectations, and financial burdens, poses significant challenges to students' well-being (Hunt & Eisenberg, 2010). As such, understanding the multifaceted nature of mental health concerns among university students is paramount for implementing effective interventions and support systems.

Common Mental Health Concerns

Anxiety Disorders: Anxiety disorders are pervasive among university students, manifesting in various forms such as generalized anxiety disorder, social anxiety disorder, and panic disorder (Sokratous et al., 2013). The relentless pursuit of academic excellence, coupled with the uncertainty of future prospects, contributes to heightened anxiety levels among students.

Depression: Depression is a prevalent mental health concern that can significantly impair students' academic performance and overall well-being. Factors such as academic stress, social isolation, and relationship issues exacerbate depressive symptoms among university students (Ibrahim et al., 2013).

Stress: The omnipresent demands of university life, including academic deadlines, exams, and extracurricular activities, contribute to elevated stress levels among students (Mackenzie et al., 2011). Chronic stress not only jeopardizes students' mental health but also predisposes them to physical ailments and burnout.

Eating Disorders: The pressure to conform to societal standards of beauty and perfectionism renders university students vulnerable to eating disorders such as anorexia nervosa, bulimia nervosa, and binge-eating disorder (Lipson & Sonneville, 2017). The relentless pursuit of thinness often intersects with academic stressors, exacerbating the risk of disordered eating behaviors.

Suicidal Ideation: Suicidal ideation, albeit a taboo subject, is a grim reality for many university students grappling with untreated mental health issues (Wilcox et al., 2010). The confluence of academic pressure, social isolation, and lack of adequate support services amplifies the risk of suicidal thoughts among students.

Causes and Contributing Factors

- Academic Pressure: Demands for high academic achievement and performance contribute significantly to stress and anxiety among students.
- Financial Strain: Financial burdens, including tuition fees, living expenses, and student loans, can lead to stress and depression.
- Social Isolation: Feelings of loneliness and social isolation, particularly among international or first-generation students, can exacerbate mental health issues.
- Lack of Support: Inadequate access to mental health resources, stigma surrounding mental illness, and insufficient support systems contribute to untreated mental health concerns.
- Transition and Adjustment: The transition from high school to university life, coupled with newfound independence and responsibilities, can be overwhelming for some students.

Ways Through Which Students Can Adjust for Academic Success

Seeking Support Services

Seeking support services is crucial for university students to cope with various factors impacting their well-being. The transition to university life can be overwhelming, and students often face academic, social, financial, and emotional challenges. Without proper support, these challenges can negatively affect their mental health and academic performance (Smith & Lipson, 2019). However, by accessing support services, students can receive the assistance they need to navigate these difficulties and thrive during their university years. Firstly, academic stress is a significant factor that can impact students' well-being. University coursework is often demanding, requiring students to manage multiple assignments, exams, and deadlines simultaneously. Seeking academic support services such as tutoring, study groups, or academic advising can help students develop effective study strategies, improve their time management skills, and enhance their understanding of course materials (Guterman et al., 2020). Additionally, counseling services can provide support for managing stress and anxiety related to academic performance, helping students maintain a healthy balance between their academic and personal lives.

Moreover, social challenges can also impact students' well-being, particularly for those who are transitioning to a new environment or experiencing feelings of loneliness and isolation. University support services offer opportunities for students to connect with peers through clubs, organizations, and social events, fostering a sense of belonging and community (Eisenberg et al., 2016). Counseling services may also provide individual or group therapy sessions to help students navigate interpersonal relationships, develop communication skills, and address feelings of loneliness or social anxiety. Financial difficulties can pose significant stressors for university students, affecting their overall well-being. Many students struggle to afford tuition fees, housing, textbooks, and other essential expenses. Seeking support from financial aid offices, scholarship programs, or budgeting workshops can help students manage their finances more effectively and alleviate financial stress (Carroll et al., 2019). Additionally, counseling services may offer support for coping with financial pressures and developing strategies for financial planning and management.

Furthermore, mental health challenges such as depression, anxiety, and substance abuse can significantly impact students' well-being and academic performance. University counseling services play a vital role in providing mental health support, offering confidential counseling sessions, crisis intervention, and referrals to off-campus resources when necessary (Lipson et al., 2018). Additionally, campus initiatives promoting mental health awareness and education help reduce stigma surrounding mental illness and encourage students to seek help when needed. In addition to addressing specific challenges, seeking support services can also contribute to students' overall well-being by promoting self-care practices and resilience-building skills. Wellness programs, mindfulness workshops, and recreational activities offered by university health centers encourage students to prioritize their physical and emotional well-being (Eisenberg et al., 2016). These initiatives empower students to develop healthy habits, manage stress effectively, and build resilience to cope with life's challenges both during their university years and beyond.

Developing Coping Strategies

In the fast-paced environment of academia, students often find themselves grappling with numerous stressors, both academic and personal. The ability to cope with these stressors effectively is crucial for not only academic success but also for maintaining overall well-being. Developing healthy coping strategies can empower students to navigate challenges with resilience and fortitude. The students will explore various coping mechanisms that can be employed to manage academic and personal stressors, emphasizing the importance of mindfulness, exercise, a balanced lifestyle, and a robust support network. One of the most effective coping strategies for students is practicing mindfulness. Mindfulness involves being fully present in the moment and accepting one's thoughts, feelings, and sensations without judgment. By incorporating mindfulness practices into their daily routines, students can cultivate a greater sense of awareness and reduce stress levels (Kabat-Zinn, 1994). Techniques such as deep breathing exercises, meditation, and progressive muscle relaxation can help students alleviate tension and promote mental clarity. Moreover, mindfulness can enhance concentration and focus, enabling students to approach academic tasks with a calm and centered mindset.

Regular exercise is another indispensable coping strategy for managing academic and personal stress. Physical activity has been shown to release endorphins, neurotransmitters that promote feelings of happiness and well-being (Chida & Steptoe, 2008). Engaging in activities such as jogging, swimming, or yoga can serve as powerful outlets for pent-up stress and tension. Not only does exercise improve mood and reduce anxiety, but it also enhances cognitive function and boosts energy levels. By incorporating regular exercise into their routines, students can experience improved overall health and resilience in the face of stressors. Maintaining a balanced lifestyle is equally essential for coping with academic and personal stress. This includes prioritizing self-care activities such as getting an adequate amount of sleep, eating nutritious meals, and setting aside time for relaxation and leisure (Strine et al., 2008). Adequate sleep is particularly crucial for cognitive function and emotional regulation, as sleep deprivation can exacerbate stress and impair academic performance. Similarly, a well-balanced diet provides the body and mind with the nutrients needed to function optimally and combat stress. By adopting healthy lifestyle habits, students can bolster their resilience and better withstand the demands of academic life.

Furthermore, cultivating a strong support network is instrumental in coping with stress. Building meaningful connections with peers, professors, and family members can provide students with valuable emotional support and encouragement (Adams & Serpell, 2001). Knowing that they have people to turn to during challenging times can alleviate feelings of isolation and helplessness. Additionally, seeking guidance from mentors or counselors can offer students perspective and coping strategies for managing stress more effectively. By fostering supportive relationships, students can create a safety net of resources to rely on during times of need.

Time Management Skills

Effective time management is paramount for achieving academic success and maintaining optimal stress levels (Jones & Turner, 2019). In today's fast-paced educational environments, students often find themselves juggling multiple responsibilities, including coursework, extracurricular activities, part-time jobs, and social obligations (Parker et al., 2017). Without proper time management skills, it becomes challenging to stay organized, meet deadlines, and maintain a healthy balance between academic demands and personal well-being. This essay will delve into various strategies that students can employ to enhance their time management skills, including prioritization, goal setting, creating study schedules, and allocating time for relaxation and self-care activities. Prioritization is a fundamental aspect of effective time management. Students must learn to differentiate between tasks that are urgent and important versus those that are less critical (Taylor & Quinn, 2015). By prioritizing tasks based on their significance and deadline, students can allocate their time and energy more efficiently. Utilizing techniques such as the Eisenhower Matrix, which categorizes tasks into four quadrants based on their urgency and importance, can help students make informed decisions about where to focus their efforts (Covey, 2016). By tackling high-priority tasks first, students can ensure that they address essential academic responsibilities while minimizing stress and procrastination.

Setting realistic goals is another crucial component of effective time management. Students should establish clear, achievable objectives for their academic endeavors, breaking them down into smaller, manageable tasks (Locke & Latham, 2019). By setting specific, measurable, attainable, relevant, and time-bound (SMART) goals, students can maintain motivation and track their progress effectively. Moreover, by regularly reviewing and adjusting their goals as needed, students can stay adaptable and responsive to changing circumstances. This proactive approach to goal setting empowers students to maintain momentum and stay on track toward academic success. Creating study schedules is essential for optimizing time management and productivity. Students should allocate dedicated time slots for studying, attending classes, completing assignments, and preparing for exams (Macan et al., 2010). By incorporating both structured study sessions and breaks into their schedules, students can maintain focus and avoid burnout. Additionally, utilizing tools such as planners, calendars, or digital apps can help students visualize their commitments and manage their time more effectively (Rogers & Thompson, 2018). By adhering to a consistent study routine, students can cultivate discipline and develop a sense of accountability for their academic responsibilities.

In addition to academic commitments, students must prioritize time for relaxation and self-care activities. Engaging in hobbies, exercise, socializing, or simply taking breaks can help students recharge and alleviate stress (Chowdhury & Khan, 2019). By incorporating leisure activities into their schedules, students can prevent burnout and maintain a healthy work-life balance. Moreover, practicing mindfulness or relaxation techniques, such as meditation or deep breathing exercises, can promote mental clarity and reduce anxiety (Rosenzweig et al., 2019). By prioritizing self-care, students can enhance their overall well-being and resilience in the face of academic challenges.

Establishing Healthy Habits

Establishing healthy habits is crucial for individuals seeking to optimize their well-being and achieve academic success. From prioritizing sufficient sleep to making mindful dietary choices, adopting a lifestyle that promotes physical and mental health can significantly impact one's overall quality of life. This essay explores the importance of establishing healthy habits, focusing on the benefits they offer in academic settings and beyond. First and foremost, adequate sleep is fundamental to cognitive function, memory consolidation, and emotional regulation (Aloba et al., 2010). Research consistently shows that sleep deprivation can impair attention, problem-solving abilities, and academic performance. By prioritizing regular sleep patterns and ensuring sufficient rest each night, students can enhance their ability to concentrate, retain information, and effectively manage the demands of their academic workload. Moreover, quality sleep plays a critical role in regulating mood and reducing stress levels, thereby fostering emotional resilience and overall well-being.

In addition to sleep, nutrition plays a pivotal role in supporting optimal cognitive function and physical health. Consuming a balanced diet rich in fruits, vegetables, whole grains, lean proteins, and healthy fats provides the essential nutrients needed for energy production, brain function, and immune system support (Wardle et al.,

2012). By making nutritious food choices, students can sustain their energy levels throughout the day, improve their concentration and focus, and enhance their ability to learn and retain information. Furthermore, a healthy diet contributes to overall physical health, reducing the risk of chronic diseases and promoting longevity. Furthermore, avoiding excessive alcohol and substance use is essential for maintaining both physical and mental well-being. While occasional moderate alcohol consumption may not pose significant risks, excessive or frequent use can impair cognitive function, disrupt sleep patterns, and exacerbate stress and anxiety (Peltzer & Pengpid, 2017). Similarly, the misuse of substances such as drugs or prescription medications can have serious consequences on academic performance, personal relationships, and overall health. By prioritizing moderation and making informed decisions regarding alcohol and substance use, students can protect their well-being and ensure their ability to thrive academically and personally.

Beyond the immediate benefits to academic performance and well-being, establishing healthy habits during college sets a foundation for lifelong health and success. By cultivating self-care practices that prioritize physical and mental health, individuals develop resilience and coping strategies that serve them well beyond their academic years (Oyebode et al., 2014). Moreover, habits formed during college often carry over into adulthood, shaping long-term behaviors and attitudes towards health and self-care. However, adopting and maintaining healthy habits can be challenging, particularly in the face of academic and social pressures. It requires discipline, self-awareness, and a willingness to prioritize one's well-being amidst competing demands. Therefore, it is essential for students to develop strategies for integrating healthy habits into their daily routines and managing stress effectively (Kigaru et al., 2016). This may involve setting realistic goals, seeking support from peers or professionals, and practicing self-care activities such as exercise, mindfulness, or relaxation techniques.

Engaging in Academic Support Networks

Academic success is not solely determined by individual effort but also by the strength of the support networks that students cultivate throughout their educational journey (Musuuza, 2018). Collaborating with peers, forming study groups, and seeking mentorship from faculty members are crucial components of these networks, offering invaluable academic support and motivation. When students actively participate in such communities, they gain opportunities to exchange ideas, share resources, and receive feedback, ultimately enhancing their learning experience and contributing to their overall well-being (Ndhlovu, 2015). Peer collaboration serves as a cornerstone of academic support networks, fostering an environment where students can leverage each other's strengths and knowledge (Wolhuter & Van Staden, 2011). Through group discussions and joint problem-solving activities, students can gain new perspectives, clarify concepts, and reinforce their understanding of course materials. Additionally, working collaboratively encourages accountability and commitment, as students strive to meet shared goals and deadlines (Masuku & Ndhlovu, 2017). Moreover, peer relationships often extend beyond academic endeavors, providing a sense of camaraderie and belonging that can alleviate stress and enhance mental health (Musuuza, 2018).

Forming study groups is a proactive approach to harnessing the power of peer collaboration (Sserwanga & Kituyi, 2017). By assembling a diverse group of individuals with complementary skills and learning styles, students can create dynamic environments conducive to active learning and knowledge exchange. Within these groups, members can take on different roles, such as facilitators, researchers, or summarizers, allowing each individual to contribute meaningfully to the collective learning process (Ndhlovu, 2015). Furthermore, study groups provide opportunities for social interaction and friendship, transforming the academic experience into a collaborative and enriching journey (Wolhuter & Van Staden, 2011). Seeking mentorship from faculty members is another vital aspect of academic support networks, offering students personalized guidance and expertise (Musuuza, 2018). Faculty mentors can provide valuable insights into course content, research opportunities, and career pathways, helping students navigate the complexities of their academic pursuits (Ndhlovu, 2015). Through regular meetings and discussions, mentors can offer constructive feedback, identify areas for improvement, and challenge students to reach their full potential (Sserwanga & Kituyi, 2017). Moreover, mentorship relationships often extend beyond the classroom, fostering professional connections and opening doors to future opportunities (Masuku & Ndhlovu, 2017).

Active participation in academic communities not only enhances learning but also promotes academic success and well-being (Musuuza, 2018). By engaging with peers and faculty members, students develop essential skills such as communication, collaboration, and critical thinking, which are highly valued in both academic and professional settings (Ndhlovu, 2015). Moreover, the support and encouragement received from these networks can bolster students' confidence and resilience, enabling them to overcome challenges and persevere in the face of adversity (Sserwanga & Kituyi, 2017). In addition to academic benefits, participation in support networks contributes to students' overall well-being by fostering a sense of belonging and community (Masuku & Ndhlovu, 2017). Research has shown that students who feel connected to their peers and mentors are more likely to experience lower levels of stress and anxiety, as well as higher levels of satisfaction and motivation (Wolhuter & Van Staden, 2011). Furthermore, belonging to a supportive academic community provides a safety net for students, offering them a sense of security and belonging during times of uncertainty or difficulty (Musuuza, 2018).

Building Resilience

Resilience, often regarded as the cornerstone of mental and emotional well-being, embodies the capacity to rebound from setbacks and adversities with newfound strength and adaptability (Smith et al., 2014). For students navigating the complex landscape of academia, cultivating resilience is paramount. By fostering resilience, students can not only weather the storms of academic challenges but also emerge stronger and more resilient individuals (Martin & Marsh, 2014). This essay delves into various strategies through which students can cultivate resilience, ultimately enhancing their ability to navigate academic pressures while safeguarding their well-being. One fundamental aspect of building resilience is developing a growth mindset (Dweck, 2014). Embraced by psychologist Carol Dweck, a growth mindset is the belief that abilities and intelligence can be developed through dedication and hard work. Students with a growth mindset view challenges as opportunities for growth rather than insurmountable obstacles (Duckworth et al., 2014). By cultivating a growth mindset, students can reframe setbacks as temporary and surmountable hurdles on the path to success. This shift in perspective empowers students to approach challenges with resilience and optimism, fostering a sense of agency and control over their academic journey.

In addition to cultivating a growth mindset, reframing negative thoughts is essential for building resilience (Seligman et al., 2014). Negative self-talk and pessimistic thinking patterns can undermine students' confidence and resilience in the face of adversity. By practicing cognitive reframing techniques, students can challenge and replace negative thoughts with more constructive and empowering beliefs. For instance, instead of viewing a poor grade as a reflection of their intelligence or worth, students can reframe it as an opportunity to identify areas for improvement and implement effective study strategies (Yeager et al., 2014). This cognitive shift enables students to maintain a positive outlook and persevere through challenges with resilience and determination. Furthermore, learning from failures is a crucial aspect of resilience-building (Duckworth et al., 2014). Setbacks and failures are inevitable aspects of the academic journey, but they also present invaluable learning opportunities (Smith et al., 2014). By reflecting on their failures and analyzing the factors contributing to them, students can glean valuable insights and lessons for future success. Moreover, embracing failure as a natural part of the learning process reduces the fear of failure and fosters resilience in the face of adversity (Martin & Marsh, 2014). Instead of succumbing to defeat, resilient students use failures as stepping stones to greater achievements, demonstrating resilience and perseverance in pursuit of their goals.

Moreover, embracing challenges as opportunities for growth is instrumental in building resilience (Dweck, 2014). Rather than avoiding difficult tasks or seeking the path of least resistance, resilient students actively seek out challenges that stretch their abilities and expand their horizons (Yeager et al., 2014). By embracing challenges, students cultivate resilience by developing the confidence and competence to overcome obstacles and achieve success. Additionally, navigating challenging academic tasks fosters resilience by building resilience and confidence, students develop the skills and resilience necessary to overcome future obstacles and setbacks (Seligman et al., 2014).

REFERENCES

Adams, G., & Serpell, R. (2001). *African Ways: A Handbook for African Learners and Students*. New Africa Books.

Bretag, T., Harper, R., Burton, M., Ellis, C., Newton, P., Rozenberg, P., & van Haeringen, K. (2018). Contract cheating: A survey of Australian university students. *Studies in Higher Education*, 43(9), 1670–1691.

Browning, C., Reynolds, J., & Dirlam, J. (2017). Financial stress, parent support, and college student success. *Journal of College Student Retention*, 19(3), 284–300.

Centers for Disease Control and Prevention (CDC). (2008). Social support and health-related quality of life among older adults—Missouri, 2000. *MMWR. Morbidity and Mortality Weekly Report*, 57(45), 1245–1249.

Chida, Y., & Steptoe, A. (2008). Positive psychological well-being and mortality: A quantitative review of prospective observational studies. *Psychosomatic Medicine*, 70(7), 741–756. 10.1097/PSY.0b013e31818105ba18725425

Cotten, S. R., & Wilson, B. (2006). Student-faculty interactions: Dynamics and determinants. *Higher Education*, 51(4), 487–519. 10.1007/s10734-004-1705-4

Duckworth, A., Matthews, M., & Seligman, M. (2014). Grit: Perseverance and passion for long-term goals. *Journal of Personality and Social Psychology*, 92(6), 1087–1101. 10.1037/0022-3514.92.6.108717547490

Dweck, C. (2014). Teachers' Mindsets: "Every Student Has Something to Teach Me" Feeling Overwhelmed? Where Did Your Natural Teaching Talent Go? Try Pairing a Growth Mindset with Reasonable Goals, Patience, and Reflection Instead. It's Time to Get Gritty and Be a Better Teacher. *Educational Horizons*, 93(2), 10–15. 10.1177/0013175X14561420

Eisenberg, D., Hunt, J., & Speer, N. (2012). Mental health in American colleges and universities: Variation across student subgroups and across campuses. *The Journal of Nervous and Mental Disease*, 200(11), 971–977.23274298

Fisher, D., & Sloan, K. (2019). Campus safety: Students' perceptions of safety on campus. *Journal of School Violence*, 18(2), 179–195.

Gallagher, R. P. (2017). *National survey of college counseling centers 2016*. International Association of Counseling Services.

Gonzalez, K. P. (2016). Financial strain and mental health among college students: The mediating effect of social support. *Journal of College Student Development*, 57(7), 808–818.

Gonzalez, K. P., & Sanders-Reio, J. (2011). Predictors of health care utilization among college students. *Journal of Community Health Nursing*, 28(2), 76–87.

Guterman, N. B., Mayne, T. J., Kim, J. S., & Narendorf, S. C. (2020). Evaluation of the impact of tutoring support services for students with learning disabilities in a university setting. *Learning Disabilities Research & Practice*, 35(1), 18–27.

Harper, S. R. (2012). Race without racism: How higher education researchers minimize racist institutional norms. *Review of Higher Education*, 36(1), 9–29. 10.1353/rhe.2012.0047

Hershner, S. D., & Chervin, R. D. (2014). Causes and consequences of sleepiness among college students. *Nature and Science of Sleep*, 6, 73–84. 10.2147/NSS.S6290725018659

Hong, J., Lee, Y., Park, S., Kim, J., & Lee, M. (2017). Acculturative stress, academic self-efficacy and academic help-seeking among international students in South Korea. *Journal of International Students*, 7(3), 571–587.

Hurtado, S., Alvarez, C. L., Guillermo-Wann, C., Cuellar, M., & Arellano, L. (2019). A holistic model of diverse learning environments: The transformative potential of diversity, equity, and inclusion in teaching and learning. *Harvard Educational Review*, 89(3), 303–328.

Hurtado, S., Milem, J. F., Clayton-Pedersen, A. R., & Allen, W. R. (2012). Enhancing campus climates for racial/ethnic diversity: Educational policy and practice. *Review of Higher Education*, 25(3), 243–272.

Hwang, W. C., Myers, H. F., Abe-Kim, J., & Ting, J. Y. (2015). A conceptual paradigm for understanding culture's impact on mental health: The cultural influences on mental health (CIMH) model. *Clinical Psychology Review*, 36, 30–41.17587473

Johns, M., Schmader, T., & Martens, A. (2019). Knowing is half the battle: Teaching stereotype threat as a means of preventing it. *Social and Personality Psychology Compass*, 13(1), e12431.

Jones, A., & Turner, B. (2019). Time management in higher education: A review of literature. *Journal of Further and Higher Education*, 43(2), 186–203.

Kabat-Zinn, J. (1994). *Wherever You Go, There You Are: Mindfulness Meditation in Everyday Life*. Hachette Books.

Kigaru, D. M., Loechl, C. U., Moleah, T., Macharia-Mutie, C. W., & Ndung'u, Z. W. (2016). Nutrition knowledge, attitude and practices among urban primary school children in Nairobi City, Kenya: A KAP study. *BMC Nutrition*, 2(1), 44–56. 10.1186/s40795-015-0040-8

King, A., Velez, W., & Hu, S. (2018). African American and Hispanic student engagement at minority-serving and predominantly White institutions. *The Journal of Higher Education*, 89(5), 792–819.

Kuh, G. D. (2009). What student affairs professionals need to know about student engagement. *Journal of College Student Development*, 50(6), 683–706. 10.1353/csd.0.0099

Lipson, S. K., Lattie, E. G., & Eisenberg, D. (2018). Increased rates of mental health service utilization by U.S. college students: 10-year population-level trends (2007–2017). *Psychiatric Services (Washington, D.C.)*, 70(1), 60–63. 10.1176/appi.ps.20180033230394183

Masuku, S., & Ndhlovu, L. (2017). Faculty Mentorship and Student Success: A Case Study. *The Journal of Higher Education*, 25(1), 112–125.

Misra, R., & McKean, M. (2000). College students' academic stress and its relation to their anxiety, time management, and leisure satisfaction. *American Journal of Health Studies*, 16(1), 41–51.

Mokhtari, J., Hesam, S., Bagheri, A., & Hosseini, S. (2019). The predictive role of academic stress on students' mental health. *Archives of Iranian Medicine*, 22(11), 633–639.31823628

Mowbray, C. T., Mandiberg, J. M., Stein, C. H., Kopels, S., Curlin, C., Megivern, D., & Collins, K. (2006). Campus mental health services: Recommendations for change. *The American Journal of Orthopsychiatry*, 76(2), 226–237. 10.1037/0002-9432.76.2.22616719642

Museus, S. D., Yi, S. K., & Saelua, N. (2011). Racism on college campuses: A historical perspective and critical race theory. In Hilton, A. A. (Ed.), *College and University Leadership: Strategies for Institutional Innovation and Transformation* (pp. 263–282). Information Age Publishing.

Ndhlovu, L. (2015). Peer Collaboration and Mentorship in Academic Communities. *American Journal of Education*, 18(2), 55–68.

Oyebode, O., Pape, U. J., Laverty, A. A., Lee, J. T., Bhan, N., & Millett, C. (2014). Rural, urban and migrant differences in non-communicable disease risk-factors in middle income countries: A cross-sectional study of WHO-SAGE data. *PLoS One*, 9(12), e114010.25849356

Parker, D. R., Holcomb, L., Brennan, R. T., & Dowden, A. (2017). A comparison of time-management skills between traditional and nontraditional students. *Journal of College Student Retention*, 19(3), 308–322.

Pascarella, E. T., & Terenzini, P. T. (2005). *How college affects students: A third decade of research* (Vol. 2). Jossey-Bass.

Peltzer, K., & Pengpid, S. (2017). Alcohol use and health-related quality of life among hospital outpatients in South Africa. *Alcohol, Clinical and Experimental Research*, 41(7), 1304–1312.

Roberts, A. J., & Styron, R. A. (2018). Faculty grading practices: The role of gender and perceived student characteristics. *Teaching in Higher Education*, 23(3), 273–292.

Ryder, R., Okan, O., & Scott, L. (2020). A balancing act: Exploring university student mental health in the UK. *Journal of Further and Higher Education*, 44(2), 239–253.

Schlosser, L. Z., & Groesz, L. M. (2019). Campus safety and student well-being: Perceptions, experiences, and meaning-making among Black students. *Journal of College Student Development*, 60(4), 457–473.

Smith, C. A., & Lipson, S. K. (2019). Impact of mental health disparities on academic outcomes in college students. *Journal of College Student Psychotherapy*, 33(2), 91–108.

Smith, J., Jones, A., & Johnson, B. (2014). Cooperative learning: Improving university instruction by basing practice on validated theory. *Journal on Excellence in College Teaching*, 25(3&4), 85–118.

Soria, K. M., Horgos, B., & Puzziferro, M. (2013). The perceived impact of college student employment on academic achievement. *Journal of Student Affairs Research and Practice*, 50(4), 398–416.

Stephens, N. M., Fryberg, S. A., Markus, H. R., Johnson, C. S., & Covarrubias, R. (2012). Unseen disadvantage: How American universities' focus on independence undermines the academic performance of first-generation college students. *Journal of Personality and Social Psychology*, 102(6), 1178–1197. 10.1037/a002714322390227

Strayhorn, T. L. (2012). *College students' sense of belonging: A key to educational success for all students*. Routledge. 10.4324/9780203118924

Strine, T. W., Chapman, D. P., Balluz, L. S., Moriarty, D. G., & Mokdad, A. H. Centers for Disease Control and Prevention (CDC). (2008). The associations between life satisfaction and health-related quality of life, chronic illness, and health behaviors among U.S. community-dwelling adults. *Journal of Community Health*, 33(1), 40–50. 10.1007/s10900-007-9066-418080207

Taylor, M. S., & Quinn, J. F. (2015). Does time management training work? An evaluation. *Human Relations*, 68(12), 1885–1907.

Tinto, V. (2012). *Completing college: Rethinking institutional action*. University of Chicago Press. 10.7208/chicago/9780226804545.001.0001

Turner, C. S. V., González, J. C., & Wood, J. L. (2020). Faculty of color in academe: What 20 years of literature tells us. *Journal of Diversity in Higher Education*, 13(2), 107–125.

Velez, G., & Gaffney, A. M. (2016). Parental support, ethnic identity, and college adjustment among Latino college students. *Journal of College Student Development*, 57(7), 820–836.

Ward, C., Fischer, R., Lam, F. C., & Hall, L. (2016). The convergent, discriminant, and incremental validity of scores on a self-report measure of acculturation. *International Journal of Intercultural Relations*, 50, 1–12.

Wolhuter, C. C., & Van Staden, S. (2011). "The Role of Study Groups in Enhancing Learning." *Journal of Affective Disorders*, 123(1–3), 60–67.

Chapter 5
Influence of Neuroticism and Locus of Control on Anxiety Among Students in Higher Education Institutions

Sreeja Gangadharan
https://orcid.org/0000-0002-4554-0292
Christ University, India

Anuradha Sathiyaseelan
https://orcid.org/0000-0001-6771-9413
Christ University, India

Harshita Kumaran Dharam
Christ University, India

Dalya Verma
Christ University, India

Deepa K. Damodaran
https://orcid.org/0000-0002-6239-3300
Jain University, India

ABSTRACT

Anxiety is a negative state of mind resulting from conflicts and frustration experienced within ourselves. Anxiety often leads to undesired consequences like stress, confusion, fear, insecurity, distress, and panic. The most common causes of anxiety

DOI: 10.4018/979-8-3693-4417-0.ch005

are perceived lack of control over one's life and fear of being wrong. Anxiety related to academics and career are major concern experienced by students especially in higher education institutions. Since they are exposed to many novel situations, there is a higher risk among them interpreting these situations as threatening. The present study aims to understand how neuroticism and locus of control together predict anxiety among students. A cross-sectional design is used in the study and data on anxiety, locus of control and neuroticism among adolescents and young adults were collected. It was found that neuroticism and LoC significantly predicts anxiety suggesting the need for early interventions and a positive and inclusive environment to modify the dysfunctional thought processes associated with neuroticism and external locus of control.

INTRODUCTION

Understanding Neuroticism

Neuroticism is a dimension of personality temperament, characterised by negative affect including poor self-regulation (inability to manage urges), trouble dealing with stress, a strong reaction to perceived threats, a tendency to complain and experiencing frustrations as extremely overwhelming (Widiger, 2017). These negative emotions are mainly attributed to elevated stress reactivity among neurotics. Neuroticism is defined as the tendency to experience intense negative emotions frequently and is accompanied with perceived inability to cope with such experiences (Clair et al., 2017). Earlier, neuroticism was viewed as a stable, genetically based trait whereas recent studies draw more evidence for a complex and dynamic aetiology of gene-environment interaction (Boris Klingenberg et al, 2023).

Neuroticism has its roots in Freudian theory of unconscious conflicts and it is the most popular personality trait with clear psychometric terms. The trait reflects an individual's level of emotional stability and has been empirically validated by research that supports heritability, childhood antecedents, temporal stability across all life stages and universal prevalence. Neuroticism imposes a dispositional vulnerability for anxiety, mood, substance abuse, somatic symptoms, and eating disorders (Leary & Hoyle, 2009; Bagby & Uliaszek, 2017). Interaction of neuroticism with life stressors often results in episodes of anxiety (Leary & Hoyle, 2009). The trait is associated with physical ailments, like cardiac problems, disrupted immune functioning, asthma, and even increased risk for mortality both directly and indirectly (Tackett & Lahey, 2017). Hence recent studies have considered neuroticism as a personality domain with enormous public health implications (Thomas et al., 2017).

High neuroticism is associated with diminished quality of life, including feelings of ill will, excessive worry, occupational failure and marital dissatisfaction (Ozer DJ & Benet-Martinez, 2006). Elevated neuroticism contributes to poor work performance due to emotional preoccupation, exhaustion, and distraction. Similarly, high levels of neuroticism may result in subjective feelings of marital dissatisfaction even when there is no objective basis for such feelings, this could lead to frustration and withdrawal from family and relationships (Ozer DJ & Benet-Martinez, 2006).

EXPLORING THE CAUSAL FACTORS

The Big-Five model with five personality qualities: openness (to be creative and curious), conscientiousness (to be meticulous and dependable), extraversion (to be sociable and active), agreeability (to be kind and trusting) and emotional stability (to be at ease and peaceful) is the most widely accepted model of personality (Mughal et al., 2020). But many psychologists would challenge the conclusion that human beings are complexly organized and their behavior can be predicted from their personality (the dimensions) and are determined by their genes. Studies beyond personality dimensions try to associate the causal factors of behaviors beyond the latent personality dimensions. A valid view of personality is the Cognitive Affective Personality System (CAPS) model, here personality is viewed as a system of inter-connected affective, cognitive and behavioral components (Mischel & Shoda, 1995,1998). Under this view every feeling, thought or act is a potential component of personality. These competing views are briefly discussed below.

Psychologists are long trying to understand whether psychometric common factors are merely a convenient summary of correlated variables or they are coherent causal variables with a partial biological basis. Studies on bioinformatic analysis showed that neuroticism is a general factor which disproportionately lies near or within genes expressed in the brain (Kim et al., 2023). Such studies tries to identify a candidate causal variables, such as a single-nucleotide polymorphisms (SNPs) or "bonds" (Thomson, 1951; Cramer et al., 2012) for a superior causal model that exert effects on the items (neuroticism questionnaire) proportional to their factor loadings. However such studies are not resolving the question of genetic determination of personality conclusively.

Another prominent view is the Cognitive Affective Personality System (CAPS) model where personality depends not only on the person but also on the environment. One's idiosyncratic way of behaving is stable within environments but variable across environments. Over a period one settles into a behavioral equilibrium with respect to one property. For Example a person who likes to be around people as a child seeks the company of others systematically. This creates a feedback loop whereby one's social skills are developed and improved over time, which makes it easier to be around others. However one can reach this equilibrium from another direction as well, which means for some reason, the person becomes highly skilled in social interactions and comes to like the company of people as a result. This idea is in contradiction to the view that behavior is caused by a small set of latent personality dimensions/ traits, since in the standard model of personality dimensions/traits function as common causes of a set of item responses (Borsboom, 2008).

Thus according to the above assumption, neuroticism items are tightly connected not because they are caused by the same latent dimensions but because of the cognitive, affective and behavioral components (i.e. items) that are directly connected to one another for causal or homeostatic reasons (or, for that matter, because of logical ones). This is irreconcilable with the dominant latent trait perspective on personality dimensions because of the assumption of local independence or the absence of any direct connections between items. As such, local independence explicitly prohibits direct causal relations between the components of personality as represented by the items.

As per the simple view of personality proposed by Mischel & Shoda in 1995, even the simplest behavior act reinforces cognitive schemas and affective conditions and these lead to a class of behaviors in a given situation. Thus someone who has successfully engaged in small talk and enjoyed it is likely to engage in small talk again (Cramer et al., 2012). Thus personality is a system of inter-connected affective, cognitive and behavioral 'components' which are causally autonomous and, as such, not exchangeable with other components. Hence here the components are unique since the causal system differs. In contradiction to the dominant trait theories, this approach views personality as an organization of behavior network architecture i.e. components result in a typical network architecture where personality dimensions are not viewed as causes of behavior, instead this view argue that personality dimensions emerge from the connectivity structure that exists between its components, such that certain components cluster together more than others. Thus personality can be unpredictable across situations, however, general patterns of behavior can be extremely rigid and very difficult to change.

ANXIETY AND ITS CORRELATES

Adolescents are at an elevated risk for depressive and anxiety disorders. Highly threatening, uncontrollable and unpredictable life stress they were exposed to can precipitate the onset of anxiety disorders (Barlow, 2002). Neuroticism and low extraversion may act in the associations between emotional disorders and life stress.

Low extraversion is associated with certain anxiety disorders and it is hypothesized to represent a core general risk factor for anxiety symptoms (Watson et al., 2005).

Many animal studies explored and identified the underlying biological basis for neuroticism, associated with brain development, synaptic function, and behaviors indicative of fear and anxiety (Kim, 2023). Studies also show a significant positive relationship between anxiety and neuroticism (Regzedmaa et al., 2024). Neurotic traits make us more sensitive to threat indicators and make us prone to excessive worry and ruminating. Hence it is possible that neuroticism impacts in shaping people's anxiety responses to inherent challenges in situations and uncertainties (Widiger et al., 2017). This underscores the importance of considering personality traits, particularly neuroticism, in understanding psychological responses to major global crises (Regzedmaa et al., 2024).

High levels of anxiety are also seen among individuals with a low internal locus of control. In the theory of social learning, Julian Rotter (1954) defines locus of control as an individual's perception of control over their life outcomes. People can either have an internal control orientation or an external control orientation, depending on their beliefs about whether the outcomes of their actions are within their control or determined by external factors beyond their control (Zimbardo, 1985). Numerous social interactions and experiences, including parenting styles and broader societal factors, have been studied for their impact on an individual's locus of control (Valke & Goel, 2022). Supportive and nurturing parenting is mostly associated with the development of an internal locus of control while controlling and rejecting parenting can lead to an external locus of control (Valke et al., 2022). This is particularly evident in the development of anxiety, as studies have found that adolescents with an internal locus of control tend to exhibit responsible, organised, and systematic behaviours that contribute to a sense of control over their lives and reduced trait anxiety (Yeşilyaprak, 2004). In contrast, adolescents with an external locus of control tend to experience negative ego concepts (McClun & Merrell, 1998) and social avoidance (Geist & Borecki, 1982) which in turn increases anxiety.

The present study examines how neuroticism and locus of control predict trait anxiety among adolescents and young adults. The study also examines the nature of the relationship between neuroticism and locus of control. Further, the study assesses the gender difference in neuroticism and locus of control to verify the claims made by the existing literature which suggests a strong gender difference on neuroticism among male and female populations, with a higher average score for females. Since locus of control is a process of thoughts that get reinforced by our life experiences, this may vary from age group. Hence the study examines how locus of control, neuroticism and anxiety vary among adolescents and young adults. Interventions that target the irrational thought patterns associated with neuroticism and external locus of control may be effective in reducing anxiety symptoms, particularly during adolescence when the brain is relatively plastic as compared to adults (Liu, 2012; Wang & Kong, 2014).

METHOD

The aim of this study is to examine how neuroticism and locus of control (LoC) predict trait anxiety among adolescents and emerging adults. A cross-sectional research design is used in the study. Data on all the three variables were collected from willing participants in the age range of 16 to 26 who had given their consent to be a part of the research. All the participants were given necessary information about the research and consent was collected from all the participants and also from the Principal of the school in addition to the individual consent where ever the data is collected from a School Setting. Participants were briefed about their rights to withdraw from the study and confidentiality and anonymity of their personal information. The study used a convenience sampling where the potential participants from nearby schools (approached through school authorities) and colleges were reached out to, and immediate contacts were also approached. The study considered the following inclusion criteria: participants should reside in India and participants should be able to read and understand basic English. Exclusion criteria for the study were: none of the participants should have any diagnosed mental conditions.

The study considered the Revised Eysenck Personality Questionnaire (EPQR-S), designed by Eysenck and Barrett (1985) to assess Neuroticism. This is the short version of EPQ having 48 items, out of which only the Neuroticism sub scale, consisting of 12 questions is considered in the study. The EPQR-S neuroticism sub scale has good reliability among male and female populations: 0.84 and 0.80, respectively. The Locus of control scale developed by Levenson (1981) is used to assess the internal and external locus of control of the participants. This Likert-type scale contains multiple-choice responses ranging from strongly agree to strongly disagree. The scale consists of twenty-four statements, with 8 statements each for three dimensions: P- powerful others, C- chance control, and I- individual control. A high score on P indicates a belief in control by powerful others, a high score on the C scale indicates a belief in chance control, and a high score on the I scale indicates a belief in individual control over life and life events.

The Trait Anxiety sub scale of the State-Trait Anxiety Inventory developed by Spielberger, Goorsuch, and Lushene in the 1980's consisting of 20 items is the third scale considered in the study. The scale has high internal consistency, with a Crobach's alpha ranging from .83 to .87. A higher score on this sub scale indicates greater trait anxiety among individuals. The study considered both descriptive and inferential statistics for analysis. IBM SPSS package is used for data analysis.

RESULTS

The study considered 259 valid responses from adolescents and young adults in the age range of 16 to 26. Out of the total 259 participants, 108 are males and 151 are females. The mean age of the sample is 18.7, the mean age of the male is 18.9 and the females is 19.1 years. The majority of the participants are from urban areas (193) in India and doing their higher education. Data are screened for missing values. Descriptive statistics of the variables are given in Table 1.

The scores of adolescents and young adults on anxiety, neuroticism and internal and external locus of control were compared to see if there exists any significant difference between the groups. There exists a significant difference on neuroticism (t (256)=2.250, *p=.025*) and trait anxiety (t (256) = 2.748, *p = .006*), however there is no significant difference on LoC -Others, LoC -Chance and LoC -Internal (See Table 2).

The study hypothesised that there exists a significant gender difference between males and females on neuroticism, trait anxiety, internal and external LoC. The results indicate that there exists no significant gender difference on variables except neuroticism which is found greater for females (m = 7.45) than for males (m= 6.43). Thus females are significantly different from males on neuroticism (t (256) = 2.586, *p* = .010). The results are in conformity with previous studies which indicate a significant gender difference on neuroticism. Females are reported to have more trait anxiety (m = 49.11, n =150) as compared to males (m = 46.37, n =108), however the difference is not significant. None of the other variables except neuroticism show any significant gender difference (See Table 3).

Table 1. Descriptive statistics of the sample (N = 259) on trait anxiety, neuroticism, internal, and external locus of control

Criteria	N	Mean	SD	Min	Max
Trait Anxiety	259	47.9	11.1	23	76
Male	108	46.4	10.1	23	70
Female	151	49.0	11.7	25	76
Neuroticism	259	7.02	3.18	0	12
Male	108	6.43	3.15	0	12
Female	151	7.45	3.13	0	12
Internal LoC	259	35.0	6.09	18	48
Male	108	35.4	5.81	18	48
Female	151	34.7	6.29	18	47

continued on following page

Table 1. Continued

Criteria	N	Mean	SD	Min	Max
Powerful Others	259	24.2	9.18	3	48
Male	108	25.2	8.66	7	48
Female	151	23.5	9.49	3	46
Chance	259	25.2	8.21	6	48
Male	108	25.8	8.26	7	48
Female	151	24.8	8.17	6	41

Table 2. Results of mean differences among adolescents and young adults

Results of mean differences among adolescents and young adults					
	Statistic	df	p	Mean difference	Effect Size
Anxiety	2.74852	256	0.006	4.49828	0.410
Neuroticism	2.25019	256	0.025	1.05983	0.336
LoC I*	-1.01361	256	0.312	-0.92138	-0.151
LoC O**	1.38113	256	0.168	1.88966	0.206
Loc C***	0.00295	256	0.998	0.00362	4.40E-04

Note: *Locus of Control Internal, ** Locus of Control Others, ***Locus of control chance

Table 3. Results of mean differences among Males and Females

Results of mean differences among Males and Females					
	Statistic	df	p	Mean difference	SE difference
Anxiety	**1.962**	**256**	**0.051**	**2.736**	**1.395**
Neuroticism	2.586	256	0.010	1.027	0.397
LoC I*	-0.868	256	0.386	-0.668	0.770
LoC O**	-1.510	256	0.132	-1.747	1.157
Loc C***	-0.927	256	0.355	-0.961	1.037

Note: *Locus of Control Internal, ** Locus of Control Others, ***Locus of control chance

Trait anxiety shows a significant positive correlation with External LoC- powerful others (r (258) = .38, p <.01) and Chance (r (258) = .27, p < .01). A significant negative correlation exists between trait anxiety and internal LoC (r (258)= -0.25, p < .01). The researchers also analysed the relationship between neuroticism, Internal and External LoC. Between Neuroticism and Internal locus of control, there exists a negative correlation and is significant (r (258) = -0.17, p < .05). With External LoC (powerful others and chance), neuroticism shows a moderate positive correlation which is also significant (See Table 4). There also exists a strong positive correlation between neuroticism and trait anxiety r(258) = .723, $p < .05$).

In order to understand the predictive validity, the present study considered a multiple linear regression to see if neuroticism and locus of control significantly predict trait anxiety. The overall regression is statistically significant ($R^2 = .58$, $F(4, 254) = 88.7, p < .001$). It was found that Neuroticism ($\beta = 2.22, p = 0.001$), External LoC- Others ($\beta = 0.25, p = 0.001$) and Internal LoC ($\beta = -0.21, p = 0.005$) significantly predict Trait anxiety.

Table 4. Correlation matrix

	Trait anxiety	Neuroticism	LoC Internal	LoC Others	LoC Chance
Neuroticism	0.72**	—			
Internal LoC	-0.25**	-0.17**	—		
Others LoC	0.38**	0.25**	-0.02	—	
Chance LoC	0.27**	0.23**	0.01	0.46**	—

Note: *, significant at .05 level, **, Significant at .01 level

DISCUSSION

Culture and Gender Basis of Neuroticism

Throughout the literature, neurotic patterns of thoughts and thought processes are attributed more to females as compared to males. A study conducted by Yanna and colleagues (2011) among young adults and adolescents found gender differences in all aspects of the big 5 traits, more significantly on the sub scale neuroticism. Studies across cultures also validate the mean difference among males and females on neuroticism with females scoring significantly higher on the sub scale (Lynn, 1997). This can be associated with the social conditioning in the thought process due to the obvious differences in the biological roles of males and females. The underlying physiological differences leads to the psychological gender differences is a controversial argument but the studies attribute it either to evolutionary or socio-cultural factors. Studies identified evident differences in the way how men and women think, feel and behave. Particularly the studies in personality which attempt to examine psychological differences between gender based on personality traits (Yanna et al., 2011).

A study conducted across culture by Costa and colleagues (2001) concluded that gender differences on Neuroticism and agreeableness stemmed from stable evolutionary and biological bases. The study also noticed larger gender differences in industrialized countries where more progressive sociocultural gender roles exists. This possibly implies that gender roles are well defined and profound in industrialised counties and it gets strengthened with the sociopolitical, cultural and economic environment.This further points out that factors other than biological differences contributes to gender differences among males and females on neuroticism. However such studies warn against associating each gender with a specific trait and say the differences do not imply experiencing traits on opposing ends of the trait spectrum (Hyde, 2005).

Understanding the influence of cultural variation on personality is particularly critical in studying Neuroticism, considering the highly variable action tendencies and heterogeneous negative emotions. Behavioral manifestations of Neuroticism are indeed sensitive to social contexts (Mehl, Gosling, & Pennebaker, 2006). Studies point out that how an individual expresses negative beliefs about action may depend on whether it is practical or socially acceptable to do so (Mehl, Gosling, & Pennebaker, 2006). To strengthen this augment, we can relate to the difference in Individualism-collectivism across countries that may moderate the link between Neuroticism and inaction, particularly in international samples (Singelis, Triandis, Bhawuk, & Gelfand, 1995). In Collectivism one considers the social consequences of one's behavior before acting (Trafimow, et al., 2010), these behavioural consequences are an important determinant of attitudes (Ajzen & Fishbein, 2005). In collectivism, there is a complex and costly relationship with action and inaction leading to more emotional instability. (Molly et al., 2015; Fabrigar, MacDonald, & Wegener, 2005). Neuroticism is a collection of related intentions and behaviors, thus Neuroticism-relevant attitudes may be more predictive of Neuroticism among collectivistic individuals (Molly et al., 2015). This cultural view of neuroticism further explains why there is a gender difference in Neuroticism.

PREDICTING ANXIETY

Neuroticism is a significant predictor of anxiety and depression in diverse populations (Jefferey, 2017). The results from the present study indicate a significant, strong positive relationship between Trait anxiety and Neuroticism. The strength of the relationship remains the same even after controlling for gender (r (258) = .719, $p < .05$). Thus it indicates that neurotic individuals are more prone to anxiety.

Neuroticism and External locus of control are cognitive vulnerabilities which play an important role in the aetiology of anxiety and depressive disorders. Neuroticism is marked by emotional instability and a low tolerance for stress or aversive stimuli and is characterised by anxiety, fear, moodiness, worry, envy, frustration, jealousy, and loneliness. It is explained by differences in the level of activity primarily in the limbic system (Eysenck, 1967). Across different populations, Neuroticism is identified as a significant predictor of anxiety and depression (Jefferey, 2017). The present study also shows a strong predictive role of neuroticism and Locus of control on Anxiety. A study conducted by Yini and colleagues (2021) among adolescents and early adults identified neuroticism increases vulnerability to developing anxiety symptoms. Studies also associate external LoC as a risk factor for the onset of anxiety and depressive symptoms (Barlow, 2000, Wiersma et al., 2011).

Studies associate serious mental and physical health problems from childhood to adulthood with neuroticism (Kendler, 2005). More specifically, mood disorders, anxiety disorders, somatoform disorders, schizophrenia and eating disorders were associated. In addition to this, studies bring extensive evidence for depression, phobia, anxiety disorder, alcohol and drug dependency and antisocial personality disorder among individuals who are Neurotic (Kornør & Nordvik, 2007). A study conducted by Mark and colleagues (2004) examine the negative impacts of neuroticism on the family environment and parenting practices with increased risk for psychosocial problems among offspring. Hence it is evident from the studies that neuroticism is not only a risk at the individual level but also to the family and to the society.

Trait anxiety is the physical, emotional, and mental alterations of an individual against a non-objective danger (Aiken, 1976). It is an acquired behavioural disposition, that predisposes a person to perceive a wide range of objectively non-dangerous (physically or psychologically) circumstances as threatening and respond to these situations disproportionately in intensity and in the magnitude to the objective danger (Spielberger, 1983). Developmental theorists attribute trait anxiety to early childhood experiences and attachment processes (Bowlby, 1988). Perceived lack of control over things and fear of being wrong also makes one extremely anxious over the course of life.

Rotter conceptualised locus of control on a dynamic bipolar continuum ranging from internal to external. It is characterized by the belief that consequences are outcomes of one's own behaviour or the belief that consequences are a result of fate, luck, or powerful others. Individuals having a high internal locus of control are responsible, have the ability to solve problems effectively, they are more organised, systematic, resistant, self-assured and success-oriented (Yeşilyaprak, 2004). If we believe that the outcome depends on our own behaviour or personal characteristics, it is said that we have an internal locus of control. A sense of belief that the real power that determines our life resides in forces outside us generally increases stress. Studies conducted among chronically ill patients identify that individuals with an external locus of control adopt dysfunctional coping strategies which increase anxiety (Kohli, 2011).

IMPLICATIONS

The observed connection between neuroticism and heightened anxiety levels emphasizes the need for targeted interventions, especially for individuals with high levels of neuroticism. Evidences from longitudinal research and observations based on Cognitive Affective Personality System (CAPS) model emphasis that personality traits remain relatively stable (Wolfle and List, 2004) in general population. LoC also remains moderately stable in the general population (Cobb-Clark and Schurer, 2013), but subjected to modest and gradual changes during specific role transitions such as parenthood, among very young and old people and among patients with chronic conditions (Ormel et al., 2017; Roberts et al., 2006). This implies, long term interventions and conscious modification of the environment can bring positive changes in neurotic thought process and external LoC. Such interventions should focus on altering the thought patterns and the specific negative influences from the environment of the individual from a very young age (Lachman, 2006).

Personality does not always predicts our thoughts, feelings and behaviours accurately or our behaviours are not always consistent with our personality. Variations in life circumstances and situations may affect the ways in which we think and behave. There are evidences to say that perceptions of life events and mind set may affect personality traits (Jantje et al., 2021) and this is very evident from the mean level changes in personality among young adults (Roberts and Mroczek, 2008). In a study conducted by Niehoff and colleagues (2017) identified an increases in extraversion, agreeableness, and emotional stability among young adults living and studying in abroad after college. If environment and mind set can bring such a change, this suggest interventions at early childhood that focus on challenging the mindset (Roberts, 2009) can bring positive changes in personality. Cognitive behavioural interventions are found to be the most effective to modify dysfunctional thought processes associated with neuroticism and external locus of control (Lachman, 2006).

CONCLUSION

The study found that neuroticism and LoC significantly predict trait anxiety since both personality traits pose a certain cognitive vulnerabilities leading to behaviours which result in increased anxiety and depression. These personality traits are largely influenced by our temperament and early developmental events, it remains relatively stable in the general population. Since heightened anxiety is a potential risk for various physiological and psychological conditions it is essential to plan early interventions to alter this dysfunctional thought pattern associated with Neuroticism and External LoC.

Adolescents and emerging adults in the transitional stage are exposed to varied novel situations which trigger anxiety. By controlling neurotic thoughts and developing internal LoC they confront various demanding situations more effectively. Curriculum-based interventions aimed at bringing gradual and lasting changes to these dysfunctional cognitive patterns at the early stage are essential for considerable improvements.

ACKNOWLEDGMENTS

The authors would like to acknowledge all the participants who were involved in our study for their cooperation.

DECLARATION OF INTEREST STATEMENT

There exists no conflict of interests.

REFERENCES

Aiken, L. R.Jr. (1976). Update on Attitudes and Other Affective Variables in Learning Mathematics. *Review of Educational Research*, 46(2), 293–311. 10.3102/00346543046002293

Ajzen, I., & Fishbein, M. (2005). The Influence of Attitudes on Behavior. In Albarracín, D., Johnson, B. T., & Zanna, M. P. (Eds.), *The handbook of attitudes* (pp. 173–221). Lawrence Erlbaum Associates Publishers.

Arı, R. (1989). Üç büyük psikolojik yaklaşımda anksiyete. *Selçuk Üniversitesi Eğitim Fakültesi Dergisi*, 3, 195–219.

Awate J. N. & Khalane S. (2021). Correlation between Locus of Control and Big Five Personality Factors among Public and Private Services Officers. *International Journal of Indian Psychology*, 9(3), 2103-2109. DOI:10.25215/0903.200

Bagby, R. M., Uliaszek, A. A., Gralnick, T. M., & Widiger, T. A. (Eds.). (2017). *The Oxford handbook of the five factor model*. Oxford University Press.

Barlow, D. H. (2000). Unraveling the mysteries of anxiety and its disorders from the perspective of emotion theory. *The American Psychologist*, 55(11), 1247–1263. 10.1037/0003-066X.55.11.124711280938

Barlow, D. H. (2002). *Anxiety and its disorders: The nature and treatment of anxiety and panic. 2nd.* Guilford Press.

Barlow, D. H., Sauer-Zavala, S., Carl, J. R., Bullis, J. R., & Ellard, K. K. (2014). The Nature, Diagnosis, and Treatment of Neuroticism. *Clinical Psychological Science*, 2(3), 344–365. 10.1177/2167702613505532

Borsboom, D. (2008). Psychometric perspectives on diagnostic systems. *Journal of Clinical Psychology*, 64(9), 1089–1108. 10.1002/jclp.2050318683856

Bowlby, J. (1988). *A Secure Base: Parent-Child Attachment and Healthy Human Development*. https://doi.org/10.1604/9780465075980

Cassiello-Robbins, C., Wilner, J. G., & Sauer-Zavala, S. (2017). Neuroticism. In Zeigler-Hill, V., & Shackelford, T. (Eds.), *Encyclopedia of Personality and Individual Differences*. Springer. 10.1007/978-3-319-28099-8_1256-1

Cobb-Clark, D. A., & Schurer, S. (2012). The stability of big-five personality traits. *Economics Letters*, 115(1), 11–15. 10.1016/j.econlet.2011.11.015

Costa, P. T., & McCrae, R. R. (1985). *The NEO Personality Inventory Manual*. Psychological Assessment Resources.

Cramer, A. O. J., Van Der Sluis, S., Noordhof, A., Wichers, M., Geschwind, N., Aggen, S. H., Kendler, K. S., & Borsboom, D. (2012). Dimensions of Normal Personality as Networks in Search of Equilibrium: You Can't like Parties if you Don't like People. *European Journal of Personality*, 26(4), 414–431. 10.1002/per.1866

De Vries, J. H., Spengler, M., Frintrup, A., & Mussel, P. (2021). Personality Development in Emerging Adulthood—How the Perception of Life Events and Mindset Affect Personality Trait Change. *Frontiers in Psychology*, 12, 671421. 10.3389/fpsyg.2021.67142134234715

Ellenbogen, M. A., & Hodgins, S. (2004). The impact of high neuroticism in parents on children's psychosocial functioning in a population at high risk for major affective disorder: A family-environmental pathway of intergenerational risk. *Development and Psychopathology*, 16(1), 113–136. 10.1017/S09545794040444438151150 67

Eysenck, H. J. (1967). *The biological basis of personality*. Thomas.

Eysenck, S. B., Eysenck, H. J., & Barrett, P. M. (1985). A revised version of the psychoticism scale. *Personality and Individual Differences*, 6(1), 21–29. 10.1016/0191-8869(85)90026-1

Fabrigar, L. R., MacDonald, T. K., & Wegener, D. T. (2005). The structure of attitudes. In Albarracín, D., Johnson, B. T., & Zanna, M. P. (Eds.), *Handbook of attitudes and attitude change* (pp. 79–124). Erlbaum.

Geist, C. R., & Borecki, S. (1982). Social avoidance and distress as a predictor of perceived locus of control and level of self-esteem. *Journal of Clinical Psychology*, 38(3), 611–613. 10.1002/1097-4679(198207)38:3<611::AID-JCLP2270380325>3.0.CO;2-H7107927

He, Y., Li, A., Li, K., & Xiao, J. (2021). Neuroticism vulnerability factors of anxiety symptoms in adolescents and early adults: An analysis using the bi-factor model and multi-wave longitudinal model. *PeerJ*, 9, e11379. 10.7717/peerj.1137934221704

Hyde, J. S. (2005). The gender similarities hypothesis. *The American Psychologist*, 60(6), 581–592. 10.1037/0003-066X.60.6.58116173891

Ireland, M. E., Hepler, J., Li, H., & Albarracín, D. (2015). Neuroticism and attitudes toward action in 19 countries. *Journal of Personality*, 83(3), 243–250. 10.1111/jopy.1209924684688

Khan, A. A., Jacobson, K. C., Gardner, C. O., Prescott, C. A., & Kendler, K. S. (2005). Personality and comorbidity of common psychiatric disorders. *The British Journal of Psychiatry*, 186(3), 190–196. 10.1192/bjp.186.3.19015738498

Kim, Y., Saunders, G. R. B., Giannelis, A., Willoughby, E. A., DeYoung, C. G., & Lee, J. J. (2023). Genetic and neural bases of the neuroticism general factor. *Biological Psychology*, 184, 108692. 10.1016/j.biopsycho.2023.10869237783279

Klingenberg, B., Guloksuz, S., Pries, L., Cinar, O., Menne-Lothmann, C., Decoster, J., van Winkel, R., Collip, D., Delespaul, P., De Hert, M., Derom, C., Thiery, E., Jacobs, N., Wichers, M., Lin, B. D., Luykx, J., van Os, J., & Rutten, B. (2023). Gene–environment interaction study on the polygenic risk score for neuroticism, childhood adversity, and parental bonding. *Personality Neuroscience*, 6, E5. 10.1017/pen.2023.238107775

Kohli, S., Batra, P., & Aggarwal, H. K. (2011). Anxiety, locus of control, and coping strategies among end-stage renal disease patients undergoing maintenance hemodialysis. *Indian Journal of Nephrology*, 21(3), 177–181. 10.4103/0971-4065.8372921886977

Kornør, H., & Nordvik, H. (2007). Five-factor model personality traits in opioid dependence. *BMC Psychiatry*, 7(1), 37. 10.1186/1471-244X-7-3717683593

Lachman, M. E. (2006). Perceived Control Over Aging-Related Declines. *Current Directions in Psychological Science*, 15(6), 282–286. 10.1111/j.1467-8721.2006.00453.x

Leary, M. R., & Hoyle, R. H. (Eds.). (2009). *Handbook of individual differences in social behavior*. The Guilford Press.

Lefcourt, H. M. (1981). Research with the Locus of Control Construct. In *Elsevier eBooks*. 10.1016/C2013-0-11068-9

Levenson, H. (1981). Differentiating among internality, powerful others, and chance. In Lefcourt, H. M. (Ed.), *Research with the locus of control construct* (Vol. 1, pp. 15–63). Academic Press. 10.1016/B978-0-12-443201-7.50006-3

Liu, Y. (2012). The Relation between Neuroticism and Life Satisfaction: The Chain Type Mediating Effect of Affect and Self-Esteem. *J. Psychol. Sci.*, 35, 1254.

Lynn, R., & Martin, T. (1997). Gender differences in extraversion, neuroticism, and psychoticism in 37 nations. *The Journal of Social Psychology*, 137(3), 369–373. 10.1080/00224549709595447920097

McClun, L. A., & Merrell, K. W. (1998). Relationship of perceived parenting styles, locus of control orientation, and self-concept among junior high age students. *Psychology in the Schools*, 35(4), 381–390. 10.1002/(SICI)1520-6807(199810)35:4<381::AID-PITS9>3.0.CO;2-S

Mehl, M. R., Gosling, S. D., & Pennebaker, J. W. (2006). Personality in its natural habitat: Manifestations and implicit folk theories of personality in daily life. *Journal of Personality and Social Psychology*, 90(5), 862–877. 10.1037/0022-3514.90.5.86216737378

Mischel, W., & Shoda, Y. (1995). A cognitive-affective system theory of personality: Reconceptualizing situations, dispositions, dynamics, and invariance in personality structure. *Psychological Review*, 102(2), 246–286. 10.1037/0033-295X.102.2.2467740090

Mischel, W., & Shoda, Y. (1998). Reconciling processing dynamics and personality dispositions. *Annual Review of Psychology*, 49(1), 229–258. 10.1146/annurev.psych.49.1.2299496625

Mughal, A. Y., Devadas, J., Ardman, E., Levis, B., Go, V. F., & Gaynes, B. N. (2020). A systematic review of validated screening tools for anxiety disorders and PTSD in low to middle income countries. *BMC Psychiatry*, 20(1), 338. 10.1186/s12888-020-02753-332605551

Niehoff, E., Petersdotter, L., & Freund, P. A. (2017). International sojourn experience and perso ality development: Selection and socialization effects of studying abroad and the Big Five. *Personality and Individual Differences*, 112, 55–61. 10.1016/j.paid.2017.02.043

Oner, N., & Le Compte, A. (1983). *Durumluk Surekli Kaygi Envanteri El Kitabi*. Bogazici Universitesi Yayinlari.

Ormel, J. (2013). *Neuroticism and common mental disorders: meaning and utility of a complex relationship - PubMed*. PubMed. 10.1016/j.cpr.2013.04.003

Ormel, J., VonKorff, M., Jeronimus, B. F., & Riese, H. (2017). Set-point theory and personality development: Reconciliation of a paradox. In Specht, J. (Ed.), *Personality Development across the Lifespan* (pp. 117–137). Elsevier. 10.1016/B978-0-12-804674-6.00009-0

Ozer, D. J., & Benet-Martínez, V. (2006). Personality and the prediction of consequential outcomes. *Annual Review of Psychology*, 57(1), 401–421. 10.1146/annurev.psych.57.102904.19012716318601

Reddy, J. K., Menon, K. R., & Thattil, A. (2018). Academic stress and its sources among university students. *Biomedical & Pharmacology Journal*, 11(1).

Regzedmaa, E., Ganbat, M., Sambuunyam, M., Tsogoo, S., Radnaa, O., Lkhagvasuren, N., & Zuunnast, K. A. (2024). A systematic review and meta-analysis of neuroticism and anxiety during the COVID-19 pandemic. *Frontiers in Psychiatry*, 14(1), 1281268. 10.3389/fpsyt.2023.128126838250262

Roberts, B. W. (2009). Back to the future: Personality and Assessment and personality development. *Journal of Research in Personality*, 43(2), 137–145. 10.1016/j.jrp.2008.12.01520161194

Roberts, B. W., & Mroczek, D. (2008). Personality trait change in adulthood. *Current Directions in Psychological Science*, 17(1), 31–35. 10.1111/j.1467-8721.2008.00543.x19756219

Roberts, B. W., Walton, K. E., & Viechtbauer, W. (2006). Patterns of mean-level change in personality traits across the life course: A meta-analysis of longitudinal studies. *Psychological Bulletin*, 132(1), 1–25. 10.1037/0033-2909.132.1.116435954

Rotter, J. B. (1954). *Social learning and clinical psychology*. Prentice-Hall, Inc., 10.1037/10788-000

Singelis, T. M., Triandis, H. C., Bhawuk, D. P. S., & Gelfand, M. J. (1995). Horizontal and vertical dimensions of individualism and collectivism: A theoretical and measurement refinement. [Google Scholar]. *Cross-Cultural Research*, 29(3), 240–275. 10.1177/106939719502900302

Spielberger, C. D., Gorsuch, R. L., Lushene, R., Vagg, P. R., & Jacobs, G. A. (1983). *Manual for the State-Trait Anxiety Inventory*. Consulting Psychologists Press.

Tackett, J. L., & Lahey, B. B. (2017). Neuroticism. In Widiger, T. A. (Ed.), *The Oxford handbook of the Five Factor Model* (pp. 39–56). Oxford University Press.

Trafimow, D., Clayton, K. D., Sheeran, P., Darwish, A. E., & Brown, J. (2010). How do people form behavioral intentions when others have the power to determine social consequences? *The Journal of General Psychology*, 137(3), 287–309. 10.1080/00221301003645210207182228

Uliaszek, A. A., Zinbarg, R. E., Mineka, S., Craske, M. G., Sutton, J. M., Griffith, J. W., Rose, R., Waters, A., & Hammen, C. (2010). The role of neuroticism and extraversion in the stress-anxiety and stress-depression relationships. *Anxiety, Stress, and Coping*, 23(4), 363–381. 10.1080/10615800903377726419890753

Valke, M., & Goel, A. (2022). Perceived Parenting Style and It's Relationship to Locus of Control and Emotional Maturity Among Emerging Adults. *International Journal of Indian Psychology*, 10(2). 10.25215/1002.029

Vettingl, J. R. (2017). *Who pays the price for high neuroticism? Moderators of longitudinal risks for depression and anxiety.* PubMed., 10.1017/S0033291717000253

W. (2011). Psychological Characteristics of Chronic Depression. *The Journal of Clinical Psychiatry,* 72(03), 288–294. 10.4088/JCP.09m05735blu

Wang, Y., & Kong, F. (2014). The role of emotional intelligence in the impact of mindfulness on life satisfaction and mental distress. *Social Indicators Research*, 116(3), 843–852. 10.1007/s11205-013-0327-6

Watson, D., Gamez, W., & Simms, L. J. (2005). Basic dimensions of temperament and their relations to anxiety and depression: A symptom-based perspective. *Journal of Research in Personality*, 39(1), 46–66. 10.1016/j.jrp.2004.09.006

Weisberg, Y. J., DeYoung, C. G., & Hirsh, J. B. (2011b). Gender Differences in Personality across the Ten Aspects of the Big Five. *Frontiers in Psychology*, 2. 10.3389/fpsyg.2011.0017821866227

Widiger, T. A., & Oltmanns, J. R. (2017). Neuroticism is a fundamental domain of personality with enormous public health implications. *World Psychiatry; Official Journal of the World Psychiatric Association (WPA)*, 16(2), 144–145. 10.1002/wps.2041128498583

Wiersma, J., Van Oppen, P., Van Schaik, D. J. F., Van Der Does, W., Beekman, A. T., & Penninx, B.

Wolfle, L. M., & List, J. H. (2004). Temporal Stability in the Effects of College Attendance on Locus of Control, 1972–1992. *Structural Equation Modeling*, 11(2), 244–260. 10.1207/s15328007sem1102_6

Yeşilyaprak, B. (2004). Denetim odağı. Y. Kuzgun & D. Deryakulu (Eds.), *Eğitimde bireysel farklılıklar içinde* (s. 239-258). Ankara: Nobel Yayınevi.

Zimbardo, P. G. (1985). *Psychology and life* (11th ed.). Scott Foresman.

Chapter 6
Exploring Protective Factors for Stress Among University Students:
A Theoretical Perspective

Anna Niitembu Hako
https://orcid.org/0000-0001-6367-1969
University of Namibia, Namibia

ABSTRACT

The chapter explores protective factors that can reduce stress in university students, highlighting cultural differences in stress responses. Using a literature review and document analysis method, it emphasizes holistic stress management, highlighting the importance of resilience, self-care, social support, coping abilities, and financial stability. The study suggests creating a welcoming campus environment, promoting social interactions, and providing resources to safeguard students' well-being.

INTRODUCTION

In the dynamic and challenging environment of higher education, university students frequently face a variety of stressors that can have a substantial impact on their mental health and academic performance (Lugo & Gil-Rivas, 2019). Understanding the elements that reduce stress in university students is critical for improving their well-being and academic performance. In this context, protective factors are those features of a person's life or surroundings that protect them from the harmful impacts of stress. This theoretical perspective seeks to investigate the protective elements that lead to resilience and stress management in university students. This chapter examines theoretical frameworks and empirical evidence to offer insight on the mechanisms by which these protective factors function, as well as the implications for interventions targeted at improving university students' well-being and academic performance. By investigating this topic, we can get valuable insights into how to foster resilience and positive mental health outcomes in university settings (Nuttall et al., 2015).

This chapter is structured as follows: First, the introduction of the protective factors that can reduce stress in university students is provided, and then the methodology. Next, the background information and the theoretical framework that guided the study are discussed. This is followed by a review of relevant literature. Finally, the conclusion is presented.

BACKGROUND

Students face a unique combination of problems throughout their transition to university life, including academic stress, social adaptations, financial concerns, and increased independence (Kloos et al., 2010; Amakali-Nauiseb et al., 2021). As a result, university students frequently suffer significant levels of stress, which can have negative consequences for their mental health and overall well-being. Stress among university students has been linked to a variety of negative effects, including lower academic performance, greater dropout rates, and an increased risk of mental health disorders such as anxiety and depression (Evans et al., 2010; Yang & Mufson, 2021). However, not all students handle stress the same way. While some may succumb to its harmful consequences, others show resilience and can effectively deal with pressures (Yau et al., 2012; Fateel, 2019). Protective variables have an important role in fostering resilience and minimizing the effects of stress on university students. These protective variables include a variety of individual, interpersonal, and environmental resources that help students adapt and prosper in the face of adversity (Lugo & Gil-Rivas, 2019).

Understanding the protective characteristics that contribute to stress among university students is critical for developing interventions and providing support services targeted at improving their mental health and academic success (Nuttall et al., 2015). It is clear that by looking at theoretical perspectives on stress and resilience, researchers can uncover important mechanisms by which protective factors work and devise tailored strategies for developing resilience in university students. Furthermore, investigating the interactions of individual traits, social support networks, and environmental factors might provide important insights into the complex dynamics of stress and coping in the university setting (Nuttall et al., 2015). By combining existing data and theoretical frameworks, this chapter aims to explain how diverse protective variables promote resilience and well-being among university students. The researcher expects that this inquiry will contribute to a better understanding of successful techniques for supporting university students' well-being and academic accomplishment in today's demanding higher education landscape (Lugo & Gil-Rivas, 2019). In this chapter, wellbeing is described as a comprehensive concept that includes both physical and mental health (World Health Organization, 2023). It entails balanced eating, exercise, appropriate sleep, and basic hygiene, as well as access to medical care for both temporary and chronic diseases, to promote physical well-being. Supporting student wellbeing recognizes that students may still face stress or tough times. As a result, it does not mean that institutions are required to prevent all mental distress or to offer on-campus care for all needs. Several studies were conducted to examine cross-cultural differences in response to stress and found cultural differences in the symptoms people focus on when experiencing distress. Lee et al. (2023) examined cross-cultural differences in student's daily stress experiences and the role of social orientations in explaining their experiences and found that the situational context moderates the effect of culture on perceptions of stress, showing a different amount of stress from interpersonal situations between Japanese and European Canadian undergraduates. Further, North Americans tend to emphasize psychological symptoms like sadness, anxiety, or anger. They value recognizing and expressing their emotions. East Asians (Chinese, Korean, Japanese) often focus on physical symptoms like headaches, stomach-aches, or fatigue. They may view these as signs of emotional distress and prioritize social harmony by keeping emotions reserved (Kirmayer & Ryder, 2016; Zhou et al., 2015). A study by Hashimoto and colleagues in 2012 found that Japanese college students were more likely to experience stressful interpersonal situations often and to feel more psychological distress as a result. In North American community health surveys, 20% of Canadians perceived most days in their life as "quite a bit" or "extremely" stressful (Statistics Canada, 2017), and 75% of Americans experienced at least one symptom of stress in the past month (American Psychological Association, 2015). Research has shown that while blacks (or African Americans) often have higher rates of psychological distress than whites, some studies also find that whites have elevated levels of depressive and anxiety symptoms compared to blacks (Williams, 2018).

METHODOLOGY

The technique utilized in this chapter included a literature review and document analysis aimed at identifying protective factors important to stress reduction among university students (Creswell & Pluno-Clark, 2018). The evaluation procedure included scanning electronic resources such as Google Scholar, ERIC, SpringerLink, Wiley

Online Library, Internet Archives, and ProQuest for pertinent research. Following the search, 600 publications from 2010 to 2023 were retrieved during April-June 2024. There were, however, a few related publications (2000 to 2007) that I looked at but do not fall between the specified period (2010 to 2023). The study's search terms included "protective measures," "coping skills," "self-efficacy," "resilience, academic support, communication channels, sense of belonging, and higher institutions individually." The studies were included if they focused on protective factors for stress among university students, were published in peer-reviewed journals, and were written in English. Exclusion criteria included papers that were unrelated to the research topic or published in non-peer-reviewed journals. Thematic content analysis of a large dataset was used to uncover protective variables that postsecondary students face throughout their academic careers and how applicable they are to the current student cohort (Braun & Clarke, 2006). For instance, I familiarised myself with the data retrieved, and the retrieved data were coded, categorised and reviewed before being grouped into emerged themes.

THEORETICAL FRAMEWORK

This chapter applies resilience theory to explore protective factors impacting student well-being in higher education. Resilience theory, which Norman Garmezy, Emmy Werner, Ann Masten, Michael Rutter, and Urie Bronfenbrenner created in 1974, emphasises people's capacity to adapt and thrive in the face of adversity. It identifies social support, coping methods, self-efficacy, and positive connections as important protective variables. According to Masten (2001), resilience is a dynamic process that depends on both personal and environmental factors. The approach stresses developing resilience at multiple levels in order to achieve positive results and psychological well-being. Overall, resilience theory offers useful insights for developing interventions to boost resilience and help people face life's obstacles. The following section examines the key factors that contribute to reduced stress among university students, maximize learning, and increase the likelihood of academic achievement and success.

SOCIAL SUPPORT

Social support is described as help made available to an individual through social ties with other people, groups, and the larger community (Klainin-Yobas et al., 2016). The National Cancer Institute's Dictionary of Cancer Terms defines social support as "a network of family, friends, neighbours, and community members that is available in times of need to provide psychological, physical, and financial assistance." Additionally, social support, identified as an external protective factor, refers to individuals' perception of sufficient and valuable support that influences their adjustment (Panani et al., 2016).

Numerous studies show that social support is critical for sustaining both physical and psychological health (Cho & Yu, 2015; Panani et al., 2016; Bartholomew et al., 2016; Klainin-Yobas et al., 2016). Panani et al. (2016) and Bartholomew et al. (2016) argue that social support is one of the most important variables impacting students' psychological well-being. They feel that solid relationships with friends, family, classmates, or mentors can help them cope with stress. Tang et al. (2019) concur that supportive relationships provide possibilities for emotional expression, advice, and practical aid. New studies show that having good positive social support can help you deal with stress better, keep you from developing trauma-related mental disorders, make it easier to function when you have a disorder like post-traumatic stress disorder (PTSD), and lower your risk of getting sick or dying (Klainin-Yobas et al., 2016; Cho & Yu, 2015; Bartholomew et al., 2016). However, Ryff (2023) claims that, despite strong evidence of the positive effects of social support on medical and psychological well-being, the field of psychiatry has made little progress in developing, testing, and implementing evidence-based interventions to increase social support for patients and at-risk populations. Lessard et al. (2014) claim that organizational support has a considerable influence on members' cognitive and emotional results, such as job satisfaction.

Students can benefit from university-based services that improve their psychological well-being and life happiness. According to the literature on social support, helpful social ties and strong social networks with close friends improve the mental health of students at higher education institutions (Cho & Yu, 2015). Significant others, including family members, friends, and lecturers, can provide students with social support (Tang et al., 2019). Klainin-Yobas et al. (2016) studied determinants predicting psychological well-being among university students in the Philippines and discovered that social support from family and friends was strongly associated with positive individual psychological well-being. It has been suggested that strong social networks can reduce the likelihood of participating in dangerous activities, avoid bad behaviour, and promote compliance. In theoretical models of social support, two critical dimensions are highlighted: (1) a structural dimension, which considers network size and frequency of social interaction, and (2) a functional dimension, which includes both emotional (such as receiving love and empathy) and instrumental elements. While both aspects are important, most studies find that the functional dimension, or the quality of connections, is a better predictor of good health.

It is vital to remember that the usefulness of social support varies according to the individual's developmental stage. For example, parental assistance tends to be more useful in early adolescence than in later adolescence. In older people, the perception of social support is related to their level of social involvement, whereas in younger ones, it is associated with instrumental aid. Furthermore, social support appears to play a role in increasing stress resilience. Overall, high-quality positive social support can boost stress resilience, delay the onset of trauma-related psychopathology, increase coping abilities, and normalize the adjustment process. As a result, university student counsellors can help students build coping skills by teaching them how to recognize and use social supports, as well as how to create networks of constructive contacts that help with the coping process.

SELF-EFFICACY

Błachnio et al. (2013) define self-efficacy as an individual's conviction in their ability to reach particular levels of performance and influence events in their lives. In simple terms, it is our belief in our ability, particularly in tackling problems and performing things successfully. While self-efficacy refers to our overall belief in our potential to succeed, it can take many other forms, including academic, parenting, and sports-related self-efficacy. As Fatima et al. (2018) emphasize, self-efficacy attempts to create a broad and long-lasting sense of personal competence in dealing with a variety of stressful situations. Individuals who experience low levels of pleasure and life satisfaction, as well as high levels of depression, are thought to benefit from strong self-efficacy, which can enable the adoption of suitable behaviours and good attitudes toward academic efforts and life in general. As a result, it is expected that self-efficacy will moderate the relationship between psychological elements and students' behaviour and attitudes in higher education.

Furthermore, students navigating higher education institutions may often feel vulnerable and helpless, which might lower their self-efficacy. Prior research has, however, proven a strong link between self-efficacy and academic success, habits, attitudes, and overall student wellbeing. For example, Andretta et al. (2020), Fatima et al. (2018), Tommasi et al. (2018), and De Caroli & Sagone (2014) found a favourable relationship between self-efficacy and student well-being, indicating a lack of psychological difficulties. Furthermore, Naeemi and Tamam (2017) found that excessive emotional reliance on platforms such as Facebook may have a negative influence on several areas of psychological well-being, even if self-efficacy is strong. In addition, Fatima et al. (2018) found that self-efficacy mediated the links between religious coping mechanisms, religious practices, and various student well-being outcomes in the context of perceived social support.

According to Maddux (2016), students with high levels of self-efficacy and emotional intelligence, as well as overall happiness, are more motivated to engage in academic activities and have positive attitudes that lead to university success. It has been noted that cheerful students with high satisfaction levels are more likely to demonstrate flexibility and efficiency in problem-solving, to be committed to academic goals, and to pursue achievement rather than simply avoiding failure. Furthermore, Greenleaf et al. (2014) underlined the importance of emotional self-efficacy in determining mental health, academic performance, social interaction, and emotion. It is critical to recognize that self-efficacy is an important factor in defining an individual's resistance to adversity as well as vulnerability to stress and depression.

RESILIENCE

According to Simons et al. (2018), who defined resilience as "the process of adapting well in the face of adversity, trauma, tragedy, threats, or significant sources of stress, such as family and relationship problems, serious health issues, or workplace and financial pressures," it is a concept that defies a single definition. As a result, the current body of research lacks a universally agreed-upon operational definition for resilience. However, it has been proposed that resilience includes both behavioural characteristics, such as maintaining effectiveness and resisting destructive behaviours (Robertson & Cooper, 2013), and psychological traits, such as the ability to maintain good mental health in the face of adversity (Bonanno, 2004). In summary, resilience is defined as the ability to recover from adversity. Resilient people are thought to be better suited to deal with stress and adversity, frequently relying on their personal qualities, adaptability, and positivity. Within an educational framework, resilience has emerged as an essential skill for students to succeed in higher education settings. For example, Fuller et al. (2020) defined resilience as a set of attitudes and behaviours related to a student's ability to recover from and actively adapt to adversity. Resilience is regarded as critical for supporting students in handling academic demands, promoting good progress, and dealing with the pressures of studying, working, and personal life (Caruana, 2014).

Durso et al. (2021) define a "resilient student" as someone who completes their undergraduate degree despite severe stress or difficulties while remaining satisfied and committed to their chosen field of study. Durso et al. (2021) used the Academic Resilience Model (ARM) to identify important protective mechanisms or determinants of resilience, including flexibility, self-control, personal organization, positive interactions with teachers, peer integration, and family support. Robbins et al. (2018) evaluated the predictive impacts of resilience, stress, mindfulness, and self-efficacy on undergraduate student well-being and discovered that resilience was the strongest predictor. Resilience, particularly in the face of stress, can protect people against severe bad life outcomes and contribute to higher lifetime happiness.

Similarly, research reveals that internal variables may influence the development of resilience. While Johnson et al. (2017) identified internal factors like optimism, self-efficacy, and psychological well-being as being crucial to young people's resilience, other scholars contend that protective traits like self-esteem, exposure to stressful events, attachment patterns in parental relationships, positive thinking, problem-solving skills, and support from family, friends, and teachers can also have an impact. Furthermore, a secure attachment status, which is regarded to persist throughout maturity, is thought to enhance long-term resilience. Secure attachment has been linked to protective resilience against the risk of substance abuse and criminal behaviour in adults (Black-Hughes & Stacy, 2013). Furthermore, attachment security has been identified as a source of resilience for adults facing the consequences of educational disadvantage in the workplace, contributing to improved health behaviours and long-term health outcomes via effective coping mechanisms (Bartley et al., 2007; Harding et al., 2019). As a result, higher education institutions play an important role in developing student resilience by adopting programs customized to individual needs or small groups. The literature confirms that such activities have a significant impact on enhancing self-esteem (Fennell, 2016; Longworth et al., 2016), underscoring the relevance of proactive resilience-building efforts in school settings.

COPING SKILLS

Exercise, creative hobbies, social support, and meditation are examples of coping mechanisms that students can use to deal with the ups and downs of life. Incorporating these diverse coping skills into students' daily lives will help them build resilience and improve their mental health. According to Algorani and Gupta (2023), coping strategies are the beliefs and activities used to deal with stressors, both internal and external. The same authors define 'defence mechanisms' as adaptive subconscious or unconscious reflexes that work to reduce or tolerate stress; this term is explicitly used to describe the mobilisation of conscious and voluntary acts. People's diverse responses to stressors are referred to as "coping styles," which are a collection of relatively consistent qualities that impact how they react under duress. It is thought that acquiring good coping mechanisms, such as problem-solving abilities, relaxation techniques, time management tactics, and positive reframing, might help students manage stress more effectively. The study by Ganesan et al. (2018) found that undergraduates prefer to rely on others as a coping method. Coping strategies include meeting with friends, seeking advice, and seeking emotional support. Productive coping, such as playing sports or focusing on the positive, is preferred over non-productive coping, such as avoiding social situations, feeling guilty, or worrying about the present situation when coping with stress. Another study by Logel et al. (2021) examined students' experiences and coping mechanisms and found that about 40% of respondents wanted to start a new daily routine and engage in physical activity as a coping mechanism. According to the findings of this survey, 64% of students reported using social or group activities as their primary coping technique. Students also emphasized the necessity of adopting good sleeping habits, eating a nutritious diet, practising meditation, and exploring new interests or learning new skills. Similar to this, Hasanah, Tribrilianti, and Oktaviani (2023) investigated students' coping mechanisms and identified three dimensions: approach, avoidance, and social support. The majority of respondents (89.7%) chose the approach tactic. This finding is consistent with Umar et al. (2021) research, which found that students often employ approach coping methods while experiencing problems in online learning. Approach coping entails carefully considering and making decisions when solving problems. Unlike previous studies that only described coping behaviours or conditions, this study emphasises the relationship between coping techniques and students' mental health. Another study by Nagar (2021) looked into how university students coped with adversity through problem-solving, seeking social support, and avoiding it. The objectives were to understand the many coping techniques used by students to manage stressful situations, including the usage of "coping with hope" as a coping strategy. The findings revealed that students prefer avoidance coping techniques to problem resolution and seeking social support coping strategies. While Yano et al. (2021) identified problem resolution, avoidance, distraction, and sharing one's concerns with others, Del Rosario (2023) discovered that respondents regularly chose napping as a stress management approach, while cognitive reappraisal was a popular coping mechanism. Positive reappraisal was the most commonly utilized approach by 76.86%, while confrontive coping was used the least by 55.83% (Baaleis & Ali, 2018). As a result, effective coping strategies for improving mental health may differ depending on the level of sensory sensitivity (SPS).

SELF-CARE PRACTICES

Self-care encompasses all of the routine activities and behaviours that assist students in maintaining their well-being while attending university (Younas, 2017). For university students, juggling homework, social life, and self-care can be difficult. However, by practicing self-care, students can better deal with life's unavoidable problems, such as the social, intellectual, and financial stress that they are likely to face during their time at university. Self-care frequently takes a backseat to exam preparation rather than getting enough sleep. Younas (2017) provides student self-care advice such as finding balance, practising meditation, requesting help when needed, engaging in soothing activities, connecting with friends, nourishing the body with the right foods, prioritizing adequate sleep, and being kind to oneself. Regular self-care activities, such as exercise, proper sleep, healthy food, hobbies, and relaxation, are thought to improve general well-being and stress resilience.

Among the studies that reported positive results, Horneffer (2006) discovered that 58% of 300 students exercised frequently, with only 4% not exercising. Nevins and Sherman (2016) discovered that 77.7% of 119 students ate a balanced diet, while 22.6% seldom ate a balanced diet, 62% of students reported drinking 3–8 glasses of water daily, 34% exercised regularly, and 24.5% exercised rarely, while 70% of students did not exercise enough. Chow and Kalischuk (2008) discovered that 83% of 211 students slept 6–8 hours per night; 60% reported adequate sleep, while 37% reported insufficient sleep; 65% reported drinking four to eight glasses of water or juice per day; 77% reported eating a balanced diet (49% "frequently" and 28% "consistently"); and 71% reported exercising regularly or occasionally, whereas 4% did not exercise at all. Clément et al. (2002) observed students' self-care activities for three consecutive years: 1992, 1993, and 1994. According to the authors, the majority of the students reported getting enough sleep (1992 = 73%, 1993 = 79%, and 1994 = 71%), eating a balanced diet (1992 = 88%, 1993 = 81%, and 1994 = 79%), and getting enough exercise. Other researchers observed similar findings (Stark et al., 2005; Siappo et al., 2016; and Padykula, 2016). However, of the studies reporting unfavourable findings, Ashcraft and Gatto (2015) and Haddad et al. (2004) found that students practised low-to-moderate self-care activities. The mean self-care practices for health responsibility, physical activity, and nutrition ranged from 2.07 to 2.58, indicating poor self-care practices (2004). In general, evidence suggests that students practice healthy self-care habits in terms of nutrition, sleep, water consumption, and physical activity. Siappo et al. (2016) qualitative findings support this since students in their study recognized the need for a balanced diet, an active lifestyle, appropriate sleep, and bodily hygiene in maintaining self-care.

Importantly, according to a Harvard report released in 2022, more than half of college students get less than seven hours of sleep every night, falling short of the National Sleep Foundation's suggested minimum for healthy adults. According to the study, sleep deprivation can worsen depression symptoms. However, prioritizing sleep among university students can result in favourable results such as higher academic achievement, increased concentration during study sessions, and decreased daytime sleepiness. Chronic sleep deprivation can have major long-term consequences for a student's physical and mental health. Insufficient sleep has also been linked to weight gain and obesity, cardiovascular disease, and type 2 diabetes. In 2021, the American College Health Association published worrisome findings:

48% of college students experienced moderate or severe psychological stress, 53% felt lonely, and 26% considered suicide. These findings emphasize the significance of self-care for students in lowering stress, minimizing burnout, and enhancing general health and well-being. According to the Mental Health First Aid (MHFA) curriculum, practising self-care allows people to adapt to change, build solid relationships, and recover from failures.

Finally, students should consider these self-care strategies to help them maintain their well-being throughout and after university.

- Maintain a defined schedule to promote steadiness.
- Prioritize sleep, as sleep deprivation can worsen sadness and anxiety.
- Incorporate everyday activity, such as walking instead of driving, to improve both your mental and physical health.
- Seek help from friends, family, or resident assistants as needed.
- To preserve balance, schedule time for enjoyable activities such as listening to music, reading, or being creative.
- To relieve tension and promote tranquility, use relaxation techniques in a peaceful, comfortable environment (Harvard, 2022; ACHA, 2021).

ACADEMIC SUPPORT

Access to academic resources such as tutoring services, study groups, and counselling can greatly reduce student stress about academic performance and workload (Vincent et al., 2020). Tutoring programs, for example, might help students who struggle with specific courses or schoolwork. Tutors can clarify difficult ideas, provide additional practice materials, and suggest efficient study practices (Centre for Access to Learning Opportunities, 2013). Students who receive focused academic support may feel more secure in their abilities, reducing anxiety and tension related to academic achievement (Blazer et al., 2019). Furthermore, working with peers in study groups can improve learning experiences and reduce academic stress. Study groups allow students to exchange ideas, debate course material, and collaborate to solve difficulties (Chickering & Reisser, 1993; Astin, 1993). This collaborative learning environment encourages students to actively interact with the curriculum while also instilling a sense of community and support. Furthermore, study groups can help students establish effective study strategies and time management skills, resulting in a more manageable workload and lower stress levels. Finally, university counselling services give expert support to students confronting a variety of issues, including academic stress (Evans et al., 2010; Singh & Singh, 2011). Counsellors can assist students in developing coping mechanisms for dealing with academic expectations, address underlying issues that contribute to stress or anxiety, and provide a safe space for students to voice their concerns and emotions (Pascarella & Terenzini, 2005). Students who use counselling services can learn useful techniques for preserving their mental health and well-being while navigating the demands of academic life. Overall, having access to these academic resources is critical for students' academic achievement and well-being because it provides focused support, fosters collaboration and community, and addresses the emotional and psychological aspects of academic stress.

SENSE OF BELONGING

With a large number of students having socio-emotional challenges and a requirement for students to be socially and emotionally competent and ready for their educational journeys, educators must be aware of the effects of emotional regulation and social skills on academic accomplishment (du Toit-Brits, 2022). For example, Maslow's Hierarchy of Needs (Maslow 1954) states that a child's well-being and sense of belonging must be addressed before the child can effectively study, apply knowledge, and solve problems. As a result, a comprehensive approach to development, including social and emotional skills, is critical for student's academic achievement. Furthermore, educators must be educated to incorporate the development of SEL skills into the classroom curriculum, while school administrators must focus on creating a schoolwide SEL by enhancing the school environment, policies, and practices, as well as engaging in family and community collaborations (Oberle et al., 2019). According to research, school climate is more than an organizational quality (Huang, 2020), since students' views of a safe and supportive environment influence the development of their social and emotional learning abilities (Osher et al., 2017; Choi et al., 2023).

Belonging is a sense of security and support that comes from being welcomed, included, and having a sense of self as a member of a particular group (Ruff, 2021; Nam et al., 2023). Students experience this when they feel like part of a campus community. For example, students may feel linked to the university community through their participation in clubs, groups, or campus activities, which can have a significant impact on their sense of belonging and well-being. For example, joining clubs or groups allows students to meet people who share similar interests, ambitions, or identities. This sense of belonging creates a supportive environment in which people feel accepted, appreciated, and understood. According to Parra et al. (2022), students who have a strong sense of belonging are more likely to participate actively in campus life, participate in academic and extracurricular activities, and develop meaningful relationships with their peers and faculty members. Furthermore, the university can be a difficult and sometimes alienating experience, particularly for students who are away from home or unfamiliar with new situations (Brady et al., 2020; Novick et al., 2019). Participating in college groups, organisations, or activities allows for social engagement, networking, and friendship-building (Kenney, 2023). These ties provide a sense of camaraderie and support for students, lowering feelings of loneliness and isolation. Participating in group activities also promotes a sense of companionship and shared purpose, which strengthens students' sense of belonging to the campus community.

According to Rockwell (2022), participation in clubs or groups can help students grow and develop personally. Students learn vital skills including communication, organization, problem-solving, and collaboration by participating in leadership roles, teamwork, and community service initiatives (Pratt & Crum, 2020). These experiences not only help students succeed academically and professionally, but they also boost their general self-esteem, resilience, and empowerment. According to research, students who actively participate in campus life report better levels of satisfaction, contentment, and overall well-being (Atkins et al., 2023; Novick et al., 2019).

Students feel more fulfilled and purposeful in college when they are linked to the university community and have opportunities to participate in important activities and interactions. This sense of fulfilment and connection protects students against stress, anxiety, and mental health difficulties, thus improving their general health and well-being. In summary, participation in clubs, groups, or campus events is critical for developing a sense of belonging, minimizing feelings of isolation, boosting personal growth and development, and improving overall well-being among college students. By actively participating in the university community, students can form important connections, build supportive relationships, and create lasting memories that enrich their college experience.

CLEAR COMMUNICATION CHANNELS

Open communication with professors, advisers, and administrative personnel is critical for students to successfully navigate academic and administrative concerns (Terenzini, 2013). To begin, lecturers, advisors, student counsellors, and administrative personnel are excellent sources of information for students on course requirements, academic policies (Jaschik, 2015), registration procedures (Pascarella & Terenzini, 2005), and campus .resources. By encouraging open communication channels, students can quickly acquire accurate and up-to-date information to solve academic difficulties and make educated decisions about their educational journey (Kuh, 2009). This availability of information minimises doubt and misunderstanding, allowing students to confidently handle academic requirements (Chickering &Reisser, 1993). Furthermore, instructors and advisors play important roles in guiding students through their academic careers. They can provide personalized advice mentorship (Gurin et al., 2010), and academic support based on students' specific needs and goals (Schlosser &Long, 1998). Professors and advisers act as trusted allies who aid students in navigating academic challenges and making progress toward their academic goals, whether by providing guidance on course selection, comments on assignments, or assisting with academic planning (Kuh, 2009). Similarly, administrative staff can help students with administrative tasks such as registration (Chickering & Reisser, 1993), financial aid and campus services (Kuh, 2009), easing the administrative burden and reducing students' stress (Terenzini et al., 2009). Furthermore, open communication encourages problem-solving and collaboration among students and faculty (Gurin et al., 2010). When students face academic or administrative challenges, such as scheduling conflicts), grading discrepancies (Chickering & Reisser, 1993), or enrolment issues (Pascarella & Terenzini, 2005), they can seek help from professors, advisors, or administrative staff to resolve them as soon as possible. Open communication channels enable the rapid resolution of difficulties, preventing issues from increasing and relieving students' stress and worry. Finally, constant communication with professors, advisors, and administrative personnel enables students to develop meaningful relationships and trust with key partners in their academic path. When students feel comfortable asking for help or guidance, they are more likely to seek it out and work together to solve problems (Gurin et al., 2010). These positive relationships build a sense of belonging and connection within the academic community, resulting in a supportive environment in which students feel valued, respected, and encouraged to achieve success. Indeed, open communication with professors, advisors, and administration personnel is critical in giving students the information, assistance, and support they need to successfully manage academic and administrative concerns (Kuh 2009). Universities may empower students to make informed decisions, access resources, overcome obstacles, and ultimately prosper in their academic endeavours by establishing open communication channels.

TIME MANAGEMENT SKILLS

Prioritizing work, setting realistic objectives, and efficiently managing time are essential skills for students to successfully handle the demands of academic and extracurricular activities (Sonnentag et al., 2014). First, prioritizing tasks entails determining the most critical and urgent obligations and allocating time and resources accordingly. Prioritizing tasks allows students to direct their energy and attention toward finishing vital assignments or meeting critical deadlines first, lowering the chance of feeling overwhelmed by an excessive workload (Owen et al., 2018). Prioritization allows students to approach work systematically, retain productivity, and make consistent progress toward their academic and personal goals. Second, developing realistic goals entails creating attainable targets that are consistent with students' talents, resources, and time limits (Blume et al., 2010). Unrealistic goals can lead to dissatisfaction, disappointment, and burnout, whereas attainable goals foster drive, confidence, and a sense of success (Wood, 2008). Setting realistic goals allows students to break down larger activities into smaller, more manageable steps, making it easier to track progress, stay focused, and maintain momentum toward their objectives. Third, successful time management is allocating time intelligently among diverse activities and duties, balancing academic obligations, extracurricular activities, personal interests, and self-care (Owen et al., 2018; Sonnentag and Fritz, 2014). Students who manage their time well are better able to meet deadlines, avoid procrastination, and strike a healthy work-life balance. Time management practices, such as developing calendars, utilizing planners or digital tools, setting deadlines, and practising time-blocking, can assist students in making better use of their time, increasing productivity, and reducing feelings of overload. Fourth, learning to prioritize work, create realistic goals, and manage time wisely might help students reduce stress (Burke, 2009). Students can approach their workload with a sense of control and confidence by breaking projects down into manageable chunks, rather than feeling overwhelmed by the total number of works. Effective time management also helps students schedule time for rest, relaxation, and self-care, all of which are necessary for general well-being and avoiding burnout (Locke & Latham, 2002). Fifth, when students prioritize work, create realistic goals, and efficiently manage their time, they can improve their productivity and performance (Sonnentag & Fritz, 2014). Focusing on high-priority activities allows students to better spend their time and energy, resulting in better academic outcomes, higher-quality work, and greater pleasure with their accomplishments. Effective time management also allows students to devote time to vital extracurricular activities, personal interests, and social connections, which improves their overall college experience. To summarize, students must learn to prioritize tasks, create realistic goals, and manage time effectively in order to successfully handle the demands of college life (Astin, 1993). These abilities enable students to maintain a sense of control, reduce feelings of overwhelm, and achieve academic and personal objectives with confidence and resilience.

FINANCIAL STABILITY

Higher education costs, such as tuition, living expenses, and student loans, can cause significant financial stress for students (Bettinger and Pascarella, 2000). Previous studies have shown that stress over money due to a lack of funds can have a negative impact on productivity and academic performance. Baik et al. (2019) believe that the stress of debt and the need to manage finances might cause worry and negatively impact students' general well-being. This is explicable by the fact that stressed-out students are more likely to experience health problems like anxiety and excessive stress. This limits their ability to be successful and perform at their best when learning (Sonnentag and Fritz, 2005). Additionally, studies have shown that students who are experiencing financial stress frequently display negative attitudes, which are best exemplified by a lack of commitment to and enthusiasm for their academic work (Richardson et al., 2012). This creates a vicious cycle of failure and low performance because most students are forced to study while under financial hardship, which produces despair and pain.

Given the aforementioned, financial stability and access to resources like grants, scholarships, part-time job opportunities, and financial aid are crucial in reducing the stress that financial worries cause among university students. According to Hako and Shikongo (2019), financial security gives students peace of mind because it ensures that their fundamental necessities, such as tuition, housing, food, and transportation, are sufficiently met. According to the same authors, students who have a solid financial situation are less likely to feel stress and worry caused by financial uncertainty, allowing them to focus more effectively on their academic goals and personal growth (College Board, 2023). Another study by Sonnentag and Fritz (2005) discovered that scholarships and grants provide financial support to students based on academic merit, financial need, or particular criteria. These types of financial aid can greatly lessen the financial burden of university attendance, making higher education more accessible and affordable to students from all backgrounds (Bettinger & Pascarella, 2000). Scholarships and grants allow students to pay for tuition, textbooks, and other educational expenses, lowering financial stress and enhancing their chances of academic achievement. Accordingly, (Blinn College (2023) believes that part-time employment possibilities allow students to earn money while studying, providing financial support and useful work experience. Working part-time allows students to contribute to their school fees, cover living costs, and learn practical skills that will improve their employability (Blinn College, 2023). To avoid undue stress and sustain academic success, students must strike a balance between their professional commitments and their academic responsibilities. Furthermore, financial aid programs such as student loans, grants, and work-study programs provide financial assistance to students based on their financial needs

(Bettinger & Pascarella, 2000). These programs can help students pay for tuition, housing, and other educational expenditures, easing the financial burden of attending college (Sonnentag & Fritz, 2005).

To make informed financial decisions, students must first grasp the terms and conditions of financial aid programs, including loan payback responsibilities. Financial aid offices, budgeting courses, and emergency funds are common resources and support services provided by universities to students who are concerned about their finances. These resources can assist students in navigating financial issues, obtaining eligible financial aid, and developing financial literacy skills to properly manage their funds (Federal Student Aid, 2023). Furthermore, support services can provide counseling and advocacy to students experiencing financial issues, ensuring that they get the help they need to achieve academically and personally. In conclusion, financial stability and access to resources like financial aid, part-time employment opportunities, scholarships, and grants are essential for reducing the stress that financial worries cause in college students. Colleges and universities can encourage student well-being, academic achievement, and overall student happiness by providing necessary financial support and assistance.

MENTAL HEALTH RESOURCES

Mental health services, like counselling centres staffed by certified experts, are critical for managing student mental health issues (American College Health Association, 2023). These centres provide professional assistance, assessment, diagnosis, and evidence-based interventions for a variety of disorders, including stress, anxiety, depression, and trauma (American College Health Association, 2023). Therapists can use a variety of treatments customized to individual requirements, including cognitive Behavioural therapy (CBT), mindfulness exercises, and supportive counselling (National Alliance on Mental Illness, 2023). Mental health services also include crisis intervention and emergency support (Singh &Singh, 2011). Crisis hotlines, walk-in appointments, and emergency response teams provide prompt support, assessment, and intervention to ensure student safety and well-being during a crisis (Singh & Singh, 2011). Furthermore, mental health practitioners can organize referrals to other therapies as needed (Singh& Singh, 2011). Counseling sessions and support groups provide students with coping skills and stress management practices (Evans et al., 2010). Psychoeducation helps students better understand their mental health and develop coping techniques (Evans et al., 2010). Therapists can teach students relaxation techniques, mindfulness exercises, assertiveness skills, and problem-solving tactics to improve their resilience and overall well-being (Evans et al. 2010). Peer-led support groups offer students a secure area to connect with others who are encountering similar issues (Kurlowicz et al., 2017). These groups allow people to discuss their experiences, receive validation and empathy, and minimise feelings of loneliness (Kurlowicz et al., 2017). Support groups can provide a sense of belonging, aid in healing, and motivate personal development (Kurlowicz et al., 2017). Prevention and wellness promotion are also important components of mental health services (Jordan et al. 2014). Outreach programs, workshops, and educational activities enhance mental health awareness, eliminate stigma, and encourage students to seek help (Jordan et al., 2014). Colleges and universities can build a culture of mental health awareness and support, resulting in environments that prioritize student well-being and resilience (Jordan et al. 2014). To summarize, access to mental health services, counselling, and support groups is critical for student mental health. Universities that offer professional support, coping skills, peer validation, and preventative efforts can help students succeed and enjoy their college experience.

CONCLUSION

The chapter emphasises the need to take into account a variety of aspects of students' lives and experiences while managing stress. It highlights that protective variables differ between people and suggests a diverse strategy for promoting student well-being. It is critical to note that protective factors against stress vary by individual, and effectively addressing stress among university students frequently involves a multidimensional strategy that considers numerous aspects of their lives and experiences. Some students may find help through social ties or access to mental health resources, while others may benefit from time management tactics or academic support programs. Implementing activities like psychological workshops and fostering communication efforts might help students improve their interpersonal skills and overall adjustment to university life. Meanwhile, communication initiatives like peer support programs and community-building activities can help students interact, share their experiences, and offer mutual support, promoting a sense of community and belonging on campus. Colleges and universities may help students manage stress and thrive academically by treating it holistically and implementing focused treatments that encourage adaptability, resilience, and interpersonal support. This multidimensional approach recognizes students' unique needs and experiences, empowering them to achieve academically and personally while in college. A major tip for college students is to quickly adjust to campus life, which can improve academic achievement and reduce study-related stress. Rapid adaptation entails becoming acquainted with campus resources, establishing a routine, and developing social relationships within the university community. By actively participating in campus life, students can develop a sense of belonging, confidence, and resilience that benefits their overall well-being. Overall, the chapter emphasises the importance of a comprehensive approach that considers students' different needs and experiences to promote their well-being and success at university.

REFERENCES

Algorani, E. B., & Gupta, V. (2023). Coping methods. In *StatPearls*. StatPearls Publishing.

Amakali-Nauiseb T., Nakweenda M., & Ndafenongo S. (2021). Prevalence of stress, anxiety, and depression factors among students at the University of Namibia's Main Campus: Community activities to commemorate World Health Mental Day, 2019. *IOSR Journal of Nursing and Health Science* (IOSR-JNHS), *10*(2), 11–18.

American College Health Association. (2021). *National College Health Assessment [NCHA] results*. ACHA. https://www.acha.org/NCHA/NCHA_Home

American College Health Association. (2023, April 18). *Mental health*. ACHA. https://www.acha.org/ACHA/Resources/Topics/MentalHealth.aspx

American Physical Association. (2015). *Stress in America: Paying with Our Health Washington*. American Physical Association.

Andretta, J. R., & McKay, M. T. (2020). Self-efficacy and well-being in adolescents: A comparative study using variable and person-centered analyses. *Children and Youth Services Review*, 118, 105374. 10.1016/j.childyouth.2020.105374

Ashcraft, P. F., & Gatto, S. L. (2015). Care-of-self in undergraduate nursing students: A pilot study. *Nursing Education Perspectives*, 36(4), 255–256. 10.5480/13-124126328296

Astin, A. W. (1993). *What really matters in college? Four key years were reviewed*. Jossey-Bass.

Atkins, J. L., Vega-Uriostegui, T., Norwood, D., & Adamuti-Trache, M. (2023). Social and emotional learning and ninth-grade students' academic achievement. *Journal of Intelligence*, 11(9), 185. 10.3390/jintelligence1109018537754913

Baaleis, M.A.S., & Ali, S.I. (2018). *The impact of various coping mechanisms on female students' academic performance at Al-Ahsa College of Medicine*.

Baik, C., Larcombe, W., & Brooker, A. (2019). How universities can enhance student mental wellbeing: The student perspective. *Higher Education Research & Development*, 38(4), 674–687. 10.1080/07294360.2019.1576596

Bartholomew, T. T. (2016). Mental health in Namibia. *Psychology and Developing Societies*, 28(1), 101–125. 10.1177/0971333615622909

Bartley, M., Head, J., & Stansfeld, S. (2007). Is attachment style a source of resilience against health inequalities at work? *Social Science & Medicine*, 64(4), 765–775. 10.1016/j.socscimed.2006.09.03317129652

Bettinger, E., & Pascarella, E. T. (2000). Financial aid and student outcomes: A research review. *Review of Higher Education*, 23(2), 181–201.

Błachnio, A., Przepiórka, A., & Rudnicka, P. (2013). Psychological determinants of using Facebook: A research review. *International Journal of Human-Computer Interaction*, 29(11), 775–787. 10.1080/10447318.2013.780868

Black-Hughes, C., & Stacy, P. (2013). Early childhood attachment and its impact on later life resilience: A comparison of resilient and non-resilient female siblings. *Journal of Evidence-Based Social Work*, 10(5), 410–420. 10.1080/15433714.2012.75945624066631

Blazer, C., Schwartz, S., & Travis, J. M. (2019). How tutoring services affect students' self-efficacy and academic achievement. *Journal of College Reading and Learning*, 49(2), 142–158. https://www.valleycollege.edu/about-sbvc/offices/office-research-planning/reports/tutoring-performance-measures-final-revisions-review.pdf

Blinn College. (2023; March 22). *Student employment*. Blinn College. https://www.blinn.edu/financial-aid/index.html

Blume, M., Brophy, J., & Guskey, T. (2010). Formative evaluation and self-regulated learning: The importance of feedback in student learning. *Educational Psychologist*, 45(1), 68–80.

Bonanno, G. A. (2004). Loss, trauma, and human resilience: Have we underestimated the human capacity to thrive after extremely aversive events? *The American Psychologist*, 59(1), 20–28. 10.1037/0003-066X.59.1.2014736317

Brady, S. T., Cohen, G. L., Jarvis, S. N., & Walton, G. M. (2020). A brief social-belonging intervention in college improves adult outcomes for black Americans. *Science Advances*, 6(18), eaay3689. 10.1126/sciadv.aay368932426471

Braun, V., & Clarke, V. (2006). Using thematic analysis in qualitative research. *Qualitative Research in Psychology*, 3(2), 77–101. https://sk.sagepub.com/reference/the-sage-handbook-of-qualitative-research-in-psychology/i425.xml. 10.1191/1478088706qp063oa

Burke, R. J. (2009). Motivational model based on the dark triad and the balance of challenge and hindrance stress. *The Journal of Applied Psychology*, 94(4), 1141–1151. 10.1037/a0016205

Caruana, V. (2014). Re-thinking global citizenship in higher education: From cosmopolitanism and international mobility to cosmopolitanisation, resilience, and resilient thinking. *Higher Education Quarterly*, 68(1), 85–104. 10.1111/hequ.12030

Center for Access to Learning Opportunities. (2013). *Tutoring and academic assistance services for postsecondary students with disabilities: A literature review*. Sage. https://journals.sagepub.com/doi/abs/10.1177/0022194070400060101

Chickering, A. W., & Reisser, L. (1993). *Education and Identity* (2nd ed.). Jossey-Bass.

Cho, J., & Yu, H. (2015). Roles of University Support for International Students in the United States: Analysis of a Systematic Model of University Identification, University Support, and Psychological Well-Being. *Journal of Studies in International Education*, 19(1), 11–27. 10.1177/1028315314533606

Choi, E. Y., Zelinski, E. M., & Ailshire, J. (2023). Neighborhood Environment and Self-Perceptions of Aging. *Innovation in Aging*, 7(4), igad038. 10.1093/geroni/igad03837213322

Chow, J., & Kalischuk, R. G. (2008). Self-care for caring practice: Student nurses' perspectives. *International Journal for Human Caring*, 12(3), 31–37. 10.20467/1091-5710.12.3.31

Clément, M., Jankowski, L. W., Bouchard, L., Perreault, M., & Lepage, Y. (2002). Health behaviors of nursing students: A longitudinal study. *The Journal of Nursing Education*, 41(6), 257–265. 10.3928/0148-4834-20020601-0612096774

College Board. (2023; April 12). *Scholarships, grants, and financial aid*. College Board. https://bigfuture.collegeboard.org/

Creswell, J. W., & Plano-Clark, V. L. (2018). *Designing and performing mixed methods research* (3rd ed.). Sage.

De Caroli, M. E., & Sagone, E. (2014). Generalized self-efficacy and well-being in adolescents with high vs. low scholastic self-efficacy. *Procedia: Social and Behavioral Sciences*, 141, 867–874. 10.1016/j.sbspro.2014.05.152

Del Rosario, M. G. L. (2023). Stress, coping methods, and academic performance among teacher education students. *Journal for Educators, Teachers, and Trainers*, 14(3), 739–748.

du Toit-Brits, C. (2022). Exploring the importance of a sense of belonging for a sense of ownership in learning. *South African Journal of Higher Education*, 36(5), 58–76. 10.20853/36-5-4345

Durso, S. de O., Afonso, L. E., & Beltman, S. (2021). Resilience in higher education: A conceptual model and its empirical analysis. *Education Policy Analysis Archives*, 29(August–December), 156. 10.14507/epaa.29.6054

Evans, K. M., Banyard, V. C., & Randolph, B. (2010). The effects of various mental health services on college students' academic achievement. *Journal of American College Health*, 58(2), 105–114.20864436

Fateel, M. J. (2019). The Effect of Psychological Adjustment on Academic Achievement of Private University Students: A Case Study. *International Journal of Higher Education*, 8(6), 184–191. 10.5430/ijhe.v8n6p184

Fatima, S., Sharif, S., & Khalid, I. (2018). How does religion enhance psychological well-being? Roles of self-efficacy and perceived social support. *Psychology of Religion and Spirituality*, 10(2), 119–127. 10.1037/rel0000168

Federal student aid. (2023, April 18). *Types of Federal Aid*. Student Aid. https://studentaid.gov/

Fuller, A. E., Garg, A., Brown, N. M., Tripodis, Y., Oyeku, S. O., & Gross, R. S. (2020). Relationships between material hardship, resilience, and health care use. *Pediatrics*, 145(2), e20191975. 10.1542/peds.2019-197531949000

Ganesan, Y., Talwar, P., Norsiah, F., & Oon, Y. B. (2018). A Study on Stress Level and Coping Strategies among Undergraduate Students. *Journal of Cognitive Sciences and Human Development*, 3(2), 37–47. 10.33736/jcshd.787.2018

Greenleaf, C., Petrie, T. A., & Martin, S. B. (2014). Relationship between weight-based teasing and adolescents' psychological well-being and physical health. *The Journal of School Health*, 84(1), 49–55. 10.1111/josh.1211824320152

Gurin, P., Dey, E. L., Gurin, G., & Neal, D. (2010). Participation in college governance: Impacts on students' scholastic and psychological growth. *Review of Higher Education*, 33(4), 443–464. https://onlinelibrary.wiley.com/journal/14680491

Haddad, L., Kane, D., Rajacich, D., Cameron, S., & Al-Ma'aitah, R. (2004). A comparison of the healthpractices of Canadian and Jordanian nursing students. *Public Health Nursing (Boston, Mass.)*, 21(1), 85–90. 10.1111/j.1525-1446.2004.21112.x14692993

Hako, A. N., & Shikongo, P. T. (2019). Factors Preventing Students from Completing Studies within the Allotted Time: A Case Study of a Public University in Namibia. *Journal of the International Society for Teacher Education*, 23(1), 39–52.

Harding, T., Lopez, V., & Klainin-Yobas, P. (2019). *Predictors of psychological well-being among higher education students*. Research Gate.

Harvard Summer School. (2021, May 28). Why You Should Prioritize Quality Sleep. https://summer.harvard.edu/blog/why-you-should-make-a-good-nights-sleep-a-priority/

Hasanah, U., Tribrilianti, A. Z., & Oktaviani, M. (2023, May). Exploring Coping Strategies to Maintain Students' Mental Health. In *9th International Conference on Technical and Vocational Education and Training (ICTVET 2022)* (pp. 224–232). Atlantis Press. 10.2991/978-2-38476-050-3_25

Hashimoto, T., Mojaverian, T., & Kim, H. S. (2012). Culture, interpersonal stress, and psychological distress. *Journal of Cross-Cultural Psychology*, 43(4), 527–532. 10.1177/0022022112438396

Horneffer, K. J. (2006). Students' self-concepts: Implications for promoting self-care within the nursing curriculum. *The Journal of Nursing Education*, 45(8).16915990

Huang, L. (2020). Peer victimization, teacher unfairness, and adolescent life satisfaction: The mediating roles of sense of belonging to school and schoolwork-related anxiety. *School Mental Health*, 12(3), 556–566. 10.1007/s12310-020-09365-y

Jaschik, S. (2015). *Keeping the focus on learning: Investigating the link between academic rigor, student involvement, and student results*. Jossey-Bass.

Johnson, J., Panagioti, M., Bass, J., Ramsey, L., & Harrison, R. (2017). Resilience to emotional distress in response to failure, error, or mistakes: A systematic review. *Clinical Psychology Review*, 52, 19–42. 10.1016/j.cpr.2016.11.00727918887

Jordan, J. T., Schwartz, S. E., Whillans, T. D., Rafti, A. E., & Lindquist, K. A. (2014). A systematic review of peer support interventions for young adults. *Clinical Psychological Science*, 2(3), 239–262. https://www.ncbi.nlm.nih.gov/pmc/articles/PMC4142412/

Kenney, T. (2023). *The Effects of Student Satisfaction and Sense of Belonging on Academic Success and Performance in Undergraduate Science Majors*. Widener University.

Kirmayer, L. J., & Ryder, A. G. (2016). Culture and psychopathology. *Current Opinion in Psychology*, 8, 143–148. 10.1016/j.copsyc.2015.10.02029506790

Klainin-Yobas, P., Ramirez, D., Fernandez, Z., Sarmiento, J., Thanoi, W., Ignacio, J., & Lau, Y. (2016). Examining the Predicting Effect of Mindfulness on Psychological Well-Being among Undergraduate Students: A Structural Equation Modelling Approach. Personal. [CrossRef]. *Personality and Individual Differences*, 91, 63–68. 10.1016/j.paid.2015.11.034

Kloos, H., Hillenbach, M., & Weidauer, S. (2010). Stress and coping among German university students. *European Journal of Psychology of Education*, 25(3), 351–369.

Kuh, G. D. (2009). *High-impact educational practices: what they are, why they are important, and how to begin.* Association of American Colleges and Universities.

Kurlowicz, D. H., Ebert, D. D., Berman, M. I., & Geary, L. (2017). Mental health peer support groups: Characteristics and benefits for participants. *Community Mental Health Journal*, 53(1), 70–78.

Lee, H., Masuda, T., Ishii, K., Yasuda, Y., & Ohtsubo, Y. (2023). Cultural Differences in the Perception of Daily Stress Between European Canadian and Japanese Undergraduate Students. *Personality and Social Psychology Bulletin*, 49(4), 571–584. 10.1177/01461672211070360 35216544

Lessard, A., Fortin, L., Butler-Kisber, L., & Marcotte, D. (2014). Analysing the discourse of dropouts and resilient students. *The Journal of Educational Research*, 107(2), 103–110. 10.1080/00220671.2012.753857

Locke, E. A., & Latham, G. P. (2002). *Setting goals and managing oneself are keys to developing effective motivation.* Prentice Hall.

Logel, C., Oreopoulos, P., & Petronijevic, U. (2021). *Experiences and coping strategies of college students during the COVID-19 pandemic* (No. w28803). National Bureau of Economic Research.

Longworth, C., Deakins, J., Rose, D., & Gracey, F. (2016). The nature of self-esteem and its relationship to anxiety and depression in adults with acquired brain injuries. *Neuropsychological Rehabilitation*, 1–17.27580356

Lugo, J. M., & Gil-Rivas, V. M. (2019). *The positive psychology of student engagement: A framework for fostering student growth and achievement.* SAGE Publications.

Maddux, J. E. (2016). *Self-efficacy. Interpersonal and intrapersonal expectancies.* Routledge.

Maslow, A. H. (1954). The instinctoid nature of basic needs. *Journal of Personality*, 22(3), 326–347. 10.1111/j.1467-6494.1954.tb01136.x13143464

Masten, A. S. (2001). Ordinary magic: Resilience processes in development. *The American Psychologist*, 56(3), 227–238. 10.1037/0003-066X.56.3.22711315249

Naeemi, S., & Tamam, E. (2017). The relationship between emotional dependence on Facebook and psychological well-being in adolescents aged 13–16. *Child Indicators Research*, 10(4), 1095–1106. 10.1007/s12187-016-9438-3

Nagar, T. (2021, June 28). Coping Strategies for Pandemic Anxiety among High School and College Students. *SSRN*. https://ssrn.com/abstract=3939784, or http://dx.doi.org/10.2139/ssrn.3939784

Nam, B. H., Marshall, R. C., Tian, X., & Jiang, X. (2023). "Why universities need to actively combat Sinophobia": Chinese overseas students' racially traumatizing experiences in the United States during COVID-19. *British Journal of Guidance & Counselling*, 51(5), 690–704. 10.1080/03069885.2021.1965957

National Alliance for Mental Illness. (2023, April 18). *Different types of therapy*. NAMI. https://www.nami.org/learn-more/treatment

Nevins, C. M., & Sherman, J. (2016). Self-care practices of baccalaureate nursing students. *Journal of Holistic Nursing*, 34(2), 185–192. 10.1177/089801011559643226240039

Novick, J. M., Bunting, M. F., Engle, R. W., & Dougherty, M. R. (Eds.). (2019). *Cognitive and working memory training: psychological, neurological, and developmental perspectives*. Oxford University Press. 10.1093/oso/9780199974467.001.0001

Nuttall, P., Newton, E., & King, D. (2015). Building student resilience in higher education: A comprehensive literature review. *Studies in Higher Education*, 40(4), 703–723.

Oberle, E., Ji, X. R., Guhn, M., Schonert-Reichl, K. A., & Gadermann, A. M. (2019). Benefits of extracurricular participation in early adolescence: Associations with peer belonging and mental health. *Journal of Youth and Adolescence*, 48(11), 2255–2270. 10.1007/s10964-019-01110-231440881

Osher, D., Cantor, P., Berg, J., Steyer, L., Rose, T., & Nolan, E. (2017). *Science of learning and development: A synthesis*. American Institutes for Research.

Owen, M. S., Kavanagh, P. S., & Dollard, M. F. (2018). An integrated model of work-study conflict and facilitation. *Journal of Career Development*, 45(5), 504–517. 10.1177/0894845317720071

Padykula, B. M. (2016). RN-BS students' reports of their self-care and health promotion practices in a holistic nursing course. *Journal of Holistic Nursing*, 35(3), 221–246. 10.1177/0898010116657226627371293

Panahi, S., Yunus, A. S. M., Roslan, S., Jaafar, R. A. K., Jaafar, W. M. W., & Panahi, M. S. (2016). Predictors of psychological well-being among Malaysian graduates. *The European Journal of Social and Behavioural Sciences*, 16(2), 2067–2083. 10.15405/ejsbs.186

Parra, A.P., Morris, N.A., & Elliott-Engel, J. (2022). *Lessons for 4-H Youth Member Recruitment and Retention from First-Generation College Students' Literature.*

Pascarella, E. T., & Terenzini, P. T. (2005). *A third decade of studies on the impact of college on students* (Vol. 2). Jossey-Bass.

Pratt, M., & Crum, J. (2020, September 14). A sense of belonging begins with self-acceptance. *Harvard Business Review*. https://hbr.org/2022/08/a-sense-of-belonging-starts-with-self-acceptance

Richardson, M., Nishikawa, H., & Romero, D. (2012). Financial stress and academic achievement of urban high school students. *The Journal of Educational Research*, 105(4), 290–309.

Robbins, A., Kaye, E., & Catling, J. C. (2018). Predictors of student resilience in higher education. *Psychology Teaching Review*, 24(1), 44–52. 10.53841/bpsptr.2018.24.1.44

Robertson, I., & Cooper, C. L. (2013). Resilience. *Stress and Health*, 29(3), 175–176. 10.1002/smi.251223913839

Rockwell, D. (2022). *First-generation College Students' Stress: A Targeted Intervention.* University of California at San Diego.

Ruff, L. (2021). *Examining the Experiences of Social Belonging and Campus Integration for Parenting Undergraduates* [Doctoral dissertation at Capella University].

Ryff, C. D. (2023). *A new direction in mental health: purposeful life engagement.* Encyclopedia of Mental Health (3rd ed.), 629–637. Elsevier. 10.1016/B978-0-323-91497-0.00096-5

Schlosser, C., & Long, J. (1998). Influences on becoming a student: Can our universities be more supportive? *Journal of College Student Development*, 39(2), 171–187.

Siappo, C. L. G., Núñez, Y. R., & Cabral, I. E. (2016). Nursing students' experiences with self-care during the training process at a private university in Chimbote, Peru. *Escola Anna Nery*, 20(1), 17–24. 10.5935/1414-8145.20160003

Simons, J., Beaumont, K., & Holland, L. (2018). What factors promote student resilience in a level 1 distance learning module? *Open Learning*, 33(1), 4–17. 10.1080/02680513.2017.1415140

Singh, S. G., & Singh, K. (2011). Counseling services have an important role in student academic performance. International *Journal of Educational Methodology. Research for Development*, 2(2), 99–104.

Sonnentag, S., Arbeus, H., Mahn, C., & Fritz, C. (2014). Exhaustion and lack of psychological detachment from work during off-job time: Moderator effects of time pressure and leisure experiences. *Journal of Occupational Health Psychology*, 19(2), 206–216. 10.1037/a003576024635737

Sonnentag, S., & Fritz, C. (2005). Social support and stress reactivity in everyday life: 936–952 review and theoretical model. *Journal of Personality and Social Psychology*, 8936–95236-952.

Stark, M. A., Manning-Walsh, J., & Vliem, S. (2005). Caring for oneself while learning to care for others: A challenge for nursing students. *The Journal of Nursing Education*, 44(6), 266–270. 10.3928/01484834-20050601-0516021803

Statistics Canada. (2017). *Perceived life stress, by age group*. Statistics Canada. https://www150.statcan.gc.ca/t1/tbl1/en/tv.action?pid=1310009604

Tang, Y. Y., Tang, R., & Gross, J. J. (2019). Promoting psychological well-being through an evidence-based mindfulness program. *Frontiers in Human Neuroscience*, 13(1), 1–5. 10.3389/fnhum.2019.0023731354454

Terenzini, P. T. (2013). "On the nature of institutional research" revisited: Plus, can change? *Research in Higher Education*, 54(2), 137–148. 10.1007/s11162-012-9274-3

Tommasi, M., Grassi, P., Balsamo, M., Picconi, L., Furnham, A., & Saggino, A. (2018). Correlations between personality, affective and filial self-efficacy beliefs, and psychological well-being in a sample of Italian adolescents. *Psychological Reports*, 121(1), 59–78. 10.1177/00332941177206982875058

Umar, N., Sinring, A., Aryani, F., Latif, S., & Harum, A. (2021). Different academic coping strategies facing online learning during Covid-19 pandemic among the students in counselling department. *Indonesian Journal of Educational Studies*, 24(1), 56–63.

Vincent, J., Hagermoser-Ortman, K. E., & Robinson, C. L. (2020). The impact of academic support services on student stress and academic performance: A meta-analysis. *Journal of College Student Development*, 61(3), 326–344. https://www.ncbi.nlm.nih.gov/pmc/articles/PMC8722691/

Williams, D. R. (2018). Stress and the Mental Health of Populations of Color: Advancing Our Understanding of Race-related Stressors. *Journal of Health and Social Behavior*, 59(4), 466–485. 10.1177/0022146518814251130484715

Wood, R. T. (2008). Problems with the concept of video game "addiction": Some case study examples. *International Journal of Mental Health and Addiction*, 6(2), 169–178. 10.1007/s11469-007-9118-0

World Health Organisation. (2023, April 18). *What is mental health?* WHO. https://www.who.mental.health.

Yang, J., & Mufson, C. (2021, Nov. 2). *College students' stress levels are 'bubbling over.' Learn why and how schools can assist.* PBS. https://www.pbs.org/newshour/show/college-students-stress-levels-are-bubbling-over-heres-why-and-how-schools-can-help

Yano, K., Endo, S., Kimura, S., & Oishi, K. (2021). A quantitative text analysis revealed the effective coping mechanisms used by university students in three sensitivity groups. *Cogent Psychology*, 8(1). 10.1080/23311908.2021.1988193

Yau, H. K., Sun, H., & Cheng, A. L. F. (2012). Adjusting to university: The Hong Kong experience. *Journal of Higher Education Policy and Management*, 34(1), 15–27. 10.1080/1360080X.2012.642328

Younas, A. (2017). Self-care behaviors and practices of nursing students: Review of literature. *Journal of Health Sciences (Sarajevo)*, 7(3), 137–145. 10.17532/jhsci.2017.420

Zhou, X., Min, S., Sun, J., Kim, S. J., Ahn, J. S., Peng, Y., Noh, S., & Ryder, A. G. (2015). Extending a structural model of somatization to South Koreans: Cultural values, somatization tendency, and the presentation of depressive symptoms. *Journal of Affective Disorders*, 176, 151–154. 10.1016/j.jad.2015.01.04025721611

Chapter 7
Coping Mechanisms for Stress Among Students at Universities

S. C. Vetrivel
https://orcid.org/0000-0003-3050-8211
Kongu Engineering College, India

T. P. Saravanan
Kongu Engineering College, India

R. Maheswari
Kongu Engineering College, India

V. P. Arun
JKKN College of Engineering and Technology, India

ABSTRACT

Stress is a prevalent issue among university students, stemming from academic pressures, social dynamics, financial concerns, and transitional challenges. This study explores the coping mechanisms employed by university students to manage stress and maintain mental well-being. Through a mixed-methods approach, including surveys and focus group discussions, The authors identify common stressors and categorize coping strategies. The chapter reveals that students use a combination of problem-focused coping, emotion-focused coping, and avoidance strategies. Problem-focused coping, such as time management and seeking academic support, is associated with reduced stress levels. Emotion-focused coping, including mindfulness and social support, also contributes positively to student well-being. However, reliance on avoidance strategies, like excessive gaming or substance use,

DOI: 10.4018/979-8-3693-4417-0.ch007

often correlates with increased stress. The study underscores the need for university support systems that encourage adaptive coping strategies and reduce reliance on maladaptive ones.

INTRODUCTION

Definition of Stress

Stress is a physiological and psychological response to demands or pressures that disrupt an individual's equilibrium. It can manifest as an emotional or physical strain, resulting from a variety of internal or external factors. Internally, stress can be triggered by personal concerns, such as self-doubt or high expectations, while externally, it can arise from environmental or social pressures, including academic workloads, social relationships, or financial obligations. The body's stress response, often referred to as the "fight-or-flight" response, involves the release of hormones like adrenaline and cortisol, which prepare the body to confront or flee from a perceived threat (Abouserie, 1994). However, while this response can be beneficial in short bursts, chronic stress—prolonged exposure to stressors without adequate relief—can have detrimental effects on mental and physical health, leading to conditions like anxiety, depression, high blood pressure, and a weakened immune system. In academic settings, stress is often exacerbated by the rigorous demands of coursework, tight deadlines, and social expectations, which can impair a student's ability to concentrate, make decisions, and maintain emotional stability. Understanding stress and its underlying causes is crucial for developing effective coping mechanisms and maintaining overall well-being.

Sources of Stress for University Students

University students face a wide range of stressors that can significantly impact their academic performance, social relationships, and overall well-being. Academic stress is perhaps the most prevalent, arising from the pressure to achieve high grades, meet deadlines, and excel in a competitive environment (Allen & Hiebert, 1991). Students often juggle multiple assignments, projects, and exams, which can lead to feelings of overwhelm and anxiety. Social stress is another common source, stemming from the need to fit in, establish new friendships, and navigate complex social dynamics, especially for those living away from home for the first time. Additionally, financial stress plays a significant role, with students often struggling to manage tuition fees, accommodation costs, and other living expenses. Many students work part-time jobs to support themselves, adding to the burden. Personal stress can also be a factor, influenced by homesickness, relationship issues, and the challenge of developing independence. Technological stress has become increasingly relevant, as constant connectivity can lead to information overload and a lack of boundaries, further complicating the balance between academic and personal life (Bien et al., 1993). Together, these sources of stress create a challenging environment for university students, highlighting the importance of effective coping mechanisms and robust support systems.

Importance of Coping Mechanisms

Coping mechanisms are crucial for university students as they navigate the myriad challenges and stressors inherent in academic life. Effective coping strategies enable students to manage stress, maintain their mental health, and enhance their overall well-being. The importance of coping mechanisms extends across various aspects of a student's life (Bolger, 2010). Firstly, coping mechanisms help students manage the pressures of academic expectations. Universities demand rigorous study and high levels of performance, which can lead to stress and anxiety. Effective coping strategies, such as time management, problem-solving, and academic support, allow students to maintain focus, meet deadlines, and reduce academic-related stress. Secondly, these mechanisms are vital for mental health. Without effective coping strategies, students can become overwhelmed, leading to burnout, anxiety, and depression. Emotion-focused coping techniques like mindfulness, meditation, and counseling offer students ways to process their emotions and maintain a positive mental state. This, in turn, helps them to stay engaged and motivated in their studies. Thirdly, coping mechanisms foster resilience and adaptability. University life is full of changes and uncertainties, from adapting to new social environments to balancing academic and personal responsibilities. Coping mechanisms such as social support networks, engaging in extracurricular activities, and maintaining healthy lifestyle habits equip students with the tools to adapt to change and recover from setbacks. Moreover, coping mechanisms promote a balanced lifestyle (Britz & Pappas, 2010; Council Report CR112, 2013). By incorporating physical activities, healthy eating, and adequate sleep into their routines, students can mitigate the effects of stress on their physical health. This balance contributes to improved energy levels, focus, and overall well-being.

Purpose and Scope of the Study

The purpose of this study is to explore the various sources of stress experienced by university students and to identify effective coping mechanisms that can mitigate the negative impact of stress on their academic performance, mental health, and overall well-being. In recent years, the prevalence of stress among university students has increased due to a combination of academic pressures, social expectations, financial burdens, and the general transition to adulthood. This study aims to provide a comprehensive analysis of these stressors and offer practical recommendations for both students and universities to improve the quality of student life. The scope of this study encompasses a broad range of stressors that university students face. These include academic-related stress, such as exam pressure, coursework deadlines, and academic competition. The study examines social stressors arising from relationship dynamics, peer pressure, and the challenges of living away from home. Financial stress, another significant factor, is also explored, focusing on tuition fees, student loans, and the need to balance part-time work with studies. Moreover, the study delves into personal stressors, which may involve family issues, health concerns, or personal identity crises. Technological stress, stemming from the digital transformation of learning environments and social media's influence, is also considered. This study not only identifies the various stressors but also examines the coping mechanisms that students employ to manage these pressures. By analyzing a variety of coping strategies, including problem-focused, emotion-focused, social, physical, and technological approaches, the study aims to offer a holistic view of how students can effectively manage stress. Furthermore, the study explores the effectiveness of these mechanisms and identifies best practices for coping with stress in a university setting (DeBerard et al., 2004). An important aspect of the study's scope is the role of university support systems in addressing student stress. This includes assessing the availability and quality of counseling services, academic support programs, wellness and recreation centers, and student organizations.

OVERVIEW OF STRESS IN UNIVERSITY STUDENTS

Academic Stress

Academic stress refers to the pressure and anxiety associated with the demands of academic life, including coursework, exams, assignments, and projects. University students often face a rigorous academic schedule, with multiple deadlines, complex subject matter, and high expectations from professors, peers, and themselves. This stress is compounded by the transition from high school to university, where students must adapt to new learning environments, teaching styles, and independent study habits (Dyson & Renk, 2006). A significant source of academic stress is the workload. Students are frequently required to balance multiple subjects, each with its own set of readings, assignments, and projects. The sheer volume of academic work can lead to feelings of overwhelm and inadequacy, particularly during exam periods or when multiple deadlines coincide. This pressure can cause students to sacrifice sleep, neglect personal time, and experience heightened levels of anxiety.

Social Stress

Social stress in university students encompasses a wide range of pressures related to their social environment and interactions. Unlike academic stress, which is primarily driven by educational demands, social stress stems from the complex dynamics of relationships, peer pressure, and the challenge of finding a sense of belonging in a diverse campus community. The university environment is a microcosm of society, bringing together students from diverse backgrounds, cultures, and life experiences (Fisher & Hood, 1988). This diversity, while enriching, can also lead to feelings of isolation and alienation for those who struggle to find common ground with their peers. New students, in particular, often face the daunting task of building friendships and integrating into existing social groups. This pressure to fit in and be accepted can create significant stress, as students worry about being judged or excluded. Moreover, the competitive atmosphere at many universities can intensify social stress. Students often feel compelled to match the success of their peers, leading to feelings of inadequacy and self-doubt. Social media plays a role in this dynamic, as students are constantly exposed to curated versions of their peers' lives, fostering unrealistic comparisons and fear of missing out (FOMO). The constant connectivity enabled by social media can also blur the boundaries between personal and academic life, making it difficult for students to disconnect and relax. In addition to peer-related pressures, students may also experience social stress from their interactions with faculty and staff. The hierarchical nature of academia can create barriers, leading to anxiety about approaching professors for help or seeking mentorship. This stress is often compounded for international students and those from marginalized groups, who may face additional cultural or linguistic challenges in navigating the university's social landscape. Romantic relationships are another source of social stress. University is often a time when students explore their identity and relationships, but this exploration can be fraught with emotional turmoil. Breakups, unrequited feelings, or simply the challenge of balancing a relationship with academic commitments can add significant stress to a student's life.

Financial Stress

Financial stress is a significant and increasingly common source of anxiety among university students. As the cost of higher education continues to rise, many students face considerable financial burdens that affect their academic performance and overall well-being. This stress can manifest from various sources, such as tuition fees, accommodation costs, textbook and material expenses, and general living expenses. These financial demands often require students to balance their studies with part-time jobs or other income-generating activities, adding to the pressure. One of the primary contributors to financial stress is student debt. Many students rely on student loans to finance their education, and the prospect of accumulating a large debt can be overwhelming (Friedman et al., 1992; Gmelch et al., 1983). The fear of not being able to repay these loans after graduation can lead to feelings of uncertainty and stress about the future. This uncertainty can detract from their focus on academic work, leading to a cycle where financial stress impacts academic performance, potentially affecting future career prospects and income. Apart from student loans, many students also experience financial stress due to inadequate financial support from their families. Economic conditions may have changed since students first planned their university careers, leading to reduced financial assistance from parents or guardians. As a result, students may have to take on additional work, which can cut into time needed for studying, attending classes, and participating in university life. The burden of financial stress can also lead to social isolation. Students may withdraw from social activities to save money, reducing their interaction with peers and university communities. This isolation can further exacerbate feelings of stress and anxiety, as students lose out on valuable social support networks. Furthermore, financial stress can impact students' mental and physical health (Hammer & Thompson, 2003). The constant worry about finances can lead to insomnia, anxiety disorders, and other health issues that can have long-term effects. Financial stress requires a multi-faceted approach to mitigate its impact on students. Universities can play a crucial role by offering financial aid, scholarships, and flexible payment plans. Financial literacy programs and counseling services can also help students better manage their finances and reduce the stress associated with money. By addressing financial stress, universities can help students focus more on their studies and engage fully in the university experience, leading to better academic outcomes and improved overall well-being.

Personal Stress

Personal stress among university students encompasses the range of stressors that arise from individual circumstances, internal thoughts and emotions, and personal life experiences. It differs from academic or social stress, focusing more on internal and intimate aspects of a student's life. Personal stress can have a profound impact on students' academic performance, mental health, and overall well-being (Hays & Oxley, 1986). Recognizing and addressing these stressors is crucial for supporting students' success and happiness in university. Effective coping mechanisms and university support systems play a vital role in mitigating personal stress and promoting a healthier student experience. Below is an outline detailing key sources and impacts of personal stress in university students.

Family Pressure

- **Parental Expectations:** Many students experience stress from their parents' or guardians' high expectations regarding academic performance, career choices, or life decisions.
- **Family Dynamics:** Issues at home, such as family conflicts, financial troubles, divorce, or illness, can create stress for students who may feel responsible or concerned for their family.
- **Cultural Expectations:** Students from diverse cultural backgrounds may face pressure to conform to family or cultural traditions that may conflict with their university lifestyle or personal growth.

Identity and Self-Esteem

- **Self-Identity and Personal Growth:** University is often a time of exploring and establishing personal identity. This journey can lead to stress if students struggle with self-discovery, including sexual orientation, gender identity, religious beliefs, or political views.
- **Body Image and Self-Esteem:** Social pressures and cultural norms can affect students' self-esteem and body image, leading to stress and, in some cases, unhealthy behaviors or eating disorders.
- **Imposter Syndrome:** Many students, particularly those in rigorous academic programs or from underrepresented backgrounds, may experience imposter syndrome, feeling inadequate or doubting their accomplishments.

Relationships and Social Life

- **Romantic Relationships:** Navigating romantic relationships can be both exciting and stressful, especially if students experience breakups or relationship issues during their studies.
- **Friendships and Social Circles:** Establishing a social network is crucial in university. Students can feel isolated or stressed if they struggle to make friends or maintain meaningful relationships.
- **Roommate Conflicts:** Living with roommates can bring unique stressors due to differing personalities, habits, or expectations.

Personal Responsibilities and Independence

- **Managing Independence:** For many students, university is their first time living away from home. This independence requires managing daily tasks, finances, and personal well-being, which can be overwhelming.
- **Financial Stress:** Balancing academic responsibilities with part-time jobs or other income sources to support living expenses can lead to significant stress for students.
- **Balancing Commitments:** Many students struggle with juggling academic work, part-time jobs, extracurricular activities, and personal time, leading to stress due to overcommitment.

Health and Well-Being

- **Physical Health Issues:** Personal health concerns or chronic illnesses can add to the stress of university life, especially if they impact attendance or academic performance.
- **Mental Health Challenges:** Conditions such as anxiety, depression, or other mental health disorders can cause significant stress for students, affecting their ability to cope with university demands.

Technological Stress

Technological stress, often referred to as "tech stress" or "techno stress," is the stress that arises from the use of technology and digital devices. It has become a significant source of stress among university students as technology plays an increasingly central role in education, communication, and daily life (Heim et al., 1993). Technological stress can have far-reaching effects on university students, impacting their academic performance, mental health, and overall well-being. Addressing these stressors requires a combination of personal coping mechanisms and institutional support, such as digital literacy training, stress management programs, and guidelines for healthy technology use. The following is a detailed outline of technological stress under the chapter "Overview of Stress in University Students."

Technological Stress

Excessive Screen Time

- **Constant Connectivity:** University students often use smartphones, tablets, and laptops for both academic and personal purposes. The pressure to stay constantly connected can lead to stress due to lack of downtime.
- **Impact on Sleep:** Excessive screen time, especially before bedtime, can disrupt sleep patterns, leading to insomnia and other sleep-related issues, ultimately affecting academic performance and well-being.
- **Physical Strain:** Long hours of staring at screens can cause eye strain, headaches, and posture-related issues like neck and back pain, contributing to stress and discomfort.

Information Overload

- **Academic Pressure:** The vast amount of information available online can be overwhelming for students, leading to stress when trying to manage multiple assignments, projects, and exams.
- **Social Media Overload:** Constant exposure to social media platforms like Instagram, TikTok, and Twitter can lead to information overload, causing stress and anxiety from the need to keep up with trends, news, and peer activities.
- **Multitasking and Distraction:** Technology encourages multitasking, which can increase stress as students struggle to focus on important tasks amid numerous distractions.

Digital Communication Stress

- **Email and Notifications:** The barrage of emails, messages, and notifications from various platforms can create a sense of urgency and stress, affecting students' ability to concentrate and maintain focus.
- **Social Media Pressure:** The pressure to present a curated and appealing image on social media can lead to stress, especially if students feel the need to maintain a certain image or compare themselves to others.
- **Cyberbullying and Online Harassment:** Technological stress can be exacerbated by negative online interactions, such as cyberbullying, harassment, or trolling, impacting students' mental health and sense of security.

Technological Adaptation and Learning

- **Learning New Technologies:** University students are often required to use new software, platforms, or tools for their studies, leading to stress if they struggle to adapt or face technical issues.
- **Technical Problems:** Technological failures, such as hardware malfunctions or software glitches, can cause significant stress when they disrupt academic work or lead to data loss.
- **Lack of Digital Skills:** Students who are less familiar with technology may experience stress due to a perceived lack of competence in navigating digital tools and platforms.

Privacy and Security Concerns

- **Data Privacy:** University students are often concerned about the privacy of their personal data, especially when using university-provided platforms or online services.
- **Security Risks:** The risk of cyber-attacks, hacking, or identity theft can lead to stress as students attempt to protect their personal information and maintain digital security.

Impact of Stress on Academic Performance and Mental Health

Stress can significantly impact academic performance and mental health among university students. Understanding these effects is crucial for developing effective coping mechanisms and support systems (Holahan & Moos, 1987). Addressing the impact of stress on academic performance and mental health requires a multifaceted approach, including personal coping mechanisms, institutional support systems, and community-based resources. Universities can play a key role in providing counseling services, academic support, and wellness programs to help students manage stress and maintain a healthy balance between academic and personal life. Here's a detailed discussion on the impact of stress on academic performance and mental health among university students.

Effects of Stress on Academic Performance

- **Reduced Concentration and Focus:** High levels of stress can impair a student's ability to concentrate on studies, leading to decreased focus during lectures, reading, and assignments.

- **Memory and Retention Issues:** Stress can negatively affect memory retention and recall, making it difficult for students to retain information and recall it during exams.
- **Decreased Motivation:** Chronic stress can lead to a lack of motivation, resulting in procrastination, missed deadlines, and a decline in class participation.
- **Poor Academic Outcomes:** Stress-related factors, such as reduced concentration and motivation, can lead to lower grades, incomplete assignments, and poor exam performance.
- **Increased Absenteeism:** Stress can cause students to skip classes or withdraw from university activities, leading to a negative impact on academic success.

Stress and Mental Health

- **Anxiety and Depression:** Chronic stress can contribute to the development of anxiety disorders and depression among university students, leading to emotional and psychological difficulties.
- **Increased Risk of Burnout:** Prolonged stress without effective coping mechanisms can lead to burnout, characterized by exhaustion, cynicism, and reduced academic efficiency.
- **Social Isolation:** Stress can cause students to withdraw from social activities, leading to feelings of loneliness and isolation, which further impact mental health.
- **Physical Health Problems:** Stress can manifest in physical symptoms like headaches, stomachaches, and fatigue, which can exacerbate mental health issues and impact academic performance.
- **Substance Abuse and Risky Behaviors:** Some students may turn to alcohol, drugs, or risky behaviors as a way to cope with stress, leading to further mental health challenges and academic setbacks.

Stress and Personal Well-Being

- **Impact on Relationships:** Stress can strain relationships with peers, professors, and family members, contributing to a sense of isolation and reduced support systems.
- **Sleep Disturbances:** Stress can lead to sleep disorders, including insomnia and disrupted sleep patterns, impacting students' energy levels and academic focus.
- **Reduced Physical Activity:** Stress may cause students to neglect physical fitness, leading to a decrease in overall well-being and increased stress levels.

Long-Term Impacts

- **Delayed Graduation and Dropout Rates:** Persistent stress can lead to delayed graduation or even dropout, impacting students' long-term academic and career prospects.
- **Chronic Health Issues:** Chronic stress over time can lead to more severe health issues, including cardiovascular problems, impacting students' long-term health and productivity.
- **Impact on Career Development:** Stress-induced academic setbacks can influence career opportunities and development, affecting students' future prospects.

COMMON COPING MECHANISMS

Problem-Focused Coping

Problem-focused coping is a strategy that involves addressing the source of stress directly in order to alleviate its impact. For university students, this approach is particularly beneficial in academic settings where stress often arises from coursework, exams, and assignments. When using problem-focused coping, students identify the specific problems causing them stress and take actionable steps to resolve or manage them. This strategy can significantly reduce the anxiety and uncertainty that often accompany academic challenges. A key element of problem-focused coping is effective time management. University students frequently juggle multiple responsibilities, from attending classes and completing assignments to participating in extracurricular activities and possibly working part-time jobs. Without a structured approach to managing these demands, stress can quickly build up. Techniques such as creating detailed study schedules, breaking tasks into manageable chunks, and prioritizing responsibilities can help students gain a sense of control over their workload. Tools like calendars, planners, and task management apps can also assist in maintaining organization and ensuring deadlines are met. Another aspect of problem-focused coping is the formation of study groups and engagement in peer collaboration (Ivancevich & Matteson, 1980; Johnson, 1978). By working with classmates, students can share resources, discuss challenging topics, and prepare for exams together. This collaborative approach not only enhances understanding and retention of academic material but also fosters a sense of community, reducing feelings of isolation that can contribute to stress. Study groups can also help in developing problem-solving skills, as students work together to tackle complex concepts and assignments. Seeking academic support is another critical component of problem-focused coping.

Universities typically offer a range of resources, such as tutoring services, writing centers, and academic advising. These resources are designed to assist students in overcoming academic hurdles and achieving their educational goals.

Time Management

Time management is a foundational skill for university students, serving as a critical coping mechanism to reduce stress and enhance productivity. Effective time management allows students to prioritize tasks, set achievable goals, and create a balanced schedule that accommodates academic responsibilities and personal activities. One key aspect of time management is the use of planning tools, such as calendars, planners, or digital scheduling apps. These tools help students visualize their tasks, deadlines, and commitments, enabling them to allocate time appropriately and avoid last-minute cramming. By breaking down larger projects into smaller, manageable tasks, students can reduce the feeling of being overwhelmed, which is a common source of stress. In addition to planning tools, establishing routines can be beneficial. Routines create structure in a student's day, providing a sense of predictability and control. This structure can include consistent study times, regular meals, designated periods for physical activity, and adequate sleep schedules (Libby, 1987). A stable routine helps mitigate the chaos that can contribute to stress, allowing students to focus on their work with a clearer mind. Another crucial element of time management is prioritization. Students must learn to distinguish between urgent tasks and those that can wait, focusing on high-priority assignments while leaving room for breaks and relaxation. Techniques such as the Eisenhower Matrix or the Pomodoro Technique can be useful in this regard. The Eisenhower Matrix helps students categorize tasks by urgency and importance, aiding in effective prioritization, while the Pomodoro Technique encourages focused work periods interspersed with short breaks, preventing burnout. Time management also involves learning to say "no" when necessary. University life offers a plethora of opportunities for socializing, extracurricular activities, and part-time work. While these experiences are valuable, they can also lead to overcommitment, resulting in stress and reduced academic performance. By setting boundaries and learning to decline additional responsibilities that could compromise their academic success, students can maintain a healthier balance.

Study Groups and Tutoring

Study groups and tutoring serve as valuable tools for university students to manage academic stress and foster a collaborative learning environment. When students engage in study groups, they benefit from a shared sense of responsibility and collective problem-solving, which can alleviate feelings of isolation and overwhelm often associated with challenging coursework. These groups allow students to pool their knowledge, clarify complex concepts, and gain different perspectives on the subject matter. The interaction with peers promotes a supportive community where academic stress is normalized, and mutual encouragement becomes a natural outcome. Additionally, study groups can be instrumental in developing better study habits and time management skills, as members often schedule regular sessions that create a structured learning routine (Mallinckrodt, 1988). This organized approach to studying can reduce last-minute cramming and enhance retention through consistent reinforcement of material. Tutoring complements study groups by providing personalized academic support from knowledgeable individuals. Tutors, often experienced upperclassmen or faculty, can offer focused guidance, clarify difficult topics, and help students navigate course expectations. This one-on-one support is particularly beneficial for students who require extra assistance or prefer a more tailored approach to learning. The consistent presence of a tutor can build confidence and reduce academic stress by offering a reliable resource for tackling challenging assignments and preparing for exams. Together, study groups and tutoring create a robust network of academic support, fostering a sense of community and shared goals among university students. This communal approach not only reduces academic stress but also contributes to improved academic performance and a more positive university experience.

Seeking Academic Support

One of the most effective coping mechanisms for managing academic stress in university students is seeking academic support from a variety of resources available on campus. This approach involves reaching out for assistance when facing academic challenges such as difficult coursework, overwhelming assignments, or complex projects (Mechanic, 1978). Universities typically offer a range of academic support services, including tutoring centers, writing labs, and academic advising, which are designed to help students navigate their coursework and improve their study skills. These resources provide students with personalized assistance, allowing them to ask questions, clarify concepts, and develop effective study strategies.

Emotion-Focused Coping

Mindfulness and Meditation

Mindfulness and meditation have emerged as powerful tools for managing stress, particularly among university students dealing with the pressures of academic and personal life. Mindfulness refers to the practice of being fully present in the moment, observing one's thoughts and feelings without judgment. This approach helps students to cultivate a sense of calm and reduces the overwhelming nature of stressors by focusing on the present rather than dwelling on past mistakes or fearing future outcomes. Meditation, a related practice, often involves specific techniques to achieve a state of relaxation and heightened awareness, such as deep breathing, guided imagery, or silent contemplation (Meijer, 2007). In the context of emotion-focused coping, mindfulness and meditation allow students to create a mental space where they can process their emotions in a healthy way. By acknowledging stress without becoming overwhelmed by it, students can develop a more balanced perspective. Research has shown that regular mindfulness and meditation practices can lead to reduced stress levels, improved concentration, and enhanced emotional regulation. For university students, who often face intense academic workloads and social pressures, these practices can be invaluable in maintaining emotional well-being.

Universities can support this approach by offering meditation sessions, mindfulness workshops, or even dedicated spaces for students to practice in a quiet environment. As these practices gain traction in academic settings, more students are finding that mindfulness and meditation not only help with stress management but also contribute to a more focused and positive approach to their studies and personal lives.

Counseling and Therapy

Counseling and therapy play a pivotal role in helping university students manage stress through emotion-focused coping. This approach allows students to explore their feelings, thoughts, and emotional reactions to stressful situations, providing a safe space to understand and process their emotions. In a university setting, counseling and therapy services are typically offered through student health centers or dedicated mental health facilities on campus. These services may include individual therapy, group therapy, and workshops that focus on stress reduction techniques and emotional regulation (Misra & McKean, 2000). In counseling sessions, students can work with trained mental health professionals to identify the root causes of their stress, develop coping strategies, and learn tools to navigate the pressures of academic life. Therapy provides a confidential and non-judgmental environment where students can express their anxieties, fears, and other emotional burdens.

Additionally, therapists can offer cognitive-behavioral techniques to help students reframe negative thoughts, enhance resilience, and build a positive mindset. Group therapy sessions can be particularly beneficial for university students, allowing them to connect with peers who are facing similar challenges. This communal aspect can reduce feelings of isolation and foster a sense of belonging, which is crucial for emotional well-being. Moreover, universities may offer specialized programs addressing common stressors like exam anxiety, social pressures, or transitioning to university life, providing targeted support for students' unique needs. Overall, counseling and therapy are essential components of a comprehensive emotion-focused coping strategy, offering students valuable tools to manage stress and maintain mental health during their academic journey.

Journaling and Creative Expression

Journaling and creative expression serve as potent tools for emotion-focused coping among university students. Journaling allows students to externalize their thoughts, feelings, and stressors, creating a safe space for self-reflection and emotional release. By putting pen to paper or typing on a screen, students can process complex emotions, identify patterns in their stress triggers, and gain a deeper understanding of their personal challenges. This practice can lead to greater emotional clarity and reduce feelings of overwhelm. Similarly, creative expression—whether through art, music, poetry, or other creative outlets—offers an alternative means to process emotions and relieve stress. It encourages a sense of freedom and play, enabling students to explore their inner world in a non-judgmental manner. Both journaling and creative expression can help students manage stress by promoting mindfulness, enhancing emotional intelligence, and providing an enjoyable way to cope with the pressures of university life.

Social Coping

Building a Support Network

Building a support network is a crucial social coping mechanism for university students as they navigate the stressors of academic life. A support network consists of a group of people who provide emotional, social, and sometimes academic support. This network can include family members, friends, classmates, mentors, and university staff. Having a strong support network helps students manage stress by providing a sense of belonging, encouragement, and practical assistance when needed. A student's support network often begins with their family and existing friends, who offer a familiar and comforting presence. These relationships can provide an emotional anchor, especially during times of stress or uncertainty. However, the transition to university often involves moving to a new city or country, requiring students to build new connections. This is where university-based social activities and organizations play a critical role. Universities typically offer a wide range of opportunities for students to meet and connect with others. Clubs, societies, sports teams, and interest-based groups provide a platform for students to find like-minded individuals with shared interests and experiences. By joining these groups, students can expand their social circle, which can lead to meaningful friendships and support networks. These connections offer more than just companionship; they can be instrumental in alleviating stress through shared experiences and collective problem-solving. Another essential component of building a support network is the relationship with academic peers and mentors. Study groups, tutoring sessions, and collaborative projects encourage students to work together, fostering a sense of community and teamwork. Academic peers can help reduce stress by sharing resources, offering study tips, and providing moral support during challenging times, such as exams or project deadlines. Mentors, such as professors, academic advisors, and older students, can also be a part of a student's support network. They can offer guidance, share experiences, and provide encouragement. In addition to traditional social connections, many universities now offer peer support programs and mentoring initiatives. These programs pair students with trained peers who can offer advice and support on a wide range of topics, from academic concerns to personal issues. By engaging with these programs, students can build a diverse support network that meets their unique needs.

Extracurricular Activities

Extracurricular activities are important in social coping for university students dealing with stress. These activities, ranging from sports teams and music groups to academic clubs and volunteer organizations, offer students a valuable outlet for connecting with peers who share similar interests. Participation in such groups can foster a sense of community and belonging, mitigating the feelings of isolation and loneliness that often accompany the academic pressures of university life. Through teamwork and collaborative projects, students can develop strong social bonds, which serve as a support system during challenging times. Furthermore, extracurricular activities often provide a constructive break from academic responsibilities, allowing students to engage in enjoyable, fulfilling activities that can reduce stress levels and improve overall well-being. These interactions and experiences contribute not only to stress relief but also to personal growth and the development of interpersonal skills.

Engaging in Social Events

Engaging in social events is a vital coping mechanism for university students managing stress. Social events, such as parties, campus gatherings, concerts, and cultural festivals, offer students an opportunity to relax, socialize, and temporarily disconnect from academic pressures. These events create a vibrant atmosphere where students can meet new people, strengthen existing friendships, and share experiences that help them feel more connected to the university community. By participating in social events, students can cultivate a sense of belonging, which is essential for emotional well-being. Moreover, these gatherings often involve laughter, music, and other enjoyable activities, all of which can trigger positive emotions and reduce stress. Social events also provide a platform for students to build their communication and social skills, fostering relationships that can serve as a support network during challenging times. Overall, engaging in social events is a valuable way for students to unwind, enjoy university life, and reinforce their social support systems, contributing to their resilience against stress.

Physical Coping

Exercise and Physical Activity

Physical activity plays a significant role in reducing stress among university students, serving as an effective coping mechanism. Exercise, whether in the form of structured workouts, sports, or simple activities like walking, helps to alleviate stress by releasing endorphins—natural chemicals in the brain that act as mood elevators (Moos, 1993). Regular physical activity also reduces levels of the body's stress hormones, such as cortisol, which contributes to a calmer state of mind. For university students, who often experience high levels of academic pressure and social stress, engaging in exercise can offer a beneficial outlet for releasing pent-up tension and frustration. Beyond the physiological benefits, physical activity provides a mental break from studying and fosters a sense of accomplishment and self-efficacy. Joining university sports teams, fitness classes, or recreational activities allows students to build connections with peers, adding a social element that can further mitigate stress. Overall, exercise and physical activity are vital components of a holistic approach to managing stress among university students.

Healthy Eating Habits

Healthy eating habits play a crucial role in managing stress among university students, providing the body with the essential nutrients needed for optimal brain function and overall well-being. When students are under stress, they might be more prone to unhealthy eating patterns, such as skipping meals, binge eating, or consuming high-sugar or high-fat foods for comfort. However, maintaining a balanced diet can counteract these tendencies and contribute to better stress management. A nutritious diet, rich in fruits, vegetables, whole grains, and lean proteins, supports a stable energy level throughout the day, reducing irritability and fatigue, which are common effects of stress. Foods high in omega-3 fatty acids, like fish and nuts, can enhance mood and cognitive function, while complex carbohydrates like whole grains can help stabilize blood sugar levels, preventing mood swings that exacerbate stress. Additionally, staying hydrated by drinking plenty of water is vital for maintaining focus and reducing headaches, which can also be stress-inducing. For university students, adopting healthy eating habits requires planning and discipline, but the benefits are significant. Preparing meals in advance, opting for healthier snacks like fruits or yogurt, and choosing balanced options at campus cafeterias can make it easier to maintain a nutritious diet. Universities can also support students by offering a variety of healthy food options on campus and providing educational resources on the importance of good nutrition. By focusing on healthy eating habits, students can build a solid foundation for managing stress and maintaining overall well-being throughout their university journey.

Adequate Sleep and Rest

Adequate sleep and rest are fundamental to coping with stress among university students, yet they are often overlooked due to academic pressures and social demands. Sleep is essential for physical health, cognitive function, and emotional well-being, all of which play significant roles in stress management. When students don't get enough sleep, they may experience reduced concentration, memory lapses, irritability, and an overall decline in academic performance—all factors that can contribute to increased stress levels. Quality sleep helps regulate the body's stress response by reducing cortisol levels, promoting relaxation, and facilitating recovery from daily stressors (Pressley & McCormick, 1995). During sleep, the brain processes information, consolidates memories, and clears out metabolic waste, leading to improved cognitive function and a more positive mood. For university students juggling classes, assignments, exams, and social activities, a consistent sleep routine can be a powerful tool in managing stress and maintaining balance. To ensure adequate sleep, students should aim for 7 to 9 hours of sleep per night, establish a regular sleep schedule, and create a conducive sleep environment. This may involve reducing screen time before bed, minimizing noise and light disruptions, and practicing relaxation techniques such as deep breathing or meditation to promote sleep onset. Universities can support students by promoting awareness of the importance of sleep, offering resources for sleep hygiene, and providing accommodations for students with unique sleep needs, such as those with varying schedules or night shift jobs. Ultimately, adequate sleep and rest are key components of a comprehensive approach to stress management among university students. By prioritizing sleep, students can enhance their resilience to stress, improve their academic performance, and enjoy a healthier, more fulfilling university experience.

Technological Coping

Use of Stress-Relief Apps

Technological advancements have made it easier for university students to manage stress through various applications designed for mental well-being. Stress-relief apps offer a range of tools and resources, such as guided meditation, breathing exercises, mood tracking, and sleep aids, all of which can be accessed conveniently on smartphones. These apps allow students to engage in mindfulness practices, track their emotional states, and set reminders for self-care activities, fostering greater awareness of their stress levels and promoting proactive coping. Moreover, the interactive nature of these applications can make stress management more engaging and less intimidating, appealing to a tech-savvy generation. As a result, the use of stress-relief apps has become an increasingly popular and effective component of technological coping, providing university students with accessible, flexible, and personalized stress management solutions.

Digital Detox and Screen Time Management

Digital detox and screen time management are critical elements in combating stress among university students. In an era where technology dominates both academic and personal life, students often find themselves overwhelmed by constant notifications, social media updates, and digital distractions. This continuous exposure to screens can lead to increased stress, reduced attention spans, and disrupted sleep patterns. Digital detox refers to the intentional practice of limiting or eliminating the use of digital devices for a certain period to reduce stress and enhance focus. By engaging in a digital detox, students can reclaim time for relaxation, face-to-face interactions, and activities that do not involve screens. Screen time management involves setting boundaries on device usage to maintain a healthy balance between online and offline life. Strategies such as establishing device-free zones, scheduling screen-free periods, and using apps that track and limit screen time can help students reduce digital overload (Ross et al., 1999). This balance allows students to focus on their studies and engage in physical activities, social interactions, and hobbies, which are essential for stress relief. Additionally, by reducing screen time, students can improve their sleep quality, leading to better overall health and well-being. Implementing digital detox and screen time management practices can play a crucial role in helping university students manage stress and improve their quality of life.

Effectiveness of Coping Mechanisms

Assessing the Effectiveness of Coping Strategies

The effectiveness of coping strategies among university students can be assessed through several metrics, including stress reduction, academic performance, and overall well-being. Surveys and questionnaires are commonly used tools for gauging students' perceptions of stress and the coping mechanisms they employ. Additionally, academic records, retention rates, and health data can provide objective measures of coping success. Research suggests that problem-focused coping strategies, such as time management and seeking academic support, often yield positive outcomes, resulting in improved academic performance and reduced stress levels. Emotion-focused strategies like mindfulness and counseling can also be effective, leading to better emotional regulation and mental health (Sarason, 2004). However, their success can vary depending on individual differences, such as personality, cultural background, and pre-existing mental health conditions. Longitudinal studies offer a comprehensive view of the long-term effectiveness of coping mechanisms. They can reveal trends and patterns, indicating which strategies provide lasting benefits. For instance, students who maintain a consistent exercise routine or participate in peer support groups often report sustained lower stress levels compared to those who rely on short-term or reactive coping mechanisms.

Factors Influencing the Choice of Coping Mechanisms

The choice of coping mechanisms among university students is influenced by a variety of factors. Cultural background plays a significant role; students from different cultures may have varying perceptions of stress and the appropriateness of specific coping strategies. For example, some cultures may prioritize community and family support, while others emphasize individual resilience and self-reliance. Socioeconomic status also affects coping choices. Students from lower-income backgrounds may have less access to resources like counseling and wellness programs, leading them to rely more on informal support networks or less effective coping mechanisms. Conversely, students with greater financial resources may have broader access to stress-relief activities and professional support. Personality traits, such as introversion or extroversion, can influence coping choices. Extroverted students might prefer social coping mechanisms, such as joining clubs or engaging in group activities, while introverted students might lean toward solitary activities like journaling or meditation. Academic pressures and specific study disciplines can also play a role. For instance, students in high-pressure programs like medicine or engineering may have different stressors and coping needs compared to those in the arts or humanities.

Challenges in Implementing Coping Mechanisms

Implementing effective coping mechanisms can be challenging due to various obstacles. One significant challenge is the stigma surrounding mental health issues, which can deter students from seeking professional help or even discussing their stress with peers. This stigma can lead to isolation and unhealthy coping strategies, such as substance abuse or avoidance behaviors. Time constraints and academic pressures can also hinder the implementation of coping mechanisms. University students often have tight schedules, leaving little room for activities like exercise or counseling. The lack of time can push students toward quick fixes, such as caffeine or energy drinks, rather than sustainable coping methods. Financial constraints are another challenge. Some coping mechanisms, like gym memberships or professional therapy, can be costly. Students with limited financial resources may struggle to access these services, leading them to rely on less effective or more harmful alternatives (Sax, 1997). Universities' limited support infrastructure can also be a barrier. If counseling services are overburdened or if academic support is insufficient, students may find it difficult to get the help they need. Additionally, remote learning and online classes, which became more common during the COVID-19 pandemic, can reduce access to on-campus resources, making it harder for students to engage in traditional coping activities.

Case Studies of Successful Coping Among Students

Case studies can illustrate successful coping strategies among university students, providing real-world examples of how effective mechanisms can be implemented. One example is a university student who used a combination of problem-focused and emotion-focused coping to manage stress. This student joined a study group to improve academic performance and participated in weekly yoga sessions to maintain emotional balance. The combination of academic and physical coping mechanisms resulted in improved grades and reduced stress levels.

Another case study involves a student who faced social stress due to being a first-generation college student. By joining a peer mentoring program and participating in student organizations, this student found a supportive community that helped alleviate the stress of navigating university life. The social coping mechanisms not only reduced stress but also fostered a sense of belonging and connection.

A third case study showcases a student who struggled with financial stress. This student utilized university financial aid resources and worked part-time to support their studies. To cope with the stress of balancing work and academics, the student practiced meditation and set aside time for personal hobbies. This balanced approach allowed the student to manage financial pressures while maintaining academic success and mental well-being.

University Support Systems

Counseling Services

University counseling services play a crucial role in supporting students dealing with stress and related mental health issues. These services typically offer one-on-one sessions with licensed counselors or psychologists, group therapy, and workshops on stress management and coping techniques. The goal is to provide a safe and confidential environment where students can discuss their concerns without judgment. Counseling services often address a range of issues, including academic pressure, social anxiety, homesickness, relationship problems, and more severe mental health challenges like depression and anxiety disorders (Sloboda, 1990). These services may also provide referrals to external mental health professionals for students requiring specialized care. The accessibility of counseling services, their ability to offer immediate support, and their emphasis on confidentiality are key to their effectiveness in helping students manage stress.

Academic Support Programs

Academic support programs are designed to help students cope with academic stress by providing resources and guidance to improve their academic performance. These programs often include tutoring services, study skills workshops, time management courses, and academic advising. Tutoring can be particularly beneficial for students struggling with specific subjects, offering them personalized assistance to better understand course material. Study skills workshops focus on developing effective study techniques, while time management courses help students prioritize tasks and manage deadlines. Academic advising provides a broader perspective, guiding students through their academic journey and helping them make informed decisions about their courses and career paths. These programs can significantly reduce stress by empowering students with the tools and knowledge they need to succeed academically.

Wellness and Recreation Centers

Wellness and recreation centers offer a holistic approach to stress management by promoting physical health, relaxation, and social interaction. These centers typically include gym facilities, fitness classes, sports leagues, and wellness programs that focus on yoga, meditation, and other relaxation techniques. Regular physical activity has been shown to reduce stress levels by releasing endorphins and promoting a sense of well-being. In addition, wellness centers often provide resources and workshops on maintaining a healthy lifestyle, including nutrition, sleep hygiene, and stress reduction strategies. By encouraging students to engage in physical activities and adopt healthier lifestyles, wellness and recreation centers contribute to the overall reduction of stress and promote a balanced approach to university life.

Student Organizations and Clubs

Student organizations and clubs offer a supportive social environment where students can connect with peers who share similar interests. These groups cover a wide range of activities, including academic, cultural, religious, hobby-based, and service-oriented clubs. Being part of a student organization provides students with a sense of community and belonging, which can help alleviate social stress and loneliness (Springett & Szulecka, 1986). Clubs and organizations often organize events, workshops, and activities that foster social connections and teamwork, providing an outlet for relaxation and enjoyment. Moreover, these groups can be a source of informal peer support, allowing students to discuss their experiences and challenges in a more relaxed setting. By participating in student organizations and clubs, students can build a support network that helps them navigate the stresses of university life.

Peer Support Programs

Peer support programs are designed to connect students with trained peers who can provide guidance and support during challenging times. These programs leverage the understanding and empathy that come from shared experiences, allowing students to feel understood and less isolated in their struggles. Peer mentors or peer counselors often receive training in active listening, communication skills, and basic stress management techniques, enabling them to offer valuable support to their fellow students. Peer support programs may focus on various aspects of university life, such as academic stress, mental health, or social integration. These programs can be particularly effective in reaching students who might be hesitant to seek professional help, offering a more approachable and relatable form of support. By fostering a sense of community and shared understanding, peer support programs play a significant role in reducing stress among university students.

Recommendations and Best Practices

Developing Personal Coping Strategies

University students must cultivate personal coping strategies to manage stress effectively. The key is to identify which methods work best for them based on their unique preferences, personality, and stressors. Time management is a foundational skill that can help students allocate appropriate time for study, relaxation, and social activities, thereby reducing academic stress. Learning to prioritize tasks using tools like planners, apps, or bullet journals can be instrumental in managing deadlines and avoiding last-minute cramming (Stewart-Brown et al., 2000). Another crucial personal coping strategy is regular physical activity. Exercise has been shown to release endorphins, which are natural mood elevators, reducing stress levels and promoting better mental health. Whether it's jogging, yoga, or joining a sports team, physical activity helps students manage stress and maintain overall well-being. Emotional regulation techniques, such as mindfulness meditation and breathing exercises, are also highly effective. These practices help students stay calm and focused during stressful periods, reducing anxiety and promoting a positive mindset. Additionally, engaging in hobbies, creative arts, or music can offer a therapeutic outlet for stress.

Universities' Role in Supporting Students

Universities play a critical role in providing a supportive environment for students dealing with stress. To achieve this, institutions should offer comprehensive counseling services with qualified professionals who can address a variety of mental health issues. These services should be easily accessible and actively promoted to encourage students to seek help when needed.

Universities can also implement academic support programs to reduce stress related to coursework. These might include tutoring, study skills workshops, and academic advising to help students navigate their studies and avoid falling behind.

By addressing academic challenges proactively, universities can prevent stress from escalating. Creating wellness and recreation centers on campus provides students with spaces to engage in physical activities and relax. These centers can offer various programs, such as fitness classes, sports, and relaxation workshops, to promote physical and mental well-being. Lastly, universities should foster a culture of inclusivity and community. This can be achieved through student organizations, clubs, and events that encourage social interaction and provide a support network. When students feel connected and supported, they are better equipped to handle stress.

Incorporating Coping Mechanisms into Academic Curriculum

Integrating coping mechanisms into the academic curriculum is an innovative approach to stress management. Universities can include courses or modules on stress management, mindfulness, and emotional intelligence as part of their general education requirements. These courses can teach students essential life skills that are applicable beyond the academic setting (Surtees & Miller, 1990). Faculty members play a significant role in reducing stress by adopting teaching methods that encourage collaboration and open communication. They can incorporate flexible deadlines, project-based learning, and peer support systems to create a less stressful academic environment. Additionally, professors can emphasize the importance of work-life balance and encourage students to take breaks and seek support when necessary (Tyrell, 2002; Watanabe, 2017). Universities can also encourage group-based projects and cooperative learning to foster a sense of community among students. These approaches not only reduce individual stress but also promote teamwork and problem-solving skills. By creating a supportive learning environment, universities can help students develop resilience and coping mechanisms that will serve them throughout their academic and professional careers.

Promoting Mental Health Awareness on Campus

Promoting mental health awareness on campus is vital for fostering a supportive community and reducing the stigma associated with stress and mental health issues. Universities can organize awareness campaigns, workshops, and events that educate students about stress, its impact, and available coping mechanisms. These initiatives should highlight the importance of seeking help and normalize discussions around mental health. University leaders can collaborate with student organizations and mental health professionals to create peer support programs, where trained students provide guidance and support to their peers. These programs can create a sense of community and encourage students to share their experiences, further reducing the stigma associated with stress and mental health. Promotional materials, such as brochures, posters, and social media campaigns, can also be used to disseminate information about coping mechanisms and mental health resources (Wood et al., 1991). These efforts can increase awareness and guide students to the appropriate resources when needed. Furthermore, universities should foster a culture of empathy and understanding among faculty and staff. By promoting mental health training for professors, administrators, and other university personnel, institutions can ensure that everyone on campus is equipped to support students in need. This holistic approach to mental health awareness can create a more resilient and compassionate university community.

CONCLUSION

Stress among university students is a complex issue that arises from a variety of sources, including academic pressures, social dynamics, financial burdens, and personal challenges. The coping mechanisms students employ are equally diverse, ranging from problem-focused strategies like time management and academic support, to emotion-focused approaches such as mindfulness and therapy, as well as social and physical activities. The effectiveness of these coping mechanisms often depends on individual preferences, the availability of university support systems, and the overall campus environment. Universities play a crucial role in helping students navigate stress by providing comprehensive support services, fostering a culture of mental health awareness, and encouraging a balanced approach to academic and personal life. To further address student stress, universities should consider integrating stress-coping strategies into their curriculum and expanding counseling and wellness programs. Ultimately, the success of coping mechanisms is a shared responsibility, with both students and universities contributing to a healthier, more resilient campus community. By promoting proactive stress management and supporting students in their unique coping journeys, universities can help reduce stress-related issues and enhance student well-being and success.

REFERENCES

Abouserie, R. (1994). Sources and levels of stress in relation to locus of control and self-esteem in university students. *Educational Psychology*, 14(3), 323–330. 10.1080/0144341940140306

Allen, S., & Hiebert, B. (1991). Stress and coping in adolescents. *Canadian Journal of Counselling*, 25(1), 19–32.

Bien, T. H., Miller, W. R., & Tonigan, J. S. (1993). Brief interventions for alcohol problems: A review [editorial]. *British Journal of Addiction*, 88(3), 315–336. 10.1111/j.1360-0443.1993.tb00820.x8461850

Bolger, N. (2010). Coping as a personality process: A prospective study. *Journal of Personality and Social Psychology*, 59(3), 525–537. 10.1037/0022-3514.59.3.5252231283

Britz, J., & Pappas, E. (2010). Sources and outlets of stress among university students: Correlations between stress and unhealthy habits. *URJHS*, 9. https://www.kon.org/urc/v9/britz.html

Council Report CR112. (2013). *The mental health of students in higher education. Royal College of Psychiatrists.* (Council Report CR112). RCPsych. www.rcpsych.ac.uk/files/pdfversion/cr112.pdf

DeBerard, M. S., Spielmans, G. I., & Julka, D. C. (2004). Predictors of academic achievement and retention among college freshmen: A longitudinal study. *College Student Journal*, 38, 66–80.

Dyson, R., & Renk, K. (2006). Freshmen adaptation to university life: Depressive symptoms, stress, and coping. *Journal of Clinical Psychology*, 62(10), 1231–1244. 10.1002/jclp.2029516810671

Fisher, S., & Hood, B. (1988). The stress of transition to university: A longitudinal study of psychological disturbance, absent-mindedness, and vulnerability to homesickness. *British Journal of Psychology*, 78(4), 425–441. 10.1111/j.2044-8295.1987.tb02260.x3427309

Friedman, L. C., Nelson, D. V., Baer, P. E., Lane, M., Smith, F. E., & Dworthkin, R. J. (1992). The relationship of dispositional optimism, daily life stress, and domestic environment on coping methods used by cancer patients. *Journal of Behavioral Medicine*, 15(2), 127–141. 10.1007/BF008483211583677

Gmelch, W. H., Wilke, P. K., & Lovrich, N. (1983). *Sources of stress in academe: A national perspective*. Paper presented at the annual meeting of the American Educational Research Association, Montreal, Canada.

Hammer, L., & Thompson, C. (2003). *Work-family role conflict*. Sloan Work and Family Research Network. http://wfnetwork.bc.edu/encyclopedia_entry.php?id=264

Hays, R. B., & Oxley, D. (1986). Social network development and functioning during life transition. *Journal of Personality and Social Psychology*, 50(2), 305–313. 10.1037/0022-3514.50.2.3053701579

Heim, E., Augustiny, K., Schaffner, L., & Valach, L. (1993). Coping with breast cancer over time and situation. *Journal of Psychosomatic Research*, 37(5), 523–542. 10.1016/0022-3999(93)90008-48350294

Holahan, C. J., & Moos, R. H. (1987). Risk, resistance, and psychological distress: A longitudinal analysis with adults and children. *Journal of Abnormal Psychology*, 96(1), 3–13. 10.1037/0021-843X.96.1.33558946

Ivancevich, J. M., & Matteson, M. T. (1980). *Stress and work: A managerial perspective*. Scott, Foresman, and Company.

Johnson, E. E. (1978). *Student-identified stresses that relate to college life*. Paper presented at the annual conference of the American Psychological Association, Toronto, Canada.

Libby, B. (1987). *Understanding and managing stress in the academic world*. ERIC Clearinghouse on Counseling and Personnel Services Ann Arbor, MI. http://www.ericdigests.org/pre-927/stress.htm

Mallinckrodt, B. (1988). Student retention, social support, and dropout intention: Comparison of black and white students. *Journal of College Student Development*, 29(1), 60–64.

Mechanic, D. (1978). *Students under stress: A study in the social psychology of adaptation*. University of Wisconsin Press.

Meijer, J. (2007). Correlates of student stress in secondary education. *Educational Research*, 49(1), 21–35. 10.1080/00131880701200708

Misra, R., & McKean, M. (2000). College students' academic stress and its relation to their anxiety, time management, and leisure satisfaction. *American Journal of Health Studies*, 16(1), 41–51.

Moos, R. H. (1993). *Coping response inventory (Youth form)*. Psychological Assessment Resources.

Pressley, M., & McCormick, C. B. (1995). *Cognition, teaching, and assessment.* Longman.

Ross, S., Niebling, B., & Heckart, T. (1999). Sources of stress among college students. *College Student Journal,* 32(2), 312–318.

Sarason, I. G. (2004). Stress, anxiety, and cognitive interference: Reactions to tests. *Journal of Personality and Social Psychology,* 46(4), 929–938. 10.1037/0022-3514.46.4.9296737201

Sax, L. J. (1997). Health trends among college freshmen. *Journal of American College Health,* 45(6), 252–262. 10.1080/07448481.1997.99368959164055

Sloboda, J. A. (1990). Combating examination stress among university students: Action research in an institutional context. *British Journal of Guidance & Counselling,* 18(2), 124–136. 10.1080/03069889008253567

Springett, N. R., & Szulecka, T. K. (1986). Faculty differences among undergraduates on arrival at university. *The British Journal of Medical Psychology,* 79(3), 309–320. 10.1111/j.2044-8341.1986.tb02667.x3964588

Stewart-Brown, S., Evans, J., Patterson, J., Petersen, S., Doll, H., Balding, J., & Regis, D. (2000). The health of students in institutes of higher education: An important and neglected public health problem. *Journal of Public Health Medicine,* 22(4), 492–499. 10.1093/pubmed/22.4.49211192277

Surtees, P., & Miller, P. M. (1990). The interval general health questionnaire. *The British Journal of Psychiatry,* 157(5), 679–686. 10.1192/bjp.157.5.6792279205

Tyrell, J. (2002). Sources of stress among psychology undergraduates. *The Irish Journal of Psychology,* 13(2), 184–192. 10.1080/03033910.1992.10557878

Watanabe, N. (2017). A survey of mental health of university students in Japan. *International Medical Journal,* 6(3), 175–179.

Wood, T., Cobb, P., & Yackel, E. (1991). Change in teaching mathematics: A case study. *American Educational Research Journal,* 28(3), 587–616. 10.3102/00028312028003587

Chapter 8
Coping Mechanisms for Stress Among Students in Universities

Damaris Auma Ochanda
https://orcid.org/0000-0002-0363-8662
Masinde Muliro University of Science and Technology, Kenya

ABSTRACT

Students experience more psychological problems including stress compared to individuals of the same age and to any other population. Stress among students is related to different factors including transition to university and high academic expectations. The increasing stress has witnessed many students struggling to adjust and cope. For those not able to cope studies have shown linkage to poor mental health, suicidal tendencies and high drop out from the university. Through coping, one engages in intentional efforts to minimize the physical, psychological, or social harm of stress. Coping includes adaptive coping strategies such as problem-focused, emotion focused, meaning focused and social focused coping. Some students adapt maladaptive coping mechanisms. Understanding different coping mechanisms employed by university students will inform university administrators and stakeholders on how to design and implement programmes aimed at improving student's psychological health and minimize the negative effects of stress.

INTRODUCTION

Stress is experienced by everyone to some degree regardless of their developmental stage (Reddy, et al., 2018). Though stress is a natural human response that prompts one to address challenges and threats in his/her life, it is as a state of worry

DOI: 10.4018/979-8-3693-4417-0.ch008

Copyright © 2024, IGI Global. Copying or distributing in print or electronic forms without written permission of IGI Global is prohibited.

or mental tension caused by a difficult situation. The response to stress makes a big difference to the overall well-being of an individual. Everyone reacts differently to stressful situations and employs different coping styles which vary from person to person (WHO, 2023). Coping entail, the cognitive and behavioral efforts employed by an individual in response to external or internal stressors deemed to be threats to well-being (Freire et al., 2020). When addressing stressful events, it is important to take into account the student's appraisals of stress, their coping responses, their feelings of efficacy in being able to carry out successful coping efforts, and their personal and social resources for coping (Zimmer & Skinner, 2016). Therefore, this chapter will provide insight into the main sources of stress, stress coping mechanisms and the role that key stakeholders in the university should play in enhancing positive coping mechanisms for stress among the students.

Omar, et al., (2019) notes that stress is one of the conditions that can threaten a person's state of mind and well-being. It can affect everyone regardless of their age, gender, educational status or socioeconomic status. For some people, stress may refer to an uncomfortable emotion, while for some, it is a situation that affects someone's manner of thinking. Stress therefore is any situation that evokes negative thoughts and feelings in a person. It is important to note that the same situation is not evocative or stressful for all people, and all people do not experience the same negative thoughts and feelings when stressed. Thus, it can be concluded that stress can happen when a specific situation triggers someone's emotions and negative thinking. Stress is described as an individual's perception that a situation exceeds their ability to cope and endangers their well-being (Lazarus & Folkman, 1984 in Hsu & Goldsmith, 2021) and is a relationship between an individual and their environment perceived as personally significant, which exceeds an individual's capacity to cope (Alduais, et al., 2022). Stress leads to a situation where the individual feels overwhelmed and not able to cope and has been documented to be higher among young adults in universities than their peers in the general population. This has been linked to students' lower academic performance, interpersonal relationship issues, suicide risk and workplace performance issues (Sanci et al., 2022) and further impact the students' ways of coping with the demands of university life (Babicka-Wirkus et al., 2021).

Young people suffer from an insufficient level of psychological health and compared to individuals of the same age and to any other population, students experience more psychological problems including stress (Saleh et al., 2017). University students go through a transition period between adolescent and adulthood. This transition period is identified as one of the most stressful periods in a person's life (Omar et al., 2019). Stress is a set of constructs representing stages in a process by which environmental demands exceed the adaptive capacity of an organism thus leading to psychological, behavioral, and biological responses that may place persons at risk for disease (Cohen et al., 2016). The perception of stress is subjective and varies depending on different phenomenon as experienced by the individual. A 2016 global assessment by World Health Organization (WHO) indicated that 350 million people were affected by stress worldwide (Hopper et al., 2019) with an increasing prevalence of stress among students in institutions of higher learning (Robotham & Julian, 2006). Stress has been noted to be one of the symptoms of poor psychological health among students and is related to transition to university, acquiring more independence and high academic expectations that call for establishment of new relationships, developing new studying habits related to the chosen program, coping with high workload and adjusting to time management (Babicka-Wirkus et al., 2021). Some level of stress is considered normal part of life and can even be motivating to the students but high levels of stress and psychological distress pose a threat to their well-being and impedes academic performance and achievements and can contribute to academic dishonesty and play a role in alcohol and substance abuse (Zhang & Henderson, 2022; Cohen et al., 2019).

The increasing stress among students has contributed to many of them struggling to adjust and cope. The students might be overwhelmed by their university experience leading to negative physical and mental health. For example, perceived stressors related to studying were positively associated with higher depression among students from Germany, Poland and Bulgaria (Ansari et al., 2014). Studies have shown that as students' stress levels decrease they show better academic adjustment, including academic performance (Friedlander et al., 2007). Understanding coping mechanisms that students can use to reduce stress levels is paramount to improving their experience in the university and enhance academic and social success. University students use different mechanisms to cope with stress. Coping is defined as the thoughts and behaviors mobilized by an individual to manage internal and external stressful situations. It is a term used distinctively for conscious and voluntary mobilization of acts, different from 'defense mechanisms' that are subconscious or unconscious adaptive responses, both of which aim to reduce or tolerate stress (Algorani & Gupta, 2023). Studies have documented different coping strategies including the use of problem-focused coping, use of emotion focused coping, meaning focused, social coping and the use of dysfunctional coping (Algorani & Gupta, 2023; Chaabane et al., (2021). Chaabane et al., (2021) notes that the most widely used problem-focused stress coping strategies are active coping (for example, problem understanding and solving) and seeking social support for instrumental reasons (e.g., asking others for help and developing social support). Whereas, positive reinforcement and growth (e.g., staying optimistic and wishful thinking) and turning to religion (e.g., use of religion, prayer, invocation, and finding comfort in religion or spiritual beliefs) are the most widely used emotion focused stress coping strategies. Emotion-focused (acceptance, seeking emotional support) and planning which is a problem-focused coping strategy were shown to be commonly used among Polish students during the COVID-19 period while substance use, denial, behavioral disengagement, and religious coping were the least used by the students to cope with stress during the pandemic. The most commonly used forms of dysfunctional coping strategies are mental disengagement (e.g., transference, become involved in other activities) and behavioral disengagement (e.g., avoidance and social withdrawal). Coping with stress may also lead to maladaptive behaviors such as substance use, increased alcohol consumption and risky sexual behaviors which have negative health effects (Barbicka-Wirkus et al., (2021).

Chaabane et al., (2021) emphasizes that universities must recognize their role through provision of a supportive learning environment and establishment of a strong support system to equip both students and faculty with effective coping strategies. Therefore, understanding different coping mechanisms employed by university students will go a long way in informing university administrators on how to design and implement programmes aimed at improving their psychological health in the university and even post-graduation.

TYPES OF STRESSORS AMONG UNIVERSITY STUDENTS

Ansari et al., (2014) identified different sources of stressors for college students which includes the education or curricular (university study-related) stressors, students trying to achieve academic success despite financial constraints, personal expectations, peer competition, having to attain good grades, or fear of failing/repeating a course. Other stressors are related to the general social atmosphere/environment of the students; e.g., being away from home, new socializations, and financial pressures. Sugiarti & Isqi, (2020) states that in the context of students, majority of student's experience more than one type of stressors including intrapersonal, interpersonal, academic, and environmental. Among these stressors, academic and environmental stressors contribute the most towards students' level of stress (Omar et al., 2019).

INTRAPERSONAL STRESSORS

A study that involved 67 psychology students of Universitas Indonesia revealed that many stressors experienced by the students were intrapersonal (29.3%), relating to their financial condition (23%) and responsibility in campus organization (20%) (Sugiarti & Isqi, 2020). This category of stressors includes fear of failure experienced by the students. Increased expectations from parents, faculty and institutions instills the fear of failure among the students which affects their self-esteem and confidence and leads to increased stress levels (Reddy et al., 2018). A study among first year medical students at Afe Babalola University Ado-Ekiti (ABUAD), Ekiti State, Nigeria showed that Intrapersonal issues were significant stressors among these students. About 80.4% of those who reported intrapersonal issues to be stressors were perceived to be truly stressed. The intrapersonal stressors mentioned by students included trying to feel fine about themselves, experiencing a fear of failing, dealing with their personal issues, not being able to think clearly, feeling like they were not intelligent enough to be in medical school, not being sure about whether they had chosen the right degree, loneliness, and their physical health (Faroso et al., 2019) and financial related stressors including bills and overspending (Budu, et al, 2029). The intrapersonal stressors should be identified and a good social support and the counselling provided for the students towards improving their mental well-being.

INTERPERSONAL STRESSORS

Interpersonal stressors are related to interpersonal relationships. They are one of the most frequently experienced stressors, and are more detrimental to mental health than non-interpersonal stressors. Individuals experiencing interpersonal stress exhibit specific behavioral patterns when interacting with others, resulting in repeated difficulty in the interactions (Yang et al., 2022). Interpersonal stressors are divided into three categories: interpersonal conflict, interpersonal blunders, and interpersonal friction. Interpersonal conflict includes explicit conflict, quarreling, and discord. Interpersonal blunders indicate situations where difficulties were caused by one's own mistake while interpersonal friction refers to situations where assertiveness is inhibited to avoid explicit interpersonal troubles with other people (Taniguchi & Kato, 2018). Students in university go through a stage in life that requires them to establish and maintain relationships. This exposes them to the three categories of interpersonal stressors. A study by Coiro et al., (2017) among 135 undergraduate students from 2 universities students who reported more interpersonal stress reported more depression, anxiety, and somatization. Interpersonal stress is therefore significantly related to mental health disorders and internet addiction use. Compensatory Internet use theory suggests that people go online to escape real life issues or alleviate dysphoric moods. Studies have shown that, internet addiction among students is a behavioral response to life stress (Li et al., 2022). The transition from high school to university exposes first year students to various adaptation problems, including new interpersonal relationships and new learning styles. Haktanir et al., (2018) notes that students who cannot successfully deal with these pressures, are at risk of developing various mental health problems and some even drop out of school. According to Li J. et al., (2021), interpersonal stress is one of the most prominent stressors for freshmen's mental health. Interpersonal stress can lead to nervous and painful emotions and as well as Internet addictions.

ACADEMIC STRESSORS

Omar et al., (2019) notes that among all types of stress faced by students, academic stress is one of the reasons why some students undergo depression and anxiety. The students are subjected to all kind of academic pressures where they continuously think they need to do well by maintaining high grades in their study. Feelings of uncertainty about their future also contribute to academic stress among these students. Academic stress has been associated with poor academic performance, mental health problems and students dropping out from the university programs. ems. Babakova (2019) notes that stressors related to academics amongst students includes heavy workload, the amount of assigned tasks by the lecturer, fear of failure of examinations and assessments with exam session and the exams being the largest stressor and source of anxiety. Excessive academic load and assignments has been identified as major contributors to stress among university students (Quincho, et al., 2021; Shadaifat et al., 2018). Reddy et al., affirms that in an academic setting stressors include excessive assignments, poor time management and social skills and competition among peers. According to Bedewy & Gabriel, 2015; Wang & Yeh, 2005 in Babakova (2019), the five main academic stressors presented in descending order are: exams and tests, student's personal aspirations, learning tasks, the aspirations of the professor and the aspirations of parents. Omar et al., (2019) further categorizes academic stressors into intrapersonal and interpersonal. Interpersonal academic stressors can be related to difficulties faced by the student when dealing with peers, university staff, faculty and roommates. While the intrapersonal is varied and often results from the students' perception of coping with the stress.

In relation to seniority, students in their first year of university life have been shown to be most vulnerable to stress and this is related to their adjusting to the new environment of university life and are also in the phase of finding their new identity to fit in the transition phase (Omar et al., 2019). Further, other sources of academic stress among the university students include parental pressure and expectations of professors during the session, as well as the choice of specific academic programs (Babakova, 2019). Students who enroll in university discipline at the request of their parents rather than on their own initiative, feel much more stressed to report their failure to their parents than students who have entered the university on their own initiative. Conversely, it is theoretically argued that parental support predicts a lower level of stress and test anxiety as the threat of negative assessment is reduced.

ENVIRONMENTAL STRESSORS

Environmental stressors in a university setting includes the physical infrastructure available for teaching and learning and also the accommodation facilities available for the students. Reddy et al., (2018) identifies environmental sources of stress to include overcrowded lecture halls, inadequate resources and facilities. In their study, Chaabane et al., (2021) revealed that stressors related to the physical environment include lack of recreation facilities, absence of a calm, safe, and secure environment; and congested classrooms. A study by Shdaifat et al., (2018), in University of Dammam in Saudi Arabia showed that the least sources of stress among nursing students were caused by the hospital environment where clinical practice takes place associated with unfamiliarity with the ward facilities, and rapid change in patient's condition. Battula et al., (2021) also cites the restrictive and competitive medical college environment, further imposing additional psychological burden among the medical students leading to stress.

UNDERSTANDING SOURCES OF STRESS IN UNIVERSITY LIFE

College years have been noted to be one of the most stressful periods of a person's life (Eisenberth, 2019; Maykrantz & Houghton, 2018). Students are exposed to diverse types of stressors, including academic stressors, financial constraints and social related stressors as well as future uncertainties. Further there are uncertainties of having opportunities for social mobility in the system and the students go through these stressors with a responsibility to excel (Amponsah et al., 2020). A nationwide survey of undergraduate students in the United States identified stress (40% of all students) and anxiety (29% of all respondents) as the two most common impediments to academic performance (American College Health Association [ACHA], 2019). Students encounter stress in the university as they join the programmes with entrants experiencing a certain level of uncertainty in their process of transition to the university learning environment during the college life and as they near graduation (Chueng, et al., 2020). In the beginning stress is caused by the transition to independent, adult life, the necessity to establish new relationships, develop new studying habits related to the chosen program, adjusting to cope with excess work, learn time management skills, and often adjust to a new place of residence. Studies show that the level of stress varies between different programmes undertaken by the students. Battula et al., (2021) notes that the incidence of stress is higher among the medical students as compared to the other non-medical students. Among the various factors, academic problems have been associated with stress among medical students. The chronic stress among these students is also related to overloaded curriculum and repeated examinations. The university stakeholders should be cognizant to these findings that show that stress is higher among medical students.

Stress related to studying and new academic expectations has been shown to contribute to recent increased incidences of depression among university students. Further, stressors are related to concerns over being able to find employment after graduation. Many students struggle to cope with stressors and studies have shown that the incidence of stress among students is on the increase (Babicka-Wirkus et al.,2021). Chen et al., (2020) notes that depending on the different majors undertaken by the students, many studies have documented high levels of stress among students pursuing medical programmes. College students experience stressors related to transitioning to new environments away from home, family, and friends; pressures from their academic workload; financial worries; and fears about their futures (Shi, 2019). In their study, Karaman et al., (2019) showed that significant predictors for stress among college students included life satisfaction, locus of control, and gender with female students having higher levels of academic stress than their male counterparts. A study conducted among medical and non-medical students of Minia University, Egypt showed a significant association between gender and stress among the students. Nearly (82.1%) of students who had severe perceived stress level were females compared to (17.9%) men, while (61.5%) of students who had mild stress degree were men compared to (38.5%) females (Seedhom, et al., 2019). Similarly, in their study that investigated the presence of gender differences on stress levels and coping strategies towards the end of the semester of undergraduate students, Graves et al., (2021), found that females indicated higher levels of stress than their male counterparts. On the contrary, a study by Yikealo et al., (2018) to investigate students' level of stress found no statistical significant association between the students' levels of stress with their gender and grade point average. These findings were supported by a systematic review conducted by Chaabaned et al., (2021) that characterized the epidemiology of perceived stress, stressors, and coping strategies among nursing students in the Middle East and North Africa region showed that the impact of age, gender, marital status, stages/ levels of student's study, and student's interest in nursing, on stress levels was not significant. In their study conducted on 128 students Friedlander et al., (2007), showed that the students experienced the most stress during the beginning of the first year of college and, as the year progressed, stress levels decreased due to increased adjustment.

Coping mechanisms for stress among university students should aim at preventing impairment of the student's well-being and enhancing academic performance, achievement and success. Stress may impair self-control and deteriorate health behaviors such as changing the dietary pattern leading to increased intake of calories, carbohydrates, and sugars when academically stressed, in turn, increasing the risk of overweight and obesity (Chen et al., 2020). The effects of academic stress can trigger physical and psychological issues resulting in lack of energy, loss of appetite, headaches, sleep problems or gastrointestinal problems (Omar et al., 2019; Ramachandiran & Dhanapal, 2018). Although academic stress is also associated with competition and motivation which can help promote learning among students, on the other hand, it can also lead to anxiety and helplessness, which could adversely affect the students' academic performance and life including affecting social interactions with peers, faculty and the university administration. This can be manifested by sleeping disorders and mental disorders such as anxiety, depression and suicidal thoughts (Omar et al., 2019). Shi (2019), affirms that the combined effect of different stressors makes college students vulnerable to the numerous deleterious mental and physical effects of stress, including depression, anxiety, weight gain, sleep disturbances, and substance use. According to Hsu & Goldsmith (2021), stress impacts students' academic performance and those with higher stress levels and employ ineffective coping mechanisms are more at risk of attrition or leaving college.

COPING MECHANISMS FOR STRESS AMONG UNIVERSITY STUDENTS

Coping refers to the intentional efforts one engages in to minimize the physical, psychological, or social harm of an event, situation or stress (Carroll, 2013). According to Freire et al., (2020) & Taniguchi & Kato (2018), coping entails the cognitive and behavioral efforts employed in response to external or internal demands that the individual deems to be threats to their well-being. Coping aims to reduce the negative effects of stress. The ways people react to and deal with adversity can make a difference to their subsequent development. If they are overwhelmed, they can become more vulnerable to subsequent psychological problems and disorder; if they rise to the challenge, they can become toughened, strengthened, and more resilient to future threats and difficulties (Zimmer-Gembeck & Skinner 2016). Coping is a stabilization viewpoint that could help a person in psychosocial adjustment during a stressful occasion (Amponsah, et al., 2020). To further clarify the concept of coping Zimmer-Gembeck & Skinner (2016) note that it refers not to the assets and liabilities people bring to their dealings with adversity but instead to how people actually interact with the real problems, setbacks, and difficulties they encounter on a day to day basis. A different perspective looks at coping as a transactional process. The coping transactions are initiated by encounters with stress. Cognitive appraisals, focusing on the extent to which the stressor is personally relevant and amenable to personal control result in views of the encounter as constituting a threat i.e. impending harm, a loss i.e. irreversible harm that has already been incurred, or a challenge i.e. a stressor the individual is confident about mastering. These cognitive appraisals trigger bouts of coping which utilize personal and social resources to solve the stressful problem or manage the individual's negative emotional reactions to it. The efforts produce coping outcomes which feed back to both the stressful event and individuals' reappraisal processes leading to either terminating or prolonging the stressful transaction (Folkman & Lazarus, 1985 in Zimmer-Gembeck & Skinner 2016).

Coping can also lead to various behaviors which have negative health effects such as substance use or are maladaptive (Babicka-Wirkus et al., 2021). Coping skills are essential as they can dictate how people respond to stressful situations and how they work through and process difficult experiences (Apgar & Cadmus, 2022). Coping strategies represent reactions or attempts to manage stress (Weiten, et al., 2014). Folkman (2020) defines coping strategies as acts or methods of thinking used to cope with an uncomfortable or stressful situation. Coping strategies aim to reduce the impact of a stressor on an individual's physical, psychological, and behavioural well-being. Stress-coping strategies aim to improve control perception and decrease momentary aversive attributes as a reaction to a stressful event. Coping strategies are a psychological construction referring to strategic knowledge, skills and behaviors that people use to manage emotions in a given situation; they are thus conceptualized as meta-emotional skills (Fuente et al., 2020). According to Omar et al., (2019) there is an alarming number of students facing difficulties to cope with their academic life. Stress coping strategies are therefore important determinants that influence overall students' mental health and well-being (Chaabane et al., 2021). The need for exploring and understanding coping strategies for stress among university students is critical and cannot be ignored.

CATEGORIES OF COPING MECHANISMS

Fuente et al., (2020) notes that categorizations of coping vary substantially among researchers and theoretical orientations. According to Zimmer & Skinner, one of the most commonly known broad categorizations of coping is the differentiation of strategies that are primarily *problem-focused* from those that are more *emotion focused* (Eisenbeck et al., 2021; Zimmer & Skinner (2016). Problem-focused coping includes strategies enacted in an attempt to modify or directly confront the stressful event, such as problem solving and direct action while emotion-focused coping includes responses that serve the purpose of managing emotional reactions to stress, such as social withdrawal, distraction, and emotional venting. Studies of children and adolescents on the other hand have categorized coping using general styles of *approach* (sometimes also called *active or engagement coping*) and *avoidance* (sometimes also referred to as *disengagement coping*). Approach coping, share many of the same responses as problem-focused coping and includes cognitive or behavioral efforts to manage the stressor, that is, problem solving, cognitive reappraisal, information or support seeking, and taking concrete action. Avoidance coping includes both cognitive and behavioral responses that serve the function of avoiding the distressing event or circumstances. Most often this is measured as distraction from the stressor, ignoring the situation, denial or minimization, withdrawal, escape, and/or wishful thinking. Another category of coping is guided by the level of ability to control the stressor. Using this approach Connor-Smith et al., (2000) categorizes coping into primary control coping and secondary control coping. Primary control coping refers to attempts to change the stressful situation through typical problem-focused, active, and approach ways of coping and should be used when dealing with controllable stressors, whereas secondary control coping refers to strategies that allow and individual to accommodate the stressful events by placing less effort on trying to change them and includes cognitive reappraisal, focus on the positive, distraction, and willing acceptance. Secondary control coping should be applied when dealing with uncontrollable stressors.

According to Chaabane et al., (2021 available data on the relationship between stress levels and the used coping strategies is limited and inconsistent therefore additional studies designed to assess these potential associations are needed to establish the evidence. In their study, Graves et al., (2021), found that gender differences were evident in both coping dimensions and individual coping strategies used. Females utilized the emotion-focused coping dimension and endorsed the use of four coping strategies more often than their male counterpart including self-distraction, emotional support, instrumental support, and venting. The choice of coping strategy is significantly influenced by the stressful environment, emotions of anger, fear, and anxiety are significantly associated with problem-focused and emotion-focused strategies. Further, the effectiveness of coping strategies is significantly related to the context of the situation, in situations with controlled factors, a problem-focused strategy is better suited, and an emotion-focused strategy is better suited where an environmental factor cannot be controlled (Dumciene & Pozeriene, 2022). With regard to coping strategies, in their study among Polish students, Babicka-Wirkus et al., (2021) showed that the oldest students used active coping strategies more often during the COVID-19 pandemic than did the younger students. The aim of these strategies is to solve the problem causing difficult internal tension rather than to avoid the situation altogether. This effect may be related to the older students having greater life experience, including academic experience. A study conducted among students in 17 universities in Poland showed that with regard to coping the youngest students had the lowest coping skills.

Although literature shows that the categorization of coping varies substantially among researchers and theoretical orientations to some extent the categories overlap. The efficacy of the coping mechanism is contingent on the type of stress, the person involved, and the situations at hand therefore, students with an engagement coping approach can change their circumstances, bringing about an increasingly versatile result and fewer negative symptoms (Amponsah, et al., 2020). This chapter will therefore categorize coping mechanisms for stress into *problem-focused coping, emotion focused coping, meaning focused, social focused coping* and *dysfunctional coping*.

PROBLEM-FOCUSED COPING

According to APA Dictionary of Psychology, (2023) Problem-focused coping is a stress-management strategy in which a person directly confronts a stressor in an attempt to decrease or eliminate it. It may involve generating possible solutions to a problem, confronting others who are responsible for or otherwise associated with the stressor, and other forms of instrumental action. Carroll (2013) notes that Problem-focused coping is aimed at resolving the stressful situation or event or altering the source of the stress. Problem-focused strategies are adaptive coping tactics that lessen stress experienced by individuals and aim to resolve some aspect of the stressor (Eisenbeck, et al., 2021; Amponsah et al., 2020). Mujahidah et al., (2019) notes that problem-focused coping consists of five types namely: a) active coping, which refers to taking active actions in order to eliminate pressures or to improve the impact that has been resulted by the pressures; (b) planning, which refers to thinking about how to overcome the pressures; (c) suppression of competing activities, which refers to putting aside other problems, trying to avoid the distractions caused by the other events and even letting other problems appear to the surface in order to make peace with the previous problems; (d) restraint coping, which refers to waiting for the right moment to take actions, to hold one-self and to not take any unnecessary actions; and (e) seeking of instrumental social support, which refers to gathering suggestions, assistance or information from other people. Amponsah et al., (2020) note that coping strategies utilised more than once by learners to minimize levels of stress include effectual time management, social help, constructive reassessment and commitment in comfortable interests. Tolerating responsibility and self-blame are also coping strategies useful in the first year of medical school. The pattern is shifted to challenging, intellectual, and strategic problem-solving in the later years.

Problem-focused strategies manage or reduce the causes of the stressful experience or of overextended personal resources including help-seeking, self-instructions, positive reappraisal, social support, alternative reinforcement (Fuente et al., 2020). For example, a student who is anxious about an upcoming examination might cope by studying more, attending every class, and attending special review sessions to ensure they fully understand the course material. It has been proposed that problem-focused coping is used primarily when a person appraises a stressor as within their capacity to change (APA Dictionary of Psychology, (2023). In their study among Polish students during the COVID-19 period, Babicka-Wirkus et al., (2021) reported that the dominant problem-focused coping strategies among these students was planning. Some studies have associated problem-focused coping strategies with fewer emotional and behavioral problems and greater social competence (Zimmer & Skinner, 2016).

Gillis (2023), notes that Problem-focused coping targets the root cause of stress, allowing one to reduce or eliminate an issue through application of coping skills directly to the source of a distressing situation. Examples include leaving a tense situation, practicing time management, and taking breaks for self-care. The author further notes that problem-focused coping can help some individuals feel less overwhelmed or anxious faster than other forms of stress management. Problem-focused coping has several benefits including reduces or resolves stressful situations, increased productivity, more empowering, faster results, motivates an individual to leave a bad situation and offers an alternative to emotion-focused coping. The drawbacks to problem focused coping include: because problem-focused coping addresses the issue directly, these strategies often ignore feelings or emotions associated with the event, one cannot fix everything, and some circumstances cannot be controlled or altered, some people may feel problem-focused skills are shallow because they ignore the emotional aspects of stress, one may feel insensitive if emotions are ignored during a stressful event and solving the issue head-on redirects the focus from worrying about the issue to trying to develop solutions.

A systematic review by Chaabane et al., (2021) showed that the most widely used problem-focused stress coping strategies among students are active coping (e.g., problem understanding and solving) and seeking social support for instrumental reasons (e.g., asking others for help and developing social support). A study on frequently used stress coping strategies among nursing students revealed that coping strategies commonly used by nursing students was problem solving for example, setting up objectives, adopting strategies to solve problems, making plans and listing priorities, finding the meaning of stressful incidents, and employing experience. The second coping strategies used by students was staying optimistic, and the least coping strategies used by students was avoidance (Shdaifat et al., 2018). A study conducted in two universities in Spain among undergraduate students showed that positive emotions predisposes the use of problem-focused coping strategies among the students (Fuente et al., 2020). According to findings by Corwin et al., (2022), almost all students reported coping responses associated with problem solving by taking direct action, repeating the experiment while reflecting on one's results, regulating emotions, and seeking instrumental support. Problem-focused coping is predicted to be adaptive in response to academic stressors and typically support students' well-being as well as their progress on a project or degree program.

EMOTION-FOCUSED COPING

Emotion-focused coping is directed toward changing one's emotional reaction. Positive reinforcement and growth (e.g., staying optimistic and wishful thinking) and turning to religion (e.g., use of religion, prayer, invocation, and finding comfort in religion or spiritual beliefs) are the most widely used emotion focused stress coping strategies (Chaabane et al., 2021). This coping strategy is aimed at managing the emotions associated with the situation (Carroll, 2013). Emotion-focused strategies seek to manage, minimize or avoid negative emotional states (distraction, reducing anxiety, preparing for the worst, emotional venting & resigned acceptance) (Fuente et al., 2020). These strategies represent the attempt to regulate one's emotions in the face of adversity or when dealing with stressors (Eisenbeck et al., 2021). Emotion-focused coping selectively focuses on positive aspects of the self and the stressful situation by evading or recreating the stressful situation as an effort to control the emotional state related to or resulting from stress. People use emotion-focused coping including wishful thinking, venting their emotions, etc. to manage or reduce their emotional stress. Negative emotions predispose one to the use of emotion-focused strategies (Fuente et al., 2020). Rathakrishnan et al., (2022) affirms that the presence of negative thoughts and ineffective thoughts, and in situations of extreme concern for the unknown future, that dominate a person's cognitive processes, instead of direct problem-solving actions or information for problem-solving (problem-focused coping), the person resorts to emotion-focused coping, which relieves them of high stress in the short term. This explains why people with depression, anxiety, and stress apply emotion-focused coping based on the efficacy in a short duration of time and their inability to use problem-focused coping because of their unpleasant thoughts.

Factors associated with emotion-focused coping as shown in previous research in United Arab Emirates that highlighted the inclination of females to employ a greater degree of emotion-focused coping strategies compared to men. This is supported by a similar study conducted in Pakistan during COVID-19 pandemic which showed that women reported higher religious-spiritual coping such as offering prayers regularly, deriving strength from religious beliefs, giving charity to the needy, and remembering God (Ahmad & Jafree, 2023). On the contrary, Babicka-Wirkus et al., (2021) reported that the least frequent strategies used by Polish students during the COVID-19 pandemic included religious coping among others. Chaabane et al., (2021) notes that the most widely used emotion focused stress coping strategies include positive reinforcement and growth (e.g., staying optimistic and wishful thinking) and turning to religion (e.g., use of religion, prayer, invocation, and finding comfort in religion or spiritual beliefs).

MEANING-FOCUSED COPING

Meaning focused coping involves reflecting on a stressful situation from a self-distanced stance (temporal or spatial) which allows individuals to find meaning in negative life events (Wang et al., 2019). Well-being does not simply represent a lack of stress and negative emotions but highlights their importance by incorporating an adaptive relationship with them. This therefore means that suffering associated with stress can be mitigated and transformed into something meaningful by, among other factors, adopting an attitude of positive reframing, maintaining hope, existential courage, appreciation of life, engagement in meaningful activities, and prosociality. All these elements have been recently denominated as meaning-focused coping (Eisenbeck et al., 2021). In their study, Eisenbeck et al., (2021) evaluated the protective role of meaning-focused coping on mental health during the period of COVID-19 pandemic. A sample of 12,243 participants from 30 countries across all continents participated in the study which showed that meaning-focused coping was strongly associated with diminished symptoms of stress, anxiety, and depression. The author further notes that it is important to appraise stressful situations positively to optimize affective responses. A stressor conceived as a challenge or as a threat, and appraised positively and given positive meanings influences the emotions the one experiences during the stressful encounter and can activate coping processes that support the positive affect domain.

According to Eisenbeck, et al., (2021) meaning in life seems to act as a buffer against psychological distress, foster resilience and improve well-being.

SOCIAL COPING

This entails any interpersonally based stress-management strategy where the person seeks support from family members, friends, or formal service providers to help them through a difficult event or situation (APA Dictionary of Psychology, 2023). In their study, Rathakrishnan et al., (2022) that investigated psychological distress among the students of a public University in Sabah, findings showed that perceived social support from family, friends, and significant others was negatively correlated with depression, anxiety, and stress. This study concluded that a solid social support network enables students to build self-esteem and self-efficacy more easily and reduce the likelihood of negative feelings such as depression. While when a student is stressed, social support helps them underestimate the risks and types of stress by increasing their perceived coping abilities. Hence, seeking social support enables one to receive advice from people and this improves their ability to cope with problems or stressors. Further, social support could help individuals develop problem-solving methods, minimize the severity of an issue, and lessen the negative impact of stress. Social support plays an important role in regulating the levels of depression, anxiety, and stress of university students and is therefore an essential environmental resource for students where social support could be found within people that we tend to surround ourselves with, such as our family, friends, and even significant others like boyfriends, girlfriends, husbands, wives, and fiancés. In their study Kwaah and Essilfie (2017), findings showed that students on distance education programmes utilised different coping strategies for stress management including self-diverting exercises, for example, sitting in front of the TV and listening to music.

DYSFUNCTIONAL COPING

When under stress, students often develop coping strategies that may be positive such as positive reframing, planning, and seeking support, but they may also develop dysfunctional strategies such as self-blame, denial, the consumption of alcohol, tobacco use, or illicit drugs (Zang & Henderson, 2022). Dysfunctional coping strategies are behaviors that do not always seek to resolve the problem or eliminate the stressor but are usually attempts to reduce its symptoms in the short-term leading to negative effects and increasing stress in the long term. Studies have documented students to use dysfunctional coping mechanisms (Algorani & Gupta, 2023). The relief experienced as a result of using these strategies is temporary, but they often result in negative consequences such as increased distress, physical harm, strained relationships, and worsening mental health. Dysfunctional coping further entails helplessness, hopelessness, anxious preoccupation and fatalism about the stressful phenomenon. In addition, it includes denial, behavioural and mental disengagement, concentration on and venting of emotions, humor and substance use, etc. With regard to gender, studies have shown that more males use maladaptive coping strategies, while women use more adaptive coping (Ahmad & Jafree, 2023).

In their study, Chaabane et al., (2021) found that the most commonly used forms of dysfunctional coping strategies are mental disengagement (e.g., transference, become involved in other activities) and behavioral disengagement (e.g., avoidance & social withdrawal). Shaban et al., (2012) in their study found that avoidance was the most commonly used mechanism among students in dealing with different stresses.

It is characterized by a person's efforts, conscious or unconscious, to avoid dealing with a stressor in order to protect oneself from the difficulties the stressor presents. As a dysfunctional strategy, avoidance is a temporary measure and not a sustainable solution to address underlying stressors because it involves avoiding thoughts and emotions associated with unpleasant stressors rather than managing the emotional response (Zang & Henderson, 2022). Unfortunately, avoidant coping reactions to stress tend to worsen anxiety rather than alleviate it in the long run (Rathakrishnan et al., 2022). Among university students, avoidance coping has been associated with higher levels of perceived stress, lower satisfaction with life and increased postgraduate mental health problems (de Vibe et al., 2018).

During the COVID-19 pandemic, studies show that students used dysfunctional coping mechanisms. It was revealed that some students began to use more alcohol and drugs during the pandemic, with most deteriorating in mental health. The level of mental health problems and suicide risk among students also increased significantly and the level increased with increasing periods of isolation during the pandemic. Further, anxiety, depression, and alcohol abuse increased, and the overall quality of life among students deteriorated (Dumciene & Pozeriene, 2022). This is confirmed by Rathakrishnan et al., (2022), in their study where findings showed that Avoidant coping and the subscales of depression, anxiety, and stress displayed a positive and significant correlation. In this study the relationship portrayed between avoidant coping and the psychological distress of depression, anxiety, and stress among the students of University Malaysia Sabah was that the more frequently they used an avoidant type of coping strategy such as self-distraction, denial, substance use, and behavioral disengagement, the higher their levels of depression, anxiety and stress became.

RECOMMENDATIONS FOR COPING MECHANISMS FOR STRESS AMONG STUDENTS IN UNIVERSITIES

Universities must recognize their role in improving stress management among students through provision of a conducive learning environment and to establish a strong support system to equip both students and educators with effective coping strategies. Universities are further encouraged to adopt interventions which focus on reducing the number or intensity of stressors through curriculum revision or improving students' coping response (Chaabane et al., 2021). A study by Apgar & Cadmus (2022) to assess coping and self-regulation among undergraduate socio-work students revealed the ability of students to readily apply self-care strategies learned in the classroom to enhance their own mental health, thus the recommendation of education about coping skills within the formal undergraduate educational curricula. Graves et al., (2021), affirms that students need educational interventions to develop effective and healthy coping strategies. Similarly, Babicka-Wirkus, et al., (2021) recommends that apart from universities introducing interpersonal training and stress coping workshops for individual student groups, they should also implement assessments of students' psychosocial functioning in order to determine the potential need for emotional, social, and psychological support, and establishing psychological consultation points for students requiring such support.

Studies have shown that the younger students are less likely to cope due to lack of experience therefore the university administration should pay closer attention to this group. Further a common course on coping skills should be recommended for all students to undertake in their first year curriculum. This could improve students' coping competences, wellbeing, and resilience (Babicka-Wirkus, et al., 2021). During the COVID-19 pandemic, it was found that students who felt high levels of psychological well-being were more likely to choose active coping styles, while those with lower levels of psychological well-being were more likely to choose avoidance coping strategies. Studies therefore suggest that universities should develop programs to explicate students' ability to choose active stress management strategies as opposed to dysfunctional coping mechanisms (Dumciene & Pozeriene, 2022). Universities must recognize their role in improving stress management through provision of a supportive learning environment and establishment of a strong support system to equip both students and faculty with effective coping strategies. Therefore, understanding different coping mechanisms employed by university students will go a long way in informing university administrators on how to design and implement programmes aimed at improving their psychological health in the university and even post-graduation.

FUTURE RESEARCH DIRECTION

Understanding the magnitude of stress its sources and effect on students' is important for all stakeholders in higher education institutions. Studies have shown that university life is the most stressful period for students, this is related to different factors including transitioning to adult life, high expectations from both parents and university and high demand from the workload. Students use both adaptive and maladaptive coping mechanisms and this contributes to their social and academic adjustment. Studies have shown that majority of students experience a lot of pressure from academic and environmental stressors compared to other sources of stress. The existing studies and literature are however very silent on the role of universities in helping the students to cope. Further research should therefore explore how universities can support students to cope during their university life from admission to graduation. Further, available data on the relationship between stress levels and the used coping strategies is limited and inconsistent therefore additional studies designed to assess these potential associations are needed to establish the evidence

CONCLUSION

Studies have shown an increase in the prevalence of mental health problems among students in universities associated with different stressors that they experience during their university life. The students experience stress from different sources with academic and environmental stressors being sighted as the main causes of stress. The different stressors negatively affect the students' academic and social life. Ability of the students to adapt and cope is important for their social and academic success. Different coping mechanisms including adaptive and maladaptive are used by students whenever faced by stressors. Understanding coping strategies will enable university stakeholders including the students, administrators, faculty, counsellors and parents to provide the required support and develop interventions targeted to reduce sources of stress among students and enhance use of appropriate coping strategies, which in turn will contribute towards holistic well-being of the student. The university stakeholders are encouraged to integrate coping and coping mechanisms into the curriculum as this will prepare the students to be able to face different stressors during their university life.

REFERENCES

Ahmada, S & Jafree, S.R. (2023). Influence of gender identity on the adoption of religious-spiritual, preventive and emotion-focused coping strategies during the COVID-19 pandemic in Pakistan. *Annals of Medicine,55*(2).

Alduais, F., Samara, A. I., Al-Jalabneh, H. M., Alduais, A., Alfadda, H., & Alaudan, R. (2022). Examining Perceived Stress and Coping Strategies of University Students during COVID-19: A Cross-Sectional Study in Jordan. *International Journal of Environmental Research and Public Health*, 19(15), 9154. 10.3390/ijerph1915915435954508

Algorani, E. B., & Gupta, V. (2023). *Coping Mechanisms*. StatPearls Publishing. https://www.ncbi.nlm.nih.gov/books/NBK559031/

American College Health Association. (2019). *National college health assessment III: Undergraduate reference group: Executive summary*. American College Health Association. www.acha.org/documents/ncha/NCHA III_Fall_2019_Undergraduate_Reference_Group_Executive_Summary.pdf

Amponsah, K. D., Adasi, G. S., Mohammed, S. M., Ampadu, E., Okrah, A. K., & Wan, P. (2020). Stressors and coping strategies: The case of teacher education students at University of Ghana. *Cogent Education*, 7(1), 1727666. 10.1080/2331186X.2020.1727666

Ansari, E. W., Khalil, K., & Stock, C. (2014). Symptoms and Health Complaints and Their Association with Perceived Stressors among Students at Nine Libyan Universities. *International Journal of Environmental Research and Public Health*, 11(12), 12088–12107. 10.3390/ijerph111212088825429678

Apgar, D., & Cadmus, T. (2022). Using Mixed Methods to Assess the Coping and Self-regulation Skills of Undergraduate Social Work Students Impacted by COVID-19. *Clinical Social Work Journal*, 50(1), 55–66. 10.1007/s10615-021-00790-333589848

Babakova, L. (2019). Development of the Academic Stressors Scale for Bulgarian University Students. *Eurasian Journal of Educational Research*, 19(81), 115–128. 10.14689/ejer.2019.81.7

Babicka-Wirkus, A, Wirkus, L, Stasiak, K & Kozłowski, P. (2021). University students' strategies of coping with stress during the coronavirus pandemic: Data from Poland. *PLoS ONE, 16*(7), e0255041. https://doi.org/.pone.025504110.1371/journal

Battula, M., Arunashekar, P., & John, A. (2021). ThiyagaRajan, R & Vinoth, P.N. (2021). Stress level among the final year medical students at an urban medical college: A cross-sectional study. *Biomedicine (Taipei)*, 41(1), 70–74.

Budu, I., Abalo, E. M., Bam, V., Budu, F. A., & Peprah, P. (2019). A survey of the genesis of stress and its effect on the academic performance of midwifery students in a college in Ghana. *Midwifery*, 73(June), 69–77. 10.1016/j.midw.2019.02.01330903921

Carroll, L. (2013). Problem-Focused Coping. In Gellman, M. D., & Turner, J. R. (Eds.), *Encyclopedia of Behavioral Medicine*. Springer. 10.1007/978-1-4419-1005-9_1171

Chaabane, S., Chaabna, K., Bhagat, S., Abraham, A., Doraiswamy, S., Mamtani, R., & Cheema, S. (2021). Perceived stress, stressors, and coping strategies among nursing students in the Middle East and North Africa: An overview of systematic reviews. *Systematic Reviews*, 10(1), 136. 10.1186/s13643-021-01691-933952346

Chen, Y., Liu, X., Yan, N., Jia, W., Fan, Y., Yan, H., Ma, L., & Ma, L. (2020). Higher Academic Stress Was Associated with Increased Risk of Overweight and Obesity among College Students in China. *International Journal of Environmental Research and Public Health*, 17(15), 5559. 10.3390/ijerph1715555932752122

Cheung K, Yip TL, Wan CLJ, Tsang H, Zhang LW, Parpala A (2020) Differences in study workload stress and its associated factors between transfer students and freshmen entrants in an Asian higher education context. *PLoS ONE 15*(5), e0233022. https://doi.org/. pone.023302210.1371/journal

Cohen, S., Murphy, M. L. M., & Prather, A. A. (2019). Ten surprising facts about stressful life events and disease risk. *Annual Review of Psychology*, 70(1), 577–597. 10.1146/annurev-psych-010418-10285729949726

Cohen, S., Gianaros, P. J., & Manuck, S. B. (2016, July). A Stage Model of Stress and Disease. *Perspectives on Psychological Science*, 11(4), 456–463. 10.1177/17 45691616646305274741 34

Coiro, J.M, Bettis, A.H & Compas, B.E. (2017). College students coping with interpersonal stress: Examining a control-based model of coping. *Journal of American College Health*, 65.

Connor-Smith, J. K., Compas, B. E., Wadsworth, M. E., Thomsen, A. H., & Saltzman, H. (2000). Responses to stress in adolescence: Measurement of coping and involuntary stress responses. *Journal of Consulting and Clinical Psychology*, 68(6), 976–992. 10.1037/0022-006X.68.6.97611142550

Corwin, L. A., & Ramsey, M. E. Vance, E.A, Woolner, E, Maiden, S, Gustafson‖, N & Harsh, J.A. (2022). Students' Emotions, Perceived Coping, and Outcomes in Response to ResearchBased Challenges and Failures in Two Sequential CUREs. *CBE Life Sciences Education*. 10.1187/cbe.21-05-013135580005

de Vibe, M., Solhaug, I., Rosenvinge, J. H., Tyssen, R., Hanley, A., & Garland, E. (2018). Six-year positive effects of a mindfulness-based intervention on mindfulness, coping and well-being in medical and psychology students; Results from a randomized controlled trial. *PLoS One*, 13(4), e0196053. 10.1371/journal.pone.019605329689081

Dumciene, A., & Pozeriene, J. (2022). The Emotions, Coping, and Psychological Well-Being in Time of COVID-19: Case of Master's Students. *International Journal of Environmental Research and Public Health*, 2022(19), 6014. 10.3390/ijerph1910601435627550

Eisenbarth, C. A. (2019). Coping with Stress: Gender Differences among College Students. *College Student Journal*, 53(2).

Eisenbeck, N., Carreno, D. F., & Perez-Escobar, J. A. (2021). *Meaning-Centered Coping in the Era of COVID-19: Direct and Moderating Effects on Depression, Anxiety, and Stress* (Vol. 12). Front. Psychol., Sec. Personality and Social Psychology. 10.3389/fpsyg.2021.648383

Folkman, S. (2020). Stress: Appraisal and Coping. In Gellman, M. D., & Turner, J. R. (Eds.), *Encyclopedia of Behavioral Medicine* (pp. 2177–2179). Springer. 10.1007/978-3-030-39903-0_215

Friedlander, L. J., Reid, G. J., Shupak, N., & Cribbie, R. (2007). Social support, self-esteem, and stress as predictors of adjustment to university among first-year undergraduates. *Journal of College Student Development*, 48(3), 259–274. 10.1353/csd.2007.0024

Freire, C, Ferradas, M.D.M, Regueiro, B, Rodriguez, S, Valle, A & Nunez, J. C. (2020). Coping Strategies and Self-Efficacy in University Students: A Person-Centered Approach. Sec. *Educational Psychology*. Frontiers. 10.3389/fpsyg.2020.00841

Fuente, J. D. L., Lahortiga-Ramos, F., Laspra-Solís, C., Maestro-Martín, C., Alustiza, I., Aubá, E., & Martín-Lanas, R. (2020). A Structural Equation Model of Achievement Emotions, Coping Strategies and Engagement-Burnout in Undergraduate Students: A Possible Underlying Mechanism in Facets of Perfectionism. *International Journal of Environmental Research and Public Health*. 10.3390/ijerph170632235741

Fasoro, A. A., Oluwadare, T., Ojo, T. F., & Oni, I. O. (2019, October). MSc a and Ignatius O. Oni,Perceived stress and stressors among first-year undergraduate students at a private medical school in Nigeria. *Journal of Taibah University Medical Sciences*, 14(5), 425–430. 10.1016/j.jtumed.2019.08.00331728140

Gillis, K. (2023). *Problem-Focused Coping: Definition, Examples & Strategies.* Choosing Therapy. https://www.choosingtherapy.com/problem-focused-coping/

Graves BS, Hall ME, Dias-Karch C, Haischer MH, Apter C (2021) Gender differences in perceived stress and coping among college students. *PLoS ONE 16*(8), e0255634. https://doi.org/10.1371/journal.pone.0255634

Haktanir, A., Watson, J. C., Ermis-Demirtas, H., Karaman, M. A., Freeman, P. D., Kumaran, A., & Streeter, A. (2018). Resilience, academic self-concept, and college adjustment among first-year students. *Journal of College Student Retention*, 23(1), 161–178. 10.1177/1521025118810666

Hsu, J. L., & Goldsmith, G. R. (2021). Instructor Strategies to Alleviate Stress and Anxiety among College and University STEM Students. *CBE Life Sciences Education*, 20(1), es1. 10.1187/cbe.20-08-018933635124

Karaman, M. A, Lerma, E, Vela, J.C & Watson, J.C. (2019). Predictors of Academic Stress Among College Students *Journal of College Counseling*, 22(1).

Kwaah, C. Y., & Essilfie, G. (2017). Stress and coping stra-tegies among distance education students at theUniversity of Cape Coast, Ghana. *Turkish Online Journal of Distance Education*, 18(3), 120–134. 10.17718/tojde.328942

Li, B., Zhang, K., Wu, Y., & Hao, Z. (2022). Interpersonal Relationship Stress Brings on Social Networking Sites Addiction Among Chinese Undergraduate Students. *Frontiers in Psychology*, 13, 905971. 10.3389/fpsyg.2022.90597135814166

Maykrantz S.A & Houghton, J,D. (2018). Self-leadership and stress among college students: Examining the moderating role of coping skills. *Journal of American College Health*, 68.

Mujahidah, N., Astuti, B., & Nhung, L. (2019). Decreasing academic stress through problem-focused coping strategy for junior high school students. *Psychology, Evaluation, and Technology in Educational Research*, 2(1), 1–9. 10.33292/petier.v2i1.25

Omar, M., Bahaman, A. H., Lubis, F. A., Ahmad, S. A. S., Ibrahim, F., Aziz, S. N. A., Ismail, F. D., & Tamuri, A. R. B. (2019). Perceived Academic Stress Among Students in Universiti Teknologi Malaysia. *Proceedings of the International Conference on Student and Disable Student Development 2019 (ICoSD 2019).* Research Gate.

Quincho, F. S., Rodríguez Galán, D. B., Farfán Pimentel, J. F., Yolanda Josefina, H. F., Arenas, R. D., Crispín, R. L., & Navarro, E. R. (2021). Academic Stress in University Students: Systematic Review. *Ilkogretim Online, 20*(5).

Ramachandiran, M., & Dhanapal, S. (2018). Academic Stress Among University Students: A Quantitative Study of Generation Y and Z's Perception. *Pertanika Journal of Social Science & Humanities*, 26(3), 2115–2128.

Rathakrishnan, B., Singh, S. S. B., & Yahaya, A. (2022). Perceived Social Support, Coping Strategies and Psychological Distress among University Students during the COVID-19 Pandemic: An Exploration Study for Social Sustainability in Sabah, Malaysia. *Sustainability (Basel)*, 14(6), 3250. 10.3390/su14063250

Reddy, K. J., & Karishmarajanmenon, M. S. (2018). Academic Stress and its Sources among University Students. *Biomedical & Pharmacology Journal*, 11(1), 531–537. 10.13005/bpj/1404

Robotham, D., & Julian, C. (2006). Stress and the higher education student: A critical review of the literature. *Journal of Further and Higher Education*, 30(2), 107–117. 10.1080/03098770600617513

Saleh, D., Camart, N., & Romo, L. (2017). Predictors of Stress in College Students. *Frontiers in Psychology*, 8, 19. 10.3389/fpsyg.2017.0001928179889

Seedhom, A. E., Kamel, E. G., Mohammed, E. S., & Raof, N. R. (2019). Predictors of perceived stress among medical and nonmedical college students, Minia, Egypt. *International Journal of Preventive Medicine*, 10(1), 107. 10.4103/ijpvm.IJPVM_6_1831360354

Shaban, I. A., Khater, W. A., & Akhu-Zaheya, L. M. (2012). Undergraduate nursing students' stress sources and coping behaviours during their initial period of clinical training: A Jordanian perspective. *Nurse Education in Practice*, 12(4), 204–209. 10.1016/j.nepr.2012.01.00522281123

Shdaifat, E., Jamama, A., & Al-Amer, M. (2018). Stress and Coping Strategies Among Nursing Students. *Global Journal of Health Science, 10*(5).

Shi, W. (2019). Health information seeking versus avoiding: How do college students respond to stress-related information? *American Journal of Health Behavior*, 43(2), 437–448. 10.5993/AJHB.43.2.1830808481

Sugiati, M., & Isqi, K. (2020). Description of Stress and Its Impact On College Student. College Student Journal, 54(2). link.gale.com/apps/doc/A634682859/AONE?u=anon~78135f9&sid=googleScholar&xid=19ffa26c.

Taniguchi, H., & Kato, T. (2018). The Frequencies and Effects of Interpersonal Stress Coping with Different Types of Interpersonal Stressors in Friendships on Mental Health and Subjective Well-Being among College Students. *The Japanese Journal of Personality*, 27(3), 252–258. 10.2132/personality.27.3.8

Wang, Y, Lippke, S, Miao, M & Gan, Y. (2019). Restoring meaning in life by meaning-focused coping: The role of self-distancing. *Psych J,.8*(3), 386-396. . 10.1002/pchj.296

Weiten, W., Dunn, D. S., & Hammer, E. Y. (2014). *Psychology Applied to Modern Life: Adjustment in the 21st Century*. Cengage Learning.

WHO. (2023). *Stress*. WHO. https://www.who.int//news-room/questions-and-answers/item/stress/?

Yang, Q., Shi, M., Tang, D., Zhu, H., & Xiong, K. (2022). Multiple Roles of Grit in the Relationship Between Interpersonal Stress and Psychological Security of College Freshmen. *Frontiers in Psychology*, 13, 824214. 10.3389/fpsyg.2022.82421435310215

Yikealo, D., Tareke, W., & Karvinen, I. (2018). The Level of Stress among College Students: A Case in the College of Education, Eritrea Institute of Technology. *Open Science Journal, 3*(4). 10.23954/osj.v3i4.1691

Zhang, N., & Henderson, C. N. R. (2022). Coping strategies and chiropractic student perceived stress. *The Journal of Chiropractic Education*, 36(1), 13–21. 10.7899/JCE-20-2834320658

Chapter 9
Stress Among the Undergraduate Students in Public Universities in Kenya

Peter Omae Onderi
 https://orcid.org/0000-0002-4298-9211
Maseno University, Kenya

Samson N. O. Moracha
Maseno University, Kenya

Christine Mwajuma Opondo
Maseno University, Kenya

Justine Momanyi Omare
 https://orcid.org/0000-0002-2909-9214
Jaramogi Oginga Odinga University of Science and Technology, Kenya

ABSTRACT

Stress is an emotional feeling of tension. Stress is the body's reaction to a challenge or demand. The arising struggles of life in developing countries of the world has led to the increase of stress in instructions of higher learning. The purpose of this study is to find out the major causes of stress amongst students of higher learning in public universities in Kenya. The study investigated the causes of stress. The study sample consisted of undergraduate students from public universities. Based on the study findings university students face a lot of stress. The stressors are academic stress, financial stress, relationships, family conflicts, and uncertain future. The

DOI: 10.4018/979-8-3693-4417-0.ch009

study recommended constant guidance and counseling for the students, parents, and guardians.

INTRODUCTION

In Kenya, a study conducted on medical students found 61.6% of the students to have moderate stress while another study on stress and psychosocial adjustment among non-medical students reported that 35.6% had a low score, 27.4% moderate and 37.0% were classified as having high stress levels.(WHO).

For many years' higher education institutions were envied for their financial prospects. Students worked hard to join universities so as to escape from poverty. They used to get allowance known as boom. Nowadays things have changed for the worst. Of late university students are faced with financial stress as the following studies show. Some commit suicide. World health organized carried a study on the mental health status of students in higher educational institutions. The majority of students (93.7%) reported at least some stress in at least one of the six areas. A significant dose-response association was found between extent of stress in each life area and increased odds of at least one of the six disorders. (National Institutes of Health (.gov) 2020). Further more A January 2023 report on university and college students in Kenya revealed that money and finances are the main causes of stress, with a staggering 30% of students experiencing mild to severe stress related to their financial situation. According to Muguna L.C(2021), Money will be a critical and essential resource in your life on campus and can work for or against you. It can make your life comfortable or miserable depending on how and where you use it. Research has been done to find out the causes of depression. This study has been done to find out how financial challenges cause stress to university students. The study was done using peer reviewed literature review. The objectives were to find out the causes of financial stress among students, how financial stress affects university students and coping mechanisms students use to overcome financial stress. it was found out the main cause of financial stress was family background, lack of financial literacy and many dependents. It was found out that students who lack money may work hard or may not work hard depending on the nature of the student. However, in general those who lack money are more stressed. The coping mechanisms were skipping meals, deferring studies asking for fundraising, cohabiting and borrowing. The study recommended that the government should provide food to the students and stipends for the needy students. Parents should also be sensitized on the need to provide their children with enough finances. The current study will use thematic analysis to find out the financial stressors facing students in higher education institutions.

Students in secondary and tertiary education settings face a wide range of ongoing stressors related to academic demands. Previous research indicates that academic-related stress can reduce academic achievement, decrease motivation and increase the risk of school dropout. The longer-term impacts, which include reduced likelihood of sustainable employment, cost Governments billions of dollars each year. This narrative review presents the most recent research concerning the impact of academic-related stress, including discussion of the impact on students' learning capacity and academic performance, mental health problems, such as depression and anxiety, sleep disturbances and substance use. The current study focused on identifying financial stressors affecting higher education students.

RELATIONSHIPS AMONG STRESSORS, PERCEIVED STRESS AND ANXIETY SYMPTOMS

Appraisal or perception of stress is another factor that may mediate the association between the stressors and psychological responses. Based on the transactional model of stress, stress represents an imbalance between abilities of individuals and demands of environment, and the results of the transaction could lead to negative psychological outcomes (Lazarus & Folkman, 1984). Therefore, the effect of stressors depends on the perception of stress (Lazarus, 1966). Some study results confirmed the presence of such a mechanism. For example, McCuaig Edge investigated the impact of combat exposure on psychological distress of military personnel and found the mediation effect of cognitive appraisal in the association (McCuaig Edge & Ivey, 2012). Besharat et al. conducted a survey regarding anxiety among Iranian university students, and found that perceived stress played a mediating role in the association between facing existential issues and anxiety (Besharat et al., 2020). Zhang et al. examined the relationships of sleep quality and anxiety/depression among nursing students of a public university in the United States, and found that perceived stress not only mediated the association between sleep quality and anxiety symptoms, but also the association between sleep quality and depression symptoms (Zhang et al., 2018). These results strongly suggest that the appraisal or perception of stress can be the factor that determines whether the stressors will result in psychological responses or not. As a result, we posit the following hypotheses: (H5) Stressors in university life are positively and significantly associated with perceived stress among international students; (H6) Perceived stress is positively and significantly associated with anxiety symptoms among international students; (H7) Stressors in university life have a significant indirect effect on anxiety symptoms via perceived stress among international students.

Relationship Between Self-Efficacy and Perceived Stress

A review of the literature related to self-efficacy and stress revealed a significant relationship between individuals' self-efficacy and their effectiveness in coping with stress (Houghton et al., 2012). Self-efficacy is related to experiencing less negative emotions in risky situations and appraising the stressors as challenges rather than threats (Luszczynska, Gutiérrez-Doña, & Schwarzer, 2005). Individuals with higher level of self-efficacy believe they are capable of dealing with their demands, and this belief may result in adopting positive approaches and perceiving less stress in life. According to the transactional model of stress, self-efficacy may play a significant role in the primary and secondary appraisals which will lead to a decline in perceived stress, and then result in less negative psychological outcomes. Thus, we posit the following hypotheses: (H8) Self-efficacy is negatively and significantly associated with perceived stress among international students; (H9) Stressors in university life have a significant indirect effect on anxiety symptoms via self-efficacy and then perceived stress among international students.

Based on the above mentioned theoretical assumptions and research results, we have constructed the conceptual framework of this study (Fig. 1). We hope that this conceptual framework will become the theoretical basis for exploring intervention measures to prevent or manage mental health problem such as anxiety for the international students.

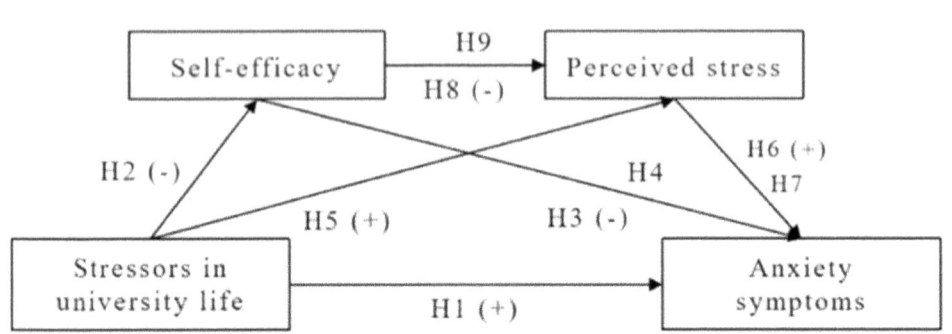

Figure 1. Conceptual framework of this study

LITERATURE REVIEW

This section represents studies which have been done on stressors among university students.

Wang et al (2023) found that Academic stress may be the single most dominant stress factor that affects the mental well-being of college students. Some groups of students may experience more stress than others, and the coronavirus disease 19 (COVID-19) pandemic could further complicate the stress response. We surveyed 843 college students and evaluated whether academic stress levels affected their mental health, and if so, whether there were specific vulnerable groups by gender, race/ethnicity, year of study, and reaction to the pandemic. Using a combination of scores from the Perception of Academic Stress Scale (PAS) and the Short Warwick-Edinburgh Mental Well-Being Scale (SWEMWBS), we found a significant correlation between worse academic stress and poor mental well-being in all the students, who also reported an exacerbation of stress in response to the pandemic. In addition, SWEMWBS scores revealed the lowest mental health and highest academic stress in non-binary individuals, and the opposite trend was observed for both the measures in men. Furthermore, women and non-binary students reported higher academic stress than men, as indicated by PAS scores. The same pattern held as a reaction to COVID-19-related stress. PAS scores and responses to the pandemic varied by the year of study, but no obvious patterns emerged. These results indicate that academic stress in college is significantly correlated to psychological well-being in the students who responded to this survey. In addition, some groups of college students are more affected by stress than others, and additional resources and support should be provided to them. The current study was done after corvid 19.

A study was done on Students stress patterns in a Kenyan socio-cultural and economic context: toward a public health intervention (Mutiso, Ndetei, Esther N Muia, Musyimi, Masake, Osborn , Sourander, Weisz, Mamah 2024). This study aimed at determining the prevalence of stress, different types of stress, their severity and their determinants in Kenyan university, college and high school students. The following tools were administered to 9741 students: (1) Researcher-designed socio-demographic tool, (2) Psychiatric Diagnostic Screening Questionnaire (PDSQ) for psychiatric disorders, (3) WERC Stress Screen for stress, (4) Washington Early Recognition Center Affectivity and Psychosis (WERCAP) screen for psychosis and affectivity, (5) Wealth Index Questionnaire for economic indicators. Descriptive analysis for the prevalence of different types of stress and inferential analysis for stress and independent variables were done. Significant variables ($p < 0.05$) were fitted into generalized linear model to determine independent predictors. The mean age of the respondents was 21.4 years (range 16-43). Money issues were the commonest stressors while alcohol and drug use were the least. The independent predictors of stress were females, college students and use of gas stove. In conclusion, up to 30% of the students suffer from mild to severe stress. The students experience a wide range of stressors. The most important stressors include money and finances, family related problems and concerns about their future. The findings suggested a public health approach to create stress awareness in students. The current study used qualitative data analysis to find the financial stressors of higher education students.

A study entitled Financial Stress and Financial Counseling: Helping College Students (Sonya, Britt, Canale, Fernatt, Stutz, & Tibbetts 2024) was done. This study had two distinct purposes. First, to determine the predictors of financial stress among college students who sought free peer-based financial counseling from a large Midwestern university (N = 675). Secondly, to determine the effectiveness of the particular financial counseling center from a subsample of those who sought help (N = 97). Results of the regression analysis indicate that students more likely to experience financial stress include freshmen, those with low perceived mastery and net worth, and those with median student loan debt as compared to those with no student loan debt. Results of t-test analyses suggest that financial counseling had positive effects on subjective financial knowledge and financial attitudes and mixed effects on financial behaviors. The current study used a conveniently sampled 10 students to identify financial stressors in higher institutions of learning.

A study was done on Sources of stress and coping strategies of Kenyan university athletes: Implications for coaches (RINTAUGU, LITABA, MUEMA &. MONYEKI). It found that the debate on whether participation in college sports is a "buffer" or "stressor" to student-athletes has not yielded conclusive consensus. The purpose of this study was to assess the sources of stress and coping strategies utilized by Kenyan university athletes. It was predicted that the sources of stress and coping strategies will not differ based on the university athletes' gender, age, and level of study. Data were collected through the use of modified version of COPE inventory from 210 university athletes (males 60.7% and females 38.9%). Data were analyzed through independent t-test and one-way ANOVA. Results showed that university athletes' sources of stress were mainly interpersonal and environmental sources. These sources of stress varied significantly based on age ($F_{3,201}=3.32$, $p<0.021$), gender ($t=2.18$, $df, 202$, $p<0.03$) and year of study ($F_{4,203}=4.00$, $p<0.04$). University athletes utilized both approach and avoidance coping strategies in equal measures and with minimal differences of the predictor variables of gender ($t=4.05$ $df=195$ $p<0.000$) and age ($F_{3, 195}=3.26$, $p<0.002$). It is concluded that Kenyan university athletes are faced with stress levels and as such coping strategic urgent intervention measures are needed from university coaches, administrators and counselors. The current study used in-depth interview to collect data on stressors among higher education students.

A study entitled Stress levels, coping strategies, and mental health literacy among secondary school students in Kenya (Ayiro Lushya, Dingili) was done. It found that mental health literacy could be a protector from stress and other mental health problems. Statistics in sub-Saharan Africa estimate that up to 20% of children and adolescents experience mental health problems due to stress. Research has also shown that there is a bidirectional association between positive coping and mental health literacy. Nonetheless, little is known about stress levels, coping strategies, and mental health literacy of secondary school students in Kenya. This study sought to answer the following questions: What is the stress level of students in secondary schools in Kenya? What is the association between stress levels and coping strategies of learners? What is the mental health literacy level of learners in secondary schools in Kenya? The study employed a sequential explanatory mixed methods research design by carrying out a quantitative study to ascertain stress levels and coping strategies and a qualitative study to explore the mental health literacy of the students. A total of 400 secondary school students aged 16–22 years participated in the study. Quantitative data were analyzed using descriptive and inferential statistics whereas qualitative data was analyzed thematically. Based on these results, the majority of students were moderately 244 (66%) and highly 112 (31%) stressed. Only 11 students (3%) reported low stress levels. The study also indicated a positive significant association between stress and avoidance coping strategy ($r = 0.11$, $p < 0.05$). Qualitative data revealed varied conceptualizations of mental health. The following themes emerged: the students conceptualized mental health as help offered to people who are stressed to help them reduce stressors, others felt that it was a state of being at peace with one's self and being able to think and act soundly, whereas others felt that mental health is severe mental disorder or illness. Students further attributed stress to school, peer, and home pressure. Lastly, although the students believed that seeking emotional, social, and psychological support was the best way to cope with stress, they feared seeking this support from teachers and peers. There was no evidence of students seeking support from parents. This study contributes to the Group Socialization Theory that suggests that peers become the primary social agents of adolescents outside the confinement of their homes. It provides essential information for developing awareness programs on mental health issues in Kenyan secondary schools. It also highlights a need to equip students with skills so that they can offer peer-to-peer support in times of distress. The current study focused on higher education students.

A study done on Prevalence and associated factors of depression among Jimma University students. A cross-sectional study(Gutema , Negash, Kerebih, Alemu & Tesfaye, 2020) found that Depression is a common health problem among university students. It is debilitating and has a detrimental impact on students psychosocial, emotional, interpersonal functioning and academic performance, however, there is a scarcity of information on this regard in higher education institutions in Ethiopia, and so the study was conducted to assess the prevalence of depression and its associated factors among Jimma University students. An institution-based quantitative cross-sectional study was conducted on a total of 556 sampled students selected by a multistage stratified sampling technique. Beck Depression Inventory (BDI-II) was used to screen depression severity. Data was collected through a pretested, structured, and self-administered questionnaire. The collected data were checked manually for completeness and entered into Epidata manager Version 2.0.8.56 data entry software then exported to SPSS version 20 Statistical software for analysis. The obtained data were described using descriptive statistics as well as logistic regression analysis was done to determine the independent predictors of the outcome variable. First bivariate analysis was done and variables significant at p value ≤ 0.25 were entered into a multivariate logistic regression analysis to control for confounders. The significance of association was determined at a 95% confidence interval and p-value < 0.05. The prevalence of depression among the students was 28.2%. Having a mentally ill family member (OR = 2.307, 95%CI 1.055–5.049), being from the college of Social science and humanity (OR = 2.582, 95%CI 1.332–5.008), having sex after drinking (OR = 3.722, 95%CI 1.818–7.619), being hit by sexual partner (OR = 3.132, 95%CI 1.561–6.283), having childhood emotional abuse (OR = 2.167, 95%CI 1.169–4.017), having monthly pocket money between 500-999 ETB (OR = 0.450, 95% CI 0.204–0.995), and promoted academic performance (OR = 2.912, 95% CI 1.063–7.975) were significantly associated with depression. The prevalence of depression among Jimma University students was high and positively associated with being from the college of social science and humanity, history of a hit by a sexual partner, having a mentally ill family member, having more monthly pocket money, promoted academic performance, having sex after drinking and childhood emotional abuse. Therefore, establishing depression screening services on the campus and designing proper mental health intervention programs is recommended to tackle the problem. The current study focused on financial stressors among students in higher education institutions in Kenya.it also used qualitative research methods which helps capture the feelings of the students

A study was done on Factors Related to Financial Stress among College Students (Heckman, Lim, Montalto, 2014). It found that Concerns that debt loads and other financial worries negatively affect student wellness are a top priority for many university administrators. Factors related to financial stress among college students were explored using the Roy Adaptation Model, a conceptual framework used in health care applications. Responses from the 2010 Ohio Student Financial Wellness Survey were analyzed using proportion tests and multivariate logistic regressions. The results show that financial stress is widespread among students – 71% of the sample reported feeling stress from personal finances. The results of the proportion tests and logistic regressions show that this study successfully identified important financial stressors among college students. Two of the most important financial stressors were not having enough money to participate in the same activities as peers and expecting to have higher amounts of student loan debt at graduation. The results also indicate that students with higher financial self-efficacy and greater financial optimism about the future are significantly less likely to report financial stress. Implications for student life administrators, policymakers, financial counselors, and financial therapists are discussed.

Figure 2. Roy adaptation model

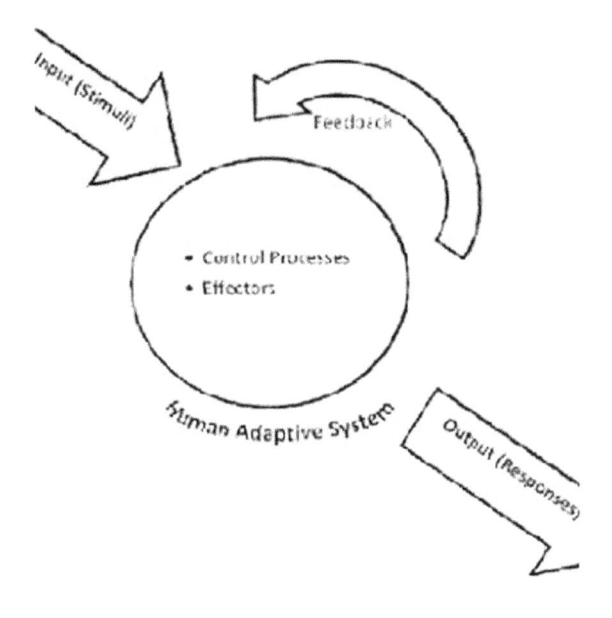

Figure 3. Conceptual framework based on the Roy adaptation model

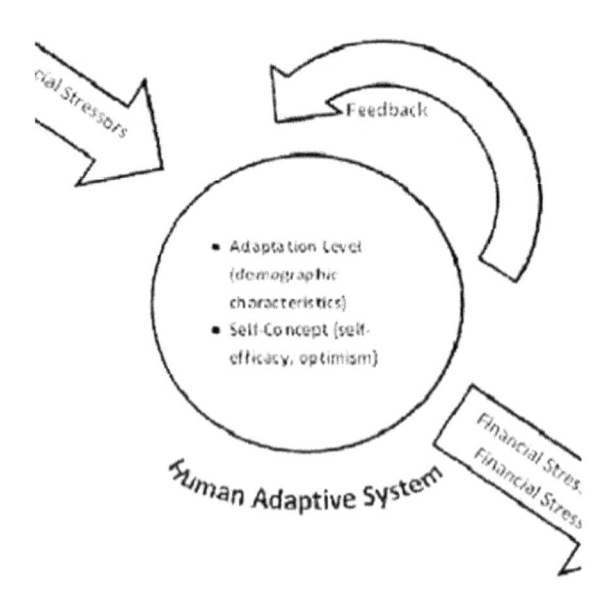

THE CURRENT STUDY USED IN-DEPTH INTERVIEW SCHEDULE TO IDENTIFY STRESSORS

A study was done entitled Financial Stress, Social Supports, Gender, and Anxiety during College: A Stress-Buffering Perspective (Alisia, Tran, Lam & Legg). The study, examined financial stress and general anxiety in college students (N = 304) with attention to the moderating roles of different types of social support (i.e., family support, social support) and gender, as assessed via moderated moderation. Results indicated that financial stress was moderately-to-strongly associated with symptoms of general anxiety. A three-way interaction revealed that perceived family support and gender were moderators of financial stress in relation to general anxiety. Consistent with a stress-buffering effect, for male college students financial strain was positively associated with general anxiety at low levels of perceived family support, but unrelated at high levels of family support. For female college students, a significant financial stress–anxiety link was present regardless of level of family support. This study highlights the potential mental health costs of financial stress faced by college students, with implications for tailoring mental health interventions that target financial stress. The current study used a sample of 8 students to identify financial stressors among higher education students.

A study by (Mbwayo, Kiarie & Ndegwa, 2020) on Factors Related to Depression among University Students in Nairobi County, Kenya. It found that Depression is a serious mental disease that affects both young and old people in the society. People who have gone through adverse life events are more likely to develop depression. Depression can, in turn, lead to more stress and dysfunction, and worsen the affected person's life situation and the depression. The objective of this study was to establish the factors related to depression among university students in Kenya. A quasi-experimental research design was adopted, where two Kenyan public universities were conveniently sampled. Experimental sample was obtained from one university and control sample from the other university. The study data was collected using questionnaires and the Beck's Depression Inventory (BDI). The prevalence of depression was determined through proportions obtained from the data from the BDI at the different stages of the study. The findings revealed that interpersonal relationships were key in determining depression levels among the students. The study concluded that various factors are related to depression among university students which include age, year of study, expenditure, friendship, dependents, leadership and club membership. The current study focused on affecting higher education students in Kenya.

EFFECTS OF STRESSORS

Stressors affect students in several ways. The first is on academic achievement. A study was done on The impact of stress on students in secondary school and higher education (Michaela C. Pascoe, Sarah E. Hetrick & Alexandra G. Parker, 2019). It found out that Students in secondary and tertiary education settings face a wide range of ongoing stressors related to academic demands. Previous research indicates that academic-related stress can reduce academic achievement, decrease motivation and increase the risk of school dropout. A study was done on the academic impact of financial stress on college students. (So-Hyun, Durband, Grable 2024) found that Staying in school and graduating on time is an important factor for students and their families. Greater financial burdens may lead students to reduce coursework or drop out of school for paid work. A Web-based survey (N = 503) was conducted in fall 2004 at a large public university to examine the characteristics of students who experienced dropping out or reducing credit hours due to financial reasons. Analyses were conducted to compare these students with those who did not drop out or reduce their coursework. Findings show the relationship between financial stress and academic performance. The current study sought to identify financial stressors among higher education students.

Another study was done on Financial Stress in Undergraduate Students Financial Stress in Undergraduate Students (Samantha Pearl Hick). It found out that Undergraduate students are a vulnerable population faced with college costs and a lack of financial management knowledge, issues that have led to high student debt, failure to repay this debt, and sometimes dropping out of college. Facing these financial matters often serves as a leading source of stress, which, according to Selye's stress theory, can negatively affect the lives of these college students, but may also be experienced differently by various demographic groups. This quantitative study compared financial stress reported on an anonymous online National Survey of Student Engagement (NSSE) financial stress survey by respondents from a stratified random sample of 2,130 undergraduate students across all 4 years of a public university in the Southeastern United States. Multiple regression analysis was used to determine if a relationship existed between financial stress and demographic characteristics including grade classification (first-year, sophomore, junior, senior), sex, race/ethnicity, and parental educational levels. The only statistically significant relationship was between NSSE financial stress index scores and grade classification (p = .039). Most literature on financial stress of college students and the findings reported by NSSE focus on first-year and senior students; however, this study showed an increase in financial stress index scores for sophomores and seniors, suggesting the need for interventions beyond those typically offered in the first and final years of college. Findings were used to develop a policy recommendation on the need for financial literacy education to address financial stress, decrease loan default rates, and improve academic outcomes such as retention and graduation, especially for demographic groups who already face multiple barriers to college success. The current study used qualitative research methods.

COPING WITH STRESS

Higher education students use a variety of methods to cope with financial stress. A study was done on Stress among higher education students: towards a research agenda (Robotham, 2008).This article has two primary aims. Firstly, it provides a critical review of previous studies into student stress and identifies several important issues that, as yet, have not been explored. There has been no consideration of the effect of students maturing during their studies on the stress that they experience and how they cope with that stress. Secondly, the article highlights limitations in the past and present literature base, where there has been a concentration on a quantitative approach, and focus on a narrow range of subject groups. There is also a need to undertake longitudinal research to investigate individuals' stress experiences during the period they study at university. Overall the key assertion here is that thus far research into student stress has not offered a complete account and explanation of students' stress experiences. The current study used qualitative research methods to get its findings.

A study done on financial stress and its impact on first-year students' college experiences (Fosnacht, Dong 2024) examined the relationship between undergraduate engagement and financial stress coping strategies. The study found that students who evidenced financial stress perceived a less supportive campus environment, but tended to participate in more academically beneficial activities. The results indicated that magnitude of the impact of financial stress varied by the type of financial stress coping strategy used. The current study sought to find out the financial stressors of students in higher education institutions in Kenya.

Another study was done on Impact of Financial Stress on Students' Academics (Usman & Banu). It found that over the last few decades, the cost of attending colleges in India have been rising steadily and students who enroll for various courses are forced to rely on some form of financial aid to finance their cost of tuition fees. The main forms of financial aids available are grants and loans that can be sourced through government or financial institutions. The main difference between the two sources is grants need not be repaid, whereas loans need to be. For families and students, it is more important for to pass/complete school and college in the same year, otherwise it increases the financial burden of the family. The students who are vulnerable to financial stress were found to earn lower grades and fewer credit hours. The students who experienced such interruption in academics have to consider reducing their course loads or dropping for a semester due to financial issues/concerns and reported higher stress from their personal finances. Students who perceived that worrying about money/ academic funding affected their academic performance were found to have poorer academic performances. In this study, the data was collected from samples by a set of research tools and analyzed using SPSS, and resulted in research findings and interpretations. The sampling technique used in this study is non-probability sampling. Convenient sampling was used to select the respondent from the samples. Accordingly, the sample size is 100 college students which were chosen by random sampling and further responses were analyzed and interpreted. The current study used 10 students and employed qualitative research methods.

METHODOLOGY

The study was carried in four higher education institutions in Kenya. Kenya is bordered by Uganda in the west Tanzania in the south Ethiopia and Sudan in the north and Somalia and Indian Ocean to the East. It lies on the equator. It was assumed that all higher education students suffer from financial stress.

Through qualitative research methods the study identified financial stressors that affect university students. The study used convenient sampling technique to select ten students to be interviewed using an interview schedule. Kothari (2009) defines an interview schedule as an outline of questions that form a basis for and guide the interviewing process. The schedule provides a structure that aids in obtaining the necessary information efficiently and business like atmosphere. The validity of the interviews was ascertained by the assistance of experts from maseno university psychology department.

Before undertaking the actual study informed consent was obtained from students. The researcher assured the target respondents that their confidentiality was to be upheld at all stages of the study by keeping their identities anonymous while the data collection tools were being administered. Permission was requested and granted.

Qualitative Data Analysis

The researcher used a thematic analysis to pinpoint examine and record patterns (or themes) within the data. Gibbs (2008) describes themes as patterns across data sets that are important to the description of a phenomenon and are associated to a specific research question. The themes become categories for analysis and according to Gibbs (2008) a thematic analysis can be used in two different fields; literature critique and qualitative analysis of data and requires the determination of the frequency of appearance of a theme or a type of data. Qualitative research reports give a vivid descriptive account of the situation under study. For Data collection in qualitative research Interview schedules and observation checklists are used to yield qualitative data. To yield rich data a qualitative researcher used in-depth interviews focus group discussions and observations.

Thematic analysis was performed through the process of coding in phases to create established and meaningful patterns. These phases consist of familiarization of data generating initial codes searching for themes among codes reviewing defining and naming themes and producing final reports (Raburu 2011) as presented in table 1.

Table 1. Coding

Transcripts	Themes/subthemes	Codes for themes/subthemes
There are no finances for food…s1. I skip meals…s2. Ninainama…s3	Financial stress	FS
Parents don't trust me…s4. Anything I tell them they say I lie…s4. My father doesn't understand… s6	Student parental conflicts	spC
There are a lot of academic demands. s1. We have to attend classes every morning…s5	Academic stress	AS
Relationships are a problem… s6. He is threatening to kill me…s4	Student relationships	R
We are not sure of being employed. s7 The future is not clear... s8	Uncertain future	F

FINDINGS DISCUSIONS AND SUMMARY

Financial Stress

There are no finances for food…s1.

I skip meals…s2. Ninainama…s3

Students need money for food and other items. The government gives allowances but this are not always enough. This agrees with Onderi, & Opondo (2023) who found that is expected that students in higher educational institutions should experience financial wellness. Contrarily a majority of them are facing financial distress. The study revealed that financial stressors arise from rent college fee student loans and cost of food has gone up, lack of financial literacy. The study recommends provision of free food accommodation and increase in subsistence. Parents should provide their children with enough finances.

>Student parental conflicts
>Parents don't trust me…s4. Anything I tell them they say I lie…s4
>Some parents feel that their children are over demanding. This creates stress.
>Academic stress
>University students that they face academic stress
>There are a lot of academic demands… s1
>The students attend classes daily sometimes in the morning when it is cold. Some classes are consecutive. They are also supposed to print and type assignments. Some of them who are kidded have challenges. This agrees with George et al (2024) who found out that Academic stress may be the single most dominant stress factor that affects the mental well-being of college students.

Student relationships
Relationships are a problem… s6. He is threatening to kill me…s4
Some students are in toxic relationships. This creates stress.
Uncertain future
We are not sure of being employed. s7
In Kenya unemployment is 80%. This reality creates stress among the students. They know their relatives who are jobless.

SUMMARY

Based on the study university students face a lot of stress. The stressors are academic stress, financial stress, relationships, family conflicts, and uncertain future.
Recommendations.
The study recommends that universities, parents, churches and other parties should counsel students adequately so that they can know how to manage their stress.

RECOMMENDATION

Prioritizing your mental health is crucial as it directly affects various aspects of your life, including finances and academic performance. Recognizing the connection between mental well-being and financial stability is key since neglecting one will inevitably affect the other. Whether you are battling financial stress or simply looking to improve your overall mental well-being, it is essential to invest in both areas and make your well-being a top priority. By nurturing your mental health and tending to your financial wellness, you create a solid foundation for a more fulfilling and balanced life. Remember, taking care of yourself holistically yields long-term benefits and paves the way for a brighter future.

REFERENCES

Abouserie, R. (1994). Sources and levels of stress in relation to locus of control and self-esteem in university students. *Educational Psychology*, 14(3), 323–330. 10.1080/0144341940140306

Ahmed, G., Negash, A., Kerebih, H., Alemu, D., & Tesfaye, Y. (2020). 2020). Prevalence and associated factors of depression among Jimma University students. A cross-sectional study. *International Journal of Mental Health Systems*, 14(1), 52. 10.1186/s13033-020-00384-532742303

Al-Dubai, S. A., Al-Naggar, R. A., Alshagga, M. A., & Rampal, K. G. (2011). Stress and coping strategies of students in a medical faculty in Malaysia*The Malaysian Journal of Medical Sciences : MJMS*, 18(3), 57–64.22135602

Alisia, G. T. T. (2018). Financial Stress, Social Supports, Gender, and Anxiety During College: A Stress-Buffering Perspective. *The COunsiling Psychologist, 46*(7). 10.1177/0011000018806687

Auerbach, R. P., Mortier, P., Bruffaerts, R., Alonso, J., Benjet, C., Cuijpers, P., Demyttenaere, K., Ebert, D. D., Green, J. G., Hasking, P., Murray, E., Nock, M. K., Pinder-Amaker, S., Sampson, N., Stein, D. J., Vilagut, G., Zaslavsky, A. M., & Kessler, R. C. (2018). WHO WMH-ICS Collaborators. WHO world mental health survey international college student project: Prevalence and distribution of mental disorders. *Journal of Abnormal Psychology*, 127(7), 623–638. 10.1037/abn000036230211576

Ayiro, L. (2023). Stress levels, coping strategies, and mental health literacy among secondary school students in Kenya. *Educational Psychology,* 8.10.3389/feduc.2023.1099020

Bandari, M. A. (2022). *Study on Academic Stress and Mental Well-Being in College Students*. NIH.

Bandura, A. (1997). Self-efficacy: the exercise of control (1st ed). New York: Worth Publishers.

Bann, T. (2018). *Financial stress and mental health among higher education students in the UK up to 2018: rapid review of evidence.* NIH.

Beiter, R., Nash, R., McCrady, M., Rhoades, D., Linscomb, M., Clarahan, M., & Sammut, S. (2015). The prevalence and correlates of depression, anxiety, and stress in a sample of college students. *Journal of Affective Disorders*, 173, 90–96. 10.1016/j.jad.2014.10.05425462401

Besharat, M. A., Khadem, H., Zarei, V., & Momtaz, A. (2020). Mediating role of perceived stress in the relationship between facing existential issues and symptoms of depression and anxiety. *Iranian Journal of Psychiatry*, 15, 80–87. 10.18502/ijps.v15i1.244232377217

Britt, S. L., Canale, A., Fernatt, F., Stutz, K., & Tibbetts, R. (2015). A study entitled Financial Stress and Financial Counseling: Helping College Students. *Financial Counseling and Planning*, 26(2), 172–186. 10.1891/1052-3073.26.2.172

Cohen, S., Kamarck, T., & Mermelstein, R. (1983). A global measure of perceived stress. *Journal of Health and Social Behavior*, 24(4), 385–396. 10.2307/21364046668417

Cohen, S., & Williamson, G. (1998). Perceived stress in a probability sample of the United States. *The social psychology of health: Claremont Symposium on applied psychology*. London: Sage.

Collier, D. A., Fitzpatrick, D., Brehm, C., & Arche, E. (2021). Coming to College Hungry: How Food Insecurity Relates to A motivation Stress, Engagement, and First-Semester Performance in a Four-Year University. *Journal of Postsecondary Student Success*, 1(1), 106–135. 10.33009/fsop_jpss124641

Davis, M., Eshelman, E. R., & McKay, M. (2008). The relaxation & stress reduction workbook (1st ed.). Oakland: New Harbinger Publications.

Dixon, S., & Kurpius, S. (2008). Depression and college stress among university undergraduates: Do mattering and self-esteem make a difference? *Journal of College Student Development*, 49(5), 412–424. 10.1353/csd.0.0024

Donker, T., van Straten, A., Marks, I., & Cuijpers, P. (2011). Quick and easy self-rating of generalized anxiety disorder: Validity of the Dutch web-based GAD-7, GAD-2 and GAD-SI. *Psychiatry Research*, 188(1), 58–64. 10.1016/j.psychres.2011.01.01621339006

Drescher, C. F., Baczwaski, B. J., Walters, A. B., Aiena, B. J., Schulenberg, S. E., & Johnson, L. R. (2012). Coping with an ecological disaster: The role of perceived meaning in life and self-efficacy following the Gulf Oil Spill. *Ecopsychology*, 4(1), 56–63. 10.1089/eco.2012.0009

Elhadi, M., Buzreg, A., Bouhuwaish, A., Khaled, A., Alhadi, A., Msherghi, A., Alsoufi, A., Alameen, H., Biala, M., Elghewi, A., Elkhafeefi, F., Elmabrouk, A., Abdulmalik, A., Alhaddad, S., Elgzairi, M., & Khaled, A. (2020). Psychological impact of the civil war and COVID-19 on Libyan medical students: A cross-sectional study. *Frontiers in Psychology*, 11, 570435. 10.3389/fpsyg.2020.57043533192858

Folkman, S., Lazarus, R. S., Gruen, R. J., & DeLongis, A. (1986). Appraisal, coping, health status, and psychological symptoms. *Journal of Personality and Social Psychology*, 50(3), 571–579. 10.1037/0022-3514.50.3.5713701593

Fosnacht, K., & Dong, Y. (2013). Financial stress and its impact on first-year students' college experiences. *Paper presented at the annual meeting of the Association for the Study of Higher Education*. Research Gate.

Fritz, M. V., Chin, D., & DeMarinis, V. (2008). Stressors, anxiety, acculturation and adjustment among international and North American students. *International Journal of Intercultural Relations*, 32(3), 244–259. 10.1016/j.ijintrel.2008.01.001

Georgia, G. (2024). Academic Stress and Mental Well-Being in College Students: Correlations, Affected Groups, and COVID-19. *PMCID: PMC9169886*.

Ghaderi, A. R., & Rangaiah, B. (2011). Influence of self-efficacy on depression, anxiety and stress among Indian and Iranian students. *Journal of Psychosomatic Research*, 6(2), 231–240.

Gibbs, G. R. (2008). *Analyzing qualitative* data. Uk. *Sage (Atlanta, Ga.)*.

Grable, J. E., & Joo, S. (2006). Student racial differences in credit card debt and financial behaviors and stress. *College Student Journal*, 40(2), 400–408.

Guillena, R. M., & Guillena, J. B. (2022). Perceived stress, self-efficacy, and mental health of the first-year college students during Covid-19 pandemic. *Indones J Multidiscip Sci.*, 2(2), 2005–2013. 10.55324/ijoms.v2i2.281

Heckman, S. J., & Montalto, H. L. C. P. (2014). Factors Related to Financial Stress among. *College Student Journal*, 5(1). 10.4148/1944-9771.1063

Hecman Stuart, H., Lim, A. & Montalto, C. (2014). Factors Related to Financial Stress among College Students. *JournCollege Student Life and Financial Stress*.

Hick, , S. (2021). *Financial Stress in Undergraduate Students Financial Stress in Undergraduate Students*. Walden University Scholar Works. Walden Dissertations and Doctoral Studies Walden Dissertations and Doctoral Studies.

Hossain, K. (2023). Determinants of Financial Stress among University Students and Its Impact on Their Performance. *Journal of Applied Research in Higher Education*, 15.

Houghton, J. D., Wu, J., Godwin, J. L., Neck, C. P., & Manz, C. C. (2012). Effective stress management a model of emotional intelligence, self-leadership, and student stress coping. *Journal of Management Education*, 36(2), 220–238. 10.1177/1052562911430205

Jafar, H. M., Salabifard, S., Mousavi, S. M., & Sobhani, Z. (2015). The effectiveness of group training of CBT-based stress management on anxiety, psychological hardiness and general self-efficacy among university students. *Global Journal of Health Science*, 8(5), 47–54. 10.5539/gjhs.v8n6p4726755483

Joo, S.-H. (2009). The Academic Impact Of Financial Stress On College Students. *J. College student retention, 10*(3) 287- 305.

Joo, S.-H., Durband, D. B., & Grable, J. (2008). The Academic Impact of Financial Stress on College Students. *Journal of College Student Retention*, 10(3), 287–305. 10.2190/CS.10.3.c

Kamardeen, I., & Sunindijo, R. Y. (2018). Stressors impacting the performance of graduate construction students: Comparison of domestic and international students. *Journal of Professional Issues in Engineering Education and Practice*, 144(4), 4018011. 10.1061/(ASCE)EI.1943-5541.0000392

Kaya, C., Tansey, T. N., Melekoglu, M., Cakiroglu, O., & Chan, F. (2019). Psychometric evaluation of Turkish version of the perceived stress scale with Turkish college students. *Journal of Mental Health (Abingdon, England)*, 28(2), 161–167. 10.1080/09638237.2017.141756629260926

Keyes, C. L. M., Eisenberg, D., Perry, G. S., Dube, S. R., Kroenke, K., & Dhingra, S. S. (2012). The relationship level of positive mental health with current mental disorders in predicting suicidal behavior and academic impairment in college students. *Journal of American College Health*, 60(2), 126–133. 10.1080/07448481.2011.60839322316409

Klein, M. C., Ciotoli, C., & Chung, H. (2011). Primary care screening of depression and treatment engagement in a university health center: A retrospective analysis. *Journal of American College Health*, 59(4), 289–295. 10.1080/07448481.2010.50372421308589

Kothari, C. R. (2009). *Research methods: methods and methods.* (2nd revision. Ed.). New Age International Publishers.

Larson, L. M., & Daniels, J. A. (1998). Review of the counseling self-efficacy literature. *The Counseling Psychologist*, 26(2), 179–218. 10.1177/0011000098262001

Lazarus, R. S. (1966). Psychological stress and the coping process. (1st ed). New York: McGraw-Hill.

Lazarus, R. S., & Cohen, J. B. (1977). Environmental Stress. In Altman & Wohlwill (Eds.) *Human Behavior and Environment*. New York: Plenum Press. 10.1007/978-1-4684-0808-9_3

Lazarus, R. S., & Folkman, S. (1984). Stress, appraisal, and coping. (1st ed). New York: Springer.

Löwe, B., Decker, O., Müller, S., Brähler, E., Schellberg, D., Herzog, W., & Herzberg, P. Y. (2008). Validation and standardization of the generalized anxiety disorder screener (GAD-7) in the general population.. *Medical Care*, 46(3), 266–274. 10.1097/MLR.0b013e318160d09318388841

Lu, W., Bian, Q., Song, Y., Ren, J., Xu, X., & Zhao, M. (2015). Prevalence and related risk factors of anxiety and depression among Chinese college freshmen. *Journal of Huazhong University of Science and Technology. Medical Sciences*, 35(6), 815–822. 10.1007/s11596-015-1512-426670430

Luszczynska, A., Gutiérrez-Doña, B., & Schwarzer, R. (2005). General self-efficacy in various domains of human functioning: Evidence from five countries. *International Journal of Psychology*, 40(2), 80–89. 10.1080/00207590444000041

Luszczynska, A., Scholz, U., & Schwarzer, R. (2005). The general self-efficacy scale: Multicultural validation studies. *The Journal of Psychology*, 139(5), 439–457. 10.3200/JRLP.139.5.439-45716285214

Ma, L., Fu, T., Qi, J., Gao, X., Zhang, W., Li, X., Cao, S., & Gao, C. (2011). Study on cross-cultural adaptation and health status in medical international students. *Chin J Med Edu Res.*, 11, 1379–1382.

Manzar, M. D., Salahuddin, M., Pandi-Perumal, S. R., & Bahammam, A. S. (2021). Insomnia may mediate the relationship between stress and anxiety: A cross-sectional study in university students. *Nature and Science of Sleep*, 13, 31–38. 10.2147/NSS.S27898833447116

McCloud, T. (2018). Fin*ancial stress and mental health among higher education students in the UK up to 2018: rapid review of evidence Epidemiol Community Health*. NIH.

McCuaig Edge, H. J., & Ivey, G. W. (2012). Mediation of cognitive appraisal on combat exposure and psychological distress. *Military Psychology*, 24(1), 71–85. 10.1080/08995605.2012.642292

McPherson, A. (2012). *Examination of the Relation Among Perception of Control and Coping Styles on Mental Health Functioning* [Dissertation, North Carolina State University]. 10.4148/1944-9771.1063

Michaela, C. (2019). The impact of stress on students in secondary school and higher education. *International Journal of Adolescence and Youth, 25*(1). 10.1080/02673843.2019.1596823

Misra, R., & Castillo, L. G. (2004). Academic stress among college students: Comparison of American and international students. *International Journal of Stress Management*, 11(2), 132–148. 10.1037/1072-5245.11.2.132

Misra, R., Crist, M., & Burant, C. J. (2003). Relationships among life stress, social support, academic stressors, and reactions to stressors of international students in the United States. *International Journal of Stress Management*, 10(2), 137–157. 10.1037/1072-5245.10.2.137

Misra, R., & McKean, M. (2000). College student's academic stress and its relation to their anxiety, time management and leisure satisfaction. *American Journal of Health Studies*, 16(1), 41–52.

Misra, R., McKean, M., West, S., & Russo, T. (2000). Academic stress of college students: Comparison of student and faculty perception. *College Student Journal*, 34(2), 236–245.

Mori, S. (2000). Addressing the mental health concerns of international students. *Journal of Counseling and Development*, 78(2), 137–144. 10.1002/j.1556-6676.2000.tb02571.x

Muguna, L.N. (2021). *Campus life simplified. A student's guide*. interCEN Books.

National Institutes of Health. (n.d.). *Home*. NIH. https://pubmed.ncbi.nlm.nih.gov

Ndegwa, J. (2020).Factors Related to Depression among University Students in Nairobi County, Kenya. *SSRG International Journal of Humanities and Social Science (SSRG-IJHSS), 7*(2). www.internationaljournalssrg.org

Olivas, M., & Li, C. (2006). Understanding stressors of international students in higher education: What college counselors and personnel need to know. *Journal of Instructional Psychology*, 32(3), 217–222.

Pereira-Morales, A. J., Adan, A., & Forero, D. A. (2019). Perceived stress as a mediator of the relationship between neuroticism and depression and anxiety symptoms. *Current Psychology (New Brunswick, N.J.)*, 38(1), 66–74. 10.1007/s12144-017-9587-7

Preacher, K. J., & Hayes, A. F. (2008). Asymptotic and resampling strategies for assessing and comparing indirect effects in multiple mediator models. *Behavior Research Methods*, 40(3), 879–891. 10.3758/BRM.40.3.87918697684

Preacher, K. J., Rucker, D. D., & Hayes, A. F. (2007). Addressing moderated mediation hypotheses: Theory, methods, and prescriptions. *Multivariate Behavioral Research*, 42(1), 185–227. 10.1080/00273170701341316268210810

Raburu, P. A. (2011). *Women academic careers in kemnya*. [Thesis, Lancaster University, United Kingdom].

Rajasekar, D. (2013). Impact of academic stress among the management students of AMET University-an analysis. *AMET J Manag.*, 5, 32–39.

Rashid, T. (2009). Positive interventions in clinical practice. *Journal of Clinical Psychology*, 65(5), 461–466. 10.1002/jclp.2058819294745

Razavi, S. A., Shahrabi, A., & Siamian, H. (2017). The relationship between research anxiety and self-efficacy. *Materia Socio-Medica*, 29(4), 247–250. 10.5455/msm.2017.29.247-25029284993

Rintaugu, E.G., Litaba, S.A., Muema, E.M. & Monyeki, M.A. (2014). Sources of stress and coping strategies of Kenyan university athletes: Implications for coaches. *African Journal for Physical, Health Education, Recreation and Dance, 20*(2), 1621-1636.

Robotham, D. (2008). Stress among higher education students: Towards a research agenda. *Higher Education*, 56(6), 735–746. 10.1007/s10734-008-9137-1

Rogers, K. D., Young, A., Lovell, K., Campbell, M., Scott, P. R., & Kendal, S. (2013). The British sign language versions of the patient health questionnaire, the generalized anxiety disorder 7-item scale, and the work and social adjustment scale. *Journal of Deaf Studies and Deaf Education*, 18(1), 110–122. 10.1093/deafed/ens04023197315

Ross, S. E., Neibling, B. C., & Heckert, T. M. (1999). Sources of stress among college students. *College Student Journal*, 33(2), 2–9.

Ruiz, M. A., Zamorano, E., Garcia-Campayo, J., Pardo, A., Freire, O., & Rejas, J. (2011). Validity of the GAD-7 scale as an outcome measure of disability in patients with generalized anxiety disorders in primary care. *Journal of Affective Disorders*, 128(3), 277–286. 10.1016/j.jad.2010.07.01020692043

Scherbaum, C. A., Cohen-Charash, Y., & Kern, M. J. (2006). Measuring general self-efficacy: A comparison of three measures using item response theory. *Educational and Psychological Measurement*, 66(6), 1047–1063. 10.1177/0013164406288171

Seligman, M. E. P., Rashid, T., & Parks, A. C. (2006). Positive psychotherapy. *The American Psychologist*, 61(8), 774–788. 10.1037/0003-066X.61.8.77417115810

Shange, N. (2018). *Experiences of students facing financial difficulties to access Higher Education in the case of the University of KwaZulu-Natal* [Thesis, University of KwaZulu-Natal].

Siu, O. L., Lu, C. Q., & Spector, P. E. (2007). Employees' well-being in greater China: The direct and moderating effects of general self-efficacy. *Applied Psychology*, 56(2), 288–301. 10.1111/j.1464-0597.2006.00255.x

Spitzer, R. L., Kroenke, K., Williams, J. B. W., & Löwe, B. (2006). A brief measure for assessing generalized anxiety disorder: The GAD-7. *Archives of Internal Medicine*, 166(10), 1092–1097. 10.1001/archinte.166.10.109216717171

Struthers, C. W., Perry, R. P., & Menec, V. H. (2000). An examination of the relationship among academic stress, coping, motivation and performance in college. *Research in Higher Education*, 41(5), 581–592. 10.1023/A:1007094931292

Usman, M. (2021). A Study on Impact of Financial Stress on Students' Academics. *Journal of Business & Economic Policy, 6*(1).

Victoria, N. (2023). *Students stress patterns in a Kenyan socio-cultural and economic context: toward a public health intervention.* Nature.com. doi:10.1038/s41598-023-27608-1. www.nature.com/scientificreports10.1038/s41598-023-27608-1

Xiao, H., Carney, D. M., Youn, S. J., Janis, R. A., Castonguay, L. G., Hayes, J. A., & Locke, B. D. (2017). Are we in crisis? National mental health and treatment trends in college counseling centers. *Psychological Services*, 14(4), 407–415. 10.1037/ser000013029120199

Zhang, M., & He, Y. (2015). Handbook of rating scales in psychiatry (1st ed.). Changsha: Hunan Science & Technology Press.

Zhang, Y., Peters, A., & Chen, G. (2018). Perceived stress mediates the associations between sleep quality and symptoms of anxiety and depression among college nursing students. *International Journal of Nursing Education Scholarship*, 15(1), 20170020. 10.1515/ijnes-2017-002029306924

Stress: a state of worry or mental tension caused by a difficult situation. Stress is a natural human response that prompts us to address challenges and threats in our lives. Everyone experiences stress to some degree. The way we respond to stress, however, makes a big difference to our overall well-being.

Chapter 10
A Systematic Literature Review for Identifying the Factors Causing Prevalences of Suicide Among Youths in India

Priya Baluni
https://orcid.org/0009-0005-8099-4766
Department of Humanities and Social Sciences, Graphic Era University (Deemed), Dehradun, India

Rishima Bhutani
https://orcid.org/0009-0007-2943-6683
Department of Humanities and Social Sciences, Graphic Era University (Deemed), Dehradun, India

Ravindra Singh
https://orcid.org/0000-0003-3062-1812
Department of Psychology, Magadh University, Bodh Gaya, India

Ajay Kumar Singh
https://orcid.org/0000-0003-0429-0925
Department of Humanities and Social Sciences, Graphic Era University (Deemed), Dehradun, India

ABSTRACT

The prevalence of suicide rate is relatively higher among the youths in India as compared to other countries. However, limited studies could examine the preva-

DOI: 10.4018/979-8-3693-4417-0.ch010

lence of suicide rate and its leading factors among the youths in India. This chapter, therefore, explains the suicide rate of youths and its causing factors in India using a systematic literature review of previous studies. The statistical results showed that suicide has contributed to 12% of total deaths in the total population of India. It is also noticed that suicide cases have increased two times more among the male population in India in last five years. More comprehensive and inclusive data would be helpful for analyses and the development of suicide prevention measures in India. This chapter provides a significant scope for further research in the area of the suicide rate of youth and its causing factors in India.

INTRODUCTION

Suicide is a serious matter and it is often side-lined by other issues. Rising trends have been observed in the number of suicide cases over the last few years at global level. Suicide is a 3rd main cause for death of youth worldwide (Radhakrishnan & Andrade, 2012). It is an unavoidable health problem and social issue among the youth in all communities (Arya, 2024). The future of a nation depends on the young adults, culture, social and economic prosperity, and mental well-being. The mental health of youths is obstructed due to family problems, mental illness, depression, lack of social and mental counselling, and competitive pressure. The youths are losing their future assets and social liabilities due to mental illness. Various attitudinal, behavioral, and cognitive variations have been explored by the existing research community in the prevalence of suicide among the youths. Different cultures have different reasons to realize the suicide rate and its affecting factors across countries. According to the data provided by WHO in 2018, 44% of all suicides around the world occurred in China and India. India has around 53% higher suicide rates than the entire Europe combined (GHE, 2023). Asia, the biggest continent of this planet consists of around 750 million youth between the ages of 15 and 24 years, where death by suicide is the third leading cause of youth mortality (WHO, 2014).

India has the highest rate of suicide and it counts 11.2 deaths per 100,000 people (WHO, 2016; GHE, 2023). Based on the data provided by NCRB, the total number of deaths due to suicide among the youth saw an increase of 4.5% in 2021. Over 13,000 students have died at the rate of 35 every day in India (Adhikari, 2023). Many mental health professionals have cited various reasons for the prevalence of suicide among Indian youths. India has a considerable young population but at the same time there is a lack of employment opportunities (Adhikari, 2023). India has the largest contribution of youths in the world, and it accounts 28% of global suicide (Arya, 2024). Therefore, high unemployment may be a significant reason for increasing the suicide rate among Indian youths. Unemployed youths do not have social dignity and self-esteem in society. Thus, it also causes an increase in mental illness and levels of depression among the youth. Demonstration effects, economic and social failures, and over-expectations of parents on their children are also major causes for increasing the incidence of suicide among the youth (Balaji et al., 2023). High expectation of parents for their children and extreme pressure also lead to increase suicides rate among the youth. There has been a consistently increasing trend in the prevalence of suicide among the youths in India and other countries during the last few years (WDI, World Bank, 2023). The emerging phenomenon of "copycat suicide" has been a cause of concern lately in the era of the internet and digitalization worldwide (Stack, 1987; Birbal et al., 2009).

Nowadays, suicide is more common for young people to contemplate death or dying. It is mainly due to change in thinking patterns of youths and their social issues. Present youths are unable bear the various social and philosophical issues to prevent them from suicides (Arya, 2024). This power enables them to ponder upon the meaning of life, and their role in society, and they do not consider a few common questions like what happens after his/her death. Who will take the responsibilities of their families? What would be the social positions of their parents after suicide? How parents and relatives would justify suicide concerns about their children in society? While questioning one's existence to a certain extent is normal, when that club together with their insecurities, work pressure, and other toils of life, often leads to deterioration of one's mental well-being (Ross & Heath, 2003).

Death caused by inflicting self-harm with the intention to end all the suffering is suicide. The foremost cause of suicide is impulsiveness at the time of crisis. Youths are driven to it when they fail in exams or their families fight, they are unable to fulfil their financial needs or are unable to fulfil their love life (Bertolote & Fleischmann, 2002). Not addressing emotions and trauma, and practicing unhealthy coping strategies is the behavior of the youth, which puts them at the risk of unresolved emotions which if left unattended, leads to the considerable possibility of suicide. India is rich in multiple cultures, languages, religions, and traditions, following which cultural discrepancies occur. Several social, religious, and political differences are there as compared to other countries in the West and Europe. These also lead to increase various missed cultural variations that might exist as a cause of suicides among youth in India. However, the existing researchers, clinical experts, and national and international organizations could not provide the authentic indicators that are most responsible for increasing the prevalence of suicide in India. This chapter, therefore, seeks to review the existing literature that investigated the factors affecting the prevalence of suicide among the youths in India.

RESEARCH METHODOLOGY

This research is a premeditated study on the phenomenon of suicide amongst Indian youth and focuses on conceivable prevention ideas to reduce the suicide rate. The data have been collected from multiple government databases namely the National Crime Records Bureau (NCRB), India which is the central agency for the collection of data on suicide in this country. NCRB has been publishing this data since 1969. We have taken data for the period of 7 years (i.e., 2014 – 2021) for this study from their section Accidental Deaths and Suicide in India (ADSIL). Thereupon, grey literature (Google Scholar), research papers, and federated articles with keywords namely "youth", "suicide in India", "developing countries", "LMIC", "suicide", "suicide prevention" and " suicide prevention in LMIC" were also taken for this study. Initially it includes 200 articles. After a full-text review and screening of 69 abstracts, 40 suitable articles were chosen and reviewed. The study deals fastidiously with the aspects of youth suicide in Indian context. However, relevant LMIC studies on the same were searched for and studied with integrity.

Rationale of the Study

Through a focus on the urgent need for greater understanding, this paper aims to explain the significance of researching prevalences of suicide among the youth in India. Suicide is a complex, multidimensional issue that nevertheless poses a serious threat to global public health. It involves multiple biological, psycho-social, and environmental aspects rather than one single factor. Surprisingly high suicide rates cases require the critical thinking for further researches to comprehend and intervene in this global problem. By integrating research findings into clinical practice, professionals can deliver more personalized and effective care to individuals struggling with suicidal ideation or behaviour. Through systematic review work, researchers can identify risk factors associated with suicidal behaviour and develop targeted prevention interventions tailored to high-risk populations (Bilsen, 2018). Moreover, effective suicide prevention relies on evidence-based strategies informed by robust research findings. Such work will also contribute to reducing stigma and promoting awareness in general population. Furthermore, research can highlight the interconnectedness of suicide and mental health, social determinants, and systemic inequities, advocating for holistic approaches to suicide prevention that address underlying structural factors. Additionally, by such research initiatives, we can also reduce the global burden of suicide and promoting mental health and well-being for all individuals and family.

SUICIDE CASES IN INDIA

Prevalence of Total Suicide Cases

The trend in suicide mortality rate in India and the world during 2000 – 2019 is given in Figure 1. The figure indicates that the suicide mortality rate is significantly declined after 2000. However, suicide mortality rate in India is higher as compared to world average during the mentioned time period. Accordingly, suicide mortality rate in female and male are also reported higher in India as compared to world's average (Figure 2 and Figure 3). While suicide mortality rate was relatively higher in males as they seemed more susceptible to committed suicides than females in India during 2000 – 2019. Therefore, increasing suicide cases among the male youth has been a serious concern in India (Senapati et al., 2024).

Figure 1. Suicide mortality rate (per 100,000 population) in India and World

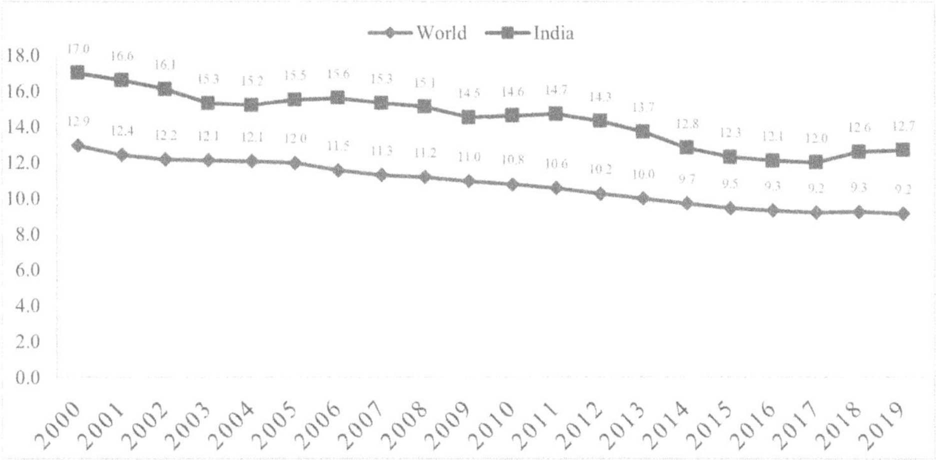

Source: WDI, World Bank (2023).

Figure 2. Suicide mortality rate, female (per 100,000 female population) in India and World

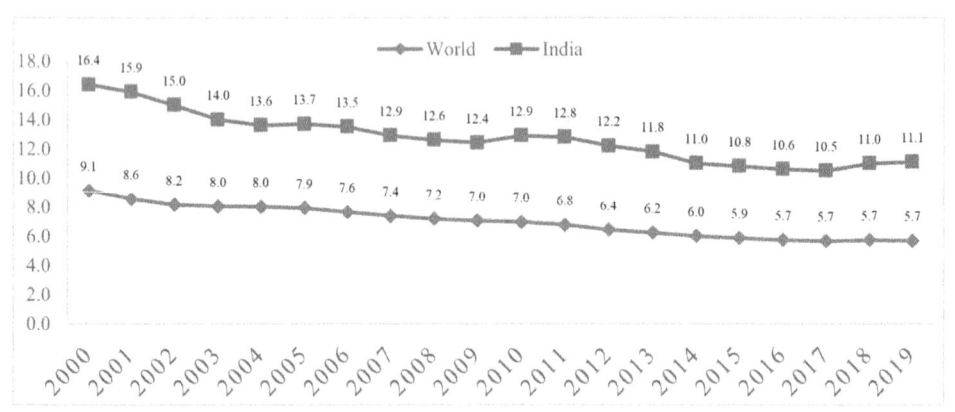

[Chart showing World and India female suicide mortality rates from 2000 to 2019. World values: 16.4, 15.9, 15.0, 14.0, 13.6, 13.7, 13.5, 12.9, 12.6, 12.4, 12.9, 12.8, 12.2, 11.8, 11.0, 10.8, 10.6, 10.5, 11.0, 11.1. India values: 9.1, 8.6, 8.2, 8.0, 8.0, 7.9, 7.6, 7.4, 7.2, 7.0, 7.0, 6.8, 6.4, 6.2, 6.0, 5.9, 5.7, 5.7, 5.7, 5.7.]

Source: WDI, World Bank (2023).

Figure 3. Suicide mortality rate, male (per 100,000 male population) in India and World

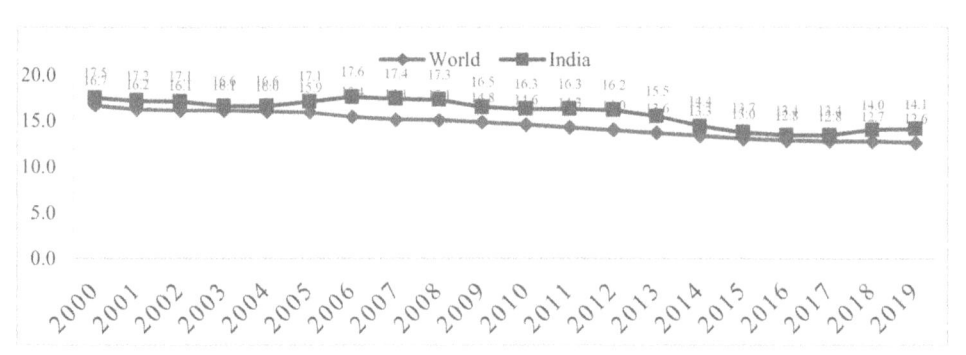

[Chart showing World and India male suicide mortality rates from 2000 to 2019. India values around 17.5–17.1 declining; World values around 14.7 declining to 12.6–12.7.]

Source: WDI, World Bank (2023).

Changes throughout millennia have been observed in several fields that have led to increase suicide. Over the years, it has been noticed that the total number of suicidal cases are growing significantly in India (Table: 1). However, a decrease of 7.85% was noticed in the year 1981 but, after that the number of suicide cases are consistently increased in India (NCRB, 1981). In a general hospital study of suicidal idolators, the age range 16–45-year likewise showed higher rates of suicidal ideation, while the average age of suicide committer is reported 25.3 years in India. (Unni & Mani, 1996).

Table 1. Total number of suicide cases in India during 1971- 2021

Year	Total Number	Rate (in %)
1971	43675	7.9
1981	40245	5.8
1991	78450	9.2
2001	108506	10.6
2011	135585	11.2
2020	153052	11.3
2021	164033	12.0

Source: NCRB (2021).

Age-Wise Suicide Cases in India

The NCRB report claimed that out of thousands of suicides in India in 2021, 35.68% (58543) of the cases were in the age group of 18 – 30 years (NCRB, 2021). The estimate of suicide cases among individuals aged 18 and older for the year 2020 is significantly higher than the previous year of 2021. A gradual increase in suicidality among youth has been observed in India (Figure 4). The highest number of suicidal cases among youth was reported in 2021 in India. The figure below shows the rate of suicidal cases in India during 2014 – 2021 (NCRB, 2014; 2021).

Figure 4. Age-wise suicide cases in India

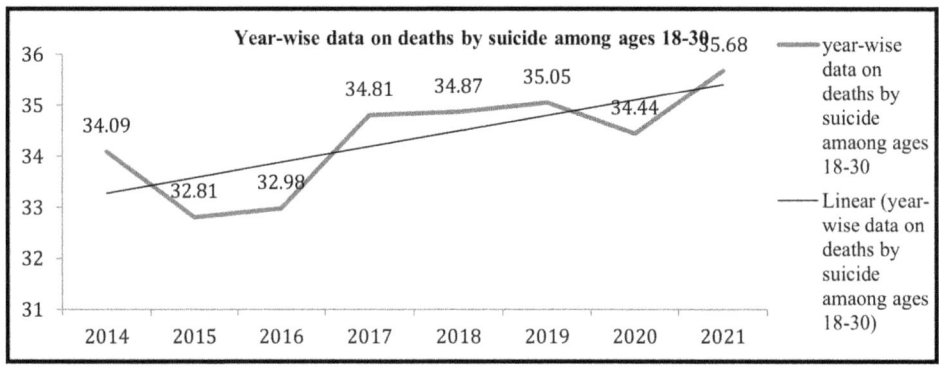

Year-wise data on deaths by suicide among ages 18-30

Year	Rate
2014	34.09
2015	32.81
2016	32.98
2017	34.81
2018	34.87
2019	35.05
2020	34.44
2021	35.68

Source: *NCRB (2021).*

Sex-Wise Suicide Cases in India

The overall male and female ratio of suicide victims for the year 2021 was observed as 12647:6196 (NCRB, 2021). Figure 5 provides the information on sex-wise suicide cases in India during 2014 – 2021. It is perceived that the prevalence of suicide cases among males and females consistently increased in India during the mentioned period. Over the 7 years of data taken, males were typically found to have higher rates of suicide than females. The World Banks also found that male is more sensitive for committed suicide that female in India. Comparing the data from that of the USA, the difference between male and female cases was found to be way lesser than India (Suicide Data and Statistics Suicide, 2021). The deaths from suicide among Indian males have increased 2 times than women in 2021 (Yadav et al., 2023). High suicide mortality rate among males in India is linked to unemployment, family problems, and health issues. (Kashyap, 2023; Arya, 2024).

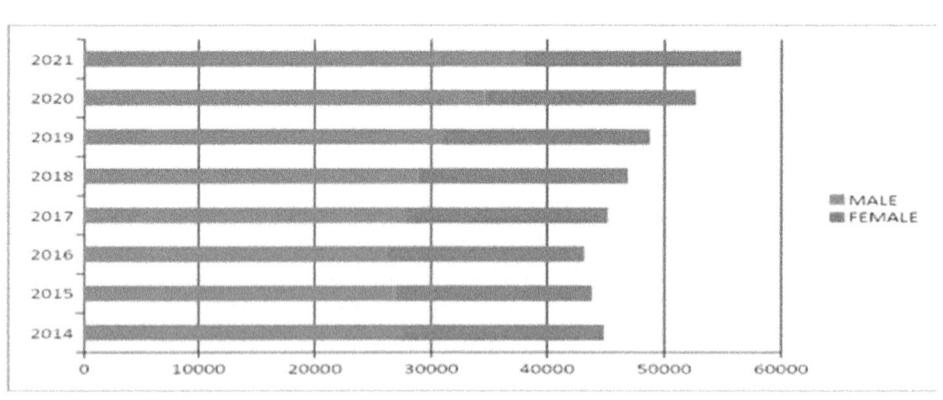

Figure 5. Sex-wise suicide cases in India

Source: *NCRB (2021)*.

Geographical Location-Wise Suicide Cases in India

After a detailed analysis of the data from NCRB, it was revealed that around 80% of suicides occurred in 5 states (i.e., Maharashtra, Tamil Nadu, West Bengal, Madhya Pradesh, and Karnataka) out of 28 states in India (NCRB, 2021). As seen in the trends established from the annual reports published by NCRB, Maharashtra has been taking the lead for the last 7 years. This figure has remained almost constant over some time. Amongst the Union Territories, Delhi followed by Puducherry is recorded to have the highest number of deaths by suicide. One of the key findings from these data was an association of southern states with a higher risk of suicide. (Patel et al., 2012). Multiple studies from the southern states of India are confirmed. These studies highlight the major contributors of suicide in southern states which include, family and interpersonal problems, social problems, financial problems, and pre-existing mental illness (Vijayakumar & Rajkumar, 1999; Borges et al., 2010; Manoranjitham et al., 2010). Ease of access to highly lethal pesticides and widespread suicidal ideation partly contribute to high rates of suicide in these states (Manoranjitham et al., 2007; Harmer et al., 2024).

CAUSES OF SUICIDE CASES IN INDIA

Causes for Suicides of Male and Female in India

According to the NCRB report of the 2014 – 2021 period, it was observed that family problems and illness are the major causes that lead to increase suicide in males and females in India (NCRB, 2014, 2021). Along with family issues, love affairs, exam failure, and drug/alcohol addiction are cited as significant reasons for youth death through suicide in India (NCRB, 2021). Under illness, suicide by insanity and other mental illness is the highest in India. An egregious gap in suicide mortality between males and females under the subheading of physical abuse can be noticed. According to estimates from psychological research carried out in developed nations, 47–74% of the population's risk of suicide is attributed due mental problems (Bachmann, 2018). At the time of the act, over 50% of suicide victims in developed nations fit the diagnostic criteria for affective illness (Harris & Barraclough, 1998; Moscicki, 2001; Cavanagh et al., 2003; Hawton & van Heeringen, 2009). Another cause for suicide was found to be physical violence, which is 2 times higher in females than males.

Even though social drinking is not part of Indian culture, alcoholism (dependence and abuse) is still one of the major risk factors for suicide in India (Vijayakumar & Rajkumar, 1999; Gururaj et al., 2011). Other risk factors include marriage-related issues (NCRB, 2014, 2021), poverty, professional/ career problems (NCRB, 2014, 2021), unemployment, and a fall in social reputation (NCRB, 2014, 2021). Figure 6 and Figure 7 are highlighted the causes for suicide of male and females, respectively in India. These highlight the need for the creation of an effective suicide prevention program that is multidimensional and addresses the social, economic interpersonal, and cultural factors in India.

Figure 6. Causes of suicides of males in India

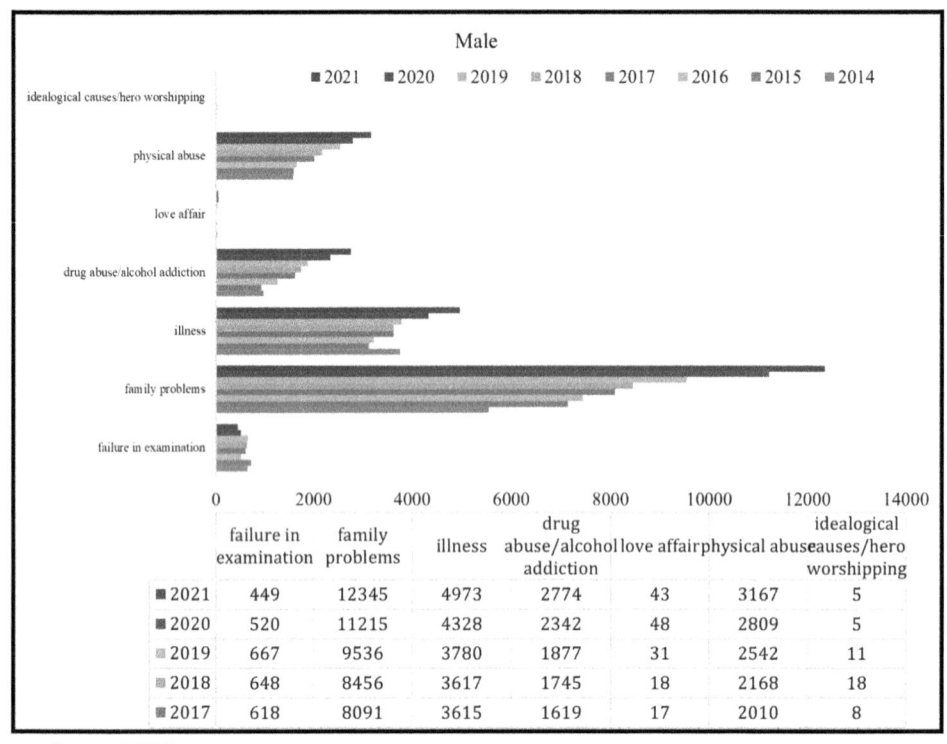

	failure in examination	family problems	illness	drug abuse/alcohol addiction	love affair	physical abuse	idealogical causes/hero worshipping
2021	449	12345	4973	2774	43	3167	5
2020	520	11215	4328	2342	48	2809	5
2019	667	9536	3780	1877	31	2542	11
2018	648	8456	3617	1745	18	2168	18
2017	618	8091	3615	1619	17	2010	8

Source: *NCRB*

Figure 7. Causes for suicides of female in India

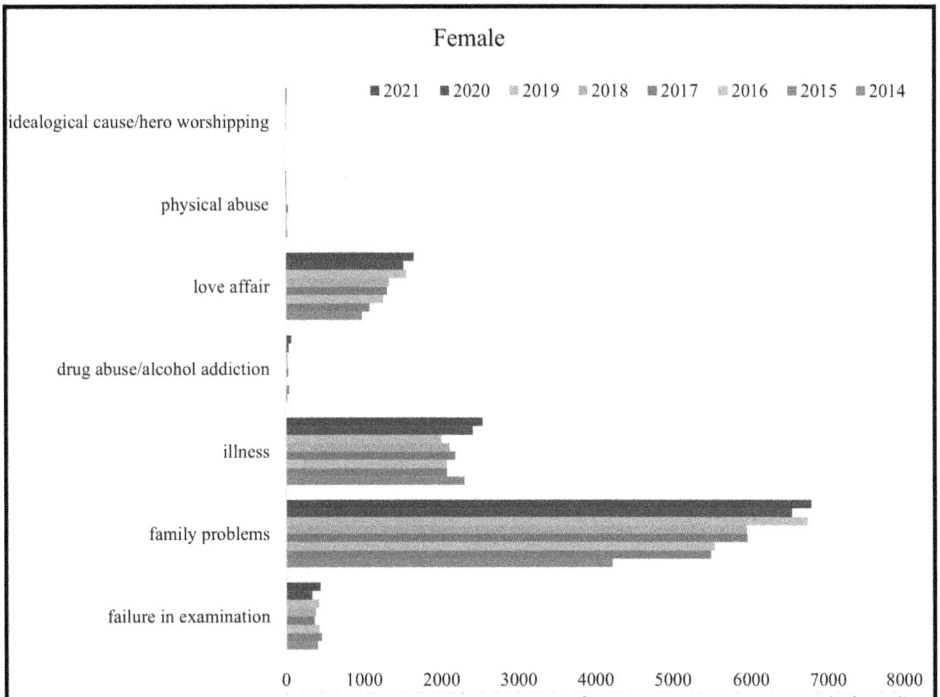

	failure in examination	family problems	illness	drug abuse/alcohol addiction	love affair	physical abuse	idealogical cause/hero worshipping
2021	444	6786	2537	78	1652	19	22
2020	340	6536	2410	38	1521	18	23
2019	424	6740	2002	31	1557	23	18
2018	386	5940	2109	28	1335	23	19
2017	366	5952	2183	34	1307	38	19
2016	433	5538	2072	19	1256	31	14
2015	457	5492	2073	44	1080	19	10
2014	407	4221	2299	24	985	29	8

Source: *NCRB.*

Common Ways of Act Out of Suicide Cases in India

Based on the data provided by NCRB for the year 2016-2021, hanging is the most preferred method of suicide for both males and females (NCRB, 2016 - 2021). In recent studies, the most frequently reported method of suicide was found to be hanging (57% of all suicides) followed by poisoning (25%), drowning (5%), and self-immolation (2.5%) (Figure 8 and Figure 9).

Figure 8. Methods of suicide adopted by females in India

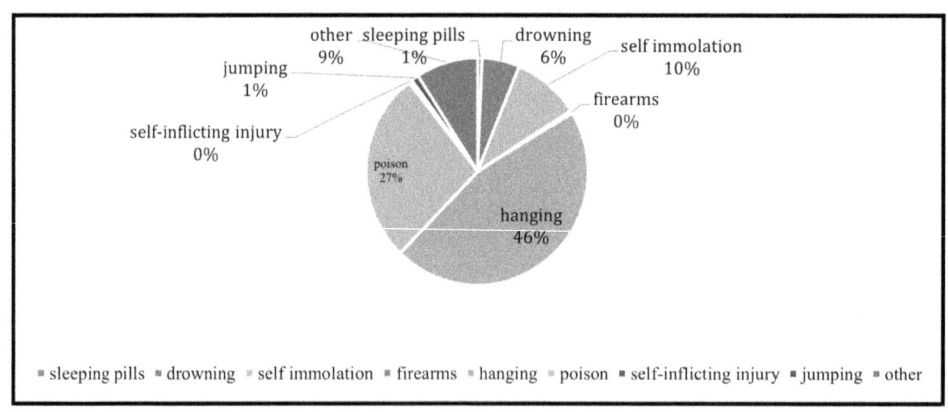

[Pie chart: sleeping pills 1%, drowning 6%, self immolation 10%, firearms 0%, hanging 46%, poison 27%, self-inflicting injury 0%, jumping 1%, other 9%]

Source: NCRB.

Figure 9. Methods of suicide adopted by males in India

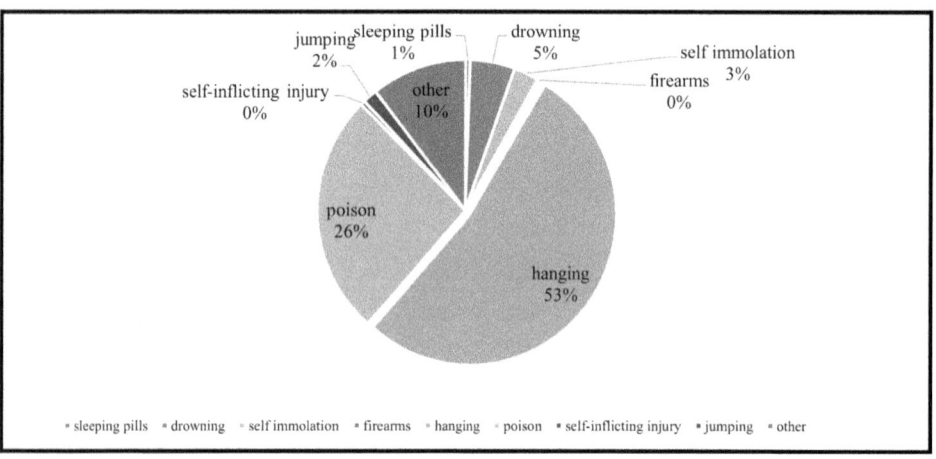

[Pie chart: sleeping pills 1%, drowning 5%, self immolation 3%, firearms 0%, hanging 53%, poison 26%, self-inflicting injury 0%, jumping 2%, other 10%]

Source: *NCRB.*

Figure 10 and Figure 11 provide the most common way that is adopted by males and females, respectively for committing suicide among youths in India. In poisoning, consumption of insecticides is also found to be the leading cause of death in India. More than half of female committed suicides through hanging their self. Compared to the male population, death by self-immolation is also a widely used method by females (NCRB, 2021). This could be due to the ease of this method or may symbolize a protest against any injustice in life as fire has an important connotation in Hindu rituals (Wu et al., 2012).

Figure 10. More common method of suicide amongst males

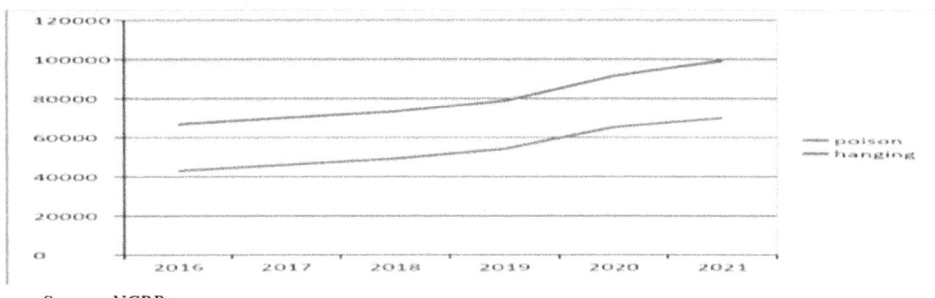

Source: NCRB

Figure 11. More common method of suicide amongst females

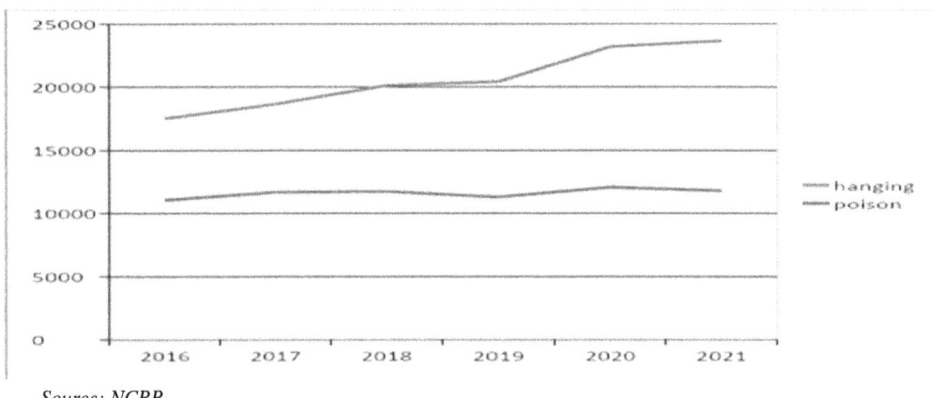

Source: NCRB.

FACTORS AFFECTING SUICIDE AND ITS PATTERNS IN INDIA

Factors Affecting Suicide

Young people are dying due to stress in economic and social changes in India (Arya, 2024). According to the NCRB, 1 student commits suicide every 42 minutes in India (Rampal, 2020). Various circumstances can trigger suicidal thoughts or influence suicidal attempts in India. Some of these reasons can be academic distress, biological factors, psychological factors, and socio-environmental factors (Arya, 2024; Senapati et al., 2024). Academic stress is found as the main cause of suicide in young adults in India. These factors alone do not have any influence, but they rather interact with each other. Suicide usually goes from depression followed by various situational events. These events can range from the death of a loved one, preparing for an entrance exam, or any open embarrassment the student might have faced. It is crucial to realize that youth are inexperienced individuals who encounter a variety of experiences every day. It is also important to understand how they deal with it daily (Deb, 2015).

Academic Distress: Education in India has been seen as a gateway to employment rather than to knowledge. Many students and their families aim to get a 'sarkari' naukari' (Government job) to get away from the current social rabbit hole they are in Academic Distress and Student Suicides in India (Sarveswar & Thomas, 2020). These projections from parents and cut-throat competition result in anxiety and stress and, therefore depressive disorders which lead to suicidal tendencies. Unable to accept their failure and fear of facing their parents or teachers due to bad results is also a major contributor to stress. Scoring fewer marks can give them get a negative idea of not achieving anything in the future. Entrance examinations like NEET, JEE and SSC have been a major contributor to increase stress among the youths in India (Pandey, 2017). For instance, Kota district of Rajasthan is hub of more suicide cases of youth male and female as compared to other cities of India. Many students committed suicides due to fear and failure in competitive examination in India.

Biological Factors: A higher suicide rate among youth is attributed to the influence of psychological and socio-environmental factors, drug use, impulsivity, and increasing threshold to tolerate pain and fear in India (Bridge et al., 2006; Samuel & Sher, 2013; Cha et al., 2018; Senapati et al., 2024). The suicide rate among women in LMIC (low-middle income countries) including India is higher than many developed nations (Pritchard, 1996; Mashreky et al., 2013). This can be associated with higher mood disorders, psychosocial stressors, and aspects of culture that violate women's rights. Researchers have found that suicidal tendencies are heritable in most countries. Monozygotic twins are noted to have higher rates of suicide (5.8%-28%) than dizygotic twins (1.8%-2.8%) with more effect on the female twin than their male counterpart. If a parent has suicidal tendencies, it gets transferred to their offspring and the child's suicide rate increases from two to six times (Brent & Mann, 2005). There is also an ample evidence which shows that the presence of mental health disorders like adjustment disorder, depression and use of perception-altering drugs are associated with increasing the prevalence of suicide rates among youth (Linker et al., 2012; Balazs & Kereszteny, 2017; Uddin et al., 2019).

Socio-Environmental Factors: A very common cause of suicide among young adults is bullying of any form (peer coercion, physical or verbal assault, etc.) and the severity of bullying. Cyberbullying (posting derogatory comments and spreading hate speech, etc.) is another emerging form of bullying that adds to suicide among young adults (Hinduja & Patchin, 2010). Glorification of suicide by media, mainly suicide by luminary individuals is linked to suicide in young adults and other types of copycat suicide. The influence of media occurs due to continuous reporting of suicide, elaborating the means of suicide, etc. India's youth are more likely to commit suicide because of inter-caste strife, caste-based discrimination, and other educational and professional disadvantages (Nath et al., 2012). Many students belong to SC, ST and marginal and weaker section the society also committed suicide due to their mental torching from their peers and faculty in educational institutions in India. Another important aspect of this is the process of sexual orientation and gender identification (Deb, 2015). Students face troubles related to gender expression and are prone to develop mental health problems and suicidal behavior due to peer victimization, lack of laws protecting their rights, and lack of family or teacher support (Shaffer et al., 1995).

Psychological Factors: Affective processes are emotionally charged psychological processes that have negative effects which include low self-esteem, feelings of worthlessness, neuroticism, and other unpleasant thoughts. Lack of access to appropriate regulatory mechanisms and difficulty identifying emotions is another reason for elevated suicide attempts among young adults (Pisani et al., 2013; Senapati et al., 2024). Psychological distress is also a significant cause for suicide among the youth (Balaji et al., 2023). One trait that has been noticed among youths who attempt suicide is impulsivity, though the transcript proposes that impulsivity only correlates with suicide intention and not suicide ideation (Mckeown et al., 1998). Youth suicide is most likely to be predicted by loneliness. Suicide attempts among young adults are predicted by feelings of unfulfilled belongingness in the case of females and a sense of burden in males (Czyz et al., 2015). Among 30-40% of those who died by suicide have shown the presence of personality disorders namely, borderline personality disorder. Suicide is also found in high numbers among people who suffer from eating disorders like anorexia nervosa as well as those with schizophrenia. Associations have been found between suicide and anxiety disorders. Substance abuse disorders also have quite an influence in such cases (Bridge et al., 2006). Further, social communication and response processing are associated with suicidality in youth (Scherer et al., 2013; Melhem et al., 2016).

Family Factors: Families are the major pillars of support for individuals while they are dealing with any stressful events. Numerous studies have pointed out that family structure and processes play a major role in suicidal behaviours (Brent & Mann, 2006). Other than just the biological inheritance of suicidal tendencies, family dynamics also have a good share in development of such behaviours (Centre for Suicide Prevention, 2022). Poor communication and direct conflicts have a great impact on a child's psyche (Portzky et al., 2005). Moreover, violence at home is found in the background history of youth suicide. It is not specific to violence against child, but also how the family members deal with the violence. Parental divorce is weakly associated with young suicide cases (Im et al., 2017).

Contagion Imitation: Youths are impressionable and thus they are more prone to contagion behavior by older adults (Gould, 2001). Contagion refers to the communication of any disease from one organism to another through close contact. Imitation is the behavior whereby; one watches and replicates the behavior of another person. It is learning by modelling. Imitation by youngsters can be done at the macro level (mass media or by contact with their direct environment (peer group). Imitating depends on 3 factors (Pirkis et al., 2016). First, the imitating effects are stronger when there is a similarity between the person and the model (age, gender, etc), there exists a strong bond between them or the model is someone they look up to (any celebrity). The second factor is reinforcement. The more the behavior is regarded as positive, understandable, or admired, the more young people are likely to imitate it. Lastly, the frequency of behavior is important i.e., how frequently it occurs in the headlines, real story or fiction. At times, this suicide imitation can take place at a large level and cause a chain of actual suicides usually among young individuals. This is also known as a suicide clusters (O'Connor & Pirkis, 2016).

Cultural Variations: Social penalties, such as laws, rules, and moral codes, can influence group members' behavior. Cultural theories of suicide acknowledge that various societies and groups have their own norms, values, and beliefs regarding all types of behaviours. Different nations, communities, civilizations, and ethnic groups have differing views on suicide and, more broadly, on death (Clinard & Meier, 1975; Williams, 1977; Retterstol, 1993; Billie-Brahe, 2000). Then the presence of subcultures also contributes greatly. The general definition of subcultures is "cultures within cultures." These are social groupings that shape the behaviours of their members through unique norms, values, and beliefs. Certain subcultures interact with the mainstream culture and hold many of its ideals in common whereas, countercultures also exist. According to Clinard and Meier, "countercultures" are those that primarily exist in opposition to the larger culture.

The Indian penal code forbids both suicide and suicide attempts in India. The majority of families choose not to disclose suicide attempts. The issue is that, out of fear of legal repercussions, families frequently conceal suicides as accidents. As a result, there must be a significant number of unidentified cases. It is clear that the legal restriction of suicide attempts and commitment to it does not address the suicide issue. Instead, out of fear of punishment and social status loss, it increases the pressure placed on the individual who tried suicide as well as their family. According to gender, since ancient times, there have been several exceptions granted for suicide in the Vedas, Upanishads, Epics, Puranas, and other works of Hindu literature. Suicide at a sacred site or while on a pilgrimage is the most well-known. Like for ascetics committing samadhi was and is glorified. For a widowed woman to perform sati was the social norm in ancient India. A few historical examples demonstrate that, despite being illegal, sati is nevertheless acceptable among the general public, who view it more as an attraction than as a religious practice. Only if they occur in a religious context are suicides accepted in certain Hindu texts. The goal or objective of religious suicide, which is to be saved from the cycle of birth and rebirth and to become immortal, justifies it (Zimmermann, 2007).

Political suicides are those that take place within the context of political actions or objectives. An example of the LTTE (Liberation Tigers of Tamil Eelam), which, under V. Prabhakaran's leadership, has been the most potent and significant guerrilla group in Sri Lanka since 1986 can be taken as an example of political suicide. The LTTE has also operated in India. The political organization's main component is its fighters' willingness to give their lives to further their political objectives. As members of a community who are always prepared to die, the fighters are initiated. That's why every fighter carries a cyanide capsule around their neck, ready to be used in the event of a capture. A symbol of bravery, boldness, and invincibility is the cyanide capsule. Even young people are happy to wear the "saving" capsule. (Zimmermann, 2007).

Within a societal setting, social suicide occurs. Nobody condones suicide. The community and the law both oppose it. A person who attempts or completes a suicide will often call for assistance in a desperate attempt. Individuals who attempt suicide often feel that it is the only way out. It could be due to lovesickness, demand for dowry, violence against women, tensions within the family, and financial burden (Zimmermann, 2007). This reflects the severity the youth take under the influence of social, religious, and political issues on the youth. While fighting for better facilities at college through hunger strikes, a student is unaware of when it has changed to striking for some political party. These causes are unique to each culture, while sati was idealized in one culture, it was criticized in another (Maskill et al., 2005).

Patterns of Suicides in India

A trend, that is quite specific to India, is that suicide rates peak among young individuals. Annual suicide rates are estimated using data from the NCRB, stratified by state and sex. According to NCRB's Accidental Deaths and Suicide in India (ADSI) reported that 8.2% of students in the country die due to suicide (NCRB, 2021). Young Indians die from suicide more frequently than from infectious diseases or heart conditions combined. A significant degree of pessimism towards the future was observed among the participants in the 1988 Australian National Youth Study, who ranged in age from 15 to 24. Their dread of nuclear war, joblessness, economic hardship, drug misuse, and family issues seemed to be the main causes of their pessimism. Such pessimism, according to Hassan (1995), is easily translated into sentiments of hopelessness, helplessness, and personal despair. It also has the potential to exacerbate mental disease, problem behaviour (such as drug and alcohol misuse), emotions of alienation, and loneliness (Beck et al., 1985; Maskill et al., 2005).

A wide spectrum of thoughts, desires, and obsessions with death and suicide are collectively referred to as suicidal ideations, sometimes known as suicidal thoughts or ideas. Clinicians, researchers, and educators face constant hurdles since there is no single, widely accepted definition of suicidal ideation. For example, it is often given distinct operational definitions in research investigations. One common drawback in suicidality-related meta-analyses is that it makes it difficult to compare results from different studies. While planning is viewed as a distinct stage in certain suicidal ideation definitions, it is included in others (Harmer et al., 2024).

In suicide literature, altruism is expressed in the adage "Not all persons who commit suicide want to die, and not all persons who want to die to commit suicide". Important characteristics that categorize the motivation behind the act are the intentionality and lethality of suicide. Motives might be more complicated than a simple cry for assistance, going beyond Durkheim's sociological typology and Freud's concepts of the "wish to kill," "wish to die," and "wish to be killed (Bhargava et al., 2001; Radhakrishnan & Andrade, 2012). Only the Hopelessness Scale and the pessimistic items on the Beck Depressive Inventory were found to be predictive of suicides by Beck et al. (1985) in a 10-year prospective study of patients admitted with suicidal intent. 91% of final suicides were properly diagnosed by those who received a Hopelessness Scale score of 10 or higher. The degree of suicidal intent has been demonstrated to positively correlate with hopelessness (Dyer & Kreitman, 1984; Beck et al., 1985).

Therefore, it is hard to predict suicide, especially among the younger population because of their unpredictable behaviour. Though some of the patterns or changes in behaviour one might experience are: (1) Cutting off contact with family and friends, (2) Feeling entrapped or hopeless. (3) Discussing a death or a suicide, (4) Affecting a donation, (5) A rise in drug abuse or use, (6) Mood swings, fury, and/or impatience that are more frequent, (7) Taking risks by doing things like consuming drugs or having sex without protection, (8) Pretending to be saying farewell to others, and (9) Feeling quite anxious.

RESULTS AND DISCUSSION

The paper highlighted the various key factors that are responsible for increasing in suicide rate among the youth in India. Moreover, the youth population specifically contribute to about 27.3% of suicides among youths in India. A premeditated study was done using the existing literature in this context. The data was taken from NCRB. It is most prevalent in the age group of 18-30. Various causes such as family problems, love affairs, exam failure, and substance abuse were highlighted through the data. Academic distress, biological factors, socio-environmental factors, psychological factors, family factors, and contagion imitation were mainly delved into. There are behavioural, attitudinal, and cognitive tendencies among individuals suffering through the phenomenon of suicide. One such concept is suicidal ideation, the thoughts of harming oneself. Altruistic suicide was also explored. These act as major indicators that can be seen in a suicidal individual.

Suicide is defined as self-inflicted death with evidence (explicit or implicit) of a desire to die (Harmer et al., 2024). A suicide attempt happens if someone harms themselves with the goal of ending their life, but does not die as a result of their actions. Many factors can either enhance or lower the risk of suicide (Bilsen, 2018). It is linked to various types of injury and violence (Yadav et al., 2023). Suicide can be driven by a variety of factors, including release/relief, a response to abnormal thinking, religion, revenge, rebirth, reunification, or reason (Harmer et al., 2024). Various cultural and demographic factors influence the occurrence of suicide. Social suicides, political suicides often take place affected by the social construct and beliefs of the society.

Mental ailments, prior suicide attempts, specific personality characteristics, genetic loading, and familial processes, in conjunction with triggering psychosocial stresses, exposure to inspiring models, and the availability of suicide means, are all significant risk factors in youth suicide (Harmer et al., 2024; Arya, 2024). The four categories of suicide were proposed by Emile Durkheim in his famous book "Le Suicide; étude de sociologie." They are namely: egoistic, which is committed when the given individual uses suicide as a means to escape facing the consequences of his actions. Second Altruistic, refers where the person is so embedded into a society that they are convinced that suicide is the only means to contribute to the given social group's existence. Third is anomic, where a person has lost all their social contacts and commits suicide as a result of not belonging anywhere; and fatalistic, where a person is believes that they cannot follow the rules of a certain social group, which they see as unchangeable and incontrovertible. Statistics have shown that suicide contributes for 12% of total deaths in India. Reported data presents that during 2021, the suicide cases have increased 2 times among the male population with 80% of the cases being from southern part of India and family problems and illness account to majority of cases.

India is a country that is deeply rooted in cultural norms. Political, religious, and social suicide often occurs in India due to the thin line between idealized and frowned upon. Youth often feel tangled in the various cultural expectations. The subsequent pressure often leads to psychopathological symptoms among them. There are certain measures such as setting up suicide clinics, efficient counselling, and restriction of chemicals used in suicide like pesticides, and so on. The importance of implementing these measures is urgent. Suicide is a pressing matter at hand. Most of the time family, friends, and society fail to realize the subsequent help one might require. This continues, often ending the lives of various capable individuals our country is in dire need to reduce suicide among the males and females.

CONCLUSION

The statistical data published by the NCRB (Government of India) infers that the prevalence of total suicide cases has consistently increased in India after 1991. Also, age-wise suicide cases are also increased in India after 2014. It is also noticed that the prevalence of suicide cases among males and females consistently increased in India during 2014 - 2021. It has also appeared that around 80% of suicide cases were reported in 5 states (i.e., Maharashtra, Tamil Nadu, West Bengal, Madhya Pradesh, and Karnataka), while males were typically found to have higher rates of suicide than females in India. It was also observed that family problems and illness are the major causes that lead to increase suicide cases in both males and females in India. Failure in the examination, family problems, terminal illness, drug abuse, ideological hero, failure in a relationship, and physical abuse are found inducive factors to increase suicide cases among youths in India.

Academic stress is found as the main cause of suicide in young adults in India. A higher suicide rate among youth is attributed to the influence of psychological and socio-environmental factors, drug use, impulsivity, and increasing threshold to tolerate pain and fear in India. This can be associated with higher mood disorders, psychosocial stressors, and aspects of culture that violate women's rights. Indian youths are committed for suicide due to inter-caste strife, and caste-based discrimination in education and their professional occupation in India. The process of sexual orientation and gender identification are also significant reasons for more suicide's cases in India. Psychological factors such as low self-esteem, anxiety, feelings of worthlessness, neuroticism, and unpleasant thoughts are also causing an increase in suicide cases among the youth in India. Family structure, social conflict, violence in the family, gender discrimination, and extensive expectations are also leading suicide cases among the youths in India. High diversity in culture is also reported to be a significant reason for suicide in India.

POLICY GUIDELINES

Suicide prevention must become a national priority, and there is a long-standing need for a plan to increase awareness of this issue. The easily available sources of data do not provide an actual picture of the cause. It may be due to various discrepancies in data collection, lack of resources or simply because of the social norm of hiding the reality of suicide. But this in turn is downplaying the severity of suicide in India. The implementation of a national strategy requiring this kind of attention will need a thorough approach covering the national, regional, and local levels of activity promotion, coordination, and support. For populations at risk, the policies would need to be customized. Therefore, it is important to develop suicide preventive strategies keeping in mind the cultural differences in India (Swain et al., 2021). Child parent relationship and school-based intervention may be effective to reduce suicide cases in India (Senapati et al., 2024). All suicide deaths cannot be prevented but, some steps can be taken to reduce it. Some suggested preventive measures are as follows:

Setting up suicide clinics in all medical colleges and hospitals (public and private), district hospitals, taluk hospitals, community health centres, and primary health centres. Special clinics for addiction counselling in all hospitals would significantly decrease the number of suicide cases. Updating the educational system with the motive to promote holistic development in children rather than just emphasizing scoring marks. A concentration in consultation-liaison psychiatry would be of great help. Restricting access to suicidal means like pesticides and certain medications. Setting up employee guidance clinics in all industries. Providing professional services at family courts as most of the family-related issues are dealt with in these centres and some sort of psychiatric intervention would help in solving the issues.

Making mental health services affordable and accessible. Time to time review, evaluation, and modification is necessary for existing policies and the formation of new policies. Educational institutions should provide opportunities to students so that they can express their emotions and learn how to manage them in a way that harms no one. Another major step towards preventing suicide should be destigmatizing mental health issues and promoting appropriate measures to deal with such issues. It is important to develop suicide preventive strategies keeping in mind the cultural differences in India (Swain et al., 2021). All suicide deaths cannot be prevented but, some steps can be taken to reduce it. Some suggested preventive measures are as follows:

- Setting up of suicide clinics in all medical colleges and hospitals (public and private), district hospitals, taluk hospitals, community health centres and primary health centres.
- Special clinics for addiction counselling in all hospitals would significantly decrease the number of suicide cases in India.
- Updating the educational system with the motive to promote holistic development in children rather than just emphasising on scoring marks in India.
- Concentration of consultation-liaison psychiatry would be of a great help in India.
- Restricting access to suicidal means like pesticides and certain medications in India.
- Setting up employee guidance clinics in all the industries in India.
- Providing professional services at family courts as most of the family related issues are dealt in these centres and some sort of psychiatric intervention would help in solving the issues in India.
- Making mental health services affordable and accessible for people in India.
- Time to time review, evaluation and modification is necessary in existing policies and formation of new policies in India.
- Educational institutions should provide opportunities to students do that they can express their emotions and learn how to manage them in a way which harms no one.
- Another major step towards preventing suicide is de-stigmatize mental health issues and promoting appropriate measures to deal with such issues.

SIGNIFICANCE AND VALUE ADDITION

The paper tried to understand and highlight the multifaceted nature of suicide. By synthesizing and analysing existing research, the literature review sheds light on the multiple factors that contribute to suicidal ideation and suicide attempts, encompassing psychological, social, economic, and cultural dimensions (Balaji et al., 2023). It emphasises the lack of existing data and studies regarding youth suicide. Moreover, it attempts to understand and display how individual vulnerabilities interact with societal structures and factors, highlighting the need for policymakers, clinicians, and researchers to move towards more effective prevention and intervention approaches. Finally, it suggests scope of further research in the domain of prevalences of suicide among the youth in India and other countries.

LIMITATIONS OF THE STUDY AND SCOPE OF FURTHER RESEARCH

It is important to highlight the limitations of the study. The first limitation of this chapter is that we completely depend on secondary data sources i.e., NCRB records. Second, we have not developed any theoretical and empirical model for the study. As we are dependent on secondary data, thus, it seems the number of cases is under-reported. In India, suicide is considered a crime at the same time exaggeration from social media. Therefore, it may affect the authenticity of number of reporting cases of suicides in India. Thus, these results should be interpreted with caution. Not much literature is available centred around youth suicidality in India. The accessible data is inadequate to reach towards any concrete result. Cultural influence and variation are a crucial factor for youth suicide, which are often overlooked in suicide related studies. Unfortunately, the related data available is scarce. Not many verified studies are available who have analysed youth suicidality in cultural context. Various factors were discovered throughout the review that act as casual factors for suicide. However, some factors, particularly some environmental and cultural variables do not have enough empirical evidence to show their correlation with suicidal ideation amongst youth. We, therefore, plan to conduct an empirical study to find correlation amongst suicide and its causing factors.

REFERENCES

Adhikari, A. (2023). *India's shocking suicide rate: More than 35 students end life every day.* WION. https://www.wionews.com/india-news/indias-shocking-suicide-rates-more-than-35-die-students-every-day-591830

Arya, V. (2024). Suicide prevention in India. *Mental Health & Prevention*, 33(1), 1–13. 10.1016/j.mhp.2023.20031631299398

Bachmann, S. (2018). Epidemiology of Suicide and the psychiatric perspective. *International Journal of Environmental Research and Public Health*, 15(7), 1425. 10.3390/ijerph1507142529986446

Balaji, M., Mandhare, K., Nikhare, K., Shah, A. K., Kanhere, P., Panse, S., Santre, M., Vijayakumar, L., Phillips, M. R., Pathare, S., Patel, V., Czabanowska, K., & Krafft, T. (2023). Why young people attempt suicide in India: A qualitative study of vulnerability to action. *SSM. Mental Health*, 3(1), 23–32. 10.1016/j.ssmmh.2023.100216

Balazs, J., & Kereszteny, A. (2017). Attention-deficit/hyperactivity disorder and suicide: A systematic review. *World Journal of Psychiatry*, 7(1), 44–59. 10.5498/wjp.v7.i1.4428401048

Beck, A. T., Steer, R. A., Kovacs, M., & Garrison, B. (1985). Hopelessness and eventual suicide: A 10-year prospective study of patients hospitalized with suicidal ideation. *The American Journal of Psychiatry*, 142(5), 559–563. 10.1176/ajp.142.5.5593985195

Bertolote, J. M., & Fleischmann, A. (2002). Suicide and psychiatric diagnosis: A worldwide perspective. *World Psychiatry; Official Journal of the World Psychiatric Association (WPA)*, 1(1), 181–185. https://www.ncbi.nlm.nih.gov/pmc/articles/PMC1489848/16946849

Bhargava, S. C., Sethi, S., & Vohra, A. K. (2001). Klingsor syndrome: A case report. *Indian Journal of Psychiatry*, 43(1), 349–350. https://www.ncbi.nlm.nih.gov/pmc/articles/PMC2956247/21407886

Billie-Brahe, U. (2000). Sociology and suicidal behavior. In: K Hawton, k van Heerington (eds.) *The International Handbook of Suicide and Attempted Suicide* (pp. 193-207). Chichester. https://www.wiley.com/en-in/The+International+Handbook+of+Suicide+and+Attempted+Suicide-p-9780470849590

Bilsen, J. (2018). Suicide and youth: Risk factors. *Frontiers in Psychiatry*, 9(1), 1–13. 10.3389/fpsyt.2018.0054030425663

Birbal, R., Maharajh, H. D., Birbal, R., Clapperton, M., Jarvis, J., Ragoonath, A., & Uppalapati, K. (2009). Cyber suicide and the adolescent population: Challenges of the future? *International Journal of Adolescent Medicine and Health*, 21(2), 151–159. https://pubmed.ncbi.nlm.nih.gov/19702194/19702194

Borges, G., Nock, M. K., & Haro, A. J. M. (2010). Twelve-month prevalence of and risk factors for suicide attempts in the world health organization world mental health surveys. *The Journal of Clinical Psychiatry*, 71(12), 16–27. 10.4088/JCP.08m04967blu20816034

Brent, D. A., & Mann, J. J. (2005). Family genetic studies, suicide, and suicidal behavior. *American Journal of Medical Genetics. Part C, Seminars in Medical Genetics*, 133C(1), 13–24. 10.1002/ajmg.c.3004215648081

Bridge, J. A., Goldstein, T. R., & Brent, D. A. (2006). Adolescent suicide and suicidal behavior. *Journal of Child Psychology and Psychiatry, and Allied Disciplines*, 47(3–4), 372–394. 10.1111/j.1469-7610.2006.01615.x16492264

Cavanagh, J., Carson, A. J., Sharpe, M., & Lawrie, S. M. (2003). Psychological autopsy studies of suicide: A systematic review. *Psychological Medicine*, 33(3), 395–405. 10.1017/S0033291702006943 12701661

Centre for Suicide Prevention. (2022). Sociology and Suicidal Behaviour. K. Hawton & K van Heeringen (eds.), *The International Handbook of Suicide and Attempted Suicide*. Centre for Suicide Prevention. https://www.suicideinfo.ca/resource/siecno-20010031/

Cha, C. B., Franz, P. J., Guzmán, M. E., Glenn, C. R., Kleiman, E. M., & Nock, M. K. (2018). Annual research review: Suicide among youth – Epidemiology, (potential) etiology, and treatment. *Journal of Child Psychology and Psychiatry, and Allied Disciplines*, 59(4), 460–482. 10.1111/jcpp.1283129090457

Clinard, M. B., & Meier, R. F. (1975). *Sociology of Deviant Behaviour* (5th ed.). Holt, Rinehart and Winston. https://www.shortcutstv.com/wp-content/uploads/2020/02/sociology-of-deviant-behavior.pdf

Czyz, E. K., Berona, J., & King, C. A. (2015). A prospective examination of the interpersonal-psychological theory of suicidal behavior among psychiatric adolescent inpatients. *Suicide & Life-Threatening Behavior*, 45(2), 243–259. 10.1111/sltb.1212525263410

Deb, S. (2015). Academic stress, parental pressure, anxiety and mental health among Indian high school students. *International Journal of Psychology and Behavioral Sciences*, 5(1), 26–34. 10.5923/j.ijpbs.20150501.04

Dyer, J., & Kreitman, N. (1984). Hopelessness, depression and suicidal intent in parasuicide. *The British Journal of Psychiatry*, 144(2), 127–133. 10.1192/bjp.144.2.1276704597

Global Health Estimates (GHE). (2023). *Life expectancy and leading causes of death and disability.* GHE. https://www.who.int/data/gho/data/themes/mortality-and-global-health-estimates

Gould, M. S. (2001). Suicide and the media. *Annals of the New York Academy of Sciences*, 932(1), 200–224. 10.1111/j.1749-6632.2001.tb05807.x11411187

Gururaj, G., Isaac, M. K., & Subba, K. D. K. (2011). Risk factors for completed suicides: A case-control study from Bangalore, India. *Injury Control and Safety Promotion*, 11(3), 183–191. 10.1080/156609704/233/28970615764105

Harmer, B., Lee, S., Rizvi, A., & Saadabadi, A. (2024). Suicidal Ideation. In *StatPearls*. Stat Pearls Publishing. https://pubmed.ncbi.nlm.nih.gov/33351435/

Harris, E. C., & Barraclough, B. (1998). Excess mortality of mental disorder. *The British Journal of Psychiatry*, 173(1), 11–53. 10.1192/bjp.173.1.119850203

Hawton, K., & van Heeringen, K. (2009). Suicide. *Lancet*, 37(3), 72–81. 10.1016/S0140-6736(09)60372-X19376453

Hinduja, S., & Patchin, J. W. (2010). Bullying, cyberbullying, and suicide. *Archives of Suicide Research*, 14(3), 206–221. 10.1080/13811118.2010.49413320658375

Im, Y., Oh, W., & Suk, M. (2017). Risk Factors for suicide ideation among adolescents: Five-year national data analysis. *Archives of Psychiatric Nursing*, 31(1), 282–286. 10.1016/j.apnu.2017.01.00128499568

Kashyap, A. (2023). Suicide deaths in Indian men increased 2 times more than women in 2021: Lancet study. *Business Line.* https://www.thehindubusinessline.com/news/national/suicide-deaths-in-ndian-men-increased-2-times-more-than-women-in-2021-lancet-study/article67250785.ece

Linker, J., Gillespie, N. A., Maes, H., Eaves, L., & Silberg, J. L. (2012). Suicidal ideation, depression, and conduct disorder in a sample of adolescent and young adult twins. *Suicide & Life-Threatening Behavior*, 42(4), 426–436. 10.1111/j.1943-278X.2012.00101.x22646517

Manoranjitham, S., Charles, H., & Saravanan, B. (2007). Perceptions about suicide: A qualitative study from southern India. *The National Medical Journal of India*, 20(2), 176–179. 18085122

Manoranjitham, S. D., Rajkumar, A. P., Thangadurai, P., Prasad, J., Jayakaran, R., & Jacob, K. S. (2010). Risk factors for suicide in rural south India. *The British Journal of Psychiatry*, 196(1), 26–30. 10.1192/bjp.bp.108.06334720044655

Mashreky, S. R., Rahman, F., & Rahman, A. (2013). Suicide kills more than 10,000 people every year in Bangladesh. *Archives of Suicide Research*, 17(4), 387–396. 10.1080/13811118.2013.80180924224672

Maskill, C., Hodges, I., McClellan, V., & Collings, S. (2005). *Explaining patterns of suicide: A selective review of studies examining social, economic, cultural and other population-level influences*. Ministry of Health. https://citeseerx.ist.psu.edu/document?repid=rep1&type=pdf&doi=a860ae0d819a6302b110d58d749fec82948ce7b5

Mckeown, R. E., Garrison, C. Z., Cuffe, S. P., Waller, J. L., Jackson, K. L., & Addy, C. L. (1998). Incidence and predictors of suicidal behaviors in a longitudinal sample of young adolescents. *Journal of the American Academy of Child and Adolescent Psychiatry*, 37(6), 612–619. 10.1097/00004583-199806000-000119628081

Melhem, N. M., Keilp, J. G., Porta, G., Oquendo, M. A., Burke, A., Stanley, B., Cooper, T. B., Mann, J. J., & Brent, D. A. (2016). Blunted HPA axis activity in suicide attempters compared to those at high risk for suicidal behavior. Neuropsychopharmacology. *Neuropsychopharmacology*, 41(6), 1447–1456. 10.1038/npp.2015.30926450815

Moscicki, E. (2001). Epidemiology of suicide. In Goldsmith, S. (Ed.), *Risk Factors for Suicide. Summary of a workshop, pp. 1–4*. National Academy Press. https://pubmed.ncbi.nlm.nih.gov/8829423/

Nath, Y., Paris, J., Thombs, B., & Kirmayer, L. (2012). Prevalence and social determinants of suicidal behaviours among college youth in India. *The International Journal of Social Psychiatry*, 58(4), 393–399. 10.1177/002076401140116421632571

National Crime Records Bureau (NCRB). (1981). *Accidental Deaths and Suicides in India*. New Delhi: Government of India. https://ncrb.gov.in/accidental-deaths-suicides-in-india-year-wise.html?year=1981&keyword=

O'Connor, R., & Pirkis, J. (2016). Suicide clusters. In *O'Connor RC, Perkis J, (Edt.), International Handbook of Suicide Prevention* (2nd ed., pp. 758–774). John Wiley & Sons., 10.1002/9781118903223

Pandey, V. (2017). Students' Suicides in Institutions of Higher Education in India: Risk Factors and Interventions. *International Journal of Social Work and Human Services Practice*, 5(1), 29–34. 10.13189/ijrh.2017.050104

Patel, V., Rama, S. C., & Vijayakumar, L. (2012). Suicide mortality in India: A nationally representative survey. *Lancet*, 37(9), 2343–2351. 10.1016/S0140-6736(12)60606-022726517

Pirkis, J., Mok, K., Robinson, J., & Nordentoft, M. (2016). Media influences on suicidal thoughts and behaviors. In *The International Handbook of Suicide Prevention* (2nd ed., pp. 743–757). John Wiley & Sons, Ltd. 10.1002/9781118903223.ch42

Pisani, A. R., Wyman, P. A., Petrova, M., Schmeelk-Cone, K., Goldston, D. B., Xia, Y., & Gould, M. S. (2013). Emotion regulation difficulties, youth-adult relationships, and suicide attempts among high school students in underserved communities. *Journal of Youth and Adolescence*, 42(6), 807–820. 10.1007/s10964-012-9884-223666604

Portzky, G., Audenaert, K., & van Heeringen, K. (2005). Suicide among adolescents. A psychological autopsy study of psychiatric, psychosocial and personality-related risk factors. *Social Psychiatry and Psychiatric Epidemiology*, 40(1), 922–930. 10.1007/s00127-005-0977-x16217594

Pritchard, C. (1996). Suicide in the People's Republic of China categorized by age and gender: Evidence of the influence of culture on suicide. *Acta Psychiatrica Scandinavica*, 93(5), 362–367. https://onlinelibrary.wiley.com/doi/abs/10.1111/j.1600-0447.1996.tb10661.x. 10.1111/j.1600-0447.1996.tb10661.x8792906

Radhakrishnan, R., & Andrade, C. (2012). Suicide: An Indian perspective. *Indian Journal of Psychiatry*, 54(4), 30–41. 10.4103/0019-5545.104793233722 32

Rampal, N. (2020). More than 90,000 young adults died by suicide in 2019 in India: NCRB report. *India Today*. https://www.indiatoday.in/diu/story/ncrb-report-data-india-young-adults-suicide-2019-india-1717887-2020-09-02

Retterstol, N. (1993). *Suicide: A European perspective*. Cambridge University Press. https://onlinelibrary.wiley.com/doi/abs/10.1111/j.1943-278X.1997.tb00509.x

Ross, S., & Heath, N. L. (2003). Two models of adolescent self-mutilation. *Suicide & Life-Threatening Behavior*, 33(1), 277–287. 10.1521/suli.33.3.277.2321814582838

Samuel, D., & Sher, L. (2013). Suicidal behavior in Indian adolescents. *International Journal of Adolescent Medicine and Health*, 25(3), 207–212. 10.1515/ijamh-2013-005424006319

Sarveswar, S., & Thomas, J. (2020). Academic distress and student suicides in India: A crisis that needs to be acknowledged. *The Wire*. https://thewire.in/rights/academic-distress-and-student-suicides-in-india

Scherer, S., Pestian, J., & Morency, L. P. (2013). *Investigating the speech characteristics of suicidal adolescents. 2013 IEEE International Conference on Acoustics, Speech and Signal Processing*, Vancouver, BC, Canada. 10.1109/ICASSP.2013.6637740

Senapati, R. E., Jena, S., Parida, J., Panda, A., Patra, P. K., Pati, S., Kaur, H., & Acharya, S. K. (2024). The patterns, trends and major risk factors of suicide among Indian adolescents – a scoping review. *BMC Psychiatry*, 24(35), 23–32. 10.1186/s12888-023-05447-838195413

Shaffer, D., Fisher, P., Hicks, R. H., Parides, M., & Gould, M. (1995). Sexual orientation in adolescents who commit suicide. Suicide Life Threat Bahaviour, 25(1), 64-71 https://pubmed.ncbi.nlm.nih.gov/8553430/

Stack, S. (1987). Celebrities and Suicide: A Taxonomy and analysis, 1948-1983. *American Sociological Review*, 52(3), 40–51. 10.2307/209535911613886

Suicide Data and Statistics. (n.d.). CDC. https://www.cdc.gov/suicide/suicide-data-statistics.html

Swain, P. K., Tripathy, M. R., Priyadarshini, S., & Acharya, S. K. (2021). Forecasting suicide rates in India: An empirical exposition. *PLoS One*, 16(7), 1–21. 10.1371/journal.pone.025534234324554

Uddin, R., Burton, N. W., Maple, M., Khan, S. R., & Khan, A. (2019). Suicidal ideation, suicide planning, and suicide attempts among adolescents in 59 low-income and middle-income countries: A population-based study. *The Lancet. Child & Adolescent Health*, 3(4), 223–233. 10.1016/S2352-4642(18)30403-630878117

Unni, S. K., & Mani, A. J. (1996). Suicidal ideators in the psychiatric facility of a general hospital - a psycho demographic profile. *Indian Journal of Psychiatry*, 38(2), 79–85. https://pubmed.ncbi.nlm.nih.gov/21584150/21584150

Vijayakumar, L., & Rajkumar, S. (1999). Are risk factors for suicide universal? A case-control study from India. *Acta Psychiatrica Scandinavica*, 99(6), 407–411. 10.1111/j.1600-0447.1999.tb00985.x10408261

Williams, M. (1977). *Cry of Pain: Understanding suicide and self-harm*. Penguin. https://www.ncbi.nlm.nih.gov/pmc/articles/PMC1296580/

Wu, K. C. C., Chen, Y. Y., & Yip, P. S. (2012). Suicide methods in Asia: Implications in suicide prevention. *International Journal of Environmental Research and Public Health*, 9(4), 1135–1158. 10.3390/ijerph904113522690187

Yadav, S., Aathavan, K. K., Cunningham, S. A., Bhandari, P., Mishra, U. S., Aditi, A., & Yadav, R. (2023). Changing pattern of suicide deaths in India. *The Lancet Regional Health. Southeast Asia*, 16(1), 10–26. 10.1016/j.lansea.2023.10026537649643

Zimmermann, M. (2007). *GRIN- Suicide in India in a religious, political and social context.* GRIN. https://www.grin.com/document/80758

Chapter 11
Study on Vulnerability to Maladjustment and Addictions in the Early Years of Student Life

Cristina-Georgiana Safta
Petroleum-Gas University of Ploiesti, Romania

Silvian Suditu
https://orcid.org/0009-0008-6538-0274
Petroleum-Gas University of Ploiesti, Romania

ABSTRACT

In a society characterized by an accentuated dynamic, by uncertainty and insecurity, with complex challenges and temptations at every step, the problem of students' well-being and the evaluation of their degree of vulnerability, respectively of the dimensions of that, represents a problem of major interest, with multiple implications both on an individual level and on a social level. This study therefore aims to evaluate the well-being and vulnerability of students in the first years of study, with the help of two standardized instruments, namely the vulnerability to maladjustment (VM) questionnaire and the vulnerability and resilience to addictions (VrA) questionnaire. The conclusions drawn from the analysis and interpretation of the results led to the formulation of a set of recommendations regarding the strategies that universities can develop with the aim of securing the emotional security of young people and cultivating well-being.

DOI: 10.4018/979-8-3693-4417-0.ch011

INTRODUCTION

This study aims to investigate how vulnerability and maladjustment influence the well-being of first year undergraduate students. To this end, the concepts: well-being, vulnerability in relation to the concepts of maladjustment, and addiction, are presented and explained from multiple perspectives (historical, sociological, psychological, etc.). We start from the premise that there is a high level of vulnerability in the first years of university, which is obviously incompatible with achieving a state of well-being. This vulnerability stems from adaptation difficulties (academic, social, personal, emotional), observed in first year students and previously analyzed in the study Adapting to the Academic Environment: A Prerequisite for Academic Success (Suditu, Safta, 2023: 67-83). The present micro research was conducted on a sample of 100 first year students at the Petrol-Gaze University of Ploiesti and its main objective was to determine the risk factors and the degree of vulnerability felt by them in relation to maladjustment and addictions. The applied research instruments are standardized questionnaires: the VM (Vulnerability to Maladjustment) Questionnaire and the VrA (Vulnerability and Resilience to Addictions) Questionnaire. The analysis of the results leads us to the idea that vulnerability, even at a low level, should engender prudence, empowerment, deep awareness of the risks and most importantly, outlining *strategies to cultivate well-being and identify sources of support for students.*

THE THEORETICAL ANALYSIS OF THE WORKING CONCEPTS

The Concept of Well-Being as it Relates to the Higher Education System: A Historical, Ecological, Sociological, and Psychological Perspective

In a broad sense, the concept of well-being refers to the general feeling of pleasure, fulfilment, and the satisfaction of both physical and mental needs. From the perspective of English literature, the concept of well-being also adds the dimensions of wealth and prosperity to its explanation. Thus, a polarization of meaning can be observed as an oscillation between income and assets on the one hand and 'utility', happiness on the other. In fact (Lafaye, 2007:127), "well-being depends on the satisfaction of desires and practices, but also on goods related to forms of common life and finally to goods related to dispositions inherent to human nature."

Throughout history the concept has been in the attention of philosophers: Plato and Aristotle understand happiness as a way of being, as a state of the soul and a form of doing good, which is the end of any action. However, although Aristotle establishes that happiness is coextensive with contemplation, considered to be the best part of happiness, he recognizes that joining virtue and pleasure to it produces an even greater good. "Bliss is found neither in the life of pleasure nor in the life of wisdom, but in a mixed life associating certain pleasures with wisdom" (Lafaye, 2007:128, apud Plato, Philebus).

In utilitarian theory, the concept of well-being is closely related to that of utility, defined as pleasure or the edge of pleasure in relation to pain. Thus, enjoying pleasure or less pain is equivalent to enjoying more utility and well-being.

J.S. Mill establishes a close link between hedonism and the principle of utility, thus adding a new dimension to the term well-being, by moving from "happiness for everyone" to "welfare for everyone" (Mill, 1988: 49).

In more complex utilitarian theories, utility and well-being are defined in terms of the satisfaction of desires, preferences, which must be neither unconscious, irrational nor contrary to our objective interest, but must reflect informed and prudent satisfaction.

Viewed through the lens of the criterion of morality, the welfare state cannot be reduced to individual happiness, but aims more than that, with optimism even, at the happiness of all or the happiness of as many people as possible, assessed from an impersonal and impartial point of view.

The concept of well-being has a composite structure that integrates the terms: needs, wants, preferences. If from a psychological point of view, desire is fundamental, from a moral point of view, needs are the determining basis for well-being. In reality, there is a subtle boundary between need and desire, so that need must be understood as that "something" whose absence would profoundly harm individual interests, while desire is an aspiration for fulfilment.

One of the best-known conceptual models of well-being was popularized by M. Seligman and is known by the acronym PERMA. According to it, well-being is based on five pillars (Seligman, 2011).

- *Positive emotions*: to experience the feeling of well-being
- *Engagement*: to become fully involved in activities
- *Relationship*: having authentic relationships with others
- *Meaning*: to live a meaningful life
- Achievement: to succeed in reaching your goals

To ensure the development of these pillars, the PERMA model constructs a set of questions useful to any institution interested in wellness: What are the elements that bring you satisfaction? What are those elements that cause you concern? Do you think colleagues feel the same way as you do about answering these questions? What might be the opinion of others on this topic?

"Well-being is a process made up of four essential elements that are intrinsically linked and that influence each other: feeling good, having a balanced life, fulfilling your goals and developing yourself."

The State of Well-Being in Higher Education: Compositional Structure

From the perspective of the World Health Organization (WHO), well-being is a holistic concept, encompassing social life, private life and physical well-being. Several facets of well-being can thus be distinguished and grouped into several categories, each of which translates into specific behaviors:

- Emotional: managing emotions effectively, asking for support when individual resources are insufficient;
- Physical: following a strict eating and sleeping schedule, participating in sports activities, maintaining good health;
- Social: building strong relationships, showing empathy and altruism;
- Spiritual: promoting harmony and balance in one's relationships with others, seeking relational meaning;
- Financial: planning financial resources in relation to the goals to be achieved;
- Professional: finding meaning in work activities and manifesting concern for the recognition of skills and their development;
- Intellectual: taking advantage of learning opportunities and showing concern for self-improvement;
- Environment: respecting the environment and understanding the relationship between people and nature.

Student well-being has a direct impact on academic performance. Students who feel well are more likely to be motivated, focused and engaged in educational activities. They are able to manage time and stress more effectively, which is critical for academic success. In addition, well-being contributes to the development of essential skills such as resilience, problem-solving and critical thinking. (see Fayaz, Aasim Ur, Danishwar, 2024).

On a personal level, optimal well-being allows students to develop healthy relationships and participate actively in the community. This facilitates the development of a strong identity and sense of belonging, which is essential for personal growth and life satisfaction.

In terms of education, there are several myths related to student well-being that can be examined (Balica, 2021):

- One of the most widely held myths is that students' well-being translates into their happiness in the institutional environment, happiness that comes either from the lack of worries about learning or from having those skills that help them succeed in academic challenges. However, research in the field shows that well-being as a whole involves much more than inner joy, but also health, balance, commitment, perseverance, etc.
- Another common myth is that students' well-being is innate. But research has shown the opposite. Well-being is dependent on a multitude of factors: interactions with others, personal life events, socio-emotional skills, adaptability/flexibility, etc.
- Last but not least, there are voices that argue that student well-being cannot be quantified. Recent studies, however, show that, although complex, this assessment is not impossible. It must, however, take into account a pre-existing framework that defines well-being, age specificity, and correlation with data from other longitudinal studies.

According to the ecological approach (Bronfenbrenner, 1992) social factors that influence students' well-being can be grouped into three categories:

- at the micro level: family, peers, teachers, school and the natural environment.
- at the meso-level: community culture, access to and participation in different services and activities.
- at the macro level: national factors and global issues that indirectly influence overall well-being.

Improving students' well-being is a key pillar for their personal, social and professional success. By fostering a healthy academic environment where students feel supported and encouraged, they can achieve better academic performance and develop important social skills. Good well-being can help reduce stress and anxiety, thus facilitating concentration and effective learning. A happy and balanced student can also build positive social relationships and develop skills essential for career success. It is important for educational institutions to provide adequate support and resources to promote student well-being.

Vulnerability: A Concept With Complex Dynamics

Vulnerability is a broad phenomenon that raises the question of the relationship between individuals and the society in which they live. Vulnerability is universal, involving the whole of society and its functioning. According to the OECD, "it constitutes (...) our initial human condition, both ontologically and psychologically or even ethically.

Little used until the 1980s, the term has seen an explosion of meanings since the 2000s, in France as in the Anglo-Saxon world. It has thus gradually spread to many fields, and today speaks of a multitude of facets of vulnerability: social, educational, legal, economic, environmental, etc. In this context, there is also a change in the understanding of health, social, economic and environmental effects, as well as in the individual, collective, institutional or political responses proposed to remedy them. Thinking about vulnerability involves recognizing its 'differential' variations and uneven distribution in social organization. Thus, the notion of vulnerability, linked to stressors and the risks they entail, becomes a practical category, a category of action, not just a category of analysis.

A HISTORY OF THE CONCEPT OF VULNERABILITY

According to the Larousse dictionary, vulnerable comes from the Latin *vulnus*, *vulneris* (wound) and *vulnerare* (to wound) and defines one "who can be hurt, struck", "who can be easily touched, who defends himself poorly" and has as synonyms the terms "fragile" and "sensitive". It claims to refer to two realities: the crack on one side (the sensitive, fragile area through which the attack will occur) and the wound on the other side (which will materialize the attack), (Thomas, 2010: 43).

Seen from a historical perspective, the concept of vulnerability has undergone wide-ranging transformations, sometimes acquiring meanings and interpretations with divergent valences. Thus, while in the Judeo-Christian world (until the 18th century), vulnerability was perceived as existential, biological, specific to man since the original fault (Martuccelli, 2014), in the "modernity" period (19th-20th century), vulnerability was understood as a problem requiring intervention with a resolving purpose, leading to the emergence of social protection services and the development of medicine, etc. The end of the 20th century brought a new perspective on vulnerability, now associated with a situation of individual, multifaceted crisis and a widespread sense of powerlessness.

In recent years, vulnerability is increasingly seen as a societal problem, with implications for job insecurity and relational fragility. We are thus witnessing the promotion of a cold individualism, far removed from any attempt at attachment, the promotion of a society in which, as R. Castel (1991) puts it, the vulnerable, marked with the 'seal of uncertainty' and disaffiliation, become 'useless in the world' before falling into 'social non-existence'. Relational vulnerability is seen as a continuum between integration and disaffiliation, as a limitation of cultural, material and social resources.

From an ethical perspective, vulnerability is defined as an increased likelihood of harm, which makes the ethics of autonomy opposed to the ethics of vulnerability.

In the human sciences, as in public policy, the notion of precariousness tends today to compete with that of vulnerability, which is used more and more widely. Thus, psychology, moving from mental illness to mental health, implicitly appeals to the concept of vulnerability as a source of mental health deterioration, calling into question its remedial systems.

From a global perspective, vulnerability is an operational concept commonly used to designate a state of fragility, warning of an increased risk of harm. If we attempt an in-depth analysis of vulnerability, we can use a number of criteria such as:

- persistence over time (it can be an occasional condition or one that manifests itself over a longer period of time);
- individual or collective character;
- the circumstances in which it occurs;
- the individual's potential to recover, to get out of the vulnerable situation;
- area/field of vulnerability (material or moral fragility, etc.).

In terms of social and medical action, vulnerability tends to designate people who are at risk, who need support, accompaniment, protection. The fact that, at some point, each of us may play the role of an autonomous person who has to take care of other people who are themselves vulnerable, does not exclude the denial of our own vulnerability. This perspective leads to an understanding of vulnerability as a relationship "bringing together two vulnerable people who can each bring something to each other". Because to recognize that we share vulnerability is to be able to recognize the dignity of others, without condescension or pity, in a spirit of equality.

For B. Brown (2013), vulnerability is both a weakness, because it is at the heart of shame and fear and of our problem with self-esteem, but also a strength because it can be the source of joy, creativity, a sense of belonging, of love. When the audacity to expose oneself to vulnerability is equated with consent, consent to one's own fragility acknowledged and accepted, it appears as a strength, a capacity to welcome the fragility, and even the wretchedness of others. Vulnerability thus takes on a new dimension, that of superiority, of empowering the individual in the struggle against external barriers.

Vulnerability: Truly a Problem for Well-Being

Today's society is characterized by the emergence of a new socio-cultural model marked by normative individualism and a conception of society that overvalues two extremely important dimensions from a relational perspective: risk and trust. This 'socio-cultural model' is characterized by a destabilization of social reference points, increasing the uncertainty of the members of a society about their identity. The individual is, in fact, forced to continually re-conceptualize their relationship with the physical and social world and to develop conditions conducive to the realization of an inter-connection with their contemporaries." (Soulet, 2005:26)

This model also generates changes in the status of institutions, in the sense that, beyond the rules of behavior and action that they impose from outside, they must accept that each individual continues to search for authenticity and self-fulfillment.

One can thus speak of the creation of social networks through the intertwining and interweaving of freely established relationships between relational individuals. Society is no longer thought of as a vast pre-existing and constraining whole in the manner of Émile Durkheim, but is conceived as a continuous productive movement that feeds on the voluntary interaction of individuals and the relationships that are woven between them. We thus speak of a need for the relentless pursuit of authenticity as a principle for affirming the identity of individuals, on the one hand, and the decline of what society has done through its institutions, on the other.

In such a social configuration, the behavior of individuals is no longer dictated by the rigor of strict institutional frameworks, but it "is always dictated from the outside, a posteriori however, from the evaluative perspective of a diversity of alter egos with whom individuals choose to enter into a relationship. One can thus speak of a fragmented heteronomy, always uncertain, because individual acts and choices developed without guarantees and without protection are subject to the judgment of those with whom specific individuals have chosen to enter into a relationship". (Soulet, 2005:26) Uncertainty is the dominant feature of these social systems whose mission is to harmonize individual aspirations for achievement with the requirement of reciprocity in relationship.

This context marked by uncertainty and the transfer of responsibility to individuals creates a world of vulnerability insofar as society is no longer so much conceived as a universe of normative control over the behavior of its members, but as a setting in which individuals have to face the most diverse challenges, many of which are generated by their own fellow human beings, and have to go through the various tests and experiences to which society subjects them. In this context, it is the individuals' relationship with others and the extent to which they manage to integrate socially that send messages with strong inner echoes about their potential, their doubts and fears, and their temporary failures; that can lead to underestimation and the suffering created by the imbalance between what they are and what they could become if they were able to make the most of the opportunities offered to them.

On the one hand, collective problems become individual tests because they test the capacity of the individual to self-manage and participate in the constitution of the social fabric. Faulty integration makes individuals vulnerable and weakens them, as they do not have the means to self-establish and self-manage themselves, to participate actively in the production of collective life.

On the other hand, individual events become collective problems, because it is important to be aware of the social costs of individual shortcomings, whether it is a lack of responsibility or a lack of skills. Vulnerability is thus defined by the inability of individuals to actively influence the production of social norms.

In this context, the promotion of a culture of well-being aims to empower the vulnerable to strengthen their capacity to manage their future trajectory, to take responsibility for personal resource management, self-care and self-efficacy. At the same time, reducing vulnerability also requires a supportive intervention, by creating a micro-climate of communication, spaces for discussion and conviviality that allow the expression of the suffering that vulnerability causes, so as to then take effective action to recover individual confidence and dignity. Social health is becoming an acute problem in contemporary society, marked by the difficulty of individuals to find and then maintain their place/role in the world, to create and develop relationships, a problem with broad psychological implications.

VULNERABILITY AND THE VULNERABILITIES PRESENT IN THE ACADEMIC ENVIRONMENT

The Relationship Between Vulnerability and Academic Adjustment

The feeling of loneliness experienced as a result of relocation is one of the main enemies of well-being felt by many first-year students. Conflicting relationships with parents and economic difficulties, cultural and sometimes even language barriers, loss of value and loss of direction among multiple challenges sometimes difficult to decipher, and the distance from loved ones, prevent sociability and limit interactions with peers, accentuating the feeling of loneliness.

The absence of a relationship with parents or living in an "incomplete", conflictual relationship, the lack of emotional and moral support from parents, exacerbate the feeling of loneliness, and in serious cases even lead to suicidal behavior.

Lack of self-confidence is widespread among the student population and is often associated with the desire to gain status, and the need for recognition at the group level. Experiencing economic hardship undermines students' self-confidence and hence their well-being, leaving room for the development of risky behaviors such as substance abuse.

Facing multiple discriminatory experiences from the first day of university, from learning to social and economic ones, makes young people with low self-esteem vulnerable and easy targets for physical and psychological violence.

The Relationship Between Vulnerability and Addictions

The use of tobacco, alcohol and banned substances could be described as the main temptations students have to resist. Involvement in learning or work activities to a greater extent, coupled with regular sports activities and the presence of role models, however, decreases the incidence of these risk factors.

A study conducted in 2019 by the National Anti-Drug Agency (ANA) highlighted the following characteristics of alcohol, tobacco and drug consumption: compared to the European average, consumption is lower in Romania for all categories of illicit drugs; tobacco consumption remains similar to the European average (41%) with an equal spread between the two sexes, which means that girls tend to adopt the same consumption behavior; alcohol consumption increases annually, reaching percentages above 80% and exceeding the European average.

Daily consumption remains, however, marginal and is most often associated with a negative perception of the quality of life, but also with socio-economic issues (lack of economic resources, isolation, etc.), while frequent but non-daily consumption is associated with a student lifestyle oriented towards sociability and entertainment. (see also Ghadiri, Sabouri Moghadam, Babapur Kheiradin, 2014).

Moving away from home and moving to new territory can lead to the loss of a network of health professionals, and students' knowledge of the health system is often partial. This is why the 19-25 age group here seems to be particularly vulnerable in terms of empowerment for initiatives related to staying healthy and developing preventive behaviors.

Aggression towards other people (hetero-aggression) is a common risk behavior among young people, which is more frequently expressed in the circle of friends, acquaintances or family. Conflicts with strangers are not lacking either, as their frequency seems to increase with age (Petrescu, Băncilă, Suciu, Vlaicu, Doroftei, 2004:6), nor is self-aggression or suicidal behavior.

RESEARCH METHODOLOGY

Evidence of adaptability to the academic environment is based on the idea that students' chances of social and academic success are directly proportional to the level of well-being embodied in good collaboration, communication, empathy, engagement and problem-solving skills.

The objectives of the study aim to investigate the degree of vulnerability present in students in their first years of study and to identify the structural-compositional elements of vulnerability. We start from the premise that a high level of vulnerability is incompatible with the achievement of a state of well-being.

Also, our hypothesis is based on qualitative observations from a previous study on students' adaptation to the academic environment. The study assessed (based on the Student Adaptation to College Questionnaire) the degree of adaptability on 4 dimensions: academic adjustment, social adjustment, personal-emotional adjustment, and attachment, and the results showed that the lowest scores were recorded on the personal-emotional adjustment and social adjustment scales. These were also the dimensions that we considered relevant, with impact on the complex analysis of students' well-being, i.e. in the identification of areas of vulnerability with consequences, cognitive emotional or behavioral effects which are felt in the academic context.

Within the above-mentioned instrument, social adjustment is the scale that measures students' success in managing the interpersonal and social demands acquired in university. The scale is divided into 4 categories: the measure and success of social activities, the involvement and relationship with other people in the university, the management of social relocation, and satisfaction with the social aspects of the academic environment. Low scores on this dimension are associated with decreased participation in social activities in university and indicate poor social skills, failure to severe home ties and establish social autonomy.

Personal emotional adjustment is the subscale that focuses on the emotional state of students during their adjustment to the academic environment. This scale also focuses on measuring the degree of general psychological discomfort, including somatic problems that students experience. The two categories of items that make up this subscale target the psychological state - the feeling of psychological well-being and the physical state - the feeling of physical well-being. Low scores indicate a higher degree of emotional dependence, low resources for managing emotional situations, toxic dependence on parents, a high degree of psychological discomfort including anxiety and depression, a more extensive experience of negative life events.

Based on these results of empirical studies, in the present study we aim to operationalize the concept of vulnerability and to capture possible correlations between the dimensions of this concept that impact students' well-being.

The research instruments in this current study are: the VM (Vulnerability to Maladjustment) Questionnaire and the VrA (Vulnerability and Resilience to Addictions) Questionnaire. These instruments are standardized, tested and validated on the Romanian population.

According to the presentation manual, the VM (Vulnerability to Maladjustment) questionnaire allows the assessment of dimensions or factors by which a personality with "vulnerability to maladjustment" can be described, specific traits and characteristics that can be associated with possible difficulties or deficiencies related to socio-professional integration, respectively:

- emotional instability (the tendency of a person to experience frequent and intense negative emotions);
- distorted experiences (a tendency towards unconventional thinking, bizarre beliefs, or distorted perceptions of reality)
- identity deficits (difficulties in self-knowledge and self-regulation);
- dysfunctional relating (difficulties in understanding others and inability to form close relationships or inadequate understanding of the dynamics of social relationships);
- uncontrolled impulsivity (inability to control impulses, which can lead to risky behavior, unwise decisions and difficulties in meeting responsibilities);
- poor empathy (inability or difficulty recognizing, understanding and responding appropriately to other people's feelings and needs);
- problematic intimacy (difficulty forming and maintaining close and long-lasting emotional bonds with others).

The tool provides relevant data for identifying people at high risk of maladjustment and can help identify vulnerabilities and define effective prevention or remedial intervention strategies.

The second instrument is the VrA Questionnaire, which, according to its accompanying presentation note, allows the assessment of dimensions that can be used to describe a personality with vulnerability to addictions, psychological traits that in empirical scientific studies have been frequently associated with different types of addictions (or addiction-related difficulties).

The psychological dimensions measured are:

- Thrill-seeking or a tendency to seek out new, often risky or intense experiences;
- Poor self-control or difficulty regulating impulses and behaviors and a reduced ability to resist temptation or pressure;

- Intolerance of discomfort or low resistance to frustration, stress or emotional and physical discomfort;
- Emotional avoidance, as the tendency to avoid or detach from difficult or painful emotions;
- Escape or the desire to escape from reality or avoid life problems through addictive behaviors;
- Immediate gratification or the predisposition to be motivated by immediate and pleasurable rewards on offer, with no tolerance for delay in order to obtain consistent long-term benefits;
- Emotional resilience or the ability to cope with stress and negative emotions;
- Social support, as a protective factor, refers to the positive social environment and the social resources a person can use to cope with stress and challenges and resist temptations or addictions;
- Self-efficacy, with reference to one's confidence in one's abilities to manage challenges and resist temptations;
- Cognitive flexibility, as associated with better mental and psychological health, avoidance of limiting situations and finding alternative solutions, which can reduce vulnerability to addictions.

The tool identifies a potential vulnerability and can be useful in preliminary screening and identification of people at high risk of addiction and also for prevention and intervention purposes.

The questionnaires were administered online by accessing an individualized link.

The target population is represented by 100 subjects, students in their first two years of university, in different fields of study. The reason why our interest is focused on students in their first two years of study is related to the numerous transitions to which they are subjected (geographical relocation, adaptation to the requirements of the academic environment, integration into a new group, etc.) which generate a higher degree of vulnerability (see Safta, Suditu, 2022).

DATA ANALYSIS

In order to achieve the above-mentioned objectives, in the data analysis we aimed to correlate the responses from the two instruments administered. Thus, for the VrA Questionnaire we assessed that obtaining high scores on the dimensions thrill-seeking, self-control, discomfort intolerance, emotional avoidance, desire for escape, desire for gratification reflects a high level of perceived vulnerability, while high scores on the dimensions self-efficacy, cognitive flexibility, and social support are associated with respondents' well-being. It should be noted that scores on each dimension are rated on a scale of 1 to 10, and high scores are considered to be those where the value is greater than five. It is also worth mentioning that high scores on one or more dimensions of the VrA questionnaire do not mean that a person will definitely develop addictions, but only indicate a potential vulnerability, which may fluctuate depending on one's own value system, entourage, and educational level and other psychosocial factors may play a decisive role in the development of addictions or in increasing resistance to addictions.

The VM questionnaire was used to reinforce and complete the information obtained on the vulnerability experienced, i.e. the areas of increased vulnerability. High scores on the VM questionnaire dimensions indicate only increased vulnerability to maladaptation and not the existence or obligatory occurrence of adaptation problems. Factors such as a person's environment (background), education, family values, life experiences (pathogenic or adaptive) or other psychosocial factors can play a decisive role in the development of effective coping mechanisms.

The qualitative analysis of the results of the Vulnerability to Maladjustment questionnaire highlighted several issues:

- In terms of emotional stability, the majority of respondents show a good ability to manage emotional challenges, remaining unaffected in the face of irritation or anger, feeling secure in potentially destabilizing circumstances, reflecting high emotional adaptability and strong resilience.
- A significant number of respondents hold ideas that are generally aligned with societal norms and expectations, without a pronounced attraction to mysterious or supernatural elements, demonstrating that their perception of reality corresponds to that accepted by the majority, reflecting a harmonious integration into the common human experience; There are, however, cases of unconventional thinking, in which subjects believe in phenomena that others consider unusual or unreal and report sensory experiences that deviate from those of the majority. We appreciate that the latter may be the result of a need for attention, patterns promoted by the media, or even a low level of culture.
- For many students in their first years of study, the common denominator is the presence of a self-image characterized by vagueness and fluctuations, which makes it impossible to establish a clear sense of direction in life. They oscillate between self-confidence and self-doubt and struggle deeply with their self-concept and personal identity. Although less common, the sense of self-worth is nonetheless present in a smaller category of subjects.
- The empathy shown towards other people's experiences and problems makes many of those interviewed succeed in building harmonious and conflict-free relationships, relationships based on trust and respect, being perceived by others as warm, close people. Insufficient self-awareness, coupled with a lack

of trust, however, means that a small percentage (18%) of first-year students report difficulties in establishing social interactions and managing relationships effectively.
- Although the majority of respondents believe that they show a high level of self-control, acting deliberately and considering the consequences of their actions, more than 30% of respondents admit that they make decisions in a hurry, without proper analysis, that they are not always consistent and responsible, and that they sometimes break the rules, deliberately or not.
- In terms of intimacy, we see a polarization of the results obtained and a relatively equal distribution of scores towards the two extremes. We thus speak of either normal intimacy, characterized by easy expression of feelings and personal information in close relationships, experiencing the openness or of problematic intimacy, characterized by discomfort and reluctance in situations requiring emotional openness, intimacy or sharing of personal information, appreciating that revealing this information makes them vulnerable to others. This type of behavior may also be due to the traditionalist upbringing that has long made topics that have privacy at their core treated as taboo subjects.

THE RESULTS OF THE VULNERABILITY AND RESILIENCE TO ADDICTIONS QUESTIONNAIRE LED TO THE FOLLOWING ASSESSMENTS

- Thrill-seeking, a preference for extreme or challenging, adrenaline-filled experiences, a desire to escape from the banality of existence, to avoid routine and the ordinary, less risky activities is a characteristic for more than half of those surveyed, with few stating that they feel comfortable in quiet, less stimulating activities, consciously avoiding situations that might be perceived as too intense or dangerous. Relative to the age segment investigated, we could not say that we are surprised by the results, especially as the scores obtained, although high in the case of some, are not taken to extremes. However, this indicates a level of risk, which implies caution and further careful monitoring of the behavior of these students, taking action to prevent risk situations and to raise awareness of the possible consequences on an individual and social level.
- Most of the time, however, subjects recognize that good impulse control means being able to resist temptation and act on the basis of rational analysis and a well-thought-out plan. Although there are times when they act spontaneously and have difficulty keeping promises because their decisions are

made based on feelings and desires on the spur of the moment, falling prey to outside influences and the desire for immediate gratification, these instances are, however, few in number.
- Resistance to stress and the ability to cope easily with tense or negative situations, dealing calmly and effectively with challenges are common to many respondents. We appreciate that this low vulnerability to physical or emotional discomfort, which many of the interviewees claim, is the fruit of the experience gained in the educational space and not only, where the rules are numerous and not always convergent with the desires, and the momentary interests of the pupils/students.
- For most subjects, talking openly about their emotions and feelings does not correlate with discomfort. They feel able to confront strong emotional feelings by understanding and exploring them in depth, thus demonstrating high self-esteem and good ownership of who they are and how they feel.
- On a declarative level, they prefer to face problems, to live in the present, actively engaging in resolving stressful situations rather than looking for ways to avoid or escape reality. They prefer a more direct and pragmatic approach to life, with an acceptance of reality as it is, with its good and bad, and have the ability to cope with everyday difficulties. They control their negative emotions well and rarely feel overwhelmed by everyday challenges, showing emotional and cognitive stability.
- In a few cases, however, overwhelmed by the multitude of problems and the inability to handle them, the subjects look for ways to escape from unpleasant situations, preferring to take refuge in the virtual world or use various methods to forget about everyday worries; this is the segment we consider to be most vulnerable to various more or less dangerous addictions.
- The focus on short-term goals, low motivation and lack of persistence in dealing with tasks, as mentioned above, are now demonstrated by the preference for immediate rewards, for activities that promise quick benefits. It is perhaps also the result of the "Live in the moment!" lifestyle, the speed of events in our lives, and of immaturity and superficiality.
- Most first year students report that they have a satisfying social life with many events and friends, have the ability to maintain diverse social connections and feel that there are people around them who are ready to help if needed, have a good social support network and feel supported by friends and family. Things are slightly different for students characterized by introversion, with a less active social life, fewer group activities to get involved in and who face some barriers in expressing themselves emotionally or in relating to others. With a less active social life and difficulty integrating into groups, they feel they have few people to turn to in times of need. In their case, they need to be made

aware of the support services available to them and to increase the number of extra-curricular activities in which they can be involved.
- Faced with many exams, some even difficult, which they have successfully completed, most respondents have a high level of self-efficacy and proactivity, manage their tasks and responsibilities effectively, and are confident in their ability to achieve their goals, showing realistic optimism about future achievements. We appreciate that the recent passing of the baccalaureate exam and the acquisition of student status have contributed significantly to building this winning attitude.
- Broadly speaking, this shows a good capacity for cognitive adaptability and openness to new experiences, an ease and preference for approaching problems and situations from different angles, a quick acceptance of different points of view, which demonstrates the ability to value diversity of opinion. There are also cases, however, where students show great resistance to change and tend to adhere to known and tested approaches, and find it harder to understand or accept different points of view. This is particularly the case for those who have a low level of academic performance, have a relatively poor cultural background and at the same time have a fear of failing, a fear of stepping out of their comfort zone, a fear of disappointing.

The correlated analysis of the results obtained from the two questionnaires shows that, at the level of the Petroleum Gas University of Ploiesti, students have a low level of vulnerability, and the dimensions that this vulnerability covers are not amongst the most dangerous. The fact that it exists, however, should push us to be cautious, to take responsibility, to be strongly aware of the risks that arise from it and, consequently, to develop strategies that help cultivate and increase well-being, to eliminate uncertainty and insecurity, and to identify sources of support and make the most of them.

SOME RECOMMENDATIONS ON HOW TO TRANSFORM THE ACADEMIC ENVIRONMENT INTO AN ENVIRONMENT THAT FOSTERS WELLNESS

Universities today are increasingly concerned with providing their beneficiaries with support and care services that are both effective and accessible, mobilizing adequate resources while intervening proactively. In recent years, "many institutions have begun to develop strategies that take into account the experience of all those involved, thus creating effective, comprehensive and accessible student support services" (Repenser le bien-être dans l'enseignement supérieur / Rethinking well-being in higher education, https://www.salesforce.org/wp-content/uploads/2022/08/edu-guide-rethinking-wellbeing-in-higher-education-fnl-fr-071822.pdf).

In this sense, the university's concerns focus on the prevention of crisis situations and risky behaviors, by empowering students to be aware of problems and find the necessary support, but especially in developing resilience over the course of their academic life. The achievement of these objectives makes it necessary to think about, design and implement spaces dedicated to coaching activities, use tools (standardized or not) to assess vulnerability and mental health, develop strength within the student community and facilitate a valuable transfer of information to produce a real enrichment of problem-solving strategies, and promote a culture of well-being.

Providing virtual counselling services, building online communities to bring together those going through more difficult times, conducting surveys on student well-being may be just some of the strategies universities can use to maintain or restore well-being in students' lives.

However, providing support services is not enough, and must be coupled with actions to promote and clarify the conditions under which they can be accessed, and to promote mental health; to stimulate cooperation between community organizations and online services.

There is also a need for mental health awareness campaigns (to help students recognize mental health problems and intervene promptly when they occur); to reduce mental health stigma; to prioritize psychological well-being alongside academic success; to empower students in positive self-care strategies, stress and anxiety management.

Promoting a caring and inclusive campus works as one of the most effective strategies through which students can be helped to achieve their educational goals. Thus, creating welcoming spaces designed for learning, but more importantly, meeting, socializing and building strong connections among members of the academic community; adapting the educational pathway by taking into account the obstacles students face; developing and implementing universal design principles in the classroom where appropriate and possible, these are all solutions to increase well-being.

Of particular importance to the equitable promotion of student health and well-being is the creation of an educational environment in which individual differences are recognized, respected and encouraged. In order to make this environment as free as possible from bullying, subjectivism, discrimination and exclusion, it is imperative to implement culturally sensitive instructional materials for all members of the community, but especially for mental health providers; to engage student support staff to help students who are in a state of heightened vulnerability with implications across multiple levels of existence; and to design educational resources that help both students and professors address systemic barriers.

Strengthening institutional commitment and promoting shared responsibility for students' mental health are thus the pillars around which all actions that encourage the active presence of student representatives with diverse needs, backgrounds and experiences in institutional decisions are built at higher education level. In this sense, in order to truly speak of an academic empowerment that can significantly reduce vulnerability, a call to action is needed to all those who want to play an active role in promoting student well-being, and promoting policies of equity, diversity and inclusion.

CONCLUSION

Mental health and equilibrium are fundamental aspects of student life and have a significant impact on personal, social and professional success. Maintaining good mental health involves managing emotions and stress as well as increasing resilience.

For a student, equilibrium means having time not only for study, but also for rest, relaxation and recreation. Harmony between academic and social life is essential, as too much stress and pressure can lead to burnout, anxiety or depression.

That's why universities and educational institutions should provide resources and support to improve students' mental health. Counselling services, mental health promotion programs and mindfulness or meditation activities can be of great help to students in managing the various challenges they face.

In conclusion, maintaining good mental health and equilibrium are essential factors for students' academic and personal success. Investing in one's own mental health and finding a balance between the different aspects of student life can have a positive impact in the long term.

REFERENCES

Balica, M. (2021). *Qu'est-ce que le bien-être? Document stratégique*. International Baccalaureate Organization.

Bronfenbrenner, U. (1992). Ecological systems theory. In VASTA, R. (sous la direction de). *Six Theories of Child Development: Revised Formulations and Current Issues*. Londres, Royaume-Uni: Jessica Kingsley Publishers.

Brown, B. (2013). *The Power of Vulnerability: Teachings on Authenticity, Connection and Courage*. Sounds True Publisher.

Castel, R. (1991). De l'indigence à l'exclusion, la désaffiliation. Précarité du travail et vulnérabilité relationnelle. In *Donzelot J (dir.), Face à l'exclusion. Le modèle français*. Éditions Esprit.

Fayaz, A. P., Aasim Ur, R. G., & Danishwar, R. D. (2024). Substance use in university students: a comprehensive examination of its effects on academic achievement and psychological well-being. In: *Social Work in Mental Health, 22*(3). https://www.tandfonline.com/doi/full/10.1080/15332985.2024.2306935

Ghadiri, F., Sabouri Moghadam, H., & Babapur Kheiradin, J. (2014). *Prediction of Vulnerability to Addiction on the Basis of Psychosocial Stressors*. In: *Practice of Clinical Psychology, 2*(4), 271-276. https://jesp.upg-ploiesti.ro/index.php?option=com_phocadownload&view=file&id=659:the-transition-to-the-academic-environment-between-difficulties-and-coping-strategies&Itemid=16

Martuccelli, D. (2014). La vulnérabilité, un nouveau paradigme? In *Axelle Brodiez, Christian Laval, Bertrand Ravon. Vulnérabilités sanitaires et sociales*. Presses Universitaires de Rennes.

Mill, J. (1988). *L'Utilitarisme, 2*. Flammarion.

Ministry of Internal Affairs, National Antidrug Agency. (2019). *Studiul în şcoli privind consumul de alcool, tutun şi droguri ilicite în România – ESPAD 2019*

Petrescu, C., Băncilă, S. P., Suciu, O., Vlaicu, B., & Doroftei, S. (2004). *Profile psihologice şi comportamente cu risc întâlnite la tineri*. In: *Revista de Igienă şi Sănătate Publică, 54*(3).

Prinsloo, P., & Slade, S. (2016). Student vulnerability, agency, and learning analytics: An exploration. *Journal of Learning Analytics*, 3(1), 159–182. 10.18608/jla.2016.31.10

Safta, C. G., & Suditu, M. (2022) The transition to the academic environment: between difficulties and coping strategies. In: *Journal of Educational Sciences and Psychology, 11*(73). 10.51865/JESP.2022.2.03

Seligman, M. E. (2011). Flourish: A visionary new understanding of happiness and well-being. New York, États-Unis: Free Press.

Soulet, M. H. (2005). Reconsidérer la vulnérabilité. In *Empan 2005/4* (no 60). Éditions Érès https://www.cairn.info/revue-empan-2005-4-page-24.htm

Suditu, M., & Safta, C. G. (2023). Adapting to the Academic Environment: A Prerequisite for Academic Success. In *Handbook of Research on Coping Mechanisms for First-Year Students Transitioning to Higher Education*. IGI Global Publishing.

Thomas, H. (2010). *Les vulnérables*. Éditions du Croquant.

Chapter 12
Transition From Virtual to Reality in Post-Pandemic Academic Environment:
Challenges of Students' Well-Being

N. Elangovan
https://orcid.org/0000-0002-4551-6081
Christ University, India

E. Sundaravel
Christ University, India

ABSTRACT

The COVID-19 pandemic triggered a significant shift in academic settings. Post-pandemic normality prompted a return to traditional face-to-face classrooms from virtual and hybrid models. This chapter explores the multifaceted challenges students encounter during this transition, drawing on existing literature and empirical observations. Findings highlight the complexities of readjusting to classroom environments, managing academic expectations, and fostering peer interactions. Moreover, it emphasizes the critical need to address mental health concerns amid performance pressures. Practical implications underscore the importance of resilience, adaptability, and community support in empowering students. It calls for educational institutions to prioritize student well-being and academic success through robust support systems and open discourse on mental health. This chapter contributes to understanding the evolving academic landscape, offering insights for stakeholders to develop targeted interventions and support mechanisms for successful transitions in the post-pandemic era.

DOI: 10.4018/979-8-3693-4417-0.ch012

INTRODUCTION

The global outbreak of COVID-19 led to disruptions in education, prompting a transition from traditional classroom settings to remote and blended learning approaches. With the return to normal, students and schools are facing daunting obstacles as they navigate the shift to physical learning environments (Rapanta et al., 2021). At the heart of this transition lies the emotional spectrum experienced by students, which encompasses a mix of excitement, apprehension, and uncertainty. Identifying the lingering effects and challenges students face in the post-pandemic academic environment is crucial (Mesmar & Badran, 2022). Many students initially anticipated a return to the familiarity of classroom settings with a sense of excitement and the prospect of reinvigorated learning experiences. However, underlying this optimism is a palpable undercurrent of apprehension and uncertainty. The abrupt shift to remote and hybrid learning during the pandemic disrupted established routines, altered social dynamics, and fundamentally transformed the academic experience for students worldwide (Turnbull et al., 2021).

One of the most significant challenges students face in the post-pandemic academic environment is reconciling past experiences with the uncertainties of the present. The prolonged period of remote learning exacerbated existing inequities, particularly concerning the digital divide. Disparities in access to technology and educational resources widened, further marginalizing already vulnerable student populations. As students return to physical classrooms, they must navigate the complexities of readjusting to traditional academic expectations and routines after adapting to the flexibility of remote instruction (Siegel et al., 2021).

The transition back to face-to-face learning necessitates a recalibration of academic expectations and social dynamics. Students must navigate the nuances of interpersonal interactions, peer relationships, and classroom etiquette, all while managing heightened academic expectations (Stoian et al., 2022). Moreover, the continued integration of technology in post-pandemic academic environments poses additional challenges as students grapple with barriers to reliable internet connectivity, access to essential hardware and software, and digital literacy skills. Addressing these inequities requires concerted efforts to bridge the digital divide and cultivate inclusive learning environments that empower all students to thrive. Educational institutions and policymakers must prioritize initiatives aimed at expanding access to technology, providing digital literacy training, and fostering equitable distribution of educational resources (Haleem et al., 2022).

The pandemic has taken a toll on students' mental health and well-being, amplifying feelings of isolation, anxiety, and stress. The disruption of social networks, loss of traditional support systems, and societal stressors have contributed to emotional exhaustion and burnout among students. As they navigate the complexities of the post-pandemic academic environment, students require comprehensive support systems, access to mental health resources, and opportunities for self-care and resilience-building to foster emotional well-being and cultivate a sense of belonging within their academic communities (Kiss et al., 2022).

For educators, the transition signifies not only a return to familiar pedagogical practices but also an opportunity to integrate insights and innovations cultivated during the pandemic. The shift back to in-person learning prompts a reevaluation of traditional pedagogical practices and instructional methodologies. Educators must adapt to evolving student needs and preferences by integrating technology, exploring innovative teaching modalities, and emphasizing student-centered approaches to promote engagement, collaboration, and enhanced learning outcomes within the post-pandemic academic environment (Ratten, 2023).

The integration of technology, asynchronous learning tools, and hybrid teaching methodologies underscores the importance of flexibility and agility in catering to diverse learning needs. Moreover, prioritizing holistic student well-being becomes imperative as the pandemic highlighted the interconnectedness of mental health, emotional resilience, and academic success. Providing access to mental health resources, fostering a culture of empathy and support, and promoting open dialogue about emotional well-being are paramount in this context. Educators must prioritize opportunities for students to engage in meaningful discussions, express their concerns, and seek support when needed (Barron et al., 2021).

The chapter's focus on students' perspectives and experiences in face-to-face classrooms serves as a foundational framework for understanding the intricacies and dynamics of the post-pandemic academic environment. By centering students' experiences, concerns, and aspirations, the chapter aims to foster empathy, understanding, and collaboration among educators, administrators, and students themselves. Ultimately, by foregrounding students' perspectives, the chapter seeks to cultivate a deeper appreciation for the complexities inherent in the post-pandemic academic landscape and empower stakeholders to navigate the transition back to in-person learning effectively. It underscores the importance of proactive planning, empathetic communication, and comprehensive support systems in fostering student well-being and academic success in the post-pandemic era.

LITERATURE BACKGROUND

The COVID-19 pandemic has significantly impacted the well-being of students in the academic environment, and it is essential to understand the challenges they face in the post-pandemic era. This literature review aims to synthesize and integrate the research findings on the challenges of students' well-being in the post-pandemic academic environment.

CHALLENGES DURING PANDEMIC

The global COVID-19 pandemic has disrupted various aspects of our lives, including education. Educators and students at all levels have had to quickly adapt to the shift from traditional face-to-face instruction to online learning (Karakose et al., 2021). This transition to emergency remote teaching and learning has presented numerous challenges for both teachers and students. As a result, the delivery of education has been permanently altered, with online education becoming a prominent alternative mode of learning (Sharaievska et al., 2022). Teachers and students have faced various challenges during the transition to remote teaching and learning, including limited access to resources, difficulties maintaining engagement and connection, and the need for increased technological proficiency (Xie et al., 2021).

Parents have also had to juggle their own work responsibilities while supporting their children's education from home. In addition to the challenges faced, the shift to online education has also brought about some positive changes. Many educators have found innovative ways to deliver content and engage students in virtual classrooms. The use of technology in education has been accelerated, leading to the development of new digital teaching tools and platforms. As the academic community continues to navigate this new landscape, it is important to consider the long-term implications of these changes and how they will shape the future of education. Adapting to this shift will require ongoing support for educators, students, and families as they embrace the opportunities and address the challenges of online learning. It is crucial to continue exploring best practices for effective online teaching and learning, as well as to prioritize equitable access to education for all students, regardless of their circumstances (Sun & Chen, 2016; Xie et al., 2021).

Bowman (2010) explored the development of psychological well-being among first-year college students. While not specific to the post-pandemic era, the study provided valuable insights into the factors that influence students' well-being during their transition to higher education. Understanding the developmental aspects of well-being can contribute to addressing challenges in the post-pandemic academic environment.

Prowse et al. (2021) investigated gender differences in stress and mental health among university students during the COVID-19 pandemic. The study highlighted the unique challenges faced by male and female students, shedding light on the intersection of gender and well-being in the academic context. This research is pertinent to understanding the nuanced impact of the pandemic on students' well-being and can inform targeted interventions in the post-pandemic academic environment.

POST-PANDEMIC ENVIRONMENT

In response to the global COVID-19 pandemic, educational institutions have shifted to virtual and hybrid models of instruction. This transition brought significant changes to the traditional face-to-face classroom model (Gupta & Yadav, 2023). As the situation improved and restrictions began to ease, schools and universities faced the complex task of transitioning back to traditional face-to-face classrooms. This transition required careful planning and coordination to ensure the safety and well-being of students, teachers, and staff.

One of the key considerations in the transition back to traditional classrooms is the implementation of health and safety protocols. Schools will need to establish guidelines for social distancing, mask-wearing, and sanitization to create a safe learning environment. Additionally, implementing screening measures and vaccination policies may be necessary to minimize the risk of COVID-19 transmission within the school community (Lordan et al., 2021).

Another crucial aspect of the transition is addressing the academic and emotional needs of students. Educators and administrators will need to provide support for students who may have faced challenges during the period of remote and hybrid learning. This could involve targeted academic interventions, mental health resources, and counseling services to help students readjust to in-person learning (Watson et al., 2022).

Additionally, exploring the role of technology in supporting students' mental health and well-being in the post-pandemic era is essential (Sato et al., 2024). Furthermore, there is a need for research that addresses the intersectionality of students' identities, such as race, gender, and socioeconomic status, in understanding and addressing well-being challenges in the post-pandemic academic environment (Blewett & Ebben, 2022). By addressing these knowledge gaps, future research can contribute to the development of evidence-based interventions and support systems to promote students' well-being in the post-pandemic academic environment (Ni & Jia, 2023).

The return to in-person learning brings about a mix of excitement, apprehension, and hope for a sense of normalcy. As schools reopen their doors and students file back into classrooms, one of the key considerations is the impact on student learning and well-being. While virtual and hybrid models offered flexibility and new opportunities for personalized learning, they also highlighted disparities in access to technology and resources among students. As educational institutions transition back to traditional classrooms, it is crucial to address these inequities and ensure that all students have the support they need to thrive academically (Ferren, 2021). The return to face-to-face learning presents an opportunity to reevaluate the role of technology in education. While digital tools have become essential during the pandemic, there is a growing recognition of the importance of human connection and social interaction in the learning process. Teachers and students alike are eager to rebuild relationships, foster collaboration, and create a sense of community that may have been lacking in virtual settings (Jia et al., 2022).

However, the transition back to traditional classrooms is not without its challenges. Teachers must adapt their instructional practices to meet the diverse needs of students who have experienced varying levels of academic progress during remote learning. School administrators must also consider the logistical aspects of reopening, such as ensuring a safe learning environment, implementing health protocols, and addressing concerns about student and staff well-being (Stoian et al., 2022).

Returning to the classroom after a prolonged period of remote learning can be daunting for students. The abrupt shift from the comfort and flexibility of virtual learning to the structured environment of a classroom can lead to various challenges. Research by Mali and Lim (2021) highlights feelings of anxiety and social awkwardness as common experiences among students readjusting to face-to-face learning. Moreover, students may struggle with attention span and concentration after being accustomed to the distractions present in home environments. These challenges necessitate a supportive transition process that acknowledges and addresses students' emotional and social needs (Jamil et al., 2023).

The pandemic has disrupted traditional academic routines, leading to uncertainties regarding academic expectations post-pandemic. Educators face the challenge of balancing the need to cover missed content with recognizing the emotional toll the pandemic has taken on students. This balancing act requires a nuanced approach to curriculum planning and assessment. Research by Dayagbil et al. (2021) emphasizes the importance of flexible teaching strategies that accommodate diverse learning paces and styles. Additionally, educators must provide students with clear guidance on academic goals and expectations, helping them regain confidence in their academic abilities.

Peer interactions play a crucial role in students' social and emotional development, yet transitioning back to traditional classrooms poses challenges in fostering meaningful peer connections. Social distancing measures and lingering concerns about health and safety may inhibit students' willingness to engage in social activities (Jessiman et al., 2022). Moreover, the reliance on digital communication during remote learning may have affected students' interpersonal skills and communication abilities (Peñalver & Laborda, 2021). Educators must proactively create opportunities for peer interactions through collaborative learning activities, group projects, and extracurricular opportunities. Building a supportive classroom community where students feel valued and connected is essential for promoting positive peer relationships.

Singh et al. (2021) examined the hybrid and blended learning approach as a response to the COVID-19 pandemic. The study focused on the post-vaccine and post-pandemic world, highlighting the importance of adapting to new learning models. The findings emphasized the need for a flexible and adaptive educational system to support students' well-being in the post-pandemic academic environment.

Ladson-Billings (2021) discussed post-pandemic pedagogy to preserve cultural equity and excellence in education. The article emphasized the need for a "hard reset" in the academic environment and proposed strategies to support students from diverse cultural backgrounds. This perspective is crucial for addressing the broader societal impact of the pandemic on students' well-being and academic experiences.

WELL-BEING OF STUDENTS

As students navigate the post-pandemic academic environment, mental health concerns have come to the forefront as a critical issue. Much literature delves into the urgent need to address mental health concerns, the impact of performance pressures on students' well-being, and potential strategies for supporting students' mental health needs.

The post-pandemic academic environment presents unique challenges that exacerbate existing mental health concerns among students. Research by Aljaberi et al. (2023) underscores the increased prevalence of anxiety, depression, and stress among students as they grapple with uncertainties surrounding academic performance, social interactions, and future prospects. The disruption caused by the pandemic has heightened feelings of isolation and loneliness, further impacting students' mental well-being (Bell et al., 2023). Additionally, the transition back to in-person learning may trigger adjustment difficulties and exacerbate pre-existing mental health conditions (Lyons et al., 2023). Addressing these mental health concerns is paramount to ensuring students' overall well-being and academic success.

Performance pressures in the academic environment contribute significantly to students' mental health challenges. The expectation to excel academically, coupled with competition and comparison with peers, can lead to heightened stress and anxiety (Jiang et al., 2022). There is a detrimental effect of excessive academic pressure on students' self-esteem and confidence. Moreover, the emphasis on standardized testing and grades as measures of success further exacerbates performance-related stressors (Goyer et al., 2022). The cumulative impact of these pressures can impede students' ability to cope effectively and negatively affect their mental health and academic outcomes.

Supporting students' mental health needs requires a multifaceted approach that addresses both individual and systemic factors. Providing access to mental health resources and support services is essential for students experiencing psychological distress (Margrove et al., 2014). Introducing initiatives such as mental health awareness campaigns, peer support groups, and counseling services can help reduce stigma and encourage help-seeking behaviors (Ahorsu et al., 2021). Additionally, integrating social-emotional learning (SEL) programs into the curriculum can equip students with coping strategies and resilience skills to navigate academic and personal challenges (Cahill & Dadvand, 2020). Furthermore, fostering a culture of care and empathy within the academic community promotes a supportive environment where students feel valued and understood (Eden et al., 2024).

Resilience, adaptability, and community support are integral components of fostering student well-being. Building resilience is important in helping students navigate challenges and setbacks effectively. By cultivating resilience skills such as problem-solving, optimism, and emotional regulation, educators empower students to bounce back from adversity and thrive in the face of challenges (Sato et al., 2024). Additionally, promoting adaptability is essential in preparing students for the dynamic nature of the modern world. Providing opportunities for experiential learning, flexibility in curriculum delivery, and exposure to diverse perspectives fosters adaptability skills crucial for success in academic and personal endeavors. Furthermore, fostering a sense of community support promotes a supportive environment where students feel connected, valued, and empowered to seek help when needed. Building strong relationships among students, educators, and the broader community fosters a sense of belonging and enhances overall well-being (Crawford et al., 2024)

Educational institutions must prioritize student well-being to ensure holistic development and academic success. Studies show the interconnectedness between student well-being and academic achievement, emphasizing the need for a balanced approach that addresses both academic and socio-emotional needs. By recognizing the impact of mental health on learning outcomes, educational institutions can create policies and practices that prioritize student well-being. This includes allocating resources for mental health services, implementing wellness initiatives, and integrating social-emotional learning into the curriculum. Moreover, fostering a culture of care and empathy within the educational community promotes a supportive environment where students feel valued and supported in their academic journey (Willis, 2024).

ROLE OF STAKEHOLDERS

In the post-pandemic academic environment, addressing student challenges and enhancing well-being requires coordinated efforts from multiple stakeholders. By leveraging their respective roles and expertise, educators, administrators, parents, policymakers, and community organizations can create a supportive ecosystem that fosters student success and well-being. Moving forward, collaborative partnerships and evidence-based interventions are essential in addressing the diverse needs of students and promoting a culture of care within educational settings.

Academics are driven by PCO (political, cultural, and organizational) factors and engage in career self-management activities to enhance social and human capital (Nam & Bai, 2023). Academic leaders and policy decision-makers must recognize potential risk factors and incidents in order to prevent crises and effectively respond to emergencies. One important aspect highlighted in the literature is the need for various stakeholders, including administrators, staff members, teachers, parents, learners, and government officials, to adapt to the abrupt changes and disruptive transformations caused by emergencies (Okoli et al., 2023). The literature emphasizes the importance of creating a secure and safe learning environment through policy development. This includes revisiting frameworks that enable administrators to devise policies that prioritize safety and security. Additionally, the literature suggests the integration of crisis-resilient pedagogy, which incorporates attributes such as adaptability, creativity, connectivity, diversity, and endurance into pedagogical components for effective teaching and learning. Another significant aspect discussed in the literature is the role of crisis communication strategies in managing post-crisis academic environments (Chow et al., 2020).

Educators play a pivotal role in supporting students' academic and socio-emotional needs. By creating inclusive learning spaces, implementing trauma-informed teaching strategies, and providing personalized support, educators can mitigate the impact of the pandemic on students' well-being. Moreover, educators can integrate social-emotional learning (SEL) into the curriculum to promote self-awareness, relationship skills, and responsible decision-making among students (Kelly et al., 2023; Perez & Bahamon Muneton, 2023).

Administrators hold the responsibility of creating policies and allocating resources to support student well-being at the institutional level. By prioritizing student well-being in strategic planning and decision-making, administrators can create a supportive infrastructure that addresses students' academic, emotional, and social needs. Additionally, administrators can collaborate with educators and community stakeholders to implement comprehensive support systems and initiatives (Montemurro et al., 2023).

Parental involvement is crucial in promoting student well-being and academic success. Studies show the impact of parental support and involvement on students' mental health and resilience. By fostering open communication, providing emotional support, and advocating for their children's needs, parents can create a supportive home environment that complements the efforts of educators and administrators. Moreover, parents can collaborate with schools to access resources and participate in workshops or training sessions on topics related to student well-being (Jeynes, 2024; Novianti & Garzia, 2020; Yang et al., 2023).

Policymakers play a significant role in shaping the educational landscape and allocating resources to support student well-being. There is an emphasis on the importance of policy initiatives that prioritize mental health services, counseling, and wellness programs in schools. By advocating for funding, legislation, and policy reforms that support student well-being, policymakers can create an enabling environment for educators and administrators to implement effective interventions. Additionally, policymakers can collaborate with stakeholders to develop evidence-based strategies and initiatives that address the diverse needs of students in the post-pandemic academic environment (CBSE, 2013; UNICEF et al., 2022; Wiedermann et al., 2023).

Community organizations serve as valuable partners in addressing student challenges and promoting well-being. Community-based initiatives provide additional support and resources to students and families. By collaborating with schools, community organizations can offer extracurricular activities, mentorship programs, and access to social services that enhance students' academic, emotional, and social development. Moreover, community organizations can facilitate partnerships between schools, families, and local stakeholders to create a holistic support network for students (Sepanik & Brown, 2021).

CHALLENGES FACED BY STUDENTS

Central to understanding the intricacies and dynamics of the post-pandemic academic environment is the focus on students' perspectives and experiences in face-to-face classrooms. Figure 1 categorizes various challenges.

Figure 1. Post-Pandemic academic challenges

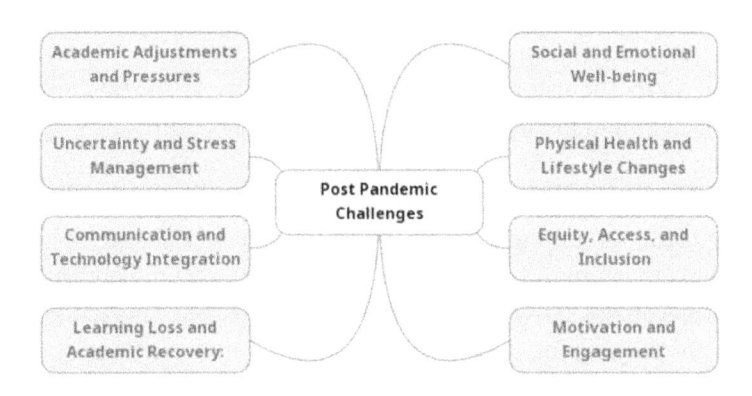

```
Academic Adjustments          Social and Emotional
   and Pressures                  Well-being

Uncertainty and Stress        Physical Health and
    Management                 Lifestyle Changes
                Post Pandemic
                  Challenges
Communication and             Equity, Access, and
Technology Integration             Inclusion

 Learning Loss and             Motivation and
 Academic Recovery:              Engagement
```

Social and Emotional Well-being: The social and emotional well-being of students post-pandemic is a critical aspect of their overall adjustment and success as they transition back to in-person learning environments. This transition presents a multifaceted challenge, encompassing various emotional and social dynamics that require careful consideration and support from educators and institutions. One of the primary challenges students face is re-establishing face-to-face social interactions after an extended period of virtual communication. For many, this adjustment may evoke feelings of anxiety, discomfort, or awkwardness as they navigate physical proximity and social cues they may have become unaccustomed to during remote learning. Students may struggle to rebuild interpersonal connections, form new friendships, and participate in group activities, particularly if they experience social isolation during the pandemic.

Managing mental health concerns exacerbated by the pandemic adds another layer of challenge. Students may be grappling with increased levels of stress, anxiety, depression, or trauma resulting from various factors such as academic pressures, family dynamics, or personal losses experienced during the pandemic. These mental health challenges can significantly impact students' ability to engage in learning and maintain emotional well-being. Concerns about health risks associated with returning to school may exacerbate students' anxiety and emotional distress. Fear of contracting or spreading the virus, coupled with uncertainties about safety protocols and vaccination status, may contribute to heightened levels of stress and apprehension among students and their families.

Academic Adjustments and Pressures: Post-pandemic, students are confronted with a myriad of academic adjustments and pressures as they navigate the transition back to traditional learning environments. Adapting to new academic expectations represents a significant challenge, particularly for those who have become accustomed to different instructional methods during virtual learning. The shift from remote or hybrid models to face-to-face instruction necessitates a reorientation towards traditional classroom dynamics, including direct interaction with instructors, peer collaboration, and participatory learning activities. For some students, this adjustment may entail overcoming feelings of disorientation or uncertainty as they recalibrate their learning strategies and study habits to align with in-person instruction. Managing time effectively within structured schedules poses another hurdle for students. The flexible nature of remote learning allowed for greater autonomy in managing one's time, but the return to structured class timetables requires students to readjust their time management skills and organizational strategies. This transition may be particularly challenging for students who thrive in remote settings but struggle to adapt to the rigidity of traditional classroom routines.

The disparities in academic resources and support services exacerbated by the pandemic amplify the challenges students face. Students from marginalized or underprivileged backgrounds may encounter unequal access to essential tools, technology, or academic assistance, further hindering their ability to succeed academically. Addressing these inequities requires a concerted effort to provide additional support and resources to students who need them most. This ensures that all students have equal opportunities to thrive in the post-pandemic academic landscape. The return to in-person learning often brings heightened academic pressures, including the need to catch up on missed coursework, adjust to the pace of face-to-face instruction, and meet academic expectations set by instructors and institutions. Balancing these demands alongside other stressors, such as personal responsibilities or extracurricular commitments, can be overwhelming for students, contributing to feelings of anxiety or burnout.

Learning Loss and Academic Recovery: Learning loss and academic recovery are pressing issues facing students in the wake of the COVID-19 pandemic, as disruptions to traditional learning environments have led to significant setbacks for many individuals. Addressing these challenges requires a multifaceted approach that encompasses targeted interventions, remedial programs, and robust academic support systems. To effectively address learning loss, educators must first identify areas of academic weakness and assess the extent of students' learning gaps. This may involve diagnostic assessments, formative evaluations, and ongoing monitoring of student progress to pinpoint specific areas where additional support is needed. Once identified, educators can tailor instruction to meet the diverse learning needs of students, providing differentiated learning opportunities and personalized interventions to address areas of weakness effectively.

Implementing evidence-based practices is essential for accelerating learning progress and promoting academic recovery. This may include incorporating research-backed instructional strategies, utilizing technology-enhanced learning tools, and offering extended learning opportunities such as after-school programs, tutoring, or academic enrichment activities. By leveraging proven methods and resources, educators can help students regain lost ground and make meaningful strides toward academic proficiency. Moreover, supporting students' socio-emotional well-being is crucial for facilitating effective academic recovery efforts. The emotional toll of the pandemic may have impacted students' motivation, confidence, and resilience, making it essential to prioritize mental health and social-emotional learning initiatives alongside academic interventions. Creating a positive and nurturing learning environment where students feel supported, valued, and empowered to succeed is essential for fostering academic resilience and promoting holistic student development.

Physical Health and Lifestyle Changes: The transition back to in-person learning poses significant challenges for students' physical health and lifestyle habits, particularly after extended periods of remote learning characterized by sedentary behaviors. Students must readjust to more active lifestyles, reintegrating physical activity into their daily routines. This adjustment can be challenging as they become accustomed to the convenience of remote learning, where physical movement may have been limited. During virtual learning, prolonged screen time and reduced physical activity may have contributed to various physical health issues, including poor posture, eye strain, and musculoskeletal discomfort. Addressing these challenges requires a concerted effort to promote physical activity, encourage breaks from screen time, and provide resources for students to prioritize their physical well-being.

Educational institutions can play a pivotal role in supporting students' physical health by implementing strategies to incorporate movement into the school day. This may involve integrating physical activity breaks, outdoor recess periods, or structured exercise programs into the curriculum. Additionally, fostering a culture of wellness within the school community can help students develop healthy habits and attitudes toward physical activity. Providing access to resources such as ergonomic seating, standing desks, and eye care initiatives can also mitigate the negative effects of prolonged screen time and promote better posture and eye health among students. Moreover, educating students about the importance of maintaining a balanced lifestyle that includes regular physical activity, proper nutrition, and adequate sleep can empower them to make healthier choices in their daily lives.

Uncertainty and Stress Management: Navigating uncertainty and managing stress post-pandemic presents formidable challenges for students as they grapple with the unknowns of the future. The lingering unpredictability surrounding the pandemic, including the potential for outbreaks and shifting public health guidelines, adds layers of stress and anxiety to students' lives. Moreover, uncertainty regarding future academic plans, career prospects, and personal safety further intensifies these challenges, leaving students feeling overwhelmed and unsettled. Coping with heightened stress and anxiety necessitates effective stress management techniques and robust mental health support systems. However, the demand for such resources may surpass available capacities, exacerbating feelings of uncertainty and distress among students. This underscores the critical importance of fostering resilience and providing students with tools to navigate uncertainty and manage stress effectively in the post-pandemic era.

Building a supportive community within educational institutions is crucial for supporting students' mental well-being. By fostering connections among peers, faculty, and support staff, students can feel a sense of belonging and access valuable social support networks. Additionally, promoting open dialogue about mental health encourages students to seek help when needed and reduces the stigma surrounding mental illness. Equipping students with coping mechanisms and resilience-building strategies is essential for navigating the challenges of uncertainty and stress. This may involve teaching mindfulness techniques, promoting healthy lifestyle habits, and providing access to mental health resources such as counseling services or support groups. By empowering students with the tools and support they need to manage stress effectively, educational institutions can help them thrive in the face of ongoing uncertainty and adversity.

Equity, Access, and Inclusion: Addressing equity, access, and inclusion within educational settings remains a critical challenge post-pandemic. Disparities in access to resources, technology, and support services persist, disproportionately impacting marginalized communities and widening existing gaps in educational attainment. These disparities not only hinder students' academic success but also perpetuate systemic inequalities in education. Promoting equity and inclusion within educational settings requires proactive measures to create an environment where all students feel valued, respected, and supported. This involves addressing systemic barriers such as socioeconomic status, race, ethnicity, gender identity, and disability that impede students' access to educational opportunities. Educational institutions must prioritize dismantling these barriers through targeted interventions and policy reforms.

Implementing inclusive policies and practices is essential for fostering a sense of belonging and ensuring that every student has equitable access to educational resources and opportunities. This may include providing additional support for marginalized groups, such as English language learners, students with disabilities, or those from low-income backgrounds. Moreover, fostering a culture of diversity and inclusion within schools promotes empathy, understanding, and mutual respect among students and staff. Also, educational institutions must prioritize the provision of support services that address the diverse needs of all students. This includes access to mental health resources, academic tutoring, counseling services, and assistance with technology and internet connectivity. By providing comprehensive support systems, schools can mitigate the impact of systemic inequalities and empower all students to thrive academically and socially.

Communication and Technology Integration: Post-pandemic, students encounter the challenge of adapting to diverse communication modes in traditional classrooms while effectively integrating technology. Having heavily relied on digital platforms for communication during remote learning, students must now readjust to in-person interactions, including verbal communication and nonverbal cues. This transition necessitates refining interpersonal skills and becoming comfortable expressing themselves face-to-face. Also, integrating technology into face-to-face learning environments presents its own challenges. Ensuring access to necessary technology, troubleshooting technical issues, and promoting digital literacy skills among students are paramount. Proficiency in navigating digital tools and discerning credible information online has become increasingly important in today's technology-driven world.

Addressing these challenges requires educators to create a balanced learning environment that incorporates both traditional and digital communication methods. This involves providing opportunities for students to practice verbal communication, active listening, and nonverbal communication skills in class. Additionally, educators should offer training and support to enhance students' digital literacy, teaching them how to effectively use technology for learning purposes and critically evaluate online information. In addition, fostering a culture of collaboration and peer learning can facilitate students' adaptation to diverse communication modes. Encouraging group discussions, collaborative projects, and peer feedback sessions promotes active engagement and helps students develop essential communication skills in both face-to-face and digital contexts.

Motivation and Engagement: Post-pandemic, sustaining motivation and engagement in traditional classrooms presents a significant challenge, particularly for students accustomed to the autonomy and novelty of remote learning. The transition from the flexibility and personalized learning experiences of virtual environments to the structured nature of face-to-face classrooms can lead to a loss of motivation for some students. Furthermore, the absence of technological tools and interactive features present in virtual learning environments may further contribute to decreased engagement. To address these challenges, educators must find innovative ways to keep students engaged and motivated in face-to-face settings. This may involve incorporating interactive teaching methods, such as group discussions, hands-on activities, and experiential learning opportunities. Providing opportunities for student collaboration and participation can also enhance engagement by allowing students to actively contribute to the learning process and interact with their peers.

Integrating real-world applications into the curriculum can make learning more relevant and meaningful for students, increasing their motivation to participate and succeed. By connecting classroom content to authentic, real-life scenarios, educators can help students see the practical applications of their learning and understand its relevance beyond the classroom walls. Also, building a supportive and inclusive classroom environment is essential for fostering motivation and engagement post-pandemic. When students feel valued, respected, and empowered to take ownership of their learning, they are more likely to be motivated and engaged in the learning process. Creating a positive classroom culture where students feel comfortable expressing themselves, asking questions, and taking risks can contribute to a more enriching and fulfilling educational experience for all.

WELL-BEING IN FACE-TO-FACE SETTINGS

Promoting Social and Emotional Learning (SEL) is indispensable for nurturing students' overall well-being and academic success, especially in the post-pandemic educational landscape. Schools play a pivotal role in implementing SEL programs and curricula tailored to support students' social and emotional development. These programs equip students with essential skills such as self-awareness, self-management, social awareness, relationship-building, and responsible decision-making, which are crucial for navigating various aspects of life effectively. Incorporating SEL into the curriculum provides students with structured opportunities to develop these skills in a supportive and nurturing environment. By engaging in SEL activities, students learn to recognize and manage their emotions, develop empathy and understanding for others, and build healthy relationships. Moreover, SEL programs foster a sense of belonging and connectedness within the school community, promoting a positive school climate conducive to learning and personal growth.

Peer interactions, group discussions, and collaborative learning experiences are integral components of SEL implementation in schools. These activities provide students with opportunities to practice social skills, communicate effectively, resolve conflicts, and work collaboratively with their peers. By engaging in collaborative activities, students develop essential interpersonal skills that are essential for success not only in academic settings but also in real-world contexts. In addition, offering counseling services and mental health resources is crucial for supporting students' emotional well-being. Access to trained counselors and mental health professionals ensures that students receive the support they need to navigate challenges, manage stress, and develop effective coping strategies. By prioritizing students' mental health and well-being, schools create a safe and supportive environment where students feel valued, supported, and empowered to thrive academically and personally.

Creating supportive learning environments is paramount for promoting student success and well-being. Educators play a crucial role in fostering a positive and inclusive classroom culture by establishing norms that prioritize respect, empathy, and acceptance. By valuing diversity and actively promoting inclusivity, educators ensure that all students feel welcome and respected in the learning environment. Encouraging open communication is fundamental in creating a safe space where students feel comfortable expressing their thoughts, opinions, and feelings without fear of judgment. This fosters a sense of belonging and empowerment among students, promoting engagement and participation in classroom activities. Additionally, it cultivates a culture of mutual respect and understanding, where students learn to appreciate and learn from each other's perspectives.

Building strong teacher-student relationships is essential for creating a supportive learning environment. By offering personalized attention, encouragement, and empathy, educators demonstrate care and support for their students, which enhances trust and rapport. Strong teacher-student relationships not only contribute to academic success but also provide a foundation for social-emotional growth and development. In addition, incorporating student voice and choice into the learning process empowers students to take ownership of their learning and fosters a sense of autonomy and agency. Providing opportunities for students to collaborate, share their interests, and contribute to decision-making processes cultivates a sense of ownership and investment in their education.

Addressing academic adjustments and pressures post-pandemic necessitates proactive measures to support students in navigating academic challenges effectively. One effective approach is to provide a range of academic support services tailored to meet the diverse needs of students. These services may include tutoring, mentoring, and academic advising, which offer personalized assistance to students, helping them overcome obstacles, clarify concepts, and develop effective study habits. Additionally, offering workshops or seminars on study skills, time management, and effective learning strategies equips students with the tools they need to succeed academically. By teaching students how to manage their time efficiently, prioritize tasks, and utilize effective study techniques, educators empower them to take control of their academic journey and perform at their best.

Implementing flexible assessment methods and grading policies that accommodate diverse learning needs is essential for alleviating academic pressures and fostering a more inclusive learning environment. By providing opportunities for alternative assessments, such as project-based assignments or portfolios, educators can assess students' understanding and progress in ways that recognize their strengths and challenges. This allows for a more comprehensive evaluation of student learning and reduces the emphasis on standardized testing, which may not accurately reflect students' abilities or potential. Also, fostering a growth mindset and promoting resilience among students is crucial for helping them navigate academic challenges and setbacks effectively. Encouraging students to embrace challenges, learn from failures, and persist in the face of adversity fosters a positive attitude toward learning and promotes academic resilience.

Prioritizing physical health and wellness in educational settings is paramount for supporting students' overall well-being and academic success. One effective strategy is to encourage regular physical activity by integrating movement breaks, outdoor activities, or sports into the school day. Physical activity not only promotes physical fitness but also enhances cognitive function and concentration, thereby improving students' ability to focus and learn. By incorporating opportunities for movement throughout the day, educators create an environment that supports both physical and mental well-being. Educating students on the importance of maintaining a balanced lifestyle is crucial. Teaching them about healthy eating habits, the importance of adequate sleep, and stress management techniques empowers them to make informed choices about their health. By providing knowledge and resources on maintaining a healthy lifestyle, educators equip students with essential skills for lifelong well-being. Integrating health education into the curriculum ensures that students have access to information that can positively impact their physical and mental health.

Offering access to resources and services that promote physical health is essential. Schools can provide wellness programs, health screenings, and counseling support for issues like substance abuse or eating disorders. By offering these resources, educators ensure that students receive the support they need to address any health-related concerns effectively. Creating a supportive environment where students feel comfortable seeking help and accessing resources is essential for promoting overall well-being.

Supporting students in managing uncertainty and stress post-pandemic is crucial for their overall well-being and academic success. One essential step is to offer guidance and resources designed to help students cope with uncertainty and navigate stress effectively. Educators play a pivotal role in empowering students by providing them with information, strategies, and support networks to develop resilience and manage challenging situations. Incorporating mindfulness practices, relaxation techniques, and stress-reduction activities into the school day can offer students valuable tools for coping with stress and promoting emotional balance. These practices encourage self-awareness, mindfulness, and relaxation, fostering a sense of calm and mental clarity amidst uncertainty. By integrating such practices into the curriculum or daily routines, educators create opportunities for students to practice self-care and build resilience.

Fostering a culture of resilience within the school community involves promoting problem-solving skills, adaptability, and positive coping strategies. Educators can encourage students to approach challenges with a growth mindset, emphasizing the importance of perseverance and flexibility. By teaching students to reframe setbacks as opportunities for growth and learning, educators help build their capacity to navigate uncertainty and stress with confidence and resilience. Also, providing a supportive and nurturing environment where students feel safe to express their concerns and seek help is essential. Educators can create space for open dialogue and encourage students to share their feelings and experiences. By validating students' emotions and offering empathy and support, educators can help alleviate stress and foster a sense of connection and belonging within the school community.

Promoting equity, access, and inclusion in educational settings is paramount for creating a supportive and enriching learning environment where all students have the opportunity to thrive. One crucial approach is to address systemic inequities and barriers to access by implementing policies and initiatives that promote diversity, equity, and inclusion. This involves actively identifying and dismantling discriminatory practices and fostering a culture of respect, acceptance, and belonging. Additionally, providing equitable access to resources, technology, and support services is essential. Ensuring that all students, regardless of their background or socioeconomic status, have the tools and support they need to succeed academically is crucial for leveling the playing field. This may include providing access to technology devices and reliable internet connection, offering tutoring and academic support services, and providing accommodations for students with disabilities.

Creating opportunities for student voice and leadership further empowers marginalized communities and promotes a sense of belonging and ownership within the school community. By amplifying student voices, facilitating meaningful participation in decision-making processes, and valuing diverse perspectives, educators create a more inclusive and equitable learning environment where every student feels valued, respected, and empowered to reach their full potential. Fostering collaboration and partnership with families and communities is essential for promoting equity and inclusion in educational settings. Engaging families and community members in decision-making processes, seeking their input and feedback, and partnering with community organizations can help address the unique needs and challenges faced by students from marginalized backgrounds.

Enhancing communication and technology integration is essential for modernizing educational practices and preparing students for success in a digital world. By leveraging technology to facilitate communication, collaboration, and engagement in the classroom, educators can create dynamic and interactive learning experiences that cater to diverse learning styles and preferences.

Providing training and support for both educators and students is crucial for effectively integrating technology into learning experiences. Educators need to be equipped with the knowledge and skills necessary to incorporate digital tools seamlessly into their teaching practices. Likewise, students require guidance and instruction to navigate digital platforms, utilize online resources, and participate in digital learning environments effectively. Fostering digital literacy skills is vital in modern education. Educators must prioritize teaching students how to critically evaluate online information, discern credible sources, and protect their digital identity. By instilling these skills, educators empower students to navigate the vast digital landscape confidently, enabling them to succeed academically and professionally in an increasingly digital society. Promoting responsible use of technology is integral to ensuring students' well-being and safety online. Educators play a crucial role in educating students about the potential risks associated with technology use and teaching them how to make informed and responsible decisions when interacting online.

Implementing strategies for motivation and engagement is crucial for fostering a dynamic and enriching learning environment where students are inspired to participate and excel academically. Offering varied and interactive learning experiences that cater to diverse learning styles and interests ensures that all students feel engaged and valued in the classroom.

Incorporating project-based learning, hands-on activities, and real-world applications into the curriculum provides students with opportunities to apply their knowledge and skills in meaningful contexts. This fosters deeper understanding and long-term retention of content, as students are actively engaged in problem-solving and critical thinking. Recognizing and celebrating students' achievements, milestones, and contributions plays a pivotal role in creating a positive and supportive learning environment. By acknowledging students' efforts and successes, educators reinforce their confidence and motivation, promoting a culture of academic excellence and intrinsic motivation. This can be achieved through verbal praise, written feedback, certificates, or public recognition ceremonies.

Fostering a sense of ownership and autonomy in learning empowers students to take control of their education and pursue topics of interest. Providing opportunities for student choice and voice in assignments, projects, and classroom activities allows students to personalize their learning experience and feel invested in their academic journey. Creating a collaborative and inclusive classroom culture where students feel safe to express their ideas, ask questions, and engage in discussions fosters a sense of belonging and encourages active participation. By valuing and respecting students' perspectives and contributions, educators cultivate a positive learning environment where all students feel valued and respected.

Figure 2 outlines the key components of student's well-being in the post-pandemic academic environment: SEL, supportive environments, proactive measures, health, resources, policies, communication, technology, motivation, and engagement.

Figure 2. Strategies for the well-being of students

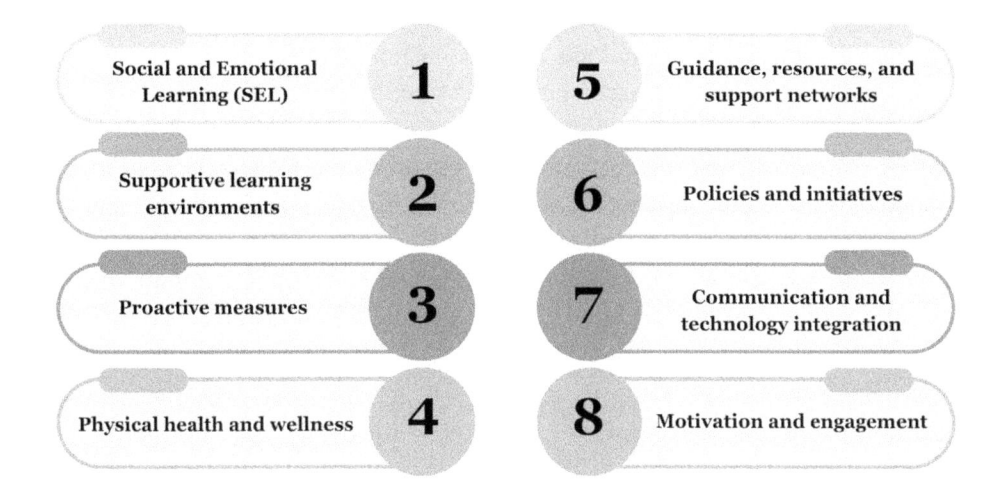

1. Social and Emotional Learning (SEL)	5. Guidance, resources, and support networks
2. Supportive learning environments	6. Policies and initiatives
3. Proactive measures	7. Communication and technology integration
4. Physical health and wellness	8. Motivation and engagement

CONCLUSION

The transition to post-pandemic face-to-face classroom settings has presented students with a myriad of challenges and adjustments. These include re-establishing routines and study habits, overcoming social and emotional barriers to in-person interactions, managing expectations amid changes in learning dynamics, accessing academic support services, and navigating the complexities of social and extracurricular reintegration. Each of these challenges requires resilience, adaptability, and support to navigate successfully in the evolving educational landscape.

As students navigate the transition to post-pandemic face-to-face learning environments, resilience, adaptability, and community support emerge as essential pillars of success. By cultivating resilience, students can overcome obstacles, embrace change, and persevere in the face of adversity. Adaptability enables students to navigate evolving learning dynamics, embrace new opportunities, and thrive in diverse academic settings. Additionally, community support fosters a sense of belonging, connection, and collaboration that empowers students to navigate challenges, access resources, and achieve their academic and personal goals.

Institutions and stakeholders have a collective responsibility to prioritize student well-being and academic success in the evolving educational landscape. This entails fostering inclusive and supportive learning environments, promoting mental health awareness and resilience-building initiatives, enhancing accessibility to academic support services, and fostering a culture of empathy, respect, and collaboration. By prioritizing student well-being and academic success, institutions and stakeholders can empower students to thrive academically, socially, and emotionally, contributing to a vibrant, inclusive, and equitable educational community.

In conclusion, by recognizing the challenges faced by students in the post-pandemic face-to-face classroom setting, emphasizing resilience, adaptability, and community support, and prioritizing student well-being and academic success, institutions and stakeholders can create a nurturing and empowering educational environment that prepares students for lifelong learning, personal growth, and professional success in the ever-changing world. Through collaborative efforts and a commitment to student-centered care, we can build a brighter future for all learners.

REFERENCES

Ahorsu, D. K., Sánchez Vidaña, D. I., Lipardo, D., Shah, P. B., Cruz González, P., Shende, S., Gurung, S., Venkatesan, H., Duongthipthewa, A., Ansari, T. Q., & Schoeb, V. (2021). Effect of a peer-led intervention combining mental health promotion with coping-strategy-based workshops on mental health awareness, help-seeking behavior, and wellbeing among university students in Hong Kong. *International Journal of Mental Health Systems*, 15(1), 1–10. 10.1186/s13033-020-00432-033422098

Aljaberi, M. A., Al-Sharafi, M. A., Uzir, M. U. H., Sabah, A., Ali, A. M., Lee, K. H., Alsalahi, A., Noman, S., & Lin, C. Y. (2023). Psychological Toll of the COVID-19 Pandemic: An In-Depth Exploration of Anxiety, Depression, and Insomnia and the Influence of Quarantine Measures on Daily Life. *Healthcare (Basel)*, 11(17), 2418. 10.3390/healthcare1117241837685451

Barron, M., Cobo, C., Munoz-Najar, A., & Ciarrusta, I. S. (2021). The changing role of teachers and technologies amidst the COVID 19 pandemic: key findings from a cross-country study. *Education for Global Development, 18*, 1–9. https://blogs.worldbank.org/education/changing-role-teachers-and-technologies-amidst-covid-19-pandemic-key-findings-cross

Bell, I. H., Nicholas, J., Broomhall, A., Bailey, E., Bendall, S., Boland, A., Robinson, J., Adams, S., McGorry, P., & Thompson, A. (2023). The impact of COVID-19 on youth mental health: A mixed methods survey. *Psychiatry Research*, 321(March), 115082. 10.1016/j.psychres.2023.11508236738592

Blewett, L., & Ebben, M. (2022). Post-Pandemic Anxiety: Teaching and Learning for Student Mental Wellness in Communication All. In *Post-Pandemic Pedagogy: A Paradigm Shift*, 129–148).

Bowman, N. A. (2010). The development of psychological well-being among first-year college students. *Journal of College Student Development*, 51(2), 180–200. 10.1353/csd.0.0118

Cahill, H., & Dadvand, B. (2020). In Midford, R., Nutton, G., Hyndman, B., & Silburn, S. (Eds.), *Social and Emotional Learning and Resilience Education BT - Health and Education Interdependence: Thriving from Birth to Adulthood* (pp. 205–223). Springer Singapore. 10.1007/978-981-15-3959-6_11

CBSE. (2013). *Mental Health and Wellbeing: A Perspective*. CBSE. https://manodarpan.education.gov.in/assets/img/pdf/CBSE_MH_Manual.pdf

Chow, R. S., Lam, C. M., & King, I. (2020). Crisis resilience pedagogy (CRP) for teaching and learning. *Proceedings of 2020 IEEE International Conference on Teaching, Assessment, and Learning for Engineering, TALE 2020,* (pp. 384–391). IEEE. 10.1109/TALE48869.2020.9368496

Crawford, J., Allen, K. A., Sanders, T., Baumeister, R., Parker, P., Saunders, C., & Tice, D. (2024). Sense of belonging in higher education students: An Australian longitudinal study from 2013 to 2019. *Studies in Higher Education*, 49(3), 395–409. 10.1080/03075079.2023.2238006

Dayagbil, F. T., Palompon, D. R., Garcia, L. L., & Olvido, M. M. J. (2021). Teaching and Learning Continuity Amid and Beyond the Pandemic. *Frontiers in Education*, 6(July), 1–12. 10.3389/feduc.2021.678692

Eden, C. A., Chisom, O. N., & Adeniyi, I. S. (2024). Cultural Competence in Education. *Strategies for Fostering Inclusivity and Diversity.*, 6(3), 383–392. 10.51594/ijarss.v6i3.895

Ferren, M. (2021). *Remote Learning and School Reopenings - What Worked and What Didn't*. ERIC. https://files.eric.ed.gov/fulltext/ED613768.pdf

Goyer, J. P., Akinola, M., Grunberg, R., & Crum, A. J. (2022). Supplemental Material for Thriving Under Pressure: The Effects of Stress-Related Wise Interventions on Affect, Sleep, and Exam Performance for College Students From Disadvantaged Backgrounds. *Emotion (Washington, D.C.)*, 22(8), 1755–1772. 10.1037/emo000102634780237

Gupta, O. J., & Yadav, S. (2023). Determinants in advancement of teaching and learning in higher education: In special reference to management education. *International Journal of Management Education*, 21(2), 100823. 10.1016/j.ijme.2023.100823

Haleem, A., Javaid, M., Qadri, M. A., & Suman, R. (2022). Understanding the role of digital technologies in education: A review. *Sustainable Operations and Computers*, 3(February), 275–285. 10.1016/j.susoc.2022.05.004

Jamil, N., Belkacem, A. N., & Lakas, A. (2023). On enhancing students' cognitive abilities in online learning using brain activity and eye movements. In *Education and Information Technologies, 28*(4). Springer US. 10.1007/s10639-022-11372-2

Jessiman, P., Kidger, J., Spencer, L., Geijer-Simpson, E., Kaluzeviciute, G., Burn, A.-M., Leonard, N., & Limmer, M. (2022). School culture and student mental health: A qualitative study in UK secondary schools. *BMC Public Health*, 22(1), 1–18. 10.1186/s12889-022-13034-x35351062

Jeynes, W. H. (2024). A Meta-Analysis: The Relationship Between the Parental Expectations Component of Parental Involvement with Students' Academic Achievement. *Urban Education*, 59(1), 63–95. 10.1177/00420859211073892

Jia, C., Hew, K. F., Bai, S., & Huang, W. (2022). Adaptation of a conventional flipped course to an online flipped format during the Covid-19 pandemic: Student learning performance and engagement. *Journal of Research on Technology in Education*, 54(2), 281–301. 10.1080/15391523.2020.1847220

Jiang, M. M., Gao, K., Wu, Z. Y., & Guo, P. P. (2022). The influence of academic pressure on adolescents' problem behavior: Chain mediating effects of self-control, parent–child conflict, and subjective well-being. *Frontiers in Psychology*, 13(September), 1–10. 10.3389/fpsyg.2022.95433036211862

Karakose, T., Polat, H., & Papadakis, S. (2021). Exploring Teachers' Perspectives on the Role of Digital Leadership in the COVID-19 Pandemic and Tech Skills of School Leaders. *Sustainability*, 13, 13448. 10.3390/su132313448

Kelly, M. L., Yeigh, T., Hudson, S., Willis, R., & Lee, M. (2023). Secondary teachers' perceptions of the importance of pedagogical approaches to support students' behavioural, emotional and cognitive engagement. *Australian Educational Researcher*, 50(4), 1025–1047. 10.1007/s13384-022-00540-5

Kiss, O., Alzueta, E., Yuksel, D., Pohl, K. M., de Zambotti, M., Műller-Oehring, E. M., Prouty, D., Durley, I., Pelham, W. E. III, McCabe, C. J., Gonzalez, M. R., Brown, S. A., Wade, N. E., Marshall, A. T., Sowell, E. R., Breslin, F. J., Lisdahl, K. M., Dick, A. S., Sheth, C. S., & Baker, F. C. (2022). The Pandemic's Toll on Young Adolescents: Prevention and Intervention Targets to Preserve Their Mental Health. *The Journal of Adolescent Health*, 70(3), 387–395. 10.1016/j.jadohealth.2021.11.02335090817

Ladson-Billings, G. (2021). I'm Here for the Hard Re-Set: Post Pandemic Pedagogy to Preserve Our Culture. *Equity & Excellence in Education*, 54(1), 68–78. 10.1080/10665684.2020.1863883

Lordan, R., Prior, S., Hennessy, E., Naik, A., Ghosh, S., Paschos, G. K., Skarke, C., Barekat, K., Hollingsworth, T., Juska, S., Mazaleuskaya, L. L., Teegarden, S., Glascock, A. L., Anderson, S., Meng, H., Tang, S. Y., Weljie, A., Bottalico, L., Ricciotti, E., & Grosser, T. (2021). Considerations for the Safe Operation of Schools During the Coronavirus Pandemic. *Frontiers in Public Health*, 9(December), 1–15. 10.3389/fpubh.2021.75145134976917

Lyons, K., Magsayo, M., & Maheshwari, R. (2023). Loneliness & College Students: A Needs Assessment Regarding Georgetown Student Experiences in a Post-Virtual World. *Georgetown Scientific Research Journal*, 3(2), 41–49. 10.48091/gsr.v3i2.70

Mali, D., & Lim, H. (2021). How do students perceive face-to-face/blended learning as a result of the Covid-19 pandemic? *International Journal of Management Education*, 19(3), 100552. 10.1016/j.ijme.2021.100552

Margrove, K. L., Gustowska, M., & Grove, L. S. (2014). Provision of support for psychological distress by university staff, and receptiveness to mental health training. *Journal of Further and Higher Education*, 38(1), 90–106. 10.1080/0309877X.2012.699518

Mesmar, J., & Badran, A. (2022). The Post-COVID Classroom: Lessons from a Pandemic. In Badran, A., Baydoun, E., & Mesmar, J. (Eds.), *Higher Education in the Arab World: New Priorities in the Post COVID-19 Era* (pp. 11–41). Springer International Publishing. 10.1007/978-3-031-07539-1_2

Montemurro, G., Cherkowski, S., Sulz, L., Loland, D., Saville, E., & Storey, K. E. (2023). Prioritizing well-being in K-12 education: Lessons from a multiple case study of Canadian school districts. *Health Promotion International*, 38(2), daad003. 10.1093/heapro/daad00336857609

Nam, B. H., & Bai, Q. (2023). ChatGPT and its ethical implications for STEM research and higher education: A media discourse analysis. *International Journal of STEM Education*, 10(1), 66. 10.1186/s40594-023-00452-5

Ni, Y., & Jia, F. (2023). Promoting Positive Social Interactions: Recommendation for a Post-Pandemic School-Based Intervention for Social Anxiety. *Children (Basel, Switzerland)*, 10(3), 1–13. 10.3390/children10030049136980049

Novianti, R., & Garzia, M. (2020). Parental Engagement in Children's Online Learning During COVID-19 Pandemic. *Journal of Teaching and Learning in Elementary Education (Jtlee)*, 3(2), 117. 10.33578/jtlee.v3i2.7845

Okoli, J., Arroteia, N. P., & Ogunsade, A. I. (2023). Failure of crisis leadership in a global pandemic: Some reflections on COVID-19 and future recommendations. *Leadership in Health Services*, 36(2), 186–199. 10.1108/LHS-06-2022-006136129236

Peñalver, E. A., & Laborda, J. G. (2021). Online Learning during the Covid-19 Pandemic: How Has This New Situation Affected Students' Oral Communication Skills? *Journal of Language and Education*, 7(4), 30–41. 10.17323/jle.2021.11940

Perez, B. R., & Bahamon Muneton, M. J. (2023). The socio-emotional dimension in education: A systematic review. *Issues in Educational Research*, 33(1), 307–326. https://search.informit.org/doi/10.3316/informit.173573406487575

Prowse, R., Sherratt, F., Abizaid, A., Gabrys, R. L., Hellemans, K. G. C., Patterson, Z. R., & McQuaid, R. J. (2021). Coping With the COVID-19 Pandemic: Examining Gender Differences in Stress and Mental Health Among University Students. *Frontiers in Psychiatry*, 12(April), 1–11. 10.3389/fpsyt.2021.65075933897499

Rapanta, C., Botturi, L., Goodyear, P., Guàrdia, L., & Koole, M. (2021). Balancing Technology, Pedagogy and the New Normal: Post-pandemic Challenges for Higher Education. *Postdigital Science and Education*, 3(3), 715–742. 10.1007/s42438-021-00249-1

Ratten, V. (2023). The post COVID-19 pandemic era: Changes in teaching and learning methods for management educators. *International Journal of Management Education*, 21(2), 100777. 10.1016/j.ijme.2023.100777

Sato, S. N., Condes Moreno, E., Rubio-Zarapuz, A., Dalamitros, A. A., Yañez-Sepulveda, R., Tornero-Aguilera, J. F., & Clemente-Suárez, V. J. (2024). Navigating the New Normal: Adapting Online and Distance Learning in the Post-Pandemic Era. *Education Sciences*, 14(1), 19. 10.3390/educsci14010019

Sepanik, S., & Brown, K. T. (2021). *School-Community Partnerships*. ERIC. https://files.eric.ed.gov/fulltext/ED616007.pdf

Sharaievska, I., McAnirlin, O., Browning, M. H. E. M., Larson, L. R., Mullenbach, L., Rigolon, A., D'Antonio, A., Cloutier, S., Thomsen, J., Metcalf, E. C., & Reigner, N. (2022). "Messy transitions": Students' perspectives on the impacts of the COVID-19 pandemic on higher education. *Higher Education*, 2022(April), 1–18. 10.1007/s10734-022-00843-735463941

Siegel, A. A., Zarb, M., Alshaigy, B., Blanchard, J., Crick, T., Glassey, R., Hott, J. R., Latulipe, C., Riedesel, C., & Senapathi, M., Simon, & Williams, D. (2021). Teaching through a Global Pandemic: Educational Landscapes Before, during and after COVID-19. *Annual Conference on Innovation and Technology in Computer Science Education, ITiCSE*, (pp. 1–25). ACM. 10.1145/3502870.3506565

Singh, J., Steele, K., & Singh, L. (2021). Combining the Best of Online and Face-to-Face Learning: Hybrid and Blended Learning Approach for COVID-19, Post Vaccine, & Post-Pandemic World. *Journal of Educational Technology Systems*, 50(2), 140–171. 10.1177/00472395211047865

Stoian, C. E., Fărca iu, M. A., Dragomir, G. M., & Gherhe , V. (2022). Transition from Online to Face-to-Face Education after COVID-19: The Benefits of Online Education from Students' Perspective. *Sustainability (Basel)*, 14(19), 12812. 10.3390/su141912812

Sun, A., & Chen, X. (2016). Online education and its effective practice: A research review. *Journal of Information Technology Education*, 15, 157–190. 10.28945/3502

Turnbull, D., Chugh, R., & Luck, J. (2021). Transitioning to E-Learning during the COVID-19 pandemic: How have Higher Education Institutions responded to the challenge? *Education and Information Technologies*, 26(5), 6401–6419. 10.1007/s10639-021-10633-w34177349

UNICEF, WHO, & UNESCO. (2022). *Five essential pillars for promoting and protecting mental health and psychosocial well-being in schools and learning environments.* UNESCO. https://unesdoc.unesco.org/ark:/48223/pf0000384614

Watson, K. R., Astor, R. A., Benbenishty, R., Capp, G., & Kelly, M. S. (2022). Needs of Children and Families during Spring 2020 COVID-19 School Closures: Findings from a National Survey. *Social Work*, 67(1), 17–27. 10.1093/sw/swab05234791495

Wiedermann, C. J., Barbieri, V., Plagg, B., Marino, P., Piccoliori, G., & Engl, A. (2023). Fortifying the Foundations: A Comprehensive Approach to Enhancing Mental Health Support in Educational Policies Amidst Crises. *Healthcare (Basel)*, 11(10), 1423. 10.3390/healthcare1110142337239709

Willis, A. (2024). Teachers prioritise relationships over curriculum for student well-being. *Pedagogy, Culture & Society*, 32(2), 473–489. 10.1080/14681366.2022.2055116

Xie, J., Gulinna, A., & Rice, M. F. (2021). Instructional designers' roles in emergency remote teaching during COVID-19. *Distance Education*, 42(1), 70–87. 10.1080/01587919.2020.1869526

Yang, D., Chen, P., Wang, K., Li, Z., Zhang, C., & Huang, R. (2023). Parental Involvement and Student Engagement: A Review of the Literature. *Sustainability (Basel)*, 15(7), 5859. 10.3390/su15075859

Chapter 13
Impact of Social Media on Student Wellbeing in Kenyan Universities

Peter Omae Onderi
 https://orcid.org/0000-0002-4298-9211
Maseno University, Kenya

Moses Oginda
Maseno University, Kenya

ABSTRACT

Students who spend much of their time on social media are likely to struggle with time management and become less productive in their studies due to distractions by constant alerts, endless scrolling feeds, and the appeal of viral material. The chapter proposed to discuss, social networking sites, academic performance, social opportunities, and challenges. The findings were that social media helps university students get necessary information for their academic achievement, it creates stress, and it exposes them to cyberbullying, is addictive, causes sleep disorders and anxiety, and can help them make money online. The study recommended that the social media use at university should be restricted to academic use only and here should be provide adequate Wi-Fi hotspots within the universities.

INTRODUCTION

Students in public universities are among the most active users of social media tools and platforms. (Annette, Simiyu& Too, 2019).Kenya was home to 13.05 million social media users in January 2024, equating to 23.5 percent of the total population. A total

DOI: 10.4018/979-8-3693-4417-0.ch013

of 66.04 million cellular mobile connections were active in Kenya in early 2024, with this figure equivalent to 118.7 percent of the total population (Digital 2024, Kenya). The population of Kenya stood at 55.65 million in January 2024. Data shows that Kenya's population increased by 1.1 million (+2.0 percent) between early 2023 and the start of 2024.50.4 percent of Kenya's population is female, while 49.6 percent of the population is male. At the start of 2024, 29.8 percent of Kenya's population lived in urban centres, while 70.2 percent lived in rural areas. *Note: gender data are currently only available for "female" and "male."* There were 22.71 million internet users in Kenya in January 2024. Kenya's internet penetration rate stood at 40.8 percent of the total population at the start of 2024. Kepios analysis indicates that internet users in Kenya increased by 445 thousand (+2.0 percent) between January 2023 and January 2024. For perspective, these user figures reveal that 32.93 million people in Kenya did *not* use the internet at the start of 2024, suggesting that 59.2 percent of the population remained offline at the beginning of the year. However, complexities associated with the collection and analysis of internet user data mean that it can often take several months before research is ready for publication. As a result, the latest *published* figures for internet use invariably *under*-represent reality, and actual adoption and growth may be higher than the figures shown here suggest. Internet connection speeds in Kenya in 2024.Connection speed: 9.78 Mbps. Ookla's data reveals that the median mobile internet connection speed in Kenya increased by 1.37 Mbps (+6.7 percent) in the twelve months to the start of 2024. Meanwhile, Ookla's data shows that fixed internet connection speeds in Kenya increased by 0.17 Mbps (+1.8 percent) during the same period.

Report's figures show that there were 13.05 million active social media user identities in Kenya in January 2024. Kepios analysis shows that social media users in Kenya increased by 3.6 million (+38.2 percent) between early 2023 and the beginning of 2024. The number of social media users in Kenya at the start of 2024 was equivalent to 23.5 percent of the total population, but it's important to stress that social media users may not represent unique individuals .Meanwhile, data published in the ad planning tools of top social media platforms indicates that there were 13.05 million users aged 18 and above using social media in Kenya at the start of 2024, which was equivalent to 41.9 percent of the total population aged 18 and above at that time. More broadly, 57.5 percent of Kenya's total internet user base (regardless of age) used at least one social media platform in January 2024. At that time, 43.2 percent of Kenya's social media users were female, while 56.8 percent were male. Data published in Meta's advertising resources indicates that Facebook had 13.05 million users in Kenya in early 2024. Figures published in Meta's own tools indicate that Facebook's potential ad reach in Kenya increased by 3.8 million (+41.1 percent) between January 2023 and January 2024. The same data show that the number of users that marketers could reach with ads on Facebook in Kenya decreased by 150 thousand (-1.1 percent) between October 2023 and January 2024. As the company states within its ad planning tools,

"Estimated audience size is not a proxy for monthly or daily active users, or for engagement. Estimates aren't designed to match population, census estimates or other sources, and may differ depending on factors such as how many accounts across Meta technologies a person has, how many temporary visitors are in a particular geographic location at a given time, and Meta user-reported demographics."

As a result, changes in ad reach may *not* necessarily indicate any change in the platform's overall user base. But despite these caveats, Meta's ad reach data still offers valuable insights into how Facebook use is evolving.

FACEBOOK ADOPTION IN KENYA

Facebook's ad reach in Kenya was equivalent to 23.5 percent of the total population at the start of 2024. However, Meta only allows people aged 13 and above to use Facebook, so it's worth highlighting that 34.5 percent of the "eligible" audience in Kenya uses Meta in 2024. For additional context, Facebook's ad reach in Kenya was equivalent to 57.5 percent of the local internet user base (regardless of age) in January 2024. At the start of 2024, 43.2 percent of Facebook's ad audience in Kenya was female, while 56.8 percent was male. Google's advertising resources indicate that YouTube had 9.79 million users in Kenya in early 2024. It's important to stress that these advertising reach figures do not necessarily represent the same thing as monthly active user figures though, and there may be meaningful differences between the size of YouTube's ad audience and its total active user base. However, the company's own data suggests that YouTube's *ad reach* in early 2024 was equivalent to 17.6 percent of Kenya's total population at the start of the year. To put those figures in perspective, YouTube ads reached 43.1 percent of Kenya's total internet user base (regardless of age) in January 2024. At that time, 43.4 percent of YouTube's ad audience in Kenya was female, while 56.6 percent was male.

YOUTUBE USER GROWTH IN KENYA

Data published in Google's own ad planning tools show that YouTube's potential ad reach in Kenya increased by 350 thousand (+3.7 percent) between the start of 2023 and early 2024. Meanwhile, the same data show that the number of users that marketers could reach with ads on YouTube in Kenya remained unchanged between October 2023 and January 2024. Numbers published in Meta's advertising tools indicate that Instagram had 3.05 million users in Kenya in early 2024. The company's regularly revised figures suggest that Instagram's ad reach in Kenya was equivalent to 5.5 percent of the total population at the start of the year. However, Meta only allows people aged 13 and above to use Instagram, so it's worth highlighting that 8.1 percent of the "eligible" audience in Kenya uses Instagram in 2024. It's also worth noting that Instagram's ad reach in Kenya at the start of 2024 was equivalent to 13.4 percent of the local internet user base (regardless of age). In early 2024, 50.0 percent of Instagram's ad audience in Kenya was female, while 50.0 percent was male.

INSTAGRAM USER GROWTH IN KENYA

Data published in Meta's planning tools show that Instagram's potential ad reach in Kenya increased by 850 thousand (+38.6 percent) between January 2023 and January 2024. On a quarterly basis, the company's data also reveal that the size of Instagram's ad audience in Kenya increased by 300 thousand (+10.9 percent) between October 2023 and January 2024. changes in the audience reach figures published in Meta's ad planning tools do not necessarily correlate with overall changes in its platforms' active user bases. Figures published in ByteDance's advertising resources indicate that TikTok had 10.60 million users aged 18 and above in Kenya in early 2024. ByteDance allows marketers to target TikTok ads to users aged *13 and above* via its advertising tools, but these tools only show audience data for users aged *18 and above*. For context, ByteDance's figures indicate that TikTok ads reached 34.0 percent of all adults aged 18 and above in Kenya at the start of 2024. Meanwhile, TikTok's ad reach in Kenya was equivalent to 46.7 percent of the local internet user base at the beginning of the year, regardless of age. In early 2024, 44.7 percent of TikTok's ad audience in Kenya was female, while 55.3 percent was male. Ad audiences often only account for a subset of a platform's total users, and given that TikTok's ad tools only publish data for users aged 18 and above, it's important to remember that trends in TikTok's ad reach figures may not necessarily match changes in the platform's overall user base.

FACEBOOK MESSENGER USERS IN KENYA IN 2024

Data published in Meta's advertising resources indicate that ads on Facebook Messenger reached 2.20 million users in Kenya in early 2024. The company's frequently revised audience numbers suggest that Facebook Messenger's ad reach in

Kenya was equivalent to 4.0 percent of the total population at the start of the year. Meta only allows people aged 13 and above to use Facebook Messenger though, so it's worth highlighting that 5.8 percent of Facebook Messenger's "eligible" audience in Kenya in 2024. Facebook Messenger's ad reach in Kenya is equivalent to 9.7 percent of the local internet user base (regardless of age). At the start of 2024, 42.0 percent of Facebook Messenger's ad audience in Kenya was female, while 58.0 percent was male.

FACEBOOK MESSENGER USER GROWTH IN KENYA

Data published in Meta's planning tools show that Facebook Messenger's potential ad reach in Kenya increased by 350 thousand (+18.9 percent) between January 2023 and January 2024. On a quarterly basis, the company's data reveal that the size of Facebook Messenger's ad audience in Kenya increased by 50 thousand (+2.3 percent) between October 2023 and January 2024. However, , changes in the audience reach figures published in Meta's ad planning tools do not necessarily correlate with overall changes in its platforms' active user bases.

LINKEDIN USERS IN KENYA IN 2024

Figures published in LinkedIn's advertising resources indicate that LinkedIn had 4.30 million "members" in Kenya in early 2024. However, note that LinkedIn's advertising tools publish audience reach data based on *total registered members*, rather than the *monthly active users* that form the basis of the ad reach figures published by most other social media platforms. As a result, these LinkedIn figures are not directly comparable with the figures for other social media platforms published on this page, or in our Digital 2024 reports. The company's advertising reach figures suggest that LinkedIn's audience in Kenya was equivalent to 7.7 percent of the total population at the start of 2024. LinkedIn prevents people below the age of 18 from using its platform though, so it's also helpful to know that 13.8 percent of the "eligible" audience in Kenya uses LinkedIn in 2024. LinkedIn's ad reach in Kenya was equivalent to 18.9 percent of the local internet user base (regardless of age) at the start of the year. In early 2024, 40.0 percent of LinkedIn's ad audience in Kenya was female, while 60.0 percent was male. *Note: LinkedIn's advertising resources only publish audience gender data for "female" and "male" users.*

LINKEDIN USER GROWTH IN KENYA

Data published in LinkedIn's planning tools show that LinkedIn's potential ad reach in Kenya increased by 800 thousand (+22.9 percent) between the start of 2023 and the beginning of 2024. On a quarterly basis, the company's data reveal that the size of LinkedIn's ad audience in Kenya increased by 300 thousand (+7.5 percent) between October 2023 and January 2024. However, because LinkedIn's ad audience figures are based on *total registered members* rather than monthly active users, it's unclear whether these trends might reflect changes in *active* LinkedIn use too.

SNAPCHAT USERS IN KENYA IN 2024

Data published in Snap's advertising resources indicate that Snapchat had 3.16 million users in Kenya in early 2024. This figure means that Snapchat's ad reach in Kenya was equivalent to 5.7 percent of the total population at the start of the year. However, Snap only allows people aged 13 and above to use the platform, so it's also worth noting that 8.4 percent of the "eligible" audience in Kenya uses Snap in 2024. For additional context, Snapchat's ad reach in Kenya was equivalent to 13.9 percent of the local internet user base (regardless of age) at the start of the year. In early 2024, 65.9 percent of Snapchat's ad audience in Kenya was female, while 30.5 percent was male.

SNAPCHAT USER GROWTH IN KENYA

Data published in Snap's own ad planning tools show that Snapchat's potential ad reach in Kenya increased by 710 thousand (+29.0 percent) between the start of 2023 and early 2024. Meanwhile, the same data show that the number of users that marketers could reach with ads on Snapchat in Kenya increased by 425 thousand (+15.5 percent) between October 2023 and January 2024. However, it's important to stress that these advertising reach figures do not represent monthly active user figures, and there may be meaningful differences between the size of Snapchat's ad audience and its total active user base.

X USERS IN KENYA IN 2024

Numbers published in X (Twitter)'s advertising resources indicate that X had 1.87 million users in Kenya in early 2024. This figure means that X's ad reach in Kenya was equivalent to 3.4 percent of the total population at the time. However, it's important to stress that these advertising reach figures are not the same as monthly active user figures, and there may be meaningful differences between the size of X's ad audience and its total active user base. Moreover, we've seen some particularly bizarre trends in the data reported in X's advertising tools over the past year, so we'd advise caution when it comes to analysing these X figures. It is worth noting that X only allows people aged 13 and above to use its platform, so the latest figures suggest that 5.0 percent of the "eligible" audience in Kenya uses X in 2024. For additional context, X's ad reach in Kenya was equivalent to 8.2 percent of the local internet user base (regardless of age) at the start of the year. In early 2024, the company's own data indicated that 25.4 percent of X's ad audience in Kenya was female, while 74.6 percent was male.

However, it's worth noting that X *infers* its users' gender, by analyzing signals such as the name that users enter in their profile, and their broader activity on the platform. This contrasts with the gender data offered in the advertising tools of platforms like Facebook, which relies on the gender that users themselves enter in their own profile. Moreover, our analysis suggests that X's inferences may not be particularly reliable in determining users' gender, especially in countries where English is *not* the dominant language. For example, consumer research findings published by GWI often offer quite a different picture of X use by gender compared with X's own audience data. But the apparent distortions that frequently appear in X's inferred gender data may be due in large part to the high number of "non-human" accounts that feature in X's active user data (e.g. accounts that represent businesses, animals, musicians, etc.), especially because X doesn't currently separate these accounts out from "real" human individuals in the ways that Facebook and Instagram do. Regardless of the cause of these anomalies though, we advise caution when analyzing or interpreting X's reported figures for use by gender.

X USER GROWTH IN KENYA

Data published in X (Twitter)'s own ad planning tools show that X's potential ad reach in Kenya decreased by 26 thousand (-1.4 percent) between the start of 2023 and early 2024. Meanwhile, the same data show that the number of users that marketers could reach with ads on X in Kenya decreased by 426 thousand (-18.5 percent) between October 2023 and January 2024. However, the figures published in X's planning tools appear to be liable to significant fluctuation – even over short periods of time – and these anomalies may impact the reliability and representativeness of this change data. Data from GSMA Intelligence shows that there were 66.04 million cellular mobile connections in Kenya at the start of 2024. However, note that many people around the world make use of more than one mobile connection – for example, they might have one connection for personal use, and another one for work – so it's not unusual for mobile connection figures to significantly exceed figures for total population. GSMA Intelligence's numbers indicate that mobile connections in Kenya were equivalent to 118.7 percent of the total population in January 2024. The number of mobile connections in Kenya increased by 1.8 million (+2.8 percent) between the start of 2023 and the start of 2024.

KEY TERMS USED IN THE STUDY

The following are the key terms used in the study.

Students' well being, as defined in this report, refers to the psychological, cognitive, social and physical functioning and. capabilities that students need to live a happy and fulfilling life.

Depression: Will refer to a common and serious psychiatric disorder that adversely influences how one feels thinks and how they act. It is also, in many cases referred to as a mood disorder and results in feeling sad and also leads to loss of interest in things once loved.

Social media: Will include a collection of virtual communication methods focused on community-based participation, interaction, sharing information and association such as Facebook, Twitter, WhatsApp and LinkedIn

Social media use: Will refer to sending and receiving information through social media sites for various reasons.

Forms of social media: Are digital channels used to pass information between individuals or groups. Some of the most common social media forms include; social networking sites (Facebook, Twitter, WhatsApp and LinkedIn), image sending and receiving apps (Instagram, Snapchat and Imgur) and video hosting sites (Youtube and Vimeo).

Functions of social media: The purpose with which social media is utilized by students. Communication, socializing, sharing academic information and entertainment are among the major functions of social media for University students. Xii

Pathological social media use: A pathological behaviour is an extreme deviation from a healthy or normal way of behaving. Pathological media use is an excessive or extreme utilization of social media platforms or it can also be described as a dependence to social networking.

Frequency of social media use: Frequency is the degree at which something takes place over a specific time or in a given population. Frequency of social media consumption is the rate at which individuals utilize social media.

The study sought to understand how university students utilise the above social media.

LITERATURE REVIEW

According to a recent report from the Pew Research Centre, 95% of teens use a smartphone, and 45% say they are online almost constantly. About 70% of teens are on Snapchat and Instagram, while 85% are on YouTube. One would think all this near constant "socializing" would make teens feel more connected than ever before. In her classroom, McAbee, the opposite is true. "Social media has crippled my students when it comes to interacting with one another in person. Their very ability to communicate is deteriorating," says McAbee (2024.The very definition of "social" media may be misleading, according to experts who are finding that the more time teens spend on social media, the lonelier and more anxious they are.

A study by Munyiva, Simiyu, and Too, (2019) found that Students in public universities are among the most active users of social media tools and platforms. There is little research data on the influence of social media on public universities in Kenya. It is critical to study how social media affects the wellbeing and academics of public university students in Kenya. The objective was to determine the influence of social media on public universities in Kenya. The research utilized a qualitative research design facilitated by a systematic literature review methodology. Findings from 12 studies were comparatively analysed to determine the degree of conformity in a bid to answer the research question. The findings included that the influence of social media on a student's wellbeing and academics depends on the student's engagement in social media activities and consumption of the corresponding content. Social media can be an educational resource, enhance engagement, communication, and participation in classroom activities, and improve professional networking. Social media can also be a source of distraction and cybercrime besides the fact that it can also lead to addiction. The influence of social media on public universities in Kenya depends on the students' engagement with social media activities and content. The increase in the use of social media among the university students motivated them for changing their behaviour and habits. Lack of face to face interactions may also lead to loneliness, depression and other mental disorder. The additional time students are involved with social media they are in higher risk of being deprived of their sleep, increment in depression or anxiety and low self-esteem. The effects of them being emotionally unhappy in one site in specific, the more pressure and anxiety may be available always.

There's a correlation between smartphone usage and lower satisfaction with life, according to Barkley, (2013) "Interaction on social media is not beneficial. It's electronic," explains Barkley, who has been studying smartphone use and students since 2013. "The higher the cell phone use, the more time spent on social media, and the higher the anxiety. Peer relationships actually get worse the more you use your phone." Twenge (2017) discovered that students who spend more time using smartphones and other electronic devices are less satisfied with their lives than students who frequently engage in face-to-face interaction."*We found that teens who spent five or more hours a day online were 71 percent more likely than those who spent less than an hour a day to have at least one suicide risk factor (depression, thinking about suicide, making a suicide plan or attempting suicide). Overall, suicide risk factors rose significantly after two or more hours a day of time online,* (2018 Children's Mental Health Report, Child Mind Institute).

If teens were to follow up high social media usage with lots of time spent socializing in person, the effects perhaps wouldn't be so adverse. But in most cases, they aren't. It turns out, liking a post, commenting "Cute," or keeping up with a "snapchat streak" isn't the same as catching up. It's not even close. Yet too many teens, according to these experts, are substituting real life interactions for Instagram posts, and paying the price. Because research into social media and education is still generally in its infancy, many educators are still trying to fully understand the effects of these technologies. Social media can be an effective teaching tool, but many educators are alarmed at the role it plays in heightening student anxiety and stress.

SOCIAL MEDIA AND ANXIETY

In 2018, the Centres for Disease Control issued some sobering statistics about student anxiety and depression. Teens are lonelier, anxious and depressed than ever. About a third of teens surveyed by the CDC said they'd felt persistent sadness or hopelessness. Social media, social media is exacerbating this trend. "*Researchers are finding that when someone develops depression and withdraws from peers, they see other people on social media smiling and at parties with friends. It magnifies their sense of isolation,*" (Richter 2018). The Child Mind Institute's 2018 Children's Mental Health Report focuses on anxiety in teenagers, spotlighting the prevalent role of social media has in their lives. The report points out that existing research does conclude that social media can be constructive, "youth with a stronger emotional investment in social media are likely to have higher levels of anxiety."

And yet, students have trouble putting their phone down for too long, says Crystal Huset, counsellor at Pardeeville High School in Wisconsin. "It seems like many students struggle to detach from their electronic devices," says Huset. "Many students do see social media as an issue, but it is also the only thing that they know."

Anne (2018) noticed the increase of mental health issues in her students. *"I never had kids diagnosed with anxiety and depression 10 years ago,"* (Anne, 2018). "They compare themselves, and it brings on bad feelings." *"They base their love of themselves on how people respond to their pictures,"* Smith (2018)." The lack of real life communication, the comparison, and the bullying are too much for some students to bear, Smith adds. Recently, she noticed a student acting out in her classroom. "She was especially agitated and disrupted the class. After working with her, I found that she had a lot more going on, and it had to do with Instagram. Her so-called friends had called her names the evening before. *Students will talk about feeling left out when they see their friends communicating on social media.* Anne (2018). They have FOMO- fear of missing out. They don't have the tools to deal with these negative emotions."(Common Sense Media, 2018.). The current study deals with university students.

A study by Saha and Guha (2024) found that Social Media is one of the most important source through which people can easily get updated information and they have easy access to online global knowledge bank. Students could utilize the social media as endless source of learning. This kind of stream is suitable for IT learning. The title survey was done on the nature of social media uses by the students of two reputed universities in Bangladesh to clarify the impact on their other daily diverse actions. The information was collected from 502 students on a random basis from both of the universities by providing questionnaire. the obtained information was assessed through descriptive statistical methods to explain the results. Some important findings in the study show that everyone possesses and uses at least one social media site and many have more than one. They spend more than one hour daily to use social media. Facebook is the most popular among all other social media activity. Students have high positive perception, low negative attitude, and moderate dependency on social media. The current study was done to find out the effects of social media on student wellbeing in Kenya.

A study on Social media use among Australian university students: Understanding links with stress and mental health (Emma, Hurley, Ian, Williams, Adrian, Tomyn, Sanci 2024) found that rapid growth in social media use among young adults has raised concerns about its possible impact on mental health and wellbeing, particularly among university student populations where the prevalence of mental health issues is also rising. Using qualitative approaches, this study identified the ways in which social media use may create stress in the lives of Australian university students. Data was drawn from an online health and wellbeing survey undertaken at a large, Australian university. Students were asked about their social media use habits and whether social media creates stress in their lives, with a follow-up question asking them to describe the source of this stress. Participants' free-text responses were examined using thematic analysis, with 3298 students providing a response for analysis (67.0% female; mean age = 24.5 years). Following data saturation, four main themes and twelve subthemes emerged about the ways that social media use was perceived to cause stress. The main themes identified were negative self-reflection, feeling overwhelmed by constant demands of social media, exposure to negativity, and addiction behaviours. Findings highlight the complex relationship between social media use and mental health among young adults, and may be used to inform development of targeted guidelines for university students on awareness and management of the aspects of SMU that appear to be driving university student distress. The current study was done in Kenya.

Emergence and rapidly change information and communication technology has a significant impact on social networking/ social media. Now just with a press on a button we can see our near and dear one on the screen does not matter where he/she lives. The use of social networking sites such as Facebook, Messenger, Imo, WhatsApp and Viber offer youth a portal for entertainment and communication which permits consumers to keep in touch with others and reshaping their daily life. Though there are many positive benefits and impacts of using social medias, the recent Cambridge Analytica scandal has lighten deliberations about our lives for the place of social media and social networking sites. Facebook is popular and its growth has been rapid around the world. As of the first quarter of 2018, the number of Facebook active users worldwide is approximately 2.19 billion (Facebook, 2018).The changes are happening exponentially in recent years. Perhaps, with the expansion of mobile technology it is playing a vital role in restructuring the social networking. Mobile devices have given an easy access in internet regardless anywhere/anytime and how it is dominating in terms of total minutes spent online. This set the resources to connect frequently on various devices in their hands.

Actually students are fond of social media for many reasons. Firstly, social networks give a feel of freedom to do whatever they want to upload what they want and talk to whom they want. They can make new friends and comment on the posts inbox by them. Social media actually has given students a place where they can create virtual community that may create conflicts in the real world. It gives them the liberty to fascinate themselves with more freedom. It was just impossible just a decade before for young attentions to generate a digital appearance of their activities through such an unprompted medium. The excess usage of social media of people diverted them from watching television and listening radio. Researchers are involved in research works on social media how people are being so attached with this day by day. They have been trying to figure out the nature and quality of the activities conducted on social media. There are significant differences between online and offline relationship.

Now students are the largest user of social media which is influencing them to change their daily life, behaviours, community approaches, public life and the bodily events. It has become an immense challenge for the society to address this issue and strongly recommended each member of the society should pay more concern in this substance.

Facebook, Messenger, Imo, WhatsApp and Viber have rapidly transform ever-present in recent couple of years among all age group particularly young groups mostly maladaptive due to extreme uses. It has been identified following a recent research that excessive browsing of social networking sites (SNS) causes an impact on interactive addiction, categorically 10% of students endorsed a set of requirement habitually thought of as being characteristic of material addiction, including acceptance, or an increase in time spent on the sites, removal, or annoyance or touchiness when incapable to access these websites, and desires for SNS use. Extreme involvement in SNS use has been connected to a different damage in psychosocial activities with loosing tolerances, showing gloomy symptoms, creating problems with interactions, and compact physical movement, lack in the real world community contribution, and decreasing academic success

Now social media has ignited as a type of online dissertation where people generate content, share it, and bookmark it, and network at a remarkable rate. As a consequence of its ease of use, rapidity and reach, social media is fast shifting the community dissertation in society and locale trends and schedule in topics that range from the situation and politics to technology and the amusement industry. The online world has improved drastically in last one decade, thanks to the creation of social media, young people share ideas, moods and audio visual materials with cheap rate. Martin, (2008) and Lusk, (2010) is aligned with the same perception with social media and according to them social media is the use of Facebook, Blogs, Twitter, My Space and LinkedIn for multi purposes such as communication, sharing photos as well as videos. The widespread use of social networking websites has converted global situation in the last couple of years. What happening out as a hobby for particular computer knowledgeable persons has become a social standard and lifestyle for people from all over the world. Young generation has particularly incorporated these sites as a way to attach with their peers, share material, reinvent their behaviors, and setting their social lives.

Person to person communication and communication through internet and social networking websites are two completely different platform of sharing ideas and views. Throughout the communication using these websites, they trail instant message (IM) and chatting as well as status or Twitter updates to conversation to friends and direct themselves. Kaitlin (2010) added opines that social networking websites likewise touch the way we obtain information and update. The sites accelerate different portals concluded which we get information and make additional various news openings.

Risk Factors Associated With Social Media Addiction: An Exploratory Study (Ting, Wang, Xiao, & Wu 2024) found that use of social media is becoming a necessary daily activity in today's society. Excessive and compulsive use of social media may lead to social media addiction (SMA). The main aim of this study was to investigate whether demographic factors (including age and gender), impulsivity, self-esteem, emotions, and attentional bias were risk factors associated with SMA. The study was conducted in a non-clinical sample of college students ($N = 520$), ranging in age from 16 to 23 years, including 277 females (53%) and 243 males (47%). All participants completed a survey measuring impulsivity, self-esteem, anxiety, depression, social anxiety, loneliness, and attentional bias. The final hierarchical regression model indicated significant risk factors for SMA with an accuracy of 38%. The identified set of associated risk factors included female gender ($\beta = -0.21$, $t = -4.88$, $p < 0.001$), impulsivity ($\beta = 0.34$, $t = 8.50$, $p < 0.001$), self-esteem ($\beta = -0.20$, $t = -4.38$, $p < 0.001$), anxiety ($\beta = 0.24$, $t = 4.43$, $p < 0.001$), social anxiety ($\beta = 0.25$, $t = 5.79$, $p < 0.001$), and negative attentional biases ($\beta = 0.31$, $t = 8.01$, $p < 0.001$). Finally, a discussion of the results is presented, followed by corresponding recommendations for future studies.

Social media (e.g., Facebook, WeChat, Tik Tok) have attracted substantial public interest to the point that they are becoming a cornerstone of modern communication. It has been argued that social media promote social interaction, help in maintaining relationships, and allow for self-expression (Baccarella et al., 2018). According to a survey by the China Internet Network Information Center, there are 900 million users of social media in China. College students are freer than others to control the use of their time and the use of social media is thus becoming an integral part of their lives. However, social media, if used immoderately, may lead to social media addiction (SMA), which refers to the excessive and compulsive use of social media platforms, resulting in severe impairment in all aspects of life (Kuss and Griffiths, 2017). Addicted users of social media tend to spend too much time on social media, to be overly concerned about social media and to be driven by uncontrollable urges to use social media (Andreassen and Pallesen, 2014). SMA can be viewed as a specific form of digital technology addiction, in which the conceptualizations all center on these addictive behaviors as pathological forms of necessary and normal behaviors (Moreno et al., 2021). SMA may affect users' mental health, leading to anxiety, depression, lower subjective wellbeing, and poor academic performance (Lin et al., 2016). The study examined potential risk factors associated with SMA focusing on demographic factors, impulsivity, self-esteem, emotions, and attentional bias. The current study examined impact of social media on student wellbeing in Kenyan public universities.

In general, the impact of demographic factors such as age and gender has been considered in previous studies. Young individuals maintain an online presence and develop addictive behaviors more often than older individuals (Abbasi, 2019). Furthermore, women are more likely to indulge in social media more than men in order to enhance their social connections (Andreassen et al., 2017).

Impulsivity is an important personality trait that plays a major part in the occurrence, development, and maintenance of addiction (Cerniglia et al., 2019). However, the link between impulsivity and SMA is controversial. It has been found that trait impulsivity is a marker for vulnerability to SMA (Sindermann et al., 2020). The most influential theoretical explanation for this is Dual System Theory, which is also known as reflective–impulsive theory. The reflective system includes the prefrontal cortex, which plays a key role in a wide range of executive and inhibitory behaviors, such as short-term memory, planning, attention, and resistance to immediate rewards for the sake of long-term rewards. By contrast, the impulsive system includes the subcortical brain areas, accounts for pleasure and addictive behaviors, and responds to quickly acquired cues regardless of long-term negative results. Imbalance between the reflective and impulsive systems leads to addictive behaviors (Droutman et al., 2019). However, another empirical study based on a Go/Stop Impulsivity task found impulsivity was not significantly associated with SMA (Chung et al., 2019). This inconsistency of results may be caused by the use of different measurement approaches. Therefore, the association between impulsivity and SMA needs further exploration.

Self-esteem impacts the predisposition to SMA and there is a negative association between the frequency of Facebook use, the meaning attributed to Facebook use, and users' levels of self-esteem (Błachnio et al., 2016). People with low levels of self-esteem prefer to avoid face-to-face communication and escape into the virtual world where they can behave anonymously and do what they want. Also, negative feedback from social media will reduce users' levels of self-esteem (Andreassen et al., 2017).Nowadays in every one's life social media have become an inevitable part. Multitude of students in Kenya pass a majority of valuable time by speculate about online social media sites. So it is essential to speak briefly the effects of using social media sites on the community

A study on Association between social media use and students' academic performance through family bonding and collective learning: The moderating role of mental well-being(Zhang, Abbas, Farrukh, Shankar,Ercisli & Dobhal 2024) found that the advent of the digital age represents a transformative era in which technology, primarily social media platforms, has become an integral part of the daily lives of individuals worldwide. Students are the most prolific users of social media, utilizing these platforms for a variety of purposes, including communication, information sharing, entertainment, and social networking. This study evaluated the connection between student social media use and academic performance through family bonding and collaborative learning. This research also explores how mental wellbeing moderates the link between students' family bonding, collaborative learning, and academic performance. This research article analysed a sample of 330 university students from the public and private sectors and tested the proposed hypothesized relationships. The study used the Partial Least Squares Structural Equation Modelling (PLS-SEM) methodological approach for evaluating proposed parameters. The findings indicated that social media use positively correlated with students' academic performance. Second, family bonding and collaborative learning significantly moderated the association between students' academic performance and social media use. Finally, mental well-being significantly moderated the connection between students' collaborative learning, family bonding, and academic performance. This study's findings contribute to the knowledge of global education with valuable insights into students' psychological well-being and academic performance. In theory, the research advanced the scientific understanding of education by assessing social media usage's effects on students' academic performance and psychological well-being. The current study used qualitative research methods.

METHODOLOGY

The study was carried in four higher education institutions in Kenya. Kenya is bordered by Uganda in the west Tanzania in the south Ethiopia and Sudan in the north and Somalia and Indian ocean to the east. It lies on the equator. It was assumed that all higher education students suffer from financial stress. Through qualitative research methods the study identified the impact of social media on student wellbeing among university students in Kenyan public universities. The study used saturated sampling technique to select eight students to be interviewed using an interview schedule. Kothari (2009) defines an interview schedule as an outline of questions that form a basis for and guide the interviewing process. The schedule provides a structure that aids in obtaining the necessary information efficiently and business like atmosphere. The validity of the interviews was ascertained by the assistance of experts from Maseno university psychology department. Before undertaking the actual study informed consent was obtained from students. The researcher assured the target respondents that their confidentiality was to be upheld at all stages of the study by keeping their identities anonymous while the data collection tools were being administered. Permission was requested and granted.

QUALITATIVE DATA ANALYSIS

The researcher used a thematic analysis to pinpoint examine and record patterns (or themes) within the data. Gibbs (2008) describes themes as patterns across data sets that are important to the description of a phenomenon and are associated to a specific research question. The themes become categories for analysis and according to Gibbs (2008) a thematic analysis can be used in two different fields; literature critique and qualitative analysis of data and requires the determination of the frequency of appearance of a theme or a type of data. Qualitative research reports give a vivid descriptive account of the situation under study. For Data collection in qualitative research Interview schedules and observation checklists are used to yield qualitative data. To yield rich data a qualitative researcher may therefore use in-depth interviews focus group discussions and observations.

Thematic analysis was performed through the process of coding in phases to create established and meaningful patterns. These phases consist of familiarization of data generating initial codes searching for themes among codes reviewing themes defining and naming themes and producing final reports (Raburu 2011) as presented in table 1.

Table 1. Coding

Transcript	Themes/subthemes	Coding for themes/subthemes
Definitely it impacts. It helps get information…s1. Right now I can do assignment…s2. we have classes online…s3. we send and receive cats online…s4. We read online…s5.	Students get information Assignments classes	IF A C R
They create stress…s5. There is cyberbullying…s6. No time for sleeping…s7.	Stressor Bullying Sleep disorders	ST B SD
We compare our image with others…s8	imaging	I
Somebody can post something and you take it personal. It affects you psychologically… s7. it makes me feel like killing myself…s3	Anxiety suicidal	AX SU
One becomes addicted…s5	addiction	AD
We write academic articles for pay….s4	money	M

FINDINGS AND DISCUSSIONS

Findings and discussions were done according to the objectives. The following were found to be the impact social media had on student wellbeing in universities.

Information

Students reported that they get useful information from social media.
'' it helps get information…s1.

University students need information on various areas. Social media becomes handy in providing this. This agrees with A study on The Impact of Social Media on Student Well-Being: Navigating the Digital Journey by (DiYES International School, 2023) found both positive effects and challenges. The Positive Facets of Social Media were that Social media is a potent communication tool, nurturing connections among students separated by geographical boundaries. It facilitates the sharing of ideas, experiences, and support networks, especially valuable for those facing unique challenges. Online communities provide a sense of belonging and help form friendships, positively contributing to students' mental health. Moreover, social media platforms serve as avenues for awareness and education. Mental health advocacy and support groups leverage these platforms to share information, reduce stigma, and encourage open conversations about mental health issues among students. The Challenges of Social Media were that Despite its benefits, social media poses significant challenges to student mental well-being. Continuously encountering carefully curated and idealized depictions of others' lives may result in individuals comparing themselves and experiencing a sense of inadequacy. The pressure to conform to societal standards and unrealistic beauty ideals perpetuated on these platforms can contribute to body image issues and low self-esteem among students.

The pervasive nature of social media also means that cyberbullying and online harassment are serious concerns for students. The anonymity provided by the digital landscape can embolden individuals to engage in harmful behaviour, leading to profound negative impacts on the mental health of those targeted. However, the current study was done in a third world country with different economic conditions.

While social media presents challenges, it also offers avenues for digital empowerment in the realm of mental health for students. Mental health apps and online communities provide accessible resources and support for students seeking to enhance their well-being. These digital tools empower students to take an active role in managing their mental health and foster a sense of wellbeing. Concerning the negative effects of the social media students who used it got lesser time to study. Karpinski et al (2009) stated that Facebook users devote lesser time to their studies than the on users did and consequently had poor GPA.

Stress

Students reported that social media creates stress;
"They create stress…s5."

Students reported that social media creates stress. A person may post something which may disturb the student psychologically. The findings further established that 76% of the university students had a mild level of depression. A significant relationship was found between frequency of social media use and level of depression. A significant relationship was further established between Facebook use and WhatsApp use with level of depression. This agrees with Emma, Ian, Adrian, Lena (2024) who found that Australian students are stressed.

Bullying

University students reported bullying;
There is cyberbullying...s6

University students using social media are exposed bullying. Some people abuse them online. The pervasive nature of social media also means that cyberbullying and online harassment are serious concerns for students. The anonymity provided by the digital landscape can embolden individuals to engage in harmful behaviour, leading to profound negative impacts on the mental health of those targeted.

Addiction

Students reported addiction
One becomes addicted...s5

Addiction comes because students are always online. A person may feel the compulsion to check social media platforms and experience withdrawal symptoms when they do not. Social media addiction can affect someone's mental health and result in physical problems, such as sleep problems. A person may be able to decrease social media use on their own.

Sleep Disorders

Students were found to have sleep disorders
No time for sleeping...s7.

Looking at social media in bed can make it harder for you to fall asleep. It can also reduce the amount of time you sleep for and leave you feeling unrefreshed the next day. Try to limit (or stop) social media use a couple of hours before bedtime, to allow your body to wind down and prepare for sleep.

Anxiety

Students who use social media were found to have anxiety.

Somebody can post something and you take it personal. It affects you psychologically.... s7

Social media use can affect users' physical health even more directly. Researchers know the connection between the mind and the gut can turn anxiety and depression into nausea, headaches, muscle tension, and tremors.(2)

Suicidal Tendencies

Students using social media were found to have suicidal tendencies
it makes me feel like killing myself...s3

Bullying, whether on social media or elsewhere, physical or not, significantly increases victims' risk of suicidal behaviour. Since social media was introduced some people have taken their lives as a result of cyberbullying. Furthermore, suicide rates among teenagers have increased from 2010 to 2022 as social media has become something that people interact with more throughout their day-to-day lives.(1)

Earning Money on Social Media

Some students make money using social medias
We write academic articles for pay.... s4

Some students are making money using social. This agrees with Emma et al (2024) who found that Social media seems to be growing by leaps and bounds every day. And with it come viable opportunities for individuals and business too. It is shown on research and found out that on average a person spends around two hours on social media but if the person is addicted he probably spends more.

SUMMARY AND CONCLUSION

From the research done social media has both positive and negative impacts. However, the negative impacts are more in Kenya. This is due to the fact that the social media are not monitored. The students can access any site even if it is harmful.

Social media can also be a source of distraction and cybercrime besides the fact that it can also lead to addiction. The influence of social media on public universities in Kenya depends on the students' engagement with social media activities and content.

As social media continues to shape the way students connect and communicate, it is crucial to acknowledge both its positive and negative influences on mental health. Navigating the digital landscape requires a mindful approach and striking a balance to harness the benefits of social media while mitigating its potential adverse effects on student well-being.

In conclusion, it is evident that social media plays a multifaceted role in students' lives, impacting mental health in various ways. From nurturing connections and spreading awareness to perpetuating unrealistic beauty standards and contributing to anxiety, the digital landscape presents both opportunities and challenges. To navigate this complex terrain, students must adopt strategies such as mindful consumption, periodic digital detoxes, and promoting positive content.

Moreover, recognizing the role of social media in influencing sleep patterns, relationships, and the spread of misinformation is essential for a comprehensive understanding of its impact on student mental health. As the digital realm evolves, researchers are leveraging social media data to gain insights into mental health trends, highlighting the need for responsible and ethical practices in this burgeoning field.

Recently there has been a massive evolution in social media, in the way by which people communicate or socialize. From the study we observed that the higher proportion of students accessed to internet through mobile phone leading. Social media is used on daily basis and time span in per day is one hour or higher by most of the students. A significant number of students used social media for chatting. In our findings regarding social media practices by the students Facebook is very popular social media platform among Kenyan students followed by YouTube and Twitter. Social media is taken as an entertainment task by the students and they prefer to update their status by using social media sites. The majority of the students do not feel any impact of social media on their life. Some of the respondent has positive impact, because social media may be utilizing for various communication with others and for news update. Indifferent circumstances, the negative impact of social on student life are that it badly affects their studies and wastes their time a lot.

The study also concluded that there is no seriously negative impact of social media on students' life when they are properly guided to use it for positive purpose. If the students' life has not been affected negatively this will lead to healthy life and consequently might enhance and influence the learning process, occur and meaning will be constructed. The study also recommended the encouragement of students to continue using social media to exchange social issues among them and to form social groups to collaborate on specific issues. The social media should be used such a way that it never hampers education or social lives of students.

REFERENCES

Allen, K. A., Ryan, T., Gray, D. L., McInerney, D. M., & Waters, L. (2014). Social media use and social connectedness in adolescents: The positives and the potential pitfalls. *The Educational and Developmental Psychologist*, 31(1), 18–31. 10.1017/edp.2014.2

Alonzo, R., Hussain, J., Stranges, S., & Anderson, K. K. (2021). Interplay between social media use, sleep quality, and mental health in youth: A systematic review. *Sleep Medicine Reviews*, 56, 101414. 10.1016/j.smrv.2020.10141433385767

Appel, H., Gerlach, A. L., & Crusius, J. (2016). The interplay between Facebook use, social comparison, envy, and depression. *Current Opinion in Psychology*, 9, 44–49. 10.1016/j.copsyc.2015.10.006

Astleitner, H., Bains, A., & H¨ormann, S. (2023). The effects of personality and social media experiences on mental health: Examining the mediating role of fear of missing out, ghosting, and vaguebooking. *Computers in Human Behavior*, 138, 107436. 10.1016/j.chb.2022.107436

Asur, S., & Huberman, B. A. (2010). Predicting the Future with Social Media. Social Computing Lab: HP Labs, Palo Alto, California. 10.1109/WI-IAT.2010.63

Australian Institute of Health and Welfare (AIHW). (2021). *Mental illness*. AIHW. https://www.aihw.gov.au/reports/children-youth/mental-illness

Baker, D. A., & Algorta, G. P. (2016). The relationship between online social networking and depression: A systematic review of quantitative studies. *Cyberpsychology, Behavior, and Social Networking*, 19(11), 638–648. 10.1089/cyber.2016.020627732062

Baker, Z. G., Krieger, H., & LeRoy, A. S. (2016). Fear of missing out: Relationships with depression, mindfulness, and physical symptoms. *Translational Issues in Psychological Science*, 2(3), 275–282. 10.1037/tps0000075

Berryman, C., Ferguson, C. J., & Negy, C. (2018). Social media use and mental health among young adults. *The Psychiatric Quarterly*, 89(2), 307–314. 10.1007/s11126-017-9535-629090428

Best, P., Manktelow, R., & Taylor, B. (2014). Online communication, social media and adolescent wellbeing: A systematic narrative review. *Children and Youth Services Review*, 41, 27–36. 10.1016/j.childyouth.2014.03.001

Beyens, I., Frison, E., & Eggermont, S. (2016). "I don't want to miss a thing": Adolescents' fear of missing out and its relationship to adolescents' social needs, Facebook use, and Facebook related stress. *Computers in Human Behavior*, 64, 1–8. 10.1016/j.chb.2016.05.083

Boyd, D. (2010) *Taken Out of Context: American Teen Sociality in Networked Publics*. Wikipedia. en.wikipedia.org

Chan, D. K. S., & Cheng, G. H. (2004). A Comparison of offline and online friendship qualities at different stages of relationship development. *Journal of Social and Personal Relationships*, 21(3), 305–320. 10.1177/0265407504042834

Dhaka ranked second in number of active Facebook users. Retrieved February 13, 2018, fromhttps://m.bdnews24.com/en/detail/bangladesh/1319890.

DiYES International School. (2023). *The Impact of Social Media on Student Well-Being: Navigating the Digital Journey*. IGCSE Curriculum. DiYES International School.

Gaitho, M. (2018). *What Is the Real Impact of Social Media?* Simplilearn. https://www.simplilearn.com/real-impact-social-media-article

Griffiths, M. D., Kuss, D. J., & Demetrovics, Z. (2014). Social networking addiction: An overview of preliminary findings. In Rosenberg K. P., Feder L. C., editors. (Eds.), *Behavioral addictions. Criteria, evidence, and treatment* (pp. 119–141). New York: Elsevier.

Hormes, J. M., Kearns, B., & Timko, C. A. (2014). Craving Facebook? Behavioral addiction to online social networking and its association with emotion regulation deficits. *Addiction (Abingdon, England)*, 109(12), 2079–2088. 10.1111/add.1271325170590

Internet World Stats. (2017). Internet Top 20 Countries - Internet Users. Internet World Stats. http://www.internetworldstats.com/top20.htm

Kaitlin, C. (2010). Social media changing social interactions. *Student Journal of Media Literacy Education*, 1(1), 1–11.

Karadkar, A. (2015). *The impact of social media on student life*. Technician Online. https://www.technicianonline.com/opinion/article_d1142b70-5a92-11e5-86b4-cb7c98a6e45f.html

Kuss, D. J., & Griffiths, M. D. (2011). Online social networking and addiction—A review of the psychological literature. *International Journal of Environmental Research and Public Health*, 8(9), 3528–3552. 10.3390/ijerph809352822016701

Lusk, B. (2010). Digital natives and social media behaviors: An Overview. *Prevention Researcher*, 17, 3–6.

Mark, D. (2018). Addicted to Social Media? What can we do about it problematic, excessive use? *Psychology Today*.https://www.psychologytoday.com/us/blog/in-xcess/201805/addicted-social-media

Martin, J. L., & Yeung, K. (2006). Persistence of close personal ties over a 12-year period. *Social Networks*, 28(4), 331–362. 10.1016/j.socnet.2005.07.008

Nuskiya, A. F. (2017). The impact of social media among the university students empirical study based on the South Eastern University of Sri Lanka. *Journal of Information Systems & Information Technology*, 2(1), 10–19.

Pornsakulvanich, V. (2018, January–April). Excessive use of Facebook: The influence of self-monitoring and Facebook usage on social support. *Kasetsart Journal of Social Sciences*, 39(1), 116–121. 10.1016/j.kjss.2017.02.001

Ryan, T., Chester, A., Reece, J., & Xenos, S. J. (2014). The uses and abuses of Facebook: A review of Facebook addiction. *Journal of Behavioral Addictions*, 3(3), 133–148. 10.1556/JBA.3.2014.01625317337

Saha, S. R., & Guha, A. K. (2019). Impact of social media use of university students. *International Journal of Statistics and Applications*, 9(1), 36–43. 10.5923/j.statistics.20190901.05

Samsudeen, S. N., & Kaldeen, M. (2015). Adoption of Social Media Marketing By Tourism Product Suppliers: A Study in Eastern Province Of Sri Lanka. *European Journal of Business and Management*, 448–455.

Shabir, G., Yousef Hameed, Y. M., & Safdar, G. (2014). The impact of social media on youth. A Case Study of Bahawalpur City. *Asian Journal of Social Sciences & Humanities*, 3(4), 23–34.

Shortell, T. (2001). *An introduction to data analysis & presentation*. CUNY. http://academic.brooklyn.cuny.edu/soc/courses/712/chap18.Html

Steers, M. N., Wickham, R. E., & Acitelli, L. K. (2014). Seeing everyone else's highlight reels: How Facebook usage is linked to depressive symptoms. *Journal of Social and Clinical Psychology*, 33(8), 701–731. 10.1521/jscp.2014.33.8.701

Tsitsika, A. K., Tzavela, E. C., Janikian, M., Ólafsson, K., Iordache, A., Schoenmakers, T. M., Tzavara, C., & Richardson, C. (2014). Online social networking in adolescence: Patterns of use in six European countries and links with psychosocial functioning. *The Journal of Adolescent Health*, 55(1), 141–147. 10.1016/j.jadohealth.2013.11.01024618179

Zhang, X. (2024). *A study on Association between social media use and students' academic performance through family bonding and collective learning: The moderating role of mental well-being*. Springer.

Chapter 14
Social Networking Platforms and Academic Performance of Students:
A Correlation Tests Approach

Kapil Kumar Aggarwal
https://orcid.org/0000-0002-2752-9495
Chandigarh University, India

ABSTRACT

Since college students use social media extensively, studying the link between social media use and academic achievement has become an important research topic. This study aimed to assess the impact of social networking platform usage on the academic performance of undergraduate and postgraduate students in the commerce and management fields. The chapter also aimed to determine the extent to which University students' usage of social networking sites influences their academic achievement. This chapter utilizes the correlation tests to assess and compare the impact of social networking sites on the academic achievement of the chosen students. The data has been collected from December 2023 to February 2024. This research examines the impact of social networking sites on students' academic achievement, specifically focusing on how students might utilize these platforms without negative consequences. Several tools on these platforms facilitate students in acquiring new learning techniques and exchanging thoughts and questions with students worldwide.

DOI: 10.4018/979-8-3693-4417-0.ch014

INTRODUCTION

Social networking platforms are the online space that is used by any individual for communication with friends or relatives, sharing their thoughts, forming communities with other people of the same interests, or retaining connection with others for various purposes such as academic, entertainment, communication and socialization (Taprial & Kanwar, 2012). High speed internet connectivity and the availability of smartphones have immensely increased the number of users using these platforms. Social networking platforms as communication mediums are growing rapidly, with the increase of mobile phones and other portable hand-held devices. Using Instagram, Facebook, Google +, Snapchat, LinkedIn and other social networking platforms has become a trend in the young generation, especially college-going students (Akhtar, 2017). They use these platforms and remain active by posting their photographs, audio, video status and commenting or complimenting others' posted material and enjoying their virtual life (Evans, 2010). In the last couple of years, the trend of social networking platforms such as Facebook, Instagram, Snapchat, Twitter etc. has been observed on a large scale. Some social networking platforms e.g., Facebook, LinkedIn, Google Plus, Instagram and Snapchat have some inbuilt tools with the help of which users can create dynamic virtual communities and connect easily with others. Through such groups or communities' people with common interests remain more connected (Allen et al., 2014).

Just like any individual, college students also create their profile on different social platforms, send personal and private messages to each other, interact with other students, friends, and teachers, play games, and also use audio and video call features of these platforms (Pempek et al., 2009).

Nearly all users of social media websites are young adults from 14 to 25 years old who are called "Digital Natives" of this digital world. Sometimes these digital natives use social networking platforms to make their existing relations stronger rather than making new friends or relationships. On the other hand, most of these social networking platforms are offering a medium to acquire online knowledge, if all the resources are implemented and used properly by the students (Margaryan et al., 2011). Social network websites enable students to show their inner talents and their experiences and convey and express themselves.

The benefits of using social networking platforms for educational purposes are widely applicable in today's world. The use of social networking platforms enhances student's learning prospects and allows real-time communication outside the classroom (Boyd & Ellison, 2007). Students also adopt collaborative approaches to study which improves their creativity (Kumar & Nanda, 2020). Students can watch educational videos or exchange information about what they learn and then discuss with their teachers about doubts. Social networking platforms provide a medium to contact other students and teachers even after college hours. Some social networking sites like Facebook and Instagram have features that may boost students' morale to be involved in social and creative learning that assist learners to think out of the box (Binns, 2014). Nowadays many academic institutes are using the advantages of social networking platforms in the teaching-learning process (Aggarwal et al., 2023). Many colleges and universities are using these platforms for marketing or publicity via uploading the achievements of their students in various areas, placements, guest lectures, workshops, and many other day-to-day activities. Students realised their online classes using social networking platforms were more effective and interesting as compared to face-to-face classroom sessions (Burke & Kraut, 2016). Considering the shared and interactive environment of social networking platforms, they have great opportunities and potential in the field of education. Different universities or educational institutes after understanding the potential power of social networking platforms are implementing it in education (Chen & Bello, 2017). There are huge numbers of benefits to using social networking platforms in education such as more student participation, more interest in sessions, more accountability to their education and students have better control over the learning process. Social networking platforms assist students in active participation in the session or during discussion, query, or suggestion time. It is observed that social networking has become a vital component of student's life, and it is now considered as a learning platform that can be utilized to boost student morale, performance, and participation (De Vries et al., 2018). On the other hand, social networking platform usage may give undesirable consequences such as low academic grades or performance and less engagement in real life as compared to virtual life. So, to examine this there is a need for a reliable and valid questionnaire. Thus, the point of this analysis would be to bridge this difference and then also confirm the questionnaire by defining its precision and consistency of measurement seeing its properties. Hence, this analysis is an effort to learn if these networking platforms do impact the students' performance.

LITERATURE REVIEW

A study titled "Social Media, learning and connections for international students: The disconnect between what students use and the tools learning management systems offer" tried to discover out how international students use social media for educational purposes (Jade Sleeman, Catherine Lang, 2020). This research concluded that with proper knowledge of the educational usage of social networking service, these platforms can be used to create opportunities for teachers and to engage international students in the academic learning process.

To analyse the use of social media to make the teaching and learning process smoother. The objective of the study is to find the role of a supportive environment of social media in the learning process of a foreign language. Social media can be used as an effective and efficient mode of learning any foreign language like English (Bano & Zaman, 2020).

The impact of social media on post-graduate level students and the main objectives of the study were to examine why students make use of social media, how often students of post-graduate level make use of social media and whether social media affects the cumulative grade point average (CGPA) of students or not. Researchers concluded that proper utilisation of social media can become a very beneficial source of knowledge and sharing (Kauser & Awan, 2019).

The importance of social media in communication patterns. The objectives of the study were to know the types of users of social media the rising reasons for social media and emergent trends of social media communication patterns in the context of Indian people. Researchers have also covered the flip side of social media communication such as addiction in the younger generation, over communication through messaging and chat and degradation of ethics and so on (Bharucha, 2018).

The impact of social media on Indian youth. This study also covered the pattern of understanding social networking addiction in youths and the importance of social networking sites in culture development, building self-identity, developing relationships and acquisition of social, communication, and technical skills (Bhardwaj et al., 2017).

The engagement of Indian students on social media platforms especially Facebook and examined the patterns of engagement of students in terms of time, privacy, advertisements etc. on Facebook (Utpal, 2017). The researcher also analysed the usage patterns, network patterns and routine activities of the students.

A study titled "Impact of Social Networking Sites on Social Interactions Study of college students" tried to find out the impact of the use of social networking sites on the social relationships of college students (Kumari & Verma, 2015). This study also covered the impact of the use of social networking services on adolescents concerning gender. This research concluded that although social media gives an abundance of information and exposure to an open and supportive environment to students to build relationships, students should be aware of the risks associated with social networking services.

A study on the impact of social media on the development of school students, tried to find out whether students' academic performance is impacted by social media or not. They employed questionnaires to conduct the survey (El-Badawy & Hashem, 2015). The importance of social media especially Facebook in business.

Researchers have also considered the advantages and disadvantages of Facebook in the context of business (Bhagwat & Goutam, 2013). The study concluded that communication, transparency, and new trends of marketing through Facebook have brought evolution in business.

In a study to know the impact of social media on students and studied how it is helping students in collaborative learning and improving their academic performance (Al-Rahmi & Othman, 2013). Researchers concluded that social media is helpful to create better relationships with peers and teachers but on the flip side, students must control time devotion on social media to make it more productive.

A study titled "A survey on Facebook and academic performance in Nigeria universities" tried to find out the impact of Facebook on academic performance with references to the universities based out in Nigeria. Their primary objective was to find out whether Facebook impacts the student's grade points (Yusuf et al., 2012). The author concluded the study by stating that usage of Facebook had brought lower grade points in students.

RESEARCH OBJECTIVES

- To analyse the impact of social networking platforms on student's academic performance with respect to GPA.
- To analyse whether a student's class attendance is impacted by frequent usage of social networking platforms.
- To analyse whether the usage of social networking platforms affects the class participation amongst the students.

HYPOTHESES FRAMED FOR THE STUDY

- H_{01}: The more time a student spends on social networking platforms, "lower his or her grade point average will be".
- H_{02}: The more time a student spends on social networking platforms, "less likely they are to participate in class.
- H_{03}: The more friends a student has on social networking platforms, "more time he spends on social networking platforms.
- H_{04}: The more posts a student puts on social networking platforms, the less likely they are to participate in class.

RESEARCH METHODOLOGY

Based on the above-mentioned study objective and the hypothesis the following methodology is opted.

- Method for data collection: A structured questionnaire was prepared and used for collecting data from the students of commerce and management. Hence the sample drawn from the study in 284 based on stratified simple random sampling method.
- Sampling Technique: Students of Commerce and Management were considered for the study is not homogeneous, hence stratified random samplings is used.
- Area of Study: Undergraduate and postgraduate students of Commerce and Management.
- Data Collection Period: During the month of December 2023 to February 2024.
- Research Tools: For the present study correlation is used to test the hypothesis. Pearson's Correlation is a statistical technique that can show whether and how strongly the pairs of variables are closely associated. In the present study the author is trying to find out the inter relationship between the time spend on Social Networking Platforms and academic performance.

DATA ANALYSIS AND INTERPRETATION

Hypothesis One: The More Time a Student Spends on Social Networking Platforms, the "Lower His or Her Grade Point Average Will Be"

Table 1. Correlation analysis for GPA and time spend on social networking platforms

Correlations		What is your GPA (on a 5.0 scale)	How often do you spend time on social networking platforms?
What is your GPA (on a 5.0 scale)?	Pearson Correlation	1	.056
	Sig. (2-tailed)		.639
	N	284	284
How often do you spend time on social networking platforms?	Pearson Correlation	.056	1
	Sig. (2-tailed)	.639	
	N	284	284

Source: Computed from Primary data analysis

Interpretation: As per the first hypothesis, students who spend too much on social networking platforms are more likely to have lower performance and have low GPA. This hypothesis is tested with correlation and we need to see the relationship between independent and dependent variables such as time spend and GPA. The results show that the variables are weakly correlated (0.056) as shown in the above table. Hence, we conclude that there is no significance difference between the two variables. Hence the hypothesis is rejected. By this result we also see that students do have many responsibilities and activities during that academic year and their mindset and performance is showing inclined performance.

Hypothesis Two: The More Time a Student Spends on Social Networking Platforms, the "Less Likely They Are to Participate in Class"

Table 2. Correlation analysis for active participation and time spent

Correlations		In general, how actively do you participate in class?	How often do you spend time on social networking platforms?
In general, how actively do you participate in class?	Pearson Correlation	1	.301
	Sig. (2-tailed)		.971
	N	284	284
How often do you spend time on social networking platforms?	Pearson Correlation	.301	1
	Sig. (2-tailed)	.971	
	N	284	284

Source: Computed from Primary data analysis

Interpretation: From the above table it is observed that the more time a student spends on social networking platforms, the more likely they are to participate in class. The results show that there is no significant correlation between the two variables. The study also reveals that the present generation students are good in multitasking and they are involved in many activities of the University and also, they do pay attention in the class. Hence, the correlation shows lesser value (.301) the hypothesis is rejected.

Hypothesis Three: The More Friends a Student Has on Social Networking Platforms, the "More Time He or She Spends on Social Networking Platforms"

Table 3. Correlation Analysis for Friends and Time Spent on Social Networking Platforms

Correlations		How many friends do you have on social networking platforms?	How often do you spend time on social networking platforms?
How many friends do you have on social networking platforms?	Pearson Correlation	1	-0.310
	Sig. (2-tailed)		.002
	N	284	284
How often do you spend time on social networking platforms?	Pearson Correlation	-0.310	1
	Sig. (2-tailed)	.002	
	N	284	284

Source: Computed from Primary data analysis

Interpretation: From the above table we see that the correlations between the two variables are negatively correlated (-0.310). It means that even if there are many friends and followers on social networking platforms, respondents are doing their academic work on time and they are not deviated. Hence, we conclude that there is no significant relationship between number of friends and followers and the time spent on social networking platforms. Hence, we reject the hypothesis.

Hypothesis Four: The More Posts a Student Puts on Social Networking Platforms, the "Less Likely They Are to Participate in Class"

Table 4. Correlation analysis

Correlations		In general, how actively do you participate in class?	How often do you post on other people's social networking platforms?	How often do you text during Class?	How often do you use your laptop for activities	How often do you contribute to class discussion?
In general, how actively do you participate in class?	Pearson Correlation	1	.070	-.029	-.060	.417
	Sig. (2-tailed)		.390	.774	.564	.000
	N	284	284	284	284	284
How often do you post on other people's social networking platforms?	Pearson Correlation	.070	1	.319	.150	.092
	Sig. (2-tailed)	.390		.019	.122	.415
	N	284	284	284	284	284
How often do you text during Class?	Pearson Correlation	-.029	.319	1	.281	.053
	Sig. (2-tailed)	.774	.019		.002	.425
	N	284	284	284	284	284
How often do you use your laptop for activities	Pearson Correlation	-.060	.150	.281	1	-.151
	Sig. (2-tailed)	.564	.122	.002		.145
	N	284	284	284	284	284
How often do you contribute to class discussion?	Pearson Correlation	-.417	.092	.053	-.151	1
	Sig. (2-tailed)	.000	.415	.425	.145	
	N	284	284	284	284	284

Source: Computed from Primary data analysis

Interpretation: The respondents were asked multiple questions like how active they are on social networking platforms, how often they post their videos, portraits and other information, how often they use social networking platforms during the class hours, usage of laptops and their effective class participation. It is noted that all the responses as per the analysis are low correlated (positive and negative) (.070, -.029, -.060 and.417). As a result, we may conclude that students' use of social media platforms has no effect on their performance, particularly their academic performance. As per the above statistics figures, the correlation is weak and the hypothesis is rejected.

FINDINGS

Social media platforms are currently trending more amongst the youngsters; it is high time to see whether their academic performance is affected by these social media platforms. In order to analyse the above-mentioned objective, four hypotheses were framed and tested with correlation in SPSS. From the study we see that all the hypotheses were rejected as there is no relationship existing between the independent variable and dependent variables.

First objective was framed to test the relationship between the time spent on social media platforms and their grade points, hence the results show that students spending more time the GPA is not affected.

Second hypothesis was framed to test whether the students' class participation, hence there is no relationship existing either. Although students are frequently on social networking platforms, they are actively participating in all the events and lectures conducted.

Third hypotheses were framed to test the friends and time spent on social networking platforms. Nowadays students do a lot of networking with neighbour colleges; however as per this study the students are networking for the higher performance in their academics.

In last hypothesis is test the frequent posts on social networking platforms and class participation. In this hypotheses correction between different factors are very low so its shows that the frequent posts on social networking platforms does not affect their class participation.

CONCLUSION

With the rapid advancement in ICT, students are engaged in online sources intensively and various social networking platforms have become indispensable part of their life. Continuous usage of social networking platforms may distract a student from his studies, hamper his life goals and make him addicted. But interactive classroom sessions, academic rules, guidelines and regulations and most importantly maturity of a student may be helpful for him to understand and deal with negative effects of these platforms. The present study aimed to develop and validate questionnaires to understand the purposes of usage of social networking platforms by college students in one of the selected regions of Punjab. The developed questionnaire in this study can help to improve the measurement of college student's usage of social networking platforms in today's changing environments. From the above study we concluded that most of the sampled students use social networking platforms but without affecting their academic performance. As per student's point of view, indeed there are many tools available on these platforms which help students to learn innovative learning skills and share their ideas and doubts with other students globally. Hence students should use social networking platforms to connect and improvise their academic skills.

REFERENCES

Aggarwal, K. K., Sharma, A., Kaur, R., & Lakhera, G. (2023). Algorithmic FinTech pioneering the financial landscape of tomorrow. In *Algorithmic Approaches to Financial Technology*. Forecasting, Trading, and Optimization., 10.4018/979-8-3693-1746-4.ch002

Akhtar, N. (2017). Social Networking Sites and Teens: Literature Review. *Trends in Information Management, 11*(2).

Al-Rahmi, W., & Othman, M. (2013). The impact of social media use on academic performance among university students: A pilot study. *Journal of Information Systems Research and Innovation*, 4(12), 1–10.

Allen, K. A., Ryan, T., Gray, D. L., McInerney, D. M., & Waters, L. (2014). Social Media Use and Social Connectedness in Adolescents: The Positives and the Potential Pitfalls. *The Educational and Developmental Psychologist*, 31(1), 18–31. 10.1017/edp.2014.2

Bano, A., & Zaman, S. (2020). The Use of Social Media in Facilitating the Teaching and Learning Process: A Case Study of Undergraduates at University of Bisha in Saudi Arabia. *International Journal of Linguistics. SSRN*, 3(c), 89–99. 10.2139/ssrn.3546836

Bhagwat, S., & Goutam, A. (2013). Development of social networking sites and their role in business with special reference to Facebook. *Journal of Business and Management*, 6(5), 15–28.

Bhardwaj, A., Avasthi, V., & Goundar, S. (2017). Impact of social networking on Indian youth-A survey. *International Journal of Electronics and Information Engineering*, 7(1), 41–51.

Bharucha, J. (2018). Social network use and youth well-being: A study in India. *Safer Communities*, 17(2), 119–131. 10.1108/SC-07-2017-0029

Binns, A. (2014). Twitter city and Facebook village: Teenage girls' personas and experiences influenced by choice architecture in social networking sites. *Journal of Media Practice*, 15(2), 71–91. 10.1080/14682753.2014.960763

Boyd, D. M., & Ellison, N. B. (2007). Social network sites: Definition, history, and scholarship. *Journal of Computer-Mediated Communication*, 13(1), 210–230. 10.1111/j.1083-6101.2007.00393.x

Burke, M., & Kraut, R. E. (2016). The relationship between Facebook use and well-being depends on communication type and tie strength. *Journal of Computer-Mediated Communication*, 21(4), 265–281. 10.1111/jcc4.12162

Chen, Y., & Bello, R. S. (2017). Does receiving or providing social support on Facebook influence life satisfaction? Stress as mediator and self-esteem as moderator. *International Journal of Communication*, 11, 14.

De Vries, D. A., Möller, A. M., Wieringa, M. S., Eigenraam, A. W., & Hamelink, K. (2018). Social comparison as the thief of joy: Emotional consequences of viewing strangers' Instagram posts. *Media Psychology*, 21(2), 222–245. 10.1080/15213269.2016.1267647

El-Badawy, T. A., & Hashem, Y. (2015). The impact of social media on the academic development of school students. *International Journal of Business Administration*, 6(1), 46.

Evans, L. (2010). *Social media marketing: strategies for engaging in Facebook, Twitter & other social media*. Pearson Education.

Kauser, S., & Awan, A. G. (2019). Impact of using social media on academic performance of students at graduate level: Evidence from Pakistan. *Glob J Manag Soc Sci Humanities*, 5(1), 116–142.

Kumar, V., & Nanda, P. (2020). Social media as a tool in higher education: A pedagogical perspective. In *Handbook of research on diverse teaching strategies for the technology-rich classroom* (pp. 239–253). IGI Global. 10.4018/978-1-7998-0238-9.ch016

Kumari, A., & Verma, J. (2015). Impact of social networking sites on social interaction-a study of college students. *Journal of the Humanities and Social Sciences*, 4(2), 55–62.

Margaryan, A., Littlejohn, A., & Vojt, G. (2011). Are digital natives a myth or reality? University students' use of digital technologies. *Computers & Education*, 56(2), 429–440. 10.1016/j.compedu.2010.09.004

Pempek, T. A., Yermolayeva, Y. A., & Calvert, S. L. (2009). College students' social networking experiences on Facebook. *Journal of Applied Developmental Psychology*, 30(3), 227–238. 10.1016/j.appdev.2008.12.010

Sleeman, J., & Lang, C. E. D. (2020). View of Social media, learning and connections for international students: The disconnect between what students use and the tools learning management systems offer. *Australasian Journal of Educational Technology, 36*(4), 44–56. https://ajet.org.au/index.php/AJET/article/view/4384/1624

Taprial, V., & Kanwar, P. (2012). *Understanding social media*. Bookboon.

Utpal, V. K. J. (2017). A study on the engagement of Indian students on social media. *Journal of Content, Community & Communication, 6*(3).

Yusuf, M., Peter, O., & Jadesola, A. (2012). *A Survey on Facebook and Academic Performance in Nigeria Universities*. Research Gate.

Chapter 15
Spatial Dimension of Students' Well-Being:
A Gender-Sensitive Approach

Susana Rosado
https://orcid.org/0000-0003-3456-3103
University of Lisbon, Portugal

Vitória Rodrigues Jeronimo
https://orcid.org/0009-0004-9273-952X
University of Lisbon, Portugal

ABSTRACT

Human well-being depends on various factors, including the perception of spaces and architecture. For higher education students, well-being is closely linked to their experiences within institutional spaces, which affect them differently based on gender. This study focuses on students at the Lisbon School of Architecture, University of Lisbon, Portugal, to understand how physical and symbolic aspects of spaces facilitate or hinder their appropriation in a gender-sensitive manner. Using participatory methods like exploratory marches, collective maps, focus groups, and questionnaires, the authors examine how these spatial experiences impact student well-being. The research identifies deficiencies in comfort, security, and belonging, and suggests architectural improvements to enhance social well-being in higher education institutions.

DOI: 10.4018/979-8-3693-4417-0.ch015

INTRODUCTION

Human well-being is influenced by a complex interplay of intrinsic and extrinsic factors. Among these, the perception of physical spaces and the architectural design underlying those spaces significantly impact individuals' lives. When considering higher education students, their well-being is closely tied to their experiences within the institutional spaces they inhabit. However, it is essential to recognize that spaces are not neutral; they exert differential effects on different student populations. Researching about spatial dimension of student well-being focused on the Lisbon School of Architecture (LSA), University of Lisbon, physical and symbolic aspects of LSA spaces are analyzed, aiming to understand how they influence students' lives. Particularly there is a focus on female students' encounters with the physical and symbolic dimensions of LSA spaces.

Examining both qualitative and quantitative data makes it possible to understand how these spaces either facilitate or hinder students' appropriation and utilization. The qualitative analysis draws on participative methods, including exploratory marches conducted by LSA female students and focus group discussions with undergraduates. Simultaneously, a quantitative approach involves an online questionnaire distributed to the entire student community, encompassing both women and men.

The results reveal a fragmented spatial territory, inadequate spaces for living and leisure, comfort-related deficiencies, and feelings of insecurity and exclusion. These external factors significantly impact students' well-being within higher education institutions.

BACKGROUND BASES

The well-being of students in Higher Education lacks a clear definition (Douwes, 2023). Factors affecting student well-being include living conditions, emotional stability, and social interactions. Definitions vary, but they emphasize effective functioning, positive mood, and satisfaction as important factors (Fraillon, 2004; Noble et al., 2008). Also, outdoor experiences and transdisciplinary approaches enhance well-being (Rosado & Ribeiro, 2024a, 2024b). Assessments of well-being often focus on academic and social integration, but little consider the study environment and gender differences. Likewise, green spaces impact mental health (Vidal et al., 2020). The importance of students perception of campus landscapes (Pullman, 2022) play an important role in evaluating the quality of the spatial organization and the landscape of the campus. Well-being spaces have dimensions like security, capability, therapeutic, and integrity (Fleuret & Atkinson, 2007) that contribute to the well-being and students' well-being influences their perception of study spaces (Fleuret & Prugneau, 2014).

According to Agrawal & Yadav (2021) "the most popular methodology across campus design/planning researches to analyse impact has been user surveys (…) and have also been carried out to understand health in terms of student and teacher perspective of learning evironments" . This author also states that "there is much to study about the impact of the physical environment in helping a university achieve its overall objectives". Authors like Dober (1996) and Turner (1986) recommend that campus design should respond human needs. This is also recommended by Hajrasouliha (2017) and Hajrasouliha & Ewing (2016) stating that "most works focus on teaching-learning or research environments on the micro-scale and less on the contextual condition of the campus environments".

Our research intends to contribute to attenuate this existing gap in research regarding the impact of spaces (physical planning and design) on the quality of student life in higher education. Also, gender plays a role in these perceptions. Marcela Lagarde (1996) explains that the gender perspective, rooted in gender theory and the historical-critical paradigm of feminism, allows us to analyze how women and men are defined in specific ways within a social context. This perspective is used in urban studies to examine gender asymmetries in city spaces and their reinforcement. It also applies to students' perception of space and well-being within campus environments.

The intersection of architecture, urbanism, and gender gained prominence in the United States and England during the 1960s. European experiences include feminist collectives like Matrix Feminist Design Co-operative and the Women Design Service. In Portugal, efforts are emerging to discuss gender in public spaces, led by associations like *Mulheres na Arquitectura* and the feminist collective *MAAD – Mulheres, Arte, Arquitetura e Design*. MAAD conducts feminist tours in Porto, Portugal, highlighting symbolic representations of women and critiquing historical erasure and patriarchal structures (Col.lectiu Punt6, 2019; Fávero, 2020).

The current city model, shaped by the sexual division of labor, organizes spaces into public and private spheres (Col.lectiu Punt6, 2019). The Industrial Revolution played a pivotal role in defining public and private spaces. Silvia Federici (2017) highlights how this division emerged during the transition from feudalism to capitalism, impacting gender roles. While this spatial configuration is not universally constant, it primarily applies to Europe and the United States, especially since the Industrial Revolution. Women from popular classes have historically participated in productive spheres. Pre-industrial societies blurred boundaries between production and reproduction, coexisting in communal villages. Industrialization led to spatial separation: men engaged in public, urban activities, while women focused on domestic and care roles (Col.lectiu Punt6, 2019).

Disputes over public space have historically occurred in highly unequal ways. Reversing the traditional allocation of public space to men and private space to women changes the symbolism: 'public woman' sounds pejorative, while 'public man' conveys power and authenticity (Abreu, 2021). Throughout history, socialization (including formal and informal education) and media have perpetuated the public-male and private-female dichotomy through objectification and hypersexualization of the female body in public life. Women who engaged in public life faced attacks, devaluation of their work, questions about qualifications, and legitimization of their experience—all aimed at maintaining male dominance in the public sphere (Col. lectiu Punt6, 2019).

Emerging as a response to the crisis of industrial cities, the modern city model is rooted in a capitalist and patriarchal logic, overemphasizing productive activities at the expense of other aspects of daily life and conditioning its planning to the productive system. The goal was to create a universal city model for a "standard subject" based on the segregation of human functions: living, moving, working, and recreating. This led to expansive and monofunctional growth, reliant on private vehicles as the main mode of transportation. Jane Jacobs (1993) criticized orthodox urbanism, advocating for cities as dynamic ecosystems shaped by human interactions. She emphasized diverse uses and urban density to promote community vitality, economic development, and safer spaces. Jacobs advocated streets, sidewalks, parks, and neighborhoods as essential for socialization, challenging specialist planners' detachment from local experience, which she believed also applied to the local economy.

The lack of representation of women in cities and poorly planned spaces create a sense of not belonging. Women who do not identify with city spaces become alienated, reinforcing gender ideologies. Addressing gender inequalities in spaces requires considering aspects beyond spatial configuration (Abreu, 2021). Women's socialization shapes their bodily experiences differently from men, even in shared spaces. Childhood behavioral restrictions persist into adulthood, impacting how women navigate public spaces. When these limitations exist in spaces marked by gender oppression, they affect people's ability to appropriate those spaces. Spaces communicate norms and perpetuate systems of female body manipulation.

Feminist groups have emerged as alternatives to traditional urban thinking, addressing challenges faced by women in cities. British collectives like the Matrix Feminist Design Co-operative and the Women Design Service analyzed women's relationship with urban spaces and architecture. In Spain and Catalonia, feminist collectives like Col.lectiu Punt 6 and Equal Saree prioritize people's daily lives in urban decisions, recognizing the importance of reproductive and care tasks carried out mainly by women. Feminist Urbanism challenges androcentric and patriarchal city paradigms, advocating for more democratic, equal, and community-oriented urban models. It emphasizes interdisciplinary approaches and opposes new predatory global city models.

In Portugal, traditional socialization has historically confined women to the private sphere and men to the public sphere, influenced by conservative and Catholic values. However, recent decades have seen significant shifts due to social and legal reforms, education, and global feminist movements, leading to increased female participation in the workforce, politics, and higher education.

In higher education institutions in Portugal, there has been a recent increase in participation in gender equality projects, with the University of Beira Interior (UBI) and the University of Trás-os-Montes and Alto Douro (UTAD) being pioneers. UBI launched the UBIgual project in 2011 to promote equal opportunities (UBIgual, 2011), and UTAD followed with a similar plan in 2016/17, focusing on personnel management and equality in decision-making (Universidade de Trás-os-Montes e Alto Douro, 2016). Other institutions such as ISCTE- Instituto Superior de Ciências do Trabalho e da Empresa, Universidade do Minho, Universidade de Coimbra, Universidade do Porto, and Universidade Nova de Lisboa have also developed equality plans with funding from the European Union, showing a continuous effort in the area.

Despite these advances, the implementation of gender equality strategies is still slow. The Lisbon School of Architecture at the University of Lisbon, for example, has yet to formalize the existence of Commissions for Gender Equality, Inclusion and Non-Discrimination. The study highlights the importance of addressing gender inequalities not only through policies and plans but also by considering the physical spaces of institutions as active agents in the reproduction of inequalities. It is essential to integrate spatial analysis to promote more inclusive and equitable academic environments.

RESEARCH FOCUS

The Lisbon School of Architecture (LSA) at the University of Lisbon, noted for its complex project history, provides a basis for initiating broader discussions with other institutions in Portugal and beyond. This research aims to explore how academic and institutional architectural designs can be planned or transformed according to principles of equality, care, and support networks.

The LSA is situated within the Ajuda University Campus, Lisbon, Portugal. Designed alongside the campus, LSA emerged from a complex and gradual urban planning process. Inspired by Anglo-Saxon models, the campus aimed to centralize multiple higher education institutions in Lisbon, replacing scattered facilities for improved efficiency and collaboration. Despite political controversies and internal challenges during planning, the final 1993 Detailed Plan adopted an orthogonal grid with tree-lined avenues, maintaining a connection to the Monsanto Forest Park. However, over the years, changes and delays affected the original configuration, resulting in modifications to the planned road structure (Carvalho, 2017). This results in an incomplete and fragmented set, which fails to provide well-being to its users.

Figure 1. Orthophotomap of the Ajuda University Campus, Lisbon, Portugal

Source: adapted from Google Maps, 2023

Currently, the Ajuda University Campus (AUC), highlighted in color on the orthophoto map in Figure 1, is made up of three faculties (Lisbon School of Architecture, Faculty of Veterinary Medicine and the School of Social and Political Sciences), the Sports Pavilion, the Canteen and a set of university residences, which together serve around 9000 students. This land has a sloped topography, varying around 80 meters in height.

The AUC, shaped by a slow and troubled process, reflects a monofunctional, disconnected territory. It stands isolated between the Monsanto Forest Park to the north and the consolidated city to the south. Precarious public transport connections exacerbate its isolation. The model of the university campus promotes car dependence, rendering faculties unattractive to pedestrians. Internally, the AUC lacks cohesion, resulting in fragmented, unsafe spaces. Oversized roads prioritize cars over pedestrians, and insufficient amenities hinder community life. The absence of urban structures diminishes vitality and character, leaving uncomfortable passages for students.

Thus, the Ajuda University Campus in general, and the Lisbon School of Architecture in particular, grapple with challenges stemming from its turbulent history, outdated urban model, and insufficient infrastructure for community engagement. The outcome is a monofunctional, isolated, and unappealing space—both internally and to its surroundings. Addressing these issues is essential to enhance student well-being.

LISBON SCHOOL OF ARCHITECTURE

Born from the Department of Architecture of the Escola Superior de Belas Artes de Lisboa (ESBAL), the LSA was integrated into the Technical University of Lisbon in 1979. Due to the lack of space and adequate conditions for teaching architecture, it was moved, in 1994, to the new building dedicated exclusively to the faculty at the Ajuda University Campus, Figure 2 (Gonçalves et al., 2011).

Figure 2. Lisbon School of Architecture, University of Lisbon

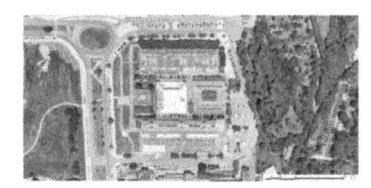

Source: adapted from Google Maps, 2023

The project design for the LSA envisaged an open, pavilion-like, and modulated form - a reflection of the author's experiences in designing primary schools (Gonçalves et al., 2011). As can be seen in Figure 3, the set is made up of 5 volumes of different sizes arranged across the land in a rectilinear mesh, forming types of pedestrian streets. The buildings in the complex are marked by a predominant horizontality that adapts to the terrain and its slope so does not interfere with the landscape (Figure 4). The central volume, commonly called the Cube, compact and massive, has brutalist characteristics, with part of the roofs in oblique planes at 45 degrees. The blocks are marked by open facades in modular semi-covered galleries, and feature a regular rhythm of glazed walls, concrete pillars painted in blue, and entrance.

Figure 3. Implementation plan of the Lisbon School of Architecture, and its circulation plan

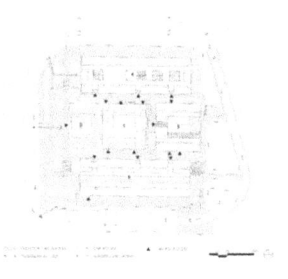

Source: adapted from Jeronimo, 2023

Figure 4: Section A-A N/S of Lisbon School of Architecture land

Source: Jeronimo, 2023

The LSA, like the Campus, underwent physical and programmatic changes. Design modifications, including block removal and course additions, aimed to transform it into a School of Arts (Gonçalves et al., 2011). However, LSA now serves over 3000 students—triple the projected number—highlighting inadequate infrastructure (FA. ULisboa, [n.d.]). Poor connectivity with surroundings, dysfunctional access points, and incomplete spaces pose challenges, as shown in Figure 3. The absence of Block 3 contributes to an uncharacterized front area, hindering accessibility and well-being (Figure 5 and Figure 6). Peripheral areas further isolate the LSA.

Figure 5. Photographic documentation of participants in the exploratory march: (a) Rear parking lot; (b) Void where Block 3 should have been built

Source: adapted from Jeronimo, 2023

Figure 6. Different accesses of Lisbon School of Architecture: (a) Central access; (b) NW access; (c) Pedestrian access in SW; (d) South access; (e) Car access in NE; (f) Car access in SE

Source: adapted from Jeronimo, 2023

The Lisbon School of Architecture (LSA) lacks connection with the rest of the campus and suffers from a fragmented territory affecting both building layout and open spaces. Inconsistent circulation between blocks, peripheral arrangement, lack of weather protection, and disproportionate connecting elements contribute to this issue. Notably, stairs and ramps are predominantly located on the outer perimeter (Figure7). While there are extensive outdoor and green spaces, their quality for everyday life is not abundant. Large cemented areas dedicated to cars and underused open green spaces contribute to a fragmented territory. These factors hinder the promotion of coexistence and permanence, impacting overall well-being.

Figure 7. Existing stairs and ramps of Lisbon School of Architecture: (a) NW stairs; (b) SW stairs; (c) Ramp in the rear of Block 6; (d) Ramp between Blocks 1 and 5

Source: adapted from Jeronimo, 2023

Currently, the functions of each block of LSA are distributed as follows, shown in Table 1. In addition to the questions raised about the open spaces of the LSA, the buildings that comprise it reveal a structural and functional complexity that directly affects the experience and well-being of users.

Table 1. Distribution of the different spaces of Lisbon School of Architecture

Spaces	Functions
Block 1	Rainha Sonja Auditorium, Library, Meeting Rooms, Offices, Laboratories and IT and Documentation Center, Technical area and Bathrooms
Block 2	Administrative Services, Governing Council, Bathrooms, Archive.
Block 3	Not built
Block 4	Classrooms for the Architecture course, Offices, Small Auditoriums and Atriums, Bathrooms and Storage.
Block 5	Classrooms for Masters Degree, Ph.D. Degree and Fashion Design Course; Ateliers; Cabinets; Students band staff room and bathrooms.
Block 6	Classrooms for Urban Planning, Interiors, and Design courses; Workshops; Cabinets; Academic Services; Commercial Services; Student Association; Pub; Space 24 and Space 25 and Garage.

The distribution of courses in the LSA blocks exhibits hierarchy and disproportion, accentuated by varying ground altitudes. A holistic approach is needed to improve university spaces and enhance student well-being. Particularly in Blocks 4, 5, and 6, intended for class accommodation, it is important to highlight how the typology used, despite raising a certain ambiguity, brings positive aspects to coexistence and the feeling of security and well-being. Both blocks are longitudinal, with open classrooms, connected by a corridor that runs through the interior of them, with double-height ceilings and a glazed facade (Figure 8).

Figure 8. Practical math class at LSA

Source: Rosado & Ribeiro, 2016

The ambiguity is caused by the mix of circulation and permanence spaces. Despite facing problems with acoustic and thermal comfort, in addition to the lighting discomfort caused by the excess light that enters through the glazed facades, this typology allows for good visibility, which is a fundamental factor for the feeling of security.

The LSA at Ajuda University Campus lacks external communication and suffers from fragmented, dysfunctional spaces internally. It fails to provide essential community exchanges and necessary social spaces for student well-being.

METHODOLOGY

To explore how the physical and spatial aspects of the LSA and its surroundings impact students, especially female students, we employed participatory methods with the student community. A purposive sampling was considered at first, since we were targeting for women. Fortunatelly also men joined the study and enriched it. Rooted in feminist urbanism, these approaches prioritize people's daily experiences, recognizing their diverse perceptions and needs. By treating users as experts in their environments, feminist urbanism empowers them as sources of knowledge and agents of change. This perspective not only enhances a sense of ownership but also fosters gender awareness and a deeper understanding of spaces. In this sense, the guides developed by Collectiu Punt 6, Mujeres Trabajando (2014), and Espacios para la Vida Cotidiana (2014) were used, which explain, respectively, the methodological tools and indicators for evaluating results. The participatory methodology adopted was the Exploratory March.

This concept has its origin in Canada in 1989 as a response to violence against women and children in Montreal (Michaud & Paquin, 2002). This feminist, participatory methodology involves group walks by public space users to analyze their needs and perceptions. Initially focused on security, it has since incorporated broader parameters to enhance urban quality and well-being. Six design principles guide this approach: signaling, visibility, concentration of people, formal surveillance, organization of spaces, and community involvement. These parameters work together to create safe environments for women (Marchas Exploratorias, [n.d.]).

The Mujeres Trabajando guide (Col.lectiu Punt 6, 2014) explains in detail the tools used in workshops carried out with communities to recognize the spaces of everyday life from the relationship between the physical characteristics of the space and the experience of the body in it. The methodological tools described in the guide are explained in Table 2.

Table 2. Methodological tools described in the Mujeres Trabajando guide. Source: adapted from Col.lectiu Punt 6, 2014

Tools	Description / Function
Questionnaires	Recognize, reflect on different elements of everyday environment - participation, public spaces for relationships and socialization, equipment and services, mobility and relationships, security and housing
Reconnaissance Visits	Collective walk with residents to recognize points relevant to life of neighborhood
Photographs of the Surroundings	Recognize urban elements that are part of lived environment
Daily Itinerary Network	Recognition, description and evaluation of participants' daily tasks to find dependencies
Daily Network	Analyze an environment from different themes – equipment, services, spaces for relationships, mobility, security, participation, housing
Photo Walk	Register, through photographs, elements, and situations considered important to describe the daily lives of participants
Community Map	Systematize collective information of a neighborhood on a map based on experience and daily needs of users
Perceptual Map	Visualize physical or social limits that limit or benefit use of spaces and point out qualities that allow them to be used and enjoyed with autonomy and safety

Inspired by the principles developed by CAFSU (Comité d'Action Femmes et Sécurité Urbaine), Col.lectiu Punt 6 developed a system of indicators to evaluate the quality of spaces (Col·lectiu Punt 6 & Ciocoletto, 2014). Five urban qualities necessary to respond to the needs of everyday life were identified, considering physical, social, and functional aspects. As Figure 9 shows the indicators are proximity, which indicates whether the location is close and accessible, concerning space and time; diversity, occurs through the promotion of social, physical, and functional mixing, embracing diversity and providing more democratic spaces, with a variation of people, activities and uses; autonomy, guarantee of planned spaces so that their urban design conveys a greater sense of security to users, without restrictions and with universal accessibility; vitality, active spaces and facades with the continuous presence of users; and representativeness, symbolic, valuing the memory, social and cultural heritage of the city, in addition to strengthening equity in urban participation and decisions. The indicators are specified for three different scales of spaces, the scale of the neighborhood and everyday network, of relational space and equipment, thus demonstrating the possibility of being adapted to the study object - LSA.

Figure 9. Diagram to evaluate the quality of urban space

Source: adapted from Col·lectiu Punt 6, 2014

As analysis tools with a feminist perspective are not universal, it was always necessary to adapt them to the context of the space studied, in this case, the LSA; and the participating public, the faculty's student community, with a special focus on female students. For this, qualitative and quantitative methods were used (Figure 10). As qualitative methods, two Exploratory Marches of LSA female students were included, carried out with interested students, with different activities of recognition and analysis of the faculty's spaces, in two periods, day and night; and a Focus Group with graduates in a work context who were unable to travel for on-site analysis, but were willing to remember and share their LSA spatial experiences. The quantitative analysis consisted of the online questionnaire "Experience of Students at LSA", aimed at the entire student community of the faculty (women, and men) to recognize differences and similarities in the use and perception of spaces between genders.

Figure 10. Structural diagram of the developed methodology

The Exploratory March of female students at LSA (Figure 11) consisted of a set of individual and collective activities developed with the main objective of qualitatively analyzing the academic space from the student's perspective.

Figure 11. Flyer for the exploratory marches

Source: Jeronimo, 2023

Held in two sessions, daytime and nighttime, the choice of schedule aimed to ensure maximum student participation without compromising their routines. The event was publicized widely, including posters on faculty panels (Figure 11), direct communication in the classroom, online posts, and on social media. Divided into four parts, the march began with an introduction about the research and continued with an individual questionnaire-filling activity (Figures 12 and 13), aiming to collect personal information about the use and feeling of comfort of the spaces.

The group walk, a central activity, facilitated space exploration and the sharing of impressions among participants. The planned route covered open spaces within the faculty and their connections to the surroundings. Additionally, the Collective Map, a cartographic exercise, represented participants' perceptions and sensations in faculty spaces. This approach not only offered a fresh perspective on spaces but also promoted ownership through student interaction.

Figure 12. Structural diagram of exploratory march

Source: adapted from Jeronimo, 2023

To accommodate final-year students in employment and former faculty students interested in participating, we incorporated the Focus Group methodology. During a lunchtime meeting, we adapted the Exploratory March activities to be conducted remotely. The Focus Group was divided into three parts: an Introductory Conversation, an Individual Activity (questionnaire), and the Collective Map.

Figure 13. Questionnaire for individual exploratory march

Source: Jeronimo, 2023

The online questionnaire complemented the main research on the female experience of LSA students. It provided a quantitative analysis of the student community, complementing the qualitative approaches of the Exploratory Marches and the Focus Group. The questionnaire covered four main categories: personal profile, journey to LSA, relationship with LSA, and perception of LSA. By allowing additional comments, it aimed to gather diverse information for more complex analyses. Responses from both genders contributed to expanding the research results and conclusions, but the bias of the sampling was always present since the number of female responses was much higher than the mens'.

By adopting this hybrid approach, the research seeks to overcome the limitations of the quantitative method, which often fails to capture the singularities and diversities of users, while raising awareness and highlighting the experiences of women (and men), historically marginalized in decision-making processes about common spaces.

RESULTS AND DISCUSSION

The qualitative research, consisting of two Exploratory Marches (daytime and nighttime), conducted with FAUL students and the Focus Group, involving a group of female graduates in a work context, unfolded as detailed in Table 3.

Table 3. Table of qualitative research events

Event	Date & Time	Activities	Number of Participants
Exploratory Walk (day session)	March 9th, 2023 (1:00h)	• Individual Questionnaire • Collective Walk / photo documentation • Collective Mapping	7

continued on following page

Table 3. Continued

Event	Date & Time	Activities	Number of Participants
Exploratory Walk (night session)	March 14th, 2023 (19:00h)	• Individual Questionnaire • Collective Walk / photo documentation • Collective Mapping	7
Focus Group	March 20th, 2023 (14:00h)	• Individual Questionnaire • Collective Mapping	5

The participants' profiles exhibited significant diversity in terms of backgrounds, nationalities, ages, and years of study. Erasmus students, a doctoral candidate, and external guests allowed for comparisons between female experiences at LSA and those at other institutions. The participation of a mature student (51 years old) highlighted the range of experiences within LSA's student community. Guests from other Portuguese faculties provided an external perspective, enriching the discussions.

During the development of the nighttime Exploratory March, there were slight adaptations compared to the daytime experience due to differences in thermal conditions, lighting, and the sense of vitality and comfort felt by the participants in the spaces. Both sessions, daytime, and nighttime, originally planned for 1.5 hours, were extended to 2 hours, with the first session spontaneously extending during a convivial moment.

Table 4. Table of participants profile in daytime exploratory march. Source: adapted from Jeronimo, 2023

Exploratory March (day session)					
	Course	Course year	Nationality	Days per week at LSA	Hours per day at LSA
29	MSc. Architecture	5	Brazilian	3-4	6-8
21	MSc. Architecture (Erasmus)	4	Catalan, Spanish	3-4	3-5
22	MSc. Architecture (Erasmus)	5	French	3-4	3-5
27	Ph.D. Urbanism	1	Portuguese	1-2	>8
25	MSc. Architecture	5	Portuguese	3-4	3-5
51	MSc. Architecture	5	Portuguese	3-4	6-8
22	MSc. Architecture	3	Portuguese	1-2	3-5

Table 4. Continued

Table 5. Table of participants profile in nighttime exploratory march. Source: adapted from Jeronimo, 2023

Exploratory March (night session)					
	Course	Course year	Nationality	Days per week at LSA	Hours per day at LSA
27	MSc. Architecture	5	Portuguese	3-4	6-8
24	MSc. Architecture	5	Portuguese	5-6	3-5
27	MSc. Architecture	5	Portuguese	<1	3-5
27	MSc. Architecture	5	Portuguese	5-6	6-8
31	MSc. Architecture Autónoma Univ.	graduated	Brazilian	-	-
25	MSc. Architecture ISCTE	graduated	Portuguese	-	-
29	MSc. Architecture Lusófona Univ.	graduated	Romanian	-	-

The Focus Group was organized as a solution for female graduates in a work context to participate, even if they were unable to attend in person at LSA and had limited time. Therefore, unlike the Exploratory March, the Focus Group did not include the walk and photographic documentation. Instead, it was divided into three parts: a brief introduction, a questionnaire, and a collective map. The activities lasted 40 minutes and took place together at their workplace. As shown in Table 6, the participants' profiles were quite similar.

Table 6. Table of focus group participants profile. Source: adapted from Jeronimo, 2023

Focus Group					
Age	Course	Course year	Nationality	Days per week at LSA	Hours per day at LSA
29	MSc. Architecture	Graduated	Portuguese	5-6	3-5
26					3-5
24					3-5
28					6-8
27					3-5

Considering the variety of courses offered by LSA (Architecture, Rehabilitation, Urbanism, Design, and Fashion), it would have been interesting to have a greater diversity of courses among the participants. However, the lack of such diversity reveals a fragmented reality within the student community. The spatial distribution of courses within the faculty and the absence of common gathering spaces contribute to the lack of integration among different courses.

QUESTIONNAIRE

The first activity, the Questionnaire, served as a tool for characterizing the participants and individually recognizing the spaces within LSA. It focused on the most relevant aspects related to comfort in specific areas, as well as favorable or unfavorable factors influencing that perception.

Among the spaces where participants reported feeling most comfortable were classrooms, gardens, the bar, the library, and the computer center. Reasons varied, including the vitality of communal gathering spaces, quiet environments conducive to studying, and favorable temperature, lighting, and furniture conditions. While some preferred calm spaces for concentration, others appreciated more lively areas for creative processes. This highlights the importance of diverse spaces within faculties to meet students' varying needs and well-being. Interestingly, even spaces considered comfortable by most participants had several reservations, suggesting a nuanced analysis and a certain acceptance of the faculty's overall environment.

On the other hand, spaces where participants felt most uncomfortable included the 24-hour room (Espaço 24), restrooms, the cafeteria, atriums, entrances, parking lots, and Block 6 (which worsened at night). Overall, the reasons were related to poor connections between spaces, lack of vitality and informal supervision, insufficient support structures for daily life and community interaction, as well as discomfort related to temperature, noise, lighting, and cleanliness. The faculty entrances and parking access were heavily criticized for being disproportionate, poorly positioned, and lacking quick-stopping zones and protection from the elements. All these factors negatively impact students' well-being at the faculty.

When asked about the spaces that are lacking, the following were mentioned most frequently: social spaces, places for relaxation, and a common meeting point capable of integrating the student community and different courses. There was also an emphasis on the need for quiet study and work spaces, more diverse food offerings for students (including spaces where they can eat without relying on the cafeteria), terraces that better connect classrooms and gardens, and covered walkways between buildings and parking areas. Some comments highlighted feelings of insecurity at night, a lack of infrastructure for students' daily lives, and poor quality of reception and integration, which contribute to inhibiting their use by some students.

WALK AND PHOTO DOCUMENTATION

The Group Walk was the second activity conducted during the Exploratory Marches. Its purpose was to recognize favorable and unfavorable spatial aspects for student well-being on campus through bodily experimentation. Participants were asked to share their impressions and document them with photographs during the walk. As before, there was a slight difference between daytime and nighttime routes, but this did not interfere with the main objective of exploring as many open spaces as possible. Figure 14's map displays the routes taken and the documented photographs.

Figure 14. Map of day and night exploratory marches

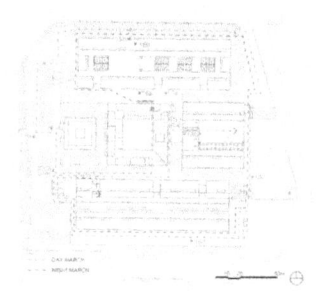

Source: adapted from Jeronimo, 2023

During the walk, three main aspects related to the body's experience in faculty spaces were discussed. The first point addressed the impact of the large, nondescript void in the main facade of the complex (Figure 15) on the student and its appropriation. Participants noted the lack of sufficient qualities for appropriation (benches, trees, shade), along with feelings of exposure, vulnerability, and disruption of the established spatial logic. The second aspect observed was the restriction imposed by poor lighting and lack of vitality in the tree corridor north of Block 4, especially at night. This was evident in the group's behavior during the walk (Figure 16): while they walked among the trees during the day, they spontaneously restricted themselves to the narrow concrete corridor adjacent to the classrooms at night. Finally, the third aspect discussed was the impact of light and shadow on the body's sense of exposure. As shown in Figure 17, the open configuration of classroom facades becomes a source of insecurity, functioning as display windows at night. These three aspects highlight the importance of considering elements together to create spaces that offer quality and well-being.

Figure 15. Photographic documentation of exploratory march: (a) North of LSA's main façade; (b) South of LSA's main facade

Source: adapted from Jeronimo, 2023

Figure 16. Photographic documentation of exploratory march at green corridor: (a) Dayttime; (b) Nighttime

Source: adapted from Jeronimo, 2023

Figure 17. Photographic documentation of exploratory march: (a) From outside looking the classrooms; (b) From the classroom looking outside

Source: adapted from Jeronimo, 2023

Finally, the group walk also allowed to observe two interesting phenomena related to student appropriation of the faculty spaces. First, there was a clear contradiction between the existing benches on campus (Figure 18(a) and (b)) and the improvised benches created by students (Figure 18(c) and (d)), highlighting the inconsistency between space design and student needs for well-being. This discrepancy arises from poor bench distribution across the campus and their user-unfriendly characteristics, such as lack of protection from sun, rain, and wind, or suboptimal materials and design.

The second phenomenon observed was the different ways in which men and women appropriated the space. Female appropriation tended to be calmer and more discreet, contrasting with the more expansive and invasive use by males (Figure 19). This gendered phenomenon results from social construction and differentiated spatial education received by men and women from childhood, which persists into adulthood (Saldaña, Goula, Cardona, & Amat, 2017). These observations underscore the need to consider spaces holistically, creating a network of features that promote equal appropriation and provide favorable conditions for student well-being.

Figure 18. Photographic documentation of participants in the Exploratory March: (a) Bench between Block 4 and Block 1; (b) Bench in front of Block 5; (c) Chair positioned in the open space on the main facade of the LSA; (d) Chairs positioned in the rear parking lot of the LSA

Source: adapted from Jeronimo, 2023

Figure 19. Photographic documentation of participants in the exploratory march: (a) Female appropriation at the rear of Block 4; (b) Female appropriation of the internal garden of Block 5; (c) Female appropriation of the stairs at the rear of Block 6; (d) Male appropriation of the south terrace

Source: adapted from Jeronimo, 2023

COLLECTIVE MAP

In the end, the Collective Map aimed to represent and locate the sensations and perceptions of the participants on a floor plan of the LSA. For this purpose, six pieces of information were suggested to be mapped: usual personal routes, spaces they use the most, spaces where they feel more or less comfortable, and areas lacking lighting and benches. Additionally, participants had the opportunity to add other ideas. The activity resulted in three maps (daytime, nighttime, and Focus Group), which were synthesized in Figure 20.

Figure 20. Summary map of the collective maps produced

Source: adapted from Jeronimo, 2023

Beyond the issues already observed and discussed in previous activities, the summary map (Figure 20) resulted in a new concept of "shadow zones." This term draws an analogy between the effect of poor lighting and the neglect of certain areas within the faculty, specifically referring to marginalized, decharacterized, and overlooked spaces (highlighted in light blue in Figure 20). The lack of attention and investment creates an unfavorable environment for student well-being, making these spaces less inviting and therefore underused. The map revealed that the introspective nature of the building complex, isolated from its surroundings, contributes to the creation of shadow zones in the peripheral areas of the faculty, which are also the most uncomfortable.

Despite this, significant potential exists for improving student well-being within and outside the faculty spaces. All these possibilities are related to creating communal and supportive spaces that cater for various student needs. Additionally, there was discussion about the need to better connect the blocks, considering the faculty as a cohesive whole, to promote balanced integration among students from different courses. Furthermore, enhancing the relationship between the faculty complex and adjacent areas would increase vitality and foster feelings of security and well-being.

In addition to spatial factors, issues related to representation and combating harassment within educational institutions were considered fundamental for fostering a sense of well-being at the faculty. The combination of individual questionnaires, group walks with photographic documentation, and the creation of the Collective Map resulted in a diverse set of information in various formats, enriching the experience and analysis for understanding LSA spaces from the student's perspective.

ONLINE QUESTIONNAIRE

The online questionnaire was available to the entire LSA student community, from March 13th to April 6th, 2023, and received a total of 207 responses. As explained previously, the questionnaire was divided into four main parts - personal profile; journey to LSA; relationship with LSA; and perception of LSA. The answers were analyzed by graphic computation of the results and with the Chi-Square test which assesses whether there is a significant association between two categorical variables[1]. In this study, the relationship between specific variables related to students' experiences within LSA spaces and mobility is analyzed.

Concerning Personal Profile (participant's gender, age, nationality, course, and year of study), 84.1% were women, and only 15.9% were men. This difference limited some analysis of the comparison between genders' answers. However, as the number of male responses exceeds 30, validates a quantitative analysis, making it possible to find some relationships. Nevertheless the male sample was considered for analysis and all comments are subject to this sample dimension discrepancy. The lack of male participation itself is quite significant, as it may represent a certain lack of interest in reflecting on faculty spaces from a gender perspective since the questionnaire was carried out online.

Regarding age, the majority responded to be between 18 and 23 years old (71%), 25% between 24 and 30 years old, and 4% over 30 years old. This shows that the student community has dispersed ages and stages of life, and, therefore, the faculty must be aware of the specificities arising from this diversity, offering comfortable and conducive environments for everyone to enjoy. Among the questions related to the profile of the participants, the nationality question was the only optional one. It was found that 86.5% were Portuguese, 10.6% were foreigners and 2.9% chose not to answer. Among the foreign nationalities were: Brazilian, Ukrainian, Chinese, Cape Verdean, Santomean, Guinean, Mozambican, Romanian, French, Peruvian, Dutch, and Mexican. It is important to highlight that some students chose not to provide information about their nationality. This choice may indicate cultural sensitivity, which is not surprising in a country with a strong colonial history.

Regarding the journey home-school, questions were asked about the means of transportation used, how long it takes, where the student lives during the school period, their perception of the quality of the route, and their feeling of safety. As shown in Figure 21, the majority use public transport (65.2%) and the most frequent route length is 30 to 60 minutes, with 48.3% of students residing in the municipality of Lisbon. When comparing the means of transport used between genders, it was found that women use public transport around 13% more than men, while they walk or cycle around three times more than women (males 18.2%; females 6.3%). This difference may be related to the feeling of insecurity, gender-related, when walking or cycling, for example, which would condition the preference for another means of transport. On the other hand, own vehicle had similar proportions for women and men, and ridesharing, and taxi were of less frequency.

Figure 21. Means of transport by gender

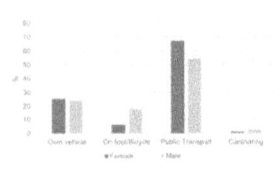

Source: adapted from Jeronimo, 2023

Regarding the quality of the route, the majority rated it as average (44.9%), while 21.8% considered it poor and 33.3% good. However, in terms of feeling safe during the journey, 85% of responding students feel secure, while 15% do not. When comparing genders, it was observed that 15.5% of women feel unsafe during the commute from home to LSA, which is approximately 3% higher than men (probably due to the smaller sample size of male respondents compared to females).

In the third category, Relationship with LSA, the majority of students who responded to the questionnaire visit LSA more than 4 days a week (72.5%), while 19.8% attend 2 to 3 days a week, and 7.7% only once a week. This suggests a strong connection with the faculty, characterized by regular and consistent attendance. Most students prefer the morning period at LSA (91.3%), as opposed to 47.3% who prefer the afternoon and 6.3% who prefer the evening. While this aligns with class schedules, the low nighttime presence may indicate inhibitions related to space quality, comfort, and security. Using the Chi-Square test to verify the statistical evidence for these assumptions, we conclude that the association between time of day and activity performed is significant ($\chi2=47.93$; p-value < 0.001).

Regarding activities, the results show, as expected, that the primary activity of students at LSA is attending classes (95.7%). Additionally, over a third engage in academic work (65.2%), have meals (50.2%), and participate in parties and other leisure activities (40.1%). However, activities related to study and research (32.9%), work within the faculty (18.8%), and conferences or workshops (11.1%) are less frequent. These data suggest that students use faculty spaces for various purposes. Notably, there is a significant difference between using LSA spaces for work versus studying or research. This disparity may relate to complaints raised during the Exploratory March and Focus Groups about the lack of quiet study spaces, which are less formal than the library. While classrooms, with their open layout and large tables, facilitate work, they can also be too busy and noisy for more focused study.

About space used by students, the main areas are classrooms (99%) and the bar/canteen (89.4%). Comparing this with data on activities conducted at LSA, it is noted that the number of students attending classes is slightly lower than those who claim to use classrooms. This suggests that classrooms serve other purposes, such as work. Additionally, the library (29%), the 24-hour room (27.1%), CIFA rooms (23.2%), and workshops (16.4%) were mentioned, though less frequently. This indicates that some students value the quiet study environment and resources available in the library. Despite complaints about the 24-hour room from the questionnaire, its usage remains considerable, likely due to the lack of better spaces for studying and work. The CIFA rooms (informatics) and workshops are mainly used by students of specific courses and years. Analyzing the association between frequented locations and activities, we find statistical significance ($\chi2=68.57$; p-value < 0.001).

The final part of the questionnaire called 'Perception of LSA,' aimed to understand the sensations and impressions that female and male students had in the faculty spaces. While the other sections sought to outline a personal profile of the users based on their utilitarian relationship with space and time, characterizing the participants, this part delved deeper into the sensations caused by the spaces. It represents a more in-depth analysis that occasionally intersects with previous information. Based on the responses, a word cloud was created (Figure 22), considering all sensations related to the LSA space. Interestingly, despite a significant number of students feeling calm, free, and secure at LSA, there is also a considerable portion that experiences insecurity, with negative sensations like embarrassment, vulnerability, and hostility.

Figure 22. Word cloud of the sensations that the LSA space transmits

HOSTILITY
EMBARRASSMENT
FREEDOM   NOSTALGIA
TRANQUILITY
SECURITY
VULNERABILITY

Source: adapted from Jeronimo, 2023

These results were separated by gender (Figure 23), with the purpose of observing differences in how spaces affect women and men. Despite the Chi-Square test not indicating significance for this relationship (as expected, since the sample dimensions are so different), an empirical analysis revealed that proportionally, male students feel more tranquil and comfortable in LSA spaces compared to female students. Female students reported experiencing more fear, insecurity, hostility, and vulnerability than male students. It is important to note that only women mentioned feeling fear and discomfort. These findings align with observations from Exploratory March and the Focus Group, highlighting that, in addition to shared adversities between genders, women also face gender-related challenges such as fear and insecurity due to the patriarchal context they live in. This influences how they perceive and experience spaces.

Figure 23. Comparative sensations of male and female students in LSA spaces

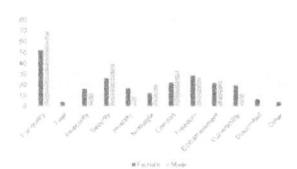

Source: adapted from Jeronimo, 2023

Additionally, cross-referencing was done between the activities carried out at LSA and the spaces used (obtained from the previous category) with the sensations conveyed by those spaces. Regarding the relationship between activities and sensations, it was found to be significant (Chi-Square = 101.297; p-value < 0.001). However, the relationship between spaces and sensations did not yield statistically significant results. Despite the question specifically addressing the sensations transmitted by the spaces, it is possible that the participating students confused these sensations with feelings arising from other reasons, such as social interactions, stress levels, or personal experiences.

Regarding the variables related to the sensations conveyed by the space and the academic year, they showed a statistically significant association (Chi-Square = 22.62; p-value = 0.012). Analyzing the variation in responses over the faculty years, it is evident that feelings of security/freedom and tranquility exhibit a more significant reduction (Figure 24). A possible explanation for this is that as students progress through their faculty years, they may encounter a reality different from their initial idealization. Given that a substantial portion of the questionnaire participants were architecture, interior design, and urban planning students, it is possible that their years of education foster a more critical view of the faculty spaces and the sensations they evoke. This critical perspective may lead to heightened awareness of space limitations and deficiencies, resulting in decreased feelings of security/freedom and tranquility.

Figure 24. Sensations at LSA spaces by course year

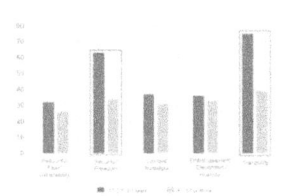

Source: adapted from Jeronimo, 2023

Regarding the perception of security (Figure 25) 85% of students feel secure during their commute from home to the faculty, 95.2% feel secure inside LSA buildings, and 86.5% feel secure in open spaces such as gardens, corridors, and parking lots. Additionally, 78.7% believe that LSA spaces inspire a sense of security. Interestingly, despite this overall feeling of security, there is a trend of decreased security perception from inside the buildings to the exterior of the faculty, including spaces between buildings.

Figure 25. Security sensations at LSA spaces

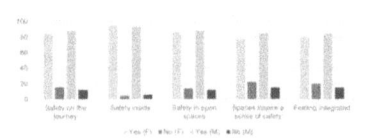

Source: adapted from Jeronimo, 2023

According to the Chi-Square test, security-related questions did not yield significant results in terms of gender. This lack of significance may be due to the low number of male responses. However, the graph indicates that women tend to feel slightly less secure than men in various spaces, except for the interior of buildings. This difference in security perceptions between genders may be related to the reality of gender-based violence that women face.

Additionally, the data shows that women (80.56%) feel less integrated than men (84.9%), which could also influence their sense of security. In summary, analyzing the feelings conveyed by the environment and the sense of integration, we conclude that this association is statistically significant ($\chi2=51.25$; p-value < 0.001).

Regarding harassment at LSA, it is observed that 12.64% of women reported experiencing harassment, while only 9.09% of men reported the same. These data underscore the concerning reality of gender-based violence that many women face in academic spaces. It is important to note that informal conversations with colleagues, as well as the Exploratory March and Focus Group, revealed that many students lack awareness of what constitutes harassment and its various forms. This highlights the urgency of addressing this issue by raising awareness, implementing appropriate policies, and fostering a culture of respect and gender equality.

In the comments section, many students emphasized the need for spaces to socialize, relax, study, work, and eat. Additionally, some students expressed a lack of belonging, which may be related to inadequate spaces that fail to cater for diverse needs and foster better integration among different individuals. Therefore, higher education institutions must provide distinct spaces that accommodate various uses and serve their diverse community. Beyond creating diverse spaces, ensuring comfort and proper maintenance is essential.

PROPOSALS AND RECOMMENDATIONS

Both methodologies employed allowed for the identification of aspects that either enhance or diminish students' sense of comfort and well-being in the LSA spaces. Overall, dissatisfaction was noted regarding the quality and diversity of the spaces, as well as the sense of safety and well-being within them. Furthermore, there is a lack of quality spaces that support students' daily lives, such as areas for socializing, staying, studying, resting, and dining. These conditions also affect the appropriation of spaces, the integration of the student community, and consequently the overall sense of well-being.

In response, six intervention proposals were developed to improve students' experience and well-being in the LSA environments, promoting more inclusive, welcoming, and safe spaces. The intervention locations (Figure 26) were chosen based on the areas of greatest dissatisfaction among students. The proposals aim to create interconnected spaces for meeting, passage, socializing, and staying, forming a network that caters to the diversity of the student community. Starting with the creation of a significant access point to the southwest of the LSA, a series of spaces were planned to extend north and east, gradually reducing the intensity of activities near the classrooms.

Figure 26. Map of intervention proposals for the LSA

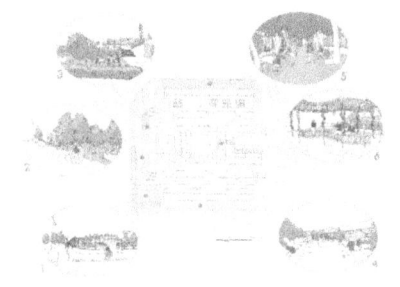

PROPOSAL ONE

For the currently disused southwest access of the faculty (Figure 27), an intervention proposal was developed to enhance the relationship between the LSA and its surroundings, improve accessibility for people with reduced mobility, and create visually connected social spaces (Figure 28). By removing the stairs, leveling the ground with the sidewalk, and installing ramps, tiered seating benches, and a covered lookout, the goal was to create a gradual transition between the exterior and interior of the faculty. This approach aims to make the area more attractive and promote vitality, offering better connections to the student residences, canteen, bar, and public transportation access.

Figure 27. Pedestrian access to the southwest of the LSA: (a) photo from outside; (b) photo from inside

Source: adapted from Jeronimo, 2023

Figure 28. Intervention proposal for the pedestrian access to the southwest of the LSA

Source: adapted from Jeronimo, 2023

PROPOSAL TWO

The proposal developed for the south space of the main facade of the LSA (Figure 29) aims to address the issues of lack of character and excessive exposure by creating a diverse social and leisure area connected with the first proposal. To achieve this, the plan (Figure 30) includes tree planting to provide shaded areas and wind protection; a variety of seating options to meet different needs; and a covered lookout facing the garden at the south entrance of the faculty, enhancing the connection between spaces and allowing for the enjoyment of the view of the National Palace of Ajuda.

Additionally, proper lighting is crucial, with lights installed at different heights among and around the trees to prevent the creation of dark areas at night.

Figure 29. Empty space to the south of the main facade of the LSA: (a) Photo angle from between Blocks 2 and 6; (b) angle from the main entrance of the LSA

Source: adapted from Jeronimo, 2023

Figure 30. Intervention proposal for the empty space to the south of the main facade of the ISA

Source: adapted from Jeronimo, 2023

PROPOSAL THREE

For the north side of the main facade (Figure 31), the aim was to create a calmer and more open environment (Figure 32). Trees are arranged on only one side, following the uneven topography, to reduce excessive noise and exposure from the street while strengthening the connection with the corridor and the access stairs to Block 4.

Figure 31. Empty space to the north of the main facade of the LSA

Source: adapted from Jeronimo, 2023

Figure 32. Intervention proposal for the empty space to the north of the main façade of the ISA

Source: adapted from Jeronimo, 2023

PROPOSAL FOUR

For the south terrace of Block 6 (Figure 33), the proposal expands on Proposal 1 by connecting the southwest access of the LSA to the faculty bar and creating social spaces to improve the area's safety. Given the proximity to classrooms, the proposal (Figure 34) includes a gradual transition in activity intensity, with busier areas to the west and quieter areas to the east. The plan includes the arrangement of game tables, benches, tables, plant pots, and adequate lighting for nighttime use. Along the length of this terrace, it is recommended to create different layouts with shaded areas, vegetation, umbrellas, or pergolas.

Figure 33. Terrace to the south of Block 6

Source: adapted from Jeronimo, 2023

Figure 34. Intervention proposal for the terrace to the south of Block 6

Source: adapted from Jeronimo, 2023

PROPOSAL FIVE

The proposal for the tree corridor north of Block 4 (Figure 35) aims to create spaces that strengthen the relationship between the classrooms and the tree corridor, as well as improve its safety. To achieve this, a calm and conducive space for studying is proposed, featuring a wooden walkway structure along the building facade for outdoor study and work (Figure 36). The corridor between the trees would be maintained to promote passage, with benches and tables arranged around it as resting and relaxation options. Once again, the importance of creating a varied lighting system with different focal points and heights is emphasized to avoid dark areas, especially at night.

Figure 35. Tree corridor to the north of Block 4: (a) Photo of the tree corridor; (b) Photo from the tree corridor to the classrooms

Source: adapted from Jeronimo, 2023

Figure 36. Intervention proposal for the tree corridor to the north of Block 4

Source: adapted from Jeronimo, 2023

PROPOSAL SIX

The intervention proposal for the bench in front of Block 5 (Figure 37) aims to promote the integration of building 5 with its surroundings, making the space more inviting and pleasant for students. Currently, the bench is excessively exposed to sunlight and rain, not fulfilling its function well as an area for staying. Therefore, it is proposed to construct a pergola, possibly made of wood, to provide shade and comfort for its users (Figure 38).

Figure 37. Bench in front of Block 5

Source: adapted from Jeronimo, 2023

Figure 38. Intervention proposal for the bench in front of Block 5

Source: adapted from Jeronimo, 2023

The results not only generated important insights for improving the well-being of students in LSA spaces but also provide parameters to be considered when thinking about student well-being in higher education institutions . Recognizing the spatial dimension of universities as a tool for transforming student well-being, it is recommended that interested institutions engage in participatory, creative, and inclusive processes with the student community to collaboratively develop effective and comprehensive formal propositions that address the needs of their users, thereby strengthening the sense of belonging.

In general, promoting diverse, connected, and vibrant spaces that foster autonomy for all students and where they feel a sense of belonging is recommended for student well-being in higher education institutions. Spatial diversity should be promoted to accommodate the different narratives and needs of students, fostering creativity. Spaces should provide the necessary conditions for their appropriation, promoting vitality and a sense of security. Creating spaces like pergolas, benches, study areas, etc. that enhance encounter and interaction strengthens the sense of community and belonging. It is crucial that all these spaces are accessible to people with reduced mobility, adequately illuminated, and visually connected.

CONCLUSION

In this chapter, the spatial dimension of students' well-being was explored. Through participatory methods, including an Exploratory March, collective mapping, Focus Group discussion, and online questionnaires, a gender-sensitive approach was adopted, and considering gender differences in space appropriation, safety, space perception, spatial experiences, and empowerment, it was shown that it is possible to transform educational spaces into environments that positively impact students' experiences and overall well-being.

The experiences of the Exploratory March and the Focus Group proved fundamental for understanding the spaces at LSA from the student's perspective. These approaches fostered an environment conducive to open dialogue and the exchange of narratives and stories, allowing for a more contextualized and enriching understanding. Through these activities, the participants' subjectivities were recognized and valued, giving voice to their experiences and perceptions. Additionally, active student engagement in the discussion promoted empowerment and transformative capacities concerning their environment.

It is important to note that the results do not fully encompass all students' perceptions, as female narratives are diverse and nuanced. Nevertheless, the creation of spaces for discussing students' experiences remains crucial, aiming to foster more inclusive and welcoming environments for students.

The online questionnaire revealed significant insights into students' experiences within LSA spaces, despite some limitations. The responses highlighted overall student dissatisfaction with faculty spaces and confirmed that ideas stemming from the female perspective benefit the entire student's community well-being. The high participation in the questionnaire underscores the interest in collaborative dialogues on these topics, with the aim of developing effective strategies for transformation and inclusion within academic environments. This realization reinforces the need for collaborative and participatory approaches to create more welcoming, equitable, and inclusive spaces that contribute to students' well-being. Proposed parameters that promote a network of diverse, vibrant and interconnected spaces offering autonomy and a sense of belonging contribute to establishing a guide of good practices in future planning for university campi.

REFERENCES

Agrawal, P., & Yadav, M. (2021). Campus Design of Universities: An Overview. *Journal of Design and Built Evironment*, 21(31), pp37–pp51. 10.22452/jdbe.vol21no3.3

Jacobs, J. (1993). *The death and life of great American cities*. New York: Vintage Books.

Punt, C. (2019). *Urbanismo feminista: Por una transformación radical de los espacios de vida*. Bilbao: Virus.

Col·lectiu Punt 6, & Ciocoletto, A. (2014). *Espacios para la vida cotidiana. Auditoría de calidad urbana con perspectiva de género*. Comanegra.

Col·lectiu Punt 6. (2014). *Mujeres trabajando. Guía de reconocimiento urbano con perspectiva de género*. Barcelona: Comanegra.

Conley, C. S., Durlak, J. A., & Kirsch, A. C. (2015). A meta-analysis of universal mental health prevention programs for higher education students. *Prevention Science*, 16(4), 487–507. 10.1007/s11121-015-0543-125744536

Conley, C. S., Shapiro, J. B., Kirsch, A. C., & Durlak, J. A. (2017). A meta-analysis of indicated mental health prevention programs for at-risk higher education students. *Journal of Counseling Psychology*, 64(2), 121–140. 10.1037/cou000019028277730

de Abreu, T. C. C. M. (2021). *Corpos insurgentes: Narrativas urbanas sob a perspectiva da mulher*. Trabalho Final de Graduação em Arquitetura e Urbanismo, Centro Universitário Christus, Fortaleza, Ceará. https://repositorio.unichristus.edu.br/jspui/handle/123456789/1109

de Carvalho, G. J. E. (2017). *Pólo Universitário da Ajuda. (Re) vitalização, integração, naturalização* Tese de Mestrado em Arquitetura, Universidade de Lisboa. http://hdl.handle.net/10400.5/13951

Dober, R. P. (1996). *Campus Planning*. Society for College and University Planning.

Douwes, R., Metselaar, J., Pijnenborg, G. H. M., & Boonstra, N. (2023). Well-being of students in higher education: The importance of a student perspective. *Cogent Education*, 10(1), 2190697. 10.1080/2331186X.2023.2190697

Federici, S. (2017). Calibã e a bruxa.*Mulheres, corpo e acumulação primitiva* (1a ed). Editora Elefante

Fleuret, S., & Atkinson, S. (2007). Wellbeing, health and geography: a critical review and research agenda. *New Zealand Geographer*, 63(2), 106–129. 10.1111/j.1745-7939.2007.00093.x

Fleuret, S., & Prugneau, J. (2014). Assessing students' wellbeing in a spatial dimension. *The Geographical Journal*, 181.

Fraillon, J. (2004). *Measuring student wellbeing in the context of Australian schooling: Discussion paper*. South Australian Department of Education and Children's Services.

Gonçalves, V. F. da C., Oliveira, M., Viana, L. P., & Fernandes, J. M. (2011). *Património Arquitectónico da Universidade Técnica de Lisboa (GAPTEC/UTL)*. UTL.

Hajrasouliha, A. (2017). Campus score: Measuring university campus qualities. *Landscape and Urban Planning*, 158, 166–176. 10.1016/j.landurbplan.2016.10.007

Hajrasouliha, A. H., & Ewing, R. (2016). Campus Does Matter. The Relationship of Student Retention and Degree Attainment to Campus Design. *Planning for Higher Education Journal*, 44(3), 1–15.

Jacobs, J. (1993). *The death and life of great American cities*. Vintage Books.

Jeronimo, V. R. (2023). *Mulheres, Arquitetura e Espaço urbano: a Vivência das Estudantes na FA-ULisboa*. [Thesis in Architecture, Lisbon School of Architecture].

Lagarde, M. (1996). El género, la perspectiva de género. Em Género y feminismo. *Desarrollo humano y democracia* (pp. 13–38). Madrid: horas y HORAS.

Michaud, A., & Paquin, S. (2002). *Pour un environnement urbain sécuritaire: Guide d'aménagement* (Ville de Montréal). Montréal. https://numerique.banq.qc.ca/patrimoine/details/52327/1985553?docref=QQ1f91Gnud9rN2mw_1M9XA

Noble, T., McGrath, H., Roffey, S., & Rowling, L. (2008). *A scoping study on student well-being*. Department of Education. Employment & Workplace Relations.

Pullman, L. (2022). *Landscape, Well-being, and Connection: A Qualitative Study of Community College Students' Perception of Campus Atributes*. [PhD Dissertation, California State University].

Rosado, S., & Ribeiro, J. (2016). A matemática na formação de arquitectos e urbanistas. *Encontro Nacional da SPM*. ResearchGate. https://www.researchgate.net/publication/320866022_A_MATEMATICA_NA_FORMACAO_DE_ARQUITECTOS_E_URBANISTAS

Rosado, S., & Ribeiro, J. T. (2024a). Outdoor Work as an ICT Tool for Teaching and Learning Maths in Lisbon School of Architecture, University of Lisbon. *EDULEARN24 Proceedings* (pp. 1742-1748). IATED Digital Library. 10.21125/edulearn.2024

Rosado, S., & Ribeiro, J. T. (2024b). *Ask New and Challenging Questions Towards Reasoning Skills: Active Approaches in Higher Education. Transdisciplinary Approaches to Learning Outcomes in Higher Education.* IRMA-International.

Saldaña, D., Goula, J., Cardona, H., & Amat, C. (2017). *El patio de la escuela en igualdad: Guía de diagnosis e intervención con perspectiva de género.* Barcelona. https://equalsaree.org/es/mediateca/

Turner, P. V. (1986). Campus: An American Planning Tradition. *Landscape Journal*, 5(1), 66–67. 10.3368/lj.5.1.66

UBIgual. (2011). Plano de Igualdade de Género da UBI, Universidade da Beira Interior. *Projeto UBIgual.* UBIgual. https://eige.europa.eu/sites/default/files/plano_igualdade_genero_da_ubi.pdf

Universidade de Trás-os-Montes e Alto Douro. (2016). *Plano Para Igualdade de Género UTAD rima com igualdade.* UTAD. https://www.utad.pt/wp-content/uploads/Plano_Igualdade.pdf

Vidal, D. G., Fernandes, C. O., Viterbo, L. M. F., Barros, N., & Maia, R. L. (2020). Espaços Verdes Urbanos e Saúde Mental: uma revisão sistemática da literatura. In *13º Congresso Nacional de Psicologia da Saúde: Melhorar o Bem-Estar Global através da Psicologia da Saúde* (pp.427-436). Covilhã, Portugal

ENDNOTE

[1] The test is used to determine whether the observed frequencies in our data significantly differ from what would be expected if the variables were unrelated (computed using the IBM SPSS Statistics software version 29.0.0.0(241)). The hypotheses tested are - Null Hypothesis (H_0): There is no association between the variables; Alternative Hypothesis (H_1): There is a significant association between the variables. A significance level (often denoted as α) of 0.05 (5%) was used. If the p-value (probability value) from the test output is less than 0.05, we reject the null hypothesis, indicating a significative association between the variables. To ensure the validity of the test more than 20% of frequencies

below 5 in the sample must be avoided. This condition ensures that the test assumptions are met and that the results are reliable.

Chapter 16
Financial Well-Being of Students at Higher Education Institutions:
A Study of Northern Zone, Tanzania

Kennedy Omondi Otieno
https://orcid.org/0000-0002-4298-9211
St. Augustine University of Tanzania, Arusha, Tanzania

Loishiye Lengaram Saiteu
Institute of Accountancy, Arusha, Tanzania

ABSTRACT

The study investigated the relationship between financial well-being of students and grade point average (GPA) scored. The study adopted sequential explanatory design. A sample size involved 151 respondents; that is, five deans of students and ten non-academic staffs purposively sampled, 36 academic staffs (AS), and 100 undergraduate students. Data was obtained using stratified and simple random sampling techniques. Research experts determined content validity of instruments. Reliability for AS questionnaire (0.877) and students' questionnaire (0.777) was established using Cronbach's Alpha method. A statistically significant relationship (R =0. 762, R2 =0.581) between financial well-being of students and GPA scored was found. Increase in financial support to students was recommended since students facing financial hardship are more likely to drop out or score a low GPA.

DOI: 10.4018/979-8-3693-4417-0.ch016

INTRODUCTION

In daily academic life, students are exposed to a wide range of potentially stressful situations which could negatively affect their academic achievement and their health. Among the factors that could be weakened by academic stress, attention has been paid to expectations of financial well-being, which is considered as one of the most important determinants for students' engagement, persistence and academic success. According to Moore et al. (2021), financial difficulties can lead to distractions, increased levels of anxiety and depression, and a decreased ability to focus on academic tasks. This can result in lower grades and a higher likelihood of academic failure. In the views of Schmid and Petko (2019), parental support towards university education is not equal in every dwelling, and some students have the disadvantage of not having parental support or learning through the support of well wishers. One of the risk factors for financial well-being among first year students at universities is the low income. Students from low income families are likely not to receive the same support and encouragement from their family members, who have limited understanding of higher education and the financial aid process (Engle & Tinto, 2008). Furthermore, students get extra responsibilities such as purchasing kitchen wares, chairs, tables and paying rent since they are living in rental houses alone. Students joining higher learning institutions in Tanzania experience similar financial challenges. Yet they are expected to settle fast and face university life (Magembe, 2018).

Students face financial challenges which results in their inability to meet basic requirement hence dropout from university. Adams et al. (2016) noted that students from low socio-economic origins are much more likely to drop out than those from high socio-economic ones. This is so because less fortunate students are less likely to be aware of the true costs associated with post-secondary education. The university loan allocated to students through Higher Education Students Loans Board (HESLB) is inadequate to cater for their rent, meals, stationery services, academic field trips and bus fare (Otieno, 2023). Due to low socio-economic family background, some students are circumstantially compelled to financially support their siblings and parents from the university loan received. Out of misinformation, some parents believe that the loan is adequate and therefore they don't give financial supplement to their sons and daughters (Mkumbo et al., 2023). Consequently, this has resulted into students' distress financially. Previous studies on financial difficulties facing university students exist but their findings and recommendations vary in different contexts. For example, a study by Garrido (2019) and Schönfeld et al. (2019) was conducted on financial challenges facing students in higher learning institution but the finding did not give a lasting solution to students' financial well-being

BACKGROUND

The financial well being of students in higher education has been a subject for discussion for decades now. Majority of students pursuing higher education particularly in developing countries rely on higher education loans and bursaries for their education (Mkumbo et al., 2023). Wangenge-Ouma (2018) asserts that students in South Africa who do not receive funding or other subsidies choose to take out students' loans, and the majority drop out to find employment to pay off the loans. Low socio-economic level among students influences their likelihood of dropping out. According to Klein (2010), while the cost of university education continues to increase, approximately 53.1% of first-year students are utilizing loans to pay for college and 73.4% of students reported receiving grants and scholarships. Once these low-income students enter their first year of university, there are a variety of obstacles they are likely to face based on their socio-economic status in addition to the standard obstacles of first year university adjustment. Bozick (2007) reiterate that low-income students are more likely to work while in university and that this additional outside work requires their focus to be split between work and university studies. Thus, university students from low-income families who do remain in university are still at a disadvantage because they are more likely to be less academically prepared due to disparities in educational opportunities. Muraskin and Lee (2004) reiterate that numerous hurdles, low-income students attending university remain at a disadvantage and often leave after their first year at higher rates than their peers. Consequently, it was necessary to carry out a study to assess if financial well-being of students in higher education could be a contributing factor towards the myriad of challenges facing their education.

THEORETICAL REVIEW

The study was anchored on Theory of Planned Behaviour (TPB) developed by Ajzen in 1991. TPB conceptualize behaviour as a result of a contribution of attitudes, subjective norms and perceived behavioural control. According to TPB, behaviour is influenced by attitudes, subjective norms and behaviour control (Ajzen, 1991). The attitude in this research is derived from financial well-being, subjective norm is financial socialization and behavioural control is financial confidence. This study uses a theoretical approach that is used to describe financial well-being of students in higher education institution and their life that involves prudent financial management that help students manage their finances and reduce stress.

LITERATURE REVIEW

Cude et al. (2006) examined US college student's overall financial management practices using quantitative and qualitative data from a multi-state research project. The findings show that parents play a key role in their children's financial management practices. In a similar study, Curran et al. (2018) examined how perceived financial socialisation (from parents, the romantic partner, and young adult's own behaviour), was associated with young adult's life outcomes and well-being (that is, physical and mental health, finances, romantic relationship). Results from hierarchical regression analyses showed that young adult's own financial behaviours were the most patterned, followed by financial socialisation from the romantic partner, and then from financial socialisation from parents.

Moore et al. (2020) conducted a study in US using a qualitative approach to gain a deeper understanding into the lived experiences of students with financial stress. Four focus groups were conducted at a large, private, urban university in the United States in September 2019. The student body, comprising 50,000 students, was approximately half undergraduate and half graduate students. About one quarter were international students, primarily from countries in Asia. The study found that 22% of incoming first-year students were the first in their family to attend college and 18% of undergraduate students were recipients of Pell Grant US federal aid provided to low income students. It may be difficult for students to receive the full benefits of a college education when their social and academic lives are impeded by financial stress. A research by Karyotaki et al. (2020) has demonstrated a link between financial stress and poorer mental health outcomes; for example, worry over finances has been correlated with mental illnesses like depression and anxiety. Similar, the study also reported an association between financial stress and general poor mental health.

Likewise, Abreu and Mendes (2011) used a survey of individual investors in education disclosed by the Portuguese Securities Commission to study the impact of investor's levels of financial literacy on portfolio diversification. The results suggest that investor's educational levels and their financial knowledge have a positive impact on investor diversification Hanson and Olson (2018) weighed in by exploring the relationship between financial literacy and family communication patterns through an online survey for a sample of 96 United States college students between the ages of 18 and 26. The results suggest that conversations within the family regarding financial matters provide important knowledge regarding financial matters and may be a factor to consider in designing any financial literacy curriculum.

In Ghana, a study was carried out by Oppong-Boakye and Kasanba (2013) on undergraduate business students, and another study by Oseifuah and Gyekye (2014) conducted on undergraduate commerce students in South Africa. The findings of all these studies, reported roles traditionally played by males and females in decision making in a typical African household where the male predominates in most decisions, including financial ones. Female students were found to be having more financial challenges than their male students. Lusardi, Mitchell (2014) reported students' perceived financial stress is correlated with negative mental health outcomes. However, the link between financial stress and debt was not substantiated, suggesting perceived stress may be a more influential factor in mental health than the amount of debt accrued.

In addition, a study by Ansong and Gyensare (2012) who used correlation analysis to examine the level of financial literacy among a sample of undergraduate and postgraduate university working-students in Ghana, and found that student's age; residing on campus or not; studying for agriculture, agribusiness, natural resources, medical sciences or midwifery appear not to account for any differences in financial literacy among participating students. These are probably variables that would not be considered important in student's decision to know about personal finance issues. Lastly, Gyimah et al. (2018) used the survey research method to investigate the financial literacy level among a sample of 480 students across public and technical universities as well as teacher-training colleges in Ghana. The findings suggest that on the average, students lack financial knowledge especially on insurance. On the contrary, the results revealed that students are financially literate in terms of savings and borrowing. Also, information technology positively influences 95% of student's financial literacy. Based on the findings, Gyimah et al. (2018) recommended that policy makers should redesign the curriculum to include financial literacy courses especially for non-business students.

AIM OF THE STUDY

The present study examined how university students' financial well-being influences their education in higher learning institution in Northern Zone, Tanzania.

METHODOLOGY

The research design adopted in carrying out this study was Sequential Explanatory Design. The design enabled the researcher to collect data in a sequential manner in which both quantitative and qualitative methods were collected in phases, then quantitative and qualitative results were later integrated (Creswell & Creswell, 2023). This research design was useful as it brought together the differing strengths of quantitative and qualitative methods (Zhou et al., 2022). The design was also employed because data collected from the sample size can be generalized to the broader population under similar settings (Wium and Louw, 2018). Moreover, the researcher was able to collect a variety of data from a large sample in a short period of time and therefore minimizing costs in terms of time and money (Creswell & Clark, 2018). Similarly, the hypothesis was tested inferentially using Pearson's Product Moment Correlation Analysis in the SPSS version 25. Linear Regression was also employed in order to ascertain the extent of relationship between financial well-being of students and Grade Performance Average (GPA) scored in higher education institutions.

The study involved a total of 151 respondents from five universities in Northern Zone, whereas five dean of students, 36 Academic staffs (AS) out of 180 which is 20%, 10 Non-academic staffs (NAS) that is, higher education students' loan officer & bursars recognized by Tanzania Commission for University (TCU) and 100 undergraduate students out of 1,000 which was 10%. According to Gay et al., (2009), a large sample size is representative enough for the research study. Similarly, the larger the sample size, the smaller the sampling error with a 95% of confidence. This study used both probability and non-probability sampling techniques for selecting respondents. Specifically, cluster technique was used to select all the five universities recognized by Tanzania Commission for Universities (TCU) in Arusha (TCU, 2022). In this study, purposive sampling was used to identify dean of students and NAS. The reason behind the use of purposive sampling was to collect specific data from specific people since they are in constant contact with students. However, both stratified and simple random sampling techniques were used to select both AS and undergraduate students. Gender formed the strata in the study. The justification for the choice of simple random sampling was based on the fact that every AS and undergraduate students were given equal chance of being selected to participate in the study. Therefore, for students (50 female & 50 male) and for AS (18 female & 18 male) from different departments were selected for the study. Five deans of students and for NAS (5 loan officers & 5 bursars) were purposively selected. Consequently, a sample size of 151 respondents provided valid and reliable data about research problem. The researcher collected both quantitative and qualitative data using different types of data collection instruments in order to address the problem under study. The current study used closed ended and open-ended questionnaires for both AS and students; interview guide was used to collect data from dean of students and NAS, while document analysis was used to collect data on financial cases reported to the dean of students in higher learning institution.

DATA ANALYSIS

Quantitative data was analyzed using descriptive statistics. Similarly, the analysis was done inferentially using Pearson's Product Moment Correlation and Linear Regression Analysis in the SPSS version 25 to test research hypothesis on relationship between students' financial well-being and their performance in academics. On the other hand, analysis of qualitative data was done using thematic analysis and verbatim reporting.

RESULTS

This section presents the results of the data analysis which discusses the statistical relationships based on correlation and linear regression procedures and tabular representations in the context of the study hypothesis and objective. Similarly, the section presents the results and analysis of the extent to which financial well-being influence students' education in the Northern Zone of Tanzania.

DEMOGRAPHIC INFORMATION OF THE RESPONDENTS

The information on the gender for undergraduate students was obtained and the results of descriptive statistics are presented in Table 1:

Table 1. Undergraduate students respondents' bio-data (n=100)

Gender	f	(%)	Cumulative %
Male	50	50	50
Female	50	50	50
Total	100	100.0	100.0

f=Frequency, %= Percentage, n=number of respondents.
Source: Field Data (2024)

The results of descriptive statistics on the bases of gender indicate that there were 100 undergraduate students respondents that included 50 (50%) males and 50 (50%) females. On the basis of the descriptive results, it is clear that both genders were represented in the study, an indication that there was no bias in capturing the views of the undergraduate students about their gender. Thus, this implies that these results from undergraduate students can easily be generalized information on their knowledge and experience on the financial well-being of university students in higher learning institution.

BIOGRAPHICAL INFORMATION OF AS

Similarly, the information on the gender for AS was obtained and the results of descriptive statistics are presented in Table 2:

Table 2. AS respondents' bio-data (n=36)

Gender	f	(%)	Cumulative %
Male	18	50	50
Female	18	50	50
Total	36	100.0	100.0

f=Frequency, %= Percentage, n=number of respondents.
Source: Field Data (2024)

The data of descriptive statistics on the bases of gender indicate that there were 36 AS participants including 18 females (50%) and 18 (50%) males. On the basis of the descriptive results, it is clear that both genders were represented in the study, an indication that there was no bias in capturing the views of AS about their gender. Consequently, this means that the information obtained from these results can easily be generalized.

RESEARCH HYPOTHESIS

The following hypothesis was formulated and tested using both Pearson's Product Moment Correlation and Linear Regression Test Analysis:

Null Hypothesis: There Is No Statistically Significant Relationship Between Financial Well-Being of Students and Grade Performance Average (GPA) Scored in Higher Education Institutions

While responding to the questionnaires, students indicated the number of times they reported financial cases to the dean. To verify the possibility of the influence of financial well-being on their performance, data were collected from 100 sampled students on a scale of how often (Very Often = 5, Often = 4, Sometimes = 3, Rarely = 2 and Never = 1) they reported financial cases to the dean. Similarly, the students recorded their reliable source of financial income. The GPA was measured in a scale of 1 to 5. The responses were presented as shown in table 3.

Table 3. Responses on frequency of financial cases reported to the dean and GPA scored (n=100)

Number of Students	Source of financial income	Frequency of financial cases reported to the dean	GPA scored
2	Guardians & well wishers	5	2.7
6	Guardians & well wishers	5	2.8
8	Guardians & well wishers	5	2.9
5	Parents	4	3.0
6	Guardians & well wishers	4	3.0
5	HESLB loan	2	3.2
5	Parents	2	3.4
10	HESLB loan	5	3.5
9	HESLB loan	3	3.6
11	HESLB loan	3	3.6
1	Parents	3	3.7
1	Salary	2	3.8
11	HESLB loan	3	4.2
10	HESLB loan	1	4.4
2	Salary	1	4.6
1	Salary	2	4.6
2	Scholarship	1	4.7
1	Scholarship	2	4.7
3	Scholarship	1	4.8
1	Scholarship	1	4.9

Source field data (2024)

Table 3 shows that the least number of times the students report financial cases to the dean, the higher the GPA scored. For instance, those who never reported any financial challenge had a GPA from 4.4 to 4.9. This implies that those who were stable financially either through scholarship, HESLB or salary had adequate time to concentrate in their education. On the contrary, those who very often reported financial difficulties to the dean had a GPA from 2.7 to 2.9.

RESULTS FROM HYPOTHESES TESTING

In order to find the relationship between financial well-being of students and their academic performance in higher education institutions, the data in table 5 on students' financial cases and GPA scored were also run through Pearson's Product Moment Correlation Test Analysis. The results are presented in table 4.

Table 4. Pearson's product moment correlation test analysis

		Frequency of financial cases reported to the dean	GPA scored
Frequency of financial cases reported to the dean	Pearson Correlation	1	-.762**
	Sig. (2-tailed)		.000
	N	100	100
GPA scored	Pearson Correlation	-.762**	1
	Sig. (2-tailed)	.000	
	N	100	100

**. Correlation is significant at the 0.01 level (2-tailed).

SOURCE FIELD DATA (2024)

Since the p-value (0.000) is less than the significance (0.01), the null hypothesis is rejected. Therefore, there is a significant relationship between students' financial cases and GPA scored. Since the two sets are significantly correlated; frequency of financial cases are likely to influence score in GPA. Further, the study established the extent to which financial cases reported to the dean influence students' academic performance using linear regression analysis.

Linear Regression Analysis

Linear regression was employed in order to ascertain the extent of relationship between frequency of financial cases reported to the dean and Grade Performance Average (GPA) scored by students in higher education institutions. The results of hypothesis testing were presented in tables; 5, 6 and 7.

Table 5. Summary of regression analysis on relationship between financial cases reported to the dean and GPA scored (n=100)

Model	R	R Square	Adjusted R Square	Std. Error of the Estimate
1	.762a	.581	.558	.95485

a. Predictors: (Constant), GPA scored

SOURCE FIELD DATA (2024)

It could be observed from table 5 that there is positive linear correlation (R =0.762) between financial cases reported to the dean and GPA scored. The study established that financial cases reported to the dean accounted for 58.1% of the total variance in the GPA score (R^2 =0.581). Thus, the study reveals a significant relationship between financial well-being of students and their academic performance in higher education institutions.

Table 6. Analysis of variance on financial well-being of students on their academic performance(n=100)

Model		Sum of Squares	df	Mean Square	F	Sig.
1	Regression	113.945	10	22.789	24.995	.000b
	Residual	82.0055	18	.912		
	Total	196.000	89			

a. Dependent Variable: Frequency of financial cases reported to the dean
b. Predictors: (Constant), GPA scored. *sig. at p<0.05
Source field data (2024)

The result in the analysis of variance in table 6 indicates that the F-ratio of the regression analysis is significant ($F_{(10,89)}$ = 24.995; p<0.05). This shows that the positive R value in table 5 is not due to probability. The study established a significant relationship between financial well-being of students on their academic performance (F=24.995). Consequently, the null hypothesis was rejected and the alternative hypothesis was accepted.

Table 7. Estimate of the relative contribution of frequency of financial cases on GPA

Model	Unstandardized Coefficients		Standardized Coefficients	t	Sig.
	B	Std. Error	Beta		
(Constant)	4.850	.462		10.492	.000
GPA scored	-.244	.049	-.762	-5.000	.000

a. Dependent Variable: Frequency of financial cases reported to the dean
Source field data (2024)

From table 7, financial cases contributes negatively towards GPA scored by students (B = -0.244 and β = -0.762). This implies that for every financial difficulty reported by a student, the GPA is likely to be negatively affected by a margin of -0.244 on Unstandardized scale and -0.762 on standardized scale. So, either way, financial difficulty as expressed in cases reported to the dean of students negatively affects GPA score.

In addition, quantitative data on the objective that investigated how university students' financial well-being influences their education in the Northern Zone of Tanzania was analyzed using descriptive statistics. The data obtained was presented in table 8.

Table 8. Response from AS on how university students' financial well-being influence their education (n=36)

Statement	Strongly Agre		Agree		Undecided		Disagree		Strongly Disagree		
	f	%	f	%	f	%	f	%	f	%	Mean
Enables them to access medical health care and promptly pay for health insurance	19	52.8	13	36.1	2	5.6	2	5.6	0	0.0	4.3611
Enhances their participation in extracurricular activities	15	41.7	17	47.2	0	0.0	2	5.6	2	5.6	4.1389
Necessary for stress management and mental health	15	41.7	16	44.4	1	2.8	2	5.6	2	5.6	4.1111
Enables them to access resources	18	50.0	7	19.4	7	19.4	4	11.1	0	0.0	4.0833
Improve quality of living conditions	14	38.9	13	36.1	4	11.1	3	8.3	2	5.6	3.9444
Contributes towards academic retention and completion of studies	14	38.9	10	27.8	0	0.0	8	22.2	4	11.1	3.8333

continued on following page

Table 8. Continued

Statement	Strongly Agree		Agree		Undecided		Disagree		Strongly Disagree		
	f	%	f	%	f	%	f	%	f	%	Mean
Helps them to access support services such as academic advice, counseling and career guidance	11	30.6	15	41.7	3	8.3	7	19.4	0	0.0	3.8333
Enable them to seek voluntary employment opportunities and unpaid internships	8	22.2	20	55.6	2	5.6	6	16.7	0	0.0	3.6111
Grand mean score											3.9894

Source field data (2024); f=frequency

The responses vary across categories, with 52.8% of academic staff strongly agreeing, 36.1% agreeing, 5.6% undecided, 5.6% disagreeing, and 0.0% strongly disagreeing that availability of finance enables students to access medical health care and promptly pay for health insurance. This item was found to have a high mean rating of 4.3611 implying that it greatly influences students' education. Concerning the availability of finances enhances students' participation in extracurricular activities, the data in table 8 show varying responses with 41.7% of the AS strongly agreeing, 47.2% agreeing, 0.0% neutral, 5.6% disagreeing, and 5.6% strongly disagreeing thereby giving a mean score of 4.1389. With regard to the availability of finances as necessary for stress management and mental health among students, the responses vary, with 41.7% of students strongly agreeing, 44.4% agreeing, 2.8% neutral, 5.6% disagreeing, and 5.6% strongly disagreeing that it influences students' education. Reflecting on the availability of finances enable students to seek voluntary employment opportunities and unpaid internships, academic staff's responses also show variation, with 22.2% strongly agreeing, 55.6% agreeing, 5.6% neutral, 16.7% disagreeing, and 0.0% strongly disagreeing that it has influence on students' education giving a mean score of 3.6111 which was below the grand mean score of 3.9894.

DISCUSSION

Table 3 shows that students with numerous financial difficulties which are very often reported to the dean post low GPA in their university examination. For example, university students who receive inadequate financial support from the guardians & well wishers frequently reported their cases to the dean and their GPA recorded was 2.7 to 2.9. While those who never reported cases at all recorded GPA score from

4.4 to 4.9. The cases reported included delay in rent payment, inability to pay for stationery services, inability to timely pay for health insurance, inadequate money to purchase food and class absenteeism due to financial embarrassment. In other words, these students take a lot of time to seek solutions to their financial difficulties leaving them with little time to concentrate in their studies. The study also found that financial well-being of students at higher education institutions can be assesses through access to basic needs such as housing, food, and healthcare, student's knowledge of budgeting, saving, investing, and managing debts, proper utilization of financial aid and resources, students' budgeting skills and student's proper time management. These results are further evidenced by Moore et al. (2020), where it was reported that it may be difficult for students to receive the full benefits of a college education when their social and academic lives are impeded by financial stress. This will certainly result in lack of concentration in education hence poor academic performance.

Using linear regression analysis to test for relationship, table 4 reveals that financial cases reported to the dean accounted for 58.1% of the total variance in the GPA scored. This implies that there is accumulative effect of financial cases reported on GPA. The results indicate a positive relationship between the two variables. Specifically, the test demonstrates that GPA depends on financial difficulties such as the debts accrued by students, inability to pay for means of transport to attend lectures and stress due to lack of financial counseling services to help students manage their finances. This significant association implies that the financial cases reported does negatively impact on the GPA of students in Tanzanian higher education institutions. Therefore, the study established that the financial cases reported to the dean influence students' academic performance by 58.1%. This study reveals that besides financial difficulties, there are other factors not considered in this study that also affect academic performance of students. These factors influence students' GPA by 41.9%. This is why Salas-Pilco et al. (2022) also stressed for institutional support, aligning with the need for improved financial aid provisions.

Data from the interviews also revealed numerous financial constraints among students. On this theme, one informant highlighted;

Yes, some students have high levels of debts. This is a clear indicator that they are struggling to cover their education expenses. Students with income sources such as employment, family support and scholarship are likely to have a higher level of financial stability. Moreover, reports of financial cases can serve as a direct indicator of financial instability. This can be seen in student's inability to pay tuition fees and cater for living expenses (Personal Interview, 14th May, 2024).

Responses from this key informant show an existing need to support students financially by all stakeholders in education sector. The financial support provided will enable students to purchase ICT equipment, cover healthcare, basic needs and travel expenses. This finding aligns with the Theory of Planned Behaviour (TPB) that guided this study. The theory conceptualizes behaviour as a result of a contribution of attitudes, subjective norms and perceived behavioural control (Ajzen, 1991). According to the TPB, financial well-being of students will help them manage their expenses and reduce stress. In further support of such discussions, an attitude towards financial products has also been shown to influence student's financial literacy levels.

Table 6 indicates that the study established a significant relationship between financial well-being of students on their academic performance (F=24.995). Consequently, the null hypothesis was rejected and the alternative hypothesis was accepted. The implication here is that the government through HESLB should continue providing loans to eligible Tanzanian students, the government should subsidize tuition fees for certain programmess or categories of students particularly those with disabilities and parents should provide financial support to cover academic progress and daily living expenses of students. Moreover, it is necessary for universities in Tanzania to offer work-study programmes where students can work part-time in campus or in related industries to enable them earn extra income that will cushion them against financial stress. This result is similar to the findings by Ansong and Gyensare (2012) who used correlation analysis to examine the level of financial literacy among a sample of undergraduate and postgraduate university working-students in Ghana, and found that among others, work income from work-study programmes and experience gathered was positively related to the level of financial literacy. Moore et al. (2021) recommended that university administrators who develop policy and allocate resources will need to consider both the downstream effects of financial stress as well as its root causes. As a result, continuous financial aid is instrumental in ensuring equitable access to necessary basic requirements for learning. Lack of adequate support in this area might lead to disparities, limiting some students' access to essential resources and potentially impacting their academic success and participation in higher learning education. Hence, universities must sustain their efforts to provide continued financial aid for education-related expenses. By prioritizing and expanding such support mechanisms, universities can ensure equal opportunities for all students, enabling them to fully engage and benefit from higher learning education.

Table 7 shows that for every financial difficulty reported by a student, the GPA is likely to be negatively affected by a margin of -0.244. To address this issue, universities need to reassess their financial strategies and ensure alignment with educational objectives. Prioritizing investments in areas that directly contribute to minimizing financial stress among students is essential. By aligning financial commitments with educational aspirations, universities can effectively channel resources to initiatives that support learning outcomes, innovation, and the overall quality of education delivered in higher learning institutions. In this regard, studies by Kwiatkowska, W. & Wiśniewska-Nogaj, L. (2022) and Zhou et al. (2022), emphasizes the challenges stemming from insufficient funding of higher learning education. This implies that institutions might struggle more with the financial demands of implementing effective learning strategies due to the absence of government subsidies, potentially affecting their ability to invest in quality education of students.

The data in table 8 shows the mean rating on how university students' financial well-being influences their education. The responses from AS indicates that availability of finance enables students to access medical health care and promptly pay for health insurance at the rate of 4.3611 which was above the grand mean score of 3.9894. According to the AS, the availability of finances enhances students' participation in extracurricular activities was rated second with a mean score of 4.1389. This implies that AS believe that good health among students should be given priority. This will enable students to dedicate their valuable time to academics and core-curriculum activities. Students with sound health will also be active in class and will be able to invest more time doing research related to their course. In this regard, research by Karyotaki et al. (2020) demonstrated a link between financial stress and poorer mental health outcomes; for example, worry over finances has been correlated with mental illnesses like depression and anxiety. Similar study by McCloud and Bann (2018) has also reported an association between financial stress and general poor mental health. According to the study, students' perceived financial stress is correlated with negative mental health outcomes, suggesting perceived stress may be a more influential factor in mental health than the amount of debt accrued.

With regard to other factors that influence students' education in the Northern Zone of Tanzania, the availability of finances as a necessary measure for stress management and mental health among students scored a mean of 4.1111 while finances enables students to access resources score 4.0833. These factors recorded mean score above grand mean score of 3.9894 indicating that they have more influence on students' education. Consequently, the study established that financial stress can also have negative effects on mental health, leading to issues such as anxiety and depression. These mental health challenges can further impede academic performance by affecting concentration, motivation, and overall well-being. To support these findings, Moore et al. (2021) in a study conducted in private and urban university in the United States on lived experiences of students with financial stress proposed Pell Grant US federal aid to be provided to low income students. This would help to address negative outcomes of financial stress.

During the interviews on how university students' financial well-being influences their education in the Northern Zone of Tanzania, one dean of students reported that;

Financial stress can significantly impact students' academic performance. Students facing financial difficulties may struggle to afford necessary resources such as textbooks, laptops, internet accessibility, transport cost, and even basic necessities like food and housing. This stress can distract their ability to focus on their studies and perform well in examinations (Personal Interview, 12th May, 2024).

The response from the respondent demonstrates that financial well-being directly impacts the quality of education received by students. Certainly, the quality of education is compromised if teaching and learning materials are not adequate. This finding collaborates with the findings from similar study by Ansong and Gyensare (2012) who pointed out that as student's financial support increases, the student's propensity to save will also be high in accordance with the theory of savings behaviour which posits that saving is a positive function of disposable income. Therefore, through saving, the student will be able to purchase basic necessities like food, textbooks, laptops, internet connectivity for personal academic progress.

In addition, some factors recorded mean score below grand mean score of 3.9894. These were; finances improve quality of living conditions among students (3.9444); availability of finances contributes towards academic retention and completion of studies (3.833); helps students to access support services such as academic advice, counseling and career guidance (3.833), and availability of finances enable students to seek voluntary employment opportunities and unpaid internships (3.6111). According to academic staff, these factors have less influence on students' education. This in further supported by Kwiatkowska & Wiśniewska-Nogaj (2022) who pin pointed the importance of students having adequate financial resources for effective implementation of virtual learning that will help them complete their studies in time. Through virtual learning, students will handle travelling inconveniences to colleges and access support services such as online academic advice from their lecturers.

Further interviews on how university students' financial well-being influences their education revealed that;

Financial difficulties may force students to engage in part-time employment thereby diverting valuable time and energy away from academic activities. This negatively impact on students' ability to complete their studies within the expected time. In some cases, financial difficulties may lead students to engage in academic misconduct, such as cheating or plagiarism, as a means of trying to improve their grades or academic standing. This could result in disciplinary action and potentially contribute to the frequency of financial cases reported to the dean of students (Personal Interview, 16th May, 2024)

The excerpt from non academic staff highlights the predicament of financial constraints experienced by students which negatively impact on their mental health and may lead to drop out from higher learning institutions. It should be pointed out that limited financial recourses may affect ability of students to fully engage in course work and research. To buttress these findings, Adams et al. (2016) noted that students from low socio-economic origins are much more likely to drop out than those from high socio-economic ones. This is so because less fortunate students are less likely to be aware of the true costs associated with post-secondary education.

CONCLUSION

The study sought to investigate the financial well-being of students at higher education institutions in Northern Zone, Tanzania. From the findings, the research study highlights the critical impact of financial stability on academic performance and overall student well-being. The findings reveal that students facing financial difficulties are more likely to experience stress, anxiety, and lower academic outcomes, which can hinder their educational achievements and future career prospects. The study underscores the importance of financial literacy programs and accessible financial support services within institutions to mitigate these challenges. By equipping students with better financial management skills and providing adequate resources, higher education institutions can play a pivotal role in enhancing student success and retention rates.

Moreover, the research emphasizes the need for systemic changes in how higher education institutions address financial well-being. Policymakers and educational leaders are urged to consider implementing more comprehensive financial aid packages and developing policies that reduce the financial burden on students. This could include measures such as increasing scholarships, offering affordable housing options, and creating work-study programmes that do not interfere with academic responsibilities. By fostering a supportive financial environment, institutions not only contribute to the personal and academic growth of their students but also promote a more equitable and inclusive educational landscape.

RECOMMENDATIONS

Based on the study findings the following recommendations were made;

i. Higher education institutions in Northern Zone of Tanzania should implement robust retention programmes that include emergency financial assistance, work-study opportunities, and flexible payment plans. Providing financial safety nets can help students stay enrolled and graduate on time.

ii. The government should increase financial support to students through HESLB since students facing financial hardship are more likely to score low GPA, drop out or take longer to complete their degrees.
iii. Institutions should provide comprehensive financial aid packages and offer financial counseling services to help students manage their finances and reduce stress.
iv. Universities should ensure equitable access to essential resources such as textbooks, laptops, and internet connectivity. Programmes like textbook lending libraries and subsidized technology access can help bridge the gap.
v. There is need to create and promote scholarships, grants, and funding opportunities specifically for extracurricular participation and global learning experiences to ensure all students can benefit.

REFERENCES

Abreu, M., & Mendes, V. (2011). Financial literacy and portfolio diversification. *Quantitative Finance*, 10(5), 515–528. 10.1080/14697680902878105

Adams, D. R., Meyers, S. A., & Boidas, R. S. (2016). The relationship between financial strain, perceived stress, psychological symptoms and academic and social integration in undergraduate students. *Journal of American College Health*, 2(5), 32–44. 10.1080/07448481.2016.115455926943354

Ansong, A., & Gyensare, M. A. (2012). Determinants of working-students financial literacy at the university of Cape Coast, Ghana. *International Journal of Business and Management*, 7(9), 126–133. 10.5539/ijbm.v7n9p126

Ajzen, I. (1991). The Theory of Planned Behavior. *Organizational Behavior and Human Decision Processes*, 50(2), 179–211. 10.1016/0749-5978(91)90020-T

Bozick, R. (2007). Making it through the first year of college: The role of students' economic resources, employment, and living arrangements. *Sociology of Education*, 80(3), 261–285. 10.1177/003804070708000304

Cude, B., Frances, L., Lyons, A., Metzger, K., LeJeune, E., Marks, L., & Machtmes, K. (2006). College students and financial literacy: What they know and what we need to learn. *Proceedings of the Eastern Family Economics and Resource Management Association*, (pp. 102-109). Research Gate.

Curran, M. A., Parrott, E., Ahn, S. Y., Serido, J., & Shim, S. (2018). Young adult's life outcomes and well-being: Perceived financial socialization from parents, the romantic partner, and young adults' own financial Behaviors. *Journal of Family and Economic Issues*, 1–12.

Creswell, J. W., & Creswell, J. D. (2023). *Research design: Qualitative, quantitative, and mixed methods approaches* (6th ed.). SAGE.

Creswell, J. W., & Creswell, J. D. (2018). *Research Design: Qualitative, Quantitative and Mixed Methods Approaches* (5th ed.). SAGE.

Engle, J., & Tinto, V. (2008). *Moving beyond access: College success for low-income, first-generation students*. Pell Institute for the Study of Opportunity in Higher Education.

Garrido, J. (2019). Stress, coping strategies and academic achievement in teacher education students. *European Journal of Teacher Education*, 42(4), 1–16. 10.1080/02619768.2019.1576629

Gyimah, P., Poku, K., & Osei-Poku, B. (2018). Financial literacy assessment on tertiary students in sub-saharan Africa: A Ghanaian perspective. *International Journal of Accounting and Financial Reporting*, 8(2), 76–91. 10.5296/ijafr.v8i2.12928

Hanson, T. A., & Olson, P. M. (2018). Financial literacy and family communication patterns. *Journal of Behavioral and Experimental Finance*, 19, 64–71. 10.1016/j.jbef.2018.05.001

Karyotaki, E., Cuijpers, P., Albor, Y., Alonso, J., Auerbach, R. P., Bantjes, J., Bruffaerts, R., Ebert, D. D., Hasking, P., Kiekens, G., Lee, S., McLafferty, M., Mak, A., Mortier, P., Sampson, N. A., Stein, D. J., Vilagut, G., & Kessler, R. C. (2020). Sources of stress and their associations with mental disorders among college students: Results of the World Health Organization world mental health surveys international college student initiative. *Frontiers in Psychology*, 11, 1759. 10.3389/fpsyg.2020.0175932849042

Klein, A. (2010). *Incoming college students rate emotional health at record low, annual survey finds*. Higher Education Research Institute.

Kwiatkowska, W., & Wiśniewska-Nogaj, L. (2022). Digital Skills and Online Collaborative Learning: The Study Report. *Electronic Journal of e-Learning*, 20(5), 510–522. 10.34190/ejel.20.5.2412

Lusardi, A., & Mitchell, O. S. (2014). The economic importance of financial literacy: Theory and evidence. *Journal of Economic Literature*, 52(1), 5–44. 10.1257/jel.52.1.528579637

Magembe, K. S. (2018). *Exploring Academic Difficulties Facing First-Year Undergraduate Students at the Institute of Adult Education, Tanzania*. Institute of Adult Education.

Moore, A., Nguyen, A., Rivas, S., & Bany-Mohammed, A. (2021). *A qualitative examination of the impacts of financial stress on college students' well-being: Insights from a large, private institution*. SAGE Publications., 10.1177/20503121211018122

Moore, Y., Koonce, J., Plunkett, S. W., & Pleskus, L. (2020). Financial information source, knowledge, and practice of college students from diverse backgrounds. *Journal of Financing Counseling & Planning*, 26(1), 63–78.

McCloud, T., & Bann, D. (2019). Financial stress and mental health among higher education students in the UK up to 2018: Rapid review of evidence. *Journal of Epidemiology and Community Health*, 73(10), 977–984. 10.1136/jech-2019-21215431406015

Mkumbo, D., Otieno, K. O., & Rufyiriza, C. G. (2023). Coping Strategies among First Year Students and its Influence on their Education: A Study of Universities in Arusha Region, Tanzania. *Journal of Research Innovation and Implications in Education*, 7(4), 480–492.

Muraskin, L., & Lee, J. (2004). *Raising the graduation rates of low-income college students*. Pell Institute for the Study of Opportunity in Higher Education.

Otieno, K. (2023). Peer Support and Adjustment Among First-Year Students at University. In Aloka, P., & Mukuna, K. (Eds.), *Handbook of Research on Coping Mechanisms for First-Year Students Transitioning to Higher Education* (pp. 315–329). IGI Global. 10.4018/978-1-6684-6961-3.ch019

Oppong-Boakye, P. K., & Kansanba, R. (2013). An assessment of financial literacy levels among undergraduate business students in Ghana. *Research Journal of Finance and Accounting*, 4(8), 36–49.

Oseifuah, E. K. (2014). Analysis of the level of financial literacy among South African undergraduate students. *Journal of Economics and Behavioral Studies*, 6(3), 242–250. 10.22610/jebs.v6i3.487

Salas-Pilco, S. Z. (2022). The Impact of COVID-19 on Latin American STEM Higher Education: A Systematic Review. *2022 IEEE World Engineering Education Conference (EDUNINE)*, (pp. 1–6). IEEE. https://doi.org/10.1109/EDUNINE53672.2022.9782354

Schmid, R., & Petko, D. (2019). Does the use of educational technology in personalized learning environments correlate with self-reported digital skills and beliefs of secondary-school students? *Computers & Education*, 136(1), 75–86. 10.1016/j.compedu.2019.03.006

Reyers, M. (2016). The role of financial literacy and advice in financial decision making. *Southern African Business Review*, 20, 388–413. 10.25159/1998-8125/6057

TCU. (2022). Guidelines for Online and Blended Delivery Modes of Courses for University Institution in Tanzania. Dar es Salaam Tanzania Commission for Universities.

Wangenge-Ouma, G. (2018). Public by Day, Private by Night: Examining the Private Lives of Kenya's Public Universities. *European Journal of Education*, 47(3).

Wium, A.-M., & Louw, B. (2018). Mixed-methods research: A tutorial for speech-language therapists and audiologists in South Africa. *The South African Journal of Communication Disorders*, 56(1), a573. 10.4102/sajcd.v65i1.57330035606

Zhou, M., Dzingirai, C., Hove, K., Chitata, T., & Mugandani, R. (2022). Adoption, use and enhancement of virtual learning during COVID-19. *Education and Information Technologies*, 27(7), 8939–8959. 10.1007/s10639-022-10985-x35340535

Chapter 17
The Impetus of Monetary Intelligence on Financial Satisfaction and Security:
A Preliminary Survey on University Students from India

K. Madhu Kishore Raghunath
https://orcid.org/0000-0002-8134-5718
GITAM University, Visakhapatnam, India

Adil Khan
https://orcid.org/0000-0002-1309-2472
GITAM University, Visakhapatnam, India

ABSTRACT

One predominant factor which has had a great influence on financial wellbeing is monetary intelligence or love for money. Different parts of the world have different perceptions towards the aspect of money/monetary intelligence/love for money. Some perceive money as not so important factor in life, whereas others believe that money is the most important part of individuals life. The desired benefits of monetary intelligence on financial well-being also depends upon the levels of hierarchical needs that people would like to satisfy. Whereas financial well-being is an abstract theory that describes the general condition of a person or society, which further differs from individual to individual. The authors in the present study aim to analyse the impact of different dimensions of monetary intelligence on the financial wellbeing of young individuals in India. The dimensions of monetary intelligence, mainly cognitive, affective, and behavioural.

DOI: 10.4018/979-8-3693-4417-0.ch017

Copyright © 2024, IGI Global. Copying or distributing in print or electronic forms without written permission of IGI Global is prohibited.

INTRODUCTION

Events such as the global financial crisis and the COVID-19 pandemic have accentuated the importance of money management. Both events have significantly disrupted the global economy and growth (Guichard and Rusticelli, 2010; Choudhry et al., 2012; Barrafrem et al., 2020; Singh and Malik, 2022). These events have reinforced the critical role which money management and thereof monetary intelligence can play in developing the financial awareness among masses. Studies suggest that monetary intelligence fosters the evolution of financial attitudes and financial satisfaction (Philippas and Avdoulas, 2020). Monetary intelligence can significantly influence investment choices and determines risk appetite. Its relevance can be linked to various strategies which individuals may employ to achieve financial well-being. Monetary intelligence is especially crucial for young adults between 25 and 35, as they form the backbone of every economy's growth (Brüggen et al., 2017).

Given that our world is frequently affected by numerous internal and external risk factors, the importance of monetary intelligence and the principles of financial satisfaction should not be overlooked. Young individuals may also lack experience, forward-thinking approach, and a strategic plan the application of monetary intelligence may not be assumed to occur naturally (Mountain et al., 2020). As in Indian context a large proportion is composed of young individuals; study of monetary intelligence among such audience can be an interesting research avenue .

India now being the worlds most populated country in the world and with large percentage of population being working youth, their money management skills will encapsulate their financial Satisfaction. Singh, R. K. (2022) based on a survey done on 600 students and their parents articulated that 96% of parents believe that their children don't have any knowledge on money management. It was further posited that only 22% of them were confident in money management and digital banking. Despite the various efforts being put in by experts and parents, financial difficulties faced by one generation are mirrored in future generations also (Lanz et al., 2020) and with a prediction of 65% of its total population being under working class, India is expected to emphasize more on creating efficient monetary intelligence among Indian youth.

One of the main drivers of the well-being of a country is based on the financial attitude of students and their expected financial attitudes are highly associated with financial knowledge, therefore students become platform to study the financial attitude (Çoşkun & Dalziel, 2020). Still students are not confident about their money matters as briefed by s (Falahati & Paim (2011).; Richter and Prawitz, 2010), which might be attributed to the fact that certain bad decisions taken by students affect the ability to become financial satisfied adults (Martin & Oliva, 2001), hence college education and their attitude towards financial awareness becomes a critical platform to shape their financial attitude. Danes, S.M (1994) & Hayhoe et al. (2000) in same sense posited that students who have better financial knowledge at university are correlated to higher future earnings, higher savings, better budgeting, better credit card usages and positive investment attitudes. Ultimately there is a mutual relationship between financial literacy, financial attitude and financial satisfaction (Çoşkun & Dalziel, 2020).

Going further, the study will be divided into the following sections: Review of Literature, Review of Literature, Need for the study, Factors influencing Monetary Intelligence, Methodology, Data Analysis, Discussions, Strategies to improve Monetary Intelligence, Importance of Monetary Intelligence, Limitations, Conclusion.

REVIEW OF LITERATURE

Beliefs and attitudes of individuals can significantly impact on their financial behaviour (Sahi & Dutta, 2015). Multiple authors such as Gasiorowska (2015), Castro-Gonzalez et al. (2020) and Sabri et al. (2020) many studies have indeed proved and established a positive relationship between monetary intelligence and financial satisfaction and financial security. Further Harnish et al (2018) & Shim et al (2009) have opined that monetary intelligence in individuals is conditioned by social and cultural factors that are acquired in life through experiences and via distinct life cycle stages. Ammerman and stueve (2019) & Ullah and Yusheng (2020) expressed that Individuals financial experiences condition their financial management behaviour in anticipation of achieving financial satisfaction.

Love for money leads to happiness is question for ages to answer and debate with inconclusive results and literature. Either ways several studies related to love for money and financial Satisfaction are largely dependent on people from different income classes. According to Jebb et al. (2018); Kahneman & Deaton, (2010) it is observed that love for money leads to happiness only when individuals are able to get their higher income levels. It is also observed that studies associating income and Satisfaction factors are stronger and well defined among economically developing samples than that of middle- and upper-class individuals in wealthier countries (Diener & Biswas-Diener 2002; Hoyt 2008). Ajzen (1991) found out in his research that the need for financial satisfaction is strongly mediated by individuals money attitudes or monetary intelligence. Based on previous studies experts have hypothesised that financial satisfaction and security are highly correlated with demographics (age, gender and education) (Malone et al., 2010), behavioural factors (Shim et al., 2009) as well as economic, political and social issues (Franko, 2021; Lyons and Yilmazer, 2005).

Monetary intelligence, financial satisfaction and financial security are interdependent elements as Monetary intelligence impacts how an individual considers his work, compensation system and motivation levels at work which in turn would influence the financial satisfaction and financial security (Tang, 1995). Monetary intelligence within itself is a multi-dimensional variable with three core elements to predict it, that are cognitive, behavioral and affective constructs. Cognitive construct measures peoples perceptions of their ability to prioritize monetary intelligence cognitive importance in terms of respect, achievement, and power. Affective construct measures peoples perception of their ability to appraise monetary intelligence for being rich, motivator and feeling important. Behavioural construct measure peoples perception of their ability to appraise monetary intelligence as factor to regulate money related intentions such as to make, donate and contribute money (Chen et al., 2014). A study by Tan & Sutarso (2013) presented that managers with high monetary intelligence focus on their intellectual virtues of prudence and fulfilment resulting in higher pay satisfaction where money is mostly associated with status, respect, freedom, control and power. In absence of proper pay or pay dissatisfaction, people become corrupt in the name of justice (Greenberg 1993) equity (Gino and Pierce, 2009) revenge (Ashforth and Anand, 2003). It was also further argued that monetary intelligence activates feeling of self-sufficiency (Vohs et al. 2006).

Studies on financial satisfaction and financial security as a separate area of research are taking a lot of momentum. Financial security as a indicator for socio-economic factor for modern society has garnered a lot of attention. Few consider financial satisfaction and financial security as a process (Nguyen and Nguyen 2020) whereas few consider it a feature of a society (Franchuk et al. 2020) or state (Shynkar et al. 2020). These two aspects are in way treated as an independent objective of a enterprise management (Stashchuk et al. 2020) which within itself entails the concepts of science and economics and financial management. Aspects of financial satisfaction and financial security for an individual or a entity also entails the dimensions of taking optimal decisions in the areas of financing and investing (Bochulia and Melnychenko 2019; Tullio and Mario 2011). Dew and Xiao (2011) & Tang et al. (2013) proposed that individuals who manage money carefully have high satisfaction with pay and life. With all being said about monetary intelligence, financial satisfaction and financial security, the present study will examine the impact of various dimensions of monetary intelligence on financial satisfaction and financial security.

NEED FOR THE STUDY

Everyone values money, be young or old, everyone has an opinion on money and the way the way they treat it is different from person to person. The present study has taken post graduation students opinion to know and evaluate their perception about money. Evidence from the past suggests that financial attitude predicts a students financial practices (Dowling et al., 2009; Shim, et al., 2009). Speaking of students especially men and women have different beliefs about money (Allen et al., 2008 & Heyhoe, et al., 2000) which majorly depends upon the financial socialization of students during their childhood (Hira and Mugenda, 1998). Different families use different strategies to socialise their children regarding financial decision making and practices that teach students the art of building their financial attitude and learning financial management skills (Newcomb and Rabow, 1999; Çoşkun & Dalziel, 2020; Yogasnumurti, 2021). Given the way students have learned to manage money or have ambitions to manage money it is key to understand their opinion about importance of money towards their financial wellbeing.

FACTORS INFLUENCING MONETARY INTELLIGENCE

Studies from different countries have been exploring the various determinants that impact monetary intelligence and eventually financial well-being of Individuals and groups. Kaur et al. (2023) in their research stressed that knowledge of various determinants of monetary intelligence can enhance individuals' capability to formulate better strategies in securing a promising financial future. The same inquisitiveness has led to the following factors being mentioned figure 1, as the determinants affecting monetary intelligence.

1. **Demographic characteristics**: Demographic factors are first set of factors that influence monetary intelligence and eventually financial wellbeing. Gender role theories and family socialization models support the fact that women are more risk averse and comparatively are less confident in taking financial decisions (Barber and Odean 2001; Fellner and Guth 2005; Hira and Mugenda 2000; Škreblin et al. 2017). The other factor is age, where it has been identified the young people tend to be more susceptible in taking wrong financial decisions in haste (Lusardi et al. 2010), whereas comparatively older people are more knowledgeable and aware while taking financial decisions leading to greater financial wellbeing. Level of education and further maritial status are also linked with factors which that have significant impact on financial decision making, monetary intelligence and financial wellbeing (Zurlo 2009)

Figure 1. Factors affecting monetary intelligence

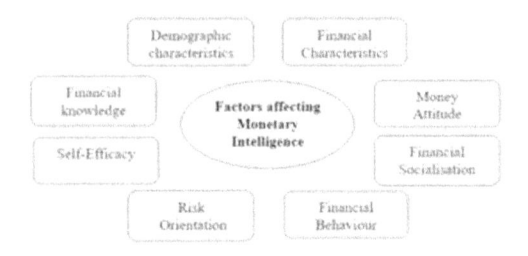

2. **Financial Characteristics**: studies in past have substantiated a positive relationship between income of a individual and financial wellbeing (Xiao 2016; Riitsalu and Murakas 2019;Kulkarni 2022; Kulshreshtha, 2019). Different income group levels (low, Moderate and High) have subsequent levels of monetary intelligence and financial wellbeing. The other aspect such as borrowings of individual such as loans, mortgages and credit cards have a total different effect on monetary intelligence, which further depends upon other factors of monetary intelligence.
3. **Financial knowledge**: Literature provides a plethora of studies where individuals scoring high on financial knowledge are found to be significantly successful in various aspects of financial decision making (Parrotta, 1996; Hilger, 2003). Financial knowledge also helps people ready themselves in economically and financially distressing situation. Coskuner (2016) and Chandra (2015) further posited that financial knowledge in both objective and subjective ways play a pivotal role in individual monetary intelligence and financial wellbeing.
4. **Money Attitude**: Money attitude talks about an individual's consistent behavioural dispositions towards money related issues. Money attitude is considered to be an instrumental factor responsible for a certain financial behaviour and perception of financial status (Akben & Aydin 2021; Abdullah et al. 2019) Money attitude predicts the success and failure of a decision further based on an persons proactive and reactive mindset towards his financial decisions (Ahmed and Limbu 2018), Eventually money attitude also governs the consumption, saving and debt behaviours (Hayhoe et al. 2012).
5. **Self-Efficacy**: An individuals capability to produce a specific performance is defined as self efficacy, which also is a key factor in strive towards financial wellbeing (Gutter and Copur 2011). Individuals self efficacy creates a resilient environment around him which drives his monetary intelligence and delivers financial satisfaction (Asebedo and Payne 2019). Self efficacy is also considered as a tools bridging gap between financial literacy and financial wellbeing by

boosting confidence among individuals to take that step towards availing and taking financial decisions (Sato 2019; Mindra et al. 2017)

6. **Risk Orientation**: Risk orientation is the measure of a significant risk appetite that an individual can accept. May studies have enunciated that individual risk tolerance is key factors propagating financial satisfaction and financial wellbeing. According to Asebedo and Payne (2019) risk tolerance is a key criteria for and individual portfolio management allocation and return calculations. Many studies have also propagated a positive relationship between risk tolerance and financial satisfaction as high risk appetite leads to higher return and monetary intelligence (Castro-Gonzalez et al. 2020).

7. **Financial Behaviour**: This indicates the various financial decisions and the way he responds to them from time to time in past and present (Joo and Grable 2004). A constant and consistent proximity with financial decisions at individual and organisational level leads to an positive monetary intelligence and better financial wellbeing (Shim e al. 2009; Oquaye et al. 2022). Financial decisions like money management, savings, investment, budgeting, risk management, future planning are all examples of financial behaviours.

8. **Financial Socialization**: Financial socialization can be defined as process of acquiring skills and developing knowledge and value that contribute to financial viability and monetary intelligence. Parent and teachers have been found to be most influential entities to shape and create this knowledge and values. Teaching and training passed to children by their parents and teachers are modelled as factors that influence financial wellbeing as they grow older. According to Ammerman and Stueve (2019) financial socialization shows a significant positive effect on individuals monetary intelligence and financial wellbeing.

RESEARCH FRAMEWORK

Figure 2, gives an idea of how the key aspect of the study will be studied based on the below mentioned hypotheses.

Figure 2. Research framework

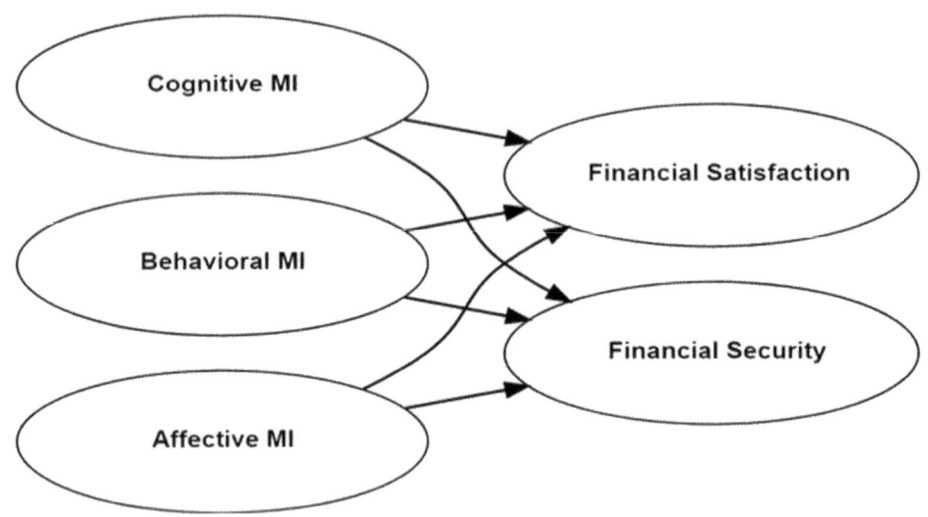

Source= Authors own elaboration, MI= Monetary Intelligence

Hypotheses

H1: Affective component of monetary intelligence has a positive influence on financial satisfaction.
H2: Behavioural component of monetary intelligence has a positive influence on financial satisfaction
H3: Cognitive component of monetary intelligence has a positive influence on financial satisfaction
H4: Affective component of monetary intelligence has a positive influence on financial security
H5: Behavioural component of monetary intelligence has a positive influence on financial security
H6: Cognitive component of monetary intelligence has a positive influence on financial security

METHODOLOGY

The data for this study have been collected through an online survey. The survey instrument was created using the Google Forms service. The sampling unit has been defined as individuals aged 18 and above. We have employed a purposing non-probability-based sampling method. The questionnaire was sent to 300 students out of which we received 150 responses and 120 complete responses were considered for study.

The instrument used in this study contains selected scales developed in the previous studies by (Chen et al., 2014; Zemtsov & Osipova., 2016). The purpose of this study was to investigate the role of money related attitudes on financial wellbeing. Financial wellbeing being has been operationalised using the concept of *"financial satisfaction"* and *"financial security"*. We have measured three variables *"monetary intelligence"*, *"financial security"*, and *"financial satisfaction"*. Monetary intelligence scale has been adopted from Tang et al (2018). The Monetary intelligence scale has three second order components *affective, behavioural, and cognitive* (these component may be termed as ABC). We have analysed the relationship between these dimensions of *monetary intelligence* with the two complementary measures of financial wellbeing, i.e. financial satisfaction, and financial security. Financial Satisfaction and financial security are measured using 1 item each and are measured using studies from Nandakishor et al (2024) respectively. Hypothesis are tested by conducting series of OLS regression in SPSS software. All hypotheses were tested at the 5% level of significance. Model fit was evaluated using R-squared values obtained from the regression results.

DATA ANALYSIS

The analysis will start with discussions over demographic variables used in the study for analyzing the relationship between dependent and independent variables. Table 1 below shows the classification of demographic variables in terms of Gender, Marital status and Educational qualification to provide a basis for understanding the demographic profile of the respondents.

Table 1. Demographic variables

		Frequency	Valid Percent
Gender	Male	66	55
	Female	54	45
	Total	120	100
Marital Status	Married	16	13.3
	Unmarried	104	86.7
	Total	120	100
Education	UG	35	29.2
	PG	85	70.8
	Total	120	100

Under gender classification, males represent 55% of the population and females represent 45% of the population, which is an ideal representation of both genders for the study. Next is marital status of the respondents which shows that 86.7% of the population are unmarried and only 13.3% of the population is married, which is justified as we are measuring the study among students. Lastly speaking of education qualification of the population, the majority of them have done their post-graduation (70.8%) and other half of the population have done their under-graduation (29.2).

Further to investigate the relationship between the variables of our interest we conducted six simple linear regressions. As the three dimensions of *monetary intelligence* are a part of same concept, we avoided doing the multiple regression due to chances of multicollinearity (Sahi, 2017).

We ran first three simple regression keeping *"financial satisfaction"* as the dependent variable and the ABC (Affective, behavioural, and cognitive) components of monetary intelligence as the independent variables. All three hypotheses were accepted. First hypothesis (H1) tests the relationship between the Affective component of monetary intelligence and the financial satisfaction. The relationship for H1 (Affective monetary intelligence →Financial Satisfaction, coefficient = .220, p= 0.016) was significant at the 95% confidence level. The results suggest that individuals with higher levels of affective monetary intelligence are more likely to be financially satisfied. Other two hypotheses H2 (Behavioural monetary intelligence →Financial Satisfaction, coefficient = .478, p= 0.000) and H3 (Cognitive monetary intelligence →Financial Satisfaction, coefficient = .319, p= 0.000) obtained highly significant results encapsulating a positive result where individuals with higher levels of behavioural monetary intelligence and cognitive monetary intelligence are more likely to be financially satisfied. Behavioural component further also has the highest explanatory power with R squared value of 0.229 which is equivalent to 22.9% explained variation, followed by R squared values of cognitive (.102) and affective components (.048).

For next set of simple regressions (H4 to H6), we used ABC (Affective, behavioural, and cognitive) components of monetary intelligence as the independent variables, as used in previous step, but with *financial security* as the dependent variable. Our first claim under financial security, Hypothesis H4 testing the relationship between Affective component of monetary intelligence was rejected (p-value>0.05). Other two dimensions (Affective and behavioural) of monetary intelligence have the positive and significant influence on *financial security*. Results of regressions are presented in the table 2 below.

The models in our analysis show reasonable level of fit; evaluated using ANOVA significance and R squared. All models were significant, except for Affective→Financial Security (Model significance > 0.05). R squared values also ranged from 2.3% to 22.9% indicating the varied proportion of explained variance in the models. Further, the R-squared values reveal that behavioural factors have the strongest impact on both financial satisfaction (R-squared = 22.9%) and financial security (R-squared = 19.1%), explaining the largest proportion of variance. Affective and cognitive factors also contribute, but to a lesser extent. This highlights the pivotal role of behaviours in shaping individuals' financial well-being, with emotions and cognitive understanding playing supporting roles.

Table 2. Results of regression analyses

Variable	R square	F statistic	Model Significance	Unstandardised coefficients (B)	Standardised coefficients (beta)	Hypothesis p-value	Result
Dependent Variable: Financial Satisfaction							
Affective	.048	5.976	.016	.320	.220	.016	*Accept*
Behavioural	.229	35.035	0.00	.804	.478	.000	*Accept*
Cognitive	.102	13.413	.000	.439	.319	.000	*Accept*
Dependent Variable: Financial Security							
Affective	.023	2.731	.101	.230	.150	.101	*Reject*
Behaviour	.191	27.829	.000	.771	.437	.000	*Accept*
Cognitive	.049	6.029	.016[b]	.319	.220	.016	*Accept*

The correlation analysis in Table 3 reveals significant relationships among affective, cognitive, and behavioural components, financial security, and financial satisfaction. The affective component is positively correlated with the cognitive component (r = .571, p < .01), behavioural component (r = .412, p < .01), and financial satisfaction (r = .220, p < .05). The cognitive component shows positive correlations with the behavioural component (r = .414, p < .01), financial security (r = .220, p < .05), and financial satisfaction (r = .319, p < .01). The behavioural component is positively correlated with financial security (r = .437, p < .01) and financial satisfaction (r = .478, p < .01). Financial security is strongly correlated with financial satisfaction (r = .695, p < .01). These findings suggest that affective, cognitive, and behavioural components significantly influence financial security and satisfaction, with financial security showing the strongest correlation with financial satisfaction. The lowest point of correlation (.150) is between financial security and affective monetary intelligence.

Table 3. Result of correlation analysis

	Affective	Cognitive	Behavioural	Financial Security	Financial Satisfaction
Affective	1	.571**	.412**	.150	.220*
Cognitive		1	.414**	.220*	.319**
Behavioural			1	.437**	.478**
Financial Security				1	.695**
Financial Satisfaction					1

**. Correlation is significant at the 0.01 level (2-tailed).
*. Correlation is significant at the 0.05 level (2-tailed).

DISCUSSIONS

In our study all the variables, Affective (p value- 0.016), Behavioural (p value- 0.000) and Cognitive ((p value- 0.000) are significant towards financial satisfaction. The present results are analogous to previous study by Arifin (2018) who posited that financial attitude variables affective, behavioural and cognitive with financial behaviour as intervening variable are positive and significant. Financial attitude has a positive relationship to financial satisfaction (Chandra and Memarista, 2015; Joo and Grable, 2004; Xiao et al., 2006; Xiao et al., 2009; Halim and Astuti, 2015; Arifin, 2018)

The overall results shows that individuals with better financial attitude have higher financial satisfaction, which further means satisfaction arises as a result of better savings and investment, effective budgeting and managing money. The results are consistent with results of Gasiorowska (2015) and Chandra et al., (2022).

As authors study the impact of financial attitude on financial security, cognitive (p value- 0.016) and behaviour components (p value- 0.000) are significant whereas affective component is insignificant (p value- 0.016) which is the only component that is not consistent with the previous studies (Ameliawati, M., & Setiyani, R. (2018), who posited that financial attitude is important contributor in achieving the success or failure of financial aspects. Without the application of a good attitude it will be difficult for students to have savings in the long term. Eventually the proposed hypotheses in the present study are similar to the previous studies as mentioned above.

STRATEGIES TO IMPROVE MONETARY INTELLIGENCE AMONG STUDENTS

Monetary Intelligence involves enhancing one's understanding of the financial concept and their ability to make informed decisions. Authors in the present have identified few strategies that would improve students' monetary intelligence as depicted in figure 3.

1. **Integrating Financial Education into Curriculum**: habits catch up to human only if they are made mandatory to us in someway or the other and for students integrating financial education into curriculum is one best way to introduce students to personal finance and its important topics like budgeting, saving, investing, credit management and taxes etc.

Figure 3. Strategies to improve monetary intelligence among students

Strategies to Improve Monetary Intelligence among Students
1. Integrating Financial Education into Curriculum
2. Using real life Examples and Simulations
3. Utilising Technology and Online resources
4. Guest Speakers and Workshops
5. Parental and Community Development
6. Incorporating financial Literacy into Extracurricular Activities.
7. Promoting Critical Thinking and Decision-Making skills.
8. Access to Financial Resources and Counselling

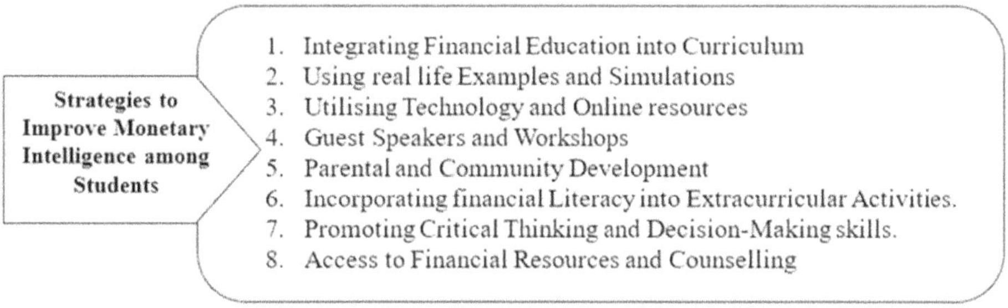

2. **Use Real life Examples and Simulations**: If integrating the concept into curriculum is one way, the other way to make it more imperative is to analyse the same concepts with the help of real world financial scenarios or it can be by the way of financial simulation games which influence the affective, cognitive and behavioural aspects of students and enhance his monetary intelligence and lastly giving students a practical exposure to financial decisions by the way of using projects and few entrepreneurial projects.

3. **Using Technology and Online Resources**: Technology has been a boon when it comes to accessing various depositories for data and information and the same can be said with regard to access of various financial apps, online course and tutorials that can be used to enlighten students monetary mindset. Learning through courses and tutorials and then implementing the concepts by tracking the same by using financial and investment app under proper supervision will work wonder for students monetary intelligence.
4. **Guest Speakers and Workshops**: These options reinforce a students monetary intelligence mindset as interaction with financial advisors, banker and entrepreneurs will give them clarity about the when, where, how aspect of investing and saving. Even few workshops on topics like tax preparation and investment strategies would benefits students.
5. **Parental and Community Development**: Schools and universities are the best place to learn about the aspects of society or money but the same knowledge in reinforced in a better way when students parents teach financial management to students in their daily chores. Students learn better and faster when the important aspects of their lives comes from their parental teachings from very young age and a society with such communities would do wonder on student confidence and monetary intelligence for future decision making.
6. **Incorporating financial Literacy into Extracurricular Activities**: Monetary intelligence among students can be effectively developed only when the process is holistic in nature. This particular step talks about providing access to monetary intelligence through extracurricular activities in schools and universities. Extracurricular activities like student clubs for various disciplines, university-national-international level financial literacy competitions will challenge and motivate students to improve their monetary intelligence.
7. **Promoting Critical Thinking and Decision-Making skills**: Above all strategies envisage student critical thinking and decision-making skills. These skills can be further strengthened by exposing students to scenario analysis games, debates and discussions to contemplate on hypothetical diverse financial scenarios to analyse and propose creative solutions.
8. **Access to Financial Resources and Counselling**: Lastly there should be a one-stop access for students to resource centres and counselling services where students can have better connect by referring to books, articles and other tools to personal finance & counselling services for personalised advice and guidance.

IMPORTANCE OF MONETARY INTELLIGENCE

Figure 4, encapsulates the various reasons for which monetary intelligence is key among young as well as old.

1. **Financial Stability:** Monetary intelligence empowers individuals to make informed decisions about their finances leading an enhanced financial stability. Understanding the Basics of the concept of simple budgeting, saving, and investment can benefit individuals to equip themselves with emergency funds, retirement plans, and overcome other financial challenges (Kim et al., 2020).
2. **Wealth Building:** Basic understanding of financial concepts like simple interest, compounding interest, portfolio diversification, and risk management among individuals can work wonders in building wealth & increased net worth (Baker et al., 2020).

Figure 4. Importance of monetary intelligence

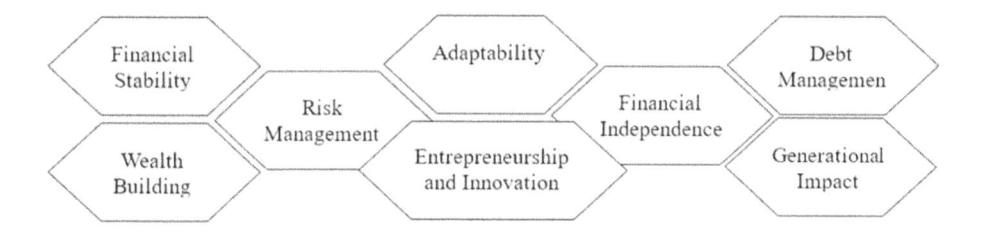

3. **Risk Management:** Financial intelligence involves understanding and managing simple risks associated with various financial decisions in day to day life, ranging from investing in the stock market to purchasing insurance. Monetary intelligence encourages to make informed choices to protect their financial well-being by assessing and managing risks (Ogundajo et al., 2020)
4. **Adaptability:** Adaptability is the willingness to change and improvise to suit different conditions and in today's rapidly changing economic environment, monetary intelligence is cruc
5. ial for adaptability. Individuals who are financially literate can navigate economic shifts, market fluctuations, and unexpected expenses more effectively than the one with no monetary intelligence (Reeves & Deimler, 2012).

6. **Entrepreneurship and Innovation:** Monetary intelligence is key for growth and survival and its very much is a driving factor towards entrepreneurs and innovation among individuals and business owners. monetary intelligence is essential for managing finances, securing funding, and driving innovation. Monetary intelligence is the factor that envisages entrepreneurial decisions while comprehending financial statements, cash flow management, and finance sources, for business growth and sustainability (Berger et al., 2021).
7. **Financial Independence:** Monetary intelligence is a subject that circumvents through ubiquitous disciplines like psychology, sociology, to economics and behavioural science. It also prepares a individual to be smart and ready to optimise finances to makes rapid and constant progress towards financial goals like saving more, spending less and investing wisely. In short monetary intelligence leads to financial independence that helps an individual to make his own decisions supported by his savings and investments (Urban et al., 2020).
8. **Debt Management:** Monetary intelligence, reciprocates into the aspect of effective debt management also. It triggers individual to make strategic decisions in matter pertaining to spending, borrowing, prioritize debt repayment, and avoid falling into debt traps (Hodula & Melecky, 2020)
9. **Generational Impact:** Monetary intelligence can be embodied from generation to generations by teaching and training younger generations onto their future financials. By imparting effective financial habits and knowledge early on, individuals can pass on a legacy of financial responsibility and success (Shankar et al., 2022).

LIMITATIONS AND FUTURE DIRECTIONS

Although utmost care was taken by the researcher to overcome omissions, errors and bias in data, there were certain limitations experienced during the various stages of the study. The main limitations of the study are:

a) The study is limited Indian states only.
b) The number of respondents were limited due to accessibility and time constraint.
c) Authors have used non probability method due with small sample which should taken into consideration before generalising the study results.

As the landscape of concepts such as financial attitude, financial satisfaction and financial wellbeing is enormous, the present results can be further explored to a larger section of audience and different other wellbeing variables can be used to make the study intensive.

CONCLUSION

Financial wellbeing was, is, and will be a crucial topic to be discussed in finance literature as individuals and families are concerned about their financial decisions and the satisfaction derived from it. The ultimate objective of this study was to investigate the association between monetary intelligence and financial wellbeing. Monetary intelligence is measured via cognitive, affective and behavioural dimensions, financial wellbeing represented via financial satisfaction and financial security variables. From the current study analysis and discussions, it can be posited that Cognitive, Affective and Behavioural variables of monetary intelligence among Indian students are significant enough in measuring the level of financial satisfaction component of well-being among respondents. While behavioural and cognitive variables of monetary intelligence are significant in measuring the financial security component of wellbeing, affective component of monetary intelligence is insignificant. The present study is vital for readers in terms of understanding the nuances of monetary intelligence and how it affects the financial wellbeing of respondents. Further, this study can be extended in terms of analysing the inherent construct of cognitive, affective and behavioural constructs of monetary intelligence upon financial well-being. Research on wellbeing can be further delved by shedding some light upon the opportunity recognition component which measures entrepreneurial motive among respondents.

REFERENCES

Abdullah, N., Fazli, S. M., & Muhammad Arif, A. M. (2019). The Relationship between Attitude towards Money, Financial Literacy and Debt Management with Young Worker's Financial Well-being. *Pertanika Journal of Social Science & Humanities*, 27(1).

Ajzen, I. (1991). The theory of planned behavior. *Organizational Behavior and Human Decision Processes*, 50(2), 179–211. 10.1016/0749-5978(91)90020-T

Akben-Selcuk, E., & Aydin, A. E. (2021). Ready or not, here it comes: A model of perceived financial preparedness for retirement. *Journal of Adult Development*, 28(4), 346–357. 10.1007/s10804-021-09387-z

Allen, R., Burgess, S., Rasul, I., & McKenna, L. (2012). *Understanding school financial decisions*. Department for Education Research Report DFE-RR183.

Ameliawati, M., & Setiyani, R. (2018). The Influence of Financial Attitude, Financial Socialization, and Financial Experience to Financial Management Behavior with Financial Literacy as the Mediation Variable. *KnE Social Sciences*, 3(10), 811. 10.18502/kss.v3i10.3174

Ammerman, D. A., & Stueve, C. (2019). Childhood financial socialization and debt-related financial well-being indicators in adulthood. *Financial Counseling and Planning*, 30(2), 213–230. 10.1891/1052-3073.30.2.213

Arifin, A. Z. (2018). *Influence factors toward financial satisfaction with financial behavior as intervening variable on Jakarta area workforce*.

Asebedo, S., & Payne, P. (2019). Market volatility and financial satisfaction: The role of financial self-efficacy. *Journal of Behavioral Finance*, 20(1), 42–52. 10.1080/15427560.2018.1434655

Ashforth, B. E., & Anand, V. (2003). The normalization of corruption in organizations. *Research in Organizational Behavior*, 25, 1–52. 10.1016/S0191-3085(03)25001-2

Baker, H. K., Nofsinger, J. R., & Spieler, A. C. (2020). *The Savvy Investor's Guide to Building Wealth Through Traditional Investments*. Emerald Publishing Limited. 10.1108/9781839096082

Barber, B. M., & Odean, T. (2001). The internet and the investor. *The Journal of Economic Perspectives*, 15(1), 41–54. 10.1257/jep.15.1.41

Barrafrem, K., Västfäll, D., & Tinghög, G. (2020). Financial well-being, COVID-19, and the fnancial betterthan-average-efect. *Journal of Behavioral and Experimental Finance*, 28, 1–5. 10.1016/j.jbef.2020.10041033042778

Berger, E. S., Von Briel, F., Davidsson, P., & Kuckertz, A. (2021). Digital o7r not– The future of entrepreneurship and innovation: Introduction to the special issue. *Journal of Business Research*, 125, 436–442. 10.1016/j.jbusres.2019.12.020

Bochulia, T., & Melnychenko, O. (2019). Accounting and analytical provision of management in the times of information thinking. *European Cooperation*, 1(41), 52–64. 10.32070/ec.v1i41.21

Brüggen, E. C., Hogreve, J., Holmlund, M., Kabadayi, S., & Löfgren, M. (2017). Financial well-being: A conceptualization and research agenda. *Journal of Business Research*, 79, 228–237. 10.1016/j.jbusres.2017.03.013

Castro-Gonzalez, S., Fernandez-Lopez, S., Rey-Ares, L., & Rodeiro-Pazos, D. (2020). The influence of attitude to money on individuals' financial well-being. *Social Indicators Research*, 148(3), 747–764. 10.1007/s11205-019-02219-4

Chandra, A. A., Manggala, F., Phurnama, R., Karystin, Y., Suade, M., & Nurfadilah, N. (2022). Financial Confidence in Financial Satisfaction Through Financial Behavior for Ciputra School of Business Makassar Students. *Hasanuddin Economics and Business Review*, 6(2), 43–51. 10.26487/hebr.v6i2.5091

Chandra, J. W., & Memarista, G. (2015). Faktor-faktor yang mempengaruhi financial satisfaction pada mahasiswa Universitas Kristen Petra. *Finesta*, 3(2), 1–6.

Chen, J., Tang, T. L. P., & Tang, N. (2014). Temptation, monetary intelligence (love of money), and environmental context on unethical intentions and cheating. *Journal of Business Ethics*, 123(2), 197–219. 10.1007/s10551-013-1783-2

Choudhry, M. T., Marelli, E., & Signorelli, M. (2012). Youth unemployment rate and impact of fnancial crises. *International Journal of Manpower*, 33(1), 76–95. 10.1108/01437721211212538

Çoşkun, A., & Dalziel, N. (2020). Mediation effect of financial attitude on financial knowledge and financial behavior: The case of university students. *International Journal of Research in Business and Social Science (2147-4478)*, 9(2), 01-08.

Danes, S. M. (1994). Parental perceptions of children's financial socialization. *Financial Counseling and Planning*, 5, 127–149.

Dew, J., & Xiao, J. J. (2011). The financial management behavior scale: Development and validation. *Financial Counseling and Planning*, 22(1), 43.

Diener, E., & Biswas-Diener, R. (2002). Will money increase subjective well-being? *Social Indicators Research*, 57(2), 119–169. 10.1023/A:1014411319119

Dowling, N., Tim, C., & Hoiles, L. (2009). Financial management practices and money attitudes as determinants of financial problems and dissatisfaction in young male Australian workers. *Financial Counseling and Planning*, 20(2).

Falahati, L., & Paim, L. H. (2011). A comparative study in money attitude among university students: A gendered view. *The Journal of American Science*, 7(6), 1144–1148.

Fellner, G., Güth, W., & Maciejovsky, B. (2005). *Satisficing in financial decision making: A theoretical and experimental attempt to explore bounded rationality* (Vol. 23). Max-Planck-Inst. for Research into Economic Systems, Strategic Interaction Group.

Franchuk, V., Omelchuk, O., Melnyk, S., Kelman, M., & Mykytyuk, O. (2020). Identification the Ways of Counteraction of the Threats to the Financial Security of High-Tech Enterprises. *Business: Theory and Practice*, 21(1), 1–9. 10.3846/btp.2020.11215

Franko, W. W. (2021). How state responses to economic crisis shape income inequality and financial well-being. *State Politics & Policy Quarterly*, 21(1), 31–54. 10.1177/1532440020919806

Gasiorowska, A. (2015). The impact of money attitudes on the relationship between income and financial satisfaction. *Polish Psychological Bulletin*, 46(2), 197–208. 10.1515/ppb-2015-0026

Gino, F., & Pierce, L. (2009). The abundance effect: Unethical behavior in the presence of wealth. *Organizational Behavior and Human Decision Processes*, 109(2), 142–155. 10.1016/j.obhdp.2009.03.003

Greenberg, J. (1993). Stealing in the name of justice: Informational and interpersonal moderators of theft reactions to underpayment inequity. *Organizational Behavior and Human Decision Processes*, 54(1), 81–103. 10.1006/obhd.1993.1004

Guichard, S. & Rusticelli, E. (2010). *Assessing the impact of the fnancial crisis on structural unemployment in OECD countries*. OECD.

Gutter, M., & Copur, Z. (2011). Financial behaviors and financial well-being of college students: Evidence from a national survey. *Journal of Family and Economic Issues*, 32(4), 699–714. 10.1007/s10834-011-9255-2

Halim, E. K. Y., & Astuti, D. (2015). Financial stressors, Financial Behaviour, risk tolerance, financial solvency, financial knowledge and financial satisfaction. *Journal of Management*, 3, 19–23.

Harnish, R. J., Bridges, K. R., Nataraajan, R., Gump, J. T., & Carson, A. E. (2018). The impact of money attitudes and global life satisfaction on the maladaptive pursuit of consumption. *Psychology and Marketing*, 35(3), 189–196. 10.1002/mar.21079

Hayhoe, C. R., Leach, L. J., Turner, P. R., Bruin, M. J., & Lawrence, F. C. (2000). Differences in spending habits and credit use of college students. *The Journal of Consumer Affairs*, 34(1), 113–133. 10.1111/j.1745-6606.2000.tb00087.x

Hilger, P. (2003). Enlargement As A Challenge To Fifth Research Framework Programme (FP5). *Changing Governance of Research and Technology Policy: The European Research Area*, 210.

Hira, T. K., & Mugenda, O. (2000). Gender differences in financial perceptions, behaviors and satisfaction. *Journal of Financial Planning-Denver*, 13(2), 86–93.

Hira, T. K., & Mugenda, O. M. (1998). Predictors of financial satisfaction: Differences between retirees and non-retirees. *Financial Counseling and Planning*, 9(2), 75.

Hodula, M., & Melecký, A. (2020). Debt management when monetary and fiscal policies clash: Some empirical evidence. *Journal of Applied Econometrics*, 23(1), 253–280.

Hoyt, J. E., Howell, S. L., Glines, L. J., Johnson, C., Spackman, J. S., Thompson, C., & Rudd, C. (2008). Assessing part-time faculty job satisfaction in continuing higher education: Implications for the profession. *The Journal of Continuing Higher Education*, 56(1), 27–38. 10.1080/07377366.2008.10400139

Jebb, A. T., Tay, L., Diener, E., & Oishi, S. (2018). Happiness, income satiation and turning points around the world. *Nature Human Behaviour*, 2(1), 33–38. 10.1038/s41562-017-0277-030980059

Joo, S. H., & Grable, J. E. (2004). An exploratory framework of the determinants of financial satisfaction. *Journal of Family and Economic Issues*, 25(1), 25–50. 10.1023/B:JEEI.0000016722.37994.9f

Kahneman, D., & Deaton, A. (2010). High income improves evaluation of life but not emotional well-being. *Proceedings of the National Academy of Sciences of the United States of America*, 107(38), 16489–16493. 10.1073/pnas.101149210720823223

Kaur, G., Singh, M., & Gupta, S. (2023). Analysis of key factors influencing individual financial well-being using ISM and MICMAC approach. *Quality & Quantity*, 57(2), 1533–1559. 10.1007/s11135-022-01422-935669163

Kim, H., Batten, J. A., & Ryu, D. (2020). Financial crisis, bank diversification, and financial stability: OECD countries. *International Review of Economics & Finance*, 65, 94–104. 10.1016/j.iref.2019.08.009

Kulkarni, V. S., Kulkarni, V. S., Imai, K. S., & Gaiha, R. (2022). Change in Subjective Well-Being, Affluence and Trust in Politicians. *Change*, 3, 30–2022.

Kulshreshtha, A., Raju, S., Muktineni, S. M., & Chatterjee, D. (2023). Income shock and financial well-being in the COVID-19 pandemic: Financial resilience and psychological resilience as mediators. *International Journal of Bank Marketing*, 41(5), 1037–1058. 10.1108/IJBM-08-2022-0342

Lanz, M., Sorgente, A., & Danes, S. M. (2020). Implicit family financial socialization and emerging adults' financial well-being: A multi-informant approach. *Emerging Adulthood*, 8(6), 443–452. 10.1177/2167696819876752

Lusardi, A. (2012). *Numeracy, financial literacy, and financial decision-making* (No. w17821). National Bureau of Economic Research.

Lyons, A. C., & Yilmazer, T. (2005). Health and financial strain: Evidence from the survey of consumer finances. *Southern Economic Journal*, 71(4), 873–890.

Malone, K., Stewart, S. D., Wilson, J., & Korsching, P. F. (2010). Perceptions of financial well-being among American women in diverse families. *Journal of Family and Economic Issues*, 31(1), 63–81. 10.1007/s10834-009-9176-5

Martin, A., & Oliva J, C. (2001). *Teaching children about money: applications of social learning and cognitive learning developmental theories.* Research Gate.

Mindra, R., Moya, M., Zuze, L. T., & Kodongo, O. (2017). Financial self-efficacy: A determinant of financial inclusion. *International Journal of Bank Marketing*, 35(3), 338–353. 10.1108/IJBM-05-2016-0065

Mountain, T. P., Cao, X., Kim, N., & Gutter, M. S. (2020). Millennials' future homeownership and the role of student loan debt. *Family and Consumer Sciences Research Journal*, 49(1), 5–23. 10.1111/fcsr.12374

Nandakishor, R. *A Study On The Service Quality Attributes Of Airport Services With Reference To Trivandrum Airport* [Doctoral dissertation, Indian Maritime University].

Newcomb, M. D., & Rabow, J. (1999). Gender, Socialization, and Money 1. *Journal of Applied Social Psychology*, 29(4), 852–869. 10.1111/j.1559-1816.1999.tb02029.x

Nguyen, V. C., & Thi, N. L. N. (2020). Financial Security of Vietnamese Businesses and Its Influencing Factors. The Journal of Asian Finance. *Economics and Business*, 7, 75–87.

Ogundajo, G. O., Adefisoye, A., & Nwaobia, A. N. (2020). Risk Management and Shareholders' Wealth Maximization. *International Journal of Business. Economics and Management*, 7(6), 387–400.

Oquaye, M., Owusu, G. M. Y., & Bokpin, G. A. (2022). The antecedents and consequence of financial well-being: A survey of parliamentarians in Ghana. *Review of Behavioral Finance*, 14(1), 68–90. 10.1108/RBF-12-2019-0169

Parotta, J. L. M. (1996). *The impact of financial attitudes and knowledge on financial management and satisfaction* [Doctoral dissertation, University of British Columbia].

Philippas, N. D., & Avdoulas, C. (2020). Financial literacy and fnancial well-being among generation-Z university students: Evidence from Greece. *European Journal of Finance*, 26(4–5), 360–381. 10.1080/1351847X.2019.1701512

Reeves, M., & Deimler, M. (2012). Adaptability: The new competitive advantage. *Own the Future: 50 Ways to Win from the Boston Consulting Group*, (pp. 19-26). Boston Consulting Group.

Richter, J., & Prawitz, A. D. (2010). Attitudes of college students toward credit cards: a comparison of credit card user types. *Proceedings of the Eastern Family Economics and Resource Management Association*. Research Gate.

Riitsalu, L., & Murakas, R. (2019). Subjective financial knowledge, prudent behaviour and income: The predictors of financial well-being in Estonia. *International Journal of Bank Marketing*, 37(4), 934–950. 10.1108/IJBM-03-2018-0071

Sabri, M., Wijekoon, R., & Rahim, H. (2020). The influence of money attitude, financial practices, self-efficacy and emotion coping on employees' financial well-being. *Management Science Letters*, 10(4), 889–900. 10.5267/j.msl.2019.10.007

Sahi, S. K. (2017). Psychological biases of individual investors and financial satisfaction. *Journal of Consumer Behaviour*, 16(6), 511–535. 10.1002/cb.1644

Sahi, S. K., & Dutta, V. K. (2015). Perceived attitudes towards sudden wealth: An exploratory study. *International Journal of Indian Culture and Business Management*, 11(2), 245–274. 10.1504/IJICBM.2015.071309

Sato, Y. (2019). Model-free reinforcement learning for financial portfolios: a brief survey. *arXiv preprint arXiv:1904.04973*.

Shankar, N., Vinod, S., & Kamath, R. (2022). Financial well-being–A Generation Z perspective using a Structural Equation Modeling approach. *Investment Management and Financial Innovations*, 19(1), 32–50. 10.21511/imfi.19(1).2022.03

Shim, S., Xiao, J. J., Barber, B. L., & Lyons, A. C. (2009). Pathways to life success: A conceptual model of financial well-being for young adults. *Journal of Applied Developmental Psychology*, 30(6), 708–723. 10.1016/j.appdev.2009.02.003

Shim, S., Xiao, J. J., Barber, B. L., & Lyons, A. C. (2009). Pathways to life success: A conceptual model of financial well-being for young adults. *Journal of Applied Developmental Psychology*, 30(6), 708–723. 10.1016/j.appdev.2009.02.003

Shynkar, S., Gontar, Z., Dubyna, M., Nasypaiko, D., & Fleychuk, M. (2020). Assessment of Economic Security of Enterprises: Theoretical and Methodological Aspects. *Business: Theory and Practice*, 21(1), 261–271. 10.3846/btp.2020.11573

Singh, K. N., & Malik, S. (2022). *An empirical analysis on household fnancial vulnerability in India: exploring the role of fnancial knowledge, impulsivity and money management skills*. Manag Financ. 10.1108/MF-08-2021-0386

Singh, R. K. (2022). Financial literacy among youth! 96% of parents feel their children lack money management knowledge; Survey. *The Logical Indian*. https://thelogicalindian.com/trending/survey-finds-96-parents-feel-their-children-lack-money-management-knowledge-37150

Škreblin Kirbiš, I., Vehovec, M., & Galić, Z. (2017). Relationship between financial satisfaction and financial literacy: Exploring gender differences. *Društvena istraživanja: časopis za opća društvena pitanja, 26*(2), 165-185.

Stashchuk, O., Vitrenko, A., Kuzmenko, O., Koptieva, H., Tarasova, O., & Dovgan, L. (2020). Comprehensive system of financial and economic security of the enterprise. *International Journal of Management*, 11(5).

Tang, T. L. P. (1995). The development of a short money ethic scale: Attitudes toward money and pay satisfaction revisited. *Personality and Individual Differences*, 19(6), 809–816. 10.1016/S0191-8869(95)00133-6

Tang, T. L. P., & Sutarso, T. (2013). Falling or not falling into temptation? Multiple faces of temptation, monetary intelligence, and unethical intentions across gender. *Journal of Business Ethics*, 116(3), 529–552. 10.1007/s10551-012-1475-3

Tang, T. L. P., Sutarso, T., Ansari, M. A., Lim, V. K. G., Teo, T. S. H., Arias-Galicia, F., Garber, I. E., Chiu, R. K.-K., Charles-Pauvers, B., Luna-Arocas, R., Vlerick, P., Akande, A., Allen, M. W., Al-Zubaidi, A. S., Borg, M. G., Canova, L., Cheng, B.-S., Correia, R., Du, L., & Tang, N. (2018). Monetary intelligence and behavioral economics across 32 cultures: Good apples enjoy good quality of life in good barrels. *Journal of Business Ethics*, 148(4), 893–917. 10.1007/s10551-015-2980-y

Tullio, J., & Mario, P. (2011). Investment in Financial Literacy and Saving Decisions. *Journal of Banking & Finance*, 37, 2779–2792.

Ullah, S., & Yusheng, K. (2020). Financial socialization, childhood experiences and financial well-being: The mediating role of locus of control. *Frontiers in Psychology*, 11, 2162. 10.3389/fpsyg.2020.02162 33132944

Urban, C., Schmeiser, M., Collins, J. M., & Brown, A. (2020). The effects of high school personal financial education policies on financial behavior. *Economics of Education Review*, 78, 101786. 10.1016/j.econedurev.2018.03.006

Vohs, K. D., Mead, N. L., & Goode, M. (2006). The psychological consequences of money. *Science*, 314(5802), 1154–1156. 10.1126/science.1132491 17110581

Xiao, J. J. (2016). Consumer financial capability and wellbeing. *Handbook of consumer finance research*, 3-17. Research Gate.

Xiao, J. J., Sorhaindo, B., & Garman, E. T. (2006). Financial behaviours of consumers in credit counselling. *International Journal of Consumer Studies*, 30(2), 108–121. 10.1111/j.1470-6431.2005.00455.x

Xiao, J. J., Tang, C., & Shim, S. (2009). Acting for happiness: Financial behavior and life satisfaction of college students. *Social Indicators Research*, 92(1), 53–68. 10.1007/s11205-008-9288-6

Yogasnumurti, R. R., Sadalia, I., & Irawati, N. (2021). The effect of financial, attitude, and financial knowledge on the personal finance management of college collage students. In *Proceedings of the 2nd Economics and Business International Conference-EBIC* (pp. 649-657). ScitePress.

Zemtsov, A. A., & Osipova, T. Y. (2016). Financial wellbeing as a type of human wellbeing: theoretical review. *European Proceedings of Social and Behavioural Sciences*. Research Gate.

Zurlo, K. A. (2009). *Personal attributes and the financial well-being of older adults: The effects of control beliefs*. Scholarly Commons.

KEY TERMS AND DEFINITIONS

Affective MI: Emotional intelligence pertaining financial matters with ability to make rational financial decisions.

Behavioural MI: the observable actions and decisions related to finance influenced by cognitive and affective factors reflecting one's financial habits and decisions.

Cognitive MI: The mental capacity to understand and process financial aspects of life to make informed decisions.

Financial Satisfaction: A feeling of contentment and fulfilment with one's financial choice made in life.

Financial Security: The assurance of having adequate resources against financial risks and uncertainties.

Financial Wellbeing: Achieving a level of state where individual gets contentment through his/her prudent financial management and planning.

Monetary Intelligence: The capacity to understand and efficiently manage financial decisions for optimal outcomes.

Compilation of References

Abdullah, N., Fazli, S. M., & Muhammad Arif, A. M. (2019). The Relationship between Attitude towards Money, Financial Literacy and Debt Management with Young Worker's Financial Well-being. *Pertanika Journal of Social Science & Humanities*, 27(1).

Abouserie, R. (1994). Sources and levels of stress in relation to locus of control and self-esteem in university students. *Educational Psychology*, 14(3), 323–330. 10.1080/0144341940140306

Abreu, M., & Mendes, V. (2011). Financial literacy and portfolio diversification. *Quantitative Finance*, 10(5), 515–528. 10.1080/14697680902878105

Adams, D. R., Meyers, S. A., & Boidas, R. S. (2016). The relationship between financial strain, perceived stress, psychological symptoms and academic and social integration in undergraduate students. *Journal of American College Health*, 2(5), 32–44. 10.1080/07448481.2016.115455926943354

Adams, G., & Serpell, R. (2001). *African Ways: A Handbook for African Learners and Students*. New Africa Books.

Adhikari, A. (2023). *India's shocking suicide rate: More than 35 students end life every day*. WION. https://www.wionews.com/india-news/indias-shocking-suicide-rates-more-than-35-die-students-every-day-591830

Aggarwal, K. K., Sharma, A., Kaur, R., & Lakhera, G. (2023). Algorithmic Fin-Tech pioneering the financial landscape of tomorrow. In *Algorithmic Approaches to Financial Technology*. Forecasting, Trading, and Optimization., 10.4018/979-8-3693-1746-4.ch002

Agrawal, P., & Yadav, M. (2021). Campus Design of Universities: An Overview. *Journal of Design and Built Evironment*, 21(31), pp37–pp51. 10.22452/jdbe.vol21no3.3

Agrawal, S., & Sharma, N. (2022). Barriers and Role of Higher Educational Institutes in Students' Mental Well-being: A Critical Analysis. In *2nd International Conference on Sustainability and Equity (ICSE-2021),* (pp. 173–180). Atlantis Press.

Ahmada, S & Jafree, S.R. (2023). Influence of gender identity on the adoption of religious-spiritual, preventive and emotion-focused coping strategies during the COVID-19 pandemic in Pakistan. *Annals of Medicine,55*(2).

Ahmed, G., Negash, A., Kerebih, H., Alemu, D., & Tesfaye, Y. (2020). 2020). Prevalence and associated factors of depression among Jimma University students. A cross-sectional study. *International Journal of Mental Health Systems*, 14(1), 52. 10.1186/s13033-020-00384-532742303

Ahorsu, D. K., Sánchez Vidaña, D. I., Lipardo, D., Shah, P. B., Cruz González, P., Shende, S., Gurung, S., Venkatesan, H., Duongthipthewa, A., Ansari, T. Q., & Schoeb, V. (2021). Effect of a peer-led intervention combining mental health promotion with coping-strategy-based workshops on mental health awareness, help-seeking behavior, and wellbeing among university students in Hong Kong. *International Journal of Mental Health Systems*, 15(1), 1–10. 10.1186/s13033-020-00432-033422098

Aiken, L. R.Jr. (1976). Update on Attitudes and Other Affective Variables in Learning Mathematics. *Review of Educational Research*, 46(2), 293–311. 10.3102/00346543046002293

Aina, B. A., & Adebowale, D. K. (2020). Knowledge and prevalence of depression among students on College of Medicine University of Lagos. *European Journal of Public Health, 30*(5), 166.

Ajzen, I. (1991). The Theory of Planned Behavior. *Organizational Behavior and Human Decision Processes*, 50(2), 179–211. 10.1016/0749-5978(91)90020-T

Ajzen, I., & Fishbein, M. (2005). The Influence of Attitudes on Behavior. In Albarracín, D., Johnson, B. T., & Zanna, M. P. (Eds.), *The handbook of attitudes* (pp. 173–221). Lawrence Erlbaum Associates Publishers.

Akben-Selcuk, E., & Aydin, A. E. (2021). Ready or not, here it comes: A model of perceived financial preparedness for retirement. *Journal of Adult Development*, 28(4), 346–357. 10.1007/s10804-021-09387-z

Akhtar, N. (2017). Social Networking Sites and Teens: Literature Review. *Trends in Information Management, 11*(2).

Al Maqbali, M. (2021). Sleep disturbance among frontline nurses during the COVID-19 pandemic. *Sleep and Biological Rhythms*, 19(4), 467–473. 10.1007/s41105-021-00337-634230810

Albani, E., Strakantouna, E., Vus, V., Bakalis, N., Papathanasiou, I. V., & Fradelos, E. C. (2022). The impact of mental health, subjective happiness and religious coping on the quality of life of nursing students during the COVID-19 pandemic. *Wiadomosci Lekarskie (Warsaw, Poland)*, 75(3), 678–684. 10.36740/WLek20220312035522878

Alduais, F., Samara, A. I., Al-Jalabneh, H. M., Alduais, A., Alfadda, H., & Alaudan, R. (2022). Examining Perceived Stress and Coping Strategies of University Students during COVID-19: A Cross-Sectional Study in Jordan. *International Journal of Environmental Research and Public Health*, 19(15), 9154. 10.3390/ijerph1915915435954508

Al-Dubai, S. A., Al-Naggar, R. A., Alshagga, M. A., & Rampal, K. G. (2011). Stress and coping strategies of students in a medical faculty in Malaysia*The Malaysian Journal of Medical Sciences : MJMS*, 18(3), 57–64.22135602

Algorani, E. B., & Gupta, V. (2023). *Coping Mechanisms*. StatPearls Publishing. https://www.ncbi.nlm.nih.gov/books/NBK559031/

Algorani, E. B., & Gupta, V. (2023). Coping methods. In *StatPearls*. StatPearls Publishing.

Alisia, G. T. T. (2018). Financial Stress, Social Supports, Gender, and Anxiety During College: A Stress-Buffering Perspective. *The COunsiling Psychologist*, 46(7). 10.1177/0011000018806687

Aljaberi, M. A., Al-Sharafi, M. A., Uzir, M. U. H., Sabah, A., Ali, A. M., Lee, K. H., Alsalahi, A., Noman, S., & Lin, C. Y. (2023). Psychological Toll of the COVID-19 Pandemic: An In-Depth Exploration of Anxiety, Depression, and Insomnia and the Influence of Quarantine Measures on Daily Life. *Healthcare (Basel)*, 11(17), 2418. 10.3390/healthcare1117241837685451

Aljohani, W., Banakhar, M., Sharif, L., Alsaggaf, F., Felemban, O., & Wright, R. (2021). Sources of stress among Saudi Arabian nursing students: A cross-sectional study. *International Journal of Environmental Research and Public Health*, 18(22), 11958. 10.3390/ijerph18221195834831714

Allen, R., Burgess, S., Rasul, I., & McKenna, L. (2012). *Understanding school financial decisions*. Department for Education Research Report DFE-RR183.

Allen, K. A., Ryan, T., Gray, D. L., McInerney, D. M., & Waters, L. (2014). Social media use and social connectedness in adolescents: The positives and the potential pitfalls. *The Educational and Developmental Psychologist*, 31(1), 18–31. 10.1017/edp.2014.2

Allen, S., & Hiebert, B. (1991). Stress and coping in adolescents. *Canadian Journal of Counselling*, 25(1), 19–32.

Alonzo, R., Hussain, J., Stranges, S., & Anderson, K. K. (2021). Interplay between social media use, sleep quality, and mental health in youth: A systematic review. *Sleep Medicine Reviews*, 56, 101414. 10.1016/j.smrv.2020.10141433385767

Al-Rahmi, W., & Othman, M. (2013). The impact of social media use on academic performance among university students: A pilot study. *Journal of Information Systems Research and Innovation*, 4(12), 1–10.

Alsaraireh, F., Al-Oran, H., Althnaibat, H., & Leimoon, H. (2023). The Determinants of Mental Health Literacy among Young Adolescents in South of Jordan. *ASEAN Journal of Psychiatry*, 24(1), 1–15.

Amakali-Nauiseb T., Nakweenda M., & Ndafenongo S. (2021). Prevalence of stress, anxiety, and depression factors among students at the University of Namibia's Main Campus: Community activities to commemorate World Health Mental Day, 2019. *IOSR Journal of Nursing and Health Science* (IOSR-JNHS), *10*(2), 11–18.

Amato, P. R. (2010). Research on Divorce: Continuing Trends and New Developments. *Journal of Marriage and Family*, 72(3), 650–666. 10.1111/j.1741-3737.2010.00723.x

Ameliawati, M., & Setiyani, R. (2018). The Influence of Financial Attitude, Financial Socialization, and Financial Experience to Financial Management Behavior with Financial Literacy as the Mediation Variable. *KnE Social Sciences*, 3(10), 811. 10.18502/kss.v3i10.3174

American College Health Association. (2019). *National college health assessment III: Undergraduate reference group: Executive summary*. American College Health Association. www.acha.org/documents/ncha/NCHA III_Fall_2019_Undergraduate_Reference_Group_Executive_Summary.pdf

American College Health Association. (2021). *National College Health Assessment [NCHA] results*. ACHA. https://www.acha.org/NCHA/NCHA_Home

American College Health Association. (2023, April 18). *Mental health*. ACHA. https://www.acha.org/ACHA/Resources/Topics/MentalHealth.aspx

American Physical Association. (2015). *Stress in America: Paying with Our Health Washington*. American Physical Association.

American Psychiatric Association. (2013). *Diagnostic and statistical manual of mental disorders: DSM-5 (5th edition)*. APA.

Ammerman, D. A., & Stueve, C. (2019). Childhood financial socialization and debt-related financial well-being indicators in adulthood. *Financial Counseling and Planning*, 30(2), 213–230. 10.1891/1052-3073.30.2.213

Amone-P'Olak, K., Kakinda, A. I., Kibedi, H., & Omech, B. (2023). Barriers to Treatment and Care for Depression among the Youth in Uganda: The Role of Mental Health Literacy. *Frontiers in Public Health*, 11, 1054918. 10.3389/fpubh.2023.1054918

Amponsah, K. D., Adasi, G. S., Mohammed, S. M., Ampadu, E., Okrah, A. K., & Wan, P. (2020). Stressors and coping strategies: The case of teacher education students at University of Ghana. *Cogent Education*, 7(1), 1727666. 10.1080/2331186X.2020.1727666

Anbesaw, T., Zenebe, Y., Necho, M., Gebresellassie, M., Segon, T., Kebede, F. & Bete, T. Prevalence of Depression among Students at Ethiopian Universities and Associated Factors: A Systematic Review and Meta-Analysis. *Plos One. 12*(10).

Andretta, J. R., & McKay, M. T. (2020). Self-efficacy and well-being in adolescents: A comparative study using variable and person-centered analyses. *Children and Youth Services Review*, 118, 105374. 10.1016/j.childyouth.2020.105374

Ansari, E. W., Khalil, K., & Stock, C. (2014). Symptoms and Health Complaints and Their Association with Perceived Stressors among Students at Nine Libyan Universities. *International Journal of Environmental Research and Public Health*, 11(12), 12088–12107. 10.3390/ijerph111212088825429678

Ansong, A., & Gyensare, M. A. (2012). Determinants of working-students financial literacy at the university of Cape Coast, Ghana. *International Journal of Business and Management*, 7(9), 126–133. 10.5539/ijbm.v7n9p126

Apgar, D., & Cadmus, T. (2022). Using Mixed Methods to Assess the Coping and Self-regulation Skills of Undergraduate Social Work Students Impacted by COVID-19. *Clinical Social Work Journal*, 50(1), 55–66. 10.1007/s10615-021-00790-333589848

Appel, H., Gerlach, A. L., & Crusius, J. (2016). The interplay between Facebook use, social comparison, envy, and depression. *Current Opinion in Psychology*, 9, 44–49. 10.1016/j.copsyc.2015.10.006

Arifin, A. Z. (2018). *Influence factors toward financial satisfaction with financial behavior as intervening variable on Jakarta area workforce.*

Arı, R. (1989). Üç büyük psikolojik yaklaşımda anksiyete. *Selçuk Üniversitesi Eğitim Fakültesi Dergisi*, 3, 195–219.

Arya, V. (2024). Suicide prevention in India. *Mental Health & Prevention*, 33(1), 1–13. 10.1016/j.mhp.2023.20031631299398

Asebedo, S., & Payne, P. (2019). Market volatility and financial satisfaction: The role of financial self-efficacy. *Journal of Behavioral Finance*, 20(1), 42–52. 10.1080/15427560.2018.1434655

Ashcraft, P. F., & Gatto, S. L. (2015). Care-of-self in undergraduate nursing students: A pilot study. *Nursing Education Perspectives*, 36(4), 255–256. 10.5480/13-124126328296

Asher, S. R., Rose, A. J., & Gabriel, S. W. (2006). Peer Rejection in Everyday Life. *Interpersonal Rejection*, 104–142. 10.1093/acprof:oso/9780195130157.003.0005

Asher, S. R., & Paquette, J. A. (2003). Loneliness and Peer Relations in Childhood. *Current Directions in Psychological Science*, 12(3), 75–78. 10.1111/1467-8721.01233

Ashforth, B. E., & Anand, V. (2003). The normalization of corruption in organizations. *Research in Organizational Behavior*, 25, 1–52. 10.1016/S0191-3085(03)25001-2

Asif, S., Mudassar, A., Shahzad, T. Z., Raouf, M., & Pervaiz, T. (2020). Frequency of Depression, Anxiety and Stress among University Students. *Pakistan Journal of Medical Sciences*, 36(5), 971–976.

Asmar, A., & Hafiz, M. (2020). Improvement students' problem solving ability through problem centered learning (Pcl). *International Journal of Scientific & Technology Research*, 9(2), 6214–6217.

Astin, A. W. (1993). *What really matters in college? Four key years were reviewed.* Jossey-Bass.

Astleitner, H., Bains, A., & Hörmann, S. (2023). The effects of personality and social media experiences on mental health: Examining the mediating role of fear of missing out, ghosting, and vaguebooking. *Computers in Human Behavior*, 138, 107436. 10.1016/j.chb.2022.107436

Asur, S., & Huberman, B. A. (2010). Predicting the Future with Social Media. Social Computing Lab: HP Labs, Palo Alto, California. 10.1109/WI-IAT.2010.63

Atkins, J. L., Vega-Uriostegui, T., Norwood, D., & Adamuti-Trache, M. (2023). Social and emotional learning and ninth-grade students' academic achievement. *Journal of Intelligence*, 11(9), 185. 10.3390/jintelligence1109018537754913

Aucejo, E. M., French, J., Araya, M. P. U., & Zafar, B. (2020). The impact of COVID-19 on student experiences and expectations: Evidence from a survey. *Journal of Public Economics*, 191, 104271. 10.1016/j.jpubeco.2020.10427132873994

Auerbach, R. P., Mortier, P., Bruffaerts, R., Alonso, J., Benjet, C., Cuijpers, P., Demyttenaere, K., Ebert, D. D., Green, J. G., Hasking, P., Murray, E., Nock, M. K., Pinder-Amaker, S., Sampson, N., Stein, D. J., Vilagut, G., Zaslavsky, A. M., & Kessler, R. C. (2018). WHO WMH-ICS Collaborators. WHO world mental health survey international college student project: Prevalence and distribution of mental disorders. *Journal of Abnormal Psychology*, 127(7), 623–638. 10.1037/abn000036230211576

Australian Institute of Health and Welfare (AIHW). (2021). *Mental illness*. AIHW. https://www.aihw.gov.au/reports/children-youth/mental-illness

Awate J. N. & Khalane S. (2021). Correlation between Locus of Control and Big Five Personality Factors among Public and Private Services Officers. *International Journal of Indian Psychology, 9*(3), 2103-2109. DOI:10.25215/0903.200

Ayhan, A. B., & Beyazit, U. (2021). The Associations between Loneliness and Self-Esteem in Children and Neglectful Behaviors of their Parents. *Child Indicators Research*, 14(5), 1863–1879. 10.1007/s12187-021-09818-z

Ayiro, L. (2023). Stress levels, coping strategies, and mental health literacy among secondary school students in Kenya. *Educational Psychology,* 8.10.3389/feduc.2023.1099020

Ayiro, L., Misigo, B. L., & Dingili, R. (2023). Stress levels, Coping Strategies, and Mental Health Literacy among Secondary School Students in Kenya. *Front. Educ. Sec. Educational Psychology*, 8, 1–10.

Baaleis, M.A.S., & Ali, S.I. (2018). *The impact of various coping mechanisms on female students' academic performance at Al-Ahsa College of Medicine.*

Babakova, L. (2019). Development of the Academic Stressors Scale for Bulgarian University Students. *Eurasian Journal of Educational Research*, 19(81), 115–128. 10.14689/ejer.2019.81.7

Babicka-Wirkus, A, Wirkus, L, Stasiak, K & Kozłowski, P. (2021). University students' strategies of coping with stress during the coronavirus pandemic: Data from Poland. *PLoS ONE, 16*(7), e0255041. https://doi.org/. pone.025504110.1371/journal

Bachmann, S. (2018). Epidemiology of Suicide and the psychiatric perspective. *International Journal of Environmental Research and Public Health*, 15(7), 1425. 10.3390/ijerph1507142529986446

Bagby, R. M., Uliaszek, A. A., Gralnick, T. M., & Widiger, T. A. (Eds.). (2017). *The Oxford handbook of the five factor model*. Oxford University Press.

Baik, C., Larcombe, W., & Brooker, A. (2019). How universities can enhance student mental wellbeing: The student perspective. *Higher Education Research & Development*, 38(4), 674–687. 10.1080/07294360.2019.1576596

Baker, D. A., & Algorta, G. P. (2016). The relationship between online social networking and depression: A systematic review of quantitative studies. *Cyberpsychology, Behavior, and Social Networking*, 19(11), 638–648. 10.1089/cyber.2016.020627732062

Baker, H. K., Nofsinger, J. R., & Spieler, A. C. (2020). *The Savvy Investor's Guide to Building Wealth Through Traditional Investments*. Emerald Publishing Limited. 10.1108/9781839096082

Baker, Z. G., Krieger, H., & LeRoy, A. S. (2016). Fear of missing out: Relationships with depression, mindfulness, and physical symptoms. *Translational Issues in Psychological Science*, 2(3), 275–282. 10.1037/tps0000075

Bakesia, G., Olayo, R., Mengich, G., & Opiyo, R. (2023). Prevalence and Sociodemographic Predictors of Depression among Adolescents in Secondary Schools in Kakamega County, Kenya. *East African Medical Journal*, 100(8).

Balaji, M., Mandhare, K., Nikhare, K., Shah, A. K., Kanhere, P., Panse, S., Santre, M., Vijayakumar, L., Phillips, M. R., Pathare, S., Patel, V., Czabanowska, K., & Krafft, T. (2023). Why young people attempt suicide in India: A qualitative study of vulnerability to action. *SSM. Mental Health*, 3(1), 23–32. 10.1016/j.ssmmh.2023.100216

Balazs, J., & Kereszteny, A. (2017). Attention-deficit/hyperactivity disorder and suicide: A systematic review. *World Journal of Psychiatry*, 7(1), 44–59. 10.5498/wjp.v7.i1.4428401048

Bale, J., Grové, C., & Costello, S. (2018). A Narrative Literature Review of Child-Focused Mental Health Literacy Attributes and Scales. *JO-Mental Health and Prevention*, 12, 26–31.

Balica, M. (2021). *Qu'est-ce que le bien-être? Document stratégique*. International Baccalaureate Organization.

Baluwa, M. A., Lazaro, M., Mhango, L., & Msiska, G. (2021). Stress and coping strategies among Malawian undergraduate nursing students. *Advances in Medical Education and Practice*, 12, 547–556. 10.2147/AMEP.S30045734093050

Bandari, M. A. (2022). *Study on Academic Stress and Mental Well-Being in College Students*. NIH.

Bandura, A. (1997). Self-efficacy: the exercise of control (1st ed). New York: Worth Publishers.

Bandura, A. (1997). *Self-efficacy: The exercise of control*. New York: Freeman. https://Psycnet.apa.org

Bann, T. (2018). *Financial stress and mental health among higher education students in the UK up to 2018: rapid review of evidence*. NIH.

Bano, A., & Zaman, S. (2020). The Use of Social Media in Facilitating the Teaching and Learning Process: A Case Study of Undergraduates at University of Bisha in Saudi Arabia. *International Journal of Linguistics. SSRN*, 3(c), 89–99. 10.2139/ssrn.3546836

Bantjes, J., Kessler, M., & Lochner, C. (2023). The mental health of university students in South Africa: Results of the national student survey. *Journal of Affective Disorders*, 321, 217–226.

Barber, B. M., & Odean, T. (2001). The internet and the investor. *The Journal of Economic Perspectives*, 15(1), 41–54. 10.1257/jep.15.1.41

Barlow, D. H. (2000). Unraveling the mysteries of anxiety and its disorders from the perspective of emotion theory. *The American Psychologist*, 55(11), 1247–1263. 10.1037/0003-066X.55.11.124711280938

Barlow, D. H. (2002). *Anxiety and its disorders: The nature and treatment of anxiety and panic. 2nd*. Guilford Press.

Barlow, D. H., Sauer-Zavala, S., Carl, J. R., Bullis, J. R., & Ellard, K. K. (2014). The Nature, Diagnosis, and Treatment of Neuroticism. *Clinical Psychological Science*, 2(3), 344–365. 10.1177/2167702613505532

Barrafrem, K., Västfäll, D., & Tinghög, G. (2020). Financial well-being, COVID-19, and the fnancial betterthan-average-efect. *Journal of Behavioral and Experimental Finance*, 28, 1–5. 10.1016/j.jbef.2020.10041033042778

Barron, M., Cobo, C., Munoz-Najar, A., & Ciarrusta, I. S. (2021). The changing role of teachers and technologies amidst the COVID 19 pandemic: key findings from a cross-country study. *Education for Global Development, 18*, 1–9. https://blogs.worldbank.org/education/changing-role-teachers-and-technologies-amidst-covid-19-pandemic-key-findings-cross

Bartholomew, T. T. (2016). Mental health in Namibia. *Psychology and Developing Societies*, 28(1), 101–125. 10.1177/0971333615622909

Bartley, M., Head, J., & Stansfeld, S. (2007). Is attachment style a source of resilience against health inequalities at work? *Social Science & Medicine*, 64(4), 765–775. 10.1016/j.socscimed.2006.09.03317129652

Battula, M., Arunashekar, P., & John, A. (2021). ThiyagaRajan, R & Vinoth, P.N. (2021). Stress level among the final year medical students at an urban medical college: A cross-sectional study. *Biomedicine (Taipei)*, 41(1), 70–74.

Beck, A. T., Steer, R. A., Kovacs, M., & Garrison, B. (1985). Hopelessness and eventual suicide: A 10-year prospective study of patients hospitalized with suicidal ideation. *The American Journal of Psychiatry*, 142(5), 559–563. 10.1176/ajp.142.5.5593985195

Beiter, R., Nash, R., McCrady, M., Rhoades, D., Linscomb, M., Clarahan, M., & Sammut, S. (2015). The prevalence and correlates of depression, anxiety, and stress in a sample of college students. *Journal of Affective Disorders*, 173, 90–96. 10.1016/j.jad.2014.10.05425462401

Belay, A. S., Guangul, M. M., Asmare, W. N., & Mesafint, G. (2021). Prevalence and Associated Factors of Psychological Distress among Nurses in Public Hospitals, Southwest, Ethiopia: A cross-sectional Study. *Ethiopian Journal of Health Sciences*, 31(6), 1247–1256.

Bell, I. H., Nicholas, J., Broomhall, A., Bailey, E., Bendall, S., Boland, A., Robinson, J., Adams, S., McGorry, P., & Thompson, A. (2023). The impact of COVID-19 on youth mental health: A mixed methods survey. *Psychiatry Research*, 321(March), 115082. 10.1016/j.psychres.2023.11508236738592

Berger, E. S., Von Briel, F., Davidsson, P., & Kuckertz, A. (2021). Digital o7r not– The future of entrepreneurship and innovation: Introduction to the special issue. *Journal of Business Research*, 125, 436–442. 10.1016/j.jbusres.2019.12.020

Berryman, C., Ferguson, C. J., & Negy, C. (2018). Social media use and mental health among young adults. *The Psychiatric Quarterly*, 89(2), 307–314. 10.1007/s11126-017-9535-629090428

Bertolote, J. M., & Fleischmann, A. (2002). Suicide and psychiatric diagnosis: A worldwide perspective. *World Psychiatry; Official Journal of the World Psychiatric Association (WPA)*, 1(1), 181–185. https://www.ncbi.nlm.nih.gov/pmc/articles/PMC1489848/16946849

Besharat, M. A., Khadem, H., Zarei, V., & Momtaz, A. (2020). Mediating role of perceived stress in the relationship between facing existential issues and symptoms of depression and anxiety. *Iranian Journal of Psychiatry*, 15, 80–87. 10.18502/ijps.v15i1.244232377217

Best, P., Manktelow, R., & Taylor, B. (2014). Online communication, social media and adolescent wellbeing: A systematic narrative review. *Children and Youth Services Review*, 41, 27–36. 10.1016/j.childyouth.2014.03.001

Bettinger, E., & Pascarella, E. T. (2000). Financial aid and student outcomes: A research review. *Review of Higher Education*, 23(2), 181–201.

Beyens, I., Frison, E., & Eggermont, S. (2016). "I don't want to miss a thing": Adolescents' fear of missing out and its relationship to adolescents' social needs, Facebook use, and Facebook related stress. *Computers in Human Behavior*, 64, 1–8. 10.1016/j.chb.2016.05.083

Bhagwat, S., & Goutam, A. (2013). Development of social networking sites and their role in business with special reference to Facebook. *Journal of Business and Management*, 6(5), 15–28.

Bhardwaj, A., Avasthi, V., & Goundar, S. (2017). Impact of social networking on Indian youth-A survey. *International Journal of Electronics and Information Engineering*, 7(1), 41–51.

Bhargava, S. C., Sethi, S., & Vohra, A. K. (2001). Klingsor syndrome: A case report. *Indian Journal of Psychiatry*, 43(1), 349–350. https://www.ncbi.nlm.nih.gov/pmc/articles/PMC2956247/21407886

Bharucha, J. (2018). Social network use and youth well-being: A study in India. *Safer Communities*, 17(2), 119–131. 10.1108/SC-07-2017-0029

Bhavana, N. & Otaki, F. (2021). *Promoting University Students' Mental Health: A Systematic Literature Review Introducing the 4M-Model of Individual-Level Interventions*. Front. Public Health, Sec. Public Mental Health.

Bien, T. H., Miller, W. R., & Tonigan, J. S. (1993). Brief interventions for alcohol problems: A review [editorial]. *British Journal of Addiction*, 88(3), 315–336. 10.1111/j.1360-0443.1993.tb00820.x8461850

Billie-Brahe, U. (2000). Sociology and suicidal behavior. In: K Hawton, k van Heerington (eds.) *The International Handbook of Suicide and Attempted Suicide* (pp. 193-207). Chichester. https://www.wiley.com/en-in/The+International+Handbook+of+Suicide+and+Attempted+Suicide-p-9780470849590

Bilsen, J. (2018). Suicide and youth: Risk factors. *Frontiers in Psychiatry*, 9(1), 1–13. 10.3389/fpsyt.2018.0054030425663

Binns, A. (2014). Twitter city and Facebook village: Teenage girls' personas and experiences influenced by choice architecture in social networking sites. *Journal of Media Practice*, 15(2), 71–91. 10.1080/14682753.2014.960763

Bintabara, D., Singo, J.B., Mvula, M., Jofrey, S. & Shayo, F.K. (2024). Mental Health Disorders among Medical Students during the COVID-19 Pandemic in the Area with No Mandatory Lockdown: A Multicenter Survey in Tanzania. *Sci Rep.*, 11 (1), 3451.

Birbal, R., Maharajh, H. D., Birbal, R., Clapperton, M., Jarvis, J., Ragoonath, A., & Uppalapati, K. (2009). Cyber suicide and the adolescent population: Challenges of the future? *International Journal of Adolescent Medicine and Health*, 21(2), 151–159. https://pubmed.ncbi.nlm.nih.gov/19702194/19702194

Birch, S. H., & Ladd, G. W. (1997). The teacher-child relationship and children's early school adjustment. *Journal of School Psychology*, 35(1), 61–79. 10.1016/S0022-4405(96)00029-5

Birkeland, M. S., Breivik, K., & Wold, B. (2013). Peer Acceptance Protects Global Self-esteem from Negative Effects of Low Closeness to Parents During Adolescence and Early Adulthood. *Journal of Youth and Adolescence*, 43(1), 70–80. 10.1007/s10964-013-9929-123435859

Biroli, P., Bosworth, S., Della Giusta, M., Di Girolamo, A., Jaworska, S., & Vollen, J. (2021). Family Life in Lockdown. *Frontiers in Psychology*, 12, 687570. 10.3389/fpsyg.2021.68757034421738

Bjørnsen, H. N., Espnes, G. A., Eilertsen, M.-E. B., Ringdal, R., & Moksnes, U. K. (2019). The Relationship between Positive Mental Health Literacy and Mental Well-Being among Adolescents: Implications for School Health Services. *The Journal of School Nursing: the Official Publication of the National Association of School Nurses*, 35(2), 107–116. 10.1177/1059840517732125

Błachnio, A., Przepiórka, A., & Rudnicka, P. (2013). Psychological determinants of using Facebook: A research review. *International Journal of Human-Computer Interaction*, 29(11), 775–787. 10.1080/10447318.2013.780868

Black-Hughes, C., & Stacy, P. (2013). Early childhood attachment and its impact on later life resilience: A comparison of resilient and non-resilient female siblings. *Journal of Evidence-Based Social Work*, 10(5), 410–420. 10.1080/15433714.2012.75945624066631

Blazer, C., Schwartz, S., & Travis, J. M. (2019). How tutoring services affect students' self-efficacy and academic achievement. *Journal of College Reading and Learning*, 49(2), 142–158. https://www.valleycollege.edu/about-sbvc/offices/office-research-planning/reports/tutoring-performance-measures-final-revisions-review.pdf

Blewett, L., & Ebben, M. (2022). Post-Pandemic Anxiety: Teaching and Learning for Student Mental Wellness in Communication All. In *Post-Pandemic Pedagogy: A Paradigm Shift*, 129–148).

Blinn College. (2023; March 22). *Student employment*. Blinn College. https://www.blinn.edu/financial-aid/index.html

Blossom, P., & Apsche, J. (2013). Effects of loneliness on human development. *International Journal of Behavioral and Consultation Therapy*, 7(4), 28–29. 10.1037/h0100963

Blume, M., Brophy, J., & Guskey, T. (2010). Formative evaluation and self-regulated learning: The importance of feedback in student learning. *Educational Psychologist*, 45(1), 68–80.

Bochulia, T., & Melnychenko, O. (2019). Accounting and analytical provision of management in the times of information thinking. *European Cooperation*, 1(41), 52–64. 10.32070/ec.v1i41.21

Bolger, N. (2010). Coping as a personality process: A prospective study. *Journal of Personality and Social Psychology*, 59(3), 525–537. 10.1037/0022-3514.59.3.5252231283

Bonanno, G. A. (2004). Loss, trauma, and human resilience: Have we underestimated the human capacity to thrive after extremely aversive events? *The American Psychologist*, 59(1), 20–28. 10.1037/0003-066X.59.1.2014736317

Booth, A., & Amato, P. R. (2001). Parental Predivorce Relations and Offspring Postdivorce Well-Being. *Journal of Marriage and Family*, 63(1), 197–212. 10.1111/j.1741-3737.2001.00197.x

Borges, G., Nock, M. K., & Haro, A. J. M. (2010). Twelve-month prevalence of and risk factors for suicide attempts in the world health organization world mental health surveys. *The Journal of Clinical Psychiatry*, 71(12), 16–27. 10.4088/JCP.08m04967blu20816034

Borsboom, D. (2008). Psychometric perspectives on diagnostic systems. *Journal of Clinical Psychology*, 64(9), 1089–1108. 10.1002/jclp.2050318683856

Botha, B., Mostert, K., & Jacobs, M. (2019). Exploring indicators of subjective well-being for first-year university students. *Journal of Psychology in Africa*, 29(5), 480–490.

Bowlby, J. (1988). *A Secure Base: Parent-Child Attachment and Healthy Human Development*. https://doi.org/10.1604/9780465075980

Bowlby, J. (1969). *Attachment and Loss*. Hogarth Press.

Bowman, N. A. (2010). The development of psychological well-being among first-year college students. *Journal of College Student Development*, 51(2), 180–200. 10.1353/csd.0.0118

Boyd, D. (2010) *Taken Out of Context: American Teen Sociality in Networked Publics*. Wikipedia. en.wikipedia.org

Boyd, D. M., & Ellison, N. B. (2007). Social network sites: Definition, history, and scholarship. *Journal of Computer-Mediated Communication*, 13(1), 210–230. 10.1111/j.1083-6101.2007.00393.x

Bozick, R. (2007). Making it through the first year of college: The role of students' economic resources, employment, and living arrangements. *Sociology of Education*, 80(3), 261–285. 10.1177/003804070708000304

Brady, S. T., Cohen, G. L., Jarvis, S. N., & Walton, G. M. (2020). A brief social-belonging intervention in college improves adult outcomes for black Americans. *Science Advances*, 6(18), eaay3689. 10.1126/sciadv.aay368932426471

Braun, V., & Clarke, V. (2006). Using thematic analysis in qualitative research. *Qualitative Research in Psychology*, 3(2), 77–101. https://sk.sagepub.com/reference/the-sage-handbook-of-qualitative-research-in-psychology/i425.xml. 10.1191/1478088706qp063oa

Brent, D. A., & Mann, J. J. (2005). Family genetic studies, suicide, and suicidal behavior. *American Journal of Medical Genetics. Part C, Seminars in Medical Genetics*, 133C(1), 13–24. 10.1002/ajmg.c.3004215648081

Bretag, T., Harper, R., Burton, M., Ellis, C., Newton, P., Rozenberg, P., & van Haeringen, K. (2018). Contract cheating: A survey of Australian university students. *Studies in Higher Education*, 43(9), 1670–1691.

Bretherton, I. (1985). Attachment theory: Retrospect and prospect. *Monographs of the Society for Research in Child Development*, 50(1/2), 3–35. 10.2307/3333824

Bridge, J. A., Goldstein, T. R., & Brent, D. A. (2006). Adolescent suicide and suicidal behavior. *Journal of Child Psychology and Psychiatry, and Allied Disciplines*, 47(3–4), 372–394. 10.1111/j.1469-7610.2006.01615.x16492264

Britt, S. L., Canale, A., Fernatt, F., Stutz, K., & Tibbetts, R. (2015). A study entitled Financial Stress and Financial Counseling: Helping College Students. *Financial Counseling and Planning*, 26(2), 172–186. 10.1891/1052-3073.26.2.172

Britz, J., & Pappas, E. (2010). Sources and outlets of stress among university students: Correlations between stress and unhealthy habits. *URJHS, 9*. https://www.kon.org/urc/v9/britz.html

Bronfenbrenner, U. (1992). Ecological systems theory. In VASTA, R. (sous la direction de). *Six Theories of Child Development: Revised Formulations and Current Issues*. Londres, Royaume-Uni: Jessica Kingsley Publishers.

Brooks, S. K., Smith, L. E., Webster, R. K., Weston, D., Woodland, L., Hall, I., & Rubin, G. J. (2020). The impact of unplanned school closure on children's social contact: Rapid evidence review. *Eurosurveillance*, 25(13). 10.2807/1560-7917.ES.2020.25.13.200018832265006

Brosschot, J., Verkuil, B., & Thayer, J. (2018a). Generalized Unsafety Theory of Stress: Unsafe Environments and Conditions, and the Default Stress Response. *International Journal of Environmental Research and Public Health*, 15(3), 464. 10.3390/ijerph1503046429518937

Brown, B. (2013). *The Power of Vulnerability: Teachings on Authenticity, Connection and Courage*. Sounds True Publisher.

Browning, C., Reynolds, J., & Dirlam, J. (2017). Financial stress, parent support, and college student success. *Journal of College Student Retention*, 19(3), 284–300.

Brüggen, E. C., Hogreve, J., Holmlund, M., Kabadayi, S., & Löfgren, M. (2017). Financial well-being: A conceptualization and research agenda. *Journal of Business Research*, 79, 228–237. 10.1016/j.jbusres.2017.03.013

Bubb, S., & Jones, M.-A. (2020). Learning from the COVID-19 home-schooling experience: Listening to pupils, parents/carers and teachers. *Improving Schools*, 23(3), 209–222. 10.1177/1365480220958797

Bubonya, M., Cobb-Clark, D. A., & Wooden, M. (2017). Job loss and the mental health of spouses and adolescent children. *IZA Journal of Labor Economics*, 6(1), 6. 10.1186/s40172-017-0056-1

Budu, I., Abalo, E. M., Bam, V., Budu, F. A., & Peprah, P. (2019). A survey of the genesis of stress and its effect on the academic performance of midwifery students in a college in Ghana. *Midwifery*, 73(June), 69–77. 10.1016/j.midw.2019.02.01330903921

Burke, M., & Kraut, R. E. (2016). The relationship between Facebook use and well-being depends on communication type and tie strength. *Journal of Computer-Mediated Communication*, 21(4), 265–281. 10.1111/jcc4.12162

Burke, R. J. (2009). Motivational model based on the dark triad and the balance of challenge and hindrance stress. *The Journal of Applied Psychology*, 94(4), 1141–1151. 10.1037/a0016205

Burns, D., Dagnall, N., & Holt, M. (2020). Assessing the impact of the COVID-19 pandemic on student wellbeing at universities in the United Kingdom: A conceptual analysis. *Frontiers in Education*, 5, 582882. 10.3389/feduc.2020.582882

Burris, J. L., Brechtin, E. H., Salsman, J., & Carlson, C. R. (2009). Factors Associated With the Psychological Well-Being and Distress of University Students. *Journal of American College Health*, 57(5), 536–543.

Bussell, D. A. (1996). A Pilot Study of African American Children's Cognitive and Emotional Reactions to Parental Separation. *Journal of Divorce & Remarriage*, 24(3-4), 1–22. 10.1300/J087v24n03_01

Cacioppo, J. T., & Cacioppo, S. (2018). The growing problem of loneliness. *Lancet*, 391(10119), 426. 10.1016/S0140-6736(18)30142-929407030

Cahill, H., & Dadvand, B. (2020). In Midford, R., Nutton, G., Hyndman, B., & Silburn, S. (Eds.), *Social and Emotional Learning and Resilience Education BT - Health and Education Interdependence: Thriving from Birth to Adulthood* (pp. 205–223). Springer Singapore. 10.1007/978-981-15-3959-6_11

Campbell, F., Blank, L., Cantrell, A., Baxter, S., Blackmore, C., Dixon, J., & Goyde, E. (2022). Factors that Infuence Mental Health of University and College Students in the UK: A Systematic Review. *BMC Public Health*, 22, 1778.

Caron, A., Weiss, B., Harris, V., & Catron, T. (2006). Parenting Behavior Dimensions and Child Psychopathology: Specificity, Task Dependency, and Interactive Relations. *Journal of Clinical Child and Adolescent Psychology*, 35(1), 34–45. 10.1207/s15374424jccp3501_416390301

Carroll, L. (2013). Problem-Focused Coping. In Gellman, M. D., & Turner, J. R. (Eds.), *Encyclopedia of Behavioral Medicine*. Springer. 10.1007/978-1-4419-1005-9_1171

Caruana, V. (2014). Re-thinking global citizenship in higher education: From cosmopolitanism and international mobility to cosmopolitanisation, resilience, and resilient thinking. *Higher Education Quarterly*, 68(1), 85–104. 10.1111/hequ.12030

Cassiello-Robbins, C., Wilner, J. G., & Sauer-Zavala, S. (2017). Neuroticism. In Zeigler-Hill, V., & Shackelford, T. (Eds.), *Encyclopedia of Personality and Individual Differences*. Springer. 10.1007/978-3-319-28099-8_1256-1

Castel, R. (1991). De l'indigence à l'exclusion, la désaffiliation. Précarité du travail et vulnérabilité relationnelle. In *Donzelot J (dir.), Face à l'exclusion. Le modèle français*. Éditions Esprit.

Castro-Gonzalez, S., Fernandez-Lopez, S., Rey-Ares, L., & Rodeiro-Pazos, D. (2020). The influence of attitude to money on individuals' financial well-being. *Social Indicators Research*, 148(3), 747–764. 10.1007/s11205-019-02219-4

Cavanagh, J., Carson, A. J., Sharpe, M., & Lawrie, S. M. (2003). Psychological autopsy studies of suicide: A systematic review. *Psychological Medicine*, 33(3), 395–405. 10.1017/S0033291702000694312701661

CBSE. (2013). *Mental Health and Wellbeing: A Perspective*. CBSE. https://manodarpan.education.gov.in/assets/img/pdf/CBSE_MH_Manual.pdf

Center for Access to Learning Opportunities. (2013). *Tutoring and academic assistance services for postsecondary students with disabilities: A literature review*. Sage. https://journals.sagepub.com/doi/abs/10.1177/0022194070400060101

Centers for Disease Control and Prevention (CDC). (2008). Social support and health-related quality of life among older adults—Missouri, 2000. *MMWR. Morbidity and Mortality Weekly Report*, 57(45), 1245–1249.

Centre for Suicide Prevention. (2022). Sociology and Suicidal Behaviour. K. Hawton & K van Heeringen (eds.), *The International Handbook of Suicide and Attempted Suicide*. Centre for Suicide Prevention. https://www.suicideinfo.ca/resource/siecno-20010031/

Ceri, V., & Cicek, I. (2021). Psychological well-being, depression and stress during COVID-19 pandemic in Turkey: A comparative study of healthcare professionals and non-healthcare professionals. *Psychology Health and Medicine*, 26(1), 85–97. 10.1080/13548506.2020.185956633320723

Chaabane, S., Chaabna, K., Bhagat, S., Abraham, A., Doraiswamy, S., Mamtani, R., & Cheema, S. (2021). Perceived stress, stressors, and coping strategies among nursing students in the Middle East and North Africa: An overview of systematic reviews. *Systematic Reviews*, 10(1), 136. 10.1186/s13643-021-01691-933952346

Cha, C. B., Franz, P. J., Guzmán, M. E., Glenn, C. R., Kleiman, E. M., & Nock, M. K. (2018). Annual research review: Suicide among youth – Epidemiology, (potential) etiology, and treatment. *Journal of Child Psychology and Psychiatry, and Allied Disciplines*, 59(4), 460–482. 10.1111/jcpp.1283129090457

Chan, D. K. S., & Cheng, G. H. (2004). A Comparison of offline and online friendship qualities at different stages of relationship development. *Journal of Social and Personal Relationships*, 21(3), 305–320. 10.1177/0265407504042834

Chandra, A. A., Manggala, F., Phurnama, R., Karystin, Y., Suade, M., & Nurfadilah, N. (2022). Financial Confidence in Financial Satisfaction Through Financial Behavior for Ciputra School of Business Makassar Students. *Hasanuddin Economics and Business Review*, 6(2), 43–51. 10.26487/hebr.v6i2.5091

Chandra, J. W., & Memarista, G. (2015). Faktor-faktor yang mempengaruhi financial satisfaction pada mahasiswa Universitas Kristen Petra. *Finesta*, 3(2), 1–6.

Chaudhry, S., Tandon, A., Shinde, S., & Bhattacharya, A. (2024). Student psychological well-being in higher education: The role of internal team environment, institutional, friends and family support and academic engagement. *PLoS One*, 19(1), e0297508. 10.1371/journal.pone.029750838271390

Chen, J., Tang, T. L. P., & Tang, N. (2014). Temptation, monetary intelligence (love of money), and environmental context on unethical intentions and cheating. *Journal of Business Ethics*, 123(2), 197–219. 10.1007/s10551-013-1783-2

Chen, Y., & Bello, R. S. (2017). Does receiving or providing social support on Facebook influence life satisfaction? Stress as mediator and self-esteem as moderator. *International Journal of Communication*, 11, 14.

Chen, Y., Liu, X., Yan, N., Jia, W., Fan, Y., Yan, H., Ma, L., & Ma, L. (2020). Higher Academic Stress Was Associated with Increased Risk of Overweight and Obesity among College Students in China. *International Journal of Environmental Research and Public Health*, 17(15), 5559. 10.3390/ijerph1715555932752122

Chickering, A. W., & Reisser, L. (1993). *Education and Identity* (2nd ed.). Jossey-Bass.

Chida, Y., & Steptoe, A. (2008). Positive psychological well-being and mortality: A quantitative review of prospective observational studies. *Psychosomatic Medicine*, 70(7), 741–756. 10.1097/PSY.0b013e31818105ba18725425

Chitanand, N., Rathilal, S., & Rambharos, S. (2018). Higher education well-being: A balancing Act. *South African Journal of Higher Education*, 32(6), 168–176.

Choi, E. Y., Zelinski, E. M., & Ailshire, J. (2023). Neighborhood Environment and Self-Perceptions of Aging. *Innovation in Aging*, 7(4), igad038. 10.1093/geroni/igad03837213322

Cho, J., & Yu, H. (2015). Roles of University Support for International Students in the United States: Analysis of a Systematic Model of University Identification, University Support, and Psychological Well-Being. *Journal of Studies in International Education*, 19(1), 11–27. 10.1177/1028315314533606

Choudhry, M. T., Marelli, E., & Signorelli, M. (2012). Youth unemployment rate and impact of fnancial crises. *International Journal of Manpower*, 33(1), 76–95. 10.1108/01437721211212538

Chow, J., & Kalischuk, R. G. (2008). Self-care for caring practice: Student nurses' perspectives. *International Journal for Human Caring*, 12(3), 31–37. 10.20467/1091-5710.12.3.31

Chow, R. S., Lam, C. M., & King, I. (2020). Crisis resilience pedagogy (CRP) for teaching and learning. *Proceedings of 2020 IEEE International Conference on Teaching, Assessment, and Learning for Engineering, TALE 2020,* (pp. 384–391). IEEE. 10.1109/TALE48869.2020.9368496

Cilar, L., Barr, O., Štiglic, G., & Pajnkihar, M. (2019). Mental well-being among nursing students in Slovenia and Northern Ireland: A survey. *Nurse Education in Practice*, 39, 130–135. 10.1016/j.nepr.2019.07.01231476545

Clément, M., Jankowski, L. W., Bouchard, L., Perreault, M., & Lepage, Y. (2002). Health behaviors of nursing students: A longitudinal study. *The Journal of Nursing Education*, 41(6), 257–265. 10.3928/0148-4834-20020601-0612096774

Clinard, M. B., & Meier, R. F. (1975). *Sociology of Deviant Behaviour* (5th ed.). Holt, Rinehart and Winston. https://www.shortcutstv.com/wp-content/uploads/2020/02/sociology-of-deviant-behavior.pdf

Cobb-Clark, D. A., & Schurer, S. (2012). The stability of big-five personality traits. *Economics Letters*, 115(1), 11–15. 10.1016/j.econlet.2011.11.015

Cobo-Cuenca, A. I., Fernández-Fernández, B., Carmona-Torres, J. M., Pozuelo-Carrascosa, D. P., Laredo-Aguilera, J. A., Romero-Gómez, B., Rodríguez-Cañamero, S., Barroso-Corroto, E., & Santacruz-Salas, E. (2022). Longitudinal study of the mental health, resilience, and post-traumatic stress of senior nursing students to nursing graduates during the COVID-19 pandemic. *International Journal of Environmental Research and Public Health*, 19(20), 13100. 10.3390/ijerph19201310036293681

Cohen, S., & Williamson, G. (1998). Perceived stress in a probability sample of the United States. *The social psychology of health: Claremont Symposium on applied psychology*. London: Sage.

Cohen, S., Gianaros, P. J., & Manuck, S. B. (2016, July). A Stage Model of Stress and Disease. *Perspectives on Psychological Science*, 11(4), 456–463. 10.1177/174569161664630527474134

Cohen, S., Kamarck, T., & Mermelstein, R. (1983). A global measure of perceived stress. *Journal of Health and Social Behavior*, 24(4), 385–396. 10.2307/21364046668417

Cohen, S., Murphy, M. L. M., & Prather, A. A. (2019). Ten surprising facts about stressful life events and disease risk. *Annual Review of Psychology*, 70(1), 577–597. 10.1146/annurev-psych-010418-10285729949726

Coie, J. D. (2004). The impact of negative social experiences on the development of antisocial behavior. *Children's Peer Relations: From Development to Intervention*, 243–267. APA. 10.1037/10653-013

Coiro, J.M, Bettis, A.H & Compas, B.E. (2017). College students coping with interpersonal stress: Examining a control-based model of coping. *Journal of American College Health*, 65.

Col·lectiu Punt 6, & Ciocoletto, A. (2014). *Espacios para la vida cotidiana. Auditoría de calidad urbana con perspectiva de género*. Comanegra.

Col·lectiu Punt 6. (2014). *Mujeres trabajando. Guía de reconocimiento urbano con perspectiva de género*. Barcelona: Comanegra.

College Board. (2023; April 12). *Scholarships, grants, and financial aid*. College Board. https://bigfuture.collegeboard.org/

Collier, D. A., Fitzpatrick, D., Brehm, C., & Arche, E. (2021). Coming to College Hungry: How Food Insecurity Relates to A motivation Stress, Engagement, and First-Semester Performance in a Four-Year University. *Journal of Postsecondary Student Success*, 1(1), 106–135. 10.33009/fsop_jpss124641

Conley, C. S., Durlak, J. A., & Kirsch, A. C. (2015). A meta-analysis of universal mental health prevention programs for higher education students. *Prevention Science*, 16(4), 487–507. 10.1007/s11121-015-0543-125744536

Conley, C. S., Shapiro, J. B., Kirsch, A. C., & Durlak, J. A. (2017). A meta-analysis of indicated mental health prevention programs for at-risk higher education students. *Journal of Counseling Psychology*, 64(2), 121–140. 10.1037/cou000019028277730

Connor-Smith, J. K., Compas, B. E., Wadsworth, M. E., Thomsen, A. H., & Saltzman, H. (2000). Responses to stress in adolescence: Measurement of coping and involuntary stress responses. *Journal of Consulting and Clinical Psychology*, 68(6), 976–992. 10.1037/0022-006X.68.6.97611142550

Corley, L. (2013). Prevalence of Mental Health Issues among College Students: How Do Advisers Equip Themselves? *The Mentor*.

Corwin, L. A., & Ramsey, M. E. Vance, E.A, Woolner, E, Maiden, S, Gustafson‖, N & Harsh, J.A. (2022). Students' Emotions, Perceived Coping, and Outcomes in Response to ResearchBased Challenges and Failures in Two Sequential CUREs. *CBE Life Sciences Education*. 10.1187/cbe.21-05-013135580005

Çoşkun, A., & Dalziel, N. (2020). Mediation effect of financial attitude on financial knowledge and financial behavior: The case of university students. *International Journal of Research in Business and Social Science (2147-4478)*, 9(2), 01-08.

Costa, P. T., & McCrae, R. R. (1985). *The NEO Personality Inventory Manual*. Psychological Assessment Resources.

Cotten, S. R., & Wilson, B. (2006). Student-faculty interactions: Dynamics and determinants. *Higher Education*, 51(4), 487–519. 10.1007/s10734-004-1705-4

Council Report CR112. (2013). *The mental health of students in higher education. Royal College of Psychiatrists*. (Council Report CR112). RCPsych. www.rcpsych.ac.uk/files/pdfversion/cr112.pdf

Cox, M. J., & Paley, B. (1997). FAMILIES AS SYSTEMS. *Annual Review of Psychology*, 48(1), 243–267. 10.1146/annurev.psych.48.1.2439046561

Cramer, A. O. J., Van Der Sluis, S., Noordhof, A., Wichers, M., Geschwind, N., Aggen, S. H., Kendler, K. S., & Borsboom, D. (2012). Dimensions of Normal Personality as Networks in Search of Equilibrium: You Can't like Parties if you Don't like People. *European Journal of Personality*, 26(4), 414–431. 10.1002/per.1866

Crawford, J., Allen, K. A., Sanders, T., Baumeister, R., Parker, P., Saunders, C., & Tice, D. (2024). Sense of belonging in higher education students: An Australian longitudinal study from 2013 to 2019. *Studies in Higher Education*, 49(3), 395–409. 10.1080/03075079.2023.2238006

Creswell, J. W., & Creswell, J. D. (2023). *Research design: Qualitative, quantitative, and mixed methods approaches* (6th ed.). SAGE.

Creswell, J. W., & Creswell, J. D. (2018). *Research Design: Qualitative, Quantitative and Mixed Methods Approaches* (5th ed.). SAGE.

Creswell, J. W., & Plano-Clark, V. L. (2018). *Designing and performing mixed methods research* (3rd ed.). Sage.

Cude, B., Frances, L., Lyons, A., Metzger, K., LeJeune, E., Marks, L., & Machtmes, K. (2006). College students and financial literacy: What they know and what we need to learn. *Proceedings of the Eastern Family Economics and Resource Management Association*, (pp. 102-109). Research Gate.

Cummings, E. M., Schermerhorn, A. C., Davies, P. T., Goeke-Morey, M. C., & Cummings, J. S. (2006). Interparental Discord and Child Adjustment: Prospective Investigations of Emotional Security as an Explanatory Mechanism. *Child Development*, 77(1), 132–152. 10.1111/j.1467-8624.2006.00861.x16460530

Curran, M. A., Parrott, E., Ahn, S. Y., Serido, J., & Shim, S. (2018). Young adult's life outcomes and well-being: Perceived financial socialization from parents, the romantic partner, and young adults' own financial Behaviors. *Journal of Family and Economic Issues*, 1–12.

Czyz, E. K., Berona, J., & King, C. A. (2015). A prospective examination of the interpersonal-psychological theory of suicidal behavior among psychiatric adolescent inpatients. *Suicide & Life-Threatening Behavior*, 45(2), 243–259. 10.1111/sltb.1212525263410

Danes, S. M. (1994). Parental perceptions of children's financial socialization. *Financial Counseling and Planning*, 5, 127–149.

Danneel, S., Bijttebier, P., Bastin, M., Colpin, H., Van den Noortgate, W., Van Leeuwen, K., Verschueren, K., & Goossens, L. (2019). Loneliness, Social Anxiety, and Depressive Symptoms in Adolescence: Examining Their Distinctiveness Through Factor Analysis. *Journal of Child and Family Studies*, 28(5), 1326–1336. 10.1007/s10826-019-01354-3

Davis, M., Eshelman, E. R., & McKay, M. (2008). The relaxation & stress reduction workbook (1st ed.). Oakland: New Harbinger Publications.

Dayagbil, F. T., Palompon, D. R., Garcia, L. L., & Olvido, M. M. J. (2021). Teaching and Learning Continuity Amid and Beyond the Pandemic. *Frontiers in Education*, 6(July), 1–12. 10.3389/feduc.2021.678692

de Abreu, T. C. C. M. (2021). *Corpos insurgentes: Narrativas urbanas sob a perspectiva da mulher*. Trabalho Final de Graduação em Arquitetura e Urbanismo, Centro Universitário Christus, Fortaleza, Ceará. https://repositorio.unichristus.edu.br/jspui/handle/123456789/1109

De Caroli, M. E., & Sagone, E. (2014). Generalized self-efficacy and well-being in adolescents with high vs. low scholastic self-efficacy. *Procedia: Social and Behavioral Sciences*, 141, 867–874. 10.1016/j.sbspro.2014.05.152

de Carvalho, G. J. E. (2017). *Pólo Universitário da Ajuda. (Re) vitalização, integração, naturalização* Tese de Mestrado em Arquitetura, Universidade de Lisboa. http://hdl.handle.net/10400.5/13951

De Kock, J. H., Latham, H. A., Leslie, S. J., Grindle, M., Munoz, S. A., Ellis, L., Polson, R., & O'Malley, C. M. (2021). A rapid review of the impact of COVID-19 on the mental health of healthcare workers: Implications for supporting psychological well-being. *BMC Public Health*, 21(1), 1–18. 10.1186/s12889-020-10070-333422039

De la Fuente, J., Fernández-Cabezas, M., Cambil, M., Vera, M. M., González-Torres, M. C., & Artuch-Garde, R. (2017). Linear relationship between resilience, learning approaches, and coping strategies to predict achievement in undergraduate students. *Frontiers in Psychology*, 8, 1039. 10.3389/fpsyg.2017.0103928713298

de Vibe, M., Solhaug, I., Rosenvinge, J. H., Tyssen, R., Hanley, A., & Garland, E. (2018). Six-year positive effects of a mindfulness-based intervention on mindfulness, coping and well-being in medical and psychology students; Results from a randomized controlled trial. *PLoS One*, 13(4), e0196053. 10.1371/journal.pone.019605329689081

De Vries, D. A., Möller, A. M., Wieringa, M. S., Eigenraam, A. W., & Hamelink, K. (2018). Social comparison as the thief of joy: Emotional consequences of viewing strangers' Instagram posts. *Media Psychology*, 21(2), 222–245. 10.1080/15213269.2016.1267647

De Vries, J. H., Spengler, M., Frintrup, A., & Mussel, P. (2021). Personality Development in Emerging Adulthood—How the Perception of Life Events and Mindset Affect Personality Trait Change. *Frontiers in Psychology*, 12, 671421. 10.3389/fpsyg.2021.67142134234715

DeBerard, M. S., Spielmans, G. I., & Julka, D. C. (2004). Predictors of academic achievement and retention among college freshmen: A longitudinal study. *College Student Journal*, 38, 66–80.

Deb, S. (2015). Academic stress, parental pressure, anxiety and mental health among Indian high school students. *International Journal of Psychology and Behavioral Sciences*, 5(1), 26–34. 10.5923/j.ijpbs.20150501.04

Deci, E. L., & Ryan, R. M. (2012). Motivation, Personality, and Development Within Embedded Social Contexts: An Overview of Self-Determination Theory. *The Oxford Handbook of Human Motivation*, 84–108. Oxford Press. 10.1093/oxfordhb/9780195399820.013.0006

Del Rosario, M. G. L. (2023). Stress, coping methods, and academic performance among teacher education students. *Journal for Educators, Teachers, and Trainers*, 14(3), 739–748.

Dew, J., & Xiao, J. J. (2011). The financial management behavior scale: Development and validation. *Financial Counseling and Planning*, 22(1), 43.

Dhaka ranked second in number of active Facebook users. Retrieved February 13, 2018, from https://m.bdnews24.com/en/detail/bangladesh/1319890.

Diener, E. (2009). *Well-being for public policy. Series in positive psychology. NewnYork.* Oxford University Press.

Diener, E., & Biswas-Diener, R. (2002). Will money increase subjective well-being? *Social Indicators Research*, 57(2), 119–169. 10.1023/A:1014411319119

Dixon, S., & Kurpius, S. (2008). Depression and college stress among university undergraduates: Do mattering and self-esteem make a difference? *Journal of College Student Development*, 49(5), 412–424. 10.1353/csd.0.0024

DiYES International School. (2023). *The Impact of Social Media on Student Well-Being: Navigating the Digital Journey.* IGCSE Curriculum. DiYES International School.

Dober, R. P. (1996). *Campus Planning.* Society for College and University Planning.

Dodd, A. L., Priestley, M., Tyrrell, K., Cygan, S., Newell, C., & Byrom, N. C. (2021). University student well-being in the United Kingdom: A scoping review of its conceptualisation and measurement. *Journal of Mental Health (Abingdon, England)*, 30(3), 375–387. 10.1080/09638237.2021.187541933567937

Dodge, K. A., Lansford, J. E., Burks, V. S., Bates, J. E., Pettit, G. S., Fontaine, R., & Price, J. M. (2003). Peer Rejection and Social Information-Processing Factors in the Development of Aggressive Behavior Problems in Children. *Child Development*, 74(2), 374–393. 10.1111/1467-8624.740200412705561

Donker, T., van Straten, A., Marks, I., & Cuijpers, P. (2011). Quick and easy self-rating of generalized anxiety disorder: Validity of the Dutch web-based GAD-7, GAD-2 and GAD-SI. *Psychiatry Research*, 188(1), 58–64. 10.1016/j.psychres.2011.01.01621339006

Douwes, R., Metselaar, J., Pijnenborg, G. H. M., & Boonstra, N. (2023). Well-being of students in higher education: The importance of a student perspective. *Cogent Education*, 10(1), 2190697. 10.1080/2331186X.2023.2190697

Dowling, N., Tim, C., & Hoiles, L. (2009). Financial management practices and money attitudes as determinants of financial problems and dissatisfaction in young male Australian workers. *Financial Counseling and Planning*, 20(2).

Drescher, C. F., Baczwaski, B. J., Walters, A. B., Aiena, B. J., Schulenberg, S. E., & Johnson, L. R. (2012). Coping with an ecological disaster: The role of perceived meaning in life and self-efficacy following the Gulf Oil Spill. *Ecopsychology*, 4(1), 56–63. 10.1089/eco.2012.0009

du Toit-Brits, C. (2022). Exploring the importance of a sense of belonging for a sense of ownership in learning. *South African Journal of Higher Education*, 36(5), 58–76. 10.20853/36-5-4345

Duckworth, A., Matthews, M., & Seligman, M. (2014). Grit: Perseverance and passion for long-term goals. *Journal of Personality and Social Psychology*, 92(6), 1087–1101. 10.1037/0022-3514.92.6.108717547490

Dumciene, A., & Pozeriene, J. (2022). The Emotions, Coping, and Psychological Well-Being in Time of COVID-19: Case of Master's Students. *International Journal of Environmental Research and Public Health*, 2022(19), 6014. 10.3390/ijerph19106014435627550

Dunn, J., & Munn, P. (1985). Becoming a Family Member: Family Conflict and the Development of Social Understanding in the Second Year. *Child Development*, 56(2), 480. 10.2307/1129735

Durso, S. de O., Afonso, L. E., & Beltman, S. (2021). Resilience in higher education: A conceptual model and its empirical analysis. *Education Policy Analysis Archives*, 29(August–December), 156. 10.14507/epaa.29.6054

Dweck, C. (2014). Teachers' Mindsets: "Every Student Has Something to Teach Me" Feeling Overwhelmed? Where Did Your Natural Teaching Talent Go? Try Pairing a Growth Mindset with Reasonable Goals, Patience, and Reflection Instead. It's Time to Get Gritty and Be a Better Teacher. *Educational Horizons*, 93(2), 10–15. 10.1177/0013175X14561420

Dyer, J., & Kreitman, N. (1984). Hopelessness, depression and suicidal intent in parasuicide. *The British Journal of Psychiatry*, 144(2), 127–133. 10.1192/bjp.144.2.1276704597

Dyson, R., & Renk, K. (2006). Freshmen adaptation to university life: Depressive symptoms, stress, and coping. *Journal of Clinical Psychology*, 62(10), 1231–1244. 10.1002/jclp.2029516810671

Eaton, S. E., Pethrick, H., & Turner, K. L. (2023). Academic integrity and student mental well-being: A rapid review. *Canadian Perspectives on Academic Integrity*, 5(2), 34-58. 10.11575/cpai.v5i2.73748

Eden, C. A., Chisom, O. N., & Adeniyi, I. S. (2024). Cultural Competence in Education. *Strategies for Fostering Inclusivity and Diversity.*, 6(3), 383–392. 10.51594/ijarss.v6i3.895

Eisenbarth, C. A. (2019). Coping with Stress: Gender Differences among College Students. *College Student Journal*, 53(2).

Eisenbeck, N., Carreno, D. F., & Perez-Escobar, J. A. (2021). *Meaning-Centered Coping in the Era of COVID-19: Direct and Moderating Effects on Depression, Anxiety, and Stress* (Vol. 12). Front. Psychol., Sec. Personality and Social Psychology. 10.3389/fpsyg.2021.648383

Eisenberg, D., Hunt, J., & Speer, N. (2012). Mental health in American colleges and universities: Variation across student subgroups and across campuses. *The Journal of Nervous and Mental Disease*, 200(11), 971–977.23274298

El-Badawy, T. A., & Hashem, Y. (2015). The impact of social media on the academic development of school students. *International Journal of Business Administration*, 6(1), 46.

Elhadi, M., Buzreg, A., Bouhuwaish, A., Khaled, A., Alhadi, A., Msherghi, A., Alsoufi, A., Alameen, H., Biala, M., Elghewi, A., Elkhafeefi, F., Elmabrouk, A., Abdulmalik, A., Alhaddad, S., Elgzairi, M., & Khaled, A. (2020). Psychological impact of the civil war and COVID-19 on Libyan medical students: A cross-sectional study. *Frontiers in Psychology*, 11, 570435. 10.3389/fpsyg.2020.57043533192858

Ellenbogen, M. A., & Hodgins, S. (2004). The impact of high neuroticism in parents on children's psychosocial functioning in a population at high risk for major affective disorder: A family-environmental pathway of intergenerational risk. *Development and Psychopathology*, 16(1), 113–136. 10.1017/S09545794040404443815115067

Ellis, W. E., Dumas, T. M., & Forbes, L. M. (2020). Physically isolated but socially connected: Psychological adjustment and stress among adolescents during the initial COVID-19 crisis. *Canadian Journal of Behavioural Science / Revue Canadienne. Science et Comportement*, 52(3), 177–187. 10.1037/cbs0000215

Engle, J., & Tinto, V. (2008). *Moving beyond access: College success for low-income, first-generation students*. Pell Institute for the Study of Opportunity in Higher Education.

Epkins, C. C., & Heckler, D. R. (2011). Integrating Etiological Models of Social Anxiety and Depression in Youth: Evidence for a Cumulative Interpersonal Risk Model. *Clinical Child and Family Psychology Review*, 14(4), 329–376. 10.1007/s10567-011-0101-822080334

Ersin, F., & Kartal, M. (2021). The determination of the perceived stress levels and health-protective behaviors of nursing students during the COVID-19 pandemic. *Perspectives in Psychiatric Care*, 57(2), 929–935. 10.1111/ppc.1263633090517

Evans, F. B. (2020). Interpersonal Theory of Psychiatry (Sullivan). *Encyclopedia of Personality and Individual Differences*, 2386–2394. Springer. 10.1007/978-3-319-24612-3_1390

Evans, K. M., Banyard, V. C., & Randolph, B. (2010). The effects of various mental health services on college students' academic achievement. *Journal of American College Health*, 58(2), 105–114.20864436

Evans, L. (2010). *Social media marketing: strategies for engaging in Facebook, Twitter & other social media*. Pearson Education.

Eweida, R. S., Rashwan, Z. I., Khonji, L. M., Shalhoub, A. A. B., & Ibrahim, N. (2023). Psychological first aid intervention: Rescue from psychological distress and improving the pre-licensure nursing students' resilience amidst COVID-19 crisis and beyond. *Scientific African*, 19, e01472. 10.1016/j.sciaf.2022.e0147236506753

Eysenck, H. J. (1967). *The biological basis of personality*. Thomas.

Eysenck, S. B., Eysenck, H. J., & Barrett, P. M. (1985). A revised version of the psychoticism scale. *Personality and Individual Differences*, 6(1), 21–29. 10.1016/0191-8869(85)90026-1

Fabrigar, L. R., MacDonald, T. K., & Wegener, D. T. (2005). The structure of attitudes. In Albarracín, D., Johnson, B. T., & Zanna, M. P. (Eds.), *Handbook of attitudes and attitude change* (pp. 79–124). Erlbaum.

Falahati, L., & Paim, L. H. (2011). A comparative study in money attitude among university students: A gendered view. *The Journal of American Science*, 7(6), 1144–1148.

Farrell, A. H., Vitoroulis, I., Eriksson, M., & Vaillancourt, T. (2023). Loneliness and Well-Being in Children and Adolescents during the COVID-19 Pandemic: A Systematic Review. *Children (Basel, Switzerland)*, 10(2), 279. 10.3390/children1002027936832408

Fasoro, A. A., Oluwadare, T., Ojo, T. F., & Oni, I. O. (2019, October). MSc a and Ignatius O. Oni,Perceived stress and stressors among first-year undergraduate students at a private medical school in Nigeria. *Journal of Taibah University Medical Sciences*, 14(5), 425–430. 10.1016/j.jtumed.2019.08.00331728140

Fateel, M. J. (2019). The Effect of Psychological Adjustment on Academic Achievement of Private University Students: A Case Study. *International Journal of Higher Education*, 8(6), 184–191. 10.5430/ijhe.v8n6p184

Fatima, S., Sharif, S., & Khalid, I. (2018). How does religion enhance psychological well-being? Roles of self-efficacy and perceived social support. *Psychology of Religion and Spirituality*, 10(2), 119–127. 10.1037/rel0000168

Fayaz, A. P., Aasim Ur, R. G., & Danishwar, R. D. (2024). Substance use in university students: a comprehensive examination of its effects on academic achievement and psychological well-being. In: *Social Work in Mental Health, 22*(3). https://www.tandfonline.com/doi/full/10.1080/15332985.2024.2306935

Federal student aid. (2023, April 18). *Types of Federal Aid*. Student Aid. https://studentaid.gov/

Federici, S. (2017). Calibã e a bruxa.*Mulheres, corpo e acumulação primitiva* (1a ed). Editora Elefante

Fellner, G., Güth, W., & Maciejovsky, B. (2005). *Satisficing in financial decision making: A theoretical and experimental attempt to explore bounded rationality* (Vol. 23). Max-Planck-Inst. for Research into Economic Systems, Strategic Interaction Group.

Ferrari, M., Allan, S., Arnold, C., Eleftheriadis, D., Alvarez-Jimenez, M., Gumley, A., & Gleeson, J. F. (2022). Digital Interventions for Psychological Well-being in University Students: Systematic Review and Meta-analysis. *J Med Internet Res., 28*(9).

Ferren, M. (2021). *Remote Learning and School Reopenings - What Worked and What Didn't*. ERIC. https://files.eric.ed.gov/fulltext/ED613768.pdf

Field, T., Diego, M., Pelaez, M., Deeds, O., & Delgado, J. (2012). Depression and related problems in university students. *College Student Journal*, 46(1), 193–202.

Fiorillo, A., & Gorwood, P. (2020). The consequences of the COVID-19 pandemic on mental health and implications for clinical practice. *European Psychiatry*, 63(1), e32. 10.1192/j.eurpsy.2020.3532234102

Fisher, D., & Sloan, K. (2019). Campus safety: Students' perceptions of safety on campus. *Journal of School Violence*, 18(2), 179–195.

Fisher, S., & Hood, B. (1988). The stress of transition to university: A longitudinal study of psychological disturbance, absent-mindedness, and vulnerability to homesickness. *British Journal of Psychology*, 78(4), 425–441. 10.1111/j.2044-8295.1987.tb02260.x3427309

Flatt, A. A. (2013). Suffering Generation: Six Factors Contributing to The Mental Health Crisis in North American Higher Education. *The College Quarterly*, 16(1).

Fleuret, S., & Prugneau, J. (2014). Assessing students' wellbeing in a spatial dimension. *The Geographical Journal*, 181.

Fleuret, S., & Atkinson, S. (2007). Wellbeing, health and geography: a critical review and research agenda. *New Zealand Geographer*, 63(2), 106–129. 10.1111/j.1745-7939.2007.00093.x

Folkman, S., Lazarus, R. S., Gruen, R. J., & DeLongis, A. (1986). Appraisal, coping, health status, and psychological symptoms. *Journal of Personality and Social Psychology*, 50(3), 571–579. 10.1037/0022-3514.50.3.5713701593

Fomby, P., & Cherlin, A. J. (2007). Family Instability and Child Well-Being. *American Sociological Review*, 72(2), 181–204. 10.1177/000312240707200203219185 79

Fosnacht, K., & Dong, Y. (2013). Financial stress and its impact on first-year students' college experiences. *Paper presented at the annual meeting of the Association for the Study of Higher Education*. Research Gate.

Fox, N. A., Henderson, H. A., Marshall, P. J., Nichols, K. E., & Ghera, M. M. (2005). Behavioral Inhibition: Linking Biology and Behavior within a Developmental Framework. *Annual Review of Psychology*, 56(1), 235–262. 10.1146/annurev.psych.55.090902.14153215709935

Fraillon, J. (2004). *Measuring student wellbeing in the context of Australian schooling: Discussion paper*. South Australian Department of Education and Children's Services.

Franchuk, V., Omelchuk, O., Melnyk, S., Kelman, M., & Mykytyuk, O. (2020). Identification the Ways of Counteraction of the Threats to the Financial Security of High-Tech Enterprises. *Business: Theory and Practice*, 21(1), 1–9. 10.3846/btp.2020.11215

Franke, F., Huffmeier, J., Montano, D., & Reeske, A. (2017). Leadership, followers' mental health and job performance in organizations: A comprehensive meta-analysis from an occupational health perspective. *Journal of Organizational Behavior*, 38(3), 327–350.

Franko, W. W. (2021). How state responses to economic crisis shape income inequality and financial well-being. *State Politics & Policy Quarterly*, 21(1), 31–54. 10.1177/1532440020919806

Freire, C, Ferradas, M.D.M, Regueiro, B, Rodriguez, S, Valle, A & Nunez, J. C. (2020). Coping Strategies and Self-Efficacy in University Students: A Person-Centered Approach. Sec. *Educational Psychology*. Frontiers. 10.3389/fpsyg.2020.00841

Friedlander, L. J., Reid, G. J., Shupak, N., & Cribbie, R. (2007). Social support, self-esteem, and stress as predictors of adjustment to university among first-year undergraduates. *Journal of College Student Development*, 48(3), 259–274. 10.1353/csd.2007.0024

Friedman, L. C., Nelson, D. V., Baer, P. E., Lane, M., Smith, F. E., & Dworthkin, R. J. (1992). The relationship of dispositional optimism, daily life stress, and domestic environment on coping methods used by cancer patients. *Journal of Behavioral Medicine*, 15(2), 127–141. 10.1007/BF008483211583677

Fritz, M. V., Chin, D., & DeMarinis, V. (2008). Stressors, anxiety, acculturation and adjustment among international and North American students. *International Journal of Intercultural Relations*, 32(3), 244–259. 10.1016/j.ijintrel.2008.01.001

Fuente, J. D. L., Lahortiga-Ramos, F., Laspra-Solís, C., Maestro-Martín, C., Alustiza, I., Aubá, E., & Martín-Lanas, R. (2020). A Structural Equation Model of Achievement Emotions, Coping Strategies and Engagement-Burnout in Undergraduate Students: A Possible Underlying Mechanism in Facets of Perfectionism. *International Journal of Environmental Research and Public Health*. 10.3390/ijerph170632235741

Fuller, A. E., Garg, A., Brown, N. M., Tripodis, Y., Oyeku, S. O., & Gross, R. S. (2020). Relationships between material hardship, resilience, and health care use. *Pediatrics*, 145(2), e20191975. 10.1542/peds.2019-197531949000

Gaitho, M. (2018). *What Is the Real Impact of Social Media?* Simplilearn. https://www.simplilearn.com/real-impact-social-media-article

Galanaki, E. (2004a). Are children able to distinguish among the concepts of aloneness, loneliness, and solitude? *International Journal of Behavioral Development*, 28(5), 435–443. 10.1080/01650250444000153

Galanaki, E. (2004b). Teachers and Loneliness. *School Psychology International*, 25(1), 92–105. 10.1177/0143034304041504

Gallagher, R. P. (2017). *National survey of college counseling centers 2016*. International Association of Counseling Services.

Ganesan, Y., Talwar, P., Norsiah, F., & Oon, Y. B. (2018). A Study on Stress Level and Coping Strategies among Undergraduate Students. *Journal of Cognitive Sciences and Human Development*, 3(2), 37–47. 10.33736/jcshd.787.2018

Garrido, J. (2019). Stress, coping strategies and academic achievement in teacher education students. *European Journal of Teacher Education*, 42(4), 1–16. 10.1080/02619768.2019.1576629

Garritty, C., Gartlehner, G., Nussbaumer-Streit, B., King, V. J., Hamel, C., Kamel, C., Affengruber, L., & Stevens, A. (2021). Cochrane Rapid Reviews Methods Group offers evidence-informed guidance to conduct rapid reviews. *Journal of Clinical Epidemiology*, 130, 13–22. 10.1016/j.jclinepi.2020.10.00733068715

Gasiorowska, A. (2015). The impact of money attitudes on the relationship between income and financial satisfaction. *Polish Psychological Bulletin*, 46(2), 197–208. 10.1515/ppb-2015-0026

Gedney-Lose, A., Daack-Hirsch, S., & Nicholson, A. (2022). Innovative Management of Nursing Student COVID-19 Cases and High-Risk Exposures. *The Journal of Nursing Education*, 61(4), 217–220. 10.3928/01484834-20220209-0735384764

Geist, C. R., & Borecki, S. (1982). Social avoidance and distress as a predictor of perceived locus of control and level of self-esteem. *Journal of Clinical Psychology*, 38(3), 611–613. 10.1002/1097-4679(198207)38:3<611::AID-JCLP2270380325>3.0.CO;2-H7107927

Georgia, G. (2024). Academic Stress and Mental Well-Being in College Students: Correlations, Affected Groups, and COVID-19. *PMCID: PMC9169886*.

Ghaderi, A. R., & Rangaiah, B. (2011). Influence of self-efficacy on depression, anxiety and stress among Indian and Iranian students. *Journal of Psychosomatic Research*, 6(2), 231–240.

Ghadiri, F., Sabouri Moghadam, H., & Babapur Kheiradin, J. (2014). *Prediction of Vulnerability to Addiction on the Basis of Psychosocial Stressors*. In: *Practice of Clinical Psychology, 2*(4), 271-276. https://jesp.upg-ploiesti.ro/index.php?option=com_phocadownload&view=file&id=659:the-transition-to-the-academic-environment-between-difficulties-and-coping-strategies&Itemid=16

Gibbs, G. R. (2008). *Analyzing qualitative* data. Uk. *Sage (Atlanta, Ga.)*.

Giles, J. (2003). Children's essentialist beliefs about aggression. *Developmental Review*, 23(4), 413–443. 10.1016/S0273-2297(03)00039-X

Gillis, K. (2023). *Problem-Focused Coping: Definition, Examples & Strategies*. Choosing Therapy. https://www.choosingtherapy.com/problem-focused-coping/

Gino, F., & Pierce, L. (2009). The abundance effect: Unethical behavior in the presence of wealth. *Organizational Behavior and Human Decision Processes*, 109(2), 142–155. 10.1016/j.obhdp.2009.03.003

Global Health Estimates (GHE). (2023). *Life expectancy and leading causes of death and disability*. GHE. https://www.who.int/data/gho/data/themes/mortality-and-global-health-estimates

Gmelch, W. H., Wilke, P. K., & Lovrich, N. (1983). *Sources of stress in academe: A national perspective*. Paper presented at the annual meeting of the American Educational Research Association, Montreal, Canada.

Golberstein, E., Wen, H., & Miller, B. F. (2020). Coronavirus Disease 2019 (COVID-19) and Mental Health for Children and Adolescents. *JAMA Pediatrics*, 174(9), 819. 10.1001/jamapediatrics.2020.145632286618

Gonçalves, V. F. da C., Oliveira, M., Viana, L. P., & Fernandes, J. M. (2011). *Património Arquitectónico da Universidade Técnica de Lisboa (GAPTEC/UTL)*. UTL.

González-García, M., Lana, A., Zurrón-Madera, P., Valcárcel-Álvarez, Y., & Fernández-Feito, A. (2020). Nursing students' experiences of clinical practices in emergency and intensive care units. *International Journal of Environmental Research and Public Health*, 17(16), 5686. 10.3390/ijerph1716568632781646

Gonzalez, K. P. (2016). Financial strain and mental health among college students: The mediating effect of social support. *Journal of College Student Development*, 57(7), 808–818.

Gonzalez, K. P., & Sanders-Reio, J. (2011). Predictors of health care utilization among college students. *Journal of Community Health Nursing*, 28(2), 76–87.

Gould, M. S. (2001). Suicide and the media. *Annals of the New York Academy of Sciences*, 932(1), 200–224. 10.1111/j.1749-6632.2001.tb05807.x11411187

Goyer, J. P., Akinola, M., Grunberg, R., & Crum, A. J. (2022). Supplemental Material for Thriving Under Pressure: The Effects of Stress-Related Wise Interventions on Affect, Sleep, and Exam Performance for College Students From Disadvantaged Backgrounds. *Emotion (Washington, D.C.)*, 22(8), 1755–1772. 10.1037/emo000102634780237

Grable, J. E., & Joo, S. (2006). Student racial differences in credit card debt and financial behaviors and stress. *College Student Journal*, 40(2), 400–408.

Graves BS, Hall ME, Dias-Karch C, Haischer MH, Apter C (2021) Gender differences in perceived stress and coping among college students. *PLoS ONE 16*(8), e0255634. https://doi.org/10.1371/journal.pone.0255634

Greenberg, J. (1993). Stealing in the name of justice: Informational and interpersonal moderators of theft reactions to underpayment inequity. *Organizational Behavior and Human Decision Processes*, 54(1), 81–103. 10.1006/obhd.1993.1004

Greenleaf, C., Petrie, T. A., & Martin, S. B. (2014). Relationship between weight-based teasing and adolescents' psychological well-being and physical health. *The Journal of School Health*, 84(1), 49–55. 10.1111/josh.1211824320152

Griffiths, M. D., Kuss, D. J., & Demetrovics, Z. (2014). Social networking addiction: An overview of preliminary findings. In Rosenberg K. P., Feder L. C., editors. (Eds.), *Behavioral addictions. Criteria, evidence, and treatment* (pp. 119–141). New York: Elsevier.

Guichard, S. & Rusticelli, E. (2010). *Assessing the impact of the fnancial crisis on structural unemployment in OECD countries*. OECD.

Guillena, R. M., & Guillena, J. B. (2022). Perceived stress, self-efficacy, and mental health of the first-year college students during Covid-19 pandemic. *Indones J Multidiscip Sci.*, 2(2), 2005–2013. 10.55324/ijoms.v2i2.281

Gupta, O. J., & Yadav, S. (2023). Determinants in advancement of teaching and learning in higher education: In special reference to management education. *International Journal of Management Education*, 21(2), 100823. 10.1016/j.ijme.2023.100823

Gurin, P., Dey, E. L., Gurin, G., & Neal, D. (2010). Participation in college governance: Impacts on students' scholastic and psychological growth. *Review of Higher Education*, 33(4), 443–464. https://onlinelibrary.wiley.com/journal/14680491

Gururaj, G., Isaac, M. K., & Subba, K. D. K. (2011). Risk factors for completed suicides: A case-control study from Bangalore, India. *Injury Control and Safety Promotion*, 11(3), 183–191. 10.1080/156609704/233/28970615764105

Guterman, N. B., Mayne, T. J., Kim, J. S., & Narendorf, S. C. (2020). Evaluation of the impact of tutoring support services for students with learning disabilities in a university setting. *Learning Disabilities Research & Practice*, 35(1), 18–27.

Gutter, M., & Copur, Z. (2011). Financial behaviors and financial well-being of college students: Evidence from a national survey. *Journal of Family and Economic Issues*, 32(4), 699–714. 10.1007/s10834-011-9255-2

Gyimah, P., Poku, K., & Osei-Poku, B. (2018). Financial literacy assessment on tertiary students in sub-saharan Africa: A Ghanaian perspective. *International Journal of Accounting and Financial Reporting*, 8(2), 76–91. 10.5296/ijafr.v8i2.12928

Haddad, L., Kane, D., Rajacich, D., Cameron, S., & Al-Ma'aitah, R. (2004). A comparison of the healthpractices of Canadian and Jordanian nursing students. *Public Health Nursing (Boston, Mass.)*, 21(1), 85–90. 10.1111/j.1525-1446.2004.21112.x14692993

Haisken-DeNew, J. P., & Kind, M. (2012). Unexpected Victims: How Parents' Unemployment Affects Their Children's Life Satisfaction. SSRN *Electronic Journal*. 10.2139/ssrn.2006040

Hajrasouliha, A. (2017). Campus score: Measuring university campus qualities. *Landscape and Urban Planning*, 158, 166–176. 10.1016/j.landurbplan.2016.10.007

Hajrasouliha, A. H., & Ewing, R. (2016). Campus Does Matter. The Relationship of Student Retention and Degree Attainment to Campus Design. *Planning for Higher Education Journal*, 44(3), 1–15.

Hako, A. N., & Shikongo, P. T. (2019). Factors Preventing Students from Completing Studies within the Allotted Time: A Case Study of a Public University in Namibia. *Journal of the International Society for Teacher Education*, 23(1), 39–52.

Haktanir, A., Watson, J. C., Ermis-Demirtas, H., Karaman, M. A., Freeman, P. D., Kumaran, A., & Streeter, A. (2018). Resilience, academic self-concept, and college adjustment among first-year students. *Journal of College Student Retention*, 23(1), 161–178. 10.1177/1521025118810666

Haleem, A., Javaid, M., Qadri, M. A., & Suman, R. (2022). Understanding the role of digital technologies in education: A review. *Sustainable Operations and Computers*, 3(February), 275–285. 10.1016/j.susoc.2022.05.004

Halim, E. K. Y., & Astuti, D. (2015). Financial stressors, Financial Behaviour, risk tolerance, financial solvency, financial knowledge and financial satisfaction. *Journal of Management*, 3, 19–23.

Hamadeh Kerbage, S., Garvey, L., Willetts, G., & Olasoji, M. (2021). Undergraduate nursing students' resilience, challenges, and supports during corona virus pandemic. *International journal of mental health nursing, 30*, 1407-1416. https://doi.org/10.1111/inm.12896

Hammer, L., & Thompson, C. (2003). *Work-family role conflict*. Sloan Work and Family Research Network. http://wfnetwork.bc.edu/encyclopedia_entry.php?id=264

Hanson, T. A., & Olson, P. M. (2018). Financial literacy and family communication patterns. *Journal of Behavioral and Experimental Finance*, 19, 64–71. 10.1016/j.jbef.2018.05.001

Harding, T., Lopez, V., & Klainin-Yobas, P. (2019). *Predictors of psychological well-being among higher education students*. Research Gate.

Harnish, R. J., Bridges, K. R., Nataraajan, R., Gump, J. T., & Carson, A. E. (2018). The impact of money attitudes and global life satisfaction on the maladaptive pursuit of consumption. *Psychology and Marketing*, 35(3), 189–196. 10.1002/mar.21079

Harper, S. R. (2012). Race without racism: How higher education researchers minimize racist institutional norms. *Review of Higher Education*, 36(1), 9–29. 10.1353/rhe.2012.0047

Harris, E. C., & Barraclough, B. (1998). Excess mortality of mental disorder. *The British Journal of Psychiatry*, 173(1), 11–53. 10.1192/bjp.173.1.119850203

Hart, C. H., Yang, C., Nelson, L. J., Robinson, C. C., Olsen, J. A., Nelson, D. A., Porter, C. L., Jin, S., Olsen, S. F., & Wu, P. (2000). Peer acceptance in early childhood and subtypes of socially withdrawn behaviour in China, Russia, and the United States. *International Journal of Behavioral Development*, 24(1), 73–81. 10.1080/016502500383494

Harvard Summer School. (2021, May 28). Why You Should Prioritize Quality Sleep. https://summer.harvard.edu/blog/why-you-should-make-a-good-nights-sleep-a-priority/

Hasanah, U., Tribrilianti, A. Z., & Oktaviani, M. (2023, May). Exploring Coping Strategies to Maintain Students' Mental Health. In *9th International Conference on Technical and Vocational Education and Training (ICTVET 2022)* (pp. 224–232). Atlantis Press. 10.2991/978-2-38476-050-3_25

Hashimoto, T., Mojaverian, T., & Kim, H. S. (2012). Culture, interpersonal stress, and psychological distress. *Journal of Cross-Cultural Psychology*, 43(4), 527–532. 10.1177/0022022112438396

Hawkley, L. C., & Cacioppo, J. T. (2010). Loneliness Matters: A Theoretical and Empirical Review of Consequences and Mechanisms. *Annals of Behavioral Medicine*, 40(2), 218–227. https://www.ncbi.nlm.nih.gov/pmc/articles/PMC3874845/. 10.1007/s12160-010-9210-820652462

Hawton, K., & van Heeringen, K. (2009). Suicide. *Lancet*, 37(3), 72–81. 10.1016/S0140-6736(09)60372-X19376453

Hayhoe, C. R., Leach, L. J., Turner, P. R., Bruin, M. J., & Lawrence, F. C. (2000). Differences in spending habits and credit use of college students. *The Journal of Consumer Affairs*, 34(1), 113–133. 10.1111/j.1745-6606.2000.tb00087.x

Hays, R. B., & Oxley, D. (1986). Social network development and functioning during life transition. *Journal of Personality and Social Psychology*, 50(2), 305–313. 10.1037/0022-3514.50.2.3053701579

Heckman, S. J., & Montalto, H. L. C. P. (2014). Factors Related to Financial Stress among. *College Student Journal*, 5(1). 10.4148/1944-9771.1063

Hecman Stuart, H., Lim, A. & Montalto, C. (2014). Factors Related to Financial Stress among College Students. *JournCollege Student Life and Financial Stress*.

Heim, E., Augustiny, K., Schaffner, L., & Valach, L. (1993). Coping with breast cancer over time and situation. *Journal of Psychosomatic Research*, 37(5), 523–542. 10.1016/0022-3999(93)90008-48350294

Hennesy, S., Ruthven, K., & Brindley, S. (2005). Teacher perspectives on integrating ICT into subject teaching: Commitment, constraints, caution, and change. *Journal of Curriculum Studies*, 37(2), 155–192. 10.1080/0022027032000276961

Hershner, S. D., & Chervin, R. D. (2014). Causes and consequences of sleepiness among college students. *Nature and Science of Sleep*, 6, 73–84. 10.2147/NSS.S6290725018659

Heshmati, S., Blackard, M. B., Beckmann, B., & Chipidza, W. (2021). Family relationships and adolescent loneliness: An application of social network analysis in family studies. *Journal of Family Psychology*, 35(2), 182–191. 10.1037/fam000066033871279

He, Y., Li, A., Li, K., & Xiao, J. (2021). Neuroticism vulnerability factors of anxiety symptoms in adolescents and early adults: An analysis using the bi-factor model and multi-wave longitudinal model. *PeerJ*, 9, e11379. 10.7717/peerj.1137934221704

Hick, , S. (2021). *Financial Stress in Undergraduate Students Financial Stress in Undergraduate Students*. Walden University Scholar Works. Walden Dissertations and Doctoral Studies Walden Dissertations and Doctoral Studies.

Hilger, P. (2003). Enlargement As A Challenge To Fifth Research Framework Programme (FP5). *Changing Governance of Research and Technology Policy: The European Research Area*, 210.

Hinduja, S., & Patchin, J. W. (2010). Bullying, cyberbullying, and suicide. *Archives of Suicide Research*, 14(3), 206–221. 10.1080/13811118.2010.49413320658375

Hira, T. K., & Mugenda, O. (2000). Gender differences in financial perceptions, behaviors and satisfaction. *Journal of Financial Planning-Denver*, 13(2), 86–93.

Hira, T. K., & Mugenda, O. M. (1998). Predictors of financial satisfaction: Differences between retirees and non-retirees. *Financial Counseling and Planning*, 9(2), 75.

Hodula, M., & Melecký, A. (2020). Debt management when monetary and fiscal policies clash: Some empirical evidence. *Journal of Applied Econometrics*, 23(1), 253–280.

Hogan, V., Hogan, M., & Hodgins, M. (2016). A study of workaholism in Irish academics. *Occupational Medicine*, 66(6), 460–465. 10.1093/occmed/kqw032

Holahan, C. J., & Moos, R. H. (1987). Risk, resistance, and psychological distress: A longitudinal analysis with adults and children. *Journal of Abnormal Psychology*, 96(1), 3–13. 10.1037/0021-843X.96.1.33558946

Hong, J., Lee, Y., Park, S., Kim, J., & Lee, M. (2017). Acculturative stress, academic self-efficacy and academic help-seeking among international students in South Korea. *Journal of International Students*, 7(3), 571–587.

Hormes, J. M., Kearns, B., & Timko, C. A. (2014). Craving Facebook? Behavioral addiction to online social networking and its association with emotion regulation deficits. *Addiction (Abingdon, England)*, 109(12), 2079–2088. 10.1111/add.1271325170590

Horneffer, K. J. (2006). Students' self-concepts: Implications for promoting self-care within the nursing curriculum. *The Journal of Nursing Education*, 45(8).16915990

Hossain, K. (2023). Determinants of Financial Stress among University Students and Its Impact on Their Performance. *Journal of Applied Research in Higher Education, 15*.

Houghton, J. D., Wu, J., Godwin, J. L., Neck, C. P., & Manz, C. C. (2012). Effective stress management a model of emotional intelligence, self-leadership, and student stress coping. *Journal of Management Education*, 36(2), 220–238. 10.1177/1052562911430205

Hoyt, J. E., Howell, S. L., Glines, L. J., Johnson, C., Spackman, J. S., Thompson, C., & Rudd, C. (2008). Assessing part-time faculty job satisfaction in continuing higher education: Implications for the profession. *The Journal of Continuing Higher Education*, 56(1), 27–38. 10.1080/07377366.2008.10400139

Hsu, J. L., & Goldsmith, G. R. (2021). Instructor Strategies to Alleviate Stress and Anxiety among College and University STEM Students. *CBE Life Sciences Education*, 20(1), es1. 10.1187/cbe.20-08-018933635124

Huang, L. (2020). Peer victimization, teacher unfairness, and adolescent life satisfaction: The mediating roles of sense of belonging to school and schoolwork-related anxiety. *School Mental Health*, 12(3), 556–566. 10.1007/s12310-020-09365-y

Hurtado, S., Alvarez, C. L., Guillermo-Wann, C., Cuellar, M., & Arellano, L. (2019). A holistic model of diverse learning environments: The transformative potential of diversity, equity, and inclusion in teaching and learning. *Harvard Educational Review*, 89(3), 303–328.

Hurtado, S., Milem, J. F., Clayton-Pedersen, A. R., & Allen, W. R. (2012). Enhancing campus climates for racial/ethnic diversity: Educational policy and practice. *Review of Higher Education*, 25(3), 243–272.

Hwang, W. C., Myers, H. F., Abe-Kim, J., & Ting, J. Y. (2015). A conceptual paradigm for understanding culture's impact on mental health: The cultural influences on mental health (CIMH) model. *Clinical Psychology Review*, 36, 30–41.17587473

Hyde, J. S. (2005). The gender similarities hypothesis. *The American Psychologist*, 60(6), 581–592. 10.1037/0003-066X.60.6.58116173891

Hymer, S. (1986). The multidimensional significance of the look. *Psychoanalytic Psychology*, 3(2), 149–157. 10.1037/0736-9735.3.2.149

Ibrahim, N., Al- Kharboush, D., El-Khatib, L., Al –Habib, A. & Asali, D. (2013). Prevalence and predictors of anxiety and depression among female medical students in King Abdulaziz University, Jeddah, Saudi Arabia. *Iranian Journal of Public Health*, 42(7), 726–736.

Im, Y., Oh, W., & Suk, M. (2017). Risk Factors for suicide ideation among adolescents: Five-year national data analysis. *Archives of Psychiatric Nursing*, 31(1), 282–286. 10.1016/j.apnu.2017.01.00128499568

Internet World Stats. (2017). Internet Top 20 Countries - Internet Users. Internet World Stats. http://www.internetworldstats.com/top20.htm

Ireland, M. E., Hepler, J., Li, H., & Albarracín, D. (2015). Neuroticism and attitudes toward action in 19 countries. *Journal of Personality*, 83(3), 243–250. 10.1111/jopy.1209924684688

Ivancevich, J. M., & Matteson, M. T. (1980). *Stress and work: A managerial perspective*. Scott, Foresman, and Company.

Jacobs, J. (1993). *The death and life of great American cities*. New York: Vintage Books.

Jacobs, J. (1993). *The death and life of great American cities*. Vintage Books.

Jafar, H. M., Salabifard, S., Mousavi, S. M., & Sobhani, Z. (2015). The effectiveness of group training of CBT-based stress management on anxiety, psychological hardiness and general self-efficacy among university students. *Global Journal of Health Science*, 8(5), 47–54. 10.5539/gjhs.v8n6p4726755483

Jamil, N., Belkacem, A. N., & Lakas, A. (2023). On enhancing students' cognitive abilities in online learning using brain activity and eye movements. In *Education and Information Technologies, 28*(4). Springer US. 10.1007/s10639-022-11372-2

Jaschik, S. (2015). *Keeping the focus on learning: Investigating the link between academic rigor, student involvement, and student results*. Jossey-Bass.

Jebb, A. T., Tay, L., Diener, E., & Oishi, S. (2018). Happiness, income satiation and turning points around the world. *Nature Human Behaviour*, 2(1), 33–38. 10.1038/s41562-017-0277-030980059

Jefferson, R., Barreto, M., Verity, L., & Qualter, P. (2023). Loneliness During the School Years: How It Affects Learning and How Schools Can Help. *The Journal of School Health*, 93(5), 428–435. Advance online publication. 10.1111/josh.1330636861756

Jeronimo, V. R. (2023). *Mulheres, Arquitetura e Espaço urbano: a Vivência das Estudantes na FA-ULisboa*. [Thesis in Architecture, Lisbon School of Architecture].

Jessiman, P., Kidger, J., Spencer, L., Geijer-Simpson, E., Kaluzeviciute, G., Burn, A.-M., Leonard, N., & Limmer, M. (2022). School culture and student mental health: A qualitative study in UK secondary schools. *BMC Public Health*, 22(1), 1–18. 10.1186/s12889-022-13034-x35351062

Jeynes, W. H. (2024). A Meta-Analysis: The Relationship Between the Parental Expectations Component of Parental Involvement with Students' Academic Achievement. *Urban Education*, 59(1), 63–95. 10.1177/00420859211073892

Jia, C., Hew, K. F., Bai, S., & Huang, W. (2022). Adaptation of a conventional flipped course to an online flipped format during the Covid-19 pandemic: Student learning performance and engagement. *Journal of Research on Technology in Education*, 54(2), 281–301. 10.1080/15391523.2020.1847220

Jiang, M. M., Gao, K., Wu, Z. Y., & Guo, P. P. (2022). The influence of academic pressure on adolescents' problem behavior: Chain mediating effects of self-control, parent–child conflict, and subjective well-being. *Frontiers in Psychology*, 13(September), 1–10. 10.3389/fpsyg.2022.95433036211862

Jithoo, V. (2018). Contested meanings of mental health and well-being among university students. *South African Journal of Psychology. Suid-Afrikaanse Tydskrif vir Sielkunde*, 48(4), 453–464. 10.1177/0081246317731958

Joanna Briggs Institute. (2017). JBI critical appraisal checklist for analytical cross sectional studies. 2017. *Diakses Pada*, 22, 2019–05.

Johns, M., Schmader, T., & Martens, A. (2019). Knowing is half the battle: Teaching stereotype threat as a means of preventing it. *Social and Personality Psychology Compass*, 13(1), e12431.

Johnson, E. E. (1978). *Student-identified stresses that relate to college life*. Paper presented at the annual conference of the American Psychological Association, Toronto, Canada.

Johnson, J., Panagioti, M., Bass, J., Ramsey, L., & Harrison, R. (2017). Resilience to emotional distress in response to failure, error, or mistakes: A systematic review. *Clinical Psychology Review*, 52, 19–42. 10.1016/j.cpr.2016.11.00727918887

Johnson, M. D., & Galambos, N. L. (2014). Paths to Intimate Relationship Quality From Parent-Adolescent Relations and Mental Health. *Journal of Marriage and Family*, 76(1), 145–160. 10.1111/jomf.12074

Jones, A., & Turner, B. (2019). Time management in higher education: A review of literature. *Journal of Further and Higher Education*, 43(2), 186–203.

Joo, S.-H. (2009). The Academic Impact Of Financial Stress On College Students. *J. College student retention, 10*(3) 287- 305.

Joo, S. H., & Grable, J. E. (2004). An exploratory framework of the determinants of financial satisfaction. *Journal of Family and Economic Issues*, 25(1), 25–50. 10.1023/B:JEEI.0000016722.37994.9f

Joo, S.-H., Durband, D. B., & Grable, J. (2008). The Academic Impact of Financial Stress on College Students. *Journal of College Student Retention*, 10(3), 287–305. 10.2190/CS.10.3.c

Jordan, J. T., Schwartz, S. E., Whillans, T. D., Rafti, A. E., & Lindquist, K. A. (2014). A systematic review of peer support interventions for young adults. *Clinical Psychological Science*, 2(3), 239–262. https://www.ncbi.nlm.nih.gov/pmc/articles/PMC4142412/

Junttila, N., & Vauras, M. (2009). Loneliness among school-aged children and their parents. *Scandinavian Journal of Psychology*, 50(3), 211–219. 10.1111/j.1467-9450.2009.00715.x19490524

Juvonen, J. (1991). Deviance, perceived responsibility, and negative peer reactions. *Developmental Psychology*, 27(4), 672–681. 10.1037/0012-1649.27.4.672

Kabat-Zinn, J. (1994). *Wherever You Go, There You Are: Mindfulness Meditation in Everyday Life*. Hachette Books.

Kahneman, D., & Deaton, A. (2010). High income improves evaluation of life but not emotional well-being. *Proceedings of the National Academy of Sciences of the United States of America*, 107(38), 16489–16493. 10.1073/pnas.1011492107208232 23

Kaitlin, C. (2010). Social media changing social interactions. *Student Journal of Media Literacy Education*, 1(1), 1–11.

Kamardeen, I., & Sunindijo, R. Y. (2018). Stressors impacting the performance of graduate construction students: Comparison of domestic and international students. *Journal of Professional Issues in Engineering Education and Practice*, 144(4), 4018011. 10.1061/(ASCE)EI.1943-5541.0000392

Karaca, A., Yildirim, N., Cangur, S., Acikgoz, F., & Akkus, D. (2019). Relationship between mental health of nursing students and coping, self-esteem and social support. *Nurse Education Today*, 76, 44–50. 10.1016/j.nedt.2019.01.02930769177

Karadkar, A. (2015). *The impact of social media on student life*. Technician Online. https://www.technicianonline.com/opinion/article_d1142b70-5a92-11e5-86b4-cb7c98a6e45f.html

Karakose, T., Polat, H., & Papadakis, S. (2021). Exploring Teachers' Perspectives on the Role of Digital Leadership in the COVID-19 Pandemic and Tech Skills of School Leaders. *Sustainability*, 13, 13448. 10.3390/su132313448

Karaman, M. A, Lerma, E, Vela, J.C & Watson, J.C. (2019). Predictors of Academic Stress Among College Students *Journal of College Counseling, 22*(1).

Karyotaki, E., Cuijpers, P., Albor, Y., Alonso, J., Auerbach, R. P., Bantjes, J., Bruffaerts, R., Ebert, D. D., Hasking, P., Kiekens, G., Lee, S., McLafferty, M., Mak, A., Mortier, P., Sampson, N. A., Stein, D. J., Vilagut, G., & Kessler, R. C. (2020). Sources of stress and their associations with mental disorders among college students: Results of the World Health Organization world mental health surveys international college student initiative. *Frontiers in Psychology*, 11, 1759. 10.3389/fpsyg.2020.0175932849042

Kashyap, A. (2023). Suicide deaths in Indian men increased 2 times more than women in 2021: Lancet study. *Business Line*. https://www.thehindubusinessline.com/news/national/suicide-deaths-in-ndian-men-increased-2-times-more-than-women-in-2021-lancet-study/article67250785.ece

Kaur, G., Singh, M., & Gupta, S. (2023). Analysis of key factors influencing individual financial well-being using ISM and MICMAC approach. *Quality & Quantity*, 57(2), 1533–1559. 10.1007/s11135-022-01422-935669163

Kauser, S., & Awan, A. G. (2019). Impact of using social media on academic performance of students at graduate level: Evidence from Pakistan. *Glob J Manag Soc Sci Humanities*, 5(1), 116–142.

Kawachi, I., & Berkman, L. (2001). Social Ties and Mental Health. *Journal of Urban Health*, 78(3), 458–467. 10.1093/jurban/78.3.45811564849

Kaya, C., Tansey, T. N., Melekoglu, M., Cakiroglu, O., & Chan, F. (2019). Psychometric evaluation of Turkish version of the perceived stress scale with Turkish college students. *Journal of Mental Health (Abingdon, England)*, 28(2), 161–167. 10.1080/09638237.2017.141756629260926

Kelly, M. L., Yeigh, T., Hudson, S., Willis, R., & Lee, M. (2023). Secondary teachers' perceptions of the importance of pedagogical approaches to support students' behavioural, emotional and cognitive engagement. *Australian Educational Researcher*, 50(4), 1025–1047. 10.1007/s13384-022-00540-5

Kenney, T. (2023). *The Effects of Student Satisfaction and Sense of Belonging on Academic Success and Performance in Undergraduate Science Majors*. Widener University.

Keyes, C. L. M., Eisenberg, D., Perry, G. S., Dube, S. R., Kroenke, K., & Dhingra, S. S. (2012). The relationship level of positive mental health with current mental disorders in predicting suicidal behavior and academic impairment in college students. *Journal of American College Health*, 60(2), 126–133. 10.1080/07448481.2011.60839322316409

Khaldoun, M. A., Nasir, A. M., & Le Navenec, C. (2014). Mental Health among Undergraduate University Students: A Background Paper for Administrators, Educators and Healthcare Providers. *Universal Journal of Public Health*, 2(8), 209–214.

Khan, A. A., Jacobson, K. C., Gardner, C. O., Prescott, C. A., & Kendler, K. S. (2005). Personality and comorbidity of common psychiatric disorders. *The British Journal of Psychiatry*, 186(3), 190–196. 10.1192/bjp.186.3.19015738498

Kiarie-Makara, M., & Ndegwa, J. (2020). Factors Related to Depression among University Students in Nairobi County, Kenya. *International Journal of Humanities and Social Science*, 7, 35–41.

Kigaru, D. M., Loechl, C. U., Moleah, T., Macharia-Mutie, C. W., & Ndung'u, Z. W. (2016). Nutrition knowledge, attitude and practices among urban primary school children in Nairobi City, Kenya: A KAP study. *BMC Nutrition*, 2(1), 44–56. 10.1186/s40795-015-0040-8

Kim, H. K., Pears, K. C., Fisher, P. A., Connelly, C. D., & Landsverk, J. A. (2010). Trajectories of maternal harsh parenting in the first 3 years of life. *Child Abuse & Neglect*, 34(12), 897–906. 10.1016/j.chiabu.2010.06.00221030081

Kim, H., Batten, J. A., & Ryu, D. (2020). Financial crisis, bank diversification, and financial stability: OECD countries. *International Review of Economics & Finance*, 65, 94–104. 10.1016/j.iref.2019.08.009

Kim, L. S., Sandler, I. N., & Tein, J.-Y. (1997).. . *Journal of Abnormal Child Psychology*, 25(2), 145–155. 10.1023/A:10257835130769109031

Kim, S. C., Sloan, C., Montejano, A., & Quiban, C. (2021). Impacts of coping mechanisms on nursing students' mental health during COVID-19 lockdown: A cross-sectional survey. *Nursing Reports*, 11(1), 36–44. 10.3390/nursrep1101000434968310

Kim, Y., Saunders, G. R. B., Giannelis, A., Willoughby, E. A., DeYoung, C. G., & Lee, J. J. (2023). Genetic and neural bases of the neuroticism general factor. *Biological Psychology*, 184, 108692. 10.1016/j.biopsycho.2023.10869237783279

King, A., Velez, W., & Hu, S. (2018). African American and Hispanic student engagement at minority-serving and predominantly White institutions. *The Journal of Higher Education*, 89(5), 792–819.

Kirmayer, L. J., & Ryder, A. G. (2016). Culture and psychopathology. *Current Opinion in Psychology*, 8, 143–148. 10.1016/j.copsyc.2015.10.02029506790

Kiss, O., Alzueta, E., Yuksel, D., Pohl, K. M., de Zambotti, M., Müller-Oehring, E. M., Prouty, D., Durley, I., Pelham, W. E.III, McCabe, C. J., Gonzalez, M. R., Brown, S. A., Wade, N. E., Marshall, A. T., Sowell, E. R., Breslin, F. J., Lisdahl, K. M., Dick, A. S., Sheth, C. S., & Baker, F. C. (2022). The Pandemic's Toll on Young Adolescents: Prevention and Intervention Targets to Preserve Their Mental Health. *The Journal of Adolescent Health*, 70(3), 387–395. 10.1016/j.jadohealth.2021.11.02335090817

Klaczynski, P. A., & Daniel, D. B. (2005). Individual differences in conditional reasoning: A dual-process account. *Thinking & Reasoning*, 11(4), 305–325. 10.1080/13546780442000196

Klainin-Yobas, P., Ramirez, D., Fernandez, Z., Sarmiento, J., Thanoi, W., Ignacio, J., & Lau, Y. (2016). Examining the Predicting Effect of Mindfulness on Psychological Well-Being among Undergraduate Students: A Structural Equation Modelling Approach. Personal. [CrossRef]. *Personality and Individual Differences*, 91, 63–68. 10.1016/j.paid.2015.11.034

Klein, A. (2010). *Incoming college students rate emotional health at record low, annual survey finds*. Higher Education Research Institute.

Klein, M. C., Ciotoli, C., & Chung, H. (2011). Primary care screening of depression and treatment engagement in a university health center: A retrospective analysis. *Journal of American College Health*, 59(4), 289–295. 10.1080/07448481.2010.5 0372421308589

Klingenberg, B., Guloksuz, S., Pries, L., Cinar, O., Menne-Lothmann, C., Decoster, J., van Winkel, R., Collip, D., Delespaul, P., De Hert, M., Derom, C., Thiery, E., Jacobs, N., Wichers, M., Lin, B. D., Luykx, J., van Os, J., & Rutten, B. (2023). Gene–environment interaction study on the polygenic risk score for neuroticism, childhood adversity, and parental bonding. *Personality Neuroscience*, 6, E5. 10.1017/pen.2023.238107775

Kloos, H., Hillenbach, M., & Weidauer, S. (2010). Stress and coping among German university students. *European Journal of Psychology of Education*, 25(3), 351–369.

Kohli, S., Batra, P., & Aggarwal, H. K. (2011). Anxiety, locus of control, and coping strategies among end-stage renal disease patients undergoing maintenance hemodialysis. *Indian Journal of Nephrology*, 21(3), 177–181. 10.4103/0971-4065.8372921886977

Kondo, A., Abuliezi, R., Naruse, K., Oki, T., Niitsu, K., & Ezeonwu, M. C. (2021). Perceived control, preventative health behaviors, and the mental health of nursing students during the COVID-19 pandemic: A cross-sectional study. *Inquiry*, 58, 00469580211060279. 10.1177/0046958021106027934915745

Korhonen, J., Axelin, A., Stein, J. D., Seedat, S., Mwape, L., Jansen, R., Groen, G., Grobler, G., & Jörns-Presentati, A. J., Katajisto & Lahti, M. (2022). Mental health literacy among primary healthcare workers in South Africa and Zambia. *Brain and Behaviour Journal.*, 12(12), 1–2.

Kornør, H., & Nordvik, H. (2007). Five-factor model personality traits in opioid dependence. *BMC Psychiatry*, 7(1), 37. 10.1186/1471-244X-7-3717683593

Koss, K. J., & Gunnar, M. R. (2017). Annual Research Review: Early adversity, the hypothalamic–pituitary–adrenocortical axis, and child psychopathology. *Journal of Child Psychology and Psychiatry, and Allied Disciplines*, 59(4), 327–346. 10.1111/jcpp.1278428714126

Kothari, C. R. (2009). *Research methods: methods and methods.* (2nd revision. Ed.). New Age International Publishers.

Kuczynski, L., & Kochanska, G. (1990). Development of children's noncompliance strategies from toddlerhood to age 5. *Developmental Psychology*, 26(3), 398–408. 10.1037/0012-1649.26.3.398

Kuh, G. D. (2009). *High-impact educational practices: what they are, why they are important, and how to begin.* Association of American Colleges and Universities.

Kuh, G. D. (2009). What student affairs professionals need to know about student engagement. *Journal of College Student Development*, 50(6), 683–706. 10.1353/csd.0.0099

Kulkarni, V. S., Kulkarni, V. S., Imai, K. S., & Gaiha, R. (2022). Change in Subjective Well-Being, Affluence and Trust in Politicians. *Change*, 3, 30–2022.

Kulshreshtha, A., Raju, S., Muktineni, S. M., & Chatterjee, D. (2023). Income shock and financial well-being in the COVID-19 pandemic: Financial resilience and psychological resilience as mediators. *International Journal of Bank Marketing*, 41(5), 1037–1058. 10.1108/IJBM-08-2022-0342

Kumari, A., & Verma, J. (2015). Impact of social networking sites on social interaction-a study of college students. *Journal of the Humanities and Social Sciences*, 4(2), 55–62.

Kumar, V., & Nanda, P. (2020). Social media as a tool in higher education: A pedagogical perspective. In *Handbook of research on diverse teaching strategies for the technology-rich classroom* (pp. 239–253). IGI Global. 10.4018/978-1-7998-0238-9.ch016

Kurlowicz, D. H., Ebert, D. D., Berman, M. I., & Geary, L. (2017). Mental health peer support groups: Characteristics and benefits for participants. *Community Mental Health Journal*, 53(1), 70–78.

Kuss, D. J., & Griffiths, M. D. (2011). Online social networking and addiction—A review of the psychological literature. *International Journal of Environmental Research and Public Health*, 8(9), 3528–3552. 10.3390/ijerph8093528 22016701

Kwaah, C. Y., & Essilfie, G. (2017). Stress and coping stra-tegies among distance education students at theUniversity of Cape Coast, Ghana. *Turkish Online Journal of Distance Education*, 18(3), 120–134. 10.17718/tojde.328942

Kwiatkowska, W., & Wiśniewska-Nogaj, L. (2022). Digital Skills and Online Collaborative Learning: The Study Report. *Electronic Journal of e-Learning*, 20(5), 510–522. 10.34190/ejel.20.5.2412

Labrague, L. J. (2021). Resilience as a mediator in the relationship between stress-associated with the Covid-19 pandemic, life satisfaction, and psychological well-being in student nurses: A cross-sectional study. *Nurse Education in Practice*, 56, 103182. 10.1016/j.nepr.2021.103182 34508944

Labrague, L. J. (2022). Specific coping styles and its relationship with psychological distress, anxiety, mental health, and psychological well-being among student nurses during the second wave of the COVID-19 pandemic. *Perspectives in Psychiatric Care*, 58(4), 2707–2714. 10.1111/ppc.13111 35582787

Labrague, L. J. (2024). Umbrella Review: Stress Levels, Sources of Stress, and Coping Mechanisms among Student Nurses. *Nursing Reports*, 14(1), 362–375. 10.3390/nursrep14010028 38391073

Labrague, L. J., McEnroe-Petitte, D. M., Gloe, D., Thomas, L., Papathanasiou, I. V., & Tsaras, K. (2017). A literature review on stress and coping strategies in nursing students. *Journal of Mental Health (Abingdon, England)*, 26(5), 471–480. 10.1080/09638237.2016.1244721 27960598

Lachman, M. E. (2006). Perceived Control Over Aging-Related Declines. *Current Directions in Psychological Science*, 15(6), 282–286. 10.1111/j.1467-8721.2006.00453.x

Ladd, G. W. (2006). Peer Rejection, Aggressive or Withdrawn Behavior, and Psychological Maladjustment from Ages 5 to 12: An Examination of Four Predictive Models. *Child Development*, 77(4), 822–846. 10.1111/j.1467-8624.2006.00905.x16942492

Lades, L. K., Laffan, K., Daly, M., & Delaney, L. (2020). Daily emotional well-being during the COVID-19 pandemic. *British Journal of Health Psychology*, 25(4), 902–911. 10.1111/bjhp.1245032573074

Ladson-Billings, G. (2021). I'm Here for the Hard Re-Set: Post Pandemic Pedagogy to Preserve Our Culture. *Equity & Excellence in Education*, 54(1), 68–78. 10.1080/10665684.2020.1863883

Lagarde, M. (1996). El género, la perspectiva de género. Em Género y feminismo. *Desarrollo humano y democracia* (pp. 13–38). Madrid: horas y HORAS.

Landers-Potts, M. A., Wickrama, K. A. S., Simons, L. G., Cutrona, C., Gibbons, F. X., Simons, R. L., & Conger, R. (2015). An Extension and Moderational Analysis of the Family Stress Model Focusing on African American Adolescents. *Family Relations*, 64(2), 233–248. 10.1111/fare.12117

Lanz, M., Sorgente, A., & Danes, S. M. (2020). Implicit family financial socialization and emerging adults' financial well-being: A multi-informant approach. *Emerging Adulthood*, 8(6), 443–452. 10.1177/2167696819876752

Larsen, L., Helland, M. S., & Holt, T. (2021). The impact of school closure and social isolation on children in vulnerable families during COVID-19: A focus on children's reactions. *European Child & Adolescent Psychiatry*, 31(8), 1–11. 10.1007/s00787-021-01758-x33770275

Larson, L. M., & Daniels, J. A. (1998). Review of the counseling self-efficacy literature. *The Counseling Psychologist*, 26(2), 179–218. 10.1177/0011000098262001

Lazarus, R. S. (1966). Psychological stress and the coping process. (1st ed). New York: McGraw-Hill.

Lazarus, R. S., & Cohen, J. B. (1977). Environmental Stress. In Altman & Wohlwill (Eds.) *Human Behavior and Environment*. New York: Plenum Press. 10.1007/978-1-4684-0808-9_3

Lazarus, R. S., & Folkman, S. (1984). Stress, appraisal, and coping. (1st ed). New York: Springer.

Leary, M. R., & Hoyle, R. H. (Eds.). (2009). *Handbook of individual differences in social behavior*. The Guilford Press.

Lee, H., Masuda, T., Ishii, K., Yasuda, Y., & Ohtsubo, Y. (2023). Cultural Differences in the Perception of Daily Stress Between European Canadian and Japanese Undergraduate Students. *Personality and Social Psychology Bulletin*, 49(4), 571–584. 10.1177/01461672211070360352l6544

Lefcourt, H. M. (1981). Research with the Locus of Control Construct. In *Elsevier eBooks*. 10.1016/C2013-0-11068-9

Lempinen, L., Junttila, N., & Sourander, A. (2017). Loneliness and friendships among eight-year-old children: Time-trends over a 24-year period. *Journal of Child Psychology and Psychiatry, and Allied Disciplines*, 59(2), 171–179. 10.1111/jcpp.1280728892142

Lessard, A., Fortin, L., Butler-Kisber, L., & Marcotte, D. (2014). Analysing the discourse of dropouts and resilient students. *The Journal of Educational Research*, 107(2), 103–110. 10.1080/00220671.2012.753857

Levenson, H. (1981). Differentiating among internality, powerful others, and chance. In Lefcourt, H. M. (Ed.), *Research with the locus of control construct* (Vol. 1, pp. 15–63). Academic Press. 10.1016/B978-0-12-443201-7.50006-3

Li, B., Zhang, K., Wu, Y., & Hao, Z. (2022). Interpersonal Relationship Stress Brings on Social Networking Sites Addiction Among Chinese Undergraduate Students. *Frontiers in Psychology*, 13, 905971. 10.3389/fpsyg.2022.90597135814166

Libby, B. (1987). *Understanding and managing stress in the academic world*. ERIC Clearinghouse on Counseling and Personnel Services Ann Arbor, MI. http://www.ericdigests.org/pre-927/stress.htm

Li, D., Zou, L., Zhang, Z., Zhang, P., Zhang, J., Fu, W., Mao, J., & Cao, S. (2021). The psychological effect of COVID-19 on home-quarantined nursing students in China. *Frontiers in Psychiatry*, 12, 652296. 10.3389/fpsyt.2021.65229633897502

Lifshin, U., Kleinerman, I. B., Shaver, P. R., & Mikulincer, M. (2019). Teachers' attachment orientations and children's school adjustment: Evidence from a longitudinal study of first graders. *Journal of Social and Personal Relationships*, 37(2), 559–580. 10.1177/0265407519874881

Lim, M. H., Rodebaugh, T. L., Zyphur, M. J., & Gleeson, J. F. M. (2016). Loneliness over time: The crucial role of social anxiety. *Journal of Abnormal Psychology*, 125(5), 620–630. 10.1037/abn000016227124713

Linker, J., Gillespie, N. A., Maes, H., Eaves, L., & Silberg, J. L. (2012). Suicidal ideation, depression, and conduct disorder in a sample of adolescent and young adult twins. *Suicide & Life-Threatening Behavior*, 42(4), 426–436. 10.1111/j.1943-278X.2012.00101.x22646517

Lippold, M. A., Glatz, T., Fosco, G. M., & Feinberg, M. E. (2017). Parental Perceived Control and Social Support: Linkages to Change in Parenting Behaviors During Early Adolescence. *Family Process*, 57(2), 432–447. 10.1111/famp.1228328271492

Lipson, S. K., Lattie, E. G., & Eisenberg, D. (2018). Increased rates of mental health service utilization by U.S. college students: 10-year population-level trends (2007–2017). *Psychiatric Services (Washington, D.C.)*, 70(1), 60–63. 10.1176/appi.ps.20180033230394183

Liu, Y. (2012). The Relation between Neuroticism and Life Satisfaction: The Chain Type Mediating Effect of Affect and Self-Esteem. *J. Psychol. Sci.*, 35, 1254.

Liverpool, S., Moinuddin, M., Aithal, S., Owen, M., Bracegirdle, K., & Caravotta, M. (2023). Mental health and wellbeing of further and higher education students returning to face-to- face learning after Covid-19 restrictions. *PLoS One*, 18(1), e0280689.

Li, Z. S., & Hasson, F. (2020). Resilience, stress, and psychological well-being in nursing students: A systematic review. *Nurse Education Today*, 90, 104440. 10.1016/j.nedt.2020.10444032353643

Locke, E. A., & Latham, G. P. (2002). *Setting goals and managing oneself are keys to developing effective motivation*. Prentice Hall.

Logan-Greene, P., & Semanchin Jones, A. (2015). Chronic neglect and aggression/delinquency: A longitudinal examination. *Child Abuse & Neglect*, 45, 9–20. 10.1016/j.chiabu.2015.04.00325910418

Logel, C., Oreopoulos, P., & Petronijevic, U. (2021). *Experiences and coping strategies of college students during the COVID-19 pandemic* (No. w28803). National Bureau of Economic Research.

Longworth, C., Deakins, J., Rose, D., & Gracey, F. (2016). The nature of self-esteem and its relationship to anxiety and depression in adults with acquired brain injuries. *Neuropsychological Rehabilitation*, 1–17.27580356

Lordan, R., Prior, S., Hennessy, E., Naik, A., Ghosh, S., Paschos, G. K., Skarke, C., Barekat, K., Hollingsworth, T., Juska, S., Mazaleuskaya, L. L., Teegarden, S., Glascock, A. L., Anderson, S., Meng, H., Tang, S. Y., Weljie, A., Bottalico, L., Ricciotti, E., & Grosser, T. (2021). Considerations for the Safe Operation of Schools During the Coronavirus Pandemic. *Frontiers in Public Health*, 9(December), 1–15. 10.3389/fpubh.2021.75145134976917

Löwe, B., Decker, O., Müller, S., Brähler, E., Schellberg, D., Herzog, W., & Herzberg, P. Y. (2008). Validation and standardization of the generalized anxiety disorder screener (GAD-7) in the general population.. *Medical Care*, 46(3), 266–274. 10.1097/MLR.0b013e318160d09318388841

Luescher, T. M., Schreiber, B., & Moja, T. (2018). Towards student well-being and quality services in student affairs in Africa. *Journal of Student Affairs in Africa*, 6(2). 10.24085/jsaa.v6i2.3317

Lugo, J. M., & Gil-Rivas, V. M. (2019). *The positive psychology of student engagement: A framework for fostering student growth and achievement.* SAGE Publications.

Luo, M., Hao, M., Li, X., Liao, J., Wu, M., & Wang, Q. (2024). Prevalence of Depressive Tendencies among College Students and the Influence of Attributional Styles on Depressive Tendencies in the Post-Pandemic Era. *Frontiers in Public Health*, 12.

Lupien, S. J., McEwen, B. S., Gunnar, M. R., & Heim, C. (2009). Effects of stress throughout the lifespan on the brain, behaviour and cognition. *Nature Reviews. Neuroscience*, 10(6), 434–445. 10.1038/nrn263919401723

Lusardi, A. (2012). *Numeracy, financial literacy, and financial decision-making* (No. w17821). National Bureau of Economic Research.

Lusardi, A., & Mitchell, O. S. (2014). The economic importance of financial literacy: Theory and evidence. *Journal of Economic Literature*, 52(1), 5–44. 10.1257/jel.52.1.528579637

Lusk, B. (2010). Digital natives and social media behaviors: An Overview. *Prevention Researcher*, 17, 3–6.

Luszczynska, A., Gutiérrez-Doña, B., & Schwarzer, R. (2005). General self-efficacy in various domains of human functioning: Evidence from five countries. *International Journal of Psychology*, 40(2), 80–89. 10.1080/00207590444000041

Luszczynska, A., Scholz, U., & Schwarzer, R. (2005). The general self-efficacy scale: Multicultural validation studies. *The Journal of Psychology*, 139(5), 439–457. 10.3200/JRLP.139.5.439-45716285214

Lu, W., Bian, Q., Song, Y., Ren, J., Xu, X., & Zhao, M. (2015). Prevalence and related risk factors of anxiety and depression among Chinese college freshmen. *Journal of Huazhong University of Science and Technology. Medical Sciences*, 35(6), 815–822. 10.1007/s11596-015-1512-426670430

Lynn, R., & Martin, T. (1997). Gender differences in extraversion, neuroticism, and psychoticism in 37 nations. *The Journal of Social Psychology*, 137(3), 369–373. 10.1080/002245497095954479200973

Lyons, A. C., & Yilmazer, T. (2005). Health and financial strain: Evidence from the survey of consumer finances. *Southern Economic Journal*, 71(4), 873–890.

Lyons, K., Magsayo, M., & Maheshwari, R. (2023). Loneliness & College Students: A Needs Assessment Regarding Georgetown Student Experiences in a Post-Virtual World. *Georgetown Scientific Research Journal*, 3(2), 41–49. 10.48091/gsr.v3i2.70

Maboe, K. A., & Tomas, N. (2023). Online Assessments and COVID-19: A Qualitative Study of Undergraduate Nursing Students in Southern Africa. *International Journal of Africa Nursing Sciences*, 100590, 100590. 10.1016/j.ijans.2023.100590

Mabrouk, A., Mbithi, G., Chongwo, E., Too, E., Sarki, A., Namuguzi, M., Atukwatse, J., Ssewanyana, D., & Abubakar, A. (2022). Mental health interventions for adolescents in sub-Saharan Africa: A scoping review. *Frontiers in Psychiatry*, 13, 937723. 10.3389/fpsyt.2022.937723

Maccoby, E. E. (1984). Socialization and Developmental Change. *Child Development*, 55(2), 317. 10.2307/1129945

Maddux, J. E. (2016). *Self-efficacy. Interpersonal and intrapersonal expectancies*. Routledge.

Maes, S. D., De Mol, J., & Buysse, A. (2011). Children's experiences and meaning construction on parental divorce: A focus group study. *Childhood*, 19(2), 266–279. 10.1177/0907568211421220

Magembe, K. S. (2018). *Exploring Academic Difficulties Facing First-Year Undergraduate Students at the Institute of Adult Education, Tanzania*. Institute of Adult Education.

Ma, L., Fu, T., Qi, J., Gao, X., Zhang, W., Li, X., Cao, S., & Gao, C. (2011). Study on cross-cultural adaptation and health status in medical international students. *Chin J Med Edu Res.*, 11, 1379–1382.

Malagodi, F., Dommett, E., Findon, J. & Gardner, B. (2024). Physical activity interventions to improve mental health and wellbeing in university students in the UK: A service mapping study. JO - Mental Health and Physical Activity. VL - 26 SP – 100563.DO - 10.1016/j.mhpa.2023.100563

Mali, D., & Lim, H. (2021). How do students perceive face-to-face/blended learning as a result of the Covid-19 pandemic? *International Journal of Management Education*, 19(3), 100552. 10.1016/j.ijme.2021.100552

Mallinckrodt, B. (1988). Student retention, social support, and dropout intention: Comparison of black and white students. *Journal of College Student Development*, 29(1), 60–64.

Malone, K., Stewart, S. D., Wilson, J., & Korsching, P. F. (2010). Perceptions of financial well-being among American women in diverse families. *Journal of Family and Economic Issues*, 31(1), 63–81. 10.1007/s10834-009-9176-5

Manoranjitham, S. D., Rajkumar, A. P., Thangadurai, P., Prasad, J., Jayakaran, R., & Jacob, K. S. (2010). Risk factors for suicide in rural south India. *The British Journal of Psychiatry*, 196(1), 26–30. 10.1192/bjp.bp.108.06334720044655

Manoranjitham, S., Charles, H., & Saravanan, B. (2007). Perceptions about suicide: A qualitative study from southern India. *The National Medical Journal of India*, 20(2), 176–179. 18085122

Manzar, M. D., Salahuddin, M., Pandi-Perumal, S. R., & Bahammam, A. S. (2021). Insomnia may mediate the relationship between stress and anxiety: A cross-sectional study in university students. *Nature and Science of Sleep*, 13, 31–38. 10.2147/NSS.S27898833447116

Margaryan, A., Littlejohn, A., & Vojt, G. (2011). Are digital natives a myth or reality? University students' use of digital technologies. *Computers & Education*, 56(2), 429–440. 10.1016/j.compedu.2010.09.004

Margrove, K. L., Gustowska, M., & Grove, L. S. (2014). Provision of support for psychological distress by university staff, and receptiveness to mental health training. *Journal of Further and Higher Education*, 38(1), 90–106. 10.1080/0309877X.2012.699518

Mariani, R., Renzi, A., Di Trani, M., Trabucchi, G., Danskin, K., & Tambelli, R. (2020). The impact of coping strategies and perceived family support on depressive and anxious symptomatology during the coronavirus pandemic (COVID-19) lockdown. *Frontiers in Psychiatry*, 11, 587724. 10.3389/fpsyt.2020.58772433281647

Mark, D. (2018). Addicted to Social Media? What can we do about it problematic, excessive use? *Psychology Today*.https://www.psychologytoday.com/us/blog/in-xcess/201805/addicted-social-media

Martin, A., & Oliva J, C. (2001). *Teaching children about money: applications of social learning and cognitive learning developmental theories*. Research Gate.

Martínez-Jiménez, M. (2023). Parental nonemployment in childhood and children's health later in life. *Economics and Human Biology*, 49, 101241. 10.1016/j.ehb.2023.10124137068451

Martin, J. L., & Yeung, K. (2006). Persistence of close personal ties over a 12-year period. *Social Networks*, 28(4), 331–362. 10.1016/j.socnet.2005.07.008

Martin, P., Tian, E., Kumar, S., & Lizarondo, L. (2022). A rapid review of the impact of COVID-19 on clinical supervision practices of healthcare workers and students in healthcare settings. *Journal of Advanced Nursing*, 78(11), 3531–3539. 10.1111/jan.1536035841328

Martuccelli, D. (2014). La vulnérabilité, un nouveau paradigme? In *Axelle Brodiez, Christian Laval, Bertrand Ravon. Vulnérabilités sanitaires et sociales*. Presses Universitaires de Rennes.

Masarik, A. S., & Conger, R. D. (2017). Stress and child development: A review of the Family Stress Model. *Current Opinion in Psychology*, 13(13), 85–90. 10.1016/j.copsyc.2016.05.00828813301

Mashreky, S. R., Rahman, F., & Rahman, A. (2013). Suicide kills more than 10,000 people every year in Bangladesh. *Archives of Suicide Research*, 17(4), 387–396. 10.1080/13811118.2013.80180924224672

Maskill, C., Hodges, I., McClellan, V., & Collings, S. (2005). *Explaining patterns of suicide: A selective review of studies examining social, economic, cultural and other population-level influences*. Ministry of Health. https://citeseerx.ist.psu.edu/document?repid=rep1&type=pdf&doi=a860ae0d819a6302b110d58d749fec82948ce7b5

Maslow, A. H. (1954). The instinctoid nature of basic needs. *Journal of Personality*, 22(3), 326–347. 10.1111/j.1467-6494.1954.tb01136.x13143464

Masten, A. S. (2001). Ordinary magic: Resilience processes in development. *The American Psychologist*, 56(3), 227–238. 10.1037/0003-066X.56.3.22711315249

Masuku, S., & Ndhlovu, L. (2017). Faculty Mentorship and Student Success: A Case Study. *The Journal of Higher Education*, 25(1), 112–125.

Mattanah, J. F., Lopez, F. G., & Govern, J. M. (2011). The contributions of parental attachment bonds to college student development and adjustment: A meta-analytic review. *Journal of Counseling Psychology*, 58(4), 565–596. 10.1037/a002463521823789

Maykrantz S.A & Houghton, J,D. (2018). Self-leadership and stress among college students: Examining the moderating role of coping skills. *Journal of American College Health, 68.*

McCloud, T. (2018). Fin*ancial stress and mental health among higher education students in the UK up to 2018: rapid review of evidence Epidemiol Community Health.* NIH.

McCloud, T., & Bann, D. (2019). Financial stress and mental health among higher education students in the UK up to 2018: Rapid review of evidence. *Journal of Epidemiology and Community Health*, 73(10), 977–984. 10.1136/jech-2019-21215431406015

McClun, L. A., & Merrell, K. W. (1998). Relationship of perceived parenting styles, locus of control orientation, and self-concept among junior high age students. *Psychology in the Schools*, 35(4), 381–390. 10.1002/(SICI)1520-6807(199810)35:4<381::AID-PITS9>3.0.CO;2-S

McCuaig Edge, H. J., & Ivey, G. W. (2012). Mediation of cognitive appraisal on combat exposure and psychological distress. *Military Psychology*, 24(1), 71–85. 10.1080/08995605.2012.642292

Mckeown, R. E., Garrison, C. Z., Cuffe, S. P., Waller, J. L., Jackson, K. L., & Addy, C. L. (1998). Incidence and predictors of suicidal behaviors in a longitudinal sample of young adolescents. *Journal of the American Academy of Child and Adolescent Psychiatry*, 37(6), 612–619. 10.1097/00004583-199806000-000119628081

Mechanic, D. (1978). *Students under stress: A study in the social psychology of adaptation.* University of Wisconsin Press.

Mehl, M. R., Gosling, S. D., & Pennebaker, J. W. (2006). Personality in its natural habitat: Manifestations and implicit folk theories of personality in daily life. *Journal of Personality and Social Psychology*, 90(5), 862–877. 10.1037/0022-3514.90.5.86216737378

Meijer, J. (2007). Correlates of student stress in secondary education. *Educational Research*, 49(1), 21–35. 10.1080/00131880701200708

Melhem, N. M., Keilp, J. G., Porta, G., Oquendo, M. A., Burke, A., Stanley, B., Cooper, T. B., Mann, J. J., & Brent, D. A. (2016). Blunted HPA axis activity in suicide attempters compared to those at high risk for suicidal behavior. Neuropsychopharmacology. *Neuropsychopharmacology*, 41(6), 1447–1456. 10.1038/npp.2015.30926450815

Memiah, P., Wagner, F. A., & Kimathi, R. (2022). Voices from the Youth in Kenya Addressing Mental Health Gaps and Recommendations. *International Journal of Environmental Research and Public Health*, 19(9), 5366.

Mesmar, J., & Badran, A. (2022). The Post-COVID Classroom: Lessons from a Pandemic. In Badran, A., Baydoun, E., & Mesmar, J. (Eds.), *Higher Education in the Arab World: New Priorities in the Post COVID-19 Era* (pp. 11–41). Springer International Publishing. 10.1007/978-3-031-07539-1_2

Michaela, C. (2019). The impact of stress on students in secondary school and higher education. *International Journal of Adolescence and Youth*, 25(1). 10.1080/02673843.2019.1596823

Michaud, A., & Paquin, S. (2002). *Pour un environnement urbain sécuritaire: Guide d'aménagement* (Ville de Montréal). Montréal. https://numerique.banq.qc.ca/patrimoine/details/52327/1985553?docref=QQ1f91Gnud9rN2mw_1M9XA

Miller, E., & Chung, H. A. (2009). Literature Review of Studies of Depression and Treatment Outcomes among U.S. College Students since 1990. *Psychiatric Services (Washington, D.C.)*, 60(9), 1257–1260.

Mill, J. (1988). *L'Utilitarisme, 2*. Flammarion.

Mindra, R., Moya, M., Zuze, L. T., & Kodongo, O. (2017). Financial self-efficacy: A determinant of financial inclusion. *International Journal of Bank Marketing*, 35(3), 338–353. 10.1108/IJBM-05-2016-0065

Ministry of Internal Affairs, National Antidrug Agency. (2019). *Studiul în şcoli privind consumul de alcool, tutun şi droguri ilicite în România – ESPAD 2019*

Mischel, W., & Shoda, Y. (1995). A cognitive-affective system theory of personality: Reconceptualizing situations, dispositions, dynamics, and invariance in personality structure. *Psychological Review*, 102(2), 246–286. 10.1037/0033-295X.102.2.2467740090

Mischel, W., & Shoda, Y. (1998). Reconciling processing dynamics and personality dispositions. *Annual Review of Psychology*, 49(1), 229–258. 10.1146/annurev.psych.49.1.2299496625

Misra, R., & Castillo, L. G. (2004). Academic stress among college students: Comparison of American and international students. *International Journal of Stress Management*, 11(2), 132–148. 10.1037/1072-5245.11.2.132

Misra, R., Crist, M., & Burant, C. J. (2003). Relationships among life stress, social support, academic stressors, and reactions to stressors of international students in the United States. *International Journal of Stress Management*, 10(2), 137–157. 10.1037/1072-5245.10.2.137

Misra, R., & McKean, M. (2000). College student's academic stress and its relation to their anxiety, time management and leisure satisfaction. *American Journal of Health Studies*, 16(1), 41–52.

Misra, R., & McKean, M. (2000). College students' academic stress and its relation to their anxiety, time management, and leisure satisfaction. *American Journal of Health Studies*, 16(1), 41–51.

Misra, R., McKean, M., West, S., & Russo, T. (2000). Academic stress of college students: Comparison of student and faculty perception. *College Student Journal*, 34(2), 236–245.

Mkumbo, D., Otieno, K. O., & Rufyiriza, C. G. (2023). Coping Strategies among First Year Students and its Influence on their Education: A Study of Universities in Arusha Region, Tanzania. *Journal of Research Innovation and Implications in Education*, 7(4), 480–492.

Mohamad, N. E., Sidik, S. M., & Akhtari-Zavare, M. (2021). The Prevalence Risk of Anxiety and its Associated Factors among University Students in Malaysia: A National Cross-Sectional Study. *BMC Public Health*, 21, 438.

Mokhtari, J., Hesam, S., Bagheri, A., & Hosseini, S. (2019). The predictive role of academic stress on students' mental health. *Archives of Iranian Medicine*, 22(11), 633–639.31823628

Montemurro, G., Cherkowski, S., Sulz, L., Loland, D., Saville, E., & Storey, K. E. (2023). Prioritizing well-being in K-12 education: Lessons from a multiple case study of Canadian school districts. *Health Promotion International*, 38(2), daad003. 10.1093/heapro/daad00336857609

Moore, A., Nguyen, A., Rivas, S., & Bany-Mohammed, A. (2021). *A qualitative examination of the impacts of financial stress on college students' well-being: Insights from a large, private institution*. SAGE Publications., 10.1177/20503121211018122

Moore, S. M., Welsh, M. C., & Peterson, E. (2019). History of Childhood Maltreatment: Associations with Aggression and College Outcomes. *Journal of Aggression, Maltreatment & Trauma*, 1–18. 10.1080/10926771.2019.1637989

Moore, Y., Koonce, J., Plunkett, S. W., & Pleskus, L. (2020). Financial information source, knowledge, and practice of college students from diverse backgrounds. *Journal of Financing Counseling & Planning*, 26(1), 63–78.

Moos, R. H. (1993). *Coping response inventory (Youth form)*. Psychological Assessment Resources.

Moreland, A. D., Felton, J. W., Hanson, R. F., Jackson, C., & Dumas, J. E. (2016). The Relation Between Parenting Stress, Locus of Control and Child Outcomes: Predictors of Change in a Parenting Intervention. *Journal of Child and Family Studies*, 25(6), 2046–2054. 10.1007/s10826-016-0370-4

Morin, A. H. (2020). Teacher support and the social classroom environment as predictors of student loneliness. *Social Psychology of Education*, 23(6), 1687–1707. 10.1007/s11218-020-09600-z

Mori, S. (2000). Addressing the mental health concerns of international students. *Journal of Counseling and Development*, 78(2), 137–144. 10.1002/j.1556-6676.2000.tb02571.x

Moscicki, E. (2001). Epidemiology of suicide. In Goldsmith, S. (Ed.), *Risk Factors for Suicide. Summary of a workshop, pp. 1–4*. National Academy Press. https://pubmed.ncbi.nlm.nih.gov/8829423/

Mountain, T. P., Cao, X., Kim, N., & Gutter, M. S. (2020). Millennials' future homeownership and the role of student loan debt. *Family and Consumer Sciences Research Journal*, 49(1), 5–23. 10.1111/fcsr.12374

Moussa, M. T., Lovibond, P., Laube, R., & Megahead, H. A. (2017). Psychometric Properties of an Arabic Version of the Depression Anxiety Stress Scales (DASS). *Research on Social Work Practice*, 27, 375–386.

Mowbray, C. T., Mandiberg, J. M., Stein, C. H., Kopels, S., Curlin, C., Megivern, D., & Collins, K. (2006). Campus mental health services: Recommendations for change. *The American Journal of Orthopsychiatry*, 76(2), 226–237. 10.1037/0002-9432.76.2.22616719642

Moya, E., Larson, L. M., & Stewart, R. C. (2022). Reliability and validity of depression anxiety stress scale (DASS)-21 in screening for common mental disorders among postpartum women in Malawi. *BMC Psychiatry*, 22, 352.

Mthiyane, N., Rapulana, A. M., & Harling, G. (2022). Effect of multi-level interventions on mental health outcomes among adolescents in sub-Saharan Africa: A systematic review. *BMJ (Clinical Research Ed.)*, 13, e066586. 10.1136/bmjopen-2022-066586

Mughal, A. Y., Devadas, J., Ardman, E., Levis, B., Go, V. F., & Gaynes, B. N. (2020). A systematic review of validated screening tools for anxiety disorders and PTSD in low to middle income countries. *BMC Psychiatry*, 20(1), 338. 10.1186/s12888-020-02753-332605551

Muguna, L.N. (2021). *Campus life simplified. A student's guide.* interCEN Books.

Mujahidah, N., Astuti, B., & Nhung, L. (2019). Decreasing academic stress through problem-focused coping strategy for junior high school students. *Psychology, Evaluation, and Technology in Educational Research*, 2(1), 1–9. 10.33292/petier.v2i1.25

Mulyadi, M., Tonapa, S. I., Luneto, S., Lin, W. T., & Lee, B. O. (2021). Prevalence of mental health problems and sleep disturbances in nursing students during the COVID-19 pandemic: A systematic review and meta-analysis. *Nurse Education in Practice*, 57, 103228. 10.1016/j.nepr.2021.10322834653783

Muraskin, L., & Lee, J. (2004). *Raising the graduation rates of low-income college students.* Pell Institute for the Study of Opportunity in Higher Education.

Museus, S. D., Yi, S. K., & Saelua, N. (2011). Racism on college campuses: A historical perspective and critical race theory. In Hilton, A. A. (Ed.), *College and University Leadership: Strategies for Institutional Innovation and Transformation* (pp. 263–282). Information Age Publishing.

Mutinta, G. (2022). Mental distress among university students in the Eastern Cape Province, South Africa. *BMC Psychology*, 10, 204.

Mutiso,, V. N., Ndetei, D.M., Muia, E.N., Musyimi, C., Masake, M., Osborn, T. L., Sourander, A., Weisz, J..R & Mamah, D. (2023). Students Stress Patterns in A Kenyan Socio-Cultural and Economic Context: Toward A Public Health Intervention. *Sci Rep., 11*(1), 580.

Naeemi, S., & Tamam, E. (2017). The relationship between emotional dependence on Facebook and psychological well-being in adolescents aged 13–16. *Child Indicators Research*, 10(4), 1095–1106. 10.1007/s12187-016-9438-3

Nagar, T. (2021, June 28). Coping Strategies for Pandemic Anxiety among High School and College Students. *SSRN*. https://ssrn.com/abstract=3939784, or http://dx.doi.org/10.2139/ssrn.3939784

Najjuka, S. M., Checkwech, G., Olum, R., Ashaba, S., & Kaggwa, M. M. (2021). Depression, anxiety, and stress among Ugandan university students during the COVID-19 lockdown: An online survey. *African Health Sciences*, 21(4), 1533–1543.

Nam, B. H., & Bai, Q. (2023). ChatGPT and its ethical implications for STEM research and higher education: A media discourse analysis. *International Journal of STEM Education*, 10(1), 66. 10.1186/s40594-023-00452-5

Nam, B. H., Marshall, R. C., Tian, X., & Jiang, X. (2023). "Why universities need to actively combat Sinophobia": Chinese overseas students' racially traumatizing experiences in the United States during COVID-19. *British Journal of Guidance & Counselling*, 51(5), 690–704. 10.1080/03069885.2021.1965957

Nandakishor, R. *A Study On The Service Quality Attributes Of Airport Services With Reference To Trivandrum Airport* [Doctoral dissertation, Indian Maritime University].

Nath, Y., Paris, J., Thombs, B., & Kirmayer, L. (2012). Prevalence and social determinants of suicidal behaviours among college youth in India. *The International Journal of Social Psychiatry*, 58(4), 393–399. 10.1177/0020764011401164 21632571

National Alliance for Mental Illness. (2023, April 18). *Different types of therapy*. NAMI. https://www.nami.org/learn-more/treatment

National Crime Records Bureau (NCRB). (1981). *Accidental Deaths and Suicides in India*. New Delhi: Government of India. https://ncrb.gov.in/accidental-deaths-suicides-in-india-year-wise.html?year=1981&keyword=

National Institutes of Health. (n.d.). *Home*. NIH. https://pubmed.ncbi.nlm.nih.gov

Ndegwa, J. (2020). Factors Related to Depression among University Students in Nairobi County, Kenya. *SSRG International Journal of Humanities and Social Science (SSRG-IJHSS)*, 7(2). www.internationaljournalssrg.org

Ndhlovu, L. (2015). Peer Collaboration and Mentorship in Academic Communities. *American Journal of Education*, 18(2), 55–68.

Nevins, C. M., & Sherman, J. (2016). Self-care practices of baccalaureate nursing students. *Journal of Holistic Nursing*, 34(2), 185–192. 10.1177/0898010115596 43226240039

Newcomb, M. D., & Rabow, J. (1999). Gender, Socialization, and Money 1. *Journal of Applied Social Psychology*, 29(4), 852–869. 10.1111/j.1559-1816.1999.tb02029.x

Newland, R. P., Crnic, K. A., Cox, M. J., & Mills-Koonce, W. R. (2013). The family model stress and maternal psychological symptoms: Mediated pathways from economic hardship to parenting. *Journal of Family Psychology*, 27(1), 96–105. 10.1037/a003111223421837

Newman, M.G, Llera, S. J., Erickson, T.M, Przeworski, A. & Castonguay, L.G. (2013). Worry and Generalized Anxiety Disorder: A Review and Theoretical Synthesis of Evidence on Nature, Etiology, Mechanisms, and Treatment. *DSM: Diagnostic and Statistical Manual of Mental Disorders*. APA.

Nguyen, V. C., & Thi, N. L. N. (2020). Financial Security of Vietnamese Businesses and Its Influencing Factors. The Journal of Asian Finance. *Economics and Business*, 7, 75–87.

Niehoff, E., Petersdotter, L., & Freund, P. A. (2017). International sojourn experience and perso ality development: Selection and socialization effects of studying abroad and the Big Five. *Personality and Individual Differences*, 112, 55–61. 10.1016/j.paid.2017.02.043

Nievar, M. A., Moske, A. K., Johnson, D. J., & Chen, Q. (2014). Parenting Practices in Preschool Leading to Later Cognitive Competence: A Family Stress Model. *Early Education and Development*, 25(3), 318–337. 10.1080/10409289.2013.788426

Ni, Y., & Jia, F. (2023). Promoting Positive Social Interactions: Recommendation for a Post-Pandemic School-Based Intervention for Social Anxiety. *Children (Basel, Switzerland)*, 10(3), 1–13. 10.3390/children1003049136980049

Noble, T., McGrath, H., Roffey, S., & Rowling, L. (2008). *A scoping study on student well-being. Department of Education.* Employment & Workplace Relations.

Novianti, R., & Garzia, M. (2020). Parental Engagement in Children's Online Learning During COVID-19 Pandemic. *Journal of Teaching and Learning in Elementary Education (Jtlee)*, 3(2), 117. 10.33578/jtlee.v3i2.7845

Novick, J. M., Bunting, M. F., Engle, R. W., & Dougherty, M. R. (Eds.). (2019). *Cognitive and working memory training: psychological, neurological, and developmental perspectives.* Oxford University Press. 10.1093/oso/9780199974467.001.0001

Nuskiya, A. F. (2017). The impact of social media among the university students empirical study based on the South Eastern University of Sri Lanka. *Journal of Information Systems & Information Technology*, 2(1), 10–19.

Nuttall, P., Newton, E., & King, D. (2015). Building student resilience in higher education: A comprehensive literature review. *Studies in Higher Education*, 40(4), 703–723.

Nyashanu, M., Nuwematsiko, R., Nyashanu, W. & Jidong, D. E. (2020). Lived experiences of stressors and problems of higher education students on teacher education course in the Eastern Highlands of Zimbabwe. *Panafrican medical journal, 36*(289).

Nyayieka, M. A., Nyagwencha, S., & Nzyuko, P. S. (2020). Prevalence of Clinical Depression and Anxiety among Adolescents in Selected Public Secondary Schools in Homabay County, Kenya. *African Journal of Clinical Psychology*, 3(01).

O'Connor, R., & Pirkis, J. (2016). Suicide clusters. In *O'Connor RC, Perkis J, (Edt.), International Handbook of Suicide Prevention* (2nd ed., pp. 758–774). John Wiley & Sons., 10.1002/9781118903223

O'Neal, C. W., Arnold, A. L., Lucier-Greer, M., Wickrama, K., & Bryant, C. M. (2015). Economic pressure and health and weight management behaviors in African American couples: A family stress perspective. *Journal of Health Psychology*, 20(5), 625–637. 10.1177/1359105315579797725903249

O'Reilly, A., Tibbs, M., Booth, A., Doyle, E., McKeague, B., & Moore, J. (2021). A rapid review investigating the potential impact of a pandemic on the mental health of young people aged 12–25 years. *Irish Journal of Psychological Medicine*, 38(3), 192–207. 10.1017/ipm.2020.10632912358

Oberle, E., Ji, X. R., Guhn, M., Schonert-Reichl, K. A., & Gadermann, A. M. (2019). Benefits of extracurricular participation in early adolescence: Associations with peer belonging and mental health. *Journal of Youth and Adolescence*, 48(11), 2255–2270. 10.1007/s10964-019-01110-231440881

Ogundajo, G. O., Adefisoye, A., & Nwaobia, A. N. (2020). Risk Management and Shareholders' Wealth Maximization. *International Journal of Business. Economics and Management*, 7(6), 387–400.

Okoli, J., Arroteia, N. P., & Ogunsade, A. I. (2023). Failure of crisis leadership in a global pandemic: Some reflections on COVID-19 and future recommendations. *Leadership in Health Services*, 36(2), 186–199. 10.1108/LHS-06-2022-006136129236

Olivas, M., & Li, C. (2006). Understanding stressors of international students in higher education: What college counselors and personnel need to know. *Journal of Instructional Psychology*, 32(3), 217–222.

Oman, D., Shapiro, S. L., Thoresen, C. E., & Plante, T. G. (2008). Flinders T. Meditation Lowers Stress and Supports Forgiveness among College Students: A Randomized Controlled Trial. *Journal of American College Health*, 56(5), 569–578. 10.3200/JACH.56.5.569-578

Omar, M., Bahaman, A. H., Lubis, F. A., Ahmad, S. A. S., Ibrahim, F., Aziz, S. N. A., Ismail, F. D., & Tamuri, A. R. B. (2019). Perceived Academic Stress Among Students in Universiti Teknologi Malaysia. *Proceedings of the International Conference on Student and Disable Student Development 2019 (ICoSD 2019)*. Research Gate.

Oner, N., & Le Compte, A. (1983). *Durumluk Surekli Kaygi Envanteri El Kitabi*. Bogazici Universitesi Yayinlari.

Oppong-Boakye, P. K., & Kansanba, R. (2013). An assessment of financial literacy levels among undergraduate business students in Ghana. *Research Journal of Finance and Accounting*, 4(8), 36–49.

Oquaye, M., Owusu, G. M. Y., & Bokpin, G. A. (2022). The antecedents and consequence of financial well-being: A survey of parliamentarians in Ghana. *Review of Behavioral Finance*, 14(1), 68–90. 10.1108/RBF-12-2019-0169

Ormel, J. (2013). *Neuroticism and common mental disorders: meaning and utility of a complex relationship - PubMed*. PubMed. 10.1016/j.cpr.2013.04.003

Ormel, J., VonKorff, M., Jeronimus, B. F., & Riese, H. (2017). Set-point theory and personality development: Reconciliation of a paradox. In Specht, J. (Ed.), *Personality Development across the Lifespan* (pp. 117–137). Elsevier. 10.1016/B978-0-12-804674-6.00009-0

Osborn, T., Venturo-Conerly, K., Gan, J., Rodriguez, M., Alemu, R., Roe, E., Arango, S., Wasil, A., Weisz, J., & Wasanga, C. (2021). Depression and Anxiety Symptoms amongst Kenyan Adolescents: Psychometric Properties, Prevalence, Psychosocial and Socio- Demographic Factors.DO-10.31234/osf.io/ze8tf.ResearchGate-https://www.researchgate.net/publication/348540829

Oseifuah, E. K. (2014). Analysis of the level of financial literacy among South African undergraduate students. *Journal of Economics and Behavioral Studies*, 6(3), 242–250. 10.22610/jebs.v6i3.487

Osher, D., Cantor, P., Berg, J., Steyer, L., Rose, T., & Nolan, E. (2017). *Science of learning and development: A synthesis*. American Institutes for Research.

Othieno, C. J., Okoth, R. O., Peltzer, K., Pengpid, S., & Malla, L. O. (2014). Depression among university students in Kenya. *Prevalence and Socio-demographic Correlates Journal of Affective Disorders*, 165, 120–125.

Otu, A., Charles, C. H., & Yaya, S. (2020). Mental health and psychosocial well-being during the COVID-19 pandemic: The invisible elephant in the room. *International Journal of Mental Health Systems*, 14(1), 38. 10.1186/s13033-020-00371-w32514302

Ouzzani, M., Hammady, H., Fedorowicz, Z., & Elmagarmid, A. (2016). Rayyan—A web and mobile app for systematic reviews. *Systematic Reviews*, 5(1), 1–10. 10.1186/s13643-016-0384-427919275

Owen, M. S., Kavanagh, P. S., & Dollard, M. F. (2018). An integrated model of work-study conflict and facilitation. *Journal of Career Development*, 45(5), 504–517. 10.1177/0894845317720071

Oyebode, O., Pape, U. J., Laverty, A. A., Lee, J. T., Bhan, N., & Millett, C. (2014). Rural, urban and migrant differences in non-communicable disease risk-factors in middle income countries: A cross-sectional study of WHO-SAGE data. *PLoS One*, 9(12), e114010.25849356

Ozer, D. J., & Benet-Martínez, V. (2006). Personality and the prediction of consequential outcomes. *Annual Review of Psychology*, 57(1), 401–421. 10.1146/annurev.psych.57.102904.19012716318601

Ozer, S., & Schwartz, S. J. (2020). Academic motivation, life exploration, and psychological well-being among emerging adults in Denmark. *Nordic Psychology*, 72(3), 199–221.

Pachucki, M. C., Ozer, E. J., Barrat, A., & Cattuto, C. (2015). Mental health and social networks in early adolescence: A dynamic study of objectively-measured social interaction behaviors. *Social Science & Medicine*, 125, 40–50. 10.1016/j.socscimed.2014.04.01524797692

Padykula, B. M. (2016). RN-BS students' reports of their self-care and health promotion practices in a holistic nursing course. *Journal of Holistic Nursing*, 35(3), 221–246. 10.1177/0898010116657226227371293

Palikara, O., Castro-Kemp, S., Gaona, C., & Eirinaki, V. (2021). The mediating role of school belonging in the relationship between socioemotional well-being and loneliness in primary school age children. *Australian Journal of Psychology*, 73(1), 24–34. 10.1080/00049530.2021.1882270

Panahi, S., Yunus, A. S. M., Roslan, S., Jaafar, R. A. K., Jaafar, W. M. W., & Panahi, M. S. (2016). Predictors of psychological well-being among Malaysian graduates. *The European Journal of Social and Behavioural Sciences*, 16(2), 2067–2083. 10.15405/ejsbs.186

Pandey, V. (2017). Students' Suicides in Institutions of Higher Education in India: Risk Factors and Interventions. *International Journal of Social Work and Human Services Practice*, 5(1), 29–34. 10.13189/ijrh.2017.050104

Parker, D. R., Holcomb, L., Brennan, R. T., & Dowden, A. (2017). A comparison of time-management skills between traditional and nontraditional students. *Journal of College Student Retention*, 19(3), 308–322.

Parkhurst, J. T., & Asher, S. R. (1992). Peer rejection in middle school: Subgroup differences in behavior, loneliness, and interpersonal concerns. *Developmental Psychology*, 28(2), 231–241. 10.1037/0012-1649.28.2.231

Park, S. U., & Kim, M. K. (2018). Effects of campus life stress, stress coping type, self-esteem, and maladjustment perfectionism on suicide ideation among college students. *Korean Journal of Clinical Laboratory Science*, 50(1), 63–70. 10.15324/kjcls.2018.50.1.63

Parotta, J. L. M. (1996). *The impact of financial attitudes and knowledge on financial management and satisfaction* [Doctoral dissertation, University of British Columbia].

Parra, A.P., Morris, N.A., & Elliott-Engel, J. (2022). *Lessons for 4-H Youth Member Recruitment and Retention from First-Generation College Students' Literature.*

Pascarella, E. T., & Terenzini, P. T. (2005). *A third decade of studies on the impact of college on students* (Vol. 2). Jossey-Bass.

Pascarella, E. T., & Terenzini, P. T. (2005). *How college affects students: A third decade of research* (Vol. 2). Jossey-Bass.

Pasteels, I., & Bastaits, K. (2020). Loneliness in Children Adapting to Dual Family Life. *Life Course Research and Social Policies*, 195–213. 10.1007/978-3-030-44575-1_10

Patelarou, A., Mechili, E. A., Galanis, P., Zografakis-Sfakianakis, M., Konstantinidis, T., Saliaj, A., Bucaj, J., Alushi, E., Carmona-Torres, J. M., Cobo-Cuenca, A. I., Laredo-Aguilera, J. A., & Patelarou, E. (2021). Nursing students, mental health status during COVID-19 quarantine: Evidence from three European countries. *Journal of Mental Health (Abingdon, England)*, 30(2), 164–169. 10.1080/09638237.2021.187542033504241

Patel, V., Rama, S. C., & Vijayakumar, L. (2012). Suicide mortality in India: A nationally representative survey. *Lancet*, 37(9), 2343–2351. 10.1016/S0140-6736(12)60606-022726517

Peltzer, K., & Pengpid, S. (2017). Alcohol use and health-related quality of life among hospital outpatients in South Africa. *Alcohol, Clinical and Experimental Research*, 41(7), 1304–1312.

Pempek, T. A., Yermolayeva, Y. A., & Calvert, S. L. (2009). College students' social networking experiences on Facebook. *Journal of Applied Developmental Psychology*, 30(3), 227–238. 10.1016/j.appdev.2008.12.010

Peñalver, E. A., & Laborda, J. G. (2021). Online Learning during the Covid-19 Pandemic: How Has This New Situation Affected Students' Oral Communication Skills? *Journal of Language and Education*, 7(4), 30–41. 10.17323/jle.2021.11940

Peplau, H. E. (1955). Loneliness. *The American Journal of Nursing*, 55(12), 1476. 10.2307/346954813268491

Pereira-Morales, A. J., Adan, A., & Forero, D. A. (2019). Perceived stress as a mediator of the relationship between neuroticism and depression and anxiety symptoms. *Current Psychology (New Brunswick, N.J.)*, 38(1), 66–74. 10.1007/s12144-017-9587-7

Perez, B. R., & Bahamon Muneton, M. J. (2023). The socio-emotional dimension in education: A systematic review. *Issues in Educational Research*, 33(1), 307–326. https://search.informit.org/doi/10.3316/informit.173573406487575

Petrescu, C., Băncilă, S. P., Suciu, O., Vlaicu, B., & Doroftei, S. (2004). *Profile psihologice şi comportamente cu risc întâlnite la tineri.* In: *Revista de Igienă şi Sănătate Publică*, 54(3).

Philippas, N. D., & Avdoulas, C. (2020). Financial literacy and fnancial well-being among generation-Z university students: Evidence from Greece. *European Journal of Finance*, 26(4–5), 360–381. 10.1080/1351847X.2019.1701512

Pirkis, J., Mok, K., Robinson, J., & Nordentoft, M. (2016). Media influences on suicidal thoughts and behaviors. In *The International Handbook of Suicide Prevention* (2nd ed., pp. 743–757). John Wiley & Sons, Ltd. 10.1002/9781118903223.ch42

Pisani, A. R., Wyman, P. A., Petrova, M., Schmeelk-Cone, K., Goldston, D. B., Xia, Y., & Gould, M. S. (2013). Emotion regulation difficulties, youth-adult relationships, and suicide attempts among high school students in underserved communities. *Journal of Youth and Adolescence*, 42(6), 807–820. 10.1007/s10964-012-9884-223666604

Popay, J., Roberts, H., Sowden, A., Petticrew, M., Arai, L., Rodgers, M., & Duffy, S. (2006). Guidance on the conduct of narrative synthesis in systematic reviews. *A product from the ESRC methods programme Version,* 1(1), b92.

Pornsakulvanich, V. (2018, January–April). Excessive use of Facebook: The influence of self-monitoring and Facebook usage on social support. *Kasetsart Journal of Social Sciences*, 39(1), 116–121. 10.1016/j.kjss.2017.02.001

Portzky, G., Audenaert, K., & van Heeringen, K. (2005). Suicide among adolescents. A psychological autopsy study of psychiatric, psychosocial and personality-related risk factors. *Social Psychiatry and Psychiatric Epidemiology*, 40(1), 922–930. 10.1007/s00127-005-0977-x16217594

Pratt, M., & Crum, J. (2020, September 14). A sense of belonging begins with self-acceptance. *Harvard Business Review*. https://hbr.org/2022/08/a-sense-of-belonging-starts-with-self-acceptance

Preacher, K. J., & Hayes, A. F. (2008). Asymptotic and resampling strategies for assessing and comparing indirect effects in multiple mediator models. *Behavior Research Methods*, 40(3), 879–891. 10.3758/BRM.40.3.87918697684

Preacher, K. J., Rucker, D. D., & Hayes, A. F. (2007). Addressing moderated mediation hypotheses: Theory, methods, and prescriptions. *Multivariate Behavioral Research*, 42(1), 185–227. 10.1080/0027317070134131626821081

Pressley, M., & McCormick, C. B. (1995). *Cognition, teaching, and assessment*. Longman.

Preti, E., Di Mattei, V., Perego, G., Ferrari, F., Mazzetti, M., Taranto, P., Di Pierro, R., Madeddu, F., & Calati, R. (2020). The psychological impact of epidemic and pandemic outbreaks on healthcare workers: Rapid review of the evidence. *Current Psychiatry Reports*, 22(8), 1–22. 10.1007/s11920-020-01166-z32651717

Price, E. L., Mcleod, P. J., Gleich, S. S., & Hand, D. (2006). One-Year Prevalence Rates of Major Depressive Disorder in First-Year University Students. *Canadian Journal of Counselling*, 40, 68–81.

Prinsloo, P., & Slade, S. (2016). Student vulnerability, agency, and learning analytics: An exploration. *Journal of Learning Analytics*, 3(1), 159–182. 10.18608/jla.2016.31.10

Pritchard, C. (1996). Suicide in the People's Republic of China categorized by age and gender: Evidence of the influence of culture on suicide. *Acta Psychiatrica Scandinavica*, 93(5), 362–367. https://onlinelibrary.wiley.com/doi/abs/10.1111/j.1600-0447.1996.tb10661.x. 10.1111/j.1600-0447.1996.tb10661.x8792906

Prowse, R., Sherratt, F., Abizaid, A., Gabrys, R. L., Hellemans, K. G. C., Patterson, Z. R., & McQuaid, R. J. (2021). Coping With the COVID-19 Pandemic: Examining Gender Differences in Stress and Mental Health Among University Students. *Frontiers in Psychiatry*, 12(April), 1–11. 10.3389/fpsyt.2021.65075933897499

Pullman, L. (2022). *Landscape, Well-being, and Connection: A Qualitative Study of Community College Students' Perception of Campus Atributes*. [PhD Dissertation, California State University].

Punt, C. (2019). *Urbanismo feminista: Por una transformación radical de los espacios de vida*. Bilbao: Virus.

Putnick, D. L., Bornstein, M. H., Lansford, J. E., Chang, L., Deater-Deckard, K., Di Giunta, L., Gurdal, S., Dodge, K. A., Malone, P. S., Oburu, P. O., Pastorelli, C., Skinner, A. T., Sorbring, E., Tapanya, S., Tirado, L. M. U., Zelli, A., Alampay, L. P., Al-Hassan, S. M., Bacchini, D., & Bombi, A. S. (2012). Agreement in Mother and Father Acceptance-Rejection, Warmth, and Hostility/Rejection/ Neglect of Children Across Nine Countries. *Cross-Cultural Research*, 46(3), 191–223. 10.11 77/1069397112440093123024576

Quadt, L., Esposito, G., Critchley, H. D., & Garfinkel, S. N. (2020). Brain-body interactions underlying the association of loneliness with mental and physical health. *Neuroscience and Biobehavioral Reviews*, 116, 283–300. 10.1016/j.neubiorev.2020.06.01532610178

Quincho, F. S., Rodríguez Galán, D. B., Farfán Pimentel, J. F., Yolanda Josefina, H. F., Arenas, R. D., Crispín, R. L., & Navarro, E. R. (2021). Academic Stress in University Students: Systematic Review. *Ilkogretim Online, 20*(5).

Raburu, P. A. (2011). *Women academic careers in kemnya*. [Thesis, Lancaster University, United Kingdom].

Radhakrishnan, R., & Andrade, C. (2012). Suicide: An Indian perspective. *Indian Journal of Psychiatry*, 54(4), 30–41. 10.4103/0019-5545.104793233372232

Rajasekar, D. (2013). Impact of academic stress among the management students of AMET University-an analysis. *AMET J Manag.*, 5, 32–39.

Ramachandiran, M., & Dhanapal, S. (2018). Academic Stress Among University Students: A Quantitative Study of Generation Y and Z's Perception. *Pertanika Journal of Social Science & Humanities*, 26(3), 2115–2128.

Rampal, N. (2020). More than 90,000 young adults died by suicide in 2019 in India: NCRB report. *India Today*. https://www.indiatoday.in/diu/story/ncrb-report-data-india-young-adults-suicide-2019-india-1717887-2020-09-02

Rapanta, C., Botturi, L., Goodyear, P., Guàrdia, L., & Koole, M. (2021). Balancing Technology, Pedagogy and the New Normal: Post-pandemic Challenges for Higher Education. *Postdigital Science and Education*, 3(3), 715–742. 10.1007/s42438-021-00249-1

Rasheed, N., Fatima, I., & Tariq, O. (2022). University students' mental well-being during COVID-19 pandemic: The mediating role of resilience between meaning in life and mental well-being. *Acta Psychologica*, 227, 103618. 10.1016/j.actpsy.2022.10361835588627

Rashid, T. (2009). Positive interventions in clinical practice. *Journal of Clinical Psychology*, 65(5), 461–466. 10.1002/jclp.2058819294745

Rathakrishnan, B., Singh, S. S. B., & Yahaya, A. (2022). Perceived Social Support, Coping Strategies and Psychological Distress among University Students during the COVID-19 Pandemic: An Exploration Study for Social Sustainability in Sabah, Malaysia. *Sustainability (Basel)*, 14(6), 3250. 10.3390/su14063250

Ratten, V. (2023). The post COVID-19 pandemic era: Changes in teaching and learning methods for management educators. *International Journal of Management Education*, 21(2), 100777. 10.1016/j.ijme.2023.100777

Razavi, S. A., Shahrabi, A., & Siamian, H. (2017). The relationship between research anxiety and self-efficacy. *Materia Socio-Medica*, 29(4), 247–250. 10.5455/msm.2017.29.247-25029284993

Reddy, J. K., Menon, K. R., & Thattil, A. (2018). Academic stress and its sources among university students. *Biomedical & Pharmacology Journal*, 11(1).

Reddy, K. J., & Karishmarajanmenon, M. S. (2018). Academic Stress and its Sources among University Students. *Biomedical & Pharmacology Journal*, 11(1), 531–537. 10.13005/bpj/1404

Reeves, M., & Deimler, M. (2012). Adaptability: The new competitive advantage. *Own the Future: 50 Ways to Win from the Boston Consulting Group*, (pp. 19-26). Boston Consulting Group.

Regzedmaa, E., Ganbat, M., Sambuunyam, M., Tsogoo, S., Radnaa, O., Lkhagvasuren, N., & Zuunnast, K. A. (2024). A systematic review and meta-analysis of neuroticism and anxiety during the COVID-19 pandemic. *Frontiers in Psychiatry*, 14(1), 1281268. 10.3389/fpsyt.2023.128126838250262

Renwick, L., Pedley, R., & Johnson, I. (2022). Mental health literacy in children and adolescents in low- and middle-income countries: A Mixed Studies Systematic Review and Narrative Synthesis. *European Child & Adolescent Psychiatry*. 022-01997-610.1007/s00787-

Republic of Kenya. (2016). *2017/18-2019/20 Education Sector Report*. Government Printers.

Retterstol, N. (1993). *Suicide: A European perspective*. Cambridge University Press. https://onlinelibrary.wiley.com/doi/abs/10.1111/j.1943-278X.1997.tb00509.x

Reverté-Villarroya, S., Ortega, L., Lavedán, A., Masot, O., Burjalés-Martí, M. D., Ballester-Ferrando, D., Fuentes-Pumarola, C., & Botigué, T. (2021). The influence of COVID-19 on the mental health of final-year nursing students: Comparing the situation before and during the pandemic. *International Journal of Mental Health Nursing*, 30(3), 694–702. 10.1111/inm.1282733393201

Reyers, M. (2016). The role of financial literacy and advice in financial decision making. *Southern African Business Review*, 20, 388–413. 10.25159/1998-8125/6057

Richardson, M., Nishikawa, H., & Romero, D. (2012). Financial stress and academic achievement of urban high school students. *The Journal of Educational Research*, 105(4), 290–309.

Richter, J., & Prawitz, A. D. (2010). Attitudes of college students toward credit cards: a comparison of credit card user types. *Proceedings of the Eastern Family Economics and Resource Management Association*. Research Gate.

Riitsalu, L., & Murakas, R. (2019). Subjective financial knowledge, prudent behaviour and income: The predictors of financial well-being in Estonia. *International Journal of Bank Marketing*, 37(4), 934–950. 10.1108/IJBM-03-2018-0071

Rintaugu, E.G., Litaba, S.A., Muema, E.M. & Monyeki, M.A. (2014). Sources of stress and coping strategies of Kenyan university athletes: Implications for coaches. *African Journal for Physical, Health Education, Recreation and Dance, 20*(2), 1621-1636.

Robbins, A., Kaye, E., & Catling, J. C. (2018). Predictors of student resilience in higher education. *Psychology Teaching Review*, 24(1), 44–52. 10.53841/bpsptr.2018.24.1.44

Roberts, A. J., & Styron, R. A. (2018). Faculty grading practices: The role of gender and perceived student characteristics. *Teaching in Higher Education*, 23(3), 273–292.

Roberts, B. W. (2009). Back to the future: Personality and Assessment and personality development. *Journal of Research in Personality*, 43(2), 137–145. 10.1016/j.jrp.2008.12.01520161194

Roberts, B. W., & Mroczek, D. (2008). Personality trait change in adulthood. *Current Directions in Psychological Science*, 17(1), 31–35. 10.1111/j.1467-8721.2008.00543.x19756219

Roberts, B. W., Walton, K. E., & Viechtbauer, W. (2006). Patterns of mean-level change in personality traits across the life course: A meta-analysis of longitudinal studies. *Psychological Bulletin*, 132(1), 1–25. 10.1037/0033-2909.132.1.116435954

Robertson, I., & Cooper, C. L. (2013). Resilience. *Stress and Health*, 29(3), 175–176. 10.1002/smi.251223913839

Robotham, D. (2008). Stress among higher education students: Towards a research agenda. *Higher Education*, 56(6), 735–746. 10.1007/s10734-008-9137-1

Robotham, D., & Julian, C. (2006). Stress and the higher education student: A critical review of the literature. *Journal of Further and Higher Education*, 30(2), 107–117. 10.1080/03098770600617513

Rockwell, D. (2022). *First-generation College Students' Stress: A Targeted Intervention*. University of California at San Diego.

Rogers, K. D., Young, A., Lovell, K., Campbell, M., Scott, P. R., & Kendal, S. (2013). The British sign language versions of the patient health questionnaire, the generalized anxiety disorder 7-item scale, and the work and social adjustment scale. *Journal of Deaf Studies and Deaf Education*, 18(1), 110–122. 10.1093/deafed/ens04023197315

Rohner, R. P. (2014). Parental Power and Prestige Moderate the Relationship Between Perceived Parental Acceptance and Offspring's Psychological Adjustment. *Cross-Cultural Research*, 48(3), 197–213. 10.1177/1069397114528295

Rohner, R. P., & Rohner, E. C. (1980). Antecedents and consequences of parental rejection: A theory of emotional abuse. *Child Abuse & Neglect*, 4(3), 189–198. 10.1016/0145-2134(80)90007-1

Romeo, M., Yepes-Baldó, M., Soria, M. Á., & Jayme, M. (2021). Impact of the COVID-19 pandemic on higher education: Characterizing the psychosocial context of the positive and negative affective states using classification and regression trees. *Frontiers in Psychology*, 12, 714397. 10.3389/fpsyg.2021.71439734539516

Romero-Blanco, C., Rodríguez-Almagro, J., Onieva-Zafra, M. D., Parra-Fernández, M. L., Prado-Laguna, M. D. C., & Hernández-Martínez, A. (2020). Sleep pattern changes in nursing students during the COVID-19 lockdown. *International Journal of Environmental Research and Public Health*, 17(14), 5222. 10.3390/ijerph1714522232698343

Roper, S. W., Fife, S. T., & Seedall, R. B. (2019). The Intergenerational Effects of Parental Divorce on Young Adult Relationships. *Journal of Divorce & Remarriage*, 61(4), 1–18. 10.1080/10502556.2019.1699372

Rosado, S., & Ribeiro, J. (2016). A matemática na formação de arquitectos e urbanistas. *Encontro Nacional da SPM*. ResearchGate. https://www.researchgate.net/publication/320866022_A_MATEMATICA_NA_FORMACAO_DE_ARQUITECTOS_E_URBANISTAS

Rosado, S., & Ribeiro, J. T. (2024a). Outdoor Work as an ICT Tool for Teaching and Learning Maths in Lisbon School of Architecture, University of Lisbon. *EDULEARN24 Proceedings* (pp. 1742-1748). IATED Digital Library. 10.21125/edulearn.2024

Rosado, S., & Ribeiro, J. T. (2024b). *Ask New and Challenging Questions Towards Reasoning Skills: Active Approaches in Higher Education. Transdisciplinary Approaches to Learning Outcomes in Higher Education*. IRMA-International.

Rosen, M. L., Rodman, A. M., Kasparek, S. W., Mayes, M., Freeman, M. M., Lengua, L. J., Meltzoff, A. N., & McLaughlin, K. A. (2021). Promoting youth mental health during the COVID-19 pandemic: A longitudinal study. *PLoS One*, 16(8), e0255294. 10.1371/journal.pone.025529434379656

Ross, S., & Heath, N. L. (2003). Two models of adolescent self-mutilation. *Suicide & Life-Threatening Behavior*, 33(1), 277–287. 10.1521/suli.33.3.277.2321814582838

Ross, S., Niebling, B., & Heckart, T. (1999). Sources of stress among college students. *College Student Journal*, 32(2), 312–318.

Rotter, J. B. (1954). *Social learning and clinical psychology*. Prentice-Hall, Inc., 10.1037/10788-000

Rottschaufer, W. A. (1991). Some Philosophical Implications of Bandura's Cognitive Theory of Human Agency. *The American Psychologist*, 46(2), 153–155. 10.1037/0003-066X.46.153

Rubin, K. H. & Bukowski, W. M. (2011). *Handbook of peer interactions, relationships, and groups*. Guilford.

Rubin, K. H., Burgess, K. B., & Hastings, P. D. (2002). Stability and Social-Behavioral Consequences of Toddlers' Inhibited Temperament and Parenting Behaviors. *Child Development*, 73(2), 483–495. 10.1111/1467-8624.0041911949904

Rubin, K. H., & Chronis-Tuscano, A. (2021). Perspectives on Social Withdrawal in Childhood: Past, Present, and Prospects. *Child Development Perspectives*, 15(3), 160–167. 10.1111/cdep.1241734434251

Rubin, K. H., Coplan, R. J., & Bowker, J. C. (2009). Social Withdrawal in Childhood. *Annual Review of Psychology*, 60(1), 141–171. 10.1146/annurev.psych.60.110707.16364218851686

Ruff, L. (2021). *Examining the Experiences of Social Belonging and Campus Integration for Parenting Undergraduates* [Doctoral dissertation at Capella University].

Ruiz, M. A., Zamorano, E., Garcia-Campayo, J., Pardo, A., Freire, O., & Rejas, J. (2011). Validity of the GAD-7 scale as an outcome measure of disability in patients with generalized anxiety disorders in primary care. *Journal of Affective Disorders*, 128(3), 277–286. 10.1016/j.jad.2010.07.01020692043

Ryan, T., Chester, A., Reece, J., & Xenos, S. J. (2014). The uses and abuses of Facebook: A review of Facebook addiction. *Journal of Behavioral Addictions*, 3(3), 133–148. 10.1556/JBA.3.2014.01625317337

Ryder, R., Okan, O., & Scott, L. (2020). A balancing act: Exploring university student mental health in the UK. *Journal of Further and Higher Education*, 44(2), 239–253.

Ryff, C. D. (2023). *A new direction in mental health: purposeful life engagement. Encyclopedia of Mental Health* (3rd ed.), 629–637. Elsevier. 10.1016/B978-0-323-91497-0.00096-5

Sabri, M., Wijekoon, R., & Rahim, H. (2020). The influence of money attitude, financial practices, self-efficacy and emotion coping on employees' financial well-being. *Management Science Letters*, 10(4), 889–900. 10.5267/j.msl.2019.10.007

Safta, C. G., & Suditu, M. (2022) The transition to the academic environment: between difficulties and coping strategies. In: *Journal of Educational Sciences and Psychology, 11*(73). 10.51865/JESP.2022.2.03

Saha, S. R., & Guha, A. K. (2019). Impact of social media use of university students. *International Journal of Statistics and Applications*, 9(1), 36–43. 10.5923/j.statistics.20190901.05

Sahi, S. K. (2017). Psychological biases of individual investors and financial satisfaction. *Journal of Consumer Behaviour*, 16(6), 511–535. 10.1002/cb.1644

Sahi, S. K., & Dutta, V. K. (2015). Perceived attitudes towards sudden wealth: An exploratory study. *International Journal of Indian Culture and Business Management*, 11(2), 245–274. 10.1504/IJICBM.2015.071309

Salas-Pilco, S. Z. (2022). The Impact of COVID-19 on Latin American STEM Higher Education: A Systematic Review. *2022 IEEE World Engineering Education Conference (EDUNINE)*, (pp. 1–6). IEEE. https://doi.org/10.1109/EDUNINE53672.2022.9782354

Saldaña, D., Goula, J., Cardona, H., & Amat, C. (2017). *El patio de la escuela en igualdad: Guía de diagnosis e intervención con perspectiva de género*. Barcelona. https://equalsaree.org/es/mediateca/

Saleh, D., Camart, N., & Romo, L. (2017). Predictors of Stress in College Students. *Frontiers in Psychology*, 8, 19. 10.3389/fpsyg.2017.0001928179889

Samsudeen, S. N., & Kaldeen, M. (2015). Adoption of Social Media Marketing By Tourism Product Suppliers: A Study in Eastern Province Of Sri Lanka. *European Journal of Business and Management*, 448–455.

Samuel, D., & Sher, L. (2013). Suicidal behavior in Indian adolescents. *International Journal of Adolescent Medicine and Health*, 25(3), 207–212. 10.1515/ijamh-2013-005424006319

Sani, M., Mahfouz, M. S., Bani, I., Alsomily, A. H., Alagi, D., Alsomily, N., & Asiri, S. (2012). Prevalence of stress among medical students in Jizan University, Kingdom of SaudiArabia. *Gulf Medical Journal*, 1(1), 19–25.

Sapolsky, R. M. (2015). Stress and the brain: Individual variability and the inverted-U. *Nature Neuroscience*, 18(10), 1344–1346. 10.1038/nn.410926404708

Sarason, I. G. (2004). Stress, anxiety, and cognitive interference: Reactions to tests. *Journal of Personality and Social Psychology*, 46(4), 929–938. 10.1037/0022-3514.46.4.9296737201

Sarveswar, S., & Thomas, J. (2020). Academic distress and student suicides in India: A crisis that needs to be acknowledged. *The Wire*. https://thewire.in/rights/academic-distress-and-student-suicides-in-india

Sato, Y. (2019). Model-free reinforcement learning for financial portfolios: a brief survey. *arXiv preprint arXiv:1904.04973*.

Sato, S. N., Condes Moreno, E., Rubio-Zarapuz, A., Dalamitros, A. A., Yañez-Sepulveda, R., Tornero-Aguilera, J. F., & Clemente-Suárez, V. J. (2024). Navigating the New Normal: Adapting Online and Distance Learning in the Post-Pandemic Era. *Education Sciences*, 14(1), 19. 10.3390/educsci14010019

Savitsky, B., Findling, Y., Ereli, A., & Hendel, T. (2020). Anxiety and coping strategies among nursing students during the covid-19 pandemic. *Nurse Education in Practice*, 46, 102809. 10.1016/j.nepr.2020.10280932679465

Sax, L. J. (1997). Health trends among college freshmen. *Journal of American College Health*, 45(6), 252–262. 10.1080/07448481.1997.99368959164055

Scherbaum, C. A., Cohen-Charash, Y., & Kern, M. J. (2006). Measuring general self-efficacy: A comparison of three measures using item response theory. *Educational and Psychological Measurement*, 66(6), 1047–1063. 10.1177/0013164406288171

Scherer, S., Pestian, J., & Morency, L. P. (2013). *Investigating the speech characteristics of suicidal adolescents. 2013 IEEE International Conference on Acoustics, Speech and Signal Processing*, Vancouver, BC, Canada. 10.1109/ICASSP.2013.6637740

Schermerhorn, A. C., & Mark Cummings, E. (2008). Transactional Family Dynamics: A New Framework for Conceptualizing Family Influence Processes. *Advances in Child Development and Behavior*, 36, 187–250. 10.1016/S0065-2407(08)00005-018808044

Schlosser, C., & Long, J. (1998). Influences on becoming a student: Can our universities be more supportive? *Journal of College Student Development*, 39(2), 171–187.

Schlosser, L. Z., & Groesz, L. M. (2019). Campus safety and student well-being: Perceptions, experiences, and meaning-making among Black students. *Journal of College Student Development*, 60(4), 457–473.

Schmid, R., & Petko, D. (2019). Does the use of educational technology in personalized learning environments correlate with self-reported digital skills and beliefs of secondary-school students? *Computers & Education*, 136(1), 75–86. 10.1016/j.compedu.2019.03.006

Schütte, S., Chastang, J. F., Parent-Thirion, A., Vermeylen, G., & Niedhammer, I. (2014). Social inequalities in psychological well-being: A European comparison. *Community Mental Health Journal*, 50(8), 987–990. 10.100710597-014-9725-8 PMID:24664367

Sciarrino, N. A. (2018). *Understanding Child Neglect: Biopsychosocial Perspectives*. Springer International Publishing.

Seedat, S., Stein, D., Jackson, P., Heeringa, S., Williams, D., & Myer, L. (2009). Life stress and mental disorders in the South African stress and health study. *South African Medical Journal*, 99(5), 375–382.

Seedhom, A. E., Kamel, E. G., Mohammed, E. S., & Raof, N. R. (2019). Predictors of perceived stress among medical and nonmedical college students, Minia, Egypt. *International Journal of Preventive Medicine*, 10(1), 107. 10.4103/ijpvm.IJPVM_6_1831360354

Seeman, T. E. (1996). Social ties and health: The benefits of social integration. *Annals of Epidemiology*, 6(5), 442–451. 10.1016/S1047-2797(96)00095-68915476

Seligman, M. E. (2011). Flourish: A visionary new understanding of happiness and well-being. New York, États-Unis: Free Press.

Seligman, M. E. P., Rashid, T., & Parks, A. C. (2006). Positive psychotherapy. *The American Psychologist*, 61(8), 774–788. 10.1037/0003-066X.61.8.77417115810

Seligman, M. E., & Csikszentmihalyi, M. (2014). Positive psychology: An Introduction. In Csikszentmihalyi, M. (Ed.), *Flow and the foundations of positive psychology* (pp. 279–298). Springer.

Senapati, R. E., Jena, S., Parida, J., Panda, A., Patra, P. K., Pati, S., Kaur, H., & Acharya, S. K. (2024). The patterns, trends and major risk factors of suicide among Indian adolescents – a scoping review. *BMC Psychiatry*, 24(35), 23–32. 10.1186/s12888-023-05447-838195413

Sepanik, S., & Brown, K. T. (2021). *School-Community Partnerships*. ERIC. https://files.eric.ed.gov/fulltext/ED616007.pdf

Serrano-Ripoll, M. J., Meneses-Echavez, J. F., Ricci-Cabello, I., Fraile-Navarro, D., Fiol-deRoque, M. A., Pastor-Moreno, G., Castro, A., Ruiz-Pérez, I., Zamanillo Campos, R., & Gonçalves-Bradley, D. C. (2020). Impact of viral epidemic outbreaks on mental health of healthcare workers: A rapid systematic review and meta-analysis. *Journal of Affective Disorders*, 277, 347–357. 10.1016/j.jad.2020.08.03432861835

Sevilla, A., Phimister, A., Krutikova, S., Kraftman, L., Farquharson, C., Costa Dias, M., Cattan, S., & Andrew, A. (2020). *How are mothers and fathers balancing work and family under lockdown?* IFS. 10.1920/BN.IFS.2020.BN0290

Shaban, I. A., Khater, W. A., & Akhu-Zaheya, L. M. (2012). Undergraduate nursing students' stress sources and coping behaviours during their initial period of clinical training: A Jordanian perspective. *Nurse Education in Practice*, 12(4), 204–209. 10.1016/j.nepr.2012.01.00522281123

Shabir, G., Yousef Hameed, Y. M., & Safdar, G. (2014). The impact of social media on youth. A Case Study of Bahawalpur City. *Asian Journal of Social Sciences & Humanities*, 3(4), 23–34.

Shaffer, D., Fisher, P., Hicks, R. H., Parides, M., & Gould, M. (1995). Sexual orientation in adolescents who commit suicide. Suicide Life Threat Bahaviour, 25(1), 64-71 https://pubmed.ncbi.nlm.nih.gov/8553430/

Shange, N. (2018). *Experiences of students facing financial difficulties to access Higher Education in the case of the University of KwaZulu-Natal* [Thesis, University of KwaZulu-Natal].

Shankar, N., Vinod, S., & Kamath, R. (2022). Financial well-being–A Generation Z perspective using a Structural Equation Modeling approach. *Investment Management and Financial Innovations*, 19(1), 32–50. 10.21511/imfi.19(1).2022.03

Sharaievska, I., McAnirlin, O., Browning, M. H. E. M., Larson, L. R., Mullenbach, L., Rigolon, A., D'Antonio, A., Cloutier, S., Thomsen, J., Metcalf, E. C., & Reigner, N. (2022). "Messy transitions": Students' perspectives on the impacts of the COVID-19 pandemic on higher education. *Higher Education*, 2022(April), 1–18. 10.1007/s10734-022-00843-735463941

Shdaifat, E., Jamama, A., & Al-Amer, M. (2018). Stress and Coping Strategies Among Nursing Students. *Global Journal of Health Science, 10*(5).

Shim, S., Xiao, J. J., Barber, B. L., & Lyons, A. C. (2009). Pathways to life success: A conceptual model of financial well-being for young adults. *Journal of Applied Developmental Psychology*, 30(6), 708–723. 10.1016/j.appdev.2009.02.003

Shi, W. (2019). Health information seeking versus avoiding: How do college students respond to stress-related information? *American Journal of Health Behavior*, 43(2), 437–448. 10.5993/AJHB.43.2.1830808481

Shortell, T. (2001). *An introduction to data analysis & presentation*. CUNY. http://academic.brooklyn.cuny.edu/soc/courses/712/chap18.Html

Shynkar, S., Gontar, Z., Dubyna, M., Nasypaiko, D., & Fleychuk, M. (2020). Assessment of Economic Security of Enterprises: Theoretical and Methodological Aspects. *Business: Theory and Practice*, 21(1), 261–271. 10.3846/btp.2020.11573

Siappo, C. L. G., Núñez, Y. R., & Cabral, I. E. (2016). Nursing students' experiences with self-care during the training process at a private university in Chimbote, Peru. *Escola Anna Nery*, 20(1), 17–24. 10.5935/1414-8145.20160003

Siegel, A. A., Zarb, M., Alshaigy, B., Blanchard, J., Crick, T., Glassey, R., Hott, J. R., Latulipe, C., Riedesel, C., & Senapathi, M., Simon, & Williams, D. (2021). Teaching through a Global Pandemic: Educational Landscapes Before, during and after COVID-19. *Annual Conference on Innovation and Technology in Computer Science Education, ITiCSE*, (pp. 1–25). ACM. 10.1145/3502870.3506565

Simons, J., Beaumont, K., & Holland, L. (2018). What factors promote student resilience in a level 1 distance learning module? *Open Learning*, 33(1), 4–17. 10.1080/02680513.2017.1415140

Singelis, T. M., Triandis, H. C., Bhawuk, D. P. S., & Gelfand, M. J. (1995). Horizontal and vertical dimensions of individualism and collectivism: A theoretical and measurement refinement. [Google Scholar]. *Cross-Cultural Research*, 29(3), 240–275. 10.1177/106939719502900302

Singh, R. K. (2022). Financial literacy among youth! 96% of parents feel their children lack money management knowledge; Survey. *The Logical Indian*. https://thelogicalindian.com/trending/survey-finds-96-parents-feel-their-children-lack-money-management-knowledge-37150

Singh, J., Steele, K., & Singh, L. (2021). Combining the Best of Online and Face-to-Face Learning: Hybrid and Blended Learning Approach for COVID-19, Post Vaccine, & Post-Pandemic World. *Journal of Educational Technology Systems*, 50(2), 140–171. 10.1177/00472395211047865

Singh, K. N., & Malik, S. (2022). *An empirical analysis on household fnancial vulnerability in India: exploring the role of fnancial knowledge, impulsivity and money management skills.* Manag Financ. 10.1108/MF-08-2021-0386

Singh, S. G., & Singh, K. (2011). Counseling services have an important role in student academic performance. International *Journal of Educational Methodology. Research for Development*, 2(2), 99–104.

Siu, O. L., Lu, C. Q., & Spector, P. E. (2007). Employees' well-being in greater China: The direct and moderating effects of general self-efficacy. *Applied Psychology*, 56(2), 288–301. 10.1111/j.1464-0597.2006.00255.x

Skeens, M. A., Hill, K., Olsavsky, A., Ralph, J. E., Udaipuria, S., Akard, T. F., & Gerhardt, C. A. (2023). Family functioning buffers the consequences of the COVID-19 pandemic for children's quality of life and loneliness. *Frontiers in Psychology*, 13, 1079848. 10.3389/fpsyg.2022.107984836710839

Škreblin Kirbiš, I., Vehovec, M., & Galić, Z. (2017). Relationship between financial satisfaction and financial literacy: Exploring gender differences. *Društvena istraživanja: časopis za opća društvena pitanja, 26*(2), 165-185.

Sleeman, J., & Lang, C. E. D. (2020). View of Social media, learning and connections for international students: The disconnect between what students use and the tools learning management systems offer. *Australasian Journal of Educational Technology, 36*(4), 44–56. https://ajet.org.au/index.php/AJET/article/view/4384/1624

Sloboda, J. A. (1990). Combating examination stress among university students: Action research in an institutional context. *British Journal of Guidance & Counselling*, 18(2), 124–136. 10.1080/03069889008253567

Smith, B., & Lim, M. (2020). How the COVID-19 pandemic is focusing attention on loneliness and social isolation. *Public Health Research & Practice*, 30(2). 10.17061/phrp302200832601651

Smith, C. A., & Lipson, S. K. (2019). Impact of mental health disparities on academic outcomes in college students. *Journal of College Student Psychotherapy*, 33(2), 91–108.

Smith, J., Jones, A., & Johnson, B. (2014). Cooperative learning: Improving university instruction by basing practice on validated theory. *Journal on Excellence in College Teaching*, 25(3&4), 85–118.

Smith, K. E., Graf, E., Faig, K. E., Dimitroff, S. J., Rockwood, F., Hernandez, M. W., & Norman, G. J. (2023). Perceived control, loneliness, early-life stress, and parents' perceptions of stress. *Scientific Reports*, 13(1), 13037. 10.1038/s41598-023-39572-x37563259

Sokolova, L. (2024). *Mental health literacy and seeking for professional help among secondary school students in Slovakia: A brief report.* Front. Public Health. Sec. *Public Mental Health.*, 12(10). 10.3389/fpubh.1333216

Son, C., Hegde, S., Smith, A., Wang, X., & Sasangohar, F. (2020). Effects of COVID-19 on college students' mental health in the United States: Interview survey study. *Journal of Medical Internet Research*, 22(9), e21279. 10.2196/2127932805704

Sonnentag, S., & Fritz, C. (2005). Social support and stress reactivity in everyday life: 936–952 review and theoretical model. *Journal of Personality and Social Psychology*, 8936–95236-952.

Sonnentag, S., Arbeus, H., Mahn, C., & Fritz, C. (2014). Exhaustion and lack of psychological detachment from work during off-job time: Moderator effects of time pressure and leisure experiences. *Journal of Occupational Health Psychology*, 19(2), 206–216. 10.1037/a003576024635737

Soria, K. M., Horgos, B., & Puzziferro, M. (2013). The perceived impact of college student employment on academic achievement. *Journal of Student Affairs Research and Practice*, 50(4), 398–416.

Soulet, M. H. (2005). Reconsidérer la vulnérabilité. In *Empan 2005/4* (no 60). Éditions Érès https://www.cairn.info/revue-empan-2005-4-page-24.htm

Spielberger, C. D., Gorsuch, R. L., Lushene, R., Vagg, P. R., & Jacobs, G. A. (1983). *Manual for the State-Trait Anxiety Inventory*. Consulting Psychologists Press.

Spitzer, R. L., Kroenke, K., Williams, J. B. W., & Löwe, B. (2006). A brief measure for assessing generalized anxiety disorder: The GAD-7. *Archives of Internal Medicine*, 166(10), 1092–1097. 10.1001/archinte.166.10.109216717171

Springett, N. R., & Szulecka, T. K. (1986). Faculty differences among undergraduates on arrival at university. *The British Journal of Medical Psychology*, 79(3), 309–320. 10.1111/j.2044-8341.1986.tb02667.x3964588

Stack, S. (1987). Celebrities and Suicide: A Taxonomy and analysis, 1948-1983. *American Sociological Review*, 52(3), 40–51. 10.2307/209535911613886

Stark, M. A., Manning-Walsh, J., & Vliem, S. (2005). Caring for oneself while learning to care for others: A challenge for nursing students. *The Journal of Nursing Education*, 44(6), 266–270. 10.3928/01484834-20050601-0516021803

Stashchuk, O., Vitrenko, A., Kuzmenko, O., Koptieva, H., Tarasova, O., & Dovgan, L. (2020). Comprehensive system of financial and economic security of the enterprise. *International Journal of Management*, 11(5).

Statistics Canada. (2017). *Perceived life stress, by age group*. Statistics Canada. https://www150.statcan.gc.ca/t1/tbl1/en/tv.action?pid=1310009604

Steers, M. N., Wickham, R. E., & Acitelli, L. K. (2014). Seeing everyone else's highlight reels: How Facebook usage is linked to depressive symptoms. *Journal of Social and Clinical Psychology*, 33(8), 701–731. 10.1521/jscp.2014.33.8.701

Stephens, N. M., Fryberg, S. A., Markus, H. R., Johnson, C. S., & Covarrubias, R. (2012). Unseen disadvantage: How American universities' focus on independence undermines the academic performance of first-generation college students. *Journal of Personality and Social Psychology*, 102(6), 1178–1197. 10.1037/a002714322390227

Sterner, A., Hagiwara, M. A., Ramstrand, N., & Palmér, L. (2019). Factors developing nursing students and novice nurses' ability to provide care in acute situations. *Nurse Education in Practice*, 35, 135–140. 10.1016/j.nepr.2019.02.00530818117

Stewart-Brown, S., Evans, J., Patterson, J., Petersen, S., Doll, H., Balding, J., & Regis, D. (2000). The health of students in institutes of higher education: An important and neglected public health problem. *Journal of Public Health Medicine*, 22(4), 492–499. 10.1093/pubmed/22.4.49211192277

Stoian, C. E., Fărca iu, M. A., Dragomir, G. M., & Gherhe , V. (2022). Transition from Online to Face-to-Face Education after COVID-19: The Benefits of Online Education from Students' Perspective. *Sustainability (Basel)*, 14(19), 12812. 10.3390/su141912812

Strayhorn, T. L. (2012). *College students' sense of belonging: A key to educational success for all students*. Routledge. 10.4324/9780203118924

Strine, T. W., Chapman, D. P., Balluz, L. S., Moriarty, D. G., & Mokdad, A. H. Centers for Disease Control and Prevention (CDC). (2008). The associations between life satisfaction and health-related quality of life, chronic illness, and health behaviors among U.S. community-dwelling adults. *Journal of Community Health*, 33(1), 40–50. 10.1007/s10900-007-9066-418080207

Strohschein, L. (2005). Parental Divorce and Child Mental Health Trajectories. *Journal of Marriage and Family*, 67(5), 1286–1300. 10.1111/j.1741-3737.2005.00217.x

Struthers, C. W., Perry, R. P., & Menec, V. H. (2000). An examination of the relationship among academic stress, coping, motivation and performance in college. *Research in Higher Education*, 41(5), 581–592. 10.1023/A:1007094931292

Suditu, M., & Safta, C. G. (2023). Adapting to the Academic Environment: A Prerequisite for Academic Success. In *Handbook of Research on Coping Mechanisms for First-Year Students Transitioning to Higher Education*. IGI Global Publishing.

Sugiati, M., & Isqi, K. (2020). Description of Stress and Its Impact On College Student. College Student Journal, 54(2). link.gale.com/apps/doc/A634682859/AONE?u=anon~78135f9&sid=googleScholar&xid=19ffa26c.

Suicide Data and Statistics. (n.d.). CDC. https://www.cdc.gov/suicide/suicide-data-statistics.html

Sun, A., & Chen, X. (2016). Online education and its effective practice: A research review. *Journal of Information Technology Education*, 15, 157–190. 10.28945/3502

Surtees, P., & Miller, P. M. (1990). The interval general health questionnaire. *The British Journal of Psychiatry*, 157(5), 679–686. 10.1192/bjp.157.5.6792279205

Swain, P. K., Tripathy, M. R., Priyadarshini, S., & Acharya, S. K. (2021). Forecasting suicide rates in India: An empirical exposition. *PLoS One*, 16(7), 1–21. 10.1371/journal.pone.025534234324554

Tackett, J. L., & Lahey, B. B. (2017). Neuroticism. In Widiger, T. A. (Ed.), *The Oxford handbook of the Five Factor Model* (pp. 39–56). Oxford University Press.

Tang, T. L. P. (1995). The development of a short money ethic scale: Attitudes toward money and pay satisfaction revisited. *Personality and Individual Differences*, 19(6), 809–816. 10.1016/S0191-8869(95)00133-6

Tang, T. L. P., & Sutarso, T. (2013). Falling or not falling into temptation? Multiple faces of temptation, monetary intelligence, and unethical intentions across gender. *Journal of Business Ethics*, 116(3), 529–552. 10.1007/s10551-012-1475-3

Tang, T. L. P., Sutarso, T., Ansari, M. A., Lim, V. K. G., Teo, T. S. H., Arias-Galicia, F., Garber, I. E., Chiu, R. K.-K., Charles-Pauvers, B., Luna-Arocas, R., Vlerick, P., Akande, A., Allen, M. W., Al-Zubaidi, A. S., Borg, M. G., Canova, L., Cheng, B.-S., Correia, R., Du, L., & Tang, N. (2018). Monetary intelligence and behavioral economics across 32 cultures: Good apples enjoy good quality of life in good barrels. *Journal of Business Ethics*, 148(4), 893–917. 10.1007/s10551-015-2980-y

Tang, Y. Y., Tang, R., & Gross, J. J. (2019). Promoting psychological well-being through an evidence-based mindfulness program. *Frontiers in Human Neuroscience*, 13(1), 1–5. 10.3389/fnhum.2019.0023731354454

Taniguchi, H., & Kato, T. (2018). The Frequencies and Effects of Interpersonal Stress Coping with Different Types of Interpersonal Stressors in Friendships on Mental Health and Subjective Well-Being among College Students. *The Japanese Journal of Personality*, 27(3), 252–258. 10.2132/personality.27.3.8

Taprial, V., & Kanwar, P. (2012). *Understanding social media*. Bookboon.

Taylor, M. S., & Quinn, J. F. (2015). Does time management training work? An evaluation. *Human Relations*, 68(12), 1885–1907.

TCU. (2022). Guidelines for Online and Blended Delivery Modes of Courses for University Institution in Tanzania. Dar es Salaam Tanzania Commission for Universities.

Terenzini, P. T. (2013). "On the nature of institutional research" revisited: Plus, can change? *Research in Higher Education*, 54(2), 137–148. 10.1007/s11162-012-9274-3

The American College Health Association. (2006). American College Health Association, National College Health Assessment. *Journal of American College Health*, 54(4), 195–206.

Theurel, A., Witt, A., & Shankland, R. (2010). Promoting University Students' Mental Health through an Online Multicomponent Intervention during the COVID-19 Pandemic. *International Journal of Environmental Research and Public Health*, 19, 10442.

Thomas, H. (2010). *Les vulnérables*. Éditions du Croquant.

Thomson, E., Hanson, T. L., & McLanahan, S. S. (1994). Family Structure and Child Well-Being: Economic Resources vs. Parental Behaviors. *Social Forces*, 73(1), 221–242. 10.2307/2579924

Thomson, E., & McLanahan, S. S. (2012). Reflections on "Family Structure and Child Well-Being: Economic Resources vs. Parental Socialization.". *Social Forces*, 91(1), 45–53. 10.1093/sf/sos11923378674

Tinto, V. (2012). *Completing college: Rethinking institutional action*. University of Chicago Press. 10.7208/chicago/9780226804545.001.0001

Tomas, N., Awala-Nashima, A. N., & Tomas, T. N. (2024). Gender Differences in Stress Among Students of Higher Education During the COVID-19 Pandemic: A Textual Narrative Meta-Synthesis. In *Mental Health Crisis in Higher Education* (pp. 209-225). IGI Global. 10.4018/979-8-3693-2833-0.ch012

Tomas, N., & Hausiku, L. (2024). Stress and Coping Strategies Among Nursing Students at the University Campus in Namibia. In *Student Stress in Higher Education* (pp. 91–107). IGI Global. 10.4018/979-8-3693-0708-3.ch006

Tomas, N., Munangatire, T., & Iihuhua, S. N. (2022). Effectiveness of online assessments in higher education during the COVID-19 pandemic: Nursing students' reflections in Namibia. In *Teaching and Learning with Digital Technologies in Higher Education Institutions in Africa* (pp. 106–119). Routledge. 10.4324/9781003264026-9

Tommasi, M., Grassi, P., Balsamo, M., Picconi, L., Furnham, A., & Saggino, A. (2018). Correlations between personality, affective and filial self-efficacy beliefs, and psychological well-being in a sample of Italian adolescents. *Psychological Reports*, 121(1), 59–78. 10.1177/0033294117720698287505 84

Trafimow, D., Clayton, K. D., Sheeran, P., Darwish, A. E., & Brown, J. (2010). How do people form behavioral intentions when others have the power to determine social consequences? *The Journal of General Psychology*, 137(3), 287–309. 10.1080/00221301003645210207 18228

Tran, T. D., Tran, T., & Fisher, J. (2013). *Validation of the depression anxiety stress scales (DASS) 21 as a screening instrument for depression and anxiety in a rural community-based cohort of northern Vietnamese women*. BioMed Central. http://www.biomedcentral.com/1471-244X/13/24

Tricco, A. C., Langlois, E., Straus, S. E., & World Health Organization. (2017). *Rapid reviews to strengthen health policy and systems: A practical guide*. World Health Organization.

Troop-Gordon, W., & Ladd, G. W. (2005). Trajectories of Peer Victimization and Perceptions of the Self and Schoolmates: Precursors to Internalizing and Externalizing Problems. *Child Development*, 76(5), 1072–1091. 10.1111/j.1467-8624.2005.00898.x16150003

Tsitsika, A. K., Tzavela, E. C., Janikian, M., Ólafsson, K., Iordache, A., Schoenmakers, T. M., Tzavara, C., & Richardson, C. (2014). Online social networking in adolescence: Patterns of use in six European countries and links with psychosocial functioning. *The Journal of Adolescent Health*, 55(1), 141–147. 10.1016/j.jadohealth.2013.11.01024618179

Tullio, J., & Mario, P. (2011). Investment in Financial Literacy and Saving Decisions. *Journal of Banking & Finance*, 37, 2779–2792.

Tullius, J. & Beukema, L. (2021). Importance of Mental Literacy in times of Crisis: Adolescent Mental Health during the COVID – 19 pandemic. *European Journal of Public Health*, 31(3), 164.

Tully, L. A., Hawes, D. J., Doyle, F. L., Sawyer, M. G., & Dadds, M. R. (2019). A National Child Mental Health Literacy Initiative is needed to Reduce Childhood Mental Health Disorders. *The Australian and New Zealand Journal of Psychiatry*, 53(4), 286–290.

Turnbull, D., Chugh, R., & Luck, J. (2021). Transitioning to E-Learning during the COVID-19 pandemic: How have Higher Education Institutions responded to the challenge? *Education and Information Technologies*, 26(5), 6401–6419. 10.1007/s10639-021-10633-w34177349

Turner, C. S. V., González, J. C., & Wood, J. L. (2020). Faculty of color in academe: What 20 years of literature tells us. *Journal of Diversity in Higher Education*, 13(2), 107–125.

Turner, P. V. (1986). Campus: An American Planning Tradition. *Landscape Journal*, 5(1), 66–67. 10.3368/lj.5.1.66

Tyrell, J. (2002). Sources of stress among psychology undergraduates. *The Irish Journal of Psychology*, 13(2), 184–192. 10.1080/03033910.1992.10557878

UBIgual. (2011). Plano de Igualdade de Género da UBI, Universidade da Beira Interior. *Projeto UBIgual*. UBIgual. https://eige.europa.eu/sites/default/files/plano_igualdade_genero_da_ubi.pdf

Uddin, R., Burton, N. W., Maple, M., Khan, S. R., & Khan, A. (2019). Suicidal ideation, suicide planning, and suicide attempts among adolescents in 59 low-income and middle-income countries: A population-based study. *The Lancet. Child & Adolescent Health*, 3(4), 223–233. 10.1016/S2352-4642(18)30403-630878117

Uliaszek, A. A., Zinbarg, R. E., Mineka, S., Craske, M. G., Sutton, J. M., Griffith, J. W., Rose, R., Waters, A., & Hammen, C. (2010). The role of neuroticism and extraversion in the stress-anxiety and stress-depression relationships. *Anxiety, Stress, and Coping*, 23(4), 363–381. 10.1080/10615800903377726419890753

Ullah, S., & Yusheng, K. (2020). Financial socialization, childhood experiences and financial well-being: The mediating role of locus of control. *Frontiers in Psychology*, 11, 2162. 10.3389/fpsyg.2020.02162331329444

Umar, N., Sinring, A., Aryani, F., Latif, S., & Harum, A. (2021). Different academic coping strategies facing online learning during Covid-19 pandemic among the students in counselling department. *Indonesian Journal of Educational Studies*, 24(1), 56–63.

UNESCO. (2020, March 4). *Education: From disruption to recovery*. UNESCO. https://en.unesco.org/covid19/educationresponse#durationschoolclosures

UNICEF, WHO, & UNESCO. (2022). *Five essential pillars for promoting and protecting mental health and psychosocial well-being in schools and learning environments*. UNESCO. https://unesdoc.unesco.org/ark:/48223/pf0000384614

Universidade de Trás-os-Montes e Alto Douro. (2016). *Plano Para Igualdade de Género UTAD rima com igualdade*. UTAD. https://www.utad.pt/wp-content/uploads/Plano_Igualdade.pdf

Unni, S. K., & Mani, A. J. (1996). Suicidal ideators in the psychiatric facility of a general hospital - a psycho demographic profile. *Indian Journal of Psychiatry*, 38(2), 79–85. https://pubmed.ncbi.nlm.nih.gov/21584150/21584150

Urban, C., Schmeiser, M., Collins, J. M., & Brown, A. (2020). The effects of high school personal financial education policies on financial behavior. *Economics of Education Review*, 78, 101786. 10.1016/j.econedurev.2018.03.006

Usher, K., Wynaden, D., Bhullar, N., Durkin, J., & Jackson, D. (2020). The mental health impact of COVID-19 on pre-registration nursing students in Australia. *International Journal of Mental Health Nursing*. https://hdl.handle.net/1959.11/31619

Usman, M. (2021). A Study on Impact of Financial Stress on Students' Academics. *Journal of Business & Economic Policy, 6*(1).

Utpal, V. K. J. (2017). A study on the engagement of Indian students on social media. *Journal of Content, Community & Communication, 6*(3).

Vaez, M., & Laflamme, L. (2008). Experienced Stress, Psychological Symptoms, Self-rated Health and Academic Achievement: A Longitudinal Study of Swedish University Students. *Social Behavior and Personality*, 36(2), 183–196.

Valke, M., & Goel, A. (2022). Perceived Parenting Style and It's Relationship to Locus of Control and Emotional Maturity Among Emerging Adults. *International Journal of Indian Psychology*, 10(2). 10.25215/1002.029

Vazquez, C. Hervas, G.R., Rahona, J., & i Gómez, D. (2009). Psychological well-being and health: Contributions from Positive Psychology. *Annu Clin Health Psychol*, 5, 15–27.

Velez, G., & Gaffney, A. M. (2016). Parental support, ethnic identity, and college adjustment among Latino college students. *Journal of College Student Development*, 57(7), 820–836.

Verhagen, M., Derks, M., Roelofs, K., & Maciejewski, D. (2022). Behavioral inhibition, negative parenting, and social withdrawal: Longitudinal associations with loneliness during early, middle, and late adolescence. *Child Development*. 10.1111/cdev.1387436449019

Vettingl, J. R. (2017). *Who pays the price for high neuroticism? Moderators of longitudinal risks for depression and anxiety.* PubMed., 10.1017/S0033291717000253

Victoria, N. (2023). *Students stress patterns in a Kenyan socio-cultural and economic context: toward a public health intervention.* Nature.com. doi:10.1038/s41598-023-27608-1. www.nature.com/scientificreports10.1038/s41598-023-27608-1

Vidal, D. G., Fernandes, C. O., Viterbo, L. M. F., Barros, N., & Maia, R. L. (2020). Espaços Verdes Urbanos e Saúde Mental: uma revisão sistemática da literatura. In *13º Congresso Nacional de Psicologia da Saúde: Melhorar o Bem-Estar Global através da Psicologia da Saúde* (pp.427-436). Covilhã, Portugal

Vijayakumar, L., & Rajkumar, S. (1999). Are risk factors for suicide universal? A case-control study from India. *Acta Psychiatrica Scandinavica*, 99(6), 407–411. 10.1111/j.1600-0447.1999.tb00985.x10408261

Vincent, J., Hagermoser-Ortman, K. E., & Robinson, C. L. (2020). The impact of academic support services on student stress and academic performance: A meta-analysis. *Journal of College Student Development*, 61(3), 326–344. https://www.ncbi.nlm.nih.gov/pmc/articles/PMC8722691/

Visser, M., & Wyk, E. L. (2021). University students' mental health and emotional wellbeing during the COVID-19 pandemic and ensuing lockdown. *South African Journal of Psychology. Suid-Afrikaanse Tydskrif vir Sielkunde*, 51(2), 229–243.

Vohs, K. D., Mead, N. L., & Goode, M. (2006). The psychological consequences of money. *Science*, 314(5802), 1154–1156. 10.1126/science.113249117110581

W. (2011). Psychological Characteristics of Chronic Depression. *The Journal of Clinical Psychiatry,* 72(03), 288–294. 10.4088/JCP.09m05735blu

Wade, M., Prime, H., & Browne, D. T. (2020). Why we need longitudinal mental health research with children and youth during (and after) the COVID-19 pandemic. *Psychiatry Research*, 113143, 113143. 10.1016/j.psychres.2020.11314332502829

Waghachavare, V. B., Dhumale, G. B., Kadam, Y. R., & Gore, A. D. (2013). A study of Stress among Students of Professional Colleges from an Urban Area in India. *Sultan Qaboos University Medical Journal*, 13(3), 429–436.

Wang, Y, Lippke, S, Miao, M & Gan, Y. (2019). Restoring meaning in life by meaning-focused coping: The role of self-distancing. *Psych J,.*8(3), 386-396. . 10.1002/pchj.296

Wang, A. H., Lee, C. T., & Espin, S. (2019). Undergraduate nursing students' experiences of anxiety-producing situations in clinical practicums: A descriptive survey study. *Nurse Education Today*, 76, 103–108. 10.1016/j.nedt.2019.01.01630776531

Wangenge-Ouma, G. (2018). Public by Day, Private by Night: Examining the Private Lives of Kenya's Public Universities. *European Journal of Education*, 47(3).

Wang, Y., & Kong, F. (2014). The role of emotional intelligence in the impact of mindfulness on life satisfaction and mental distress. *Social Indicators Research*, 116(3), 843–852. 10.1007/s11205-013-0327-6

Ward, C., Fischer, R., Lam, F. C., & Hall, L. (2016). The convergent, discriminant, and incremental validity of scores on a self-report measure of acculturation. *International Journal of Intercultural Relations*, 50, 1–12.

Watanabe, N. (2017). A survey of mental health of university students in Japan. *International Medical Journal*, 6(3), 175–179.

Watson, D., Gamez, W., & Simms, L. J. (2005). Basic dimensions of temperament and their relations to anxiety and depression: A symptom-based perspective. *Journal of Research in Personality*, 39(1), 46–66. 10.1016/j.jrp.2004.09.006

Watson, K. R., Astor, R. A., Benbenishty, R., Capp, G., & Kelly, M. S. (2022). Needs of Children and Families during Spring 2020 COVID-19 School Closures: Findings from a National Survey. *Social Work*, 67(1), 17–27. 10.1093/sw/swab05234791495

Wei, C., Karunanithy, D., Khairul, S., Mohan, S. & Kavitha, S. (2022). The prevalence of depression among students in higher education institution: a repeated cross-sectional study. *Journal of Public Mental Health*, 21. DO - .10.1108/JPMH-12-2021-0152

Weisberg, Y. J., DeYoung, C. G., & Hirsh, J. B. (2011b). Gender Differences in Personality across the Ten Aspects of the Big Five. *Frontiers in Psychology*, 2. 10.3389/fpsyg.2011.0017821866227

Weissman, D. G., Rodman, A. M., Rosen, M. L., Kasparek, S., Mayes, M., Sheridan, M. A., Lengua, L. J., Meltzoff, A. N., & McLaughlin, K. A. (2021). Contributions of Emotion Regulation and Brain Structure and Function to Adolescent Internalizing Problems and Stress Vulnerability During the COVID-19 Pandemic: A Longitudinal Study. *Biological Psychiatry Global Open Science*, 1(4), 272–282. Advance online publication. 10.1016/j.bpsgos.2021.06.00134901918

Weiss, R. S. (1983). *The Experience of Emotional and Social Isolation*. Massachusetts Institute Of Technology.

Weiten, W., Dunn, D. S., & Hammer, E. Y. (2014). *Psychology Applied to Modern Life: Adjustment in the 21st Century*. Cengage Learning.

Wheaton, B. (1990). Life Transitions, Role Histories, and Mental Health. *American Sociological Review*, 55(2), 209. 10.2307/2095627

WHO. (2023). *Stress*. WHO. https://www.who.int//news-room/questions-and-answers/item/stress/?

Widiger, T. A., & Oltmanns, J. R. (2017). Neuroticism is a fundamental domain of personality with enormous public health implications. *World Psychiatry; Official Journal of the World Psychiatric Association (WPA)*, 16(2), 144–145. 10.1002/wps.2041128498583

Wiedermann, C. J., Barbieri, V., Plagg, B., Marino, P., Piccoliori, G., & Engl, A. (2023). Fortifying the Foundations: A Comprehensive Approach to Enhancing Mental Health Support in Educational Policies Amidst Crises. *Healthcare (Basel)*, 11(10), 1423. 10.3390/healthcare1110142337239709

Wiersma, J., Van Oppen, P., Van Schaik, D. J. F., Van Der Does, W., Beekman, A. T., & Penninx, B.

Williams, D. R. (2018). Stress and the Mental Health of Populations of Color: Advancing Our Understanding of Race-related Stressors. *Journal of Health and Social Behavior*, 59(4), 466–485. 10.1177/0022146518814251 30484715

Williams, M. (1977). *Cry of Pain: Understanding suicide and self-harm*. Penguin. https://www.ncbi.nlm.nih.gov/pmc/articles/PMC1296580/

Willis, A. (2024). Teachers prioritise relationships over curriculum for student wellbeing. *Pedagogy, Culture & Society*, 32(2), 473–489. 10.1080/14681366.2022.2055116

Wium, A.-M., & Louw, B. (2018). Mixed-methods research: A tutorial for speech-language therapists and audiologists in South Africa. *The South African Journal of Communication Disorders*, 56(1), a573. 10.4102/sajcd.v65i1.57330035606

Wolfle, L. M., & List, J. H. (2004). Temporal Stability in the Effects of College Attendance on Locus of Control, 1972–1992. *Structural Equation Modeling*, 11(2), 244–260. 10.1207/s15328007sem1102_6

Wolhuter, C. C., & Van Staden, S. (2011). "The Role of Study Groups in Enhancing Learning." *Journal of Affective Disorders*, 123(1–3), 60–67.

Wood, R. T. (2008). Problems with the concept of video game "addiction": Some case study examples. *International Journal of Mental Health and Addiction*, 6(2), 169–178. 10.1007/s11469-007-9118-0

Wood, T., Cobb, P., & Yackel, E. (1991). Change in teaching mathematics: A case study. *American Educational Research Journal*, 28(3), 587–616. 10.3102/00028312028003587

World Health Organisation. (2023, April 18). *What is mental health?* WHO. https://www.who.mental.health.

World Health Organization. (2018). *Mental Health Atlas 2017*. WHO Regional Office for the Eastern Mediterranean.

Worsley, J., Pennington, A., & Corcoran, R. (2020). What interventions improve college and university students' mental health and wellbeing? A review of review-level evidence. *J-O Students Mental Health, Vl*, 1(1), 1–54.

Wu, K. C. C., Chen, Y. Y., & Yip, P. S. (2012). Suicide methods in Asia: Implications in suicide prevention. *International Journal of Environmental Research and Public Health*, 9(4), 1135–1158. 10.3390/ijerph904113522690187

Xiao, J. J. (2016). Consumer financial capability and wellbeing. *Handbook of consumer finance research*, 3-17. Research Gate.

Xiao, H., Carney, D. M., Youn, S. J., Janis, R. A., Castonguay, L. G., Hayes, J. A., & Locke, B. D. (2017). Are we in crisis? National mental health and treatment trends in college counseling centers. *Psychological Services*, 14(4), 407–415. 10.1037/ser000013029120199

Xiao, J. J., Sorhaindo, B., & Garman, E. T. (2006). Financial behaviours of consumers in credit counselling. *International Journal of Consumer Studies*, 30(2), 108–121. 10.1111/j.1470-6431.2005.00455.x

Xiao, J. J., Tang, C., & Shim, S. (2009). Acting for happiness: Financial behavior and life satisfaction of college students. *Social Indicators Research*, 92(1), 53–68. 10.1007/s11205-008-9288-6

Xie, J., Gulinna, A., & Rice, M. F. (2021). Instructional designers' roles in emergency remote teaching during COVID-19. *Distance Education*, 42(1), 70–87. 10.1080/01587919.2020.1869526

Yadav, S., Aathavan, K. K., Cunningham, S. A., Bhandari, P., Mishra, U. S., Aditi, A., & Yadav, R. (2023). Changing pattern of suicide deaths in India. *The Lancet Regional Health. Southeast Asia*, 16(1), 10–26. 10.1016/j.lansea.2023.10026537649643

Yang, J., & Mufson, C. (2021, Nov. 2). *College students' stress levels are 'bubbling over.' Learn why and how schools can assist.* PBS. https://www.pbs.org/newshour/show/college-students-stress-levels-are-bubbling-over-heres-why-and-how-schools-can-help

Yang, D., Chen, P., Wang, K., Li, Z., Zhang, C., & Huang, R. (2023). Parental Involvement and Student Engagement: A Review of the Literature. *Sustainability (Basel)*, 15(7), 5859. 10.3390/su15075859

Yang, Q., Shi, M., Tang, D., Zhu, H., & Xiong, K. (2022). Multiple Roles of Grit in the Relationship Between Interpersonal Stress and Psychological Security of College Freshmen. *Frontiers in Psychology*, 13, 824214. 10.3389/fpsyg.2022.82421435310215

Yano, K., Endo, S., Kimura, S., & Oishi, K. (2021). A quantitative text analysis revealed the effective coping mechanisms used by university students in three sensitivity groups. *Cogent Psychology*, 8(1). 10.1080/23311908.2021.1988193

Yau, H. K., Sun, H., & Cheng, A. L. F. (2012). Adjusting to university: The Hong Kong experience. *Journal of Higher Education Policy and Management*, 34(1), 15–27. 10.1080/1360080X.2012.642328

Yeşilyaprak, B. (2004). Denetim odağı. Y. Kuzgun & D. Deryakulu (Eds.), *Eğitimde bireysel farklılıklar içinde* (s. 239-258). Ankara: Nobel Yayınevi.

Yikealo, D., Tareke, W., & Karvinen, I. (2018). The Level of Stress among College Students: A Case in the College of Education, Eritrea Institute of Technology. *Open Science Journal, 3*(4). 10.23954/osj.v3i4.1691

Yogasnumurti, R. R., Sadalia, I., & Irawati, N. (2021). The effect of financial, attitude, and financial knowledge on the personal finance management of college collage students. In *Proceedings of the 2nd Economics and Business International Conference-EBIC* (pp. 649-657). ScitePress.

Younas, A. (2017). Self-care behaviors and practices of nursing students: Review of literature. *Journal of Health Sciences (Sarajevo), 7*(3), 137–145. 10.17532/jhsci.2017.420

Yusuf, M., Peter, O., & Jadesola, A. (2012). *A Survey on Facebook and Academic Performance in Nigeria Universities*. Research Gate.

Zemtsov, A. A., & Osipova, T. Y. (2016). Financial wellbeing as a type of human wellbeing: theoretical review. *European Proceedings of Social and Behavioural Sciences*. Research Gate.

Zhang, M., & He, Y. (2015). Handbook of rating scales in psychiatry (1st ed.). Changsha: Hunan Science & Technology Press.

Zhang, X. (2024). *A study on Association between social media use and students' academic performance through family bonding and collective learning: The moderating role of mental well-being*. Springer.

Zhang, N., & Henderson, C. N. R. (2022). Coping strategies and chiropractic student perceived stress. *The Journal of Chiropractic Education, 36*(1), 13–21. 10.7899/JCE-20-2834320658

Zhang, Y., Peters, A., & Chen, G. (2018). Perceived stress mediates the associations between sleep quality and symptoms of anxiety and depression among college nursing students. *International Journal of Nursing Education Scholarship, 15*(1), 20170020. 10.1515/ijnes-2017-002029306924

Zhou, M., Dzingirai, C., Hove, K., Chitata, T., & Mugandani, R. (2022). Adoption, use and enhancement of virtual learning during COVID-19. *Education and Information Technologies, 27*(7), 8939–8959. 10.1007/s10639-022-10985-x35340535

Zhou, X., Min, S., Sun, J., Kim, S. J., Ahn, J. S., Peng, Y., Noh, S., & Ryder, A. G. (2015). Extending a structural model of somatization to South Koreans: Cultural values, somatization tendency, and the presentation of depressive symptoms. *Journal of Affective Disorders, 176*, 151–154. 10.1016/j.jad.2015.01.04025721611

Zhu, Y., Wang, H., & Wang, A. (2021). An evaluation of mental health and emotion regulation experienced by undergraduate nursing students in China during the COVID-19 pandemic: A cross-sectional study. *International Journal of Mental Health Nursing*, 30(5), 1160–1169. 10.1111/inm.12867

Zimbardo, P. G. (1985). *Psychology and life* (11th ed.). Scott Foresman.

Zimmermann, M. (2007). *GRIN- Suicide in India in a religious, political and social context.* GRIN. https://www.grin.com/document/80758

Zurlo, K. A. (2009). *Personal attributes and the financial well-being of older adults: The effects of control beliefs*. Scholarly Commons.

About the Contributors

Peter Aloka is currently a senior lecturer at the Wits School of Education, University of the Witwatersrand, South Africa. He holds PhD in Educational Psychology from the University of the Western Cape. He has published widely and supervised several postgraduate students. He has research interests in positive psychology, adjustment among students, students' problem behaviours and resilience.

***

Kapil Kumar Aggarwal is Professor of Finance at the University School of Business, Chandigarh University. He has earned PhD, M. Phil, MFC, MBA & M. Com. He has more than 16 years of teaching and research experience. His research experience is inclusive of 22 research papers published in National journals, International Journals, Edited Books, ABDC-listed journals, Scopus Indexed, Web of Sciences and Peer Reviewed journals, 32 research papers presented in National/International conferences and two books published in his account. His teaching interest is primarily focused on finance, management sciences, quantitative techniques, business mathematics, and business statistics. He is the reviewer of the International Journal of Educational Development Journal, indexed in Scopus Elsevier, Social Sciences Citation Index and Educational and Information Technologies Journal indexed in SCOPUS, Social Science Citation Index, and UGC-CARE List (India) and Editorial Board member of International Journal of Accounting, Finance and Risk Management (IJAFRM) of He is also a pioneer in the field of SPSS and R and has delivered multiple lectures and workshops on the same.

Arnisha Aman is currently pursuing a Master's Degree in Clinical Psychology. She holds a Bachelor of Science degree in Psychology from Christ University, where her work on child psychology and emotional intelligence in young adults resulted in a psychology bestseller titled "Precursors of Childhood Anxiety" and a publication in the leading journal "Rowman and Littlefield" This is one of her three publications as a budding psychology student. Arnisha is a two-time recipient of the meritorious scholarship at Christ University, awarded for her research skills and academic accolades fueled by her passion for psychology. She is an all-rounder who takes great pride in her communication and leadership skills, complementing her academic achievements. In her leisure time, Arnisha enjoys cooking, reading crime thrillers, taking nature walks, and caring for dogs. Her close relationship with the dichotomy of science and nature makes her an inspiration to her peers.

Harshita K Dharam is a second-year BSc Psychology (Hons) student at Christ (Deemed to be University), Bangalore. She completed her schooling at BVM Global @ Perungudi in 2022, where she studied Biology, Chemistry, Physics, Psychology, and English. Her interests lie in the interdisciplinary fields of psychology and business.

Sundaravel E is currently working as a CX Consultant at Oracle. He is also a Doctoral Scholar at Christ University, Bangalore, India. Previously, he pursued postgraduate studies in MBA (Marketing) at Christ University, Bangalore, India. He holds an undergraduate degree in Electrical and Electronics Engineering from Amrita University, Bangalore, India. Before his current roles, he gained experience as a Content Writer at Zoho Corp, Chennai, India and Tata iQ, Bangalore, India.

Anna Niitembu Hako, PhD., is a Senior Lecturer for Guidance and Counselling at the University of Namibia, Hifikepunye Pohamba Campus-Namibia. She holds a PhD in Educational Psychology from the University of the Western Cape and a Master's degree in Counsellor Education from Emporia State University, USA. She also holds a Bachelor of Education degree from the University of Namibia. Her research areas are general education, guidance and counselling, psycho-social support and inclusive education.

Vitória Jeronimo has a master's in architecture from the Lisbon School of Architecture (2020-2023), Portugal; with Erasmus at the Technische Universität Graz (2021-2022), Austria; academic exchange at the Escuela Técnica Superior de Arquitectura de Valladolid (2018), Spain; and 7 semesters at the Federal University of Ouro Preto,(2014-2019), Brazil. Research focused on spatial experience of students at the Lisbon School of Architecture, University of Lisbon, from a gender perspective, with a focus on participatory methodologies. She actively participated in the Socio-Environmental Studies and Research Group (GEPSA) and was a volunteer in the Extension Project Narrativas Atingidas (2017). She worked as an intern at Aldrava Arquitetura e Urbanismo (2016-2017, 2020), Brazil, in the area of Architectural and Interior Projects, at CroixMarieBourdon (2019), in France, in the phases of architectural studies and competitions; at the Sylvain Grasset office (2021) and Contacto Atlântico (2022-2023), in Portugal.

Deepa K Damodaran currently serves as the Associate Professor in Psychology at the JAIN (Deemed-to-be University), Kochi Campus, Kerala. The broad areas of her interest include Teaching, Administration, Research, Coaching & Training whereas areas of her research interest include Child, Adolescent & Youth mental health; Personality; Workplace mental health; Stress; Well-being, and, Positive Psychology.

K. Madhu Kishore Raghunath has obtained his Ph.D. in Management from the National Institute of Technology-Warangal and he is currently working as an Assistant Professor in the Department of Finance, GITAM institute of management, in GITAM (Deemed to be University) Visakhapatnam Campus. He has a Post-graduate degree in Management with Finance and Marketing specializations from Jawaharlal Nehru Technological University and has over 5 years of teaching experience in higher education along with CBSE-NET & AP & TS- SLET qualification. His research interests include subjects like Finance, Marketing, Risk Management.

Elangovan N is a Professor in the School of Business and Management at Christ (Deemed to be University), Bangalore, India. He also coordinates the PhD Programme at the School and serves as the Associate Director of the Research and Development Cell at the university. He was earlier the Director of National Institute of Fashion Technology (NIFT), Kannur Campus. He comes to academics after a long experience in running a textile business. He earned a PhD in Management Science from Anna University, Chennai, India. He holds an MBA in Marketing and an MSc in Psychology. He also holds a BE in Mechanical from Bharathiar University and a BA in psychology from Madras University. He has published in journals including International Journal of enterprise resource planning, MethodsX, Journal of International Technology and Information Management and International Journal of Innovation and Technology Management. His research interest is in the areas of Strategic Information Systems, Entrepreneurship, Consumer behaviour studies, Design and innovation. His book chapters have appeared in "Research into Design for a Connected World, Smart Innovation, Systems and Technologies" published by Springer and "Handbook of Research on Remote Work and Worker Well-Being in the Post-COVID-19 Era" published by IGI Global.

Hileni Nangulohi Niikondo is an accomplished professional nurse with over 30 years of experience in clinical nursing, complemented by over 15 years of dedicated teaching service at the University of Namibia. Throughout her career, she has mentored numerous novice nurses, guided them into the nursing profession, and fostered their academic advancement. Her areas of expertise and passion include student welfare, leadership, and research in palliative care and disability studies. Mrs. Niikondo has pursued post-graduate studies in both nursing and public health, demonstrating her commitment to continuous learning and professional development. She has also taken on leadership roles, actively contributing to the advancement of nursing practice and education. She consistently upholds the core values of nursing professionalism, embodying traits such as integrity, trustworthiness, accountability, and transparency.

Damaris Ochanda is the current Chairperson, Department of Nursing Research, Education and Management in the School of Nursing, Midwifery and Paramedical Sciences of Masinde Muliro University of Science and Technology, Kenya. She holds Bsc (Nursing) from University of Nairobi, Hons. BA (Health Studies) and MA (Health Studies) from University of South Africa (UNISA) and a doctorate in Public Health from Jaramogi Oginga Odinga University of Science and Technology. She is a registered nurse with over eight (8) years clinical nursing experience and her experience in teaching of nursing programmes in higher education for both undergraduate and postgraduate spans over 15 years. Her research interests include public health nursing, higher education & research. She has published several articles in peer reviewed journals and has participated in collaborative research focusing on interventions that address public health issues including mental health.

Christine Opondo is a lecturer in the Department of Psychology, at Maseno University in Kenya. She holds a PhD degree in Guidance & Counseling at Jaramogi Oginga Odinga University of Science & Technology, Kenya. She has published widely, and supervised several postgraduate students at University.

R Maheswari has completed her Graduation Bachelor of Computer Applications from Kongu Arts and Science College, Erode and secured University Gold Medal. She did her Post Graduation Master of Business Administration at Kongu Arts and Science College, Erode. Secured University 8th Rank. NET Qualified faculty. Completed PhD in Management from Bharathiar University, Coimbatore. She has teaching experience of 11 years and presently working as Assistant Professor at Kongu Engineering College, Erode. She also has Industrial Experience of 2 years and Entrepreneurial Experience of 3 years. She holds 2 patents. She is author of various book chapters and has published articles in various academic journals. She has cleared NISM Equity and Derivatives trader certification and Mutual Funds Distributor certification. She has conducted Management Development Faculty for various organizations across the state. She is a Motivational Speaker and Trainer for various organization and institutions. Posted articles in her Blog and Facebook Page. Certified Trainer at Lions Club International and JCI. She has completed Neuro Linguistic Program (NLP) – Basic level and Certified Adolescence students' handler.

Susana Maria Gouveia Rosado has a PhD in Statistics and Operational Research (2007, FCUL - Faculty of Sciences, University of Lisbon) MSc in Probabilities and Statistics (1998, FCUL). Probability and Statistics degree (1995, FCUL). Is an Assistant Professor in the University of Lisbon, Lisbon School of Architecture, a Researcher in CIAUD- Architecture, Ubanism and Design Reseach Center. Integrated in the research group DUAlab - Urban and Environmental Dynamics. Research focused on applied mathematics and statistics. Applications using data analysis, information management and optimization. Also researches in the domain of ICT (Information and Communicaton Techniques) and STEAM in Higher Education with an emphasis on the Challenge Based learning format.

Cristina Georgiana Safta is associate professor, director of the Educational Sciences Department of the Petroleum-Gas University of Ploiesti. A graduate of the Faculty of Sociology, Psychology and Pedagogy of the University of Bucharest, majoring in Pedagogy and the master's program in School Counseling, she obtained a doctorate in Educational Sciences at the University of Bucharest in 2009. Leads the courses of Introduction to Counseling, Career Development, Human Resources Management, Student Class Management and coordinates the career counseling activity of students. He is involved as a researcher in numerous national and international projects that have topics of interest in the counseling field. Among the published works we mention: On Restraining the Feeling of Self-Efficacy in the Academic Environment: Some Aspects of Institutional Violence (2019); Choosing a Career in Teaching, between Informed Decision and Happenstance (2019); Gender Stereotypes–Dimension of the Hidden Curriculum (2017); Career Decisions – A Test of Courage, Responsibility and Self-Confidence in Teenagers (2015); Cross-Curricular Competencies - Access Path to Professional Development (2015); Counseling and Assistance for Women Victims of Domestic Violence in Romania - Case Study (2010).

SC Vetrivel is a faculty member in the Department of Management Studies, Kongu Engineering College (Autonomous), Perundurai, Erode Dt. Having experience in Industry 20 years and Teaching 16 years. Awarded with Doctoral Degree in Management Sciences in Anna University, Chennai. He has organized various workshops and Faculty Development Programmes. He is actively involved in research and consultancy works. He acted as a resource person to FDPs & MDPs to various industries like, SPB ltd, Tamilnadu Police, DIET, Rotary school and many. His areas of interest include Entrepreneurship, Business Law, Marketing and Case writing. Articles published more than 100 International and National Journals. Presented papers in more than 30 National and International conferences including IIM Bangalore, IIM Kozhikode, IIM Kashipur and IIM Indore. He was a Chief Co-ordinator of Entrepreneurship and Management Development Centre (EMDC) of Kongu Engineering College, he was instrumental in organizing various Awareness Camps, FDP, and TEDPs to aspiring entrepreneurs which was funded by NSTEDB – DST/GoI

Ajay K. Singh is working as an Associate Professor (Research) in the Department of Humanities and Social Science, Graphic Era (Deemed to be University) Dehradun. He has worked as Assistant Professor (Economics) in the School of Liberal Arts & Management, DIT University Dehradun for 6 years. He did Post-Doctorate Research with EDI of India, Ahmedabad, Gujarat (India). He received MPhil (Economics) from DAVV Indore (India), and PhD (Economics) from IIT Indore (India. He has published several research papers in the diversified area such as climate change, agricultural productivity, assessment of food security; estimation of GFSI, development of environmental sustainability index (ESI) and its association with socio-economic indicators; measurement and determinants of entrepreneurship ecosystem, and dimension of sustainable development and its interlinkages with economic development.

Ravindra Singh has completed his Ph.D. from Banaras Hindu University (Institute of eminence). Currently he is working as an Assistant Professor Psychology Graphic Era Deemed to be University, Dehradun. Earlier he was Indian Youth Ambassador at BRICS. Beijing China 2017 during Indian deligation. Dr. Singh has also worked as Junior Project Fellow, NCERT funded project, New Delhi in 2018. He worked as the Former Teaching Assistant at IIT, BHU. Recently he was the Youth Member at G20 Youth for India's G-20 Presidency. He served as an Independent Reviewer in Frontiers in Psychology Journal and Member at APA, International Affiliate, Washington DC and also the member of prestigious National Academy of Psychology, (NAOP) India. He has 7 Years of teaching experience and supervising 3 PhD candidate along with many posts' graduate thesis supervision.

Silvian Suditu is a university lecturer at the Well Drilling, Extraction and Transportation of Hydrocarbons chair and vice-dean of the Faculty of Petroleum and Gas Engineering from 2022. In 2008 he obtained the title of doctor in the field of Engineering Sciences, Mines, oil and gas. He is the author of 5 books, 30 scientific papers, published in magazines or presented in national and international conferences, 15 professional research contracts. Since 2005 and currently he is a member of the Romanian Society of Thermotechnics

Nestor Tomas is currently employed as a Senior Lecturer in the department of General Nursing Science, School of Nursing, at the University of Namibia. He possesses a deep passion for research and publication, particularly in the fields of Nursing education, clinical nursing, public health, nursing leadership, mental health, and gender-based violence.

V.P. Arun is a driven and accomplished professional with a diverse educational background and extensive hands-on experience across various industries. Graduating with honors, Arun earned his Master of Business Administration (M.B.A) with a specialization in Human Resources and Marketing from the renowned Sona School of Management in Salem in 2018, where he excelled academically with an impressive 8.3 Cumulative Grade Point Average (CGPA). Before pursuing his MBA, Arun laid a solid foundation by obtaining a Bachelor of Engineering degree from Kongu Engineering College in 2014. Throughout his academic journey, Arun displayed an unwavering commitment to learning and personal growth, actively seeking opportunities to expand his knowledge and skills beyond the confines of traditional education. He sought practical experiences to complement his theoretical understanding, such as a 45-day summer internship focused on conducting a feasibility study for R-Doc Sustainability in the market. Additionally, Arun broadened his horizons through a 7-day industrial visit to Malaysia and Singapore, immersing himself in diverse cultural and professional environments. Arun's academic pursuits were further enriched by his involvement in hands-on projects, including a comprehensive study on Employee Job Satisfaction at Roots Cast Private Limited. These practical experiences not only honed his analytical and problem-solving skills but also showcased his proactive approach to learning and professional development.

Index

A

Academic assistance 148, 300
Academic environment 88, 89, 182, 268, 271, 275, 277, 279, 283, 287, 289, 290, 291, 292, 293, 295, 297, 298, 308
academic factors 81
academic performance 9, 44, 47, 84, 85, 86, 87, 88, 90, 92, 93, 95, 96, 97, 104, 127, 128, 133, 137, 142, 146, 148, 154, 158, 159, 161, 162, 163, 164, 165, 166, 167, 169, 170, 175, 176, 177, 178, 179, 188, 189, 192, 193, 194, 195, 207, 215, 219, 220, 224, 225, 228, 270, 271, 283, 295, 317, 330, 331, 332, 341, 343, 346, 347, 348, 353, 354, 355, 356, 357, 408, 409, 412, 413, 414, 415, 416
Adaptive Coping 158, 187, 198, 202
addictions 192, 267, 268, 276, 278, 279, 280, 281, 282, 339, 340
adolescents 3, 7, 10, 11, 13, 21, 22, 23, 24, 25, 26, 27, 31, 64, 66, 67, 72, 73, 75, 108, 110, 111, 112, 113, 114, 115, 117, 119, 121, 146, 148, 149, 152, 154, 184, 196, 219, 262, 263, 264, 265, 313, 338, 339, 346, 355
Affective MI 448
Anxiety 1, 2, 3, 4, 5, 6, 7, 8, 10, 14, 15, 16, 17, 19, 20, 21, 23, 25, 26, 27, 28, 38, 40, 42, 43, 44, 45, 47, 51, 53, 54, 61, 63, 65, 66, 67, 69, 72, 75, 81, 82, 83, 84, 85, 87, 91, 92, 93, 94, 96, 97, 98, 103, 107, 108, 110, 111, 112, 113, 114, 115, 116, 117, 118, 119, 120, 121, 122, 123, 124, 125, 128, 129, 137, 138, 139, 142, 143, 146, 150, 151, 152, 158, 159, 160, 161, 162, 164, 165, 167, 168, 172, 179, 181, 185, 186, 191, 192, 193, 195, 197, 200, 201, 202, 203, 208, 209, 215, 216, 222, 229, 230, 231, 232, 233, 234, 235, 236, 250, 251, 256, 261, 271, 277, 284, 285, 290, 294, 295, 299, 300, 301, 302, 311, 314, 317, 325, 326, 327, 330, 333, 336, 337, 400, 402, 414, 416
Architecture 110, 355, 359, 360, 361, 362, 363, 364, 365, 367, 368, 374, 375, 385, 396, 397
Avoidance Strategies 157

B

Behavioural MI 448

C

Cognitive MI 448
College Students 6, 7, 9, 10, 24, 25, 26, 27, 52, 54, 88, 102, 103, 104, 105, 129, 136, 137, 139, 143, 144, 149, 151, 152, 153, 155, 185, 186, 190, 194, 195, 207, 208, 209, 210, 211, 214, 217, 218, 220, 221, 222, 223, 224, 225, 227, 229, 230, 231, 232, 234, 235, 292, 311, 312, 313, 330, 343, 344, 346, 354, 356, 396, 402, 418, 419, 420, 442, 443, 445, 447
Coping 6, 11, 12, 13, 23, 32, 33, 39, 40, 42, 44, 45, 46, 48, 49, 50, 51, 52, 53, 54, 81, 93, 94, 95, 97, 118, 122, 124, 127, 128, 130, 132, 134, 135, 137, 143, 144, 146, 148, 149, 150, 151, 152, 154, 155, 157, 158, 159, 160, 162, 164, 166, 167, 168, 169, 170, 171, 172, 173, 174, 175, 176, 177, 178, 179, 181, 182, 183, 184, 185, 187, 188, 189, 190, 192, 194, 195, 196, 197, 198, 199, 200, 201, 202, 203, 204, 205, 206, 207, 208, 209, 210, 211, 214, 216, 218, 219, 224, 225, 229, 230, 231, 232, 233, 235, 236, 239, 280, 286, 287, 296, 302, 304, 306, 311, 315, 418, 420, 445
Coping Mechanisms 6, 32, 40, 50, 51, 94, 132, 134, 135, 137, 146, 155, 157, 158, 159, 160, 162, 164, 166, 167, 168, 170, 177, 178, 179, 182, 183, 187, 188, 189, 190, 194, 195, 196,

198, 202, 203, 204, 205, 206, 214, 280, 287, 302, 420
Coping Strategies 11, 13, 23, 33, 44, 45, 46, 48, 49, 51, 52, 53, 54, 81, 94, 95, 97, 118, 122, 134, 135, 149, 150, 151, 152, 154, 157, 158, 159, 160, 171, 177, 178, 181, 183, 187, 189, 190, 194, 196, 197, 198, 199, 200, 202, 203, 204, 205, 206, 207, 208, 210, 211, 218, 219, 225, 229, 235, 239, 287, 296, 304, 306, 418, 420
correlation test 408
COVID-19 4, 5, 10, 24, 25, 26, 28, 29, 31, 33, 34, 35, 36, 38, 39, 40, 41, 42, 43, 44, 45, 46, 47, 48, 49, 50, 51, 52, 53, 54, 56, 66, 67, 68, 69, 71, 72, 73, 75, 78, 79, 80, 124, 151, 152, 154, 178, 190, 197, 199, 200, 201, 203, 204, 206, 208, 210, 217, 230, 231, 289, 290, 291, 292, 293, 295, 300, 311, 313, 314, 315, 316, 420, 421, 424, 441, 444
Culture 81, 82, 85, 89, 91, 102, 115, 116, 129, 144, 150, 182, 183, 238, 245, 250, 252, 253, 256, 257, 264, 271, 275, 280, 284, 291, 296, 297, 301, 302, 303, 304, 305, 306, 307, 308, 310, 312, 313, 316, 346, 386, 445

D

DASS-21 5, 10, 15, 16
Depression 1, 2, 3, 4, 5, 6, 7, 8, 9, 10, 11, 14, 15, 16, 17, 18, 19, 20, 21, 23, 24, 25, 26, 27, 28, 29, 32, 38, 40, 41, 42, 43, 44, 45, 47, 48, 58, 61, 63, 66, 67, 72, 81, 82, 84, 92, 93, 116, 117, 119, 124, 125, 128, 132, 133, 136, 143, 146, 151, 158, 159, 164, 167, 179, 189, 191, 192, 194, 195, 200, 201, 202, 203, 208, 214, 215, 219, 220, 223, 229, 230, 231, 232, 233, 234, 236, 238, 239, 250, 262, 277, 285, 295, 299, 311, 324, 325, 326, 327, 330, 335, 336, 338, 400, 402, 414
Dysfunctional Coping 118, 189, 190, 198, 202, 203, 204

E

Emotion-Focused Coping 157, 159, 171, 172, 178, 196, 197, 199, 200, 206
engagement 6, 8, 39, 40, 48, 83, 87, 90, 91, 103, 139, 151, 153, 168, 196, 198, 201, 208, 224, 225, 230, 232, 269, 277, 291, 292, 303, 304, 305, 307, 308, 313, 314, 316, 319, 325, 336, 345, 346, 357, 364, 394, 400
environmental factors 14, 81, 128, 130, 250, 251, 255, 256
external locus of control 108, 111, 112, 113, 117, 118

F

Face-to-face learning 290, 294, 303, 309, 315
Feminist Urbanism 362, 369
Financial Satisfaction 423, 424, 425, 426, 428, 429, 430, 431, 432, 433, 434, 439, 440, 441, 442, 443, 445, 446, 448
Financial Security 142, 425, 426, 430, 431, 433, 434, 439, 442, 445, 448
Financial stability 39, 87, 127, 142, 143, 228, 412, 416, 437, 444
Financial Well-being 399, 400, 401, 403, 404, 405, 406, 408, 409, 410, 412, 413, 414, 415, 416, 423, 424, 427, 433, 437, 439, 440, 441, 442, 444, 445, 446, 447
Financial Wellbeing 423, 427, 428, 429, 431, 439, 447, 448

G

Gender-Sensitive Approach 359, 394

H

Higher education 2, 3, 4, 5, 6, 8, 10, 12, 21, 25, 27, 29, 31, 48, 53, 54, 81, 82, 83, 86, 87, 88, 89, 101, 102, 103, 104, 105, 107, 108, 113, 127, 129, 130, 131, 132, 133, 134, 142, 146, 147, 148, 149, 150, 152, 153, 154, 155, 161,

184, 186, 204, 207, 210, 214, 215, 218, 219, 220, 223, 224, 225, 226, 229, 231, 233, 234, 235, 236, 263, 268, 270, 284, 285, 287, 292, 312, 314, 315, 316, 332, 356, 359, 360, 361, 363, 386, 393, 395, 396, 397, 399, 400, 401, 404, 406, 408, 409, 412, 416, 418, 419, 420, 443
higher education institutions 4, 21, 54, 81, 83, 107, 108, 131, 132, 134, 204, 214, 220, 225, 226, 316, 332, 359, 360, 363, 386, 393, 399, 404, 406, 408, 409, 412, 416
Higher learning institutions 1, 3, 4, 15, 18, 21, 22, 400, 414, 415

I

inclusivity 91, 182, 305, 312
internal locus of control 59, 111, 114, 117, 118

L

Lisbon School of Architecture 359, 360, 363, 364, 365, 367, 368, 396, 397

M

Maladaptive Coping 187, 202, 204
maladjustment 52, 62, 75, 267, 268, 278, 280
meaning 12, 13, 21, 22, 53, 76, 104, 123, 187, 189, 198, 199, 201, 208, 211, 230, 239, 268, 269, 270, 331, 337
mental disorders 2, 13, 22, 26, 27, 28, 70, 123, 131, 195, 229, 232, 419
mental health 1, 2, 3, 4, 5, 6, 7, 8, 10, 11, 12, 13, 15, 17, 18, 21, 22, 23, 24, 25, 26, 27, 28, 29, 32, 33, 34, 36, 40, 41, 42, 43, 44, 45, 46, 47, 48, 49, 50, 51, 52, 53, 54, 55, 66, 67, 69, 71, 73, 74, 77, 78, 79, 80, 81, 82, 83, 84, 85, 86, 87, 88, 89, 91, 92, 93, 96, 97, 98, 101, 102, 103, 104, 127, 128, 129, 131, 133, 134, 135, 136, 137, 138, 139, 143, 144, 146, 149, 150, 151, 152, 153, 155, 159, 162, 164, 165, 166, 167, 171, 172, 177, 178, 179, 181, 182, 183, 184, 186, 187, 189, 191, 192, 196, 201, 202, 203, 205, 211, 214, 215, 216, 217, 219, 220, 223, 228, 229, 231, 232, 233, 234, 236, 238, 240, 250, 251, 257, 258, 260, 261, 273, 284, 285, 286, 289, 290, 291, 292, 293, 295, 296, 298, 299, 301, 302, 304, 306, 309, 311, 312, 313, 314, 315, 316, 326, 327, 328, 330, 334, 335, 337, 338, 360, 395, 402, 403, 410, 411, 414, 415, 419
Mental well-being 1, 2, 3, 4, 10, 11, 13, 23, 24, 31, 32, 33, 34, 36, 38, 40, 42, 43, 45, 46, 49, 53, 62, 91, 97, 157, 176, 179, 182, 191, 217, 227, 228, 229, 231, 238, 239, 295, 302, 306, 331, 332, 334, 341
Monetary Intelligence 423, 424, 425, 426, 427, 428, 429, 430, 431, 432, 433, 434, 435, 436, 437, 438, 439, 441, 446, 447, 448

N

neuroticism 107, 108, 109, 110, 111, 112, 113, 114, 115, 116, 117, 118, 119, 120, 121, 122, 123, 124, 125, 234, 251, 256
Northern Zone 399, 403, 404, 405, 410, 414, 416
nursing students 31, 32, 33, 34, 35, 36, 38, 39, 40, 41, 42, 43, 44, 45, 46, 47, 48, 49, 50, 51, 52, 53, 54, 146, 148, 149, 152, 153, 154, 155, 193, 194, 199, 207, 210, 215, 236

P

pandemics 34, 36, 46
Parent-child relationships 55
Participatory Methodology 369
policy 11, 24, 31, 32, 33, 37, 54, 84, 85, 102, 149, 155, 224, 236, 257, 273, 297, 298, 302, 403, 413, 442, 443
positive emotions 4, 174, 199, 269
Post-pandemic 25, 289, 290, 291, 292,

293, 294, 295, 297, 298, 299, 300, 301, 302, 303, 304, 305, 306, 308, 309, 310, 311, 314, 315
Prevalence 1, 2, 3, 4, 5, 6, 7, 8, 9, 18, 19, 21, 23, 24, 25, 26, 27, 28, 29, 52, 82, 108, 146, 160, 189, 205, 217, 219, 220, 223, 229, 233, 237, 238, 239, 241, 244, 250, 256, 261, 263, 295, 327
Problem-Focused Coping 45, 157, 168, 177, 189, 196, 197, 198, 199, 200, 207, 209
Psychological distress 3, 4, 5, 9, 10, 13, 14, 15, 17, 18, 20, 21, 22, 24, 32, 40, 41, 44, 50, 51, 62, 82, 86, 129, 150, 185, 189, 201, 203, 210, 215, 233, 251, 296, 314
psychological factors 81, 250, 251, 255, 256
Public Space 362, 369

R

relationship 3, 11, 14, 20, 21, 24, 40, 49, 50, 51, 55, 56, 58, 59, 60, 61, 64, 65, 70, 74, 77, 92, 111, 114, 116, 117, 123, 125, 132, 133, 135, 149, 151, 152, 159, 160, 161, 163, 173, 179, 184, 188, 197, 201, 203, 205, 209, 211, 216, 224, 225, 230, 232, 233, 234, 235, 236, 256, 257, 269, 270, 271, 273, 274, 275, 276, 277, 297, 304, 313, 328, 329, 335, 338, 339, 348, 349, 351, 353, 356, 362, 369, 373, 381, 383, 384, 385, 388, 391, 396, 399, 402, 404, 405, 406, 408, 409, 412, 413, 418, 425, 428, 429, 431, 432, 433, 434, 440, 442, 446
Resilience 10, 12, 13, 33, 39, 40, 41, 42, 44, 45, 46, 47, 49, 50, 51, 53, 83, 84, 89, 94, 95, 96, 97, 98, 99, 100, 127, 128, 129, 130, 132, 133, 134, 136, 139, 141, 143, 144, 145, 147, 148, 149, 150, 152, 153, 154, 159, 172, 174, 176, 177, 182, 201, 204, 209, 267, 268, 270, 278, 279, 280, 281, 284, 285, 289, 291, 296, 298, 301, 302, 305, 306, 307, 309, 310, 311, 312, 444

S

Sense of belonging 81, 86, 88, 89, 90, 93, 98, 104, 130, 138, 139, 140, 144, 145, 148, 150, 153, 161, 172, 174, 179, 270, 273, 291, 296, 302, 304, 305, 307, 308, 309, 312, 334, 393, 394
Social dignity 239
social factors 81, 271
social networking platforms 343, 344, 345, 347, 348, 349, 350, 351, 352, 353, 354
Social relationships 55, 56, 59, 63, 67, 144, 158, 271, 278, 346
Societal influences 55
Socio-demographic factors 14, 15
Space Perception 394
Spatial Experiences 359, 371, 394
Stress 1, 2, 3, 4, 5, 6, 7, 8, 9, 10, 11, 14, 15, 16, 17, 18, 19, 20, 21, 23, 26, 27, 28, 29, 31, 32, 33, 38, 39, 40, 41, 42, 43, 44, 45, 46, 47, 48, 49, 51, 52, 54, 59, 61, 67, 68, 69, 71, 72, 75, 76, 77, 78, 79, 80, 82, 83, 84, 85, 86, 87, 92, 93, 94, 95, 96, 97, 98, 101, 102, 103, 107, 108, 110, 117, 118, 124, 127, 128, 129, 130, 131, 132, 133, 134, 135, 136, 137, 138, 139, 140, 141, 142, 143, 144, 146, 147, 148, 149, 150, 151, 153, 154, 155, 157, 158, 159, 160, 161, 162, 163, 164, 165, 166, 167, 168, 169, 170, 171, 172, 173, 174, 175, 176, 177, 178, 179, 180, 181, 182, 183, 184, 185, 186, 187, 188, 189, 190, 191, 192, 193, 194, 195, 196, 197, 198, 199, 200, 201, 202, 203, 204, 205, 206, 207, 208, 209, 210, 211, 213, 214, 215, 216, 217, 218, 219, 220, 221, 222, 223, 224, 225, 226, 227, 228, 229, 230, 231, 232, 233, 234, 235, 236, 249, 250, 256, 261, 270, 271, 279, 282, 284, 285, 290, 292, 295, 299, 301, 302, 304, 306, 307, 312, 315, 317, 318, 319, 322, 323, 326, 327, 328, 332, 333, 334, 335, 339, 356, 385, 400, 401, 402, 403, 410, 411, 412, 413, 414, 415, 416, 417, 418, 419

Stressors 4, 5, 8, 9, 10, 27, 33, 39, 44, 67, 68, 84, 91, 92, 93, 94, 108, 127, 134, 155, 157, 158, 159, 160, 162, 163, 164, 171, 172, 175, 178, 181, 188, 189, 190, 191, 192, 193, 194, 195, 197, 200, 202, 203, 204, 205, 206, 207, 209, 211, 213, 214, 215, 216, 217, 218, 219, 220, 221, 222, 223, 224, 225, 226, 227, 228, 231, 232, 234, 250, 256, 272, 286, 290, 295, 300, 443

Student challenges 297, 298

Students 1, 2, 3, 4, 5, 6, 7, 8, 9, 10, 11, 12, 13, 15, 16, 17, 18, 19, 20, 21, 22, 23, 24, 25, 26, 27, 28, 29, 31, 32, 33, 34, 35, 36, 38, 39, 40, 41, 42, 43, 44, 45, 46, 47, 48, 49, 50, 51, 52, 53, 54, 65, 67, 81, 82, 83, 84, 85, 86, 87, 88, 89, 90, 91, 92, 93, 94, 95, 96, 97, 98, 99, 100, 101, 102, 103, 104, 105, 107, 108, 123, 124, 127, 128, 129, 130, 131, 132, 133, 134, 135, 136, 137, 138, 139, 140, 141, 142, 143, 144, 145, 146, 147, 148, 149, 150, 151, 152, 153, 154, 155, 157, 158, 159, 160, 161, 162, 163, 164, 165, 166, 167, 168, 169, 170, 171, 172, 173, 174, 175, 176, 177, 178, 179, 180, 181, 182, 183, 184, 185, 186, 187, 188, 189, 190, 191, 192, 193, 194, 195, 196, 197, 198, 199, 200, 201, 202, 203, 204, 205, 206, 207, 208, 209, 210, 211, 213, 214, 215, 216, 217, 218, 219, 220, 221, 222, 223, 224, 225, 226, 227, 228, 229, 230, 231, 232, 233, 234, 235, 236, 238, 250, 251, 253, 257, 258, 260, 261, 263, 264, 267, 268, 270, 271, 275, 276, 277, 279, 280, 281, 282, 283, 284, 285, 286, 287, 289, 290, 291, 292, 293, 294, 295, 296, 297, 298, 299, 300, 301, 302, 303, 304, 305, 306, 307, 308, 309, 310, 311, 312, 313, 314, 315, 317, 324, 325, 326, 327, 328, 329, 330, 331, 332, 333, 334, 335, 336, 337, 340, 341, 343, 344, 345, 346, 347, 348, 349, 350, 353, 354, 355, 356, 357, 359, 360, 361, 364, 366, 368, 369, 371, 372, 373, 374, 376, 378, 381, 382, 383, 384, 385, 386, 387, 392, 393, 394, 395, 396, 399, 400, 401, 402, 403, 404, 405, 406, 407, 408, 409, 410, 411, 412, 413, 414, 415, 416, 417, 418, 419, 420, 423, 424, 425, 427, 431, 432, 435, 436, 439, 441, 442, 443, 445, 447

Student well-being 31, 32, 36, 49, 51, 81, 85, 86, 87, 88, 90, 104, 130, 132, 134, 143, 144, 157, 183, 270, 271, 284, 285, 289, 291, 296, 297, 298, 309, 310, 316, 334, 337, 339, 359, 360, 364, 368, 369, 376, 380, 381, 393, 396, 416

Suicide 52, 137, 188, 203, 214, 237, 238, 239, 240, 241, 242, 243, 244, 245, 247, 248, 249, 250, 251, 252, 253, 254, 255, 256, 257, 258, 259, 260, 261, 262, 263, 264, 265, 266, 326, 336

support networks 69, 83, 84, 88, 89, 90, 91, 97, 98, 128, 159, 162, 173, 178, 302, 306, 334, 363

T

Tanzania 8, 24, 226, 332, 399, 400, 403, 404, 405, 410, 413, 414, 416, 419, 420

Transition 7, 82, 83, 91, 92, 93, 128, 160, 173, 184, 185, 187, 188, 189, 191, 192, 193, 286, 287, 289, 290, 291, 292, 293, 294, 295, 299, 300, 301, 303, 309, 315, 361, 388, 390

U

universities 1, 5, 7, 9, 11, 12, 13, 15, 21, 23, 41, 43, 44, 46, 47, 48, 82, 83, 84, 85, 86, 87, 88, 89, 90, 91, 101, 104, 140, 143, 144, 146, 151, 152, 153, 157, 159, 160, 161, 162, 166, 169, 170, 171, 172, 173, 175, 176, 178, 181, 182, 183, 187, 188, 190, 191, 197, 199, 203, 204, 205, 206, 213, 214, 223, 228, 267, 283, 284, 285, 293, 317, 325, 327, 331, 332, 333, 336, 345, 347, 357, 393, 395, 400,

403, 404, 413, 417, 420, 436

University Students 3, 4, 5, 6, 7, 8, 9, 10, 13, 23, 24, 25, 26, 27, 28, 29, 50, 53, 82, 84, 87, 91, 92, 93, 101, 124, 127, 128, 129, 130, 131, 135, 136, 142, 144, 149, 151, 155, 157, 158, 159, 160, 161, 162, 163, 164, 165, 166, 167, 168, 169, 170, 171, 172, 173, 174, 175, 176, 177, 178, 181, 183, 184, 186, 187, 188, 189, 190, 192, 194, 195, 196, 202, 203, 204, 206, 208, 210, 213, 214, 215, 217, 219, 220, 223, 226, 227, 228, 229, 231, 232, 233, 234, 286, 292, 311, 315, 317, 324, 325, 327, 328, 332, 334, 335, 340, 343, 355, 356, 400, 401, 403, 405, 410, 411, 414, 415, 423, 441, 442, 445

V

vulnerability 7, 80, 108, 117, 121, 133, 184, 260, 267, 268, 271, 272, 273, 274, 275, 276, 277, 278, 279, 280, 281, 282, 283, 284, 285, 286, 331, 377, 384, 446

W

Well-Being 1, 2, 3, 4, 10, 11, 13, 23, 24, 27, 28, 31, 32, 33, 34, 35, 36, 38, 39, 40, 42, 43, 44, 45, 46, 47, 48, 49, 50, 51, 52, 53, 55, 56, 58, 60, 61, 62, 63, 65, 66, 68, 69, 70, 72, 73, 77, 79, 81, 82, 83, 84, 85, 86, 87, 88, 89, 90, 91, 92, 93, 94, 95, 96, 97, 98, 99, 101, 104, 127, 128, 129, 130, 131, 132, 134, 135, 136, 137, 138, 139, 141, 142, 143, 144, 145, 146, 148, 149, 150, 151, 152, 153, 154, 157, 158, 159, 160, 161, 162, 164, 165, 167, 171, 172, 173, 174, 175, 176, 177, 179, 180, 181, 182, 183, 188, 189, 191, 194, 195, 196, 200, 201, 204, 205, 208, 211, 217, 227, 228, 229, 231, 236, 238, 239, 240, 267, 268, 269, 270, 271, 273, 275, 277, 279, 283, 284, 285, 286, 287, 289, 290, 291, 292, 293, 294, 295, 296, 297, 298, 299, 301, 302, 304, 305, 306, 308, 309, 310, 311, 313, 314, 316, 331, 332, 334, 337, 339, 341, 355, 356, 359, 360, 361, 364, 366, 367, 368, 369, 376, 378, 380, 381, 387, 393, 394, 395, 396, 399, 400, 401, 402, 403, 404, 405, 406, 408, 409, 410, 412, 413, 414, 415, 416, 418, 419, 423, 424, 427, 433, 437, 439, 440, 441, 442, 443, 444, 445, 446, 447

Y

Youth 23, 26, 67, 70, 72, 78, 79, 146, 152, 153, 185, 233, 238, 239, 240, 241, 243, 245, 250, 251, 252, 253, 254, 255, 256, 258, 259, 260, 261, 263, 264, 311, 327, 328, 338, 340, 346, 355, 424, 441, 446

Publishing Tomorrow's Research Today

Uncover Current Insights and Future Trends in Education
with IGI Global's Cutting-Edge Recommended Books

Print Only, E-Book Only, or Print + E-Book.
Order direct through IGI Global's Online Bookstore at www.igi-global.com or through your preferred provider.

Artificial Intelligence Applications Using ChatGPT in Education: Case Studies and Practices
ISBN: 9781668493007
© 2023; 234 pp.
List Price: US$ 215

Generative AI in Teaching and Learning
ISBN: 9798369300749
© 2024; 383 pp.
List Price: US$ 230

Dynamic Curriculum Development and Design Strategies for Effective Online Learning in Higher Education
ISBN: 9781668486467
© 2023; 471 pp.
List Price: US$ 215

Illuminating and Advancing the Path for Mathematical Writing Research
ISBN: 9781668465387
© 2024; 389 pp.
List Price: US$ 215

Cases on Economics Education and Tools for Educators
ISBN: 9781668475836
© 2024; 359 pp.
List Price: US$ 215

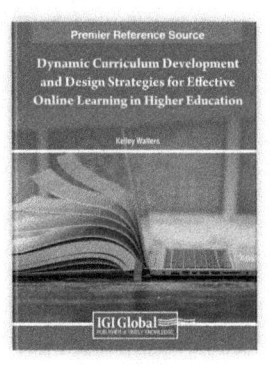

Emerging Trends and Historical Perspectives Surrounding Digital Transformation in Education: Achieving Open and Blended Learning Environments
ISBN: 9781668444238
© 2023; 334 pp.
List Price: US$ 240

Do you want to stay current on the latest research trends, product announcements, news, and special offers? Join IGI Global's mailing list to receive customized recommendations, exclusive discounts, and more.
Sign up at: www.igi-global.com/newsletters.

Scan the QR Code here to view more related titles in Education.

www.igi-global.com | Sign up at www.igi-global.com/newsletters | facebook.com/igiglobal | twitter.com/igiglobal | linkedin.com/igiglobal

Ensure Quality Research is Introduced to the Academic Community

Become a Reviewer for IGI Global Authored Book Projects

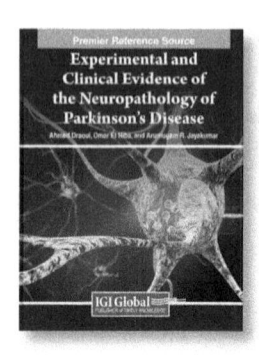

The overall success of an authored book project is dependent on quality and timely manuscript evaluations.

Applications and Inquiries may be sent to:
development@igi-global.com

Applicants must have a doctorate (or equivalent degree) as well as publishing, research, and reviewing experience. Authored Book Evaluators are appointed for one-year terms and are expected to complete at least three evaluations per term. Upon successful completion of this term, evaluators can be considered for an additional term.

If you have a colleague that may be interested in this opportunity, we encourage you to share this information with them.

IGI Global's Open Access Journal Program

Publishing Tomorrow's Research Today

Including Nearly 200 Peer-Reviewed, Gold (Full) Open Access Journals across IGI Global's Three Academic Subject Areas: Business & Management; Scientific, Technical, and Medical (STM); and Education

Consider Submitting Your Manuscript to One of These Nearly 200 Open Access Journals for to Increase Their Discoverability & Citation Impact

| Web of Science Impact Factor | 6.5 | Web of Science Impact Factor | 4.7 | Web of Science Impact Factor | 3.2 | Web of Science Impact Factor | 2.6 |

JOURNAL OF Organizational and End User Computing

JOURNAL OF Global Information Management

INTERNATIONAL JOURNAL ON Semantic Web and Information Systems

JOURNAL OF Database Management

Choosing IGI Global's Open Access Journal Program Can Greatly Increase the Reach of Your Research

Higher Usage
Open access papers are 2-3 times more likely to be read than non-open access papers.

Higher Download Rates
Open access papers benefit from 89% higher download rates than non-open access papers.

Higher Citation Rates
Open access papers are 47% more likely to be cited than non-open access papers.

Submitting an article to a journal offers an invaluable opportunity for you to share your work with the broader academic community, fostering knowledge dissemination and constructive feedback.

Submit an Article and Browse the IGI Global Call for Papers Pages

We can work with you to find the journal most well-suited for your next research manuscript.
For open access publishing support, contact: journaleditor@igi-global.com

Publishing Tomorrow's Research Today
IGI Global
e-Book Collection

Including Essential Reference Books Within Three Fundamental Academic Areas

Business & Management
Scientific, Technical, & Medical (STM)
Education

- Acquisition options include Perpetual, Subscription, and Read & Publish
- No Additional Charge for Multi-User Licensing
- No Maintenance, Hosting, or Archiving Fees
- Continually Enhanced Accessibility Compliance Features (WCAG)

| Over **150,000+** Chapters | Contributions From **200,000+** Scholars Worldwide | More Than **1,000,000+** Citations | Majority of e-Books Indexed in Web of Science & Scopus | Consists of Tomorrow's Research Available Today! |

Recommended Titles from our e-Book Collection

Innovation Capabilities and Entrepreneurial Opportunities of Smart Working
ISBN: 9781799887973

Advanced Applications of Generative AI and Natural Language Processing Models
ISBN: 9798369305027

Using Influencer Marketing as a Digital Business Strategy
ISBN: 9798369305515

Human-Centered Approaches in Industry 5.0
ISBN: 9798369326473

Modeling and Monitoring Extreme Hydrometeorological Events
ISBN: 9781668487716

Data-Driven Intelligent Business Sustainability
ISBN: 9798369300497

Information Logistics for Organizational Empowerment and Effective Supply Chain Management
ISBN: 9798369301593

Data Envelopment Analysis (DEA) Methods for Maximizing Efficiency
ISBN: 9798369302552

Request More Information, or Recommend the IGI Global e-Book Collection to Your Institution's Librarian

For More Information or to Request a Free Trial, Contact IGI Global's e-Collections Team: eresources@igi-global.com | 1-866-342-6657 ext. 100 | 717-533-8845 ext. 100

Are You Ready to Publish Your Research?

IGI Global
Publishing Tomorrow's Research Today

IGI Global offers book authorship and editorship opportunities across three major subject areas, including Business, STM, and Education.

Benefits of Publishing with IGI Global:

- Free one-on-one editorial and promotional support.
- Expedited publishing timelines that can take your book from start to finish in less than one (1) year.
- Choose from a variety of formats, including Edited and Authored References, Handbooks of Research, Encyclopedias, and Research Insights.
- Utilize IGI Global's eEditorial Discovery® submission system in support of conducting the submission and double-blind peer review process.
- IGI Global maintains a strict adherence to ethical practices due in part to our full membership with the Committee on Publication Ethics (COPE).
- Indexing potential in prestigious indices such as Scopus®, Web of Science™, PsycINFO®, and ERIC – Education Resources Information Center.
- Ability to connect your ORCID iD to your IGI Global publications.
- Earn honorariums and royalties on your full book publications as well as complimentary content and exclusive discounts.

Join Your Colleagues from Prestigious Institutions, Including:

Australian National University
Massachusetts Institute of Technology
JOHNS HOPKINS UNIVERSITY
HARVARD UNIVERSITY
COLUMBIA UNIVERSITY IN THE CITY OF NEW YORK

Learn More at: www.igi-global.com/publish
or by Contacting the Acquisitions Department at: acquisition@igi-global.com